FROM CHRISTIANITY TO JUDAISM

THE LITTMAN LIBRARY OF
JEWISH CIVILIZATION

Dedicated to the memory of
LOUIS THOMAS SIDNEY LITTMAN
*who founded the Littman Library for the love of God
and as an act of charity in memory of his father*
JOSEPH AARON LITTMAN
and to the memory of
ROBERT JOSEPH LITTMAN
who continued what his father Louis had begun
יהא זכרם ברוך

'*Get wisdom, get understanding:
Forsake her not and she shall preserve thee*'

PROV. 4: 5

*The Littman Library of Jewish Civilization is a registered UK charity
Registered charity no.* 1000784

From Christianity to Judaism

◆

The Story of Isaac Orobio de Castro

◆

YOSEF KAPLAN

Translated by
RAPHAEL LOEWE

London
The Littman Library of Jewish Civilization
in association with Liverpool University Press

The Littman Library of Jewish Civilization
Registered office: 4th floor, 7–10 Chandos Street, London WIG 9DQ

in association with Liverpool University Press
4 Cambridge Street, Liverpool L69 7ZU, UK
www.liverpooluniversitypress.co.uk/littman

Managing Editor: Connie Webber

Distributed in North America by
Oxford University Press Inc., 198 Madison Avenue,
New York, NY 10016, USA

First published 1989 by Oxford University Press on behalf of
The Littman Library of Jewish Civilization
First issued in paperback 2004

English translation
© The Littman Library of Jewish Civilization 1989

All rights reserved.
No part of this publication may be reproduced,
stored in a retrieval system, or transmitted, in any form or by
any means, without the prior permission in writing of
The Littman Library of Jewish Civilization

This book is sold subject to the condition that it shall not,
by way of trade or otherwise, be lent, re-sold, hired out or
otherwise circulated without the publisher's prior consent in any
form of binding or cover other than that in which it is published
and without a similar condition including this condition
being imposed on the subsequent purchaser

Catalogue records for this book are available from the
British Library and the Library of Congress

ISBN 978-1-904113-14-0

Preface to the Hebrew Edition

Towards the close of 1662 a Portuguese physician, born in Braganza, arrived at Amsterdam and settled in a house on Breestraat, the main artery of the Portuguese Jewish community in the city. His name was Isaac Orobio de Castro; but his fellow-students in Spain at Madre de Dios, the school of theology in the university of Alcalá de Henares, had known him as Baltazar Alvares, his students in the faculty of medicine at Seville as Dr Baltazar de Orobio, and his professorial colleagues in France at the university of Toulouse as Dr Baltazar Orobio de Castro. On arrival in Amsterdam, he returned to Judaism and changed his name to Isaac—under which name he was to be buried in 1687 in the cemetery of the Amsterdam Portuguese-Jewish Congregation *Talmud Torah* at Ouderkerk.

It was not merely a change of name, but one of identity: a Portuguese crypto-Jew, who had been the pupil of Carmelite friars and Franciscans at Alcalá, had openly joined the house of Israel. Nor, indeed, was there anything in such a metamorphosis to surprise his contemporaries or his environment. Every year throughout the seventeenth century dozens of crypto-Jews had been arriving in Amsterdam from Spain and Portugal and publicly reverting to Judaism. Thus, Manoel Dias Soeiro became Menasseh ben Israel; the Dominican Fray Vicente de Rocamora became Dr Isaac de Rocamora, preacher to the community; Pablo de Pina became Reuel Jessurun, Tomás Rodrigues Pereyra became Abraham Israel Pereyra, and Captain Miguel de Barrios became Daniel Levi de Barrios.

What was it that made possible this popular wave of return from crypto-Judaism to the Jewish fold, after many generations of forced separation from the ancestral religion and the sources of Jewish culture? What impelled these crypto-Jews to forsake the land of their birth and the scenes of childhood that they loved so well? What motivated them to go forth to a strange land, whose language they did not know and whose culture was alien to them, in order to begin a new page in their life-history? How successfully did they became absorbed into their newly adopted community, and what made them willing to submit to the religious discipline of the Torah and its commandments?

After eight or more generations' residence in lands of persecution and enforced conformity, did these refugees bring with them any knowledge at all regarding the Jewish religion and its traditions? Was there no clash between the Christian (and specifically Catholic) values that they had absorbed in the universities and monasteries of the Iberian peninsula and those concepts of normative Judaism which they discovered when, for the first time in their lives, they encountered a regularly organized Jewish community?

This book considers the life and thought of one of the foremost spokesmen of Sephardic Judaism in western Europe in the seventeenth century. The life of Isaac Orobio de Castro was packed with drama and exemplified the fate of a whole community of crypto-Jews—their hopes, their tribulations, and their aspirations. Orobio's manifold literary activity expressed the tug-of-war—psychological, spiritual, and cultural—that accompanied the public re-entry into Judaism of many 'New Christians' from Spain and Portugal: those victims of the two Iberian Inquisitions who had been lucky enough to escape.

Before Isaac Orobio reached the secure haven of Amsterdam, his life had been one long, scarcely interrupted series of wanderings. The many staging-posts on his road may each be viewed individually, but it was all of them together that fashioned his character. Not only was he subject to upheavals and persecution but he also absorbed new cultural values and became acquainted with philosophers of various schools, all of which served to extend his intellectual horizons.

His earliest memories were of Braganza, his birthplace, which were steeped in the trauma inspired by the terror of the Portuguese Inquisition, which at the beginning of the seventeenth century brought low many a 'New Christian' victim in the district, including not a few members of his own family. Whilst still a child he arrived with his parents in Spain, where he was to spend half of his life. In Málaga he learned how to present a mask to the world—a way of life that had been the heritage of his community for generations: the secret of how to be a Christian as he walked abroad whilst preserving his Judaism at home and in the inner recesses of his heart. It was a secret to be closely guarded amongst his kin and his most intimate friends only. At the university of Osuna he took his first steps in the study of medicine; from there he headed northwards towards Alcalá, there to continue his studies and supplement medicine with philosophy and theology. And it

Preface to the Hebrew Edition

was there that he became acquainted with the fundamental principles of Spanish neo-scholasticism.

Schooled like his ancestors in suffering, Orobio likewise lived as a wandering Jew, harried because of his ancestors' religion. From Seville to Cádiz; from Cádiz, where he was arrested by the Inquisition, once more back to Seville; and then on to Lorca, a small town in what had been, long before, the kingdom of Valencia, where he entertained the forlorn hope of at last finding a resting-place. But still his wanderings were not at an end. In 1660, when he was already forty-three, he reached Bayonne, from which point onward he was free of his fetters. During his two years' sojourn in France he came into close contact with the circles of the Prince de Condé, and could be said (with perhaps a little licence, that he subsequently granted himself) to have been one of the medical counsellors of Louis XIV. He also taught in the medical faculty of the university of Toulouse. There Baltazar's resolve to revert openly to observance of the Jewish Torah matured, and for this purpose he proceeded onward to Amsterdam, where at last he joined the Portuguese Congregation *Talmud Torah*.

This burden of his earlier life he brought with him to Amsterdam, where he spent his remaining twenty-five years becoming one of the most important thinkers of the Sephardi diaspora of western Europe. During this period he took his stand as the champion of normative traditional Judaism against enemies from within and without. His polemic against Juan de Prado and Barukh Spinoza was the most significant attempt made from within the Amsterdam congregation to reply to these two thinkers, who cast aspersions upon the traditions of Israel and its uniqueness as a people. His disputations with Christian theologians of various confessions and schools of thought became the stock-in-trade of apologetic literature of subsequent generations, earning him the sobriquet of 'the modern Josephus' among the members of his own congregation. His name became well known among Christian intellectual circles, including some of the most outstanding minds of the period such as Philip van Limborch, John Locke, Jean le Clerc, and Pierre Bayle.

The life of Isaac Orobio, his struggles and literary achievements, displays every problematic element affecting the spiritual existence of the Sephardi diaspora of western Europe in his day. That scattering of communities was uniquely distinguished from the Sephardi-Jewish settlements in Islamic lands by one cardinal feature: as against the majority of Sephardi centres in the Near and Middle East, founded at the end of the fifteenth century by openly Jewish exiles from Spain and Portugal, almost all the Sephardi communities of Christian Europe (including that of Amsterdam) were founded by former crypto-Jews. In most cases they had been born generations after the edicts of expulsion and had received a Christian religious education, being cut off physically no less than spiritually from the centres of Jewish life. This fundamental distinction also explains the great cultural difference between the two Sephardi diasporas, the western and the eastern. The Sephardi communities in the East maintained, in one way or another, a continuity with pre-expulsion Iberian Jewish life—its institutions, customs, liturgical forms, and characteristic Spanish vernacular. In contrast, the Sephardi communities of the West had, on the other hand, to bridge the gulf, stretching over the generations, that separated them from the quarry whence they had been hewn. On the other hand, thanks both to their own protracted residence in lands where they were persecuted and to their deep involvement in the cultural life of Spain and Portugal, on settling elsewhere they brought with them, as former crypto-Jews, cultural values qualitatively different from the spiritual baggage which the original exiles had taken with them when they were expelled.

A specific hallmark that characterizes this western Sephardi diaspora in its entirety is the sense of collective internal identity which was the legacy of their fate. They saw themselves as belonging to 'the [Judaeo-] Spanish and Portuguese folk', which is what they meant when they referred to themselves as 'members of the *Nación*'. The close family links permeating this diaspora reinforced their own feeling of collective identity. The testamentary dispositions, numbered in hundreds, that have come down to us from the seventeenth and eighteenth centuries indicate that neither national frontiers nor distance vitiated these ties. Even regarding individuals or whole branches of families who had been left behind in Spain or Portugal, and who continued to live outwardly as Christians in lands where Judaism was proscribed, kinship with relatives dispersed in many countries was in no way compromised. Those former crypto-Jews continued to regard their family connections in the 'lands of persecution' as members no less than themselves of the Spanish and Portuguese *Nación*.

Right across the Sephardi diaspora there stood out an élite consisting of merchants with international connections—entrepreneurs and investors whose energetic prosecution of business extended to many different countries. Because of the standing that this élite enjoyed with the government and in Christian society wherever its domicile happened to be, it came to wield the dominant social influence within the various Sephardi communities. Moreover, those in the Sephardi diaspora of western Europe who possessed intellectual abilities aroused the interest of Christian scholars, with whom in many cases they forged close links arising out of their shared interests. Naturally, thanks to their status in European society, the influence of this intelligentsia grew within their own parent communities, and the social and cultural values which this small class endorsed came to be guiding values, generally acknowledged by the Sephardi-Jewish communities of western Europe.

All the foregoing and everything that it implies is reflected in the personality of Isaac Orobio. As a consequence this book, which describes his life and intellectual achievements, aims at opening a window upon the social and cultural world of the unique community of which he was a member. His route from Christianity to Judaism exemplifies the changes that were occurring in the manner of living, the consciousness, and the sense of identity of Spanish and Portuguese crypto-Jews as, in the seventeenth century, they openly rejoined the Jewish fold.

Jewish historiography has not ignored the significance of Isaac Orobio, whom already Graetz recognized as 'more important that the whole of the circle [of Amsterdam Sephardi literati]' (*History of the Jews*, English translation by Bella Löwy, vol. v, p. 115). Since Graetz' time several attempts have been made to delineate his character and to analyse and assess his literary achievements. Of major importance in this field is the work of the late Israel S. Révah, who published Isaac Orobio's polemics with Juan de Prado. In his research into the Spinozan chapter of the history of the Spanish and Portuguese community of Amsterdam, Révah paid full regard to the part played in the story by Orobio. During his latter years he discovered important facts about Orobio's origins and family history, as also about his life before he left Spain: but his work was cut off in its prime by his untimely death.

This work is the first attempt at covering the life and literary achievements of Isaac Orobio as a whole, and at putting them into their contemporary social, historical, and intellectual context. It began as a

Preface to the Hebrew Edition

study undertaken for the degree of Ph.D., the subject being 'Isaac Orobio de Castro and his Circle'. The thesis was written under the supervision of Professor Ḥayyim Beinart and was presented, and approved, for the award of the doctorate by the Hebrew University of Jerusalem in 1978. The present volume incorporates new source-material that has since become available to the author, and the scope of the book has been extended.

It is a pleasant task to express my gratitude to all those who have assisted and otherwise sustained me throughout my work in producing this book and seeing it reach print. First and foremost among these stands my teacher Professor Ḥayyim Beinart, who with sustained dedication has guided me at all stages of my research and the writing up of my findings and who likewise has given me both advice and encouragement. Thanks are also due to my teachers, Professor Shmuel Ettinger and Professor Joseph Barukh Sermoneta, both of whom made important observations on my drafts and drew my attention to matters of substance.

I owe a particular debt of gratitude to my friends and colleagues Professor Robert Bonfil and Professor Michael Heyd, both of the Hebrew University of Jerusalem, to Professor Richard H. Popkin of Washington University, Saint Louis, to Professor Carlos Carrete Parrondo of Madrid, Professor Gérard Nahon of Paris, and M. H. Gans of Amsterdam, who helped clarify various problems dealt with in the work.

I am likewise very much in the debt of those responsible for the care of libraries and archives who made it possible for me to carry out research on manuscripts and other documents held by them: to the University and National Library of Jerusalem and in particular to Dr M. Nadav, its keeper of manuscripts, and to the staff of the microfilmed manuscripts department; to Drs Wilhelmina Ch. Pieterse, Director of the Municipal Archives of Amsterdam; to Daniel da Silva Solis, one of the directors of the *'Eṣ Ḥayyim*-Montezinos library belonging to the Amsterdam Synagogue; to A. Offenberg, Director of the Bibliotheca Rosenthaliana in Amsterdam, and his deputy F. Hoogewoud; to the University Library of Leiden, the Royal Library of Brussels, and the Municipal Archives of Antwerp: to the Diocesan Archives of Cuenca, the British Library in London, and the Bibliothèque Nationale in Paris.

I am also indebted to the Jewish Memorial Foundation in New York, the Warburg Fund, and the humanities fund of the Hebrew University, for material support that enabled me to carry out the research that has gone into this volume.

Finally my thanks go to Mrs Yael Kaplan, who typed the manuscript (of the original Hebrew edition), and to I. Avineri who edited it. Ben-Zion Yehoshua, director of the Magnes Press, and his assistant D. Benovitz contributed tremendously to the publication of the book, as did the printing firm of Menahem and its staff.

Y.K.

Jerusalem
'Ab 5742/July 1982

Preface to the English Edition

Nine years have passed since the completion of the Hebrew edition of this book. In that time, many valuable studies and articles have appeared on various aspects of the history of the Crypto-Jews, New Christians, and the Sephardi diaspora in Western Europe during the early modern period, particularly on the Spanish and Portuguese community in Amsterdam in the seventeenth century. My teachers, colleagues, and friends Haim Beinart, Jonathan Israel, David Katz, Henry Méchoulan, Gérard Nahon, Richard Popkin, Herman P. Salomon, Daniel Swetchinski, and Yosef Hayim Yerushalmi have published works which have deepened our insight into the problems of the Spanish and Portuguese Jews of the West in the first centuries following the expulsion from Spain in 1492 and the forced conversion in Portugal in 1497. I am grateful to all of them for what I have learnt from their works and from personal conversations. However, despite the changes and new discoveries which have taken place in the field, and despite my own continued research in the area, I have not altered the structure of the Hebrew original, nor have I introduced far-reaching changes. I have merely corrected a number of regrettable errors which found their way into the Hebrew text, and here and there I have added new bibliographical comments. I hope to return and expand upon several issues treated by this work in a forthcoming book about deviance and punishment in the Western Sephardi diaspora in early modern times.

It is my pleasant duty to thank, first of all, Raphael Loewe for his excellent translation of this book and for his valuable comments. I have included a number of his notes in square brackets followed by his initials. I would also like to thank my friends Jeffrey Green and Richard Cohen for their help at various stages of preparing this work for press, as well as Bernard Cooperman, Benjamin Ravid, and David Ruderman. I owe a particular debt of gratitude to my student and friend Tirtsah Levie for making me aware of errors in the Hebrew edition, and to Bertram Schwarzbach for his comments regarding the appendix on the French translations of the works of Orobio de Castro. The regents of the Portuguese Jewish Rabbinical Seminary 'Ets Haim' and the heads of the Portuguese Jewish Community in Amsterdam have been particularly generous in permitting me to publish photographs of manuscripts from their library and of monuments from the Ouderkerk cemetery. Likewise I am grateful to the Littman Library of Jewish Civilization, and in particular to Vivian D. Lipman, for taking on the difficult task of publishing this book.

Y. K.

Jerusalem
Tammuz 5748/June 1988

Contents

List of Plates	xvi
Maps and Tables	xvii
List of Abbreviations	xviii
1. From Portugal to Spain: The Alvares de Orobio Family	1
University Studies: Osuna and Alcalá	8
The Plague at Málaga, 1637: Baltazar Alvares' Account	15
2. A Long Brush with the Inquisition, 1639–1643	25
Isabel Luis and Andrés de Narváez	29
Violante de Paz, her Children, and her Brother José de Castro	35
Manuel Alvares and Santiago Luis	42
3. Building a Career in Andalusia	64
Professor at Seville and Service to the Duke of Medinaceli	64
Scientific Discussion of Phlebotomy	67
Cádiz	75
4. Imprisoned by the Seville Inquisition	79
5. Freedom	93
The Last Years in Spain	93
Toulouse	97
Associations with the Prince de Condé and the King of France	103
Amsterdam: The Dutch Jerusalem	106
6. Doubt and Certainty	110
Orobio de Castro's Questions to Rabbi Moses Raphael d'Aguilar	110
Isaac Orobio and Juan de Prado: Intellectual Ferment in Sephardi Amsterdam	122

Contents

7. Philosopher, Communal Leader, Physician — 179
   Raymond Lull's Philosophy Debated — 179
   Communal Activity within the Portuguese Congregation — 189
   Medical Practice in Amsterdam — 200
   Personal Standing and Material Circumstances — 205

8. Isaac Orobio and Sabbateanism — 209

9. Facing Calvinists and Catholics — 235
   Debate with a Huguenot on Salvation — 239
   'Divine Forewarning' against Catholic 'Idolatry' — 243
   Tracts on the 'Seventy Weeks' and the 'Suffering Servant' — 249
   Judaism *vis-à-vis* Christianity — 252

10. Philosophers, Theologians, and Poets — 263
    Spinoza and Metaphysics: Meeting the Challenge — 263
    A 'Friendly Conversation': Isaac Orobio and Philip van Limborch — 270
    Poets, Poetasters, and Patrons: *The Academia de los Floridos* — 286
    Last Days — 302

11. The Intellectual World of Isaac Orobio de Castro — 308
    The Hispanic Heritage — 308
    Between Scholasticism and Fideistic Scepticism — 313
    Political and Social Attitudes — 322

12. From Crypto-Judaism to Open Judaism — 326
    A New Jewish Perspective on *Converso* Life — 326
    The Jewish World: From Dreams to Reality — 343
    Israel and the Gentiles — 353
    The Jewish Fate: Exile and Redemption — 362

Epilogue — 378

APPENDICES

A. The Iconography of Isaac Orobio — 385
B. Poetical Account of the Plague at Málaga, 1637, by Baltasar Alvares (Isaac Orobio de Castro) — 387

C. Schedule of Moveable Property of Baltasar (Isaac) Orobio Sequestrated by the Inquisition at Cádiz, August 1654	402
D. Membership of the *Academia de los Floridos*	418
E. Manuscripts of Works by Isaac Orobio de Castro	431
F. Orobio's Letter to Prado's Son: A Textual Comparison	441
G. Translations of Orobio's Works in the Eighteenth and Nineteenth Centuries	451
H. Works Attributed to Orobio	465
Bibliography	469
Name Index	507
Place Index	521
Subject Index	527

List of Plates

The plates are between pp. 254 and 255

1. Alleged portrait of Isaac Orobio, artist unknown
2. J. Groenwolt's portrait, wrongly described as that of Isaac Orobio
3. Portrait of Alonso de Zepeda
4. Gravestones of Isaac and Esther Orobio, at Ouderkerk, The Netherlands
5. Title-page of Orobio's *Respuesta a un Predicante Francés*, copied by Jacob Guedelha (Gadella). MS 'Eṣ Ḥayyim-Montezinos 49 A 16
6. Title-page of G. de la Torre's Spanish translation of Orobio's *Certamen Philosophicum*, copied in The Hague in 1741. MS 'Eṣ Ḥayyim-Montezinos 48 C 16
7. Page of Orobio's *Respuesta Apologética* against Zepeda, apparently corrected (and perhaps entirely written) in his own hand. MS 'Eṣ Ḥayyim-Montezinos 48 E 42
8. Title-page of Orobio's *Respuesta Apologética* against Zepeda, copied by Abraham Machorro in 1707. MS 'Eṣ Ḥayyim-Montezinos 48 B 12²

Maps

1. Spain, Portugal, and southern France   26
2. The Low Countries   108
3. Detail of the Amsterdam Jewish quarter   419

Tables

A   Pedigree of the Family of Alvares de Orobio de Castro   2
B   The Children of Manuel Alvares and Mencia Fernández Núñez   2
C   Alvares Collaterals   28

Abbreviations

AA	*Antwerpsch archievenblad*
ACF	*Annuaire du Collège de France*
AJA	*American Jewish Archives*
AZGW	*Archief Zeewsch Genootschap der Wetenschapen*
BH	*Bulletin hispanique*
BMGJWN	*Bijdragen en mededelingen van het Genootschap voor de Joodsche Wetenschap in Nederland*
EJ	*Encyclopaedia Judaica* (English), 16 vols., Jerusalem, 1972
EUIEA	*Enciclopedia universal ilustrada europea americana*
HB	*Hebräische Bibliographie*
HJ	*Historia Judaica*
HUCA	*Hebrew Union College Annual*
JAPCS	*Journal of the American Portuguese Cultural Society*
JE	*The Jewish Encyclopedia*, New York and London, 1901–6
JJLG	*Jahrbuch der Jüdisch-literarischen Gesellschaft*
JJS	*Journal of Jewish Studies*
JQR	*Jewish Quarterly Review*
JSS	*Jewish Social Studies*
MEAH	*Miscelánea de estudios árabes y hebraicos*
MGWJ	*Monatsschrift für Geschichte und Wissenschaft des Judentums*
MLR	*Modern Language Review*
NIW	*Nieuw israelietisch weekblad*
NRFH	*Nueva revista de filología hispánica*
PAAJR	*Proceedings of the American Academy for Jewish Research*
PAJHS	*Publications of the American Jewish Historical Society*
REJ	*Revue des études juives*
RHMH	*Revue d'histoire de la médecine hébraïque*
RHR	*Revue de l'histoire des religions*
RMI	*La rassegna mensile di Israel*
SR	*Studia Rosenthaliana*
TJHSE	*Transactions of the Jewish Historical Society of England*
VA	*De vrijdagavond*
ZGJD	*Zeitschrift für die Geschichte der Juden in Deutschland*
ZHB	*Zeitschrift für hebräische Bibliographie*
ZT	*Zeeuws tijdschrift*

I

From Portugal to Spain: The Alvares de Orobio Family

Around the year 1617 Braganza, in the north of Portugal, witnessed the birth of Baltazar de Orobio.[1] Braganza was well known as one of the principal centres of Portuguese crypto-Judaism, and many 'New Christians' there were sentenced by the tribunals of the Portuguese Inquisition during the sixteenth, seventeenth, and eighteenth centuries.[2] The family of Baltazar, which was apparently of Spanish origin, had been settled there for at least four generations and had had its taste of tribulation at the hands of the Portuguese Inquisition. More than 500 Braganzan crypto-Jews had suffered harassment and imprisonment, having been tried and sentenced by the Holy Tribunal at the gruesome *autos-da-fé* staged at Coimbra in the years 1593–1602, including Baltazar's paternal grandparents, Melchor Rodrigues and Leonor Alvares, as well as his maternal grandparents, Antonio

---

[1] The exact date cannot be determined. Some scholars have placed it in 1620: Kayserling, *Biblioteca*, p. 81; S. Kagan, *Jewish Medicine*, Boston, 1852, p. 132, but Kayserling gives it as 1616 elsewhere (*Geschichte*, p. 303). Investigation of the matriculation records of the university of Alcalá de Henares reveals that he must have been born c.1617, since in Oct. 1635 he figures as aged 18, in Nov. 1626 and Feb. 1637 as 19, and in Dec. 1638 as 21. See Madrid, AHN, universities section, Alcalá 448F, list of medical students for 1635 (f. 56'), and that for 1636–8 (unpaginated). Cf. Révah, *rupt. spin., nouvel examen,*70, p. 565, who fixes Baltazar's birth at 1618, followed by N. Koren, *Jewish Physicians*, Jerusalem, 1973, p. 34. In various publications it is alleged that he was born in Spain, some specifically locating his birthplace as Málaga; thus Locke, his earliest biographer (*Bibliothèque universelle*, vii, 1687, pp. 289 f.), followed by Basnage (v, pp. 2112 f.), and the Dutch translator of Limborch's colloquy with Orobio, *De Veritate Rel. Christ.* (unpaginated). Amelander, writing in Yiddish, states that he was born in Spain to a crypto-Jewish father. Franco Mendes, '*Orovyo*, pp. 213–23, states that he was born in Seville; cf. Brugmans and Frank, p. 517. These assertions are incorrect, and derive from Baltazar Alvares de Orobio's own attempts to camouflage his origins in Portugal at the period when he was a student at the universitites of Osuna and Alcalá. See below, p. 11. The name *Orobio* or *Orovio* is known in Spain from the year 935, and points to the family's being indigenous; see J. Godoy Alcántara, *Ensayo Histórico-Etimológico sobre los apellidos castellanos*, Madrid, 1871 (fac. Barcelona, 1975), p. 135.

[2] Révah (*rupt. spin., nouvel examen,* 71, p. 584) describes Braganza as being the 'métropole du crypto-judaïsme'. Regarding the local community in the Middle Ages see Kayserling, *Geschichte*, pp. 18 f., 41 f., 56 f.; Mendes dos Remedios, *Judeus em Port.*, pp. 138 f.; Alves (generally), whose book contains much information regarding crypto-Jews in the city of Braganza and the towns of its environs.

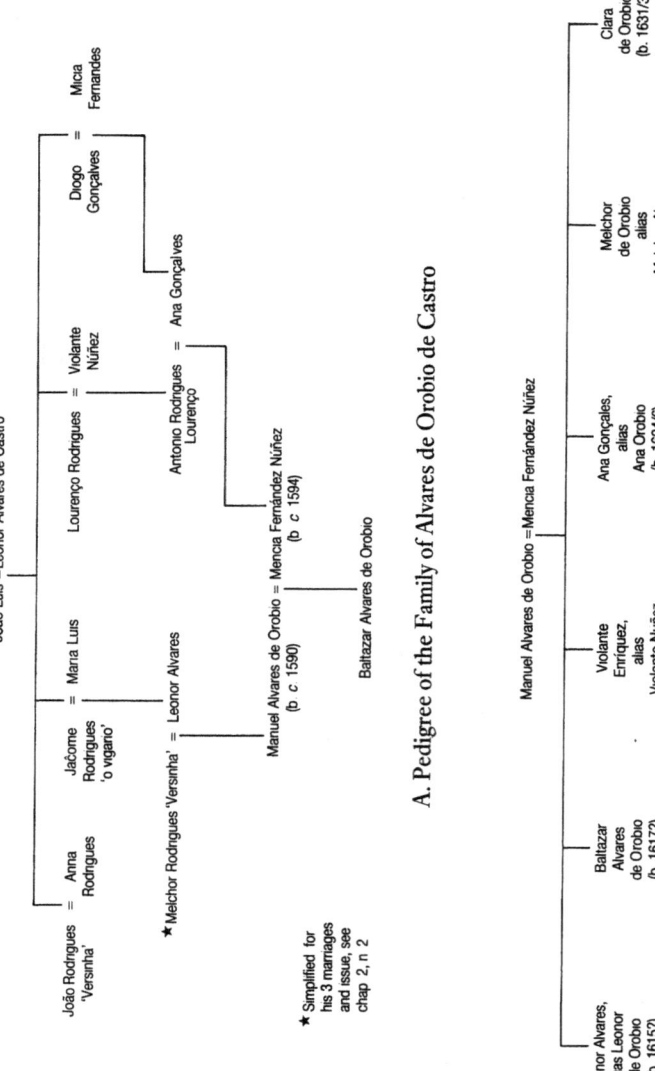

A. Pedigree of the Family of Alvares de Orobio de Castro

B. The Children of Manuel Alvares and Mencía Fernández Núñez

From Portugal to Spain 3

Rodrigues Lourenço and Ana Gonçalves (see Table A).[3] His father, Manuel Alvares de Orobio, and his mother, Mencia Fernández Núñez, were married in about 1614, and of their six children two were born in Braganza—the eldest, Leonor Alvares (de Orobio) almost certainly in 1615, and Baltazar Alvares some two years later (see Table B).[4]

During the second decade of the century members of the family were beginning to emigrate to Spain, as were many other Portuguese crypto-Jews at the same period, in an endeavour to escape the clutches of the Lusitanian Inquisition, the range of whose activities reached its zenith at the end of the sixteenth and the beginning of the seventeenth centuries. From 1580, after the crown of Portugal had become integrated in that of Spain, the flow of emigration was substantially increased.[5] In Spain the tide of inquisitional persecution had slackened towards the end of the sixteenth century, and crypto-Jews were hoping to find a refuge there from the penalties to which they had been subjected. They took advantage of the circumstance that before 1630 there were no formal extradition arrangements between the inquisitional tribunals of Spain and Portugal, the union of the crowns not having brought in its wake the union of the two Inquisitions, which continued to act independently. They did, however, have a system for the exchange of information, and many files in the Spanish inquisitional records preserve copies of trials involving crypto-Jews in Portugal. Nevertheless, the Spanish tribunals for the most part turned a deaf ear to requests for extradition laid before them on the authority of the Portuguese Inquisition.[6] Furthermore, many Portuguese crypto-Jews regarded Spain as a mere staging-post on their route to the lands of freedom, where they intended to revert to the open profession of Judaism.[7]

[3] See Révah, *rupt. spin., nouvel examen*, 72, pp. 645 f., and cf. Alves, pp. 59 f. Baltazar's forebears included members of the Alvares, Castro, Luis, Gonçalves, Fernandes, Nunes, and Rodrigues families. Of those convicted at the *autos-da-fé* held at Coimbra from 1584 to 1607 no less than 76 crypto-Jews from the Braganza area bore at least one of these surnames, and it may be assumed that some of them were Baltazar's kin. One Antonio Rodrigues of Braganza was sentenced at the *auto-da-fé* of 19 Dec. 1599 to six years in the galleys (Alves, p. 59, no. 617): possibly he was the maternal grandfather of Baltazar. The Diogo Gonçalves sentenced on the same occasion (ibid., no. 621) to a second term was conceivably his maternal great-grandfather, the father of Ana Gonçalves (see Table A). Most of these crypto-Jews were artisans—17 shoemakers, 4 tradesmen, 3 weavers, 2 goldsmiths, 1 landworker, 1 attorney, 1 doctor, etc.
[4] See Révah, *rupt. spin., nouvel examen*, 71, p. 585.
[5] See Beinart, *Te'udoth*, pp. 150 f., Révah, *Marranes et l'Inquisition*, p. 522.
[6] See Yerushalmi, *Isaac Cardoso*, pp. 8 f.
[7] See Beinart, *Conversos*, pp. 474 f.

From Portugal to Spain

The first member of Baltazar's family to reach Castile was his uncle Mateo Rodríguez, the younger brother of his mother Mencia, a merchant who settled in Alcázar (apparently Alcázar de San Juan, in the district of la Mancha) not later than 1614/15. From this base he assisted his brother-in-law Manuel Alvares to come and join him together with all his family. The exact date of their arrival in Spain is unknown, but it can be established that they were already settled in Alcázar de San Juan in 1623. Around that year the couple's family was increased by the birth of a third child, their daughter Violante; and by the beginning of the thirties they had produced a further three children—Ana, Melchor, and Clara.[8]

The early movements of the family in Spain are shrouded in darkness, and we do not know when exactly it was that they settled in Andalusia at Málaga, where they were domiciled until 1640. There was a Portuguese named Manuel Alvares living in Jaén in 1622 — conceivably identical with Baltazar's father. It may be surmised that the Alvares family will have resided for some time in Madrid. At the end of his life, after Baltazar had openly reverted to Judaism and had changed his name to Isaac, he recorded in his disputation with Philip van Limborch that he had personally witnessed the events surrounding the trials known as those of 'the Patient Christ' *(el Cristo de la Paciencia)* which took place in 1632, when Portuguese crypto-Jews were found guilty of insulting the cross and subjecting it to scourging.[9] Possibly the

---

[8] See Révah, *rupt. spin.*, *nouvel examen*, 72, pp. 647 f.: Antonio Rodrigues Lourenço and Ana née Gonçalves had 2 sons and 2 daughters—Diogo Rodrigues (b. 1584/5), Violante Núñez (b. 1588), Mencia Fernández Núñez (Baltazar's mother, b. 1594), and Mateo Rodríguez Núñez (b. 1593).

[9] Regarding the Portuguese Manuel Alvares resident in Jaén in 1622 see Jaén Archives, Leg. 1354, ff.cccxxx^v—cccxxxii^r, where he is referred to as a witness in a notarial document of 15 June 1622. For Baltazar's presence in Madrid during the events of 'the Patient Christ' see Limborch, *De Veritate Rel. Christ.*, p. 719: 'Similiter Matriti, ubi judaei accusati quod Christi imaginem verberaverant, eamque ipsos allocutam: Si sum Deus vester quare me verberatis? Quod aliqui in tormentis confessi ad triremes damnati, alii, qui negarunt, vivi concremati, et templum ibi christi ab injuriis titulo constructum. Huic spectaculo ego fui praesens.' Further evidence for the sojourn of the Alvares family in Madrid is found in the testimony of doña Flor de Ayala, who was examined in Málaga on 11 Sept. 1641, see below, chap. 2, p. 52. On 'the Patient Christ' see Isaac Cardoso, *Excel.*, pp. 405 f., who relates how schoolchildren aged 5 or 6 were tricked by sweetmeats, etc. into 'confessing' that their crypto-Jewish parents had scourged the image of Christ in secret: 'Mas por que se vea quanto puede el odio implacable contra una Nacion humilde, y quan inciertas son las pruevas que se toman de la propria confession en los tormentos, sellemos estos successos infelizes con el que succedió en Madrid el año de mil seyscientos treinta y dos, vinieron de Portugal unos Judios Portugueses à la Corte con sus mugeres y hijos pequeños, que embiandolos à las escuelas, y conversando con los otros muchachos, estos les davan confites, y golosinas, y los ivan inquiriendo si eran

family had endeavoured to become assimilated into the population of the capital city of Spain, where during the time of the Conde Duque de Olivares there was discussion regarding the possibility of again permitting Jewish settlement in Spain in general and particularly in Madrid itself.[10] However, the recrudescent persecution connected with 'the Patient Christ' affair might have dissuaded them from remaining in Madrid. It would not have been the first time that the Alvares family had fallen foul of the Spanish Inquisition. In 1623 Mateo, Baltazar's uncle, had been arrested in Cuenca, and in the course of his year-long investigation had succeeded in concealing the Jewish adherence of his own parents Antonio Rodrigues and Ana Gonçalves, who had themselves been apprehended by the Coimbra Inquisition, and had confessed to Judaism in 1593 and 1595. Mateo had not uttered the slightest word to cast suspicion on those of his kin who had already settled in Spain. On the contrary, he had imputed responsibility for his own Judaizing to two crypto-Jews who had got away from Spain—one to Antwerp and the other, it seems, to Glückstadt. He further admitted that he had been in the custom of visiting Dax (in southern France) every other year, where he had links with the local crypto-Jews as well as with those around Bayonne. Mateo succeeded in escaping the penalty that might be expected for offences of such heinousness: he submitted to the forms of reconciliation with the church, and during the 1630s he continued to support his sister's family. He even extended his financial aid to Baltazar to enable him to continue with his studies at the university—a matter to

Judios, y si sus padres en casa maltratavan, ò açotavan un Xpo. negavan ellos al principio, mas persuadidos de las golosinas que les davan, y del maestro poco affecto à esta Nacion, que tenia mas de finguido santeron, que de entero, y piadoso, [p. 406] sin saber lo que dizian vinieron à confessar lo que les imputavan, y aunque eran de menor edad de cinco ò seys años, quando son invalidos, y nulos los testimonios, por estos dichos persuadidos y aconsejados prenden los padres, que estavan enfermos en la cama de tercianas ocasionadas del ardor del Estio, y del trabajo del viage, ponenles à tormento viejos, pobres y enfermos, y exortandolos à que confesassen, y se uzaria con ellos de piedad no pudiendo sufrir los dolores, confessaron quanto les acusavan, y quemaron seys ò siete personas, leyendoles primero las sentencias en un acto publico, que relatavan que açotavan à un Xpo. que despues quemaron, y que entre los açotes que le davan les dizia, porque me maltratais . . . ' For these inquisitional trials see Caro Baroja, *Sociedad criptoj.*, pp. 105 f., Yerushalmi, *Isaac Cardoso*, pp. 105 f., and cf. Beinart, *Conversos*, pp. 118, 231.

[10] See Beinart, *Yisshuv Ḥadash*, pp. 13 f.; Caro Baroja, *Judíos*, pp. 42 f.; Marañón, p. 180; Yerushalmi, *Isaac Cardoso*, pp. 164 f. The improvement in the fortunes of the 'Portuguese' men of business (i.e. of crypto-Jewish businessmen coming from Portugal) is in some measure connected with the reluctance, from 1626, of the Genoese financiers active at the court of Philip IV to give credit; cf. Dom. Ortiz, *Saravia*, p. 560.

which we shall revert. By 1648 Mateo, his wife, and his children had escaped to Italy, where they made open profession of Judaism.[11]

There are grounds for surmise that some of those convicted at the *auto-da-fé* held in Córdoba on 21 December 1627 were likewise related to Baltazar Alvares. Francisco Alvarez, a Portuguese resident of Priego, was condemned to six months' imprisonment and to wear the *sanbenito*;[12] Diego Alvarez, a Portuguese resident in Andújar, and Ana Alvarez of Aguilar were posthumously condemned to be burned in effigy;[13] and Isabel Alvarez, a Portuguese living in Andújar, was actually burned at the stake.[14] Thus, during their first years of residence in Spain, Manuel Alvares and his family had consequently very good reason to sense that the ground was quaking beneath their feet, and that their hopes of finding secure refuge had rapidly been dashed. They were obliged to exercise extreme circumspection, since their Portuguese origins and their family connections were liable at any moment to excite the suspicions of the Spanish inquisitorial officials.

There can be no doubt that already in his childhood Baltazar had had experience of the double life of the crypto-Jew — secret adherence to his faith in the Mosaic law, beneath a scrupulous attention to the preserving in public of a Christian appearance in every detail. In 1654, at thirty-seven, he was apprehended by the Inquisition in Seville, and endeavoured to cast responsibility for his Judaizing on various persons who, according to his own statement, had exercised influence upon him at a relatively mature age. In his deposition of 13 January 1656 he maintained that he had not begun to practise the Jewish commandments until 1640, i.e. at the age of twenty-three.[15] This testimony is loosely corroborated by a tract composed after his return to Judaism,

[11] Révah, *rupt. spin., nouvel examen*, 72 pp. 647 f.

[12] See Matute i Luquin, pp. 106 f.: 'observantes de la lei de Moisen', p. 112: 'Franisco Alvarez, portugués, Vecino de Priego, hábito i cárcel por seis meses.'

[13] Ibid., p. 113: 'Diego Alvarez, portugués, vecino de Andújar, hijo de Madre reconciliada por judía, estatua con hábito de reconciliada; Doña Ana Alvarez, vezina y natural de Aguilar, estatua con hábito de reconciliada.'

[14] Ibid., pp. 117 f: 'Isabel Alvarez, portuguesa, vecina de Andújar, que por ser tullida i ciega vino en una silla i le dieron hábito de aspa i abjuró de vehementi.' At the *auto-da-fé* celebrated at Córdoba on 3 May 1655 two other crypto-Jews, likewise members of an Alvarez family, were convicted: 'Doña Beatriz Alvarez, natural y vecina de la villa de Cabra, mujer de Diego Fernández Paez, confitero de veinte y seis años, por judaizante, salió reconciliada en forma con hábito i cárcel perpetua, i destierro de Cabra, Córdoba y Madrid, i ocho leguas en contorno.' One 'Diego Alvarez, Cajero de Manuel Núñez Bernal por seis años', was burned in effigy (p. 180). All were resident in the townlets of Andalusia, where the family of Alvares de Orobio was likewise domiciled; cf. Gracia Boix, pp. 403, 404, 440, 443.

[15] See below, chap. 4, p. 86.

viz. that crypto-Jews educate their children as Catholics 'until the age of twenty, and thereafter they quite fearlessly endeavour to induce the neophytes to submit themselves to circumcision and to embrace the law of Moses'.[16] However, on 15 January—a mere two days after the foregoing testimony—Baltazar confessed that he had begun to practise Jewish rites in 1632, i.e. at the approximate age of thirteen— the very age at which a Jewish boy takes upon himself the obligation to fulfil the commandments.[17] Furthermore, his physical examination by the doctors retained by the Seville Inquisition on 9 September 1654 found that Baltazar had been circumcised. One may therefore be justified in concluding that it was customary in the Alvares family to introduce sons into the Covenant of Abraham—which Judaism marks by circumcision on the eighth day after birth—at a tender age.[18] His parents, who had brought with them from Portugal a venerable tradition of dedicated adherence to the Jewish law, gave the young Baltazar the foundations of his Jewish education. At an early age he learned from his environment about the commandments and those Jewish

[16] *Israel Vengé* (based on Orobio, *Expl. Is. 53*), p. 233: 'Les perquisitions qu'on a toujours faites depuis leur conduite, les obligerent à se cacher de leur enfans qu'ils faisoient élever dans la Religion catholique jusqu'à l'âge de vingt ans après lequel tems les pères engageoint sans peine ces nouveaux convertis à se faire circoncire et à embrasser la loi de Moise.' Cf. Sokolow, p. 167.

[17] See below, chap. 4, p. 88. Certainly it was the custom amongst many crypto-Jews to reveal to their children their Jewish identity at the age of 13; cf. Roth, *Marranos*, pp. 173 f. Beinart is, however, nearer the truth in asserting (*on Trial*, p. 266) that for so decisive a step individual circumstances dictated the timing, as assessed by the parents and other relatives of the 'neophyte'. Some instances are attested of children being introduced to the secret of Jewish observance at a very early age; cf. Abraham Cardoso's Hebrew letter: 'when I was six years old my parents informed me that I was a Jew' (Bernheimer, p. 112).

[18] See Madrid, AHN, Inquisition section, Leg. 2987, f. 2ʳ (*Méritos del Dor. Don Balthasar de Orobio, Medico, de nazion portugues, vezino de la Çiudad de Cadiz):* 'En 9 de septiembre de dicho año de 1654 se hizo Inspecçión por los Medicos y Zirujano deste Santo Ofiçio que con juramento declararon que en la punta del prepuzio por la parte derecha inferior y por la parte de afuera tenia una zicatriz con perdimiento manifiesto de sustanzia, y en la parte inferior de afuera en la raiz del frenillo del mismo miembro viril otra çicatriz con perdimiento de sustanzia y en la cabeza de la glande en la parte derecha otra zicatriz longitudinal en la superfiçie de dicha substançia del miembro y asi su parezer asentado es segun en la persona tan sospechossa y sujeto que ez zeremonia judayca de çircunçission.' Regarding those who underwent circumcision whilst still leading a crypto-Jewish existence, cf. the *Responsa* of R. Joseph Moses Trani ('Maharit') *'Even ha-'ezer* 18: 'some put themselves at risk in getting themselves circumcised whilst in the lands of their enemies.' Regarding Jews who even during the 17th cent. were jeopardizing themselves by proceeding to Spain in order to circumcise crypto-Jews, see Beinart, *Yehudey Maroqo*, p. 26, and cf. Yerushalmi, *Isaac Cardoso*, p. 37 n. 54; cf. below, chap. 12, p. 335 f.

customs which were so sedulously maintained amongst crypto-Jews. We shall have occasion to fill in this picture at a later stage.[19]

UNIVERSITY STUDIES: OSUNA AND ALCALÁ

In the year 1633, at the approximate age of sixteen, Baltazar Alvares was registered as a medical student at the university of Osuna in Andalusia. This university had been founded on 8 December 1548 by Juan Téllez Girón, the fourth conde of Ureña, whose object had been to establish a university principally concerned with the education of needy scholars and those who had to depend on the patronage of others. Its original range of studies embraced theology, canon law, civil law and medicine; study of the arts was provided for only later, with the founding of an additional faculty.[20] Theological studies were entrusted to members of the Carmelite and Franciscan orders, who were extremely zealous in maintaining standards at the university: but in regard to the other faculties (including that of medicine), by the beginning of the seventeenth century standards of scholarship had fallen into decline.[21] 'One of the inmates of the Seville mad-house has been maintained there, at his relatives' expense, ever since he lost his sanity; he holds a degree in canon law—of Osuna.' So the barber informed Don Quixote, and Cervantes' subtly restrained irony would not have been lost on seventeenth-century readers.[22] Sancho Panza likewise speaks for Cervantes in directing scorn against the incompetence of an Osuna-trained physician.[23] The name of the university was a byword

---

[19] See below, chap. 2, pp. 42 f.

[20] On the history of the university of Osuna see Ajo de Zúñiga, ii, pp. 101 f.; Merry y Colón (generally); Beltrán de Heredia, pp. 145–73; Soledad Rubio, which contains (pp. 48 f.) a critical bibliography. Osuna and Gandia (near Valencia) were the only two universities in Spain founded by members of the nobility; see Kagan, *Universities*, p. 46. The faculty of arts was conventionally styled in Spain, as elsewhere, *artes liberales*.

[21] See Beltrán de Heredia, pp. 151 f.

[22] On Cervantes' attitude towards Osuna see Rodríguez Marín; Cervantes, *Don Quijote*, in *Obras Completas[16]*, Madrid, 1970, p. 1491.

[23] Cervantes, ibid., p. 1667: 'Yo, señor Gobernador, me llamo el doctor Pedro Recio de Agüero, y soy natural de un lugar llamado Tirteafuera, que está entre Caracuel y Almodóvar del Campo, a la mano derecha, y tengo el grado de doctor por la Universidad de Osuna. A lo que respondió Sancho, todo encendido en cólera: Pues, señor doctor Pedro Recio de Mal Agüero, natural de Tirteafuera, lugar que está a la derecha mano como vamos de Caracuel a Almodóvar del Campo, graduado en Osuna, quíteseme luego de delante; si no, voto al sol que tome un garrote y que a garrotazos, comenzando por él, no me ha de quedar médico en toda la ínsula, a lo menos, de aquellos que yo entienda que son ignorantes.' Some claim that Cervantes himself studied at Osuna, but Soledad Rubio, p. 50, casts grave doubt upon this.

for backwardness in the first half of the seventeenth century, although one of the leading neo-scholastics of the period, Gabriel Vásquez, had studied there and was himself chancellor of the university from 1624 to 1627.[24] Of the disorder characteristic of Osuna, and the degeneration of its standards of scholarship, we are informed by the memorandum prepared by the Franciscan Tomás Muñoz y Espinosa, who in addition to being himself a lecturer in the university was also one of the inquisitors at Córdoba. In 1627 he was asked by the Duke of Osuna (another Juan Téllez Girón) for his opinion regarding the way in which the university was run and the nature of the instruction that it offered. He presented his findings in 1631, after an investigation that had extended over four years.[25]

The medical faculty of Osuna at that time comprised two chairs, known respectively as *prima* (sc. first class) and *visperas* (sc. 'evening', i.e. afternoon class), attendance at which was obligatory on the student throughout four years. The first of these, held from 7.30 to 9 a.m., was devoted to the study of the corpus of Avicenna; the second, from 3 to 4 p.m. (during the winter months only),[26] to the *Art*[27] of Galen and the *Aphorisms* of Hippocrates. The other Spanish medical schools—those of the universities of Valladolid, Salamanca, Valencia, and (to some extent) Alcalá—by contrast opened their doors to the medical advances of the age: but the authorities of the university of Osuna were meticulous in preserving the traditional contents of medical education.[28] One of the results of the aforesaid Fray Tomás Muñoz' involvement was the institution of a third medical chair, for anatomy and surgery, but even after the introduction of these subjects to the medical curriculum instruction in them remained purely theoretical.[29]

Most of the student body at this period came from the cities of Andalusia, although enrolments were not lacking from as far away as Catalonia, Saragossa, Calahorra, Burgos, Santander, and Astorga.[30]

---

[24] Beltrán de Heredia, p. 163; cf. Soledad Rubio, p. 290.
[25] Soledad Rubio, pp. 73–7.
[26] This was ordained in §§21–2 of the statutes of the university of 1549; Soledad Rubio, pp. 354 f.
[27] [A Latin version of Hippocrates' *Aphorisms* was printed in 1473 was subsequently; a Greek, Latin, and Hebrew edition was published in Rome in 1647. By the *Art* of Galen is meant the *Ars parva micro Tegni*, of Hunein ibn Ishaq, translated into Latin by Gerard of Cremona and frequently called *Galeni ars medicinalis*. A Latin version was printed together with the Latin of Hippocrates' *Aphorisms*, etc. in Paris, 1539, etc. R.L.]
[28] Soledad Rubio, pp. 194 f.
[29] Ibid., p. 195.
[30] Soledad Rubio (fig. 12 at the end of the book) prints a map showing the localities whence the student body of Osuna came.

Students were divided into three groups. (*a*) The *colegiales*, i.e. those who were members of the colleges and enjoyed special privileges, receiving lodging and free commons from the college of their affiliation: these were regarded as being in a class of their own. (*b*) *Sopistas*, i.e. those in receipt of charitable subvention, numbering thirty-six in each year's intake: these, as their title indicates, were poor scholars and those dependent on patronage in whose interest the university had been founded. They were supported by the university authorities during term-time. (*c*) The ordinary students, who resided in rooming-houses, some of them being clerics from the religious houses in the vicinity. These were responsible for finding their own maintenance.[31] Baltazar Alvares will certainly have belonged to the third category. With the assistance of his uncle Mateo Rodríguez he was enrolled in the medical faculty of Osuna, giving it preference over the other Andalusian universities (e.g. Granada, Seville) because of its proximity to Málaga, where he lived.

The choice of medicine as a profession was characteristic among the youth of the crypto-Jewish community. The possibilities for 'New Christians' to integrate themselves into the public service, whether as governmental or municipal officials, or in the Church or the universities, were extremely tenuous, because of the ordinances for ensuring 'purity of blood' *(estatutos de limpieza de sangre)*, which discriminated severely against Christians of Jewish ancestry. Those who came from this background saw in the medical profession their one and only means of securing social advancement within the orbit of academic livelihood. In seventeenth- and eighteenth-century Spain medical studies had lost their capacity to attract recruits, largely because medicine had become labelled as a 'Jewish profession'.[32] Scions of the securely established classes preferred to study law—a discipline which offered them a foothold upon the ladder of the royal administration. Those who took up medicine came from the less well established segments of society, amongst them 'New Christians'.[33] This decline in the numbers of students opting for medicine meant that doctors were in great demand, and a 'New Christian' who took up the medical profession could count on a career and a livelihood.

Whilst Baltazar was at Osuna some 177 students were registered

[31] Ibid., pp. 141 f.
[32] See Kagan, *Universities*, p. 60. Regarding the enforcement of the statutes concerning 'blood-purity' in 16th- and 17th-cent. Spain see Sicroff, and cf. Dom. Ortiz, *Conversos*, pp. 26–50.   [33] Kagan, *Universities*, pp. 51 f.

From Portugal to Spain

there, only seventeen in the faculty of medicine as against eighty-two who were studying canon law.[34] Few details have been preserved concerning his time there since a sizeable portion of the university's archives have disappeared, including as it happens the main part of the documents relating to the years when Baltazar was a student.[35] All that survives concerning his personal studies is a letter of certification, dated 13 March 1638, which Baltazar laid before the authorities of the university of Alcalá, in the hope of being given credit by them for his earlier studies. This document, which bears the signature of Juan Bravo de Morales, registrar of Osuna between 1624 and 1657, is preserved in the archives of the university of Alcalá. Thanks to its contents we are in a position to reconstruct Baltazar's studies in one of the southernmost universities of Spain in the years 1633–5. It states that Baltazar Alvares had been registered for two years in the Osuna faculty of medicine, first from 1 October 1633 to the end of the academic year on 18 April 1634, and then again for his second-year course between the analogous dates 1634–5. During these two years' study he had attended classes of the *prima* and *visperas* (see above, p. 9), as well as anatomy-with-surgery, and he had participated 'in the majority of lectures in conformity with the statutes of the university'.[36] In this document Málaga is given as his birthplace rather than

[34] Kagan, *Students*, p. 234. The figures given here are for 1630, but it may be assumed that they will not have been materially different in the years 1633–5 when Baltazar Alvares was a student at Osuna. In 1625 students in the medical faculty had numbered 21 as against 103 reading canon law, out of a total student body of 240 in that year. So steep a drop in intake over a 5-year period underscores the critical phase through which the university of Osuna was then passing.

[35] See Beltrán de Heredia, pp. 145 f., and esp. Soledad Rubio, pp. 45 f., 219 f.

[36] The Alcalá archives have been transferred to Madrid, AHN, see universities section, Alcalá 495F, at the end of the academic year 1637/8 (unpaginated): 'Yo el doctor Joan Bravo de Morales notario ap[odera]do: y secretario del mui insigne Collegio Maior y Unibersidad de la Limpia y Pura Concepçion de N[uest]ra Señora en esta billa de Osuna doy por berdadero testimonio a lo quel Presente bieren como el bachiller don Baltasar Alvarez de Orobio natural de Malaga, dioçesis eius dem tiene probado aber cursado en esta dicha Unibersidad el Prim[er]o curso en la Facultad de Mediçina siendo matriculado en prim[er]o de otubre de mill y seisçientos y treinta y tres años hasta diez y ocho dias del mes de abril de mil y seisçientos y treinta y quatro y el segundo curso en la dicha Facultad de Mediçina siendo matriculado en prim[er]o de otubre de mil y seisçientos y treinta y quatro años hasta diez y ocho de abril de seisçientos y treinta y çinco oyendo de los lectibos tres lecçiones, prima, bisperas y anatomia y çirugia, la maior parte de oras cada lecçion conforme a las constituçiones de esta dicha Unibersidad lo qual probo con Ju[li]o de Luque y con Miguel de Fuente sus condiçipulos que lo juraron en forma de dicho y lo firmaron en el registro de pruebas que queda en mi poder a que me refiero para que conste dello de Pedim[ien]to del suso dicho de este en la dicha Unibersidad en treze dias del mes de março de mil y seis çientos y treinta y ocho y se lo firme i signé. doctor Joan Brauo de Morales, notario.'

Braganza, and it is to be supposed that Baltazar preferred to conceal his Portuguese origins. During these years in Spain, Portuguese origins meant one thing only—membership of the community of 'New Christians', i.e. crypto-Jews, who had been escaping in hordes to Spain since the end of the sixteenth century, and were avoided and regarded with suspicion by 'old Christians'.[37]

It seems clear that Baltazar would also have studied arts at Osuna, since any student intending to read medicine there was required first to receive a bachelor of arts degree.[38] As we shall see below, Baltazar received his licentiate degree in arts at Alcalá as early as 1636, i.e. immediately on completion of his first year there. It is therefore a fair assumption that he left Osuna with his bachelor of arts degree from that university. As a student in the arts faculty of Osuna he would have been obliged during his first year to study logic according to the *Summulæ* of Fray Domingo de Soto (1494–1560), the *Introduction*[39] of Jacobus Faber (Jacques le Fèvre) and the *Prædicabilia*[40] of Porphyry; and in the second year, Aristotle's *'Predicaments'* (i.e. *Categories*), followed by Faber's *topicorum et elenchorum*.[41] He would likewise have had to attend lectures on Duns Scotus by the professor of philosophy, whose chair bore Scotus' name.[42]

It is not clear what induced the eighteen-year-old Baltazar to break off his studies at Osuna and to matriculate in 1635 in Castile at the university of Alcalá de Henares. One may assume that he was influenced on the one hand by the mediocre academic standards at the

---

[37] See below, pp. 18 f. The various writers who accepted that Orobio was born in Málaga are listed above, n. 1. Regarding the stream of crypto-Jews reaching Spain from Portugal, see above, n. 5.

[38] See Soledad Rubio, pp. 207 f.

[39] *Introductiones in diversos Aristotelis libros* (including the *Praedicabilia*), Paris, 1520.

[40] i.e. on Aristotle's Organon: *Organum ... Porphyrii communium quinque vocum sive praedicabilium liber*, Venice, 1564 (and earlier).

[41] [Presumably we should understand Jacques Le Fèvre's commentary to the two Aristotelian treatises *Libri Topicorum* (edn. 1520 f. 208ʳ) and *Elenchorum Sophisticorum* (f. 253ʳ). R.L.]

[42] Soledad Rubio, p. 354, regarding the university statutes §19. The chair of philosophy was not instituted until 1557, and was only subsequently styled the Scotus Chair, apparently under the influence of Alcalá; see ibid., pp. 207 f. The syllabus here given was characteristic of most of the Spanish universities; cf. Yerushalmi, *Isaac Cardoso*, p. 77, for the syllabus of the arts faculty of Valladolid. In his *Cart. Apol.* (MS Paris, BN Fonds éspagnoles 41, p. 880) Orobio records his own interest in Scotus ('Para esto vi mucho en Thomas, muchissimo en Scoto (particular en sus sentencias)'). If, after studying in the faculty of arts, Baltazar proceeded bachelor in 1635, there is reason to assume that he will have matriculated as a freshman no later than 1632: possibly he was registered in the medical faculty after completing a first year in arts.

From Portugal to Spain

university of Osuna, and on the other by the reputation enjoyed by the university of Alcalá—a reputation that became somewhat dimmed in the seventeenth century, though that institution had been rapidly acknowledged as one of the most important centres of enlightenment and intellectual creativity in the Iberian peninsula after its foundation in 1498 by Cardinal Francisco Ximenes de Cisneros.[43]

Baltazar's name first figures on the rolls of the university of Alcalá on 18 October 1635, amongst those registered for medical studies.[44] Elsewhere he appears as number forty-seven in a list of fifty-nine candidates for the licentiate in arts.[45] Alongside his medical work he was registered for a course in theology. His studies were crowned with success, and in 1636, having received his licentiate in arts, he was registered for an additional year in the faculty of medicine.[46]

In this same year Baltazar was admitted to one of the theological schools of the university. This school, known as Madre de Dios, was one of the eighteen smaller institutions operating as satellites of the principal college of Alcalá, which bore the name of San Idelfonso.[47] For the most part these smaller houses were intended for indigent students, the custom being that elections for places in them were left to the student body of the principal college.[48] Baltazar Alvares was elected on 20 April 1636, taking the place of Jacinto de Almazán, a student who had graduated.[49] Baltazar might have enjoyed the support of another 'New Christian' who had preceded him at the same little

---

[43] Strictly speaking, the foundation-stone was laid in 1498, but instruction did not commence until the autumn of 1509: on 22 January 1510 the first statutes of the university were drawn up. See Bataillon, pp. 11 f. For the decline of Alcalá, see Ajo de Zúñiga, iii, pp. 293–305. A special committee set up by the rector on 7 May 1623 summarized the causes leading to the university's parlous state, and the consequent steep decline in its student numbers, under 4 heads: (*a*) numerous epidemics affecting the locality because of its severe climatic conditions—intensity of heat and humidity—occasioned a high mortality rate in the city (500 per annum, mostly students); (*b*) soaring prices, which 'nowhere else in these kingdoms have risen to such proportions'; (*c*) the city having become a place of refuge for members of the underworld who, escaping from Madrid, were terrorizing university personnel; and (*d*) riots in the city, aimed at the rector and his university staff, in the course of which many students had been killed.

[44] Madrid, AHN, universities section, Alcalá Matrículas 448F, f. 56^v: 'Mediçi[na] ... En dies y ocho dias del mes de octubre D. Valtazar Alvarez, de Málaga, 18 años.'

[45] Ibid., f. 73^r.

[46] Ibid., 494F, f. 31^r, 495F (for 1636/7, unpaginated); cf. Révah, *rupt. spin., nouvel examen*, 71, pp. 582 f.

[47] Madrid, AHN (n. 44 above), 1046F, f. 34, cf. Révah, loc. cit.

[48] On the principal and minor colleges at Alcalá de Henares see Rújula de Ochotorena, pp. vii f.; Lascaris Comneno, pp. xi–xxix. On schools within the university in Spain generally at this period, see Kagan, *Students*, pp. 109–58.

[49] See Révah, *rupt. spin., nouvel examen*, 71, pp. 582 f.

college, Juan de Prado, who had himself been a student at Madre de Dios in 1633–5.⁵⁰ Prado later attained notoriety, for he was one of those excommunicated as 'heretics' by the congregation of Portuguese Jews in Amsterdam. It is probable that Baltazar had been acquainted with Prado even before attending the faculty of Alcalá. Both were sons of Portuguese crypto-Jewish families who had settled in Andalusia; and even whilst engaged in controversy with Prado in Amsterdam, Orobio did not neglect to mention the help which the latter had afforded him in his youth.⁵¹ They succeeded first in gaining admission to Madre de Dios and then in evading the investigations into racial purity that were normal in all the colleges of the university of Alcalá.⁵²

The annual intake of the college of Madre de Dios was twenty-four students, eighteen of whom read theology and six medical science.⁵³ Baltazar was one of these medical students, his name figuring on the student roll until the academic year 1640/1.⁵⁴ The curriculum was identical with that in the main university, save that students in the smaller colleges were obliged to go over what they had learned in university lectures and to deepen their grasp of the subject with the aid of senior students and professors who made themselves available to them. All courses at Alcalá opened on the feast of St Luke, patron saint of physicians (18 October), and continued until April. From five in the morning every day the students went over their university work, until at eight o'clock they joined the remainder of the medical faculty at the *prima* class. During the midday break they would go over the lecture in their chambers, and one of them would read aloud a chapter from whatever book had been selected by the rector. After the midday meal an hour was allowed for recreation, at the end of which they would

⁵⁰ For Prado's studies at Alcalá see below, chap. 6, p. 125.
⁵¹ See *Cart. Apol.* (MS Paris, see above n. 42), p. 876; cf. below, chap. 6 n. 51.
⁵² See Rújula de Ochotorena, pp. xxix f. The colleges at Spanish universities were, in point of fact, the first to institute investigations as to 'blood purity' within their walls, the earliest of all being the College of S. Bartolomé in Salamanca, which conducted such investigations from its very beginnings in 1414–18. In the main school at Alcalá, that of S. Idelfonso, investigations were conducted on 9 Aug. 1519. It seems clear that the statutes regarding *limpieza de sangre* will have been insisted upon likewise in the minor college at which Orobio was a student. At any rate, the deed of amalgamation of six of the minor colleges at Alcalá, including that of Madre de Dios, dated 13 Mar. 1779, refers explicitly to the statutes of *limpieza de sangre* as having full force.
⁵³ Rújula de Ochotorena, p. xviii.
⁵⁴ Madrid, AHN, universities section, Alcalá 1046F, ff. 34ᵛ, 37ᵛ, 40ʳ, 42ᵛ, 44ᵛ, 46ʳ, 49ʳ, 52ʳ, 53ᵛ, 55ᵛ, 61ᵛ, 62ᵛ, 63ʳ, 67ᵛ, 74ᵛ, 77ʳ⁻ᵛ, and 448F (unpaginated), roll of students registered for 1636–9.

From Portugal to Spain 15

proceed to take part in the *visperas* class. At the end of the day's teaching programme there was another short interval, and then students had to attend their various college chapels; they would then retire to rooms where they would study until nine o'clock at night. After their meal they were expected to gather for discussion with the rector or course-leader until ten, and at the conclusion of this session they would retire to bed in their cubicles. Once or twice a week a discussion would be scheduled at which one of the students would deliver a discourse on some subject specified in advance by the rector, at the end of which he had to respond to questions put by his teachers and fellow-students.[55]

This was the rigorous regimen under which the young Baltazar passed his adolescent years, moulding his mind and spirit. Like the rest of his fellow-students, he held forth on the medical topics which were prescribed for him and gave expositions on theological and philosophical subjects.[56] Together with his contemporaries, he was present when high mass was said in the college chapel; and like them, he went to confession, took part in religious ceremonies, and, in accordance with the custom ordained by the college, took his exercise by going for walks in the company of one other student.[57] Baltazar's medical studies progressed, and, having obtained his certificate from Osuna, he passed the successive examinations that marked each stage of his course—the first, second, and third principal topics—*en route* to his graduation as a licentiate in medicine.[58]

THE PLAGUE AT MÁLAGA, 1637: BALTAZAR ALVARES' ACCOUNT

To these years belong Baltazar Alvares' earliest literary venture. In the year 1637 at Málaga, where his family was living, there was a serious outbreak of plague which claimed many victims. Baltazar composed a poetical account of it running to sixty-five octets, which was printed in the same year under the title *Epílogo de lo que passó en la peste de la ciudad de Málaga este año de 1637*.[59] As a student at the university of Alcalá still

[55] See Rújula de Ochotorena, p. xviii.
[56] See Madrid, AHN (n. 54 above), 1046F. Thus e..g. in 1637 Orobio discoursed on Aristotle, *Physics*, v (f. 37ʳ).   [57] Rújula de Ochotorena, p. x.
[58] Révah, *rupt. spin., nouvel examen*, 71, pp. 582 f.
[59] Orobio, *Peste Mál.*, repr. below, Appendix B, from Kaplan, *peste de Málaga*. It was printed in 1637 by Juan Serrano de Vargas y Urueña. To date, only one copy has been

in his twenties he begins with an encomium on his Alma Mater, the college of Madre de Dios.[60]

From Baltazar's vivid description, which is of historical significance in view of its wealth of detail, it may be gathered that he was a first-hand witness of the tribulations to which Málaga was subjected whilst the plague was raging. One may surmise that he was resident there at the time, perhaps being unwilling to leave his family on their own at a time when the city was exposed to such great danger.[61] He already had behind him four years of medical studies, and one may assume that he had opportunities to assist the physicians in their attendance on patients. The poem is replete with information about hospital practice at the time, arguing for much contact on his part with what was actually happening in the infirmaries during the plague.[62]

Spain suffered severely from attacks of the plague during the seventeenth century. A number of factors contributed to this, the most important being the languishing state of the economy which meant that most of the population was living on a sub-standard diet. This does more than anything else to explain the lethal character of the outbreaks which affected the Iberian peninsula at this period. To it must be added the contemporary conditions of hygiene, which had then reached their nadir in most parts of Spain.[63]

Baltazar's poem provides excellent evidence regarding the plight of this Andalusian city during the plague. He begins with a sketch of its outbreak, the first casualties, its contagiousness, and the measures adopted to stem its advance. At first there was some uncertainty about what was occurring, but at the death of the first victims rumours began to run wild through the city populace.[64] Orobio gives a detailed description of the food shortage during the plague and of everything that followed in its wake.[65] The poem also describes the reaction of the

---

traced, in the library of the Hispanic Society of America, New York. Révah was the first to draw attention to its existence, see *rupt. spin.*, *nouvel examen*, 70, p. 568. The poem consists of octaves of 11-syllable lines, rhyming *a b a b a b c c*: this scheme, known as the *Octava Real* or *Octava Heroica*, and originating in 15th–16th-cent. Italy (*ottava rima*) was introduced to Spain by Boscán and Garcilaso.

[60] The first two stanzas, forming the dedication (see p. 387 f.), are *Liras* (cf. l. 16 'Inculta Lyra, à descrivir se atreve') of 11 and 7 syllables, interchanging at the whim of the writer, and with a rhyme-scheme different from that of the octaves.

[61] On the plague at Málaga see Hernández Morejón, v, p. 63, who however dates it in 1636. [62] See Appendix B, ff. 3ʳ, 7ʳ⁻ᵛ, 8ʳ⁻ᵛ, 9ʳ, 12ʳ.

[63] See Vinces Vives, pp. 394 f.; Lynch, ii, p. 147; J. Reglá, 'La Época de los dos últimos Austrias', in J. Vinces Vives (ed.), *Historia de España y América*, Barcelona, 1961, iii, p. 261.   [64] f. 2ʳ, ll. 9–16.   [65] f. 3ʳ, ll. 1 f.

From Portugal to Spain

townsfolk as the plague spread, and how they subjected their actions to the scrutiny of conscience and took to conducting themselves in a subdued manner of exaggerated humility.[66]

The Conde le la Rosa stood at the head of the municipal administration, giving support to those who turned to him in their hour of need. Nor did he shrink from exposing himself to the risks involved in coming into contact with those affected.[67] A special dispensary was established for distributing medicines and food,[68] and similarly a fund was organized for coping with the poverty which afflicted the bulk of the population. It would seem that the conde himself headed the fund.[69]

The *regidores*, i.e. members of the city council, 'moved by considerations of Christian charity' concerned themselves with everything which afforded some means of alleviating the sufferings of the townspeople.[70] Great indeed was their distress: the sick left in hospital isolated from parents, children, and kinsfolk who, fearful of coming into contact with the disease, forbore to visit them; husbands fleeing their homes and abandoning their wives as they lay dying; and refugees from the city returning from the countryside infected by the plague, and throwing themselves upon the mercy of heaven.[71]

In his account of an incident that took place in Málaga Baltazar opens a window on the strained relations then obtaining in the city between Christians and the residual Moorish population. A Muslim woman decided to accept baptism in the hope that doing so would keep her safe from the plague. Another Moor happened to be present when the priest was preparing himself to perform the sacramental rite, and attempted to get the woman away from him. The cries of the priest on finding himself being assaulted excited the fury of the Christian rabble, who proceeded to fall upon the Moors in the city, attacking and killing many of them. This account confirms what was previously known from other sources, that even after the Moors had been compelled to turn Christian in 1502 and the *moriscos* had been expelled in 1609, there was still a Muslim element in the Spanish population. Quite apart from those *moriscos* who had remained despite the edict of

---

[66] f. 2ᵛ, ll. 19–24.
[67] f. 3ʳ, ll. 17 f.
[68] f. 3ᵛ, l. 7. When, as the plague continued to spread, it became clear that a single infirmary was insufficient, the Conde set up an additional one, see f. 9ʳ, ll. 17 f.
[69] f. 3ʳ, l. 6.
[70] f. 3ᵛ, ll. 17 f.
[71] f. 3 v, ll. 9–14, see also f. 4ʳ, ll. 17–24.

expulsion (many of whom made no bones about their continued adherence to Islam), there were also to be found prisoners of war, Berbers, and other Muslims who had been reduced to slavery. Some of these last had succeeded in manumitting themselves and thus becoming free residents; and it seems likely that such was the status of the Moors mentioned in Orobio's poem.[72]

Nor was this the end of Málaga's calamities. Suspicion gave rise to a rumour that ran through the local Christian population to the effect that a Moorish-owned galley, apparently out of some North African port, had been equipped to set Málaga ablaze and so destroy the city. Once again passions and the lust for vengeance swept through the town's demoralized mob, many of whom formed bands of vigilantes to frustrate the danger allegedly lurking offshore.[73]

The poem is not without a 'Portuguese' motif. On the very day that a galley was being fitted out to meet the supposed Moorish threat, a group of Portuguese were getting ready to leave port and return to the country of their birth. No sooner were they aboard than they were overpowered by local assailants, i.e. Castilians, who plundered their property and subjected a number of them to bodily assault.[74] When news of the outrage reached the ears of the Conde he had two of the marauders hanged and the rest of them flogged.[75] One may well speculate as to just who these 'Portuguese' were. As a result of the substantial tide of emigration of the so-called 'New Christians', i.e. crypto-Jews from Portugal to Spain in the seventeenth century, the term 'Portuguese' came to be used in Spanish as the equivalent of 'Jew'.[76] And it cannot be doubted that the group of *Lusitanos* whose misfortunes were recounted by Baltazar, writing self-consciously as a student of the Castilian university of Alcalá, was none other than a group of crypto-Jews of Portuguese origin that had settled in southern Spain exactly as had the family of Alvares de Orobio at the beginning of the seventeenth century. Baltazar's entire sympathy is on the side of the Conde who had asserted the rule of law and punished the excesses

---

[72] ff. 4ᵛ, ll. 9–24, 5ʳ, ll. 5–8. Regarding the expulsion of the *moriscos* from Spain see Lapeyre, *passim*, and Elliot, *Spain*, pp. 305 f. For the evasion of the expulsion order by numerous *moriscos* who remained in Spain see Lapeyre, pp. 209 f. For the presence of Berbers in Andalusia and particularly in Seville, see Dom. Ortiz and Ag. Piñal, pp. 46 f.

[73] ff. 4ᵛ, 5ᵛ.

[74] f. 5ᵛ, ll. 9–21.

[75] f. 6ʳ, ll. 1–5.

[76] See Yerushalmi, *Issac Cardoso*, pp. 10 f.; Herrero García, pp. 137 f.; Beinart, *Conversos*, p. 474.

of the mob. In his account of the 'Portuguese' to whom he refers, nowhere does he mention their connection with the 'New Christian' community, and to be sure there is not the slightest hint in what he writes at any Judaizing activity amongst them. Despite this, there can hardly be a shadow of a doubt that the attack on this alien group at the time of the plague has to be seen against the background of the struggle against the 'Moorish infidel'. This struggle, which aroused the religious passions of the local Christian rabble against all those suspected of heresy, was directed, it would seem, also against the 'Portuguese'. Furthermore, the presumption of a link between war against the Moor and the outrage perpetrated against the *Lusitanos* is rendered the more plausible by Baltazar's choice of language in the poem, whence it appears that the attack on the Portuguese was carried out on the very day that the galley set sail to engage the enemy at sea.[77]

There is nothing surprising in the circumstance that Baltazar refrained from implying any connection between the causes of the struggle against the Moors and the riotous onslaught on the Portuguese. Such a thing could only serve to complicate his own situation by raising questions as to any link on his part with the 'New Christians'. As a student in one of the theological colleges at Alcalá, a college moreover in which the writ of the ordinances regarding *limpieza de sangre* ran unquestioned, it is doubtful whether Baltazar could have permitted himself to give vent to his feelings any more openly, since such expressions could have been construed as implying that his own origins were identical with theirs. But it seems clear to me that it is precisely his silence on the subject, in the very years when we are informed of his lively attachment to the Judaism that he was secretly practising in the bosom of his family, which furnishes a key to our understanding of the author's situation as a crypto-Jew living simultaneously in two worlds—making a parade of his Christianity in public, whilst covertly maintaining his links with his own persecuted and execrated community. The poem is part of the public face of Baltazar the university student, but between the lines we may catch a glimpse of his position *qua* crypto-Jew: his feelings of compassion for the sufferings endured by the 'Portuguese' at the time of the plague, and the sympathetic view that he takes of them as constituting a group on their own, are part and parcel of this. In order to forestall any suspicions on the part of the Inquisition (for whose accusations of heresy he

---

[77] f. 5ᵛ, l. 9: 'Quando unos Lusitanos este dia . . .'

was, in virtue of his origins, himself a potential candidate), he does not stint his praise of Christianity or his adulation of its priesthood. Right through the poem he refers to the devotion evinced by both secular and enclosed clergy, who were risking their lives in the attempt to save the masses from the great peril which threatened the city. The bishop lent his support to the Conde in looking after those ridden by the disease;[78] the local cathedral chapter dispatched two emissaries to bring aid to those in need;[79] the Capuchins did not flinch from danger in the face of death but distributed charity to the poor, eighteen of their order actually dying in the infirmary in the course of bringing succour to victims of the plague.[80] Likewise the Carmelites.[81] As priests fell victims to the disease themselves, others came forward to take their place in holding out a hand to the sick.[82] Nor does Baltazar omit to mention the mystical power hidden in the consecrated bread of communion.[83] He waxes eloquent about the wave of religious sentiment that took hold of the inhabitants of Málaga, who set up street altars to Mary the Mother of Jesus in her character as 'Mother of Mercy'.[84] The couplets which he devotes to St Bernard and to St Francis of Assisi, whose intercession brought the terrible scourge to an end, are imbued with an air of faith uncompromised by doubt.[85] On the day of the feast of St Anne the city could at last breathe freely, thanks to the supplications made by the saint to Jesus, her own grandson.[86] And it was on the day of 'the holy virgin, the mother undefiled' that the first infirmary to have been opened during the emergency could be closed—a circumstance which in itself symbolized the survival of Málaga from this most terrible of visitations of the plague.[87]

The King of Spain (Philip IV) also merits praise on account of the great things that he did for casualties amongst the citizenry. At a time when he was financially hard pressed to find money for his military operations he nevertheless contributed 30,000 ducats to the indigent of the city and those affected by the disease; and amidst their own calamities the whole population expressed their thanks to him for his action.[88] Whilst the city was licking its wounds and its life was gradually returning to normal, attempts were made to calculate the number of

---

[78] f. 7ʳ, l. 16.   [79] f. 7ᵛ, ll. 17-24.   [80] ff. 8ʳ, ll. 13 f., 8ᵛ. ll. 9–10.
[81] f. 8ᵛ, ll. 17–18.   [82] f. 8ᵛ, ll. 1–8.
[83] f. 8ʳ, ll. 17–18; 'El Pan divino . . .'   [84] f. 10ᵛ, l. 17–11ʳ.
[85] ff. 11ʳ, ll. 19 f. (St Bernard), 11ᵛ, ll. 1 f. (St Francis).
[86] f. 12ʳ, ll. 1 f. The feast of St Anne falls on 26 July.
[87] f. 12ʳ, ll. 17–20. The reference is to 15 Aug. i.e. the feast of the Assumption.
[88] ff. 6ʳ, l. 17–6ᵛ, l. 8.

From Portugal to Spain 21

the plague's victims. Some estimated the dead at 15–16,000, but many claimed that the total was much higher.[89]

This poem by Baltazar Alvares is rich in detail that reveals much concerning the customs and beliefs that were current amongst the Christian populace during the plague. Frequently at night religious processions would be held, those participating in them beating themselves with thorns, whilst many others bound themselves with cords, and others again crept along upon their knees.[90]

How are we to understand this poem? Was Baltazar truly overwhelmed by the exigencies of the epidemic, or must the poem be taken as a deliberate piece of camouflage, intended to present its author as a Christian of unwavering devotion to his faith? Is it, in fact, no more than a mask, whose purpose was to conceal the true identity of Baltazar the crypto-Jew? Doubtless the answer to this question must be in the affirmative: the prominence of the Christian imagery with which the *epílogo* is replete leaves no room for any alternative explanation.[91] However, it does seem to me that in one passage the young Baltazar, aware of himself as a university student, is summoning the conscience of the city and of the Christian community within it to account:

> La Causa inmensa, y Causa no causada,
> por delitos humanos ofendida,
> pretende a esta Ciudad, ya dessolada,
> dar con justicia mas constante vida:
> y en medio de sus gustos olvidada
> de quien la busca, quando mas perdida;
> rigorosa permite, que influencia
> castigue tanto error con pestilencia.[92]

The author here claims—unambiguously, and, so to speak, *ex cathedra*—that the plague by which the city of Málaga had been afflicted was an act of God in punishment of the sin of its inhabitants. And in order to make it quite clear to what sins he is alluding, Orobio makes use of the word *error*, i.e. perverse opinion. At the period with which we are concerned *error* generally meant perversity of religious opinion, and in Catholic Spain it is often used as a virtual synonym of

[89] f. 12ᵛ, ll. 5–6.
[90] f. 6ᵛ, ll. 9–20.
[91] Cf. Révah, *rupt. spin.*, *nouvel examen*, 70, p. 568: 'nous avons soigneusement étudié cet exercise littéraire typiquement marranique dont l'auteur avait alors dix-neuf ans. Il va sans dire que le poème aurait pu être signé par le plus fervent devôt du Christ, de la Vierge et de tous les Saints, par la fidèle le plus soumis de l'Église catholique.'
[92] f. 2ᵛ, ll. 1–8.

heresy or sectarianism.[93] In precise analogy to this usage it is likewise found in the apologetic writings of the Sephardi Jews of western Europe in the seventeenth century, mainly to indicate what, in the Jewish view, constitutes the perverseness of the Christian religion.[94] Some thirty years later, after Baltazar had reverted to Judaism in Amsterdam and had changed his name to Isaac Orobio, he would write:

en los cinco libros de la Ley, como en los Propheticos se advirtio contra los *errores* de la gentilidad, y muy particularmente del Christianismo.[95]

Was it the perversity of opinion inherent in Christianity itself that Baltazar was alluding to when he wrote in his poem on the plague at Málaga that it was because of her perseverance therein that God had brought punishment to bear as it were on the whole city? Remarkably, this is one of the few stanzas in the whole poem in which Baltazar uses a concept of the Deity that is innocent of any Christian symbolism involving the incarnation. God is here referred to as *Causa causarum*: and it is apparently no coincidence that the author here prefers this expression to the conventional Christian formulas which he does not hesitate to employ in other passages of the poem.[96] Possibly he does so in order to distinguish what he is saying in his peroration, as being concerned with the true God and consequently itself true, from what is said in other passages, where, through force of circumstances peculiar to his own life, Baltazar had concealed himself behind beliefs that were not in fact his own. Perhaps there is here the faintest of hints at his own

---

[93] This likewise conforms to Spanish usage of the 15th cent. A number of documents refer to the *errores* of the 'New Christians', e.g. Pedro Sarmiento's indictment of crypto-Jews in Toledo on 5 June 1449: 'e parece evidentemente ser personas muy sospechosas en la santa fe catholica de tener e creer grandissimos errores contra los articulos de la santa fe catholica' (Baer, *Christ. Span.*, ii, p. 316). Inquisitional documents contain the same term, e.g. Beinart, *Ciudad Real*, i, p. 71 (trial of María Gonzales): 'e yo nunca quise yr con el, temiendo que me faria beuir en el error que beuia.' See S. de Covarrubias, *Tesoro de la lengua española o castellana*, ed. M. de Riquer, Barcelona, 1943, p. 531, s.v. *errar*: 'yo pecador mucho errado.'

[94] See e.g. the *Contra Christianos* by a Marrano (Halkin, p. 412): 'Vean aquy vmds., como apartandose de la Ley de Dios y de lo que ella manda, todos van errados.' Already in the 15th cent. crypto-Jews were using *error* as a term to describe the deviations which they identifed as characteristic of Christianity. See e.g. the prayer quoted by Mencia Suares of Ocaña, who was tried by the Inquisition at Toledo in 1487–90: 'Ca a ti, sennor, digo mi culpa e propongo, sennor, en mi coraçon de non errar contra ti de aqui adelante e de fazer emienda de lo que he errado ...'(Baer, *Christ. Span.*, ii, p. 482).

[95] See Orobio, *Prev. Div.*, MS Amsterdam, *EH* 48 D 6, f. 287^r.

[96] ff. 5^r, 8^r–^{v}, 10^v, 11^r, 12^r, where occur such expressions as *sacro Pan, Pan divino, Olio y Dios Sacramentado, Madre de Piedad, nieto Dios en carne humana*, etc.

From Portugal to Spain 23

deep-seated psychological bond with what is stated in this stanza, viz. that the plague at Málaga was the divine visitation on a city steeped in iniquity—a city whose sin consisted in her adherence to a religion that was essentially corrupt.

If this conjecture could be substantiated, we could assert that despite the mask that circumstances compelled him to wear, the young Alcalá student succeeded in giving expression to some part of those sentiments locked away in his heart regarding the Christianity amid which he perforce lived his life, and to the religious values to which he was constrained to represent himself as being loyally devoted.

During the years 1638–40 Baltazar was still a student at the college of Madre de Dios.[97] In the college list of lectures and expositions there are recorded the subjects on which he had been directed to prepare discourses in the academic year of 1640/1; but his signature is missing, and his name is not mentioned amongst the students who were actively participating in their programme of studies.[98] There is a further significant lacuna: Baltazar's name is likewise missing from the roll of students who were actually registered as being in residence for that academic year. It looks very much as though Baltazar Alvares had left Alcalá by the spring of 1640, before receiving his licentiate in medicine. The cause of his sudden departure was not connected with any lack of progress in his university studies. The rumour had reached his ears that a certain 'New Christian' had denounced his parents and some of his other kinsfolk to the inquisitional authorities, testifying to Judaizing behaviour on their part. The halter of the Holy Office was beginning to close round the neck of the Orobio family: and in an institution which was meticulous in its application of the ordinances regarding *limpieza de sangre* his position could no longer be regarded as assured.[99]

---

[97] In 1638 Baltazar gave evidence on behalf of his fellow-student Francisco Sibiller, whose documents of registration for the academic year 1637/8 had got lost. See Madrid, AHN, univerisities section, Alcalá 449F, at the end of the course-list for 1634/5 (unpaginated).

[98] See ibid., 1046F, report for 1640/1, f. 74ᵛ: 'Don Baltasar de Orobio eligira una de las materias siguientes: de sanguinis missione, de ratione virtus statuenda in morbis acutis, etc'; also f. 77ᵛ: 'Elecçion de Oraçiones de los Sres Medicos . . . Sr. Don Baltasar eligio del jazmin y lo firmó.'

[99] It is to be noted that the editor of the register of students of the College of Madre de Dios between 1543 and 1777 omitted the name of Baltazar Alvares, being aware of his origins and of his having been investigated by an inquisitional tribunal in 1654–6. See Révah, *rupt. spin., nouvel examen*, 71, p. 583, and cf. Rújula de Ochotorena, p. 300.

We may mention at this point that a number of writers state that Baltazar studied at

Salamanca. Amelander, who writes (in Yiddish) that he became there a master in theology (f. 133ᵛ), follows Basnage (see above, n. 1). Cf. Rodríguez de Castro, i, pp. 605 f.; R. Landau, *Geschichte der jüdischen Ärzte*, Berlin, 1895, p. 81; Carvalho, p. 91; Amzalak, *Resp. Pred. franc.*, p. x; A. d'Esaguy, *Médicine Hébraique*, ii, 1948, p. 16. Others have asserted that Baltazar actually taught at Salamanca: Koenen, p. 189; Landau, loc. cit.; S. Kagan, *Jewish Medicine*, Boston, 1952, p. 132, etc. Baltazar Orobio neither studied nor taught at Salamanca at any time, and the statements of those here cited to that effect lack all foundation. [It may, however, be noted in passing that of the medical students at Salamanca during the 16th cent. bearing the family name *Alvarez* 7 originated from Braganza, and a Pedro Vaez de Castro also came from there. The published register stops at 1600 (Teresa Santander [Rodríguez], *Escolares Médicos en Salamanca (Siglo XVI)*, Salamanca, 1984). R.L.]

2
A Long Brush with the Inquisition, 1639–1643

In December 1639 testimony was laid before the Inquisition in Valdepeñas, a small township to the south-east of Almagro. The witness who deposed it was Pedro Rodríguez, alias Manuel Sarmiento, a crypto-Jew who had previously been restored to the bosom of the church by reconciliation. He had been born at Dax, in southern France, around 1617 to a family of 'New Christians' that had escaped thither from the Portuguese Inquisition, and it seems probable that this family was distantly connected with that of Baltazar Alvares. Sarmiento had, in his youth, crossed the border into Spain and had settled at Valdepeñas, but he was also an occasional resident in nearby Manzanares.[1] In his deposition made before the Holy Office he brought to notice the Judaizing activities of upwards of ten members of the Alvares family: Manuel Alvares, father of Baltazar, and Manuel's brother[2] Santiago Luis; Violante de Paz, wife of Santiago Luis, and five of their six children;[3] José de Castro, brother of Violante, Isabel Luis (a cousin of Manuel Alvares) and her husband Andrés de Narváez. As a consequence, the inquisitional court of Toledo in 1640

---

[1] For Sarmiento see Révah, *rupt. spin., nouvel examen*, 71, pp. 586 f., and the evidence of Gonzalo Luis before the Toledo tribunal on 5 June 1640, Madrid, AHN, Inquisition section, Leg. 163 no. 14, f. 14ʳ: 'Manuel Sarmiento, primo hermano de su madre' (sc. Violante de Paz); cf. ibid., f. 2ʳ, 'que como abia salido niño de França', as well as the evidence (ibid., f. 5ʳ) before the same court of José de Castro on 8 Feb. 1640: 'y declara que ansimismo en la çiudad de Berganza abra tres años poco mas o menos se declaro con Manuel Sarmiento pariente deste que bibe en Mansanares unas veçes y otras veçes en Val de Peñas por observante de la ley de Moisen.' Manuel Sarmiento had a brother named Juan in Málaga (ibid.).

[2] Melchor Rodrigues 'Versinha', father of Manuel Alvares, had 6 children (the family tree in Table A above, chap. 1, is simplified); two by his first wife Joana Gonçalves, viz. Isabel Gonçalves and Baltazar Rodrigues Versinha; his second marriage, to Justa de Leão, was without issue; and by his third wife, Leonor Alvares, Bastián (born c.1587, died young), Manuel Alvares, Santiago (also known as Jacome) Luis (born c.1594), and Ana, who also died young. Cf. Révah, *rupt. spin., nouvel examen*, 71, p. 584.

[3] Violante de Paz had been born in Braganza c.1598, and was there married to Santiago Luis in 1618. Their 6 children—Melchor Rodríguez, Leonor Alvares, Gonzalo Luis, María Núñez, Isabelica, and Manuel—were all born in Braganza. See below.

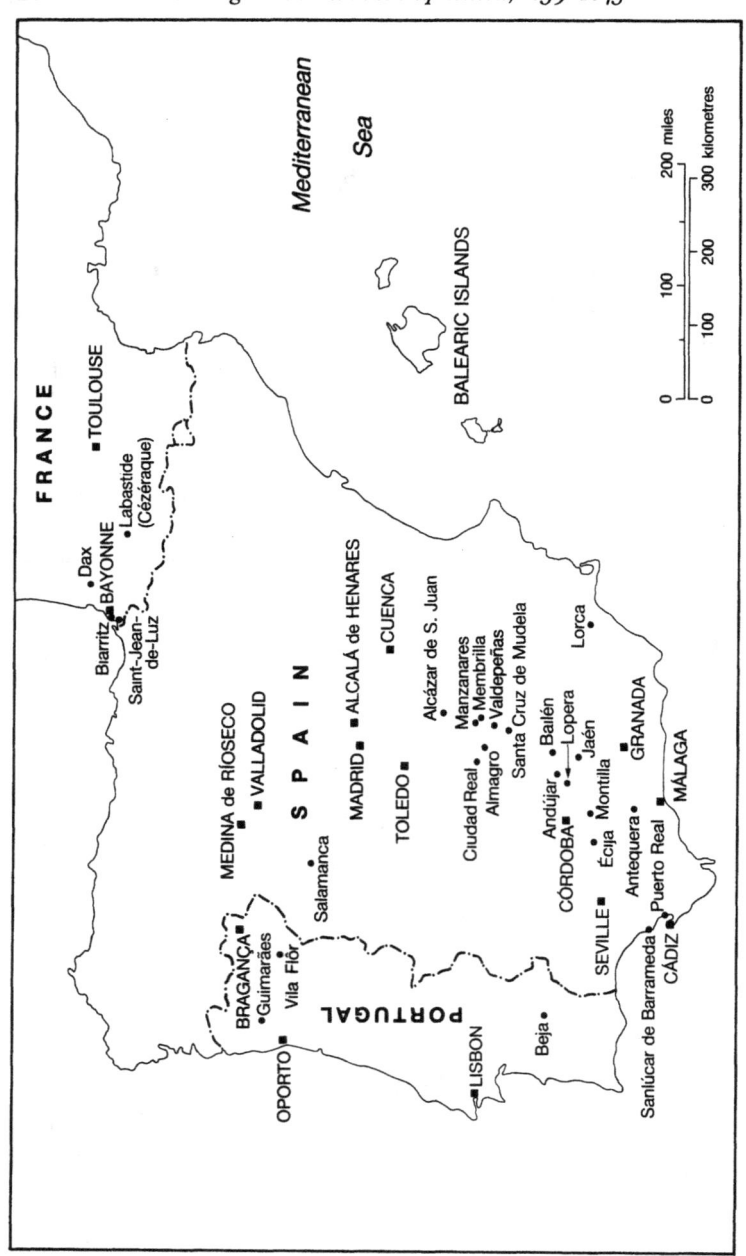

1. Spain, Portugal, and southern France

imprisoned Isabel Luis and Andrés de Narváez, then resident in Santa Cruz de Mudela, a small town in the region of Calatrava, together with José de Castro, Melchor Rodríguez and Gonzalo Luis (two of the sons of Santiago Luis and Violante de Paz), all being resident in Valdepeñas. The Granada Inquisition incarcerated Violante and three of her daughters—Leonor Alvares, María Núñez, and Isabelica, resident in Málaga. At this stage the two brothers Manuel Alvares and Santiago Luis managed to evade investigation by the Inquisition, which proceeded to publicize their names as fugitives from ecclesiastical justice. Manuel made his way to Portugal, and Sanitago lay low in some unknown locality within Spain. The two of them met in May 1641 at Medina de Ríoseco,[4] north of Valladolid, and decided to give themselves up to the Cuenca Inquisition and confess their offences. The prosecutor, Dr Alonso de Vallejo, having received the detailed and incriminating evidence collected against the two of them in trials that had taken place over the previous two years in Toledo and Granada,[5] demanded their imprisonment.

Two trials were therefore set in motion in Cuenca in 1642, against Manuel and Santiago respectively, an additional charge being brought against Manuel for concealment of property; a file was also opened on Manuel's wife, Mencia Fernández Núñez, who had escaped to Seville. The endeavours of the Cuenca prosecutor to secure the incarceration of Mencia and her sons (including Baltazar Alvares) came to nothing. The Seville court rejected his requests that they arrest Mencia and investigate her and her sons, on the grounds that the sole incriminatory evidence against them had been taken from Isabelica, daughter of Santiago Luis and Violante de Paz, a child of eight or nine who in subsequent testimony denied her earlier statements regarding Judaizing activities in the household of Mencia Fernández Núñez. On this occasion fortune smiled on Manuel Alvares' family. Not only did his wife Mencia succeed in escaping trial by the Inquisition, but all members of the family who had been arrested in Granada and Cuenca regained their liberty until 1642, having been reconciled with the church. Their relatives in Toledo had already been released, some in 1640 and others in 1641.[6]

---

[4] This little town formed a transit stage for crypto-Jews fleeing from Portugal into Spain. The family of Isaac Cardoso settled there in 1627, and it was there that Abraham Michael Cardoso was born. See Yerushalmi, *Isaac Cardoso*, pp. 68 f.

[5] See Révah, *rupt. spin., nouvel examen*, 71, pp. 587 f.

[6] The details of these trials are given below, in this chapter.

A Long Brush with the Inquisition, 1639–1643

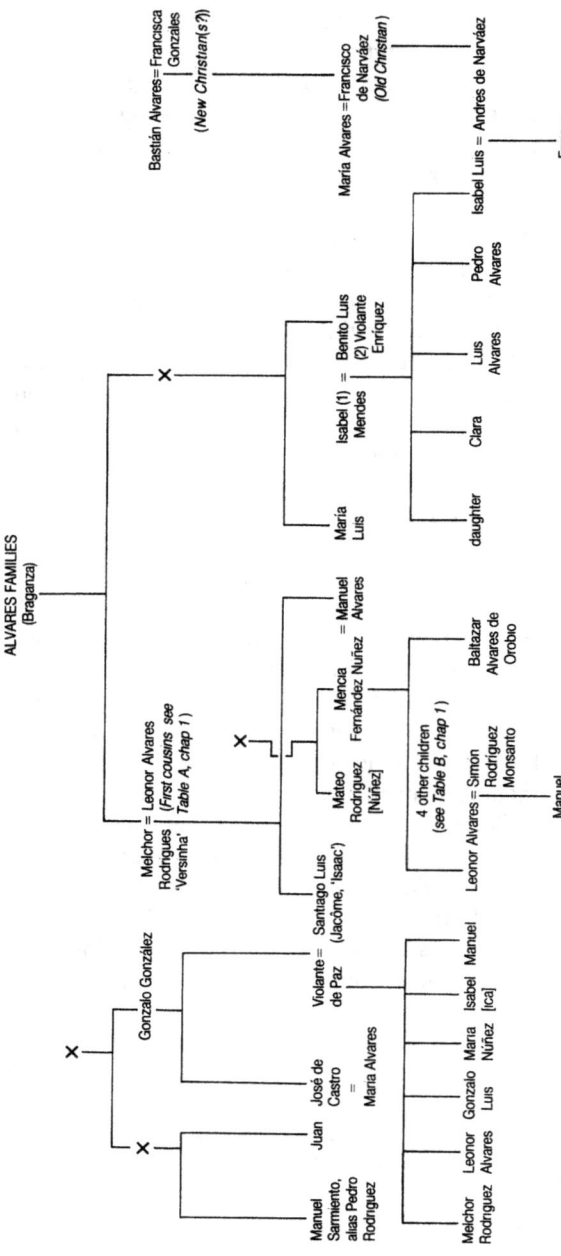

C. Alvares Collaterals

On this occasion the wave of troubles that swept over this crypto-Jewish family left no casualties as it receded; it did, however, shatter their sense of security. Clearly, a heavy cloud of suspicion would henceforth be hanging over them, one that they would not easily be able to dispel. Some of them decided that the best means of securing their future was by emigration from Spain, and Isabel Luis and Andrés de Narváez crossed the border to Bayonne in southern France. José de Castro and his family too flight to Turkey, where they openly reverted to Judaism.[7] A similar course was apparently adopted by Santiago Luis and Violante de Paz, who escaped from Spain together with their sons and daughters to an unknown destination. Manuel Alvares and his immediate family were the only ones to attempt to reconstruct their lives in Spain itself, despite the threat of the Inquisition.

Some of the files containing the records of trials to which this family were subjected between 1639 and 1643 are lost. Such is the case regarding those of Manuel Sarmiento and José de Castro in Toledo, and of family members who were arrested by the Granada court.[8] But the files of the processes which have come down to us open up a broad vista of the life of this Portuguese crypto-Jewish family, showing the tenacity with which it clung to its ancestral traditions. It had not forgotten them through generations of active persecution, suppression, and enforced conformity—the outward dissemblance of their true identity and religious allegiance. Examination of these files teaches us much regarding the Judaism preserved by the family, the religious practices which they secretly maintained, and about the particular customs that were widespread amongst the crypto-Jews of the Iberian peninsula at that period. The stories, so full of riveting incident, which these files have preserved enrich our knowledge of the atmosphere surrounding the life of Baltazar's family, and of the Jewish values which he absorbed during his youth.

ISABEL LUIS AND ANDRÉS DE NARVÁEZ

The evidence of Manuel Sarmiento before the inquisitors at Valdepeñas led to the immediate arrest of Isabel Luis and of her

---

[7] José de Castro married María Alvares before leaving Spain. From Turkey he returned to Bayonne, where he settled in 1661. See Révah, *rupt. spin., nouvel examen*, 72, p. 649.

[8] Révah, ibid., 71, p. 587.

husband Andrés de Narváez, resident in Santa Cruz de Mudela. Andrés, a shopkeeper dealing in linen and spices, had been born in about 1605; he was the son of Francisco de Narváez, an old Christian, and María Alvares, a 'New Christian' (daughter of Bastián Alvares and Francisca González) who had died when Andrés de Narváez was still a child.[9] Andrés had fled to Spain and settled in Andújar, where he became acquainted with a crypto-Jew named Martín Gómez under whose influence he commenced secret observance of Jewish religious precepts.[10] Gómez also persuaded him to accompany him to Bayonne, where he apparently arrived in 1632,[11] coming into contact with many of the local crypto-Jews in the quarter of St Esprit. In the house of Violante Enriques, where he was lodging, he made the acquaintance of her stepdaughter Isabel Luis and married her.[12] Around 1633 he returned with his wife to Andújar. When Isabel Luis' two brothers Luis and Pedro Alvares were arrested by the Inquisition in Madrid, the Narváez couple fled to Málaga and thence to Santa Cruz de Mudela.[13] Meanwhile the two Alvares brothers had been released by the Holy Office, and with the assistance of relatives they got out of Spain. Pedro made his way to Flanders and from there to Venice, where he openly reverted to Judaism. Luis returned to France.[14]

Isabel Luis, wife of Andrés de Narváez, had been born in Bayonne

[9] See the file of the process to which he was subjected in Toledo, Madrid, AHN, Inquisition section, Leg. 168 no. 2, f. 14ᵛ f., evidence deposed by him on 17 Feb. 1640. Cf. also the evidence laid by Manuel Sarmiento on 6 Dec. 1639 before the inquisitors in Valdepeñas (f. 10ʳ).

[10] Ibid. The orgins of Andrés de Narváez, and the family names of his maternal grandparents, point to their probable affinity with the family from which Baltazar Alvares sprang. See the confessional statement of Andrés de Narváez, dated 22 and 24 Feb. 1640, ibid., f. 20ʳ f.

[11] Andrés maintained that prior to his meeting Martín Gómez he had been about to marry the daughter of a certain Antonio de Santiago. With the object of deflecting indictments from those who had allegedly brought influence to bear on him to identify himself with Judaism, he went as far as to claim that Martín Gómez and the Luis family in Bayonne had deceived him, by concealing the circumstance that at the time of her marriage Isabel was not a virgin. See ibid.

[12] Ibid. (evidence of Sarmiento, f. 10ʳ): 'fue el dicho Andres de Narvaez a la çiudad de Vayona en el Reino de Françia a casar y caso con Ysauel Luis que al presente es su muger y es hija de Bento Luis Alvarez, portugues y de su muger que no saue como se llama y biuen en Vayona en el Varrio de Santi Yspiritu donde viven todos los portugueses judios . . .' Cf. the evidence of Andrés de Narváez on 24 Jan. 1640, Leg. 163 no. 15, f. 4ʳ.

[13] Evidence of Sarmiento on 6 Dec. 1639, Leg. 168 no. 2, f. 10ʳ.

[14] When Isabel Luis was examined regarding her family, out of all her brothers and sisters she mentioned only Pedro and Clara. Of Pedro she stated that he resided in Bayonne, and suppressed the fact that he had fled to Italy. Clara, aged 13 or 14, lived in Bayonne. Of her other sister, likewise living openly in Venice as a Jewess, she said nothing. See Leg. 163 no. 15, f. 12ʳ.

in about 1612 to Benito Luis, a cloth merchant of Braganza, and his wife Isabel Mendes.[15] Orphaned of both parents at an early age, she was brought up in the house of her paternal aunt María Luis, who initiated her into the secret of her Jewish identity when she was ten years old.[16] At the time of their arrest the couple had a son named Enrique, and Isabel was six months into her second pregnancy.[17] The records of their files provide revealing evidence about the life of a crypto-Jewish married couple of the seventeenth century, their family connections, their customs and beliefs. The marriage in Bayonne had been solemnized according to traditional Jewish rites. Andrés gave evidence at his investigation that 'Salvador Mendes held two full wineglasses, one in each hand, and all those present, viz. the aforesaid Salvador Mendes, Martín Gómez, Jacôme Luis [i.e. Santiago Luis, brother of Manuel Alvares], his cousin Tomé Luis, María Luis, Violante Enriques and Isabel Luis his bride, all stood and uttered a few words and prayers that he did not recall. Afterwards Salvador Mendes had tasted the wine in one of the glasses and had passed it to him the one presently confessing [sc. Andrés de Narváez] to his wife, and to the remainder of the company; and, when they had all drunk, had thrown down the glasses with their remaining contents, the said Salvador Mendes thereby pronouncing them man and wife.'[18]

On his way from Spain to France Andrés had been in the habit of washing his hands before meals, 'this being an ordinance of the law of Moses'.[19] In France the couple had observed the sabbath, 'and were accustomed to kindle a light on Fridays at four-thirty p.m. which they would not extinguish until [after] the sabbath'. They would likewise change their dress, donning freshly laundered clothes.[20] 'When they addressed their God, whose name is *Adonai*, they would utter the prayer commonly called *La Sama* [i.e. the *Shema'*],[21] and would say the

---

[15] Ibid., f. 11ʳ.
[16] Ibid., f. 13ʳ: 'dijo que esta naçio en Bayona de Francia como tiene dicho donde estubo en casa de sus padres asta la edad de diez años que murio su padre, que su madre murio mucho antes y en muriendo su padre la recojio una tia suya que se llama M[ari]a Luis donde estubo con ella asta edad de beinte años que el dicho Andres de Narbaez su marido . . . se fue a . . . Bayona.' Similarly f. 15ʳ.
[17] Ibid., f. 12ʳ.
[18] Leg. 168 no. 2, f. 23ʳ f. (Evidence of Andrés de Narváez, 24 Feb. 1640).
[19] Ibid., f. 21ᵛ.
[20] Evidence of Manuel Sarmiento, before the Valdepeñas inquisitors, 6 Dec. 1639, Leg. 163 no. 15, ff. 2ʳ, 4ʳ.
[21] The *Shema'* prayer comprises Deut. 6: 4–9 ('Hear, O Israel . . . the Lord is One . . .') which, together with certain other passages from the Pentateuch, is recited daily as a kind of credal formula by Jews.

Almida [i.e. '*Amidah*][22] out of a book called *La Reza* [i.e. the Prayer (-book)]. On completing the '*Amidah* they would stand on tiptoe and take three steps backwards, as if they wished to raise themselves higher.'[23] 'On many days in the year they would fast for the entire day until nightfall as marked by the appearance of the stars; and on the day of great devotion, called by them "the great day", they would fast in the aforesaid manner.'[24] Isabel Luis also declared that when she was 'at Santa Cruz de Mudela she had observed the fast called by them the fast of "the great day", but she did not recollect its date—she thought that it was when grapes were in season. She had likewise fasted in company with Manuel Alvares [the father of Baltazar], resident of Málaga, who had come to the aforementioned townlet of Santa Cruz from Valdepeñas where he was then staying. The aforesaid Manuel Alvares had admitted in her presence that he practised [the law of Moses]; they had in fact first met in France, where he was temporarily residing, and whilst there they were both self-professed observers of the law of Moses. In the evening they had partaken of a meal together in her own house, consisting of fish and not of meat. They had fasted that day, because the said Manuel Alvares had arrived early in the morning and had informed her that that day was "the great day".'[25] From Isabel's evidence it transpires that she had first met Manuel Alvares in Bayonne sixteen years before, i.e. in approximately 1624.[26] It seems that Manuel Alvares was in the habit of paying regular visits to his kinsfolk in southern France. In 1639 they had organized 'the great fast' in Santa Cruz on 8 October, which was, in point of fact, the exact date of the Day of Atonement.[27] One might well wonder how it was that these crypto-Jews, for all practical purposes cut off from the

---

[22] '*Amidah*, i.e. standing (-prayer) of 18 (strictly of 19) benedictions, recited in the three weekday services and in an abbreviated form on sabbaths and other holy days.

[23] Ibid., Sarmiento's evidence (see above, n. 20), f. 2ʳ. Regarding the dissemination of these prayers amongst crypto-Jews see Beinart, *Conversos*, pp. 463 f.

[24] Ibid.: 'y que muchos dias del año ayunan todo el dia hasta la noche que ven estrellas y el dia de la mayor su devoçion que ellos llaman el dia grande le ayunan en la forma referida...'

[25] Ibid., f. 35ᵛ (evidence of Isabel Luis on 13 June 1640).

[26] Ibid., f. 36ʳ: 'Preguntada que otras cosas a echo con el dicho Manuel Albarez en obserbançia de la dicha ley de Moysen o saue que las aya echo el dicho Manuel Albarez y desde quanto tienpo a esta que se guarda la ley de Moysen. Dijo que sierta ves... que le dijo que le guardaua le dicha ley y que era judio y no le dijo el tienpo que avia que lo guardaua pero supuesto que se declararon en Françia y que sauia que sus padres desta eran judios desde entonçes lo seria el, que abra mas de diez seis años...'

[27] Ibid., evidence of Sarmiento, f. 2ʳ: 'y el dia de la mayor su devoçion que ellos llaman el dia grande... cayo este año Presente a ocho de Otubre.'

Jewish world, were able to ascertain the proper dates on which the Jewish festivals fell. From the testimony deposed by Manuel Sarmiento (see above) we discover that Manuel Alvares' brother Santiago Luis (already known, within the intimacy of his family, as Isaac) possessed a Jewish calendar, 'in which were noted all the festival dates of the law of Moses'.[28]

The Narváez pair likewise kept 'Queen Esther's Fast'[29] (immediately preceding the festival of *Purim*); also an alleged 'fast of the feast of Tabernacles', when they were accustomed to fast for 'two or three days'. 'Apart from their fasting, they were in the habit of eating unleavened bread, their festive meals being celebrated at night after the appearance of the [first] star, when they would eat fish but not meat. He (i.e. Andrés) had the impression that this festival occurred after the resurrection of Our Lord (i.e. Easter Sunday), and before the Feast of the Holy Ghost' (i.e., the Christian Pentecost: it would seem that Andrés was confused in his evidence, and mixed up Passover with the festival of Tabernacles).[30] He also knew by heart the opening words of the morning prayers according to the Sephardic rite that he had learned during his stay in France — *mi dios la alma que me diste tu la*

---

[28] Ibid., Leg. 163 no. 14, f. 2ᵛ., evidence deposed on 23 Dec. 1639: 'Isac Luis alias Santiago Luis marido de la dicha Violante v[eçin]o ansi mismo de la dicha çiudad de Malaga tiene un calendario en guarismo en que tiene sentadas todas las fiestas de la ley de Moysen y a este confesante se le mostro en ocasion que le dixo que si queria ver todas las fiestas que tenian los de la naçion hebrea . . .'

[29] See the testimony of Andrés de Narváez, 24 Jan. 1640, Leg. 163 n. 15, f. 4ʳ: 'y este por guarda de la dicha ley los ayunos de judios que son el ayuno grande . . . y es de la Reina Ester.' Beinart, *Conversos*, pp. 471 f., states the fast-days that were observed by crypto-Jews in Spain in the 16th and 17th cents., and their particular attachment to observance of the fast of Esther — which they maintained for three days, instead of one (cf. Esther 4: 16). Especial importance was attached by crypto-Jews to the character of Esther, who 'did not declare her people and ancestry' (Esther 2: 10) any more than they themselves avowed their own ethnic identity. Cf. Révah, *Marranes et l'Inquisition*, pp. 500 f. In this article Révah gives a complete list of religious ordinances observed by crypto-Jews in Portugal in the 16th cent., and his remarks hold good for the 17th cent. likewise. For the Jewish regimen and daily round of Spanish crypto-Jews in the 15th cent. cf. Beinart, *on Trial*, pp. 237 f.

[30] Andrés de Narváez' evidence of 24 Jan. 1640, Leg. 163 no. 15, f. 4ʳ: '. . . y pascua de las cavanuelas y no se acuerda por que tiempo de el año hera y al fin del ayuno çenaban todos juntos . . .' Cf. what he said on 17 Apr. 1640, ibid., f. 34ᵛ: 'Preguntado que çeremonias se açen y este açia para la guarda de la dicha pasqua y en que tiempo del año cae la dicha pasqua. Dijo que las çeremonies que se açian para la guarda de la pasqua eran ayunos que le pareçe arian dos o tres e no saue quantos dias tenia la pasqua mas de que en ella por rrito y çeremonia de la ley de Moysen demas de los ayunos comian pan sin lebadura y la comida era a la noche salida la estrella y çenavan cosa de pescado y no carne y le pareçe que pasqua cae despues de la de resureçion y antes de la del espiritu santo.'

criaste limpia y tu la formaste. i.e. *'elohai neshamah*: 'Lord, the soul which Thou didst place in me is pure; it was Thou that didst create it, Thou that didst fashion it, etc.'[31] As noted, the evidence contained in these depositions provides a good idea of the sort of Judaism with which this group of crypto-Jews was familiar.

The two files on which we have drawn also preserve some of the idiosyncratic beliefs of these crypto-Jews. Manuel Sarmiento had heard Isabel and Andrés say that 'Christians are in error in reckoning Jesus Christ to be possessed of celestial sanctity and to be a [divine] emissary. Their own God, *Adonay*, was the true God: and the reason why Jesus Christ, allegedly a saint, was the object of such veneration, is connected with a certain star. Whenever it rises, the first person to observe it will be granted by *Adonay* whatever he asks of God. It once chanced that Jesus was the first to observe it, and he asked his God, namely *Adonay*, that he should be accorded veneration on earth just as God is the object of veneration in heaven; and this is the reason that people do in fact venerate him and prostrate themselves to him . . .'[32]

Manuel Sarmiento had good grounds to suspect that his life might be in danger as a result of his denunciation of all these crypto-Jews. A report given to the Toledo court on 22 December 1639 by a monk named Francisco de Córdoba stated that

after the Portuguese residents of Valdepeñas had learned that Manuel Sarmiento had conversations with him [sc. the witness] they were thrown into a state of confusion and began to have their suspicions. They got in touch with all the rest of the Portuguese in the district, as also with Fernando Alvares, a wealthy Portuguese domiciled in Madrid but at the time resident in Membrilla apart from his wife, who came to their assistance. On Wednesday last, being the twelfth of the present month [December], Fernando Alvares and witness had met in Valdepeñas where a conversation took place between them in the presence of Simón Rodríguez,[33] who was himself one of the witnesses cited to appear. After an exchange of courtesies, [Fernando Alvares] enquired with some circumspection whether witness had noticed Manuelillo Sarmiento at the previous day's bull-fight. On witness replying affirmatively, Manuel Alvares [i.e. Baltazar's father] said that it would have been better if the bull had

[31] Ibid., Leg. 168 no. 2, f. 26ᵛ (evidence given on 24 Feb. 1640).

[32] Ibid., Leg. 163 no. 15, f. 2ᵛ (Sarmiento's evidence on 6 Dec. 1639). There is possibly here a garbled echo of the *sepher toledoth Yeshuʿ*, a derogatory Jewish tract that purports to set forth the historical circumstances of the birth of Jesus. For the attitude towards Jesus of crypto-Jews in general, and in particular the approach of Baltazar Orobio himself, see below chap. 9, pp. 252 f.

[33] i.e. Rodríguez de Monsanto, brother-in-law of Baltazar as being the husband of his eldest sister Leonor Alvares. On him see below, pp. 57 f.

gored him to death—humanity would hardly have been the poorer. The said Manuel Alvares and the Portuguese residents in Valdepeñas had tried hard to get the said Manuel Sarmiento out of harm's way, on terms that he should abjure the realm and never be heard of again.[34]

Manuel Alvares had also sent Sarmiento the sum of thirty *reales*, apparently as a quid pro quo for his undertaking to get himself out of the way;[35] 'Melchor Luis, Rodrigo de Castro, José de Castro, and Gonzalo Luis, all of them resident in Valdepeñas, extended help to the aforesaid Manuel Sarmiento and assisted him to leave this land: in particular, they sent him an ass, and a letter of credit drawn on Fernando Alvares, which witness had taken from him.'[36]

This amazing testimony throws light on the strenuous efforts of this group of crypto-Jews that included Baltazar's father Manuel Alvares to inhibit Sarmiento, by all means at their disposal, from giving evidence and so denouncing them to the Inquisition. Such efforts, however, proved unavailing. Andrés de Narváez and his wife were put on trial, and after an investigation that lasted approximately six months they were condemned to a year's imprisonment at the *auto-da-fé* staged on 24 June 1640 in Toledo at the church of San Vicente: they were also obliged to wear the *sanbenito*.[37] Nor was this all: as a consequence of the evidence given against them the inquisitors had acquired a mass of proofs of the Jewish links of other 'New Christians' belonging to their wider family group.

VIOLANTE DE PAZ, HER CHILDREN, AND HER BROTHER JOSÉ DE CASTRO

Santiago Luis and his wife Violante de Paz had arrived in Spain from Braganza in about 1638. They settled in Málaga, where Santiago's brother Manuel Alvares and his family were then living.[38] Santiago seems to have joined his brother in business, trading in linen in the south of Spain, together with Manuel's well-to-do brother-in-law Mateo Rodríguez Núñez,[39] likewise resident in Málaga, and also, it seems, with Andrés de Narváez whose misfortunes have just been

[34] See Leg. 168 no. 2, ff. 11ʳ f.
[35] Ibid., f. 12ʳ.
[36] Ibid.
[37] Ibid., ff. 61ʳ f., and similarly Leg. 163 no. 15, ff. 55ᵛ f.
[38] See testimony of José de Castro on 8 Feb. 1640, Leg. 163 no. 14, f. 4ᵛ.
[39] See above, chap. 1, p. 4.

recounted. Manuel and Santiago frequently travelled to Valdepeñas and Santa Cruz de Mudela in connection with their business, and they maintained close connections with their crypto-Jewish kinsfolk who had settled in these two country towns. Of the children of Santiago and Violante, four—their daughters Leonor Alvares, María Núñez, and Isabelica, as also their youngest son Manuel, who had been born in their last year in Braganza—were living in their parents' house in Málaga.[40] Their two other sons, Melchor Rodriguez and Gonzalo Luis, moved to Valdepeñas towards the end of 1639,[41] where they were in charge of the family's local business interests.[42] Melchor and Gonzalo were later joined by their youthful uncle José de Castro, himself likewise from Braganza.[43]

As soon as news reached José de Castro and the brothers Melchor and Gonzalo that Manuel Sarmiento had testified to the inquisitors at Valdepeñas, their anxieties were aroused. They knew Manuel Sarmiento from Braganza, where he had been accustomed to visit his aunt Violante: and he had joined with her and other members of her family in her house to observe fasts and other religious celebrations customary in crypto-Jewish circles. Had Sarmiento included their names as well in the evidence that he had laid before the inquisitional tribunal? The question was one to disturb the slumbers of these newly arrived refugees who had scarcely had time to strike roots in Spain, and for whom the terrors of the Portuguese Inquisition still remained fresh in their memory. Once again, the Holy Office's policy of intimidation bore fruit. The two crypto-Jewish lads, experienced beyond their years, understood their situation all too well. If their Judaizing activities had been brought to the attention of the inquisition, they had best come forward with a voluntary confession, and the sooner the better.[44] That is exactly what José de Castro and Melchor Rodríguez did. On 8 October the former appeared before the examining inspectors at Valdepeñas, and made confession in their presence that at the time when he lived in Braganza he had been in the habit of observing the precepts of the Jewish law, together with his sister and brother-in-law and their two aforementioned sons, Melchor and Gonzalo.[45] In the

---

[40] Ibid. (n. 38 above), evidence of Manuel Sarmiento on 23 Dec., f. 2ʳ.
[41] Ibid., evidence of José de Castro, f. 4ʳ.
[42] See the response of Andrés de Narváez to the inquisitors on 4 June 1640, in which he endeavoured to impugn the evidence against him deposed by Melchor Rodríguez.
[43] See n. 41.
[44] For the means of investigation and intimidation to which the Inquisition resorted see Beinart, *on Trial*, pp. 106 f.
[45] See Madrid, AHN, Inquisition section, Leg. 181 no. 1, f. 5ʳ.

A Long Brush with the Inquisition, 1639–1643

hope of palliating the seriousness of his deeds, he claimed that since arriving at Valdepeñas some four months earlier he had not fulfilled the 'external ceremonies of the law of Moses', and that neither had his two nephews done so, with the exception of putting on clean linen on Saturdays. This they had done because in Valdepeñas they were lodging in the house of the widow Matea Sánchez, an old Christian, in whom they were at pains not to arouse suspicion of any Jewish identity.[46] On 15 January Melchor Rodríguez made a voluntary confession before the *'Suprema'*; and the following day he was placed in confinement by the inquisitional authorities together with his brother Gonzalo Luis and his uncle José de Castro, the property of all three of them being confiscated.[47] There is proof that at exactly the same date Violante de Paz and her three daughters were arrested by the inquisitional court of Granada.[48] As stated above, the files from Granada have disappeared:[49] but some of the proofs that were advanced against the wife of Santiago Luis and her three daughters are to be found in the files of the proceedings concerning the two of her sons who were living in Valdepeñas.

Study of these inquisitorial files enlarges our knowledge of the members of this branch of the Alvares family, of their attachment to Jewish law whilst still in Braganza, of how they came to settle in Spain, and of their stubborn endeavours to maintain their Jewish way of life. The house of Violante de Paz in Braganza had afforded a meeting-place where local crypto-Jews could meet others coming from elsewhere, including from Spain; they would arrange to foregather there in order to practise Jewish ceremonies in each other's company, and to gain inspiration from the staunch Jewish loyalty of their hostess. In describing her household, Manuel Sarmiento saw fit to expatiate. On one occasion when he was staying with her in Portugal, she had asked him

> whether he knew any prayers at all that formed part of the religion of Moses. He had replied that he did not, having left France when still but a child. She thereupon said that she would give him [one], and had in fact done so; she had fetched paper and ink, and he had written down in Portuguese what she had dictated to him. Since, however, he could not read [Portuguese], he had asked his cousin Gonzalo Luis, presently resident in the township of Valdepeñas, to write out a Spanish translation . . . When asked [sc. by the inquisitors] how that

---

[46] Ibid.
[47] Ibid,. f. 6ʳ, and Leg. 163 no. 14, f. 11ʳ.
[48] Cf. Révah, *rupt. spin.*, *nouvel examen*, 71, p. 587, and see Leg. 163 no. 14, f. 4ʳ.
[49] See above, p. 29.

prayer began, and what its contents were, he replied that all that he could remember was the concluding words, *'for the sake of the righteous seed of our forefathers Abraham, Isaac, and Jacob'*. There had been present on that same occasion Violante's son Luis, and her daughters Leonor (aged about sixteen), María (aged eight or ten), and Isabelica (aged seven or eight). They had been accustomed for a number of years to observe numerous fasts, and the said Violante had told him to take note how Isabelica, despite being so young a child, observed the said fast-days.[50]

At the beginning of his investigation Gonzalo Luis, who was aged seventeen when arrested by the Inquisition,[51] endeavoured to emphasize his loyal Christian faith, and declared that

he had been baptized at the church of San Juan in Braganza, and had been confirmed—he did not recall by whom, but he had heard his parents say that it was the bishop of Miranda. He had been present at mass, he had made confession, and he had received communion on the days ordained by the holy church, having last gone to confession in Málaga during the previous Lent . . . with the Jesuits. . . . He crossed himself, and repeated the four prayers and the catechism, reciting them well. When asked if he could read and write, and whether he had studied any discipline, he replied that he was indeed literate, and had been taught to read and write by the Theatines . . .[52]

He also indicated that 'he had heard tell that one of his grandfathers was an old Christian';[53] he himself was 'a good Catholic . . . and had been one all his life'.[54] However, when it was proved that his brother and his uncle had admitted their Judaizing activities and had included his own name in their confessions, Gonzalo conceded that his maternal grandfather Gonzalo González had let him into the secret of his Jewish identity by the time he was ten or eleven.[55] Since that revelation 'he had observed some twenty fasts, in Braganza and in Málaga, in company with man named Manuel Sarmiento. In Braganza he had fasted with his aunt Mencia Alvares, a widow living in Braganza . . . he did not know on how many occasions, but in the evening [sc. at the

---

[50] Evidence of Manuel Sarmiento on 23 Dec. 1639, Leg. 163 no. 14, ff. 2ʳ f.

[51] Ibid., f. 10ʳ.

[52] Ibid., ff. 11ʳ f. The Theatines were so called after their founder, Giovanni Pietro Caraffa, bishop of Chieti (Theate), later Pope Paul IV.

[53] Ibid. On this point his evidence was absolutely flawed: his paternal grandfather was Melchor Rodrigues, father of Manuel Alvares and Santiago Luis (see above, Table A, chap. 1); and not only was his maternal grandfather Gonzalo Gonzales a 'New Christian', but it was he who had introduced his grandson and namesake to the secret of his Jewish identity. See below.

[54] Ibid., f. 14ʳ.　　　　　　　　　　　　　　　　　　　　　　　　[55] Ibid., f. 15ᵛ.

A Long Brush with the Inquisition, 1639–1643

conclusion of the fast] they would eat fish and not meat; and the said Mencia had told him that it was forbidden for him to eat pork, or fish that had no scales, and indeed to eat any meat that had not been slaughtered by a certain person, but that he did not know to whom specifically she had been referring: and that on sabbath-days he must wear a clean shirt, and observe them as feast-days.'[56] He further declared that his said grandfather had warned him to fast 'in particular on a certain day at the beginning of September, known as "the great day". He had observed that fast once in Braganza, because his said aunt had told him to fast on that day, and had done so herself. In the evening the two of them had eaten alone, partaking of fish and not of meat; and his said aunt had told him that she fasted in accordance with the ordinances of the law of Moses.'[57]

This testimony reveals much instructive detail regarding the manner in which Gonzalo Luis and Manuel Sarmiento came to acknowledge to each other their Jewish loyalties. 'The occasion of his admitting to the said Manuel Sarmiento that he was an observer of the law of Moses was on a certain day whilst they were walking along the seashore. The said Manuel Sarmiento had asked him whether he had fasted all that day without eating or drinking anything at all, and he had responded affirmatively: whereupon they each acknowledged to the other that they were observers of the law of Moses.'[58] Such was, indeed, the normal procedure amongst many Spanish and Portuguese crypto-Jews. In moments when they were alone and conscious of their intimacy, they would pour out to each other the substance of the faith that they kept locked away in their hearts, thereby strengthening each other's resolve by mutual revelation of their hidden identity. Great was the significance of such a declaration, which would constitute a decisive point in the crypto-Jew's return to observance of the law of Moses, and in the development of a bond of reciprocal responsibilities between himself and another crypto-Jew—like entering into a kind of formal compact with him. Such declarations can be found recorded in many of the inquisitional files for the seventeenth century.

Whilst they were still living in Braganza, his mother Violante had told him that he 'must try to eat as little pork as possible . . . and that if he did so, he should do it to disguise himself, in order not to let it be seen that he observed the law of Moses'.[59]

The family's manner of life did not change in Spain. 'After leaving

[56] Ibid. [57] Ibid.
[58] Ibid., ff. 16ʳ f. [59] Ibid., f. 24ʳ.

Portugal, when he was in the house of his mother Violante de Paz in Málaga some twelve months previous, he once observed a fast on the instructions of his said mother, and on another occasion in accordance with the law of Moses. He did not recall the name of the fast, or at what season in the year it fell, but he did remember that he fasted together with his mother the said Violante de Paz and sisters Leonor (aged nineteen), María (aged twelve), and Isabel (aged eight) . . .'[60]

From this testimony it may be concluded that, contrary to the substance of José de Castro's confession already noted, the two brothers did, in fact, continue to observe fasts in Valdepeñas, and that on one occasion they did so in the company of their aunt.[61]

No less interesting are the details that emerge from the confession of Melchor, Gonzalo's elder brother. Whilst in Braganza he had heard from a neighbour, a widow of the name of Ginebra López, a whole series of instructions as to the manner in which he ought to fulfil the law of Moses, including his duty 'to observe the "feast of the lamb"[62] . . . and that when he ate mutton he must remove the ischiatic nerve from the leg . . . nor might he eat pork chops, nor, indeed, any swine-flesh, rabbit, or hare . . .'[63] And although he did consume pork chops from time to time he knew that this was improper, not being in accordance with the law of Moses; but he did so nevertheless, being fond of the taste . . .'[64]

From Manuel Sarmiento's evidence we learn that Melchor Rodríguez and José de Castro travelled with him from Braganza to Valdepeñas, and that on Saturday they interrupted their journey at Medina de Ríoseco, in order not to violate the sabbath.[65]

It is quite clear that the confessions of the two brothers Melchor and

---

[60] Ibid. Cf. Manuel Sarmiento's description of the ages of Violante's daughters, above, p. 38. Certainly the evidence of Gonzalo, their brother, is more reliable.

[61] Ibid., f. 26ʳ.

[62] Presumably the reference is to the feast of unleavened bread, or Passover, and alludes to the (defunct) paschal sacrifice (Exod. 12: 3 f.).

[63] Leg. 181 no. 1, f. 7ᵛ. Gonzalo mentioned a long list of names of crypto-Jews in whose company he had observed Jewish ceremonies in Braganza; see Leg. 163 no. 14, ff. 17ʳf: '. . . Felipe Rodrigues que le llaman por mal nombre el chisme del oficio, çapatero y curtidor . . . [f. 17ᵛ] . . . Clara Gonçales casada con Juan Gonçales veçinos de Bergança de oficio curtidor—. . . (loc. cit); Isavel Alvarez mujer de Luis Hurtado, mercador [f. 21ᵛ]; Catalina Desa mujer de Gaspar Pinto' (f. 22ʳ).

[64] Leg. 181 no. 1, ff. 8ᵛf.

[65] Ibid., f. 5ʳ (23 Dec.): '. . . que viniendo con los susodichos desde la dicha Villa de Vergança a la de Baldepeñas dexaron de caminar un dia sauado por ser fiesta . . . no olgaron mas de dicho dia sauado por auer pasado el señor arriero que los traya, paro en Ruiseco que es donde le guardaron . . .'

A Long Brush with the Inquisition, 1639–1643 41

Gonzalo provided the inquisitors with incriminating evidence not merely in regard to their mother Violante, who had been placed in custody in Granada, but also against their father Santiago Luis who had escaped from Málaga together with his brother Manuel Alvares.[66] Manuel comes in for frequent mention by Melchor and Gonzalo. They declared that he was 'an observer of the law of Moses',[67] and that he had once asked Melchor 'whether he observed the law of Moses, and when the latter replied affirmatively, they had made mutual acknowledgement of their observance'.[68] Gonzalo recounted how he had observed fasts in Málaga 'on two or three occasions, in company with the aforesaid Manuel Sarmiento: the two of them being accustomed to go to the mountain outside the city in the morning, and to remain there all day while fasting. On his return at nightfall to the house of his uncle Manuel Alvares, with whom he lodged, they would break their fast.'[69] On the other hand the inquisitors were unable to extract from them a single word that might incriminate their aunt Mencia Fernández, wife of Manuel Alvares.[70] As regards Baltazar himself, their son, they merely related that he was 'a theological student at Alcalá de Henares'.[71] Their cousin was, at this period, absorbed in his studies at the College of Madre de Dios, and from their language one must infer that they had not met him personally.

These trials present us with an amazing story of dedication and loyalty, of risks taken and subterfuges adopted by these crypto-Jews in the endeavour to keep alive the flame of their religious heritage. They observed the Sabbath and fast days, according to the Day of Atonement a character all its own. They also kept the festival of Passover and the Fast of Esther preceding *Purim*, retaining the custom of eating a communal meal at the conclusion of fasts. They copied prayers and disseminated them within the family circle, and they attempted to keep the dietary laws, with even something of a hint at observance of the laws for the ritual slaughter of meat. All of these details paint a colourful picture of an orderly and regular way of life led under extremely

---

[66] See above, p. 27.
[67] Leg. 181 no. 1, f. 10ʳ: 'Dijo que su tio deste que se llama Manuel Albarez que bibe en Malaga mercader de lienços es observante de la ley de Moysen.'
[68] Ibid., f. 12ʳ.
[69] Leg. 163 no. 14, f. 16ᵛ.
[70] Leg. 181 no. 1, f. 12ᵛ. When asked about any Jewish practises on the part of his aunt Mencia, Melchor 'dijo que este no saue nada de la pregunta ni su marido se lo dijo porque nunca a estado en Malaga ni la a tratado . . .'
[71] Ibid., f. 19ʳ (Melchor, on Alvares' children): 'saue que tienen hijos, solo a oydo deçir uno que se llama Baltasar Albarez de Orobio, collegial teologo en Alcalá . . .'

difficult circumstances, in defiance of danger, by a community under the constant surveillance of the suspicious and menacing Inquisition.

On 24 June 1640 — at the same *auto-da-fé* held in the church of San Vicente where, as related above, Andrés de Narváez and his wife Isabel were condemned[72] — the sentence against Melchor and Gonzalo was read out. They were condemned to four months imprisonment and were compelled to wear the *sanbenito*; in addition, their property was confiscated.[73] This was a relatively light penalty, and it would appear that the inquisitional authorities took into account the youth of the accused, and that they had made voluntary confession and had co-operated during the course of investigation. One may assume that the punishment inflicted on José de Castro, whose file (as stated above) has not survived,[74] was similar. The two brothers were released on 25 October of the same year after having completed their full sentence,[75] and thereafter all trace of them is lost. One may surmise that they escaped from Spain together with their parents and sisters after the latter, too, had been released from the inquisitional gaols of Granada and Cuenca.

MANUEL ALVARES AND SANTIAGO LUIS

Manuel Alvares and Santiago Luis, the two brothers who had made their escape, presented themselves voluntarily before the Cuenca Inquisition on 27 May 1641, stating that they wished to make confession of their Judaizing activities.[76] From the testimony that they gave to the court it is quite clear that they were both aware of the evidence which had been accumulated against them in the courts of Toledo and Granada.[77] Having learned of the relatively light sentences passed on members of their families by those two tribunals they had resolved to return to Spain and to make their confession before the inquisitors, assuming that their penalties would be no more severe than the sentences passed on those found guilty in Toledo and Granada. This was, in their view, the only possible route to reunion with their wives and families from whom they had been separated for about sixteen months, ever since Santiago had escaped to Bayonne and Manuel to Portugal.

[72] See above, p. 35. [73] See Leg. 181 no. 1, f. 58ᵛ, and 163 no. 14, f. 47ᵛ.
[74] See above, p. 29. [75] Leg. 181 no. 1, f. 63ᵛ, 163 no. 14, f. 52ʳ.
[76] See Cuenca, AD, Leg. 462 no. 6348, f. 94. [77] See above, pp. 32 f.

A Long Brush with the Inquisition, 1639–1643

The two brothers met in April 1641 at Medina de Ríoseco, and there they decided to proceed to Cuenca in order to register their confession, on the supposition that in view of the distance of Cuenca from their previous domicile in Spain, the inquisitors would find it difficult to assemble and confront them with the full tale of evidence for their Judaizing activities in Andalusia.[78] In this their reasoning was proved wrong. The prosecutor of the Cuenca court, Dr Alonso de Vallejo, was not convinced of the brothers' ingenuousness in coming forward with their confessions, and on 7 June 1641 he declared before the court that 'it seemed probable from their evidence that they were doing so after having been apprised of the fact that testimony had been given against them in the inquisitional courts of Toledo and Granada, at the very least'.[79] Vallejo demanded their immediate confinement in order to permit a rigorous investigation, and at the same time he recommended that the court apply to the courts of Toledo and Granada for all incriminatory evidence that had been adduced against the two in the course of trials of the members of their family.[80] Investigation lasted many months, revealing much detail about Manuel and Santiago, their links with Judaism, their family connections, their economic status, and the fate of the members of their family left behind in Spain when the two of them escaped beyond her frontiers.

Manuel did his best to prove to the inquisitors that he had not begun to practise Jewish law until he was past his youth. According to him, he first developed a Jewish consciousness in the year 1629 whilst on a visit to Portugal, under the influence of a man named Gonzalo Fernandes in Oporto, since deceased.[81] The latter had initiated him into the secrets of the law of Moses, and had told him that it was only through its fulfilment that he could secure salvation for his soul. From Fernandes he had learned about 'his duty to keep the fasts, which were

[78] See above, p. 27, and cf. ibid. (n. 76 above), ff. 50 f., evidence of Manuel Alvares on 27 May 1641.

[79] Ibid. (n. 76 above), f. 1 (prosecutor's statement at the session of the court on 7 June 1641: 'y porque de sus mismas confesiones pareçe que lo haçen por aver sabido que estan testificados por lo menos en las inquisiçiones de Granada y de Toledo...'

[80] Ibid: 'Pido y suplico a Vuestra Señoria mande poner a cada uno en su carçel secreta deste Santo Ofiçio porque darles las acusaçiones estando libres tendria mucho inconveniente... Otrosi pido que se embie a las inquisiçiones de Granada y de Toledo a saber si los dichos reos estan testificados por las personas conjuntas suyas que ellos diçen an salido reconçiliados en las dichas inquisiçiones o por otras algunas y que se remitan las testificaçiones...' Following up this request, on 8 July the court applied to the Granada tribunal and on 26 July to that in Toledo, asking that all information gathered by them against the two brothers be forwarded to Cuenca with dispatch.

[81] Ibid., ff. 49 f., evidence deposed on 27 May 1641.

to be commenced in the evening and kept up until the same hour on the next day, above all the fast of 10 September which was styled the "great day". Similarly he must fast on two or three further days in February or March—he did not remember the exact dates—known as [the fast of] Queen Esther. At Eastertide, throughout seven days he must eat exclusively unleavened bread, and he must keep the sabbath each week, these being the feasts that God had commanded in his law to be kept. It was forbidden to eat pork chops and other food-stuffs which he did not remember . . . in the course of the year fasts were to be observed a number of times on Mondays and Thursdays . . . at the conclusion [of each fast], on the appearance of the stars at nightfall, one would eat eggs and fish, but not meat.'[82] He stated that he had not always managed to observe the sabbath, 'because he had not [invariably] been at home on Saturdays, and he had sometimes been putting up at hostelries, since he spent much of his time away from home. He had never eaten unleavened bread on Passover, since, not having been in company [sc. with other crypto-Jews], he had had no opportunity. Although his conscience pricked him, he none the less figured that he would be pardoned because he had had no possibility of baking [unleavened bread] in accordance with the instructions given him by the said Gonzalo Fernandes.'[83] According to his own plea, it had been but four years previous, in the town of Valdepeñas, that he and his brother Santiago had made mutual acknowledgement of their Jewish identity; and they had observed a number of fasts together both there and in near-by Almagro, in accordance with the law of Moses.[84] Unlike Santiago, who stated in his confession that 'he had heard that he came on one side or other from New Christian stock',[85] Manuel maintained that 'he did not know if his parents stemmed at all from New Christian ancestry'.[86] In this way Manuel endeavoured to obscure his past, and to represent himself as having been seduced from the true faith of Christianity by a crypto-Jew whom he had encountered casually on his travels.

As against this, Manuel made a great show of the devotion to Christianity that had characterized his manner of life prior to that chance encounter with Gonzalo Fernandes.[87] Even after having become

[82] Ibid., f. 50.   [83] Ibid., ff. 50 f.   [84] Ibid., f. 51.
[85] Ibid., f. 58; a marginal note by Vallejo, the prosector, reads '. . . su ermano Santiago diçe que a oido que tenia parte de christianos nuebos . . .'
[86] Ibid.: '. . . y no saue si sus padres tuviesen alguna parte de Christianos nuevos . . .'
[87] Ibid.: 'Dijo que es christiano bautizado y confirmado y le bautizaron en la Iglesia de San Juan de la çiudad de Bergança segun le dijeron sus padres y le bautizo Sebastian

involved in the Jewish religion, 'he had been accustomed to go to mass on feast-days . . . and had made confession once a year, during Lent'; but he was at that time doing all this 'merely for form's sake, in regard to society at large, and he was concealing [his loyalty to] the law of Moses, according to the precepts of which he was arranging his life. He attended mass, despite his not believing in the real presence of the body of our Lord Jesus Christ in the host, and despite [his opinion that] the host was no more than a piece of bread. He likewise did not believe that the priest had authority to consecrate it, or to pronounce absolution from sin.'[88] When questioned by his investigators he had 'crossed himself and had recited the *Pater Noster*, *Ave Maria*, *Credo*, and *Salve regina*, and had repeated the [ten] commandments of the divine law, the general confession, and the articles of faith: and he stated that he could recognize all the principles of the Christian faith, but that he had forgotten them'.[89]

Being fully apprised of the testimony given to the Toledo court by Isabel Luis and Andrés de Narváez her husband, by Manuel Sarmiento, Melchor Rodríguez, Gonzalo Luis, and José de Castro, Manuel himself referred to meetings that had taken place between him and all those named, in Málaga, Valdepeñas, and Santa Cruz de Mudela, admitting that he had made acknowledgement to them of his belief in the law of Moses.[90]

In order to allay the suspicions of the inquisitors, Manuel tried to prove that he had abandoned his family and fled from Málaga at the beginning of 1640, not on account of any uneasiness lest the Inquisition might be interested in him, but in consequence of financial complications, 'because of pledges for which he was responsible for the *alcabala* tax'.[91] Later on he went so far as to declare that before his flight he had been in prison for his many debts.[92] From Málaga he had

---

Rodriguez cura de aquella parrochia y en ella la auia confirmado un obispo de Miranda de que el se acuerda y no del nombre del obispo y que oya missa, confesaua y comulgaba asta el año pasado de mill y seisçientos y veinte y ocho o veinte y nueue que comenzo a seguir la ley de Moysen . . .'

[88] Ibid.   [89] Ibid., f. 59.   [90] Ibid., ff. 52 f.

[91] Ibid., f. 57: 'que les dejo este en Malaga abra diez y seis meses . . . huyendo de una fiansa que este auia echo de las alcabalas.' The *alcabala* was a sales tax; for its range at the period with which we are concerned see Elliot, *Spain*, pp. 231, 269, 285 f. For Manuel's employment as an assistant collector of taxes see below, p. 53.

[92] Cuenca, AD, Leg. 462 no. 6346 (unpaginated), evidence deposed on 8 Oct. 1641: '. . . que antes debe muchas deudas en la çiudad de Malaga como tiene declarado que quando se salio della estaba preso por deudas'.

gone abroad, to Lisbon, where he had stayed about two months, thence on to Oporto, and from there to Guimarães and various other places until arriving at Medina de Ríoseco, where he and his brother resolved to turn penitent.[93] He also told his investigators that 'people had informed him' that his wife Mencia, his sons, and his daughters 'were [now] staying in or near Seville', whither they had fled after failing to settle the many debts which he had left behind him in Málaga.[94]

Dr Vallejo was unconvinced by the statements of Manuel and Santiago. In the indictment which he presented on 4 July 1640 he maintained that both of them had merely 'turned themselves in posing as penitents'.[95] He claimed that Manuel had taken flight after being informed that many of his kinsfolk had been arrested in Toledo and Granada, and for that reason 'he induced his wife and children to flee from Málaga'.[96] Manuel had 'anticipated that the said prisoners would be reconciled to the bosom of the Church and released, in the same way as they had been released from the aforementioned gaol. It seemed likely that he had been in touch with them, and that they had intimated that their evidence could be used against him. Consequently, in fear of himself being put under lock and key, he had come forward to the court to confess and to make himself out to be penitent; being unwilling to confess either in Toledo or in Granada, since he was aware that plenty of proofs of his offence had been assembled there and that there were witnesses against him who could be cited.'[97] The prosecution further argued that Manuel was not telling the truth when he alleged that his wife and daughters had left for Seville on account of the debts that he had left behind him, 'since the women had no cause to flee, be their debts never so great, it not being lawful to imprison them for such a cause. The truth was that they had run away in stealth, because of the likelihood of their being held by the Inquisition, and that they fled acting on the instruction of the said Manuel Alvares.' Vallejo dismissed the two brothers' assertion that it had been but four years since they had made mutual acknowledgement of their Judaism, 'it being certain—and, indeed, natural—that their parents would have initiated them and all their other children into the said law as soon as

---

[93] Leg. 462 no. 6348, f. 60.
[94] Ibid., f. 57.   [95] Ibid., ff. 75 f.
[96] Ibid.: 'en espeçial le pongo acusaçion de que aviendo prendido por la Inquisiçion de Toledo y de Granada muchas personas conjuntas suyas, al tiempo que las prendieron o poco antes o despues, se huyo por que tambien no le prendiesen e hizo que su muger y hijos por la misma razon se huyesen de la ciudad de Malaga . . .'   [97] Ibid.

they had reached years of understanding; and that they would thereafter have practised its requirements'.[98] The prosecutor therefore demanded that Manuel and Santiago should be handed over to the secular arm, and that their property should be confiscated 'in order to deter all who might follow the same path'.[99]

On 19 August 1641 evidence was heard by the tribunal from the doctor and surgeon who, on the instructions of the inquisitors, had conducted a physical examination of the two brothers: and their findings were that they had been circumcised.[100] Three days later Vallejo advanced his second indictment, in which he maintained that it had been proved, beyond a doubt, that the confessions of Manuel and Santiago rested on nothing but falsity; and he demanded that they both be questioned in order to establish when they had been circumcised, and by whom.[101] In response to the repeated and importunate requests of Manuel and Santiago they were submitted to further medical examinations on 26 September and 30 October of the same year, on each occasion by different doctors and surgeons. The results of the later examinations contradicted the conclusions drawn from the earlier one — to Vallejo's astonishment and chagrin.[102]

With the assistance of counsel placed at his disposal, Manuel attempted to refute the proofs advanced against him by his investigators.[103] Isabel had stated before the Toledo court that Manuel had

[98] Ibid. [99] Ibid., f. 77.
[100] Ibid., ff. 99 f. They were examined on this occasion by a doctor and a surgeon nominated by the Inquisition, viz. Dr Pedro Caballero and Tomás Pérez.
[101] Ibid., ff. 103 f.
[102] Ibid., ff. 136 f. The second examination was carried out by Dr Diego de Salçedo, the surgeon being Alonso Loçano, both of Cuenca. Salçedo reported that he had examined the prisoner L (presumably meaning Santiago Luis), and had found no evidence of his foreskin having been removed ('no esta çircunçidado ni apareçe çicatriz ni señal que lo muestre ni diminuçion de carne en el balaño ni en el perpuçio que son señales de tener la çircunçiçion'); and that he had likewise examined the prisoner M (apparently Manuel Alvares), 'ombre de edad, cano', again without discovering any proof of his having been circumcised ('no lo esta tampoco por las raçones dichas'). Dr Salçedo indicated that this prisoner had impressed upon him his concern 'that he should examine him with great care', for 'his life and honour were at stake' ('Dixo que solo el preso questa en la dicha carçel de la letra eme encargo que le mirase este declarante con mucho cuidado . . . que le importaba la bida y la honra . . .'). The third examination was conducted by Miguel Valero and Miguel Martínez, both of them Cuenca surgeons (ibid., ff. 142 f.). In the margin of the transcript of the session of the court on 7 Nov. Vallejo observed '. . . por que los çirujanos se an desconformado que es harta maravilla que en lo que ven los ojos aya diversidad de opiniones'.
[103] Manuel conducted his defence, advised by his counsel Miguel Chaves, at sessions of the court held on 5 and 9 July, 23 and 31 Aug., and 11 Sept. 1641. Ibid., ff. 83 f., 99 f., 105 f., 123 f., 127 f.

already been practising the precepts of the Jewish law whilst staying at Bayonne eighteen years earlier—that is to say, four years before his meeting with Gonzalo Fernandes, to whom he imputed sole responsibility for his own Judaizing. Manuel claimed that Isabel's statement was false, 'because at the time when I went to the Bayonne fair, over eighteen years ago, the said Isabel Luis was a child of about ten. I hardly saw her, I had no conversation with her, but simply saw her coming home from school amongst a group of other children, when she was carrying a book on the principles of the Christian faith—that being, as far as I know, the religion which was practised by those who were living there.'[104] He further added that Isabel and her husband Andrés de Narváez 'were his mortal enemies', because in 1639 there had been two lawsuits arising out of business complications in which he had been at odds with them.[105] Manuel Sarmiento's testimony against him in Toledo he endeavoured to overthrow by claiming that Sarmiento hated him for having refused to entertain Sarmiento's brother as his suggested son-in-law.[106] Finally, Manuel Alvares complained about his state of health and the severe pains to which he was subject in his head and in one of his arms, and he requested the court to extend to him some merciful consideration.[107]

Vallejo ignored the plea for mercy, and did his best to exploit the full rigour of the law. He stuck to his case, insisting that Manuel and Santiago were doing no more than pose as penitents, and that throughout the investigation they had been lying. On 7 November he demanded that they be taken to the torture-chamber in order to force out the truth about their Judaizing activities.[108] The files of the Cuenca Inquisition contain no evidence that physical torture was in fact ever applied in the investigation of these two suspects, and it is possible that the prosecutor's demand was turned down by the inquisitors. On the other hand psychological torture continued, with no term set to it, and their investigation was carried on right up to the end of the year 1641. But before we consider its outcome, and the sentences of the court passed on Manuel and Santiago when it was completed, we have to turn our attention to two other trials pertinent to our subject: first, the investigation of Manuel's wife Mencia Núñez, who had escaped from Málaga with her sons and daughters and had settled in Seville, and

---

[104] Ibid., f. 130.
[105] Ibid.: '... por quanto ella y su marido son mis enemigos mortales...'
[106] Ibid., f. 123: 'porque le quito que un hermano deste no casasse una hija de el...'
[107] Ibid, f. 131. [108] Ibid., ff. 145 f.

A Long Brush with the Inquisition, 1639–1643   49

secondly the investigation of Manuel Alvares himself in connection with his alleged concealment of property from the Inquisition.

In the first indictment brought against Manuel Alvares, on 4 July 1641, Vallejo had already maintained that Mencia's flight from Málaga was not on account of her husband's debts, but in order to evade imprisonment by the Inquisition.[109] Two weeks later the avid prosecutor advanced the theory that Mencia had escaped following on the imprisonment in Granada of her sister-in-law Violante, wife of Santiago Luis, and her three daughters—themselves likewise resident in Málaga at that time. He requested that stringent enquiries be instituted, both in Granada and in Málaga, as to the exact dates on which Violante and her daughters had been put in gaol, and the date and circumstances of the escape of Mencia and her children to Seville.[110]

From Granada Vallejo obtained transcripts of the evidence given by Isabelica, the youngest daughter of Santiago Luis and Violante de Paz, a child of eight or nine.[111] On 12 July 1640 the girl had informed the inquisitors of the court that her parents were 'New Christians'. 'On being asked what "New Christians" meant, she replied that it meant "that one was Jewish".'[112] She also declared that her parents

> had taught her and her sisters Leonor and María not to believe in Our Lord Jesus Christ and Our Lady the Holy Virgin: and that neither she herself, nor her said parents, nor her sisters did in fact believe in Our Lord Jesus Christ or in his Virgin Mother. However, at the present juncture, being confined in prison and experiencing a time when Our Lord was extending his bounties, she wished to believe in them: at which point she had burst into tears.[113]

Vallejo sought to use the child's evidence to help secure the conviction of Manuel Alvares and his wife Mencia, inasmuch as she had gone on to say that

> her uncle Manuel Alvares, a merchant resident in Málaga, was a Jew; for so she had been told by her aunt Mencia Núñez his wife, in the presence of her

---

[109] See above, p. 46.   [110] Leg. 462 no. 6351, f. 1, court session of 19 July 1641.
[111] Isabelica's age at the time that she deposed her testimony cannot be stated with certainty. The inquisitors noted that she was aged 12 (ibid., f. 3), but she herself stated that in 1639 she had been 8 or 9 (f. 7). Possibly the Granada inquisitors added a few years to her age in order to lend greater credibility to her evidence; or conceivably, *per contra*, Isabelica represented herself as being somewhat younger than she actually was, in order to win the inquisitors' sympathy and to minimize the extent of her own accountability for her actions.
[112] Ibid., ff. 3 f.: 'Dixo que son de casta de Cristianos nuebos ... y preguntada que era el ser christiano neuvo ... dijo que ser judio.'   [113] Ibid., f. 4.

said mother and of her sisters Leonor and María... This had occurred after she had come away from Portugal with her parents and sisters, at the time that they were lodging in the house of her said aunt Mencia Núñez.[114]

In the evidence which she gave before the court on 27 October 1640 Isabelica had said that on some occasion in 1639 she had observed a fast in Málaga, in the company of a Portuguese named Miguel Fernández, his wife and two daughters, as well as her uncle Manuel Alvares and his wife Mencia.[115] On 28 June 1641 Isabelica was brought back before the Granada court, this time with the object of getting her to confirm the evidence which she had given the year before. When the record of her testimony was read out, she stated that

what had been read was her own words and her own declarations, that they had been fairly written down and she recollected having said them in the course of her confession: but what she did not remember was whether the things that she had stated in her declaration ever actually happened. The court had frequently scolded her and had warned her to pay careful attention to what she was saying; and that since she had affirmed that what had been read out to her was correct, it was reasonable to suppose that the events had taken place as she had declared. Whereupon she repeated that she did not remember whether it had all really happened, on saying which she broke down in tears.[116]

The Granada inquisitors had then abandoned the examination, and in the covering letter which they sent to the Cuenca court on 7 July 1641 they asserted that 'the said woman [i.e. Violante de Paz] and her daughters had not been good confessants, and not much confidence could be placed on the testimony of Isabel [Isabelica] Alvares, in view of her being but a child...'[117]

Vallejo was not convinced. At the session of the Cuenca inquisitional court on 24 October 1641 he launched into a long tirade criticizing the manner in which the Granada court had handled this part of the process, and expressed his own confidence in Isabelica's evidence, 'on the basis of the popular adage *los niños y los locos dicen las verdades*' (children and madmen tell the truth).[118]

---

[114] Ibid.: '... dijo que su tio Manuel Aluarez, veçino de Malaga, mercader, es judio porque se lo dijo a esta su tia Mençia Nuñez, muger del dicho Manuel Aluarez en presençia de la dicha su madre y ermanas Leonor y Maria... lo qual passo luego questa y sus padres y hermanas vinieron de Portugal, viuiendo en casa de la dicha su tia Menzia Nuñez.'

[115] Ibid., ff. 6 f.

[116] Ibid., ff. 7 f.

[117] Ibid., ff. 65.

[118] Ibid., f. 38. 'No importa lo que la Inquisiçion de Granada escrivia de que alla no se hiço caso desta testificaçion por ser menor y persona de poco credito, porque si el poco

A Long Brush with the Inquisition, 1639–1643

In accordance with instructions received from the Cuenca court, the inquisitional commissary at Málaga, a priest called Francisco Maldonado de Galdo, began inquiries with the neighbours of the Alvares family.[119] Pablo de la Cruz gave evidence before him that he knew Manuel Alvares and the members of his household, they having previously lived in the neighbouring house in the calle de los Almacenes,[120] whence they had moved to a house in the plaza doña Marquesa. According to his own words, he had no first-hand knowledge of where they had gone on leaving Málaga, but he had heard from others that they had settled in Alcalá de Henares, 'where they had a son who was a medical student. Witness had met him, approximately two years previous in that city (i.e. in Málaga), in the house of his father the said Manuel Alvares—either before the plague or shortly thereafter, whilst he was staying in his father's house in the calle Manzanares. After that, he (sc. the son) had returned to Alcalá, and his parents remained in the city.'[121] Another neighbour, doña Barbarrida Paez, said that 'she had heard (she did not remember from whom, but it was one of the young men around) that the said Mencia Núñez and her daughters had gone away in the middle of the night taking all their clothes with them, but witness had not seen them nor hear any noise, although she lived in the house adjoining theirs: it was only the following morning that she realized that they were not there...'[122] Yet another neighbour, doña Ana Mateos, had heard 'that they had run away from the Inquisition'.[123] The fourth witness, doña Flor de Ayala, recounted that 'approximately two years previous, the aforesaid parties had left the said house and gone away, after Christmas. She recalled that on Christmas they had baked flapjacks in their house; and she thought that they had left before the passage of a full month after the Christmas of 1639. But she did not know where they

---

credito se funda en ser menor ... se le deve mas credito que a un ombre mayor conforme a nuestro vulgar probervio: *Los niños y los locos diçen las berdades*' (emphasis in original).

[119] Ibid., ff. 27 f. He began his inquiries on 30 Aug. 1641.

[120] The reference is to the calle Manzanares (see below). Either there is confusion here, or possibly it was sometimes so called.

[121] The son here referred to was, of course, Baltazar Alvares.

[122] She was questioned on 8 Sept. 1641, ibid., ff. 30 f.: 'Dixo que oyo decir y no se acuerda a quien, sino a unos muchachos que la dicha Menzia Nuñez y sus hijas se auian ydo a media noche llebandose toda su ropa, mas esta testigo no los a visto ni tampoco oydo el ruido, con estar su cassa junto a la donde vivian las sussodichas, solo que una mañana despues que las sussodichas faltaron...'

[123] Examined on 10 Sept. 1641, ibid., ff. 31 f.: 'dixo que se fueron huiendo de la Inquisiçion...'

were staying, merely that they had left the said house suddenly... she similarly gathered... from what the said daughters [of Mencia Núñez] had said to her that they were desirous of moving to Madrid, where they had previously lived, because they had not been able to settle down in Málaga. It was therefore possible that they had gone to stay in Madrid...'[124]

Up to this point the investigation had not succeeded in establishing the date when Mencia and her daughters had departed from Málaga. Did they leave the city before February 1640, i.e. before Violante de Paz and her daughters had been held by the Granada Inquisition, or was it after February? From Vallejo's point of view, the date was of very great moment, since if Mencia did not in fact leave Málaga until after Violante had been arrested by the Inquisition, this was enough to substantiate his case that the wife of Manuel Alvares had fled out of fear lest her sister-in-law would reveal to the inquisitors that she and her daughters were adherents of the Jewish law.

On 25 October 1641, when asked by the Cuenca inquisitors the address of the house where he had lived in Málaga, Manuel Alvares replied that 'he had resided in the said city at three addresses: first in the street known as Manzanares or La Oliva, half-way down the street, in a property belonging to Salvador de Vaesa... he had lived in this house for approximately six or seven years, after which he had moved to another house in the same street, three doors away; that house belonged to an unmarried lady called doña Gerónima de Manzanares. After he had lived there for nearly six years, he had moved to the plaza doña Marquesa, into a house the property of the *regidor* Juan López de Viloslada. Here he had been living for about two or three years, and it was in that house that he had left his wife and children when he went away from Málaga for the reason that he had stated: and he still owed about 100 ducats' rent...'[125]

As soon as the Cuenca Inquisition had heard this from Manuel, considering the detailed information to be significant they wrote the very same day to the Granada Inquisition, asking them to arrange for the inquisitional commissary in Málaga to question the landlord of the house in the plaza doña Marquesa, as well as a number of other acquaintances of the Alvares family.[126] After three days a Portuguese

---

[124] She was questioned on 11 Sept. 1641, ibid., ff. 33 f. This is further evidence that the Alvares family had previously resided for a space of time in Madrid; cf. above, chap. 1, p. 4.

[125] Leg. 462 no. 6346 (unpaginated).

[126] Leg. 462 no. 6351, ff. 39 f.

named Manuel Fernández was questioned in Málaga. He stated in evidence that Manuel Alvares had intended to move to Antequera, since 'in Málaga he was unable to keep going and to support his family'.[127] He also stated—either through lack of knowledge of the true facts, or in order to cover his former neighbours' trail—that Manuel Alvares, his wife, and sons had departed for Antequera 'about a year past, and he had remained there (according to witness) for but a few days; he had later heard that the whole family had gone off to Lisbon, after which he had heard no more of them.'[128] Another neighbour, named Miguel Herrera (also Portuguese) stated in testimony deposed by him on 1 November that Manuel Alvares 'was a very poor man'.[129] Two weeks later don Juan López de Viloslada, owner of the house in plaza doña Marquesa, was interrogated. He said 'he had let the houses[130] regarding which he was being questioned to Manuel Alvares at a rent of 100 ducats per annum . . . he did not know whether he had let the said houses for a higher rent, because no contract between them had ever been signed. He had let them to the aforementioned party because Mateo Rodríguez . . . had taken the properties and paid the rent.'[131] When the Alvares family had left the house and departed from Málaga for the area of La Mancha, 'they had not returned him the keys, which had been left with Mateo Rodríguez who had been seeking a tenant for the houses'.[132]

It seems clear that fortune had not smiled on Manuel Alvares in Málaga, and that at this period he was hard put to it to maintain his family. His brother-in-law Mateo Rodríguez,[133] the brother of his wife Mencia, tried in various ways to get them out of their troubles. As *tesorero* (collector) of the *millones*[134] for Málaga he found employment for Manuel in collecting tax-payments for the *millones* and the *Sisa*[135] from the local inhabitants. Mateo, too, was interviewed by the Málaga

[127] Ibid., ff. 46 f.
[128] Ibid.
[129] Ibid., ff. 50 f.
[130] It would seem that what is really meant is rooms, i.e. an apartment.
[131] Ibid., ff. 59 f.
[132] Ibid.
[133] For him see above, chap. 1, p. 4.
[134] The *millones* tax was introduced in Castile in 1590, being so called because its yield was reckoned in millions of ducats. It was essentially a tax on consumer goods (meat, wine, oil, etc.) and was designed to offset the cost of maintaining the king's guard and the salaries of government officials. See Elliot, *Spain*, pp. 285 f.
[135] Ibid. (n. 126 above), ff. 60 f. The *sisa*, which combined a number of indirect taxes, had already been instituted in Spain in the Middle Ages: see Baer, *History*, i, p. 231, ii, pp. 21, 63, 126.

commissary of the Inquisition, and in evidence given on 15 October 1641 he painted a dark picture of the dearth of material resources that affected his brother-in-law at the time of his residence there.[136]

When Vallejo was apprised of all this testimony, he gained the distinct impression that the witnesses 'had come forward to testify knowing very well the circumstances owing to which they had been cited'.[137] The Cuenca prosecutor was convinced that all four were guilty of perjury and that they had suppressed material items which would inevitably have revealed the date of Mencia's flight and the causes that had prompted her to leave Málaga so suddenly. On 19 December 1641 he recommended that the inquisitors of the Cuenca court ask the Granada inquisitors to place Mencia under arrest, on the strength of the evidence against her emanating from the trials of Violante de Paz and her daughters.[138] By then Vallejo knew that Mencia and her children were living in Seville, in a house situated in the calle de la Carpintería.[139]

The Cuenca court did not accede to Vallejo's recommendation, but decided to close the file of the investigation of Mencia Núñez for lack of reliable proof.[140] On the following day, 20 December, Vallejo appealed to the Inquisitor General in Madrid, Antonio de Sotomayor, and complained about the court's decision.[141] His complaint was upheld, and on 11 February 1642 the Granada court was ordered by the Superior Council of the Inquisition to recommence the investigation of Mencia Núñez.[142]

Four letters sent to Manuel Alvares, impounded by the inquisitors, contained indications of certain financial involvements on his part. They consequently opened an additional file of documents to assemble a case against him. The name of the addressee on these letters was 'Francisco Días Coronel', but the experienced investigators of the

---

[136] Ibid.: (n. 126 above), ff. 60 f.: 'dixo que era un hombre pobre y que nunca tubo conpañia con nadie desta çiudad sino tan solamente comisiones deste testigo y otros particulares y en faltando compraba algunos lienzos de poco valor y los yba a vender por los lugares comarcanos . . . '

[137] Ibid., f. 63.

[138] Ibid., f. 64.

[139] He knew this from the testimony deposed before the inquisitors of the Cuenca court on 7 Oct. 1641 by Núñez de Gobea with reference to Baltazar Alvares: 'que no sabe como se llama pero sabe que bibe en la calle de la Carpinteria . . . ' (Leg. 462 no. 6346, unpaginated).

[140] Leg. 462 no. 6351, ff. 65 f.   [141] Ibid., f. 66.   [142] Ibid., f. 69.

A Long Brush with the Inquisition, 1639–1643 55

tribunal soon showed this up as an assumed name, concealing the identity of Manuel Alvares himself. It had also become clear to them that two of the letters had been written by his son, Baltazar Alvares, though they bore the pseudonymous signature of 'Francisco Enríquez Villacorta'. Of the remaining two letters, one was unsigned and the signature on the other had been scrawled through: but they had been written by Mateo Rodríguez.[143]

Part of each of the four letters was in covert language, by means of which the correspondent had intended to convey to Manuel information about his family's situation, about the developments in the trials of his kin held in Toledo and Granada, and regarding financial matters in which Manuel was involved.

Mateo Rodríguez had written both his letters from Madrid, on 3 July and 27 July 1641: and from their contents it is clear that the *tesorero de los millones* of Málaga had been exploiting his connections with the authorities in order to discover the substance of the evidence that had been assembled against Manuel and Santiago at the inquisitional tribunals of Toledo and Granada. In his first letter he wrote: 'I am sorry that the dispatches [*despachos*] have not arrived, and until they do, you yourself will be unable to get away [*no le an de despachar*]. Let us wait and see whether those from Granada come; if those from Toledo fail to materialize, one will consider how best to get information about

---

[143] All the relevant documents are to be found in Leg. 462 no. 6346, of which the folios are not only unpaginated but in part are in chronological disorder. Copies of the 4 letters here referred to are located at the beginning of the file, and the originals of the two from Mateo Rodríguez are amongst the folios at the end. The copy of the first letter written by Baltazar Alvares under the pseudonym of Francisco Enríquez Villacorta bears the following annotation by the prosecutor: 'esta carta fue la que se le cogio que venia con cubierta para Gaspar de Gobea y ella con un sobrescrito diffraçado y el mismo preso a reconoçido es de su hijo.' For Gaspar de Gobea see below, p. 59. The copy of Baltazar's second letter is endorsed by Vallejo 'otra carta del mismo su hijo'. Amongst the contentions put forward by Simón Núñez de Gobea in his evidence before the Cuenca tribunal on 7 Oct. 1641, in which he maintained that he was not the writer of the letters, he observed that he would have been incapable of writing them since he did not know Portuguese—implying that that was the language used in them. It is, however, doubtful how much weight can be placed upon this testimony. As regards the pseudonym Francisco Enríquez Villacorta, Révah had noticed that such was the name of one of the students in the college of Madre de Dios at Alcalá during Baltazar's time there: he would, in due course, become well known as a professor of medicine and as court physician to Philip IV. Jan Rieuwerts, first printer of Spinoza's *Tractatus Theologico-Politicus*, availed himself of this same pseudonym for one part of it in the 2nd edn. (1673). See Révah, *rupt. spin., nouvel examen*, 71, pp. 582 f., and [J. C. E. Belinfante, J. Kingma, A. K. Offenberg], *Spinoza: troisième centenaire de la morte du philosophe*, Paris, 1977, p. 58.

them.'¹⁴⁴ It is obvious that what Mateo meant by 'dispatches' was the contents of the depositions at Granada and Toledo against Manuel and Santiago. This conclusion is substantiated by the second letter, in which Mateo was at less pains to be circumspect and wrote more explicitly: 'the district attorney [*fiscal*] of Toledo has been here, and accompanied by a friend I went to have a talk with him. He received us in a most kindly way, and took a note to write without delay to Toledo that they should send the papers . . . let me know whether they have yet done so from Granada.'¹⁴⁵

Clearly Mateo had succeeded—thanks to his connections in high places and thanks also, perhaps, to a little bribery—in persuading the officials of the tribunals in Toledo and Granada to pass information to Manuel. He thus learned the substance of the incriminating evidence relative to himself that had been assembled in the trials of members of his family. That Dr Vallejo, the Cuenca prosecutor, was very well aware of this is shown by the spluttering fury of the following words, penned by him in the margin of the transcript of the two letters: 'these "papers" can be nothing other than the evidence which was called for in a communication from Cuenca. How could he inform him [Manuel] [about the papers] unless he had been in touch with those possessed of confidential information?'¹⁴⁶

The two remaining letters were written by Baltazar on 25 June and 2 July 1641. Although he purported to have dispatched them from Córdoba, the inquisitors at Cuenca had no trouble in showing that this detail was contrived, and that he had in fact written them from Seville, where he and other members of his family were staying.¹⁴⁷ Baltazar was doing his best to sustain his father's spirits, and related to him how the family were settling down at Seville. In his first letter he wrote:

Simón had arrived in good health, bringing with him the furniture in two waggons. Although he had disposed of some things there at a good price, he

---

¹⁴⁴ Mateo Rodríguez' 1st letter (see above n. 143): 'Los despachos me pesan no baya y en quanto no fueren no le an de despachar; beamos si ban de Granada y sino ubieren ydo los de Toledo se bera el medio que se a de tomar para inteligencia.'

¹⁴⁵ Ibid.: 'Aqui estaba el fiscal de Toledo y le fuy hablar con un amigo y nos hiço mucha merçed y tomo de memoria el escribir a Toledo luego al punto remitiesen los papeles . . . abiseme si de Granada lo an hecho . . . '

¹⁴⁶ Ibid.: 'estos papeles no pueden ser otros sino las testificaçiones que se avia embiado a pedir de Cuenca. Cómo le podia avisar sin comunicarse con los del secreto?'

¹⁴⁷ Ibid., examination of Manuel Alvares on 8 Oct. 1641 (the words are those of the investigators): 'En la carta de 25 de junio deste año diçe "Simon vino con salud y trajo en dos carretas todos los trastos" en que claramente se ve que habla de Simon Rodriguez su yerno, marido de Leonor Albarez su hija . . . ' See continuation, ibid.

has brought both writing-desks and practically all the wooden items, save for some chairs.[148]

He also wrote that

God willing, we shall be moving within four days to a house situated in a good district, costing seventy-four *reales* [in rent] ... Simón is already installed in his shop, pray God he will do well. Doña Luisa enjoys good health; as for the rest of us—Leonor is pregnant, Manuelico is a fine little fellow. They all send you many expressions of remembrance ... and many greetings also to your companion, from all of us.[149]

This letter informed Manuel that his son-in-law Simón Rodríguez[150] had joined up with the family in Seville, and that he had opened a shop. 'Luisa' could be none other than his wife Mencia. Leonor was his eldest daughter,[151] wife of Simón, and Manuel, his grandson, was their child.

In his second letter Baltazar repeated himself: 'Simón is in his shop, thank God he is very happy, and his business is going well ... Leonor is pregnant, and the children are fine; Manuel has a nursemaid ... Doña Luisa sends you many many remembrances ... I had forgotten to say that Melchor [Baltazar's younger brother] was very ill with raging fever for six days. He was bled four times—it pleased God that he should have such a rash of measles ... he is quite well now, and quite a gallant young man, thank God...'[152]

Naturally Baltazar did not neglect to write about himself in either letter, and he refers to his problems as a fledgling professional physician and his plans for the future:

Professionally, things are not much good; this is not just because I am a beginner, but because it is difficult to make oneself known in such a confusing city;

---

[148] Ibid., 1st letter: 'Simon vino con salud y trajo en dos carretas los trastos, si bien bendio alla algunas cosas vien bendidas, trujo anbos escritorios y toda casi la madera, menos algunas sillas ...'
[149] Ibid.: 'Nos mudamos de aqui a quatro dias con el favor de Dios a una casa que aunque esta en buen barrio es buena y de setenta y quatro reales ... Simon esta ya en su tienda quiera Dios darle provecho en ella; Doña Luisa esta con salud y los demas, Leonor preñada y Manuelico gran muchacho; todos envian a Vm. muchos recaudos al conpañero de Vm. muchas encomiendas de todos nosotros.' Manuel's 'compañero' was, of course, his brother Santiago Luis.
[150] On whom, see above, p. 34.   [151] See above, Table B, chap. 1.
[152] Ibid.: 'Simon esta en su tienda muy contento y negoçia muy vien graçias a Dios ... Leonor con su preñado y los niños muy lindos; Manuel tiene ama ... Doña Luisa envia a Vm. muchos recaudos ... olvidavaseme de dezir, Melchor estuvo muy malo seis dias, con grande calentura ardiente, sangrado quatro vezes, quiso Dios que arrojo tanto sarampion ... ya esta muy bueno y muy galan graçias a Dios ...'

and although I have no doubt that, given time, I shall do all right in it, now is not the time to be going along incurring expenses without bringing in any income. I have consequently decided to do the same as you, because that is the soundest course to take,[153] but I will not take it until you come unless don Jorge[154] comes here first, as he told me he would, in order to visit his uncle in Écija and on his way takes me to Alcalá: there, he assures me, I can make a comfortable living. You ask if the mule was stolen from me and I do not know who could have told you any such thing—some mindless person—as if one can lose a mule as easily as mislaying a pin![155]

In this vein the young Baltazar described to his father his difficulties and struggles in the early days of his residence in Seville, whilst he was trying to make his way as an unknown, would-be doctor in a city where, as a stranger, he did not know his way around.

In his second letter he wrote:

Professionally, there is very little improvement so far, and what I earn is just enough to keep the mule in fodder. I do not mean to complain, because up till now I have been living in a very isolated house without getting myself known; however, I am now resolved to leave town when Jorge comes, but I shall not do anything until the happy day when you return, and meanwhile may it be God's will that things will improve.[156]

Baltazar also mentioned 'the journey which the Tesorero had made to the capital', hinting at the endeavours of Mateo Rodríguez in Madrid on behalf of Manuel and Santiago.[157]

[153] i.e., he hints that he proposes to try his luck elsewhere, in the same way that Manuel Alvares had done.

[154] Don Jorge = Dr Jorge Correa, as Manuel indicated in his testimony during the afternoon session of the court on 8 Oct. 1641.

[155] Ibid., Baltazar's 1st letter: 'es que se marca mal el ofiçio y no es tanto por ser yo moderno, como por la dificultad de darme a conozer en una çiudad tan confusa, aunque no dudo que pasando algun tienpo, tendria mucho en ella, pero no esta el tienpo para andar pasando tiempo con gasto y sin ganançia y asi yo estoy resuelto a hacer lo que a Vm. echo ques lo mas seguro lo qual no hare asta que Vm. venga, si don Gorge [sic] no llega antes cuia venida segun me auisa solamente es a ver un tio que tiene en Eçija y de camino llebarme a Alcala con seguridad de tener luego partido acomodado. Diçe Vm. que si me han hurtado la mula y no se quien le dijo eso, algun sonso, como si fuera perder una mula dejar caer un alfiler . . .'

[156] Ibid.: 'el ofiçio por agorra [sic] corre muy poco, que lo solamente se gana para la mula. No deçeo quexarme por auer estado asta agora en tan retirada casa sin darme a conozer, aunque esta ya determinado a yrme en llegando el Jorge, no hare cossa asta que Vm. venga en buena ora y entre tanto querra Dios que se sanee la cossa . . .'

[157] Ibid., 1st letter: 'Ya Vm. abra tenido aviso del viaje del Tesorero a la Corte y del sentimiento que tubo de lo mal que el Salinero huso con Vm., de adonde jusgo que no dexan de negoçiarse a gusto aquella partida porque el Tesorero va resuelto a eso tanvien . . .'

A Long Brush with the Inquisition, 1639–1643

As indicated above, in these four letters the inquisitors found various items of information regarding Manuel's economic activities. Part of that 'information' was no more than a cover by means of which Baltazar Alvares and Mateo Rodríguez intended to bring Manuel up to date about developments in the two inquisitional investigations in Toledo and in Granada that could have an influence on the fate of Manuel himself and Santiago.[158] However, the correspondence also contained references to substantial sums of money received by Manuel and his family from Fernando Alvares,[159] whom we have already mentioned in connection with the investigation of Manuel Sarmiento in Toledo.[160] There was also reference to the sale by Mateo Rodríguez of a piece of jewellery belonging to the family,[161] to an amount held by the family in sterling,[162] and to business dealings in which members of the Alvares family had been involved.[163]

On 2 October 1641 the Cuenca inquisitors commenced the investigation of a certain Gaspar de Gobea, a Portuguese resident of Cuenca, who had lent Manuel money when he and his brother had arrived there. In his evidence, Gaspar confirmed that it was from him that Manuel had received the letters addressed to Francisco Días Coronel, and that on one occasion Manuel had unburdened his soul to him 'because he had had no news of his son, and had been informed that some accident had befallen him and he had been killed in a place near Manzanares—he did not recall whether Manuel had mentioned Las Peñas [sc. Valdepeñas?] but that the letters which he had brought him contained the good news that he had been found alive'.[164]

From the evidence contained in this file it is clear that Manuel and Santiago were not placed behind bars by the Inquisition immediately on their presenting themselves before the Cuenca tribunal. For a month or more they were free to move around the city, although their investigation had already commenced.[165] During this time Manuel

---

[158] See above, n. 144 (Mateo Rodríguez), and cf. Baltazar's 2nd letter: 'juzgando que ya avia Vmd. salido de esa çiudad quiera Dios que sea con la brevedad que deseo que por tener dependençia de otros mercaderes de Toledo y Granada me da arto cuidado'.

[159] Ibid., Mateo Rodríguez' 1st letter: 'Fernando Albarez me abisa haçeto la letra de los 200 Reales que Vm. le saco y que su yerno no abia querido haçetar una de mill Reales . . .'   [160] See above, p. 34.

[161] Ibid., Baltazar's 1st letter: 'y estoy informado de çierto que vendio la prenda . . .'

[162] Ibid.: 'Las esterlinas estan en poder de Prinçipe . . .'

[163] Ibid.: 'y tengo la ropa en el lugar que suele ponerse. Fio en Dios que en viniendo la flota a de tener buen despacho porque agora no dan cossa de ganançia . . .'

[164] Ibid., testimony of Gaspar de Gobea.

[165] Ibid., transcript of examination of Mateo Rodríguez in Málaga on 1 Dec. 1641.

received some of the letters that had been sent to him, viz. the ones which had been brought to Cuenca by Gaspar de Gobea's son, Simón Núñez de Gobea. Simón was summoned before the inquisitorial tribunal, and he told how he had received one letter in Seville, at the inn of San Cristóbal, 'from a dark-skinned young man, in his judgement aged about twenty-six or twenty-eight, who had come to the inn on foot and whose name he did not know . . . After [Simón] had told him that he was from Cuenca and was the son of Gaspar de Gobea, he had asked him to do him the favour of taking the said letter with him: he never told him who the sender was, nor to whom it was addressed.'[166]

The inquisitors did not accept Simón's contention that he had been prepared to accept, from a party of whose identity he was ignorant, a letter 'the contents of which gave grounds for concluding that the party was none other than Baltazar Alvares, by profession a physician, now staying in Seville, son of Manuel Alvares, of the Portuguese nation, resident in Málaga'.[167] Simón was held in confinement, and when he was interrogated a second time he stated that 'the man who had given him the letter in Seville was a physician whose name he did not know, but he did know that he resided in the calle de la Carpintería, in a house on the corner'.[168] He further stated that 'he had stayed about two months [in Seville], having gone there with his kinsman Duarte Enríquez Alvares who had proceeded there in his capacity as Tesorero of the Canary Islands, and the latter's brother Daniel Enríquez, and some others of his party'.[169] One may surmise that this Duarte Enríquez Alvares — at that time principal collector of the royal revenues in the Canaries, and destined for subsequent fame as one of the earliest Jewish settlers in London publicly to avow their Judaism before Oliver Cromwell and the Council of State on 22 April 1656 — was a family connection of the Gobeas of Cuenca. Indeed, it would

---

[166] His examination commenced on 7 Oct. 1641: ibid.: 'le dio estando este declarante en la çiudad de Sevilla en la Posada de San Cristobal con otras personas y luego dixo que estaba solo un ombre mançebo moreno que a su pareçer seria de asta bentiseis o bentiocho años y que no sabe el nombre y llego a pie . . . y diçiendole que era de Cuenca y que era hijo de Gaspar de Gobea le dixo que le içiera merçed de encaminar aquella carta sin deçirle de quien ni para quien . . .'

[167] Ibid.: 'y que no es de creer que no conoçiese la persona que se las dio lo qual consta por dichas cartas que es Baltasar Albarez hijo de Manuel Albarez, portuguez, veçino de Malaga, de profesion medico y veçino de la Çiudad de Sevilla . . .'

[168] Ibid.: 'dixo que la persona que le dio la carta en la çiudad de Sevilla es un medico que no sabe como se llama pero sabe que bibe en la calle de la Carpiteria [sic] en una casa en una esquina . . .'   [169] Ibid., evidence on 8 Oct. 1641.

A Long Brush with the Inquisition, 1639–1643

hardly be rash to conjecture on the basis of his surname that Duarte Enríquez Alvares himself belonged to one of the branches of the greater Alvares clan that stemmed from Braganza.[170]

On 8 October 1641 Manuel Alvares was brought from the inquisitional prison of Cuenca to give evidence regarding his property. To begin with, he refused to admit that the letters had been intended for him, but as in the course of his examination he was broken down he conceded that 'Francisco Días Coronel' was a pseudonym for himself, and that 'Francisco Enríquez Villacorta' was in fact his son Baltazar. On the other hand, he vehemently denied the accusation of concealment of property with which the inquisitors confronted him.[171] He claimed that the sums of money mentioned in the letters were merely evidence of his own pitiful financial position, and of the vast sum for which he was indebted—to Fernando Alvares, to his brother-in-law Mateo Rodríguez, and to Simón, his own son-in-law.[172] He further added that 'he had only come to Cuenca to find salvation for his soul: and that of one thing he was certain, that he had not concealed anything at all in the matter of faith, and that he was minded to declare the truth; but that in the matter of property, he had nothing on his conscience [for not having disclosed the whole of the truth], inasmuch as he had three daughters and such heavy obligations, and [must be ever conscious of] the dangers to which they were exposed in virtue of their sex should they find themselves in need ... He consequently asked pardon of God, and of the holy tribunal, should any offence [in this connection] be found in him.'[173]

---

[170] His official title was *Recaudador mayor de las rentas y almoxarifasgo de las islas*. He had been born in Fundão, in the district of Beira in Portugal. See Beinart, *London*, pp. 16 f. Gobea's evidence confirms Beinart's supposition that Duarte Enríquez occupied the office of *recaudador* during the 1640s.

[171] Manuel had already been questioned about this matter on 4 July 1641, Leg. 462 no. 6348, ff. 68 f. On 6 July he claimed that he had left property worth 4,000 *reales* in Valdepeñas. According to him, he had lost most of his property in Málaga at the time of the plague; ibid., ff. 86 f.

[172] Amongst those to whom he owed money he mentioned 'Adrien Paez, de naçion ingles ... Juan Caldenn, flamenco': ibid., f. 87, also ff. 68 f.: 'Dixo que Gaspar de Gobea le a dado a este mil Reales y para açerle pago della le dio tres letras y luego dixo que eran quatro como consta abia del memorial que montan mil y çinquenta reales en Fernando Albarez de Amezquita, vezino de Madrid, por aberle ofreçido a este el dicho Fernando Albarez, estando en Madrid ... ' Cf. the evidence that he gave at the afternoon session of the court on 8 Oct. 1641, Leg. 462 no. 6346.

[173] Leg. 462 no. 6346. evidence at the morning session of the same date: 'Dixo que el no bino sino con intençion de salbar su anima y que lo que sabe de çierto es que no a encubierto nada de cosas de la fee, que su animo a sido de deçir la berdad y que en materia de la açienda como tiene tres hijas y tantas obligaçiones y peligro que podian

Vallejo requested the court to send instructions for the interrogation of Fernando Alvares in Madrid, of Mateo Rodríguez in Málaga, and Baltazar Alvares in Seville. The court assented and instructions were in fact dispatched, but of the three mentioned only Mateo Rodríguez was investigated.[174] For it would seem that Fernando and Baltazar managed to evade the grasp of the inquisitors.

On 1 December 1641 Mateo Rodríguez was interrogated in the chamber of the inquisitorial commissary in Málaga. He maintained to his investigators that Manuel Alvares had written to him from Cuenca that 'since he had some business there with the Holy Inquisition and, not being in confinement, was moving about freely but was not known by his real name, [Mateo] should write to him as "Francisco Días Coronel" '.[175] He likewise maintained that he had neglected to sign his first letter out of absent-mindedness, and that it was not he who was responsible for defacing the signature of the second.

The inquisitors in Málaga conducted a meticulous search of Mateo's house, but found nothing in his ledgers to incriminate either him or Manuel. Mateo explained that what he had written in his letters about 'dispatches' from Toledo and Granada had nothing to do with business affairs, but referred to trials that were being conducted in the inquisitorial courts against members of their family.[167] It is astonishing that Mateo's frankness did not prompt the inquisitors to attempt to clarify how it was that he had succeeded in conveying such confidentially safeguarded information to Manuel. Could it be that Mateo's connections with the authorities stood him in such good stead that he succeeded in hushing the whole affair up?

It looks as though the inquisitors of the Cuenca tribunal were satisfied with the information that had accumulated in their hands after six months of continuous and exhausting inquiry. On 16 December 1641 they resolved to reconcile Manuel Alvares and Santiago Luis to the bosom of the Church, to impose upon them the penalty of one year's imprisonment, to compel them to wear the *sanbenito*, and to confiscate their property.[177]

---

correr por ser mugeres y berse con neçesidad ... le pareçia que no encargaba su conçiençia y que asi pide perdon a Dios y a este Santo Tribunal si en alguna cosa se a encontrado ... ' Manuel here mentions 3 of his daughters only, referring to the 3 that were still unmarried. His daughter Leonor was already married, as has been stated, to Simon Rodríguez Monsanto.

[174] Ibid. Instructions were dispatched on 24 Oct. 1641.
[175] See above, p. 59.
[176] Ibid.   [177] Leg. 462 no. 6348, ff. 147 f.

A Long Brush with the Inquisition, 1639–1643

Vallejo lodged an objection to the decision of the Cuenca court with the Inquisitor General and, in consequence of his objection, on 4 February 1642 the Superior Council of the Inquisition addressed a request to the Cuenca tribunal to set into operation a further inquiry into the case.[178] The reopened inquiry did not last long, and at its conclusion the decisions of the court were upheld. The two brothers were reconciled to the Church at ceremonies held in the church of San Pedro in Cuenca: Santiago Luis on 10 February, and Manuel Alvares on 24 March. Their performance of the specified penalties was then commenced.[179]

However, on 25 June the convicted brothers were set free before completing their full sentence, at the instigation of Antonio de Sotomayor, the Inquisitor General. The court even remitted the penalty of wearing the *sanbenito*, substituting for it the obligation to fast on Fridays for a whole year, to say over the rosary of the Blessed Virgin Mary every week, and, once a month, to attend service at the principal church in whatever place they were living.[180]

What was it that induced Sotomayor to extend mercy to Manuel and Santiago? It would seem that once again the *tesorero de los millones* of Málaga had interested himself on their behalf with the inquisitional authorities, in the same way that he had done during the course of their investigation.

The release of Manuel and Santiago did not quite mark the end of the chapter since, as a consequence of Vallejo's objection and recommendations to the Inquisitor General noted above,[181] the investigation of Mencia Núñez, wife of Manuel Alvares, was still pending. Not until 22 November 1643, the inquisitors having reached the conclusion that the proofs assembled against her did not warrant a conviction, did they resolve to reaffirm their decision of December 1641, closing her file and concluding her investigation.[182]

At last, after having endured four years of terror, the Alvares family could breathe freely. In Seville, new hopes were opening up before them.

[178] Ibid., ff. 149 f.
[179] Ibid., ff. 167 f., 175.
[180] Ibid., ff. 175 f.
[181] See above, p. 54.
[182] Leg. 462 no. 6351 ff. 65 f.

3
Building a Career in Andalusia

PROFESSOR AT SEVILLE AND SERVICE TO THE
DUKE OF MEDINACELI

Baltazar's plans for leaving Seville to try his fortune elsewhere were not realized. Possibly he decided to stay at his family's side once it had become clear that his father's investigation before the inquisitional tribunal at Cuenca was getting ever more complex, and hopes of his early release and reunion with his wife and children had been dashed. He consequently took the decision to make his home base in the capital city of Andalusia, and on 12 October 1641 he entered himself as a candidate for the chair of medical method which was then vacant. There being no other applicants for the post, the university authorities (after considerable procrastination and delay) gave him the appointment.[1]

The falling-away in standards of scholarship that was noticeable at this time in other Spanish universities had left its mark also on the university of Seville. The Jesuit college of St Hermenegildo, and that of the Dominicans named after St Thomas, vied with the university successfully enough to be able to skim off the most able potential students in the city and its environs. The low salaries paid to the professors contributed not a little to the decay of academic quality, making it impossible to attract superior talent. Only the medical faculty stood any chance of changing for the better, since apart from the university there was no institution in the city that could train future physicians; but the conservatism in which the university itself was swathed inhibited all progress.[2]

It is not clear what certificate of professional qualifications Baltazar laid before the university authorities when he entered himself as a candidate for the professorship. We have seen above that he left Alcalá

[1] Révah, *rupt. spin., nouvel examen*, 71, pp. 583 f.
[2] For a general survey of the history of the university of Seville, see Campelo y Allueva; for its decadence in the 17th cent. see Dom. Ortiz and Ag. Piñal, pp. 116 f. For the resistance offered by the medical faculty to the experimental approach that the Spanish Royal Society of Medicine in Seville was endeavouring to establish in the 17th cent. see ibid., pp. 118 f., and, esp., Soledad Rubio, pp. 197 f.

Building a Career in Andalusia 65

without a medical degree,[3] and it is not to be assumed that he would have found opportunity thereafter to complete his studies in another institution. Moreover, it appears that in France in 1660, when he was registered in the medical faculty at Toulouse, all he possessed was his degree of bachelor of arts from the university of Alcalá.[4] This circumstance lends plausibility to the assumption that he was accepted by the university of Seville without producing evidence of any formal degree in medicine. Révah has suggested two possibilities. Conceivably, Baltazar presented a forged certificate—not an unknown phenomenon at this period—or perhaps he had succeeded in procuring some document from the university of Osuna, where he had taken the first steps in his specialization in his chosen subject.[5] Whatever the facts, Baltazar got his appointment mainly because the heads of the university had been stymied in their search for another candidate; and they consequently did not examine his credentials too closely.

After two years Baltazar voluntarily relinquished his chair at Seville, in circumstances not known to us.[6] By now he had made his name as a doctor of some professional standing and he was consequently no longer dependent upon the paltry sum that his university professorship could bring him. At this time he was retained as personal physician by don Antonio Juan Luis de Cerda, Duke of Medinaceli, whose place of residence was Seville.

The period that Baltazar spent at the ducal court is enshrouded in darkness, no details at all being preserved.[7] Medinaceli was one of the most influential members of the nobility in Spain, famous for his love of letters and his scholarship and as a patron of poets and artists. In his entourage Baltazar probably encountered an intellectual challenge unlike anything that he could find within the walls of the university of Seville.[8] The Duke was keenly interested in classical languages and antiquities, and in 1636 the story went the rounds of Madrid that 'the Duke of Medinaceli was applying himself assiduously to learning Hebrew, and with this object in view he had installed a rabbi [*rabí*] in his house; he had, indeed, made such progress that he could read

---

[3] See above, chap. 1, p. 23.   [4] See below, chap. 5, pp. 101.
[5] Révah, loc. cit. (n. 1 above).   [6] Ibid., p. 589.
[7] Orobio de Castro himself later recorded this detail of his career in his writings, where he also claimed to have attended (or at any rate to have been retained professionally by) the house of Burgundy: 'médico de Cámara de el Duque de Medinaçeli y de la familia de Borgoña de el Rey Phelipe Quarto'.

[8] On the Duke of Medinaceli see *EUIEA* 34, p. 137, and cf. Dom. Ortiz and Ag. Piñal, p. 27.

[Hebrew] without vowel-points.[9] There can be little doubt that this picture of a Christian nobleman who was expert in the holy tongue would have intrigued Baltazar and indeed have aroused his warm interest, and possibly he found opportunity, during his period of service with the Duke, to lay the beginnings of a foundation of knowledge of the Hebrew language.

The Alvares family left Seville at an unknown date. They were business people, and perhaps the successive economic crises that hit the city in the 1630s and 40s had affected them.[10] Or possibly they hesitated to remain for a long stretch of time in a locality where one of the keenest tribunals in the whole of the Spanish Inquisition had its centre of operations.[11] Or again, fresh commercial possibilities may have opened up for them elsewhere.

A document dated 1654 suggests that in about 1647 Baltazar was in Écija, where he was on the point of marrying a daughter of Francisco Rodríguez Almeida, a Portuguese resident there, but that at the last moment he changed his mind and the wedding was cancelled—to the intense indignation of the intended bride's father.[12] But the source does not make it clear whether Baltazar was actually resident in Écija, or whether he had merely gone there to make arrangements for his projected marriage.[13] At all events, by 1648 at the latest the family was living at Sanlúcar de Barrameda, a small town near to Jerez de la Frontera and Cádiz.[14] But here again they found no peace of mind, and

[9] See A. Rodríguez Villa (ed.), *La corte y la monarquía de España en los años de 1636 a 1637*, Madrid, 1886, p. 38: 'El Duque de Medinaceli estudia valientemente la lengua hebrea, teniendo en su casa un rabi para este efecto, y ha hecho tan grandes progresos que ya sabe leer sin puntos.'   [10] See Dom. Ortiz and Ag. Piñal, pp. 12 f., 71 f.

[11] Ibid., pp. 110 f., and see Montero de Espinosa, pp. 94 f.

[12] See Madrid, AHN, Inquisition section, Leg. 2067 no. 100, f. 5ʳ (Simón Rodríguez Monsanto before the Seville Inquisition, 14 Dec. 1654): 'Dijo quanto abra seys o siete años que el dicho doctor su cuñado se trato de casarse en Ezija con una hija de Françisco Rodriguez Almeyda y estaua ajustado y auia prendas y correspondençia y el dicho doctor no se quisso cassar y por esta caussa ubo muchos disgustos . . .' Simón alleged that he had been held in confinement by the Inquisition, together with Baltazar Orobio his brother-in-law, in consequence of denunciation by Francisco Rodríguez, who wanted to get even with them because of the affair; see below, chap. 4, p. 80.

[13] Ibid., Simón Rodríguez' testimony: 'Dijo que si conozia al dicho Françisco Rodriguez Almeida a este y que en San Lucar viuian en una cassa al tiempo que se tratauan los cassamientos referidos pero con este no auia tenido disgusto . . .' From this it appears that at the material time Simón Rodríguez and his family were resident in Sanlúcar de Barrameda, but there is no specific statement regarding Baltazar; possibly he was himself living in Écija.

[14] Madrid, AHN (as n. 12 above), Leg. 2987, 'Mérito del Dor. Balthasar de Orobio', f. 1ʳ: 'este reo fue testificado en la Inquisiçion de Valladolid por un testigo menor formal de que por el mes de Agosto de quarenta y siete o quarenta y ocho estando en la çiudad de San Lucar . . .'

Building a Career in Andalusia 67

they moved on southward, to Cádiz itself. Here Baltazar met Isabel Pérez de la Peña, daughter of Francisco Pérez, merchant of Puerto Real, and married her.[15] The marriage was a source of much blessing to the Alvares family, because as a result of it Baltazar became a partner in the business affairs of his well-to-do father-in-law, and had enough to support the entire family.[16]

SCIENTIFIC DISCUSSION OF PHLEBOTOMY

In 1653—some ten years after resigning his chair at Seville—Baltazar published there a medical treatise written in Latin, under the title *Controvertitur, utrum materialibus morbis inchoantibus sang[uinis] missio revulsiva juxta Hippocratis et Galeni dogmata per distantissimas venas effici debeat?* The work was dedicated to Pedro Miguel de Heredia, Baltazar's teacher at Alcalá, the doctor of Philip IV, who was one of the few physicians in Spain in the seventeenth century whose name meant anything beyond the confines of his own country.

This tract was composed in the very midst of a controversy regarding the appropriate part of the body to which bleeding should, when necessary, be applied. Discussion of this medical question took place in Seville in 1652 to 1653, not less than eleven physicians taking part, including several who were colleagues of Baltazar's.[17] The debate

[15] Leg. 2067 no. 95, f. 13ʳ (evidence of Baltazar before the Seville tribunal, 14 Aug. 1654): 'Dijo que este se casso tres años con Doña Isauel Perez de la Peña y esta yja de el dicho Françisco Perez vezino de la Villa de Puerto Real.' The editor of the Dutch translation of Orobio's disputation with Limborch (see above, chap. 1, n. 1) stated in his introduction that Isabel Pérez came of old Christian forebears ('Kort daar na heeft hy zig in de Houwelyken Staat begeven met eene juffrouw van St. Lucar, genoemt Dona Isabella zynde van Christen afkomst'). Possibly he learned this detail from members of the Orobio de Castro family in Amsterdam at the beginning of the 18th cent. who were *au fait* with the genealogy of Esther Orobio de Castro, née Isabel Pérez.

[16] See Baltazar's evidence, ibid., f. 13ᵛ: 'Item declara que al tiempo que este se casso no tenia hazienda alguna y que lo que ganaua no hera mucho y las amistades que haçia si era poco y haçia mucho en sustentarse y a sus padres y hermanos pobres . . .' His language makes it clear that prior to his marriage his economic situation was severely cramped, and that already then he was constrained to support his parents and siblings because of their reduced circumstances. His wife brought him a dowry of 6,000 *solidos* (ibid., f. 13'); for Baltazar's business association with his father-in-law Francisco Pérez, see ibid., f. 12ʳ.

[17] Baltazar's treatise is mentioned by Révah, *Spinoza et Prado*, p. 14. As far as I am aware, it is preserved in a unique copy in the British Library, pressmark 783 g. 21(9), where it is bound up in a convolute as the last of 8 medical items. Inspection of these has led me to conclude that they all form part of a single scientific debate on a medical topic, various details regarding which are given by Hernández Morejón, iv, pp. 165 f.; v, pp. 87, 150, 357 f., 363 f.; cf. G. Marañón, 'La Literatura científica en los siglos XVI y

provides insight into the medical world of seventeenth-century Spain, and is instructive in regard to its links with contemporary European scientific thought. In particular, it is valuable evidence of the struggle that was then going on between the conservative physicians and the standard-bearers of new ideas in medicine.

Bleeding was an extremely common form of medical treatment in Europe in the Middle Ages, being practised in various ways—by phlebotomy proper, i.e. opening a vein, by the application of leeches, by scoring of the skin, etc. The underlying assumption was that in cases of general sickness it is possible, by means of bleeding, to remove the pathogenetic factor, and where localized ailments are concerned, to 'release' the inflammation. In course of time individual methods of application were developed, consideration being given to the points in the body from which the bleeding should best be undertaken. At the beginning of the modern age, and indeed right up to the middle of the nineteenth century, the letting of blood remained one of the principal methods of medical treatment.[18]

In the sixteenth and seventeenth centuries bleeding was widely accepted amongst doctors as an appropriate treatment. It was customary, in the case of localized sickness, to open a vein on the opposite side of the body from the afflicted part, and at a distance away from it. The first medical scientist to question the value of this approach, which was anchored in Arabian medicine and the methods advocated by Avicenna, was Pierre Brissot, who stirred up a storm of controversy

---

XVII', in G. Díaz-Plaja (ed.), *Historia general de las literaturas Hispánicas*, iii, Barcelona, 1953, pp. 946 f. G. Marañón's comprehensive monograph mentions neither this debate nor the various contributors to it in print. For Pedro Miguel de Heredia see *EUIEA* 27, p. 1163.

[18] On clinical bleeding see J. Bauer, *Geschichte der Aderlässe*², Munich, 1966, and cf. J. Leibowitz, art. *Haqqazah*, *'Ensiqlopedia 'ivrith*, 15, pp. 148 f. The real turning-point in regard to the resort to it occurred only after 1835, with the publication of research carried out by the French physician Pierre C. A. Louis, who proved through study of the statistics of its application in cases of pulmonary fever that it was medically inefficacious; bleeding then gave way to other treatments with a sounder basis. See F. H. Garrison, *An Introduction to the History of Medicine*³, Philadelphia and London, 1921, pp. 428 f. Bleeding was a recognized clinical practice in Jewish medicine, but the sources indicate the prevalent opinion that it is not to be used in excess. Thus the Talmud (*Gittin* 70a): '8 things are harmful in excess but beneficial in moderation, viz. travelling, sexual intercourse, wealth, work, wine, sleep, hot water [baths], and blood-letting.' Maimonides declares that one should not get into the habit of being bled regularly, but should submit thereto in case of urgent necessity only (*Hilkoth de'oth*, 4, 18). M. Perlman, *Midrash harephu'ah*, i, Tel Aviv, 5686 [1926], pp. 85 f., assembles source-material from the Talmud, *midrashim*, and the *Zohar* regarding the Jewish attitude towards clinical bleeding.

amongst contemporary practitioners by coming out in favour of bleeding from a point close to the affected part, basing himself in this on Hippocratic teaching.[19]

In 1652 there appeared in Seville a treatise by Dr Diego de Valverde Horozco on the question of the optimal location for bleeding. He argued against the new view which, according to him, had gained ground in some medical circles, and which ran counter to the conventional notion that in case of any resort to bleeding it must first be applied at the heel, regardless of the class of disease that it was proposed to treat.[20] According to Valverde the representative of the new view was 'a great scholar, who, thanks to the wealth of his learning, has secured (and deservedly so) a great reputation in society at large'.[21] Although he does not mention him by name, the language that he uses indicates that for some time there had been a running debate between the two of them about the new method and its influence.[22] Valverde's main contention was that the clinical innovator was in fact deviating from the very teachings of Hippocrates and Galen upon which he claimed to be basing himself. In his own view, all subsequent medical science and experience over a period of more than two millennia followed in their footsteps, and substantiated the correctness of their views. Valverde attacked his opponent with great forcefulness, but also with the most urbane courtesy, and warned the medical profession against his contentions which (he alleged) could imperil the equilibrium of Spain as a Christian state.[23] Regarding himself as a

[19] For Brissot (1478–1522) and his attitude, see Garrison, op. cit., pp. 226 f.
[20] For Valverde Horozco and his medical writings see Hernández Morejón, v, p. 150. His contribution to the debate was entitled *Controversia Médica, en que se disputa, si conforme al Arte y Méthodo de Medicina, se ha de variar la parte do se ha de sangrar, según las diferencias de las enfermedades, y partes afectas: o si siempre en qualquiera enfermedad, se aya de començar sangrando del touillo*. Hernández Morejón could not locate a copy, and despite search I have not so far found a copy of the 1st edn. Baltazar Alvares reprinted it as an introduction to his own treatise in 1653, Valverde's name there appearing in the title in initial form only, D.D.D.V.H. (Doctor Diego De Valverde Horozco).
[21] *Apud* Baltazar Alvares (unpaginated): 'hombre muy docto ha alcançado por sus muchas letras (con mucha razón) grande opinión entre todos . . .'
[22] Ibid., the 4 last pages: 'Esto nos sucedió curando a un personage muy grave de esta cuidad . . . Al tercero día fuymos llamados el autor de la nueva opinion, y yo . . . Conuenimos todos en la sangria, pero en quanto al lugar, diferenciamos, por querer el autor que fuesse del touillo; mas el compañero, y yo votamos se hiziesse de el braço . . .'
[23] Ibid., 3rd page: 'y temiendo el daño graue que en callar, y dissimular tal practica, le amenaça a esta República, y que llegando a los oídos de los hombres doctos y eminentes, que assisten en la casa Real, y Universidades de España, y de otros Reynos, no entiendan que en esta de Sevilla (donde tan célebres sujetos ha auido, y cuya práctica siempre ha sido tan estimada en todas partes) siguen opinión contra todo buen méthodo . . .'

faithful disciple of the masters of classical medical science, Valverde maintained that the spot from which bleeding must take place must be determined according to the class of disease concerned, the parts affected, and the causes.[24]

There is no difficulty in identifying the learned physician who was the object of Valverde's attack, since in the same year of 1652 there appeared, likewise printed at Seville, the reply of the representative of the new method, containing a reasoned defence of his position. His name was Luis Pérez Ramírez, sometime lecturer in medicine at the university of Seville, who had retired from teaching on account of his age.[25] In his reply he argued that his conception of the subject was, on the contrary, indeed anchored in classical medical writing and the medical experimentation of the ancients. In his view, nothing in his own approach deviated from Galen. However, Pérez Ramírez was not content to leave it at that. With much emphasis he launched himself into the defence of the propriety of scientific innovation, and of the right of doctors in each generation to subject their predecessors to criticism in the light of their own experience, as well as the light of experience accumulated in the treatment of patients down the ages. 'Time', wrote Pérez Ramírez, 'reveals much to us, being in fact the best of masters; and given another hundred years—or even fifty—it will reveal yet other things, which to-day do not enter into our thinking at all. It follows that if there is a matter on which Galen had nothing to say but we have, there is nothing in this to scare us, or to cause mystification.'[26] And again,

Even if [what we have to say] runs clean contrary to Galen . . . that is no reason to disallow reasoning that carries conviction, the clear [results of] experimentation, and the facts which underlie such an opinion. An opinion does not cease being true merely because Galen did not accept it, nor ought it be accepted [definitively] as correct just because Galen did include it in his writings. There is no one who entertains a greater reverence for Galen than I . . . but

[24] Ibid.; see his 4 *conclusiones*, beginning at the 7th page.
[25] For him see Hernández Morejón, v, p. 87. His tract, entitled *Defensa de las sangrías de el tobillo*, is the 1st item bound up in the London convolute (see above, n. 17). The title-page states that the author was 'Cathedrático de Prima de Medicina jubilado en la Universidad de Sevilla'; for his age, see his own statement, f. 2ᵛ, where he declares that he had been in medical practice for 40 years. Similarly f. 14ʳ: 'que por auer yo leido Medicina en esta Universidad treinta años continuos', and Orobio's own tract, p. 46: 'per triginta annos Hispalis primarius magister medicinam . . .'
[26] Ibid: 'El tiempo va descubriendo mucho, porque es el mejor Maestro y de aqui a cien años, o cinquenta, aura descubierto otras cosas que aora no nos passan por el pensamiento. Y assi aun que Galeno no huuiesse dicho una cosa, y la digamos nosotros, no ay que espantar, ni hazer mysterios.'

Building a Career in Andalusia

despite this, I do not believe that everything that can be known in medicine was already known to Galen, or that it is inconceivable that he ever erred ... nor shall I be overcome by astonishment if someone emerges who goes against his teaching. St Thomas, the divine *doctor angelicus*, enjoys a greater authority than does Galen, but nevertheless there arose the school of the acute-minded Duns Scotus, that took its stand against him.[27]

It is almost impossible to avoid being struck by the fact that some twenty-five years after the appearance of William Harvey's *De motu cordis et sanguinis* in 1628 — a work which brought about a fundamentally changed understanding of the way in which the system of the blood operates — there is not the slightest reference to it by either of these two Sevillian physicians, or by any of the others who participated in the controversy about phlebotomy.[28] But in the approach of Dr Pérez Ramírez, who gives preference to experimentation over the authority of much-revered classical writers, there is at any rate a faint echo of the criticism of classical medicine voiced by Paracelsus in 1527 — a clarion-call that proclaimed the beginning of the scientific revolution that took place in the field of medicine in the seventeenth century.[29]

Of the other participants in the debate only two took the part of Pérez Ramírez, the first of these being Alonso de Granado, his successor in the chair of medicine at the university of Seville, and the other a doctor named Juan Moyano de Medina about whom nothing further is known.[30] All of the rest took their stand behind Valverde Horozco: Duarte Núñez de Acosta, a doctor from Sanlúcar de Barrameda — himself, it would seem, a member of a crypto-Jewish family, who served as physician in the court of the prince don Juan and also in that

[27] Ibid., f. 13ʳ. Valverde replied controversially, in his 2nd tract, *Protección de la Doctrina de Hipócrates y Galeno acerca del méthodo de curar por sangrías, según las diferencias de las enfermedades, y partes afectas: y aniquilación de la nueva opinión de sangrar de los touillos*. The book was printed at Seville in 1653, and constitutes the 4th item in the London convolute. Valverde again emphasizes his own adherence to the medical doctrine of antiquity: see p. 43: 'ni cosa alguna se escrivió por nosotros, ni por nuestros preceptores, en esta Universidad de Alcalá de Henares, ni en otras Universidades que no se refiera lo auer enseñado Galeno.'
[28] On Harvey's *De motu cordis* and the influence that it exercised, see A. G. R. Smith, *Science and Society in the Sixteenth and Seventeenth Centuries*, London, 1972, pp. 140 ff.
[29] Ibid, pp. 134 f.
[30] For Granado see Hernández Morejón, v, pp. 364 f. His treatise, *Dudas a la Anquilación y defensa de las Sangrías del touillo* is the 5th item in the London convolute (n. 17 above). For Moyano de Medina and his pamphlet see Hernández Morejón, v, pp. 362 f.; it is not included in the convolute and I have not traced a copy. Hernández Morejón was of the opinion that Moyano was attacking Duarte Núñez de Acosta (see next note), who adhered to Valverde's view. Alvaro de Tenorio (see below, n. 36) wrote against him and he rejoined with another tract, *Rayos contra el papel de los átomos de D. Alvaro de Tenorio*, which I have likewise failed to trace.

of the Duke of Medinaceli;[31] Francisco Duarte de Tavora, doctor of the Conde de Palma, and formerly lecturer in philosophy in the university of Seville;[32] Pedro de Ahumada, likewise a doctor in Seville;[33] Pablo Arias Luna, a doctor from Utrera;[34] Miguel Pérez, lecturer in anatomy in the university of Salamanca:[35] and Alvaro Tenorio de León, a Cádiz physician.[36]

This supporting phalanx was joined by Dr Baltazar Alvares, by now

[31] On him see Hernández Morejón, v, pp. 357 f. His tract, printed in Jerez in 1653, is the 2nd item in the London convolute (*Tratado Practico del Uso de las Sangrias assi en las enfermedades particulares como en las calenturas*). From what he wrote we learn that he had studied at Salamanca (f. 1ʳ: '... y aunque veo oponerse a lo que en Salamanca me enseñaron'). After he had finished writing his tract there came to his notice that of Granado (see above, n. 30), and he found it necessary to add a rejoinder thereto (f. 22ʳ): 'Estando ya este papel dado a la imprenta, vino a mis manos uno muy docto, y muy elegante del S. Doctor Alonso Granado en apoyo de la opinión nueba y para explicación de algunos lugares que en otro eruditissimo el S. Doctor Diego de Valverde auia traido en su contra ...' As to his possible links with the well-known crypto-Jewish Núñez de Acosta family, see below, chap. 4, n. 39.

[32] Printed Seville, 1653; 3rd item in the London convolute. The title-page recites his appointments: 'Copia de un Parecer que dio el Doctor Francisco Duarte de Tauora, Médico del Exmo S. Conde De Palma, Marqués de Almenara, y Montes Claros, Castil de Bayuela, etc. y Cathedrático que fue de Philosophía en la Universidad de Sevilla. *Acerca del uso de las sangrías del tovillo en todas las mas enfermedades que piden sangría.*' The tract is arranged in the form of a memorandum written at the request of a doctor who was accustomed to practise phlebotomy according to the method of Pérez Ramírez; see the beginning, f. A2: 'Porque V.M. me mando le remitiesse mi parecer de lo que sentia ... y porque à seguido la practica de las sangrias de los touillos todo este año.' From this tract it may be concluded that a decision in regard to phlebotomical practice had become a matter of great urgency in Andalusia as the result of an epidemic rife there in the same year: '... unos dolores de costado que an corrido muy agudos en toda esta Andaluzia ... de los quales murio tanta gente.'

[33] His tract, the 6th in the London convolute, was printed in Seville in 1653: *Question en la qual: se intenta averiguar como, y de que venas y de que partes se debe sangrar en las enfermedades que curamos*. Details of his life and literary activity are unknown.

[34] The 7th item in the London convolute, it appeared in 1653, without indication of the place of printing: *Tratado de la Defensa de la Vena Basilica para la cura de las Enfermedades Agudas.*

[35] The 8th tract in the London convolute; it was formulated as an opinion, and written on 9 May 1653 (p. 34): *Parecer y Eruditíssima censura del muy docto y experimentado Doctor Miguel Perez, Catedrático de Anatomía, en la Universidad de Salamanca acerca de las sangrías de touillos*. It would appear that one of the disputants at Seville, possibly Valverde Horozco himself, approached him with a view to getting an authoritative opinion from a member of the Salamanca medical faculty.

[36] His treatise has not, apparently, survived; on him see Hernández Morejón, v, pp. 363 f. He was the son-in-law of Dr Núñez de Acosta, and came to his defence after he had been attacked by Dr Juan Moyano (see above, n. 30). His tract, s.l.e.a., is entitled *Atomos que nuevamente se han descubierto en las luces de Apolo, en la controversia célebre del uso de las sangrías, así en los afectos superiores como en las calenturas*. Moyano having issued a rejoinder, Tenorio replied with a tract, likewise undated, *Laurel precioso que de los rayos defiende, y á los triunfantes corona*. Tenorio de León's work has not come down to us.

Building a Career in Andalusia

using the surname de Orobio that he had already put on the title-page of his poem about the plague in Málaga of 1637: there can be no question but that his treatise is the most full of detail and the most scholarly of all those which contributed to the debate, and it is the only one to be written in Latin. Baltazar, who wrote with great respect of both Valverde Horozco and Pérez Ramírez, endeavoured to present Valverde's case—i.e. the traditional position—and that of Ramírez without himself taking sides; and in so doing he evinced an extremely competent familiarity with the medical literature of all periods.[37] He begins by analysing the traditional view, citing the various arguments that may be advanced in support of it, as well as a justification for it resting on sheer common sense, after which he presents Pérez Ramírez' view on similar lines.[38] Having set out both sides of the controversy he lists the weak points in Pérez Ramírez' case by indicating sources which Pérez had, for some reason, seen fit to ignore, and by throwing into relief the dangers which its practice involved.[39] In outlining his own position in the argument he establishes four principles, the general tenor of which is close to the traditional view that Valverde had set out to defend.[40] It was only when Baltazar had finished writing his own work that there fell into his hands the tract of Granado in defence of Pérez Ramírez, and he therefore judged it necessary to add a special appendix whilst his work was in press, in which he dealt with points in the new contribution that were liable to give rise to doubts in regard to the principles which he had himself established.[41]

---

[37] I refrain from listing all the authorities that he cites, since they are too numerous. Contemporaries and others of recent date whom he mentions include Fernelius, i.e. Jean François Fernel (1497–1588), and Zacutus Lusitanus, i.e. Abraham Zacuth, alias Manuel Alvares de Tavara, who died in Amsterdam in 1642 after leaving Portugal to revert to Judaism. See Orobio's tract (n. 17 above), pp. 32, 89.

[38] For his presentation of the conventional view see chaps. iii and iv, pp. 10–46; for that of Ramírez, chaps. v and vi, pp. 46–81.

[39] Chaps. viii–ix; see p. 108: 'Ex dictis satis probatum reor fundamentum, que sapientiss. Doct. nititur, ut in universalium morborum praecipue febrium principio, a sang. missione per talum curatio inchoanta sit, non solum debile, sed prorsus improbabile esse, et prorsus nocivum qua propter ob id sang. missio ex talo ne quaquam conveniet . . .'

[40] Ibid., pp. 115–35.

[41] Ibid, pp. 137–54, 'De Loco, per quem sanguinis emissio revulsiva methodice et regulariter exercetur.' Appendix. See p. 137: 'Opusculum hoc thypis mandabatur, quando ad me inopinus libellus pervenit, quem nuper ediderat doctor Ildephonsus Granados vir doctus et in operibus artis excercitatus, Hispalencis Medicinae primarius qui parva mole scientificam ostendit exuberantiam . . . et quanquam in mea controversia, plura, que retulit fuerint impugnata, quae noviter obijciuntur noviter expugnabo.'

Baltazar's part in the controversy shows clearly that he enjoyed a position of prestige in academic circles in Andalusia. But it would seem that that is not the only conclusion which is to be drawn from this chapter in his career. There are grounds for supposing that his tract, composed as it was *sine ira et studio*, was not written with purely scientific and clinical considerations in mind. In it, he not only praises Valverde Horozco and stands beside him to defend the latter's case, but he actually reprints Valverde's own tract as an introduction to what he has to say himself.[42] Valverde, who belonged to one of the most highly esteemed families in Seville and who had also made a name in his own right, was at the time the doctor whose services were retained by the local inquisitional tribunal. Judging from the style in which he writes, he was a man who infused whatever positions he adopted with his own zeal; and we may surmise that he saw his dispute with Pérez Ramírez not as a purely academic discussion, but rather as an occasion calling for a national mission—almost a crusade—the importance of which was of the very first order: why else should he see fit to define the views of his opponent as being 'revolutionary' opinions, fraught with danger to the well-being and the integrity of a Christian state?[43] From a sentence in Duarte de Tavora's tract noted above it appears that governmental authorities intervened, and, at the height of the controversy, went so far as actually to prohibit doctors from adopting the clinical practice of Pérez Ramírez: and one may guess that Baltazar saw good reason to stay on the right side of a man in Valverde's position.[44] At the time when his pamphlet was published, a year before his own confinement by the Seville Inquisition, Baltazar was already aware that some of his crypto-Jewish kinsfolk had been placed under arrest, and this must certainly have undermined his confidence.[45] Perhaps he considered the possibility that association with a man of Valverde's status and position could help save his skin. It is pertinent to

[42] Ibid., p. 12: '... ultimus et si doctrina nulli secundus, pro viribus hanc opinionem tuetur sapientissimus Doctor Didacus Valverde Horosco, vir clarissimus, admirabili prudentia praeditus, longissima experientia decoratus et Galeni dogmatum, si quis alius ex corde fectator, qui tractatu vernaculo sermone nuper edito, hanc communem sententiam adeo firmavit, ut dictis aliquid addere dificilimum videatur.' For Orobio's reprinting of Valverde's text see above, n. 20.

[43] Cf. above, n. 23. See his *Controversia Médica* (n. 20 above), p. 6 from end, 'grave daño en la república christiana', and similarly in his *Protección de la Doctrina de Hipocrates* (n. 27 above), introd.: 'la amistad que profeso con el Autor que impugno en est tratado interponiendose la salud de la Patria.'

[44] See Tavora's tract (n. 32 above), f. A2: 'interpuso la justicia su autoridad auisando a V. M. no sangrasse de los touillos como lo defendia en su papel el Doctor Ramirez...'

[45] See below, chap. 4, pp. 79 f.

observe that of all those who participated in this battle in print, only Baltazar found it appropriate to conclude his tract with a dedication to the Trinity and to the Virgin Mary—*In laudem, et Gloriam Omnipotentis Dei Patris, Filii et Spiritus Sancti, et Angelorum Reginæ Virginis Mariæ sine culpæ originalis macula conceptæ.*[46] In the same way that he had done in his poem about the plague at Málaga, here again he found a method of obscuring his real identity.

CÁDIZ

Thanks to an inquisitional inventory,[47] we are exceptionally well informed about Baltazar's Cádiz house, its appointments and contents, and we may thus form a picture of his standard of living. The residence that he and his wife Isabel occupied at this period was large and spacious: built on two floors, it comprised seven rooms—a dining-room, reception-room, two bedrooms, two closets, a study containing a library of approximately 250 volumes, kitchen, courtyard, cellar, and a stable housing an ass and a mule.[48] Everything about it points to Baltazar's easy circumstances. The furniture was of good quality, and not sparse; every corner had its decorative feature, there were boxes and drawers containing jewellery, and in the chests and presses was to be found a fashionable wardrobe.

The young couple owned two female slaves, one named María de la Encarnación and the other María Manuela. Baltazar 'declared that he had purchased them both at a public sale in the house of the *licenciado* (i.e. university graduate) Francisco Antonio Claros, formerly *alcalde mayor* (i.e. chief municipal magistrate) of this city'.[49] He also owned

---

[46] p. 135.
[47] The inquisitional officials in Cádiz having been instructed by the Seville tribunal to sequestrate the chattels of Baltazar Orobio, on 1 Aug. 1654 they drew up a detailed inventory of all the property in his house; see below, Appendix C. On 4 Aug. of the same year they likewise sequestrated the property of his brother-in-law Simón Rodríguez, husband of his sister Leonor, and that of his mother and his sisters Violante and Clara. See Madrid, AHN, Leg. 2067 nos. 100–1. Violante was by now also married, in Cádiz, to a chocolate merchant named Pascual Núñez. He had agreed to marry her despite her inability to bring him a dowry, 'because her brother, Dr Orobio, had effected his cure in her house, and out of gratitude he undertook to marry her without dowry'. See ibid., no. 101, f. 15^r.
[48] See below, Appendix C.
[49] Ibid. f. 7^r. It would seem that these female slaves were of Moorish origin. On the availability of Moorish slaves, both male and female, in Andalusia at this period, see Dom. Ortiz and Ag. Piñal, pp. 45 f. See above, chap. 1, pp. 17 f.

one male slave, 'a hunchback moor, white and with marks of the iron beside his nose, aged twenty'.[50]

The subjects of the pictures on the walls of the main room of the house—St Thomas, Jesus, John the Baptist, St Mary Magdalene, and other saints, together with the picture of Christ in the reception room, would have left a visitor with the impression that those who lived in the house were good Christians of conventional piety.[51] There were other objects, too, the purpose of whose presence was to contribute to the veil of Christianity that the Alvares de Orobios threw over their Jewish identity: a number of rosaries, jewels bearing figures of saints, etc.[52]

On one of the walls of the principal room there hung a large picture of Jacob wrestling with the angel.[53] That particular picture will have been of great symbolic meaningfulness to the Alvares family, for in it they will have been able to recognize an epitome of their own fate, as children of a people the secret of whose unique character was spelled out in the heroism of its struggle to secure its own survival. It is no coincidence that a picture of the same subject was to be found in the house of Baltazar's brother-in-law, Simón Rodríguez.[54] There was also to be found in the house a brass candlestick for two lights (*velonçillo de azofar con dos candeleros para velas*), which they presumably used for lighting candles on the eve of the sabbath.[55] The inquisitional officers found a similar pair in the house of Baltazar's parents.[56]

In the study there was arranged 'a library of medical books, in one case there being five shelves of volumes in large and small format. The first shelf contained thirty-two volumes; the second, forty-six; the third, fifty-two; the fourth, again forty-six, and the fifth and last sixty-five. On the day when the inventory was taken five other large volumes were piled on a stool, and there were three more on the writing-desk.

[50] Ibid. Baltazar's parents' household likewise included two female slaves: see Leg. 2067 no. 101, f. 6ᵛ.

[51] See below, pp. 402 f. Pictures of the same genre were also to be found in the house of his brother-in-law Simón Rodríguez Monsanto: Leg. 2067 no. 100, f. 1ʳ f.: 'En la saleta prinzipal de arriua un santo Cristo en la cruz; ... vn quadro de San Juan Baptista ...' Likewise in the home of his parents Manuel Alvares and his wife Mencia, ibid., no. 101, f. 1ʳ: 'En la sala prinzipal estaua vn quadro de nuestro Señor otro de San Gerónimo con guarnizion; otro pequeño de Cristo muerto en manos de Dios Padre ...'

[52] See f. 2ᵛ. His parents' home included similar effects, see Leg. 2067 no. 101, f. 1ᵛ, 'vn rosario de frutilla negro', f. 2ᵛ, 'en otra gaveta un papel con insiensso y unas oritas doradas de deuoçion ...', f. 3ʳ, 'dos rosarios de pasta'.

[53] See below, p. 402.

[54] Leg. 2067 no. 101, f. 1ᵛ.

[55] See f. 4ᵛ.

[56] Leg. 2067 no. 100, f. 10ʳ, '... dos candeleros quadrados ...'

Building a Career in Andalusia

In a press to hold files of documents there was a number of thin dockets [*papeles menudos*] and fourteen books of small format. On the floor there lay a large book that included tables [*tablillas*]. On the writing-desk referred to there stood three small portraits, of Galen, Hippocrates, and Avicenna, together with a city plan of Lisbon on paper. The room contained three chairs: two old ones, upholstered in cowhide, and one new one.'[57]

The inventory of Baltazar's property did not, unfortunately, include a catalogue of his books, most of which (it seems safe to conclude) must have been medical works; but there were certainly some that had to do with religion and philosophy.[58] Other books were listed that were found in other rooms of the house—the second part of the well-known work by Alonso de Villegas Selvago entitled *Flos Sanctorum*,[59] and Fray José Laínez' *El Privado Cristiano*. The interest which Baltazar must have taken in these books flew in the face of their authors' own intentions. In the first-named he could read accounts of the 'pre-incarnation saints' of the Old Testament, and in the second of them he would find descriptions of the status enjoyed by Joseph and Daniel as royal counsellors of Jewish stock wielding political influence at the court of Gentile rulers.[60] His library also contained a volume of Seneca's writings in Latin;[61] and we shall have occasion below to consider the significance of Seneca in Baltazar's thought and that of other members of his circle. There were also 'a number of unbound volumes, written by Dr Baltazar Orobio, as well as the book of Dr Alonso Núñez'.[62]

---

[57] See f. 6ʳ.

[58] On the private libraries of physicians in Spain in the 15th and 16th cents., see A. García, *Tres Bibliotecas de Médicos Valencianos Renacentistas (Luis Alcañiz, Pere Pintor y Pere Martí)*, pp. 527–45.

[59] See f. 2ʳ. The inventory lists merely *Florum Sanctorum* without giving the name of the author, viz. Alonso de Villegas Selvago (1534–1615). The book appeared in five parts, the second, in 1588, being entitled *Flos Sanctorum, segunda parte y Historia general en que se escrive la Vida de la Virgen Sacratissima madre de Dios, y las de los Santos antiguos que fueron antes de la venida de nuestro Salvador al mundo, collegidos assi de la Divina escriptura como de lo que escriven acerca desto los sagrados doctores y otros autores graves y fidedignos*. A revised edn. appeared in Toledo in 1591.

[60] Laínez' work was published in Madrid, in 1641: *El Privado Christiano, deducido de las vidas de Joseph y Daniel, que fueron balanzas de los validos en el fiel contraste del pueblo de Dios*. Once again the inquisitional officers neglected to record the name of the author.

[61] For the place occupied by Seneca in the thought of Baltazar Alvares de Orobio and of some other crypto-Jews see below, chap. 11, pp. 310 f.

[62] The reference is to Baltazar's own medical work on phlebotomy (see above, pp. 67 f.) printed in Seville in 1653, and that of Duarte Núñez de Acosta on the same subject: see above, p. 71.

Further items listed in the inventory indicate that Baltazar's entire livelihood did not derive from what he might earn as a doctor. Many cupboards and chests containing chocolate were found in the house, showing clearly that he had a share in the business activities of his brother-in-law Simón Rodríguez, who during his period of residence in Cádiz was dealing in chocolate imported from New Spain and Guiana.[63] There were also four chests containing scarlet cloth which, he maintained, were not his property but that of his father-in-law Francisco Pérez, who had purchased it from a resident in Ceuta named Tomás de Quintanilla. But we may suspect that Baltazar himself had a hand not only in this transaction, but in other business-dealings between his father-in-law and de Quintanilla.[64]

Baltazar's financial position enabled him to advance money to the needy. He had in pledge a silver vessel deposited with him as security for a loan of 100 *reales* by someone described (somewhat intriguingly) as a 'Jesuit inn-sign-painter' (?) (*tavernero pintor*).[65] But most of the sums advanced by him were loans to members of his own family. When he was brought before the inquisitional tribunal of Seville on 14 August 1654 in order to make declaration of his property, he stated that his father Manuel Alvares owed him money, 'but that he had no document or other record of the amount of the sum involved, but that it would certainly be noted in his father's ledgers'.[66]

The officers of the Inquisition totalled the value of the silver jewellery sequestrated in Baltazar's house at an estimated 20,320 *reales*, and the value of the other silver effects at 22 marks.[67]

If Baltazar had hoped that in his spacious residence in Cádiz he had finally reached a position of assured ease, harsh reality was soon to shatter his illusions. He was to be left with neither status nor property. The inventory from which the above picture of his domestic circumstances has been created shows that evidence was taken before the tribunal of Seville regarding his indulging in Judaizing practices: and on this occasion he did not succeed in eluding the clutches of the Holy Office.

[63] See f. 3ᵛ etc. and Leg. 2067 no. 100, f. 2ᵛ.
[64] See ff. 7ʳ, 12ʳ.
[65] See f. 4ᵛ.
[66] See ff. 12ᵛ f.
[67] See ff. 7ᵛ f. The inquisitional bailiffs likewise found cash in Baltazar's house, viz. 327 pesos together with a further 4,750 which, he claimed, belonged to his father-in-law: see f. 6ʳ. On 3 Aug.—two days after their sequestration of his effects—the officers discovered (thanks to information laid by an informer) further silver ornaments to the value of 47½ marks that had been concealed in a cistern near the house.

4
Imprisoned by the Seville Inquisition

On 21 July 1654 the Seville tribunal of the Inquisition gave orders for the arrest of Manuel Alvares and his wife Mencia, their sons Baltazar and Melchor, their daughters Leonor, Violante, and Clara, and their two sons-in-law Simón Rodríguez (Leonor's husband) and Pascual Núñez Enríquez (husband of Violante).[1] Once again, Manuel himself managed to escape, together with his son Melchor and his son-in-law Pascual Núñez,[2] but the others were all taken in Cádiz at the beginning of August 1654 and brought to Seville, where they were placed in confinement to await their hearing.

Philip van Limborch, in his *Historia Inquisitionis* which appeared in Amsterdam in 1692, gives an extended account of the imprisonment, investigation, and condemnation of Baltazar Orobio de Castro, and it may be presumed that the remonstrant theologian heard the bare facts from Baltazar himself during the period of their acquaintanceship.[3] According to Limborch, it was the Orobios' Moorish slave who informed upon him to the inquisitors in order to get even with his master who once had him flogged for stealing. Four days later someone else who entertained feelings of hostility towards Baltazar and who wished to give vent to them reported his links with Judaism. It was these denunciations (as Limborch asserts) that led to his being put behind bars.[4]

---

[1] See Madrid, AHN, Inquisition section, Leg. 2987, 'Méritos del Doctor Don Balthasar de Orobio', f. 1ᵛ; 'Méritos de Menzia Nuñez', f. 1ᵛ; 'Méritos de Leonor de Orobio', f. 1ᵛ; 'Méritos de Violante Enriquez Nuñez y Orobio', f. 1ᵛ, 'Méritos de Clara de Orovio', f. 1ᵛ. For Pascual Núñez, see above, chap. 3, n. 47.

[2] Ibid., 'Relacion del estado que tienen las causas de fee que estan pendientes en el Santo Ofiçio de la Inquisiçion de Sevilla, remitido en 2 de Abril de seis çientos y çinquenta y seis.' See also, ibid., the list of those who had evaded arrest: 'Ausentes fugitivos: 1. Manuel Alvares ... estando votado a prision con sequestro de bienes al tiempo de querer executarse se hallo haberse ausentado ... 2. Don Melchor de Orouio, su hijo, se ausento en la mesma ocasion ... 3. Pascual Nuñez Enriques ... marido de Violante de Orobio ... se ausento al tiempo que su suegro y cuñado ...'

[3] See below, chap. 10, pp. 270 ff.

[4] See Limborch, *Inqu.*, Book iv, chap. 29, p. 323: '... qui a quodam Mauro servo suo, antehac ob furtum jussu suo verberato, delato fuit Inquisitioni quasi Judaeus, et post quadriennium ab alio inimico suo de alio facto unde judaeus agnosceretur iterum delatus fuit ...'

His brother-in-law Simón Rodríguez was more explicit about the causes of Baltazar and other members of his family being placed in the inquisitional gaol, in the evidence which he gave before the Seville tribunal on 14 August 1654. When asked if he knew what had brought it about, he replied that he suspected that Francisco Rodríguez Almeida, who had been placed under arrest by the Córdoba Inquisition, had denounced the Alvares family and had pinned false charges on them, out of a desire to revenge himself on Baltazar for having jilted his daughter.[5]

A substantial portion of the archives of the Seville Inquisition has been lost, including the files of the investigations conducted regarding members of the Alvares family between 1654 and 1656.[6] For Dr Baltazar Alvares, his mother Mencia, and his three sisters, we have summaries only; these were dispatched to the Supreme Council of the Inquisition in Madrid on 1 September 1656, after the conclusion of the judicial procedures and the conviction of each of the accused.[7] From these summaries it is possible to reconstruct the course of their investigation during their long imprisonment.

It is quite clear that what set the ball rolling was evidence given before the Valladolid Inquisition in 1654, by a youngster who declared that

> in August 1647 or 1648 he had been in Sanlúcar, where he had been a guest for forty days in the household [of Baltazar], who confided to the witness. One day, it being the date of the fast observed in the month of September, [Baltazar] told him that he and the members of his family would be fasting, it being the fast-day according to the law of Moses, and that he was saying this because he was aware that witness observed Jewish practices. Witness had, in point of fact, kept the fast in the company of the accused [reo] and his other relatives. They had neither eaten nor drunk throughout the day, in order to fulfil the [prescriptions of the] said law of Moses. At nightfall, witness, the accused, and his other relatives had entered a room, whereupon the accused had told them to wash their hands. He then went close to the wall and sat down on a stool, the remainder taking their places opposite and around him—the men on stools, wearing hats, and the women on the ground, swathed in their veils ... The accused had begun to read prayers out of a book which he held in his hand, bound in black vellum with gold-tooled ornamentation ... For half an hour he had read prayers consisting of psalms and prayers of the law of

---

[5] See above, chap. 3, p. 66, and Leg. 2067 no. 100, f. 6ʳ.
[6] See Révah, *rupt. spin.*, *nouvel examen*, 71, pp. 577 f.
[7] See above, n. 1. The summary of the case against Simón Rodríguez Monsanto has not survived.

Moses, in some of which there had occurred the word 'Adonai' [the Hebrew surrogate for the divine name], 'the offering of lambs', and 'the offering of a yearling lamb'. When witness had asked whether [the rest of them] were obliged to pray as well, the accused had replied that to hear the prayers read and to utter them oneself came to the same thing. When [Baltazar] had finished praying, witness observed that the prayer-book was printed in Spanish—the language in which the prayers had been offered—and that in sundry places it contained the words *Prayer and Psalms for the Sabbath, Prayer and Psalms for the First Day*, and so on for all the remaining days of the week. The said book had been sent to them by a relative from Florence. On leaving the room referred to, they had proceeded to the dining-room where the table was laid with clean linen, dishes, and everything requisite for a meal. They had all taken their places at the table and had dined of fish, eggs, and fruit, but had not had any meat. At the centre of the table were two loaves, each weighing three pounds, that had been placed one on top of the other. These were not eaten, nor indeed touched. An although [the company] had not explained to him why they had put them there, witness had understood that it was one of the commandments of the law of Moses ... [He also observed] that the accused and his kin were wearing fresh clothes, that they observed Saturdays as feast-days, that they did not eat pork chops; and that they observed all these matters as being precepts of the law of Moses.[8]

From this detailed evidence the Seville inquisitors could perceive the Alvares family's determined adherence to the Jewish law, their links with their kinsfolk in Italy, who had actually supplied them with a prayer-book in Spanish,[9] and the central role of Dr Baltazar de Orobio as spiritual leader of this family group of crypto-Jews.

The Seville inquisitors addressed themselves to the inquisitional commissary in Sanlúcar de Barrameda, with orders to take the Alvares family into custody. The commissary, having satisfied himself that they had moved to Cádiz, contacted the Holy Office's commissary there; and in the early hours of Saturday, 1 August 1654 the two of them arrested Dr Baltazar de Orobio and sequestrated his property.[10]

---

[8] Loc. cit., 'Méritos del Doctor Don Balthasar de Orobio', f. 1ʳ⁻. The same testimony is cited in the summary of the cases against Baltazar's mother and sisters; see above, n. 1.

[9] For prayer-books (of the Sephardic rite) that were being printed in Italy not in Hebrew, but in a Spanish translation, mainly at Ferrara and Venice, from the middle of the 16th cent., see Kayserling, *Biblioteca*, pp. 81 f. Kayserling also deals with those printed in Amsterdam from the middle of the 17th cent., ibid.; on these see also Silva Rosa, *Ergänzung zu Kayserling*, pp. 213 f.

[10] Both Sanlúcar de Barrameda and Cádiz lay within the jurisdiction of the Seville tribunal: see Leg. 2067 no. 95, f. 1ʳ. The inquisitional commissary in Sanlúcar de Barrameda at the time was the *licenciado* don Julio Caballero de los Olivos; his opposite number in Cádiz was the *licenciado* don Julio de Cetina. See below, Appendix C.

Within three days his mother Mencia, his three sisters, and his brother-in-law Simón Rodríguez had been caught and all their property likewise sequestrated.[11] As stated above, Manuel Alvares, his son Melchor, and his son-in-law Pascual Núñez had managed to get away from Cádiz some days earlier—a circumstance that points to the probability that arrest and sequestration of their property did not take the Alvares family completely by surprise. They may have learned of the arrest of other crypto-Jews to whom they were linked by ties of kinship, and whom the Inquisition could force to inform upon them.

A few days after their arrest the members of the Alvares family were brought back to Seville and confined in the inquisitional gaol, to await their investigation. Mencia, Baltazar's mother, was placed in confinement on 7 August, together with her two married daughters Leonor and Violante;[12] on the following day, Baltazar and Clara, his youngest sister, were locked up, and probably their brother-in-law Simón Rodríguez as well.[13]

Shortly after their being gaoled additional evidence against Dr Baltazar de Orobio and his family was received by the Seville Inquisition, this time from their opposite numbers in Córdoba. This testimony was taken from a man aged twenty-five, who declared that

the said accused and other Judaizers had made fun of Catholics as worshippers of images and as beseeching them to grant acts of mercy, despite their lifeless quality and their not being endowed with any capacity to do anything at all. Should the images [of saints] really have power to perform miracles, they would themselves (so they maintained) join in worship of them, but this was something impossible, since they were nought but sculpted forms . . . whereat the accused and others had laughed, and had declared that it was impossible for the holy sacrament to comprise the body and soul of our Saviour Jesus Christ, and that a priest had not the power or authority to cause the descent of God from heaven to [find embodiment] within the host: that so long as they had no actual visual evidence of such a thing, they neither could believe it nor wished to do so. The accused, and others who were members of his confidential circle had fasted on the great day, not eating from sunset until the appearance of the [first] star on the next day . . . The accused and other members of his confidential circle had frequently said that the Cross which Catholics

[11] Leg. 2067 no. 100, f. 1ʳ; no. 101, f. 1ʳ.
[12] Leg. 2987 (see above, n. 1).
[13] Ibid. It may be surmised that Baltazar and Simón Rodríguez remained in Cádiz for an extra day in order to complete their respective declarations regarding sequestrated property. The expenses incidental to the sequestration of that of Baltazar, his arrest in Cádiz, and his transport to Seville, which amounted to 88 pesos, were recovered from the property sequestrated. See below, Appendix C, f. 10ᵛ.

venerate is but an absurdity and, so far as they themselves were concerned, no more than a gibbet.[14]

That piece of evidence was of particular importance, since it contained proof that the Alvares family, and especially Baltazar, did not merely observe the precepts of the law of Moses, but that they were also in the habit of casting aspersions on the Christian faith and of treating its saints and its images with scorn.

On 19 August Baltazar was brought before the tribunal for his first investigation. On being asked about his family origins, he replied that 'he knew nothing of his origins, or the ancestry of his parents and grandparents. He thought that his father had once been convicted by the Cuenca Inquisition, but he did not know what penalty had been inflicted on him.' He likewise maintained that 'he himself had received Christian baptism, and that he did not know, nor could he conjecture, what was the reason for his being placed under arrest'.[15] At his interrogations by the inquisitional tribunal on 21 and 22 August Baltazar again refused to confess to any practice of Judaism.[16]

His sister Leonor, who was examined on 27 August, likewise denied her origins, and claimed that 'she had always heard that her parents and grandparents and [all her] other [relatives] whom she had referred to [in her testimony] were old Christians'.[17] Mencia and her two other daughters, Violante and Clara, did the same in their first examination before the inquisitors, likewise denying their Jewish origins.[18]

[14] See Leg. 2987, 'Méritos del Doctor Don Balthasar de Orobio', ff. 2ᵛ f. A marginal note reads: 'este testigo en 13 de Mayo [de 1655] en la Inquisiçion de Cordova revoco lo referido ... ', from which it appears that the witness concerned deposed before the Córdoba court but subsequently retracted his evidence before the same tribunal. Conceivably the witness was one of the sons of Francisco Rodríguez Almeida, already referred to, who had been held in Córdoba together with his father.

[15] Ibid., f. 2ʳ: 'que no sauia de que casta y generazion era el ni sus padres y abuelos y que a su padre juzga que en la Inquisiçion de Cuenca le devieron de dar alguna penitenzia, pero no sauia qual. Y que era christiano bautizado y confirmado y que no sauia, ni presumia, la causa de su prision.' [16] Ibid.

[17] Ibid., 'Méritos de Leonor de Orobio', f. 1ʳ. On 9 Sept. it transpired that Leonor had been arrested in error; the inquisitors were searching for *Isabel* de Orobio, sister of Dr Baltazar de Orobio, i.e. his sister Ana Gonçales, who had been married in Jaén to a linen-merchant named Manuel (Antonio) de Castro but she had died prior to 1654. However, once Leonor had been taken, proofs of her Judaizing activities rapidly came into the hands of the inquisitors, and it was consequently decided to keep her under arrest and investigate her, together with the other members of her family (ibid).

[18] Ibid., 'Méritos de Menzia Nuñez', f. 1ᵛ (her statement at the session of the court on 1 Sept. 1654): '... y que no sauia de que casta y generazion era, ni sus padres y abuelos ...'; also ibid., 'Méritos de Violante Enriquez' (her statement on 2 Sept.), and 'Méritos de Clara de Orovio', f. 1ᵛ.

Even after having been physically examined by the tribunal's surgeons when it was revealed that he had been subjected to circumcision, Baltazar still denied the accusations which the prosecutor had confronted him with, and was consistently and stoutly to maintain that denial right up to 13 January 1656.[19] On that date he was taken into the torture-chamber, and it was only here that the inquisitors succeeded in screwing his confession out of him.[20] However, before we come to that stage in Baltazar's story, we have to go back in time and consider the progress of the investigation of the other members of the family during the intervening period of 1654–6. Mencia was the first of them to concede a partial confession of her links with Judaism. On 11 September 1654 she told the inquisitors of the tribunal that 'approximately fifteen years ago . . . when she had been in Madrid, someone — a relative since deceased — had told her that she ought to observe Saturdays as feast-days . . . the accused had so observed them, in the said fashion, for about six months until the death of the said relative, and had thereafter continued to maintain their observance, until the time of her arrest.'[21] In her endeavour to shield her children who shared her imprisonment, Mencia added that 'she had been particularly careful that her sons and daughters should not notice'[22] how she observed Saturdays as feast-days in accordance with the law of Moses. More than that the inquisitors could not get out of her. On 16 September the first bill of indictment was presented against her and against her son Baltazar; but both of them — with the assistance of counsel placed at their disposal — denied the charges levelled against them.[23]

Meanwhile the Cádiz commissary of the Inquisition had forwarded some fresh evidence, taken there from an Armenian pedlar who reported on a casual encounter that he had had with Baltazar. The latter had once accosted him in the street and had taken him into a house, 'and, when they were alone, had asked him in strict confidence whether he was a Jew, since his style of dress was so very similar to Jewish costume. After the Armenian had said that he was a Christian

---

[19] See above, chap. 1, pp. 6 f., and ibid., summary of his case, f. 2ʳ.
[20] See below.
[21] See ibid., 'Méritos de Menzia Nuñez', f. 2ʳ. This testimony corroborates the assumption (see above, p. 4) that the Alvares family where in Madrid in 1632, at the time when crypto-Jews from Portugal were being subjected to trials arising out of the alleged 'Patient Christ'.
[22] Ibid., ' . . . por esta causa se recataua de sus hijos y hijas porque no lo advirtieran . . .'
[23] Ibid., and 'Méritos del Doctor Don Balthasar de Orobio', f. 2ʳ.

and a Catholic, the accused had replied, "you need not worry or be afraid, for I am a Hebrew, and travel the same road". In order to be sure that he [sc. the Armenian] believed him, [the accused] had partially removed his [outer] garments and had showed him a round, green symbol made of velvet or silk stitched to his under-garment; he had given him three *reales* . . . and had instructed, indeed implored him not to mention it to a soul.'[24] We shall hardly be taking to flights of fancy if we conjecture that what the Armenian saw stitched on to Baltazar's under-shirt was nothing other than some substitute for the 'lesser fringed garment' (*ṭalith qaṭan 'arba' kanfoth*). Since the Armenian did not know what the object referred to was, and had had no proper opportunity to see the shape of the 'symbol', he gave an inaccurate description of it. If this conjecture is correct, we may learn from this piece of testimony not only of the intensity of Baltazar's attachment to Judaism, but also something about the wide spectrum of religious practices that the crypto-Jews of Spain succeeded in maintaining even after having been submerged in a vigorously hostile environment over not a few generations.[25]

On 27 April 1655 there was presented the second bill of indictment against Baltazar: but, once again, advised by his counsel, he denied all the accusations advanced against him.[26] The inquisitors, having realized that all their attempts to induce the Alvares family to admit their links with Judaism had come to nothing, decided to send them to the torture-chamber in order to extract by application of physical force what they had failed to bring out by conventional methods of investigation.[27] On 12 January 1656 Mencia and Violante were taken into the chamber. Mencia, a woman of sixty, fainted as soon as her limbs were shackled to the block:[28] the surgeons examined her, and advised that

[24] Ibid., f. 2ᵛ.
[25] There is no other evidence from the 17th cent. regarding the fulfilment by crypto-Jews of the Jewish ordinance concerning the wearing of fringes on the (male) garment (Num. 15: 37–41). For crypto-Jews in 16th cent. Spain who would pray swathed in the fringed *ṭaleth* (prayer-shawl), see Beinart, *on Trial*, pp. 212, 217, 230, 251.
[26] Ibid., Summary of Baltazar Orobio's case.
[27] The decision was taken regarding Mencia on 3 May 1655, regarding Clara on 27 Sept., and regarding Baltazar and Violante on 20 Nov.; but there is no evidence in the summary of Clara's case that she was actually subjected to torture. The others were all taken into the torture-chamber, but not until Jan. 1656: see below.
[28] [By the block [? and tackle] what is presumably meant is the apparatus for applying the first method of torture, in which the accused was raised on a rope fastened round the wrists that had been doubled back behind the shoulders. After being hoisted by pulley and remaining suspended for a period, the victim would be suddenly dropped to within a few inches of the ground, thereby suffering severe dislocation. John Joseph Stockdale, *The History of the Inquisitions*, London, 1810, p. 190, gives a description of the process

torture should be stopped.²⁹ Violante, who was aged twenty-eight, held out rather longer. She heroically underwent torture on the machine until she, too, lost consciousness.³⁰ The endeavours of the inquisitors to force confessions out of these two stout-hearted women by means of physical torment bore no fruit. Neither of them revealed anything at all about their own Judaism, or uttered a single word that might incriminate their kin.

The next day it was Baltazar's turn. On being introduced into the torture-chamber and placed on the pulley-block 'he began to scream, and said that he was prepared to tell the truth, and that they should take him out of the machine'. But when they stopped the torture, he declared that 'he had nothing to say'.³¹ When torture was re-applied Baltazar was overcome by the terrible pain, and confessed 'that it was indeed true that he was a Jew, and he had begun to practise the precepts of the law of Moses approximately sixteen years previous: that a certain man had advised him to observe the said law, and had told him that he would teach him its contents in order that he might be a Jew; since when he had begun to observe the said law, and believed that therein he would be saved, and not in the [law] of Jesus Christ our Lord . . . He had maintained it until five years ago, when having read [the works of] Paul of Burgos he had been converted, and had been brought back to the true faith of our Lord Jesus Christ.'³² He stated

---

together with an illustration by his own artist. Although he lists (p. vi) a not insignificant bibliography, including Limborch's work (see above, n. 4) from the English translation by S. Chandler (London, 1731), Stockdale does not cite his sources for specific items. Limborch, *Inqu.*, Book iv, chap. 29, pp. 323 f., in describing the torturing of Isaac Orobio which the latter had himself related to him, refers to the use of ropes and pulleys (*parvae trochleae ferreae*) fixed to the wall, and to the removal of the stool upon which the trussed victim stood; but there is no reference to any sudden jerking of the ropes to cause dislocation. R.L.]

²⁹ Ibid., 'Méritos de Menzia Nuñez', f. 2ᵛ.
³⁰ Ibid., 'Méritos de Violante Enrriquez', f. 2ᵛ.
³¹ Ibid., 'Méritos del Doctor Don Balthasar de Orobio', f. 3ʳ: 'y en 13 de Henero de 656 se executo y aviendosele hecho la moniçion hordinaria y pronunziado y notificado la sentenzia del tormento estubo negativo y fue mando [sic] lleuar a la Camara del tormento donde fueron los Señores Inquisidores y hordinario y siendo amonestado dixese la verdad por amor de Dios y no se quiera ver en tanto trabajo estubo negativo y asi mismo lo estubo al atarle la zincha, poner en el Potro, atar a las argollas, ligar los braços, pies, espinillas y dedos pulgares, y aviendole dado la primera buelta de la mancuerda dio grandes voçes y dixo que queria dezir la verdad que le quiten del tormento. Y aviendo mandado afianzar la buelta y a el ministro de justiçia que saliese fuera, dixo que no tenia que dezir . . .'

³² Ibid., 'Y aviendole mandado entrar para que continuase la buelta y estandolo dixo que queria dezir la verdad. Y que era çierto que es judio y auria vivido judayzando en la ley de Moysen aura diez y seys años, poco mas o menos, y que çierta persona le auia

that during the time that he had observed the law of Moses 'he had fasted the fasts prescribed in the law of Moses twice a year, once in the month of September and once in the month of March'. He likewise revealed the names of other crypto-Jews to whom he had made acknowledgement of his own adherence to Judaism, and in whose company he had implemented the precepts of the law of Moses.[33] He conceded that during those years he had kept up the pretence of conformity, by participating in the ceremonies of the Church without believing in the sacred quality of her sacraments or in the principles of the Christian faith: 'but after his return from the devious path that he had taken, he had come to believe that it was all true, and he had actually made confession of his denial of Christianity, on numerous occasions, as well as for the aforementioned sins, but they had not been willing to grant him absolution'.[34] In this manner Baltazar sought to minimize the gravity of what he had done. He represented his Judaizing as having been a temporary affair, all responsibility for setting which in train he attributed to a casual encounter with someone in the course of his travels. He gave the credit for his restoration to faith in Christianity to Pablo de Santa María, the well-known converted Jew of Burgos, with whose writings he was, in fact, familiar. As we shall see below, he had in fact examined them closely.[35]

All the same, Baltazar's confession failed to convince the inquisitors. After twenty-four hours, when he had still not recovered from the

aconsejado que observase la dicha ley, y le dixo que se la enseñaria que fuesse judio; y desde entonzes comenzo a serlo y a obseruar la dicha ley, creyendo se auia de saluar en ella y no en la de Jessuchristo Nuestro Señor ... y asi la auia obseruado desde entonzes hasta de çinco años a esta parte que auiendo leydo a Pablo Burgense se convirtio y reduxo a la verdadera fee de Jessuchristo Señor Nuestro.'

[33] Ibid.

[34] Ibid., f. 3. Limborch, *Inqu.*, gives a detailed description of the torture to which Baltazar was subjected, in order to highlight the cruelty inherent in the procedures followed by the Spanish Inquisition: 'Erat locus subterraneus satis amplus, fornice structus, parietes undique velamine nigri coloris tecti; muro affixa erant candelabra, totumque conclave illuminabant candelae iis impositae: Ab una parte erat locus quidam, camerae instar, separatus; illic mensae assidebat Inquisitor cum Notario: ita ut locus hic ipsi visus fuerit domicilium mortis, tetro aspectu undiquaque terribilis.' According to Limborch, despite torture the Inquisition failed to extract any confession from him ('Quoniam in tormentis nihil confessus fuerat ... '). Locke, followed by Basnage, wrote that Baltazar's sufferings in the inquisitional gaol disturbed the balance of his mind (*Bibliothèque Universelle*, 1687, pp. 289 f.; Basnage, 5, pp. 2112 f.). In their wake Amelander, f. 133, stated (in Yiddish) that Orobio was imprisoned by the Inquisition for three years, and whilst under arrest went out of his mind ('er iz ... bald narrsch un meshugge geworn ... '), to the point of asking himself whether he was in fact Dr Orobio.

[35] Regarding his interest in the works of Paul of Burgos, see below, chap. 6, pp. 114 f., and chap. 9, p. 237.

pain, he was brought once again before the tribunal of investigators. At this interrogation he amended his earlier statement, saying that he had lived a Jewish life for the last twenty-four years; and he revealed the names of a further number of crypto-Jews in whose company he had been in the habit of observing Jewish precepts.[36]

From a letter addressed by the Seville tribunal on 21 February 1656 to the Supreme Council of the Inquisition in Madrid we learn the identity of those crypto-Jews whose names were betrayed by Baltazar in the course of his two confessions.[37] Six physicians were involved, who were numbered amongst Baltazar's close friends. Their names were (Gerónimo Gómez) Pereda, Simón de Silva Calbo, (Miguel) Reynoso,[38] Núñez,[39] Juan de Prado, and the *licenciado* Serrano.[40] It may be surmised that Baltazar was aware that some of these, including Reynoso and Prado, had already managed to escape from Spain.[41] Prado, he declared, he had met in Lopera, a small town in the district of Jaén, in 1643, on which occasion Prado had declared to him that all men may be saved, each in whatever his particular religion happens to be, since the source of all religions lies in natural law.[42] This is one of the earliest pieces of evidence of Prado's links with deism; we shall return below to the roots, and the first indications of the turning-point in his speculative thinking.

On 18 March 1656 Violante was broken down, and for the first time she confessed her links with the law of Moses 'which she had begun to fulfil approximately fifteen years previous, from the time when she first reached an age of understanding'.[43] Nine days later, Mencia of her

---

[36] Ibid. (see above n. 14), summary of Baltazar Orobio's case, f. 3ʳ: '... y enmendo que auia veynte y quatro años que era observante y declaro nuevos complices.'

[37] Ibid., preceding the summaries of the cases of the individual members of the family. At the head of the letter there is a note of the date when it was received in Madrid, viz. 2 Mar. 1656. It has been published in full by Révah, *Rupture Spinozienne*, pp. 430 f., together with the confirmation by the supreme council of the decision of the Seville court to open proceedings against all those mentioned in the letter.

[38] i.e. Miguel Reynoso who settled in Amsterdam in the mid-1650s. See below, chap. 6, p. 134.

[39] Apparently = Dr Duarte Núñez de Acosta, who together with Baltazar had participated in the scientific debate regarding phlebotomy: see above, chap. 3, p. 71.

[40] The reference is to Diego Duarte Serrano, who was related to Dr Juan de Prado: see Révah, *rupt. spin., nouvel examen*, 72, p. 651. The little town of Bailén is in Andalusia, east of Andújar. From 3 documents preserved in the district archives of Jaén, all dated 13 Jan. 1643, we learn that he was at that time resident in Bailén and dealing in tobacco and pepper. See Jaén archives, Leg. 1373, ff. 1xʳ–1xiiiᵛ.

[41] See below, chap. 6, pp. 128, 134.

[42] See below, p. 126.

[43] Madrid, AHN, Inquisition section, Leg. 2987, 'Méritos de Violante Enrriquez', f. 2ʳ f.

Imprisoned by the Seville Inquisition 89

own accord sought permission to appear before the tribunal; and when she was brought in front of the inquisitors, she conceded that she had been practising the law of Moses during the last twenty-four years. She gave an extended account of the feasts and fasts that she had observed during all that period, 'and besought our Lord God and this holy tribunal for pardon for the denials'.[44] She also explained that she had not admitted the whole truth earlier 'out of a desire to protect her own good name and that of her children'.[45] Her youngest daughter, Clara, confessed on 1 April,[46] and on 12 May Leonor did the same. The latter stated that 'a certain man had read to her from the *Flos Sanctorum* the story of a female saint who had fasted for three continuous days, and in virtue of that fast had delivered the people of Israel from extermination. He had persuaded the accused that it would be an excellent thing in regard to her own salvation were she to fast in the way that that saintly woman had done, and to observe the law which she had observed, namely the law of Moses, the patriarchs, and the prophets.'[47] One may guess that the man to whom she referred was none other than her own brother, Baltazar de Orobio, whose library contained, as we have seen, the second volume of the *Flos Sanctorum* containing a description of the lives of 'the early saints who lived before the coming of Jesus'.[48] It was thus from a book written by a Christian that Baltazar taught his sister about the significance and the importance of the Fast of Esther. Thus it was that through their reading in the classics of Christian literature this group of crypto-Jews found the means of deepening their attachment to Judaism, and of learning how to live a Jewish life.

On 27 May 1656, the deliberations of the tribunal being completed, verdicts were pronounced on Mencia, her son Baltazar, and her three daughters. The tribunal resolved to reconcile them all to the bosom of the Church after they had made public confession of their sins and had expressed their remorse for them. They were condemned to perpetual imprisonment, which was reckoned to be one of the most severe penalties that the Inquisition imposed on those whom it convicted.[49] For

---

[44] Ibid., 'Méritos de Menzia Nuñez', f. 2ᵛ.
[45] '... y que por su reputaçion y la de sus hijos no lo auia hecho hasta aora ...'
[46] Ibid., 'Méritos de Clara de Orovio', f. 2ʳ.
[47] Ibid., 'Méritos de Leonor de Orovio', f. 2ʳ: '... y que çierta persona le auia en un Flor Sanctorum leydo la vida de una santa que auia ayunado tres dias y que por dicho ayuno auia librado a el Pueblo de Ysrael de la muerte y que le persuadio a esta Rea que era muy bueno para saluarse el ayunar como lo auia hecho la santa y guardar la ley que ella guardaua que era la ley antigua de Moysen y de los Patriacas y Profetas.'
[48] See above, chap. 3, p. 77.
[49] Ibid., 'Méritos del Doctor Don Balthasar de Orobio', f. 3ᵛ. The same formulation appears in the summaries of the cases of his mother and 3 sisters.

practical purposes perpetual imprisonment generally meant confinement to prison for a fixed term only, after which the convicted party went free in return for payment of a substantial fine. The place of confinement prescribed was not always the inquisitional gaol, but might be the convicted party's own house, or the house of relatives, or of Christians known to the Holy Office to be trustworthy. In some cases 'perpetual confinement' merely meant that the convicted party was not allowed to leave the locality where he was confined for the duration of the term of imprisonment to which he had been sentenced.[50]

The tribunal clearly had no intention of keeping the Alvares family in perpetual confinement in the literal sense of the term, since it was explicitly stated in the sentences to which we have referred that after leaving prison they would be prohibited, for a space of six years, from residing in Seville, Cádiz, Madrid, or anywhere within twenty leagues of these, in the ports, and in any locality situated within twenty leagues of the coast.[51] Their property was confiscated, and they were compelled to wear the *sanbenito* throughout their term of confinement.[52]

The penalty imposed on Baltazar's brother-in-law, Simón Rodríguez Monsanto, who had recanted relatively easily, was slighter. He was not sentenced to confinement, but compelled to pay a fine of one thousand *reales*, and he was banished for four years from the same areas as those specified in the sentences on the other members of the family.[53]

On 11 June 1656, at an *auto-da-fé* staged in St Paul's (in the

[50] See Beinart, *on Trial*, p. 192, who states that the punishment of perpetual confinement has to be regarded as an act of mercy on the part of the tribunal towards the accused.

[51] Ibid. (see above, n. 43).

[52] Those sentenced to confinement by the inquisitional tribunals were compelled to wear the *sanbenito* throughout the period of their sentence: see Beinart, *on Trial*, loc. cit.

[53] Ibid.: 'Memorias de los Penitençiados que salieron a el auto de fee que se çelebro por el Tribunal del Santo Offiçio desta Inquisiçion de Sevilla en la Iglesia de el Real conuento de San Pablo de la Orden de Predicadores, Domingo onçe de Junio deste año de 1656', ff. 4ᵛ ff.: 'Simon Rodriguez Monsanto ... Penitençiado con abjuraçion de Levi y destierro de Sevilla, Cadiz y Madrid, veinte leguas en contorno y de los pueblos de Mar, veinte leguas la tierra adentro por quatro años preçissos y mill reales de condenaçion.' As stated above (n. 7), no summary of the case against Simón Rodríguez Monsanto has survived; but from the report of the investigations conducted by the Seville court in Apr. 1656 we learn that on 31 Jan. of that year it was resolved to introduce him into the torture-chamber, and that he was accordingly taken there on 17 Feb. He was not broken down, and the inquisitors failed to wring any confession out of him by physical torture. See ibid.: 'Relaçion del estado que tienen las causas de fee que estan pendientes en el Santo Offiçio de la Inquisiçion de Sevilla, remitida en 2 en Abril de seiçientos y çinquenta y seis'. Simón Rodríguez Monsanto figures as no. 31 on the list.

Imprisoned by the Seville Inquisition 91

Dominican friary of Seville), Mencia, her son Baltazar, her three daughters, and her son-in-law Simón Rodríguez were reconciled. At this ceremony, which lasted from six o'clock in the morning until six in the evening, forty-one people were condemned, including twenty-four who had been convicted of Judaizing. Not one was condemned to be burned, most of them being given penalities of confinement and banishment.[54] In the letter of the Seville Inquisition to the Supreme Council of the Holy Office in Madrid dated 13 June 1656, it is stated that the *auto-da-fé* had elicited great enthusiasm from the local public, and that so large a number of spectators had never been seen at a ceremony of the kind. A hundred soldiers were brought in to maintain order, and the city authorities were constrained to strengthen the bridge, in order to forestall any accident.[55]

The first of those to be reconciled at this *auto-da-fé* was Dr Baltazar de Orobio, 'physician, resident in Cádiz, native of the city of Braganza in Portugal, aged about thirty-eight, healthy in body, of dark complexion and with black hair'.[56] He was immediately followed by his mother Mencia ('approximately sixty years old, of pinched face, grey-haired'),[57] and then Leonor ('aged about twenty-nine ... dark-complexioned, black hair, with large eyes'),[58] Clara ('aged twenty-two ... with a pretty face and fair appearance'),[59] and Violante ('aged twenty-eight').[60] Baltazar's brother-in-law Simón Rodríguez ('aged forty-five ... of pinched face, average height, with a fair-coloured beard and black hair') was twenty-fifth on the list of those condemned.[61]

[54] Ibid., 'Memorias de los Penitençiados', etc.
[55] Ibid.: 'Començose a las seis de la mañana y se acauo a la misma ora de la tarde. Con grande aplauso desta çiudad y con el mayor concurso de gente que en ella se a visto y si no ubieramos prevenido 100 soldados que nos dio el Sr. Asistente se padeçiera muncho [*sic*] y fue necessario haçer reparos el mismo dia en la Puente por temerse alguna desgraçia (gloria a Dios no la ubo)...'
[56] Ibid., f. 1ʳ: 1. El Dr. Don Balthasar de Orouio, medico vezino de Cadiz, natural de la çiudad de Bergança en Portugal de edad de treinta y ocho años poco mas o menos de buen cuerpo, moreno, pelo negro...'
[57] Ibid.: '2. Mençia Nuñez, muger de Manuel Aluarez, madre del dicho Dr. Orobio ... de edad de sesenta años poco mas o menos, delgada de rostro y cana...'
[58] Ibid., f. 1ʳ: '3. Leonor de Orobio, muger de Simon Rodriguez Monsanto ... de edad de treinta y nueue años poco mas o menos ... morena de rostro, pelo negro, ojos grandes...'
[59] Ibid., f. 1ᵛ: '4. Clara de Orouio su hermana, soltera ... de edad de veinte y dos años, de buen rostro y pareçer.'
[60] Ibid.: '5. Violante Enrriquez Orouio, su hermana, muger de Pasqual Nuñez ... de edad de veinte y ocho años...'
[61] Ibid., f. 4ᵛ: '25. Simon Rodriguez Monsanto ... de quarenta y çinco años ... flaco de rostro, mediana estatura, barua rubio y cauello negro...'

When those condemned were led into the friary church of St Paul an incident occurred of which the hero was Luis Fernández Pato, a crypto-Jewish native of Villa Real in Portugal, who was resident in Seville and had been sentenced to banishment for the sin of Judaizing. When he saw that a number of women were jammed tight amid the crowd of sightseers and were begging the men near to them to let them get a sight of the condemned victims, Luis called out to the men 'give way, there . . . to those women, so that they may see how these totally innocent people who have been condemned are being humiliated, for having committed no sin at all'.[62] This crypto-Jew was not overawed by the ceremony; and he paid a price for his boldness. He was taken back to the inquisitional gaol and the inquisitors opened an additional file about his case.[63] His protest was an isolated one. All the others who had been condemned, including Baltazar and his family, submitted to their penalty meekly.

[62] Ibid., letter of 13 June 1656. Pato had previously held the office of *administrador de las salinas de la Andaluçia tierra adentro*; see 'Memorias de los Penitençiados', f. 5ʳ.
[63] Ibid.

5
Freedom

THE LAST YEARS IN SPAIN

We know little about the conditions under which Baltazar Orobio lived during his imprisonment, after he had been condemned. Limborch, in his *Historia Inquisitionis*, states that a small allowance was made to him out of his confiscated property with which to purchase food that he had to cook for himself in prison.[1] Some pieces of evidence preserved amongst documents of the Supreme Council of the Inquisition in Madrid fill out the picture with a few details regarding this chapter of his life.

On 8 February 1657 a complaint was received by the Supreme Council that 'Baltazar Orobio, physician, having been condemned by the said tribunal [sc. of Seville] to wear the *sanbenito* and to perpetual confinement, is daily seen by all and sundry walking around in the said city and in Triana[2] without his *sanbenito*: to the indignation of those who observe him, who are astonished to see how they [i.e. the officers of the Inquisition] turn a blind eye to him and permit [such flouting of his sentence]: further, that on many feast-days in the current year he did not attend mass with the others who had been condemned.'[3]

The substance of the complaint clearly shows that Baltazar was not in point of fact being held in the inquisitional gaol, but that some private residence had been determined upon as his place of confinement—the house of some relative, or of a Christian known to the Inquisition to be trustworthy.[4] Despite the risk involved, Baltazar apparently exploited the relatively comfortable conditions in which he

---

[1] Limborch, *Inqu.*, Book ii, chap. 18, pp. 158 f.: 'Illud aliquatenus convenit cum narratione Isaaci Orobio, qui cum Hispali in amplissima fortuna vixerat, se tamen in carcere Inquisitionis durissime habitum fuisse mihi narravit, et licet amplissimas possedisset opes, sibi tantum exiguam pensionem quotidie in alimenta insumendam fuisse concessam: alimentum hoc fuisse carnem, quam quandoque ipse sine ullius famuli ministerio sibi coquere et praeparare debuit.' On conditions under which those held in confinement by the Inquisition lived see Pinta Llorente, *Cárceles inquis.*

[2] A suburb of Seville, on the west bank of the Guadalquivir. The building that housed the inquisitional offices was situated there.

[3] See Madrid, AHN, Inquisition section, lib. 693, f. 75ᵛ.

[4] See above, chap. 4, p. 90.

was held, and was in the habit of going out and about. It is possible that with the assistance of relatives and friends he bribed those appointed by the Inquisition to fail to notice his behaviour. The Supreme Council of the Inquisition took a very serious view of the matter, and ordered the Seville tribunal (the Inquisitor General himself endorsing the council's decision) to give their close attention to ensuring that Baltazar should serve out all details of his sentence, without conniving at any failure on his part to do so.[5]

But Baltazar, his mother, and his sisters did not, after all, have to complete their (nominally perpetual) term of confinement. During the course of the year 1657 they addressed no less than seven pleas for mercy to Madrid, three of these emanating from Baltazar himself.[6] In them he described the material straits in which he, his mother, and his sisters found themselves, the misery of his two married sisters Leonor and Violante 'deprived of their conjugal life', and the piteous fate of his youngest sister, Clara, 'unmarried, and—thanks to her imprisonment—likely to remain so'.[7] Baltazar made a parade of the submissiveness with which all of them were satisfying the requirements of their penalties, and were fulfilling the instructions of those appointed over them to the letter: and he petitioned those who headed the Inquisition to remit their penalty of imprisonment, and to substitute for it 'spiritual penalties'.[8]

The first appeals were rejected by the Supreme Council,[9] but at Christmas 1657 they agreed to reduce the period of confinement. The leadership of the Inquisition resolved that Baltazar, Violante, and Clara should serve one more year and then be released, and that their sister Leonor should be released after but six months.[10] They were

[5] Ibid. (n. 3 above): 'y consultado con el Exmo. Sr. Obispo Inquisidor General ha pedido ordeneis se cumpla la su penitençia y estareis muy atentos a que hagan lo mismo los demas y que los ministros a quien toca no consientan cossa en contrario . . .'

[6] Madrid, AHN, Inquisition section, Leg. 2987. The letters are not holographs of the convicted parties, and were undated by the writer(s): but the Madrid officials marked them with the dates of receipt. Baltazar's appeals were received on 23 Mar., 19 May, and 5 Dec. 1657, on which last date those of Mencia and her 3 daughters were also received.

[7] See his letter received on 23 Mar.: 'Porque padeçen suma nessesidad por no tener con que sustentarse', and cf. the contents of that received on 19 May: 'y dos casadas que son Leonor de Orobio y Biolante de Orobio, no haçen vida con sus maridos por estar en la penitençia, y Clara de Orobio, donçella, deja de tomar estado por la dicha causa . . .'

[8] Ibid., cf. below, n. 12.

[9] At the foot of these earlier letters there is recorded the decision of the members of the Council: 'no a lugar', 'no ha lugar por ahora'.

[10] See the endorsement of Baltazar's appeal received in Madrid on 13 Apr. 1658: 'Por la pasqua de Nauidad del año pasado de 1657 fue seruido comutar su prision y la de Violante de Orobio y Clara de Orouio sus hermanas en un año. Y a Leonor de Orouio en seis meses.'

clearly dealing more severely with the mother, Mencia, who did not come in for mention in this resolution of the Council.[11]

Baltazar was not satisfied with this partial remission, and in early April 1658 he once again approached the Council in Madrid, asking that in view of the fact 'that they had been held in confinement for such an extended period and were suffering from extreme privation, he himself and his sisters, together with their mother, might be released forthwith in honour of the holy feast of Easter that marks the resurrection of our Lord Jesus Christ'.[12]

His pleas were accepted. On 13 April 1658 the Supreme Council of the Holy Office resolved to let the five prisoners go free, to release them from the obligation to wear the *sanbenito*, and to impose upon them penalties conducive of 'spiritual refreshment'. The Council further gave orders that 'they be banished from the city of Seville and from the localities in which they had committed their sins, also from Madrid [and from all areas] within six leagues of the places mentioned for a period of two years; nor might they settle in the ports [or in areas within] twenty leagues of them'.[13] Thus Baltazar, his mother, and his sisters obtained both the shortening of their term of imprisonment and the reduction of their period of banishment from the six years specified in their sentences to two years only.

But Baltazar remained in Seville for some little time yet, despite his order of banishment. On 4 June 1658 the supreme court received a complaint that he was walking around Seville, to the public scandal. The Seville officials were immediately instructed to enforce his departure from the city, and to be at pains to see that he fulfilled the prescriptions of the Council's resolution.[14]

Thereafter, all trace of Baltazar and his family in Spain disappears. His first-born son, later in Amsterdam to go by the name of Moses,

[11] Her appeal, received at Madrid on 5 Dec. 1657, was endorsed by the Supreme Council 'no a lugar por aora'.

[12] See above, n. 10: 'y porque ha tanto tiempo que estan en dicha prision padeçiendo estrema neçessidad y por honrra desta Santa Pascua de Resureçion [sic] de Nuestro Señor Jesuchristo, suplican a Vuestra Santa Señoria se sirva de mandar se les alçe el tiempo que les falta de la dicha prision. Y a Mençia Nuñez su madre mandarla soltar della comutandole en otra pena espiritual...'

[13] The petition was endorsed by the Supreme Council in the following terms: 'quiteseles el hauito y se les remite lo que les falta de cumplir de carçel comutandoseles en penitençias saludables. Y sean desterrados de la çiudad de Seuilla y lugares donde cometieron los delitos y villa de Madrid y seis leguas en contorno por dos años y que no lleguen a los puertos con veinte leguas en contorno...'

[14] Madrid, AHN, Inquisition section, lib. 693, f. 130ᵛ: 'El Consejo ha tenido relaçion de que el Dr. Baltasar Orobio se pasea por esa çiudad con escandalo;... had pareçido ordeneis que el susodicho y demas desterrados salgan a cumplir los destierros...'

was born about 1658. From the register-entry of the marriage of his daughter Hannah to David Sarfati in Amsterdam on 1 March 1680 one learns that she was born around 1660 in Lorca, a small town not far from Cartagena, and one may surmise that it was in Lorca that the family settled on being forced to leave Seville.[15] It was at this time that Baltazar reached the decision to leave Spain, where all sources of livelihood had become closed to him and the terror of the Inquisition lay in wait for him and for his family in every hidden corner. He knew that all hope had vanished that his father Manuel Alvares, his brother Melchor, and his brother-in-law Pascual Núñez could ever again return to Spain to rejoin their kinsfolk there, since on 15 June 1658 the Seville tribunal had decreed that the three of them, having made their escape, were to be burned in effigy.[16]

Manuel Alvares had been living all this while in France, at Bayonne, as were apparently his son and son-in-law who had escaped with him. In evidence given by Manuel de León on 3 March 1664 before the inquisitional tribunal of Toledo, he stated that whilst residing in Bayonne in 1658–9 'he had known a lot of Portuguese, who lived in the district of St Esprit; they were generally known to be Judaizers who observed the law of Moses'. He mentioned the names of several of them, including that of Manuel Alvares de Castro.[17]

No doubt Baltazar had heard from crypto-Jewish visitors to Bayonne that his father had settled there, and he must have yearned to go and join him.[18] We cannot be certain of the date when Orobio and his family left Spain, but it was certainly during the first half of 1660.

---

[15] In 1678 Baltazar's first-born son (Moses) was aged 20 at the time of his matriculation as a student of the university of Leiden: see Kaplan, *Studenṭim be-leiden*, p. 71. For Ana/Hannah, see Amsterdam, AGA, DTB 692, p. 35.

[16] Ibid., (n. 14 above), f. 131^r f.

[17] Inquisition section, Toledo, Leg. 166 no. 8, f. 2^r: 'este declarante estubo por dos veçes en Vayona de França en el Varrio de Sant Espiritus, una bez desde como media de julio asta fin de agosto del año de mil y seisçientos y çinquenta y ocho y la otra fue desde entrada de abril pocos dias despues de los primeros asta algunos dias de los de mayo de çinquenta y nuebe y en los dichos tienpos vio y conoçio en el dicho varrio de Sant Espiritus de Bayona de França a muchos y diferentes portugueses los quales comunmente se sauia y entendia que heran judayçantes obseruantes de la ley de Moysen.' See ibid., f. 2^v, list of crypto-Jews, including Manuel Alvares, and f. 6^v (evidence on 6 Mar. 1664): 'Manuel Albarez de Castro natural de Portugal, no saue de que lugar, vezino de Vayona, mercader y viene de España no saue a que parte sera; de edad de mas de çinquenta años, mediano de querpo, rostro moreno, ojos negros y grandes, pelo entre cano, barba y vigote entre cano.'

[18] Evidence strongly suggests that Baltazar had family connections elsewhere in France as well. Domingo Alvares de Castro, a member of the crypto-Jewish group at Rouen during the first third of the 17th cent., was probably a relative. Cf. Beinart, '*Inq. ḥuṣ Sepharad*, Appendix 1.

Once again this much-tried family took up the wanderer's staff and set off on the long and perilous journey to the south of France. And around the same time as their departure—to be precise, on 13 April 1660—Manuel Alvares, his son Melchor, and his son-in-law Pascual Núñez were in fact burned in effigy at the great *auto-da-fé* held in Seville.[19]

TOULOUSE

What we know of Baltazar's sojourn in France is meagre and fragmentary. From what has been stated above, it may be assumed that many members of the Alvares-Orobio clan had already settled there at the beginning of the seventeenth century. Although Jewish residence in France had been prohibited since the expulsion of 1394, the country was a centre of settlement for crypto-Jews from the Iberian peninsula who arrived wearing a thin veil of Christian conformity. Special privileges were accorded to these 'Portuguese merchants' from 1550 onwards, and they took full advantage of their rights.[20]

The date of Baltazar's arrival in France cannot be determined exactly, but he was probably living in Bayonne by 24 June 1660. In the register of baptisms of Saint-Étienne-Labourd he is recorded as having stood as godfather at the baptism of the son of Simón Gómez and Marianne Enríquez, Portuguese residents and undoubtedly crypto-Jews.[21]

[19] See Montero de Espinosa, pp. 94 f., 107. For this *auto-da-fé* cf. M. Méndez Bejarano, *Historia de la juiveria de Sevilla,* Madrid, 1922, p. 188; Adler, *Auto de Fé,* p. 103.

[20] There is an extensive literature regarding the status and situation of the 'members of the Portuguese nation' in France in the 16th and 17th cents. The most recent summaries will be found in Baron, *History,* xv, pp. 74–160; G. Nahon, *Les 'Nations' Juives Portugaises du Sud-Ouest de la France (1684–1791),* Paris, 1981; B. Blumenkranz (ed.), *Histoire des Juifs en France,* Toulouse, 1972, pp. 221 f.; Révah, *Marranes, Autobiographie,* 'Le Premier Établissement des Marranes Portugais à Rouen', *Annuaire de l'Institut de Philologie et d'Histoire Orientales et Slaves,* 13, 1953 (= *Mélanges Isidore Levy,* Brussels, 1955), pp. 539–52; Beinart, op. cit. (n. 18 above); F. Hildesheimer, 'Une créature de Richelieu: Alphonse Lopez, le "Seigneur Hebreo"', in G. Dahan (ed.), *Le Juif au miroir de l'histoire, Mélanges B. Blumenkranz,* Paris, 1985, pp. 293–9. For the economic links of crypto-Jews in France with the Iberian peninsula see Szajkowski, *Marrano Trade.* Szajkowski set out, in a whole series of articles, to refute Révah's conclusions and to prove that the great majority of crypto-Jews who settled in France from the end of the 15th to the beginning of the 17th cents. were entirely assimilated into their Christian environment: but—at least in so far as concerns the 16th and 17th cents.—he fails to convince. See his *French Marranos and Sephardim.*

[21] See Bayonne, Arch., GG suppl. 4, baptisms in the parish of Saint-Étienne-d'Arribe-Labourd, p. 18: 'Un peu après a été baptisé Baltazar, fils de Mr. Simon

That event is evidence for the rapid integration of Baltazar and his family into the circle of crypto-Jews from both Portugal and Spain who had found refuge in France from the persecution of the Inquisition. They continued to maintain their Jewish identity beneath their mask as Portuguese Christians, or rather as 'members of the Portuguese nation', as they are styled in contemporary documents. Baltazar's participation in a baptismal ceremony need occasion no surprise. As a refugee from Spain he did his best to become absorbed within the general framework of the crypto-Jewish community of the south of France, and together with his family he conformed to the way of life of the great majority of the group, who demonstrated outward loyalty to the Church.

The French towns close to the Spanish frontier—Biarritz, Bayonne, Saint-Jean-de-Luz, Labastide, and other places—constituted staging-posts for crypto-Jews who succeeded in escaping from the claws of the Inquisition. Crypto-Jewish centres of settlement grew up there, maintaining connections with the communities throughout the Sephardi diaspora.[22] There is no doubt that Bayonne formed the first station in the story of Baltazar's travels away from the Iberian peninsula. He was accompanied by his wife, Isabel Rodríguez, who had already born him a daughter in southern Spain. More than this is not known about the family's sojourn in Bayonne. Possibly they did not stay there long, since by 20 August 1660 Baltazar was already in Toulouse, as is shown by a document of the local university.[23]

It would seem that Baltazar Orobio, determined as ever to pursue a scientific career, had decided to try his luck at the university of Toulouse, where a community of crypto-Jews was established. In addition to these, there were apparently some declared Jews who had come there and remained for a period of time. On 31 May 1653, on 2 August 1679, and again on 7 July 1680 the *parlement* of Toulouse decreed the banishment of all Jews from the city, but there is doubt whether the reference is to new Christians of Portuguese origin or to others who had made open profession of their Jewish identity.[24]

Gommes et de Marian Henriques, parrin doctor Balthazar Albares de Orobio et matrine Elisabet Rodrigues, par moy de Molere, vicaire.' I am grateful to M. G. Nahon of Paris for drawing my attention to this record.

[22] For the chronology of the settlement of refugees from the Inquisition in the area of France near to the frontier with Spain, see Beinart, *Conversos*, p. 475.

[23] See below, n. 34.

[24] See Szajkowski, *Toulouse Auto da fé*, pp. 278 f., and R. Anschel, *Les Juifs de France*, Paris, 1946, pp. 144 f. The *rue des Juifs* at Toulouse still bore that name in the 17th

The university of Toulouse had been founded in 1229 on the initiative of Pope Gregory IX, to provide an intellectual bastion in the crusade against the Albigensians. From its very beginnings it was characterized by ardent zeal. Its sensitivity to the merest whisper of heresy sometimes inhibited its capacity to welcome thinkers and scholars, who were deterred by the atmosphere of bigotry.[25] In characteristically graphic style Rabelais portrayed the disappointment of Pantagruel at its poor calibre as an academic institution: 'thence he went to Toulouse, where he learned to dance, and to fence with both hands (after the manner of the students of that university). But when he saw that they roasted the members of the regent body like salted herrings, he decided to move on ...'[26] Obviously the writer's imagination has had free play here: but it is nevertheless the case that in 1531 Caturce, a member of the regent body, had been burned because of his heretical opinions. For 'New Christians' of Spanish and Portuguese origin Toulouse was far from providing a safe haven. In 1511 the corpse of Gonçalves Molina was burned, and in 1560 a Spanish student was accused of Judaizing following a debate that had degenerated into a riot. This accusation led to the departure of most of the Spanish and Portuguese students from the city.[27]

Medical studies had been treated as a step-child in the university from its very beginnings. The founders did not regard them as being a major interest, all their aspirations being bound up in dealing with the Albigensian ferment. The canons, who were incorporated into the university in 1230, deliberately sabotaged all hopes for its scholarly progress, and it was not until 1521 that a separate faculty of medicine was established. Even then it did not begin to acquire any sort of a reputation until the second half of the sixteenth century, thanks to the

---

cent., but it may be doubted whether the crypto-Jews would have lived there. See J. Chalande, 'La Rue des Juifs à Toulouse au quinzième, seizième, et dix-septième siècles', *Bulletin de la société archéologique du Midi de la France*, NS 37–9, pp. 367–72.

[25] For the history of the university of Toulouse, see Jourdain, *L'Université de Toulouse, son passé—son présent (1229–1929)*, Toulouse, 1929; Declareuil; and, for its medical faculty, Barbot.

[26] *Œvres de François Rabelais*, ed. A. Lefranc, iii, *Pantagruel*, Paris, 1922, chap. 5, pp. 55 ff.: 'De la vint à Thoulouse, où aprint fort bien à dancer et à jouer de l'espée à deux mains comme est l'usance des escholiers de la dicte université; mais il n'y demoura gueres quand il vit qu'ilz faisoyent brusler leurs regens tout vifz comme harans soretz, disant: "Jà Dieu ne plaise que ainsi je meure, car je suis de ma nature assez alteré sans me chauffer davantaige!".'

[27] See *L'Université de Toulouse* (n. 25 above), p. 137, and E. Szapiro in B. Blumenkranz (ed.), *Histoire des Juifs en France* (n. 20 above), p. 229.

scientific activity of Augier Ferrier. All the endeavours of that distinguished scholar to get himself appointed to the chair of medicine proved fruitless, because of his affiliation to Calvinism. It was not until 1581 that he succeeded in obtaining appointment as an instructor—not as professor—in the university, and only then as a result of the direct intervention of Catherine de Medici.

Things did not change much in the seventeenth century. Francisco Sánchez, the distinguished sceptic—himself the scion of a 'New Christian' family—at length succeeded in getting himself appointed to Ferrier's post after having been passed over for it for many years, and he occupied the position until his death in 1623.[28]

With the death of Sánchez decline set in. The number of students dwindled, and the professorships were assigned to physicians of mediocre ability. From the report of the commission of enquiry into the state of the universities in the Languedoc which was appointed in 1668 on the initiative of Colbert, we learn of the pitiful condition of medical studies at Toulouse. The medical faculty was the weakest in the whole university, containing but three professorships and with difficulty mustering a roll of about thirty students under instruction. Two of the chairs were of long standing. The third, that of surgery and pharmacy, was the most recently established; its teaching, somewhat surprisingly, was conducted in French. At the time of the presentation of the report in 1668 two of the chairs were vacant and the third was occupied by a professor who enjoyed very poor health. Considerable surprise was caused by the rejection, in the same year, of the candidature of François Bayle, destined to become one of the foremost prosecutors of medical studies in the seventeenth century. His attempt to join the medical faculty was again thwarted in 1676; and when, at last, he was given a professorial chair in 1679, it was in the faculty of arts.[29]

One may take it that things were not much better during the period of Baltazar's stay in Toulouse, when the most prominent personality there was Louis de Queyrats, who had been a regent since 1651.[30] Baltazar acted as professor of surgery and pharmacy, apparently occupying the chair in 1661, and from this one may deduce that he did

---

[28] See Declareuil, p. 78; *L'Université de Toulouse*, pp. 135 f. On Sánchez and his thought see Popkin, *Scepticism Erasmus–Descartes*, pp. 38 f.

[29] See Jourdain, p. 7, who prints the relevant report (pp. 11 f.).

[30] On de Queyrats see Barbot, i, pp. 145 f. He was the son of Jean de Queyrats, the well-known regent of the medical faculty of Toulouse.

actually lecture in French. He was referred to as doctor and regent for the first time on 30 March of that year, but although he had already discharged the functions of a regent at the examination for both the licentiate and the doctorate in medicine on 18 February. Further mention of him occurs in faculty documents of 9 August 1662, after which he disappears from view.[31]

If J. Barbot's conjecture is correct, Orobio got the post by succeeding in the open competition for the office of regent in surgery which was publicly advertised after its vacation by de Queyrats on 9 June 1660 upon his elevation to the chair of medicine.[32] But the earliest indication of Baltazar's presence in the university comes, as has been said, from a document of 20 August 1660 when he was admitted to the faculty as bachelor of medicine, after having presented himself as holding the same degree from Alcalá de Henares. The document recording his incorporation reads as follows:

Discretus uir Baltazar de Orobio de Castelo, Lusitanus, baccall[aureatus] in medecina in Uniuersitate Complutensi apud hispanos, fuit aggregatus bacall-[aureatus] in eadem facultate medicinae sub domino Queyratio, die uigesima mensis augusti 1661.[33]

We have already seen that Baltazar had graduated as a bachelor of medicine at Alcalá in 1636 but never attained the doctor's degree there—nor, indeed, was his first degree strictly speaking in the subject stated. When he obtained the chair of medical method at the university of Seville in 1641 he seems to have presented a forged certificate, and on arrival at Toulouse he had no university diploma beyond that recording his bachelor's degree.

It is consequently in the highest degree surprising to discover from a document preserved in the archives of the university of Toulouse that on 9 September 1660 Baltazar produced a document, dated 14 June 1640 and bearing the seal of the university of Alcalá, recording his having been granted the degree of doctor of medicine. The text is as follows:

Anno Domini 1660 et die nona mensis septembris, clarissimus uir dominus Balthazar de Orobio de Castelo, Lusitanus, in medicina doctor in Uniuersitate Complutensi apud hispanos, et olim in eadem Academia metaphisicae

---

[31] Toulouse Univ., Arch. de la Fac. de Droit, reg. 9 and 28, also Arch. hosp., Série H liasse 8. See Barbot, i, pp. 152 f., who did not know whether thereafter Orobio had left Toulouse, or had died. [32] Barbot, ibid.

[33] Toulouse Univ., Arch. de la Fac. de Droit, reg. 28, f. 178ᵛ; Barbot, i, p. 153.

propietarius regens ut nobis apparuit ex literis signatis et sigillatis die decima quarta mensis junii anni domini millesimi sescentesimi quadragesimi fuit aggregatus licenciatus et doctor in eadem facultate sub domino Queyratio medicinae professore coram domino Destopynia procancellario, anno et die praedictis.[34]

The document was received and confirmed by de Queyrats acting in the name of the medical faculty of Toulouse: and from then on Baltazar's possession of a first degree and a doctorate in medicine was acknowledged.

The question that must be asked is, if Baltazar de Orobio really held a medical doctorate, what need had he, a mere three weeks earlier, of producing evidence that he had the baccalaureate or licentiate, instead of presenting himself as a fully-fledged doctor in the first place? Could it be the case that on 20 August his doctoral diploma was not to hand, and that it only reached him from Spain at a later date? Such a suggestion is tenuous, and scarcely plausible: particularly in view of the circumstance that the Alcalá archives, which have been very well preserved, contain not the slightest confirmation of his having been awarded the doctorate. It is doubtful whether a completely satisfactory solution to the problem can be propounded, but we shall probably not be far from the truth if we adopt the view of Révah, who surmises that, once again, it was a case of a forged certificate.

It is possible that Baltazar's scientific knowledge and his experience in the field of medicine extending over many years had impressed the faculty at Toulouse, and made his task the easier. One should not forget that, at the period with which we are dealing, the obtaining of false documents was by no means regarded as a serious matter. One may conjecture that the parlous state in which the Toulouse faculty of medicine found itself, together with the necessity of filling one of the vacant chairs as a matter of urgency, added significant weight on Baltazar's side in this chapter of events. At any rate, when later he was registered at the *Collegium Medicum* of Amsterdam he produced his Toulouse diploma dated 9 September 1660, which was, in point of fact, no more than the confirmation of the 'certificate' purportedly emanating from Alcalá.[35] None of this in any way clouded the

---

[34] Ibid., reg. 9, f. 170; Barbot, ibid.

[35] Amsterdam, AGA, Collegium Medicum, file no. 20 (unpaginated). Révah was the first to draw attention to this, and was of the opinion that there was no more in it than a piece of forgery: see *rupt. spin., nouvel examen*, 71, p. 583. For Orobio's professional activity in Amsterdam as a physician, and his links with the *Collegium Medicum* there, see below, chap. 7, pp. 200 ff.

successful progress of Baltazar, this crypto-Jew schooled in so much travail and so rich in his experience of life. His short stay in Toulouse opened up new hopes for him, and prepared the way for a surprising improvement in his fortunes.

ASSOCIATIONS WITH THE PRINCE DE CONDÉ AND THE KING OF FRANCE

In a letter written to Prado about 1664 Orobio provides us with interesting details regarding his sojourn in France. We are told that he became a successful teacher at Toulouse, and that he took part in all the public discussions arranged during his stay in the city on theological and medical topics as well as other subjects.[36] He similarly records, in the same letter, the social circle in which he moved, and the names of some of the individuals with whom he came into contact—the Prince de Condé and his brother, the Prince de Conti, the Marquess of Coserans, as well as archbishops, bishops, and men of learning who became his friends.[37] He claims that when he discussed scholarly and scientific matters with them his remarks were met with attentive respect.

Baltazar's connections with the two brothers, Louis II de Bourbon, Prince de Condé, and Armand de Bourbon, Prince de Conti, ought not to pass unconsidered. Both of them were closely involved in the

[36] See Orobio, *Cart. Apol.*, MS Paris, BN Fonds éspagnoles 41, p. 888: '. . . y enseñe en España y algun tiempo en la mas insigne Universidad de la Francia, y aun decian que enseñava bien; y dispute en quantos actos publicos se hizieron en mi tiempo en Toloza [sic], que son los mas celebres de la Europa, sin encarecimiento, arguyendo en Theologia Escolastica, Philosophia, Metaphisica, Medicina, Mathematicas: aunque no todas eran de mi profession, me oyan con gusto y aun con aplauso.' Cf. Basnage (see above, chap. 1, n. 1), pp. 2113 f.; Amelander, f. 133ᵛ.

[37] *Cart. Apol.*, ibid.: 'No he comunicado con barbaros, ni siempre con plebeyos, sino con muy grandes Señores Principes: en España muchos; en Francia, el de Condé y de Conty, su hermano, admiracion de todos los ingenios y pozo de sabiduria, el Marques de Coserans, insigne en erudicion y letras y a otros muchos, tampoco me despreciaron y estimavan en algo mi conversacion, cosa bien vista de muchos de los nuestros; tambien Arzobispos, Obispos y hombres consumados en las sciencias fueron mis intimos amigos.' Cf. Franco Mendes, '*Orovyo*, p. 221, who relied on Locke and Basnage for the statement that 'after leaving prison he settled in Toulouse, and continued to reside there amongst [Christian] people, associating with them and to all appearances sharing their faith. He took part in some important discussions on scholarly topics in the presence of prominent persons and distinguished occupants of sundry chairs in the local university, vying in debate with other candidates for honorific marks . . . once again he took a prominent part in discussion . . . with one of the leading figures of the time, distinguished alike for the clarity of his expression and the depth of his understanding.' There are good grounds for assuming that the reference is to the Prince de Condé.

political life of France under Mazarin as leaders in the Fronde, each of them being both a politically significant figure and a soldier of distinction in the civil war. What, however, is important for our concerns is that at the time when Baltazar was residing in Toulouse the Prince de Condé was living at Chantilly, where he assembled around him a circle of scholars and artists to whom he afforded his patronage. The outstanding figures among this group were Molière, Racine, Nicolas Boileau, La Fontaine, Pierre Nicole, and Bossuet. On the other hand his brother the Prince de Conti had shut himself away in Languedoc after his defeat at Alessandria in Italy in 1657, to devote himself to mystical studies. He was, at this time, in close touch with Molière (whom he was later to accuse of atheism), and it was at Languedoc that he composed his *Lettres sur la grâce* and *Du devoir des grands et des devoirs de gouverneurs de province*.[38]

Baltazar was certainly in touch not only with the two brothers, but also with their respective circles of intimates. Thanks to the princes, who had both received their education from the Jesuits in the university of Bourges, the doors of the French salons where discussions on philosophical and scholarly topics took place were thrown open before the learned Dr Orobio de Castro; and possibly it was due to their representations that he became (or may have become) a medical counsellor of Louis XIV.

Baltazar's alleged associations with the King of France are shrouded in darkness. Apart from his own personal testimony in the aforementioned letter to Prado that he was 'Profesor Público de el Rey ... y su consegero ad honorem', no evidence survives of such an appointment beyond the preliminaries to some of his works preserved in manuscript.[39] One must assume that Baltazar never resided in Paris, and that whatever functions he did fulfil in his capacity as a medical counsellor he fulfilled in Toulouse, as his letter referred to above indicates. Possibly nomination to the council came his way as a result

---

[38] As is now well known, the Prince de Condé endeavoured to meet Spinoza in Utrecht; see L. Roth, *Spinoza*, p. 12. For France at this period, and the position enjoyed by the Prince de Condé and his brother de Conti see J. Boulanger, *The Seventeenth Century in France*, New York, 1963; A. Guérard, *France in the Classical Age*, New York, 1965.

[39] See Orobio, *Cart. Apol.* (n. 36 above): 'No era menor el puesto que deje en Francia: era Professor y Medico Regio, no mil leguas del pulso regio', and cf. MS Amsterdam, *EH* 48 B 12, title-page, 'Profesor Público de el Rey de Francia en la insigne universidad de Tolosa y su consegero ad honorem'. See Carmoly, i, p. 175, and C. Roth, *Marranos*, pp. 299 f.

of his name becoming more widely known through his appointment to the university of Toulouse.[40]

One cannot establish the exact date when Baltazar left France, but after 9 August 1662 his name no longer appears amongst the regents of the university of Toulouse.[41] It looks as if this time his move to a fresh country was due to a single purpose. As doctor and as philosopher he had been accorded academic degrees and honours of some significance in France, where in the course of a few years he had achieved a position of status within the social élite: but now, it seems, he resolved to move on, in order to reunite himself with his own people and make open profession of his observance of the law of Moses. Having forsaken Andalusia and having followed a chequered route that led him to Toulouse, he now continued his journey towards the north with his eyes set on Holland, where Jews from Spain and Portugal— erstwhile crypto-Jews or the children of such—had succeeded in creating a new home that afforded a place of refuge to those fleeing from the Inquisition.[42] Had he not left Toulouse, conceivably his fate would have been no different from that of the seven Portuguese merchants who were sent to the stake in 1685 after having been accused of Judaizing. On 16 April of that year—a few months before the revocation of the Edict of Nantes—the *parlement* of Toulouse

[40] See preceding note and cf. Carvalho, p. 93, who mentions a dissertation allegedly written by Orobio in Toulouse entitled *De Putrefactione*. This work is not known to survive. [Probably nomination as a medical counsellor was little more than a routine matter that followed on having one's name registered on a list of appropriately qualified physicians. In any case, the Paris medical profession exercised strict local protectionism. R.L.]

[41] See Barbot, p. 152.

[42] In his *Cart. Apol.* (n. 36 above) Orobio refers to the case of Dr Elijah Montalto, who had likewise served as court physician in France at the beginning of the century: 'Y regio pulso desprecio el Doctor Montalto, huyendo del a uña de cavallo por seguir la verdadera Religion; y ni Vmd. ni yo ni otros tantos llegamos con muchos quilates a su sciencia; mas supo despreciarlo todo, por emplearlo bien todo.' Orobio's presentation of the manner of Montalto's leaving France is, however, inaccurate. In point of fact, Montalto's first sojourn in Paris was in 1606, having been invited there by the Queen, Marie de Medici. At the time he was living in France as a Christian. He returned to Paris in 1614, after his reversion to Judaism. As far as is known, he never again left the capital during his lifetime, and it was only after his death, in 1616, that his coffin was taken for interment to the Jewish cemetery at Ouderkerk, near Amsterdam, at the instance of his disciple Saul Levi Mortera. It is possible that Orobio's version is no more than the idealization of the story of a scholar whose history and literary achievements served as a paragon for generations of Jewish writers deriving from Spain and Portugal. For Montalto's career in Paris see J. M. Pelorson, 'Le docteur Carlos García et la colonie hispano-portugaise de Paris (1613–1619)', *BH* 71, 1969, pp. 518 f.

decreed that they should be burned alive, and their ashes scattered to the four winds.[43]

AMSTERDAM: THE DUTCH JERUSALEM

Towards the end of 1662 Baltazar de Orobio arrived in Amsterdam together with his wife Isabel and their son and daughter (both still small children).[44] They were accompanied by Baltazar's parents Manuel and Mencia, his brother Melchor, his sisters Leonor, Violante, and Clara, and his two brothers-in-law Simón Rodríguez and Pascual Núñez.[45] Here in Amsterdam, for the first time in their lives the members of the Alvares de Orobio family encountered an organized Jewish community numbering about two thousand souls, the majority being former crypto-Jews or the issue of crypto-Jews who, once safely there, had commenced open observance of Judaism.[46]

[43] On the Toulouse *auto-da-fé* of 1685 see Szajkowski, *Toulouse Auto da fé*. The family names of those condemned to be burned were Mirande, Roques-Leon, Vandale, Cardoze, Sylve-Morena, Loppes, and Emanuel. The words used by Henri d'Aguesseau, counsellor of state, on the previous 27 Mar. are instructive in regard to the character of the local crypto-Jewish group: 'Ces Portugais étaient establis depuis longtemps à Toulouse et il y a eu quelques'uns qui se sont enrichis considérablement par le commerce; cela leur a attiré l'envie et la jalousie des autres marchands de la ville qui n'ont eu ni la même industrie ni la même fortune.'

[44] Orobio de Castro's name figures in documents of the Portuguese-Jewish congregation for the first time on 8 *Shebaṭ* 5423 (16 Jan. 1663), on which date he is recorded as having contributed 2 florins to the relief of the congregational poor: see Amsterdam, AGA, PA 334 no. 174, p. 538. On the following 3 *Nisan* (10 Apr.) there is recorded his contribution to the synagogue for the first half of the Jewish year that commenced in the previous autumn, viz. 3 fl. 6 stuivers (20 stuivers = 1 florin), ibid., p. 559. On 21 *'Iyyar* (28 May) the *Ma'amad* (i.e. the executive committee of the governing body of the congregation) fixed the dues for the second half-year payable by Orobio and other new members who had joined the congregation; see PA 334 no. 19, p. 518: '5423 [1662/3]. En 21 de Jyar se juntarão os Senhores do Mahamad para aver de trattar de fintar algumas peçoas vindas de fora como tambem a outras que o não estavão, tanto para gastos presiços como para Bethaim . . . (i.e. for the congregational cemetery). Dr Orobio was assessed at 8 fl., + 4 for the cemetery, which was (and still is) at Ouderkerk. Cf. Silva Rosa, *Orobio de Castro*, p. 7.

[45] See PA 334 no. 174, p. 554. Manuel Alvares, Baltazar's father, is first mentioned on 3 *Nisan* 5423 (10 Apr. 1663) in the list of contributions collected by the synagogue for the foregoing half-year, his also amounting to 3 fl. 6 st. For the others here mentioned see Amsterdam, AGA, DTB no. 687, p. 223; no. 689, p. 104; no. 695, p. 136; no. 696, pp. 106, 437. It may be presumed that the Abraham Israel Monsanto mentioned amongst the new members of the congregation on 28 May (see previous note) was Simon Rodríguez Monsanto, Baltazar's brother-in-law. From the fact that the *Ma'amad* assessed him at 40 fl. it would appear that he was well-to-do; see PA 334 no. 19, p. 518.

[46] On the Portuguese congregation in Amsterdam in general see Baron, *History*, 15, pp. 3–73, and the bibliography—an up-to-date one to 1973—mentioned in the notes,

Freedom 107

Baltazar de Orobio and the members of his family joined the congregation and threw off the cloak of Christian conformity with which they had for so long concealed their true identity. Their long-standing dream of an openly professed and full-blooded Jewish life had, at last, come true.

Baltazar changed his name to Isaac, being henceforth known as Isaac Orobio de Castro. Isabel became Esther, and they also gave their children Hebrew names; their first-born son they called Moses, and their little daughter Hannah. The other members of the family did likewise: Manuel Alvares called himself Abraham, and his wife Mencia Sarah, Melchor became Jacob, Violante Leah, Clara Rachel, Simón Rodríguez was metamorphosed into Abraham Israel, and Pascual Núñez into Jacob.[47] They all settled in Breestraat, the centre of Jewish life in the city, and became active members of the various organizations and associations ancillary to the *Talmud Torah* Congregation—that is, the congregation of Spanish and Portuguese Jews in Amsterdam.

Isaac and Esther, the early years of whose marriage had been dogged by trials and tribulations in the quagmire of Spain, had at last come home, and in the 'Dutch Jerusalem' they raised a Jewish family. Their five children—Moses and Hannah already mentioned, together with Rebecca, Abraham, and Sarah who were all born in Amsterdam[48]—were imbued with a loyalty to Judaism, and from the cradle upwards they were educated into love of the spiritual heritage that had never completely sunk into oblivion in the hearts of their parents and

---

pp. 379–411. Cf. also Menasseh b. Israel, *Esp.*, ed. H. Méchoulan and G. Nahon (*Espérance d'Israël*, Paris, 1979), introd., pp. 15–34.

[47] See above, nn. 44–5. Regarding Baltazar's sister Violante and her husband Pascual Núñez we are informed by the burial records of the congregation; Violante/Leah was buried on 5 *Tishri* 5441 (27 Sept. 1680)—PA, 334 no. 916, p. 19: '5441. 5 de tisrij em dito se enterou Lea Nunes Irma de Doitor Orobio, na careira ordinaria. Careira 2, Sepultura 5.' Ibid., no. 930, p. 18: '... donde se enterou Jacob Nunez Mendez.' It is clear beyond all doubt that Rachel de Castro Orobio, daughter of Abraham de Castro, who was married on 29 June 1668 to Moses Barukh Pérez, is identical with Baltazar/Isaac's youngest sister Clara. In the marriage register it is stated that she had been born in Málaga and was aged 28; but it is certain that at the time her age was 7 years greater than that given. Moses Barukh Pérez, a Middelburg merchant who had settled in Amsterdam at the beginning of the sixties, originated from Andújar in Andalusia. For him see PA 334 no. 854, a notarial deed from Antwerp of 11 Oct. 1657, in which he is referred to as 'Mose Perez, vezino de la ciudad de Midelburgo en Zelanda.' On the Jews of Middleburg in the 17th cent. see Smit. It seems likely that Leonor Alvares will have taken the Hebrew name of Rebecca, since her mother Mencia became Sarah and her two younger sisters Leah and Rachel respectively.

[48] Rebecca was born in 1665, Abraham in 1666, and Sarah in 1671. See Amsterdam, AGA, DTB no. 695 p. 136, no. 696 p. 437, and no. 699 p. 106.

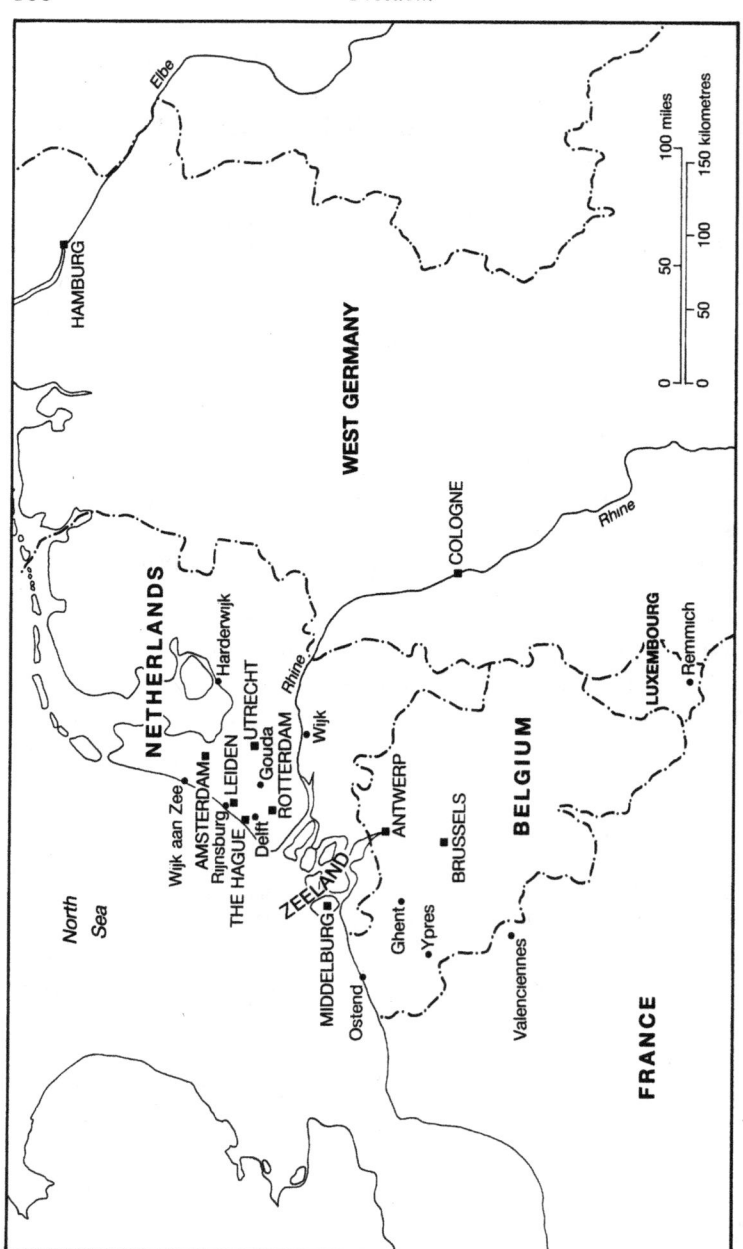

2. The Low Countries

forebears during the long years of their enforced conformity to Christian worship in Spain and Portugal.

Isaac's father Abraham (alias Manuel) and his mother Sarah (alias Mencia), who had died a few years after their reversion to open profession of Judaism, were laid to rest by Isaac in the cemetery of the 'Portuguese' community of Amsterdam at Ouderkerk, after having lived to see how their family, once cruelly cut off from the house of Israel, had rejoined the Jewish people.[49]

Isaac himself had a further twenty-five years of life before him in Amsterdam. During that quarter of a century he discovered the world of Judaism in all its wealth and depth. Jewish literary sources were available to him in the many translations into Spanish and Portuguese produced by the leaders of the Sephardi diaspora in western Europe. These scholars laboured tirelessly to bring the treasures of Israel to those returning to its bosom in languages that they could understand.[50]

In the flourishing and bustling city of Amsterdam — one of the principal centres of cultural creativity of the seventeenth century, and a 'bank of conscience', as the English poet Andrew Marvell dubbed it[51] — Isaac expanded his intellectual horizons and, for the first time, experienced the heady taste of spiritual freedom. In the pluralistic society of Amsterdam he met representatives of many different faiths, and entered into controversy with their spokesmen in regard to the fundamental issues and principles of religious faith, vindicating the unique quality of the Torah of Israel *qua* law and vocation to holiness. In the republic of letters he became acquainted with scholars, thinkers, theologians, and philosophers, including some of the seminal minds of the age.

Dr Isaac Orobio de Castro rapidly acclimatized to his new surroundings and won a name both within his own community and amongst Dutch Christians. We shall now turn our attention to what he achieved in Amsterdam, and to his standing within his own Sephardi congregation.

[49] Sarah, alias Mencia, died on *rosh ḥodesh 'Iyyar* 5426 (4–5 May 1666), Abraham alias Manuel on the first day of *rosh ha-shanah*, the Jewish new year's day, 5430 (14 Sept. 1669): information from the card-index of Ouderkerk interments.
[50] See Yerushalmi, *Isaac Cardoso*, pp. 203 f.
[51] See his poem 'The Character of Holland': *The Poems and Letters of Andrew Marvell*[3], ed. H. M. Margoliouth, Oxford, 1971, pp. 100 f. This satirical piece was composed in 1653 and first published in its entirety in 1681; but parts of it had already appeared in 1665.

6
Doubt and Certainty

OROBIO DE CASTRO'S QUESTIONS TO RABBI MOSES RAPHAEL D'AGUILAR

In Amsterdam Rabbi Moses Raphael d'Aguilar became Orobio de Castro's mentor in Jewish matters. Isaac asked him many questions regarding Jewish law and biblical exegesis, and d'Aguilar answered them conscientiously. In his *Carta Apologética* addressed to Prado, Isaac Orobio records that whenever he was assailed by any doubts he would turn to 'friends expert in scripture: and, as I have stated, some of their answers afforded me amazing satisfaction, whilst others satisfied me less, and some did not convince me at all. In such cases I adhere to my own standpoint and set forth views that are my own, yet withal I have never given cause that I should be suspected of heresy.'[1]

An instructive example of this consultative arrangement with d'Aguilar is to be seen in one such enquiry that was made a short time after Orobio's return to Judaism and his joining the Congregation *Talmud Torah* in Amsterdam. At this period, when many a gnawing doubt was robbing him of rest and clouding the happiness of his integration into Jewish religious life, Orobio addressed five questions to Moses d'Aguilar on various topics, some involving biblical exegesis and some concerned with Halakhic matters. These questions, together with the rabbi's answers, have been preserved in manuscript.[2]

Moses Raphael d'Aguilar was without doubt one of the most prominent figures in the leadership of the Portuguese community of Amsterdam in the seventeenth century. His origins and early years are

---

[1] *Cart. Apol.*, MS Paris, BN Fonds éspagnoles 40, p. 894.
[2] Orobio's questions and d'Aguilar's answers are contained in a *collectaneum* of d'Aguilar's works, MS Amsterdam, *EH* 48 A 11, ff. 85 f., 109 f., 119 f., and 131 f.; see Fuks-M., *EH*, no. 176, pp. 184 f. The questions are noted by Meijer, *Enc.*, i, p. 23; Mendes dos Remedios, *Judeus em Amst.*, p. 65; Révah, *Spinoza et Prado*, p. 19 n. 2 gives the content of but one of Orobio's questions. From the nature of these it seems probable that Orobio raised them soon after joining the Jewish community: some of them evince clear signs of confusion in face of the christological exegesis of the school of Pablo de Santa María against which he would, in due course, argue systematically in his *Prev. Div.*: see below, p. 246. On the substance of the questions, and d'Aguilar's answers to them, see Kaplan, *d'Aguilar*, pp. 101 f., and further on in the present chapter.

still unknown,³ and there is doubt as to whether he was born in Portugal or Amsterdam. However, it is known that he was already in Amsterdam whilst a child, and that it was there that he received both his Jewish and his secular education. His father, Isaac Israel d'Aguilar, was in 1620 the treasurer of the confraternity entitled *Terra Santa* which was concerned with charitable collections for Palestinian Jewry.⁴ Moses Raphael d'Aguilar's sister was the mother of both Isaac de Castro Tartas, acclaimed as a martyr after he was burned at the stake by the Inquisition in Lisbon in 1647, and Abraham de Castro Tartas, owner of the well-known Amsterdam Hebrew press.⁵ In 1642 Moses Raphael d'Aguilar had emigrated to north-eastern Brazil, then under Dutch rule, together with a large company of the Portuguese community of Amsterdam, under the spiritual leadership of Rabbi Isaac Aboab da Fonseca. It would seem that d'Aguilar acted for some time as ministerial cantor (perhaps also as local rabbi) of the Congregation *Magen Abraham* in Mauricia until, in 1654, he was compelled to return to Amsterdam as a consequence of the Portuguese military successes that spelled the end of the Dutch presence in Brazil.⁶ In 1666 he was put in charge of religious studies at the confraternity called *Gemiluth Ḥasadim*, the duties of which office he fulfilled for about a year.⁷ At the same time he was running a school in his own house, where he had

---

³ For d'Aguilar, see Kayserling, *Biblioteca*, p. 9; Meijer, *Enc.*, i, p. 23; Emmanuel, *Brazilian Jewry*, pp. 59–61; Kaplan, *d'Aguilar*, pp. 95 f.; and, most recently, E. and F. Wolff, *A Odisséia dos judeus de Recife*, São Paulo, 1979, pp. 138 f.

⁴ On this confraternity see Pieterse, *De Barrios*, pp. 74 f.

⁵ For Isaac de Castro Tartas see Cardozo de Bethencourt, 'L'Auto da Fé de Lisbonne, 15 Décembre 1647', *REJ* 49, 1904, pp. 262–9; A. Wiznitzer, 'Isaac de Castro', *PAJHS* 47, 1957, ii, pp. 63–75; *Brazil*, pp. 110–19; C. Roth, 'An Elegy of João Pinto Delgado on Isaac de Castro Tartas', *REJ* 121, 1962, pp. 355–66; Yerushalmi, *Isaac Cardoso*, pp. 397 f. For his brother Abraham see Bloom, pp. 52 f.; Meijer, *Enc.* i, pp. 139 f.

⁶ On the sojourn of Isaac Aboab da Fonseca and Moses d'Aguilar in Brazil, see Franco Mendes, *Memorias*, p.26. On the coming of Portuguese Jews to Brazil at the time of the Dutch conquest see Wiznitzer, *Brazil*, and cf. I. S. Emmanuel, *Brazilian Jewry*, Emmanuel publishes an 18th-cent. copy of a confessional and a prayer by Isaac Aboab that describe the discomforts caused by the Portuguese blockade of Brazil and the joy occasioned by its liberation at the hands of the Dutch forces in 1646: the MS is Amsterdam, *EH* 47 C 12, Fuks-M., *EH*, no. 429, p. 233. Kayserling had published these pieces in *Ha-Goren* (ed. S. A. Horodezky), 3, 5662 [1902], pp. 157 f., and cf. Kayserling in *PAJHS* 5, 1897, pp. 129 f., and *America*, pp. 14 f.

⁷ See De Barrios, *Triumpho*, pp. 203 f., his piece concerning this *Yeshiba*: 'Cinco mil quatro cientos y viente y cinco anuales bueltas dio el Luminoso Planeta al signifero circulo quando entre si formaron la Academia que en su primer año presidio el Iaxam Mosseh Raphael d'Aguilar.' On its history see Pieterse, *De Barrios*, pp. 120 f., and cf. Scholberg, *De Barrios and Amsterdam*, pp. 133 f.

upwards of twenty pupils.[8] It is clear from what Jacob Sasportas writes that during the messianic fervour aroused by Sabbatai Ṣevi, Rabbi Moses d'Aguilar was one of those who believed his messianic claims.[9] He was a member of the brotherhood *Kether Torah* founded in 1643 for the study of the Hebrew Bible by his own presumed teacher, Rabbi Saul Levi Mortera, who headed the group until his death in 1660. As a participant in its discussions he found himself alongside Dr Isaac Nahar, Dr Benjamin Musaphia, Isaac Penso, Solomon de Oliveira, and others.[10]

D'Aguilar's evident success as a teacher earned him the appointment on 8 *Tammuz* 5419 (29 June 1659) to succeed Rabbi Menasseh ben Israel as teacher in the *Yeshibah 'Eṣ Ḥayyim* on the latter's death. His contract provided that d'Aguilar would teach the Talmud with its commentaries and Hebrew grammar, his salary being fixed at 400 florins per annum.[11] He appears to have been appointed a congregational rabbi alongside Isaac Aboab, and to have joined the *beth din* (ecclesiastical court) under Aboab's presidency.[12] D'Aguilar continued to act as rabbi and preacher to the Congregation until his death on 27 December 1678 (1 *Ṭebeth* 5439); and even though he was somewhat

[8] See the *Ascamoth* (i.e. statutes and resolutions) of the Congregation *Talmud Torah*, Amsterdam, AGA, PA 334 no. 19, p. 459. The relevant document was published by Pieterse in full, *De Barrios*, Appendix 26, pp. 178 f.

[9] Sasportas, *Ṣiṣ. N. Ṣ.*, p. 47, and cf. below, pp. 211 f.

[10] See De Barrios, *Triumpho*, 'Corona de Ley' [*Kether Torah*], p. 3 (Amsterdam, *EH* pressmark 20 E 61, f. 63): 'El jaxam Rebi Mosseh de Aguilar, aplaudido Author de la Gramatica Hebrea, y admirable Maestro del Midras segundo de la Sinagoga Amstelodama, de los Españoles y Portugueses.' See also Franco Mendes, *Memorias*, pp. 53 f.: 'No A[nn]o 5403, 1643 Fundou o Insigne H[a]H[a]m Saul Levi Morteyra a famosa, Jesiba de תורה כתר [Keter tora] e dedicou sua caza p[ar]a a dita meditação o Magnanimo Ishac Penso — — Os prim[ei]ros estud[ante]s de d[i]ta ישיבה forão o H[aham] Abuaf, Dr. Is[hac] Naar, Benj[ami]n Musaphia, o H[aham] R[abi] Mos[eh] Reph[ael] d'Aguilar, Ab[raha]m Cohen Pimentel, Sem[ue]l e Sel[omoh] d'Oliveyra.' There is some doubt as to whether Isaac Aboab was also a member of this academy: see Pieterse, *De Barrios*, pp. 106 f.

[11] See the document cited above, n. 8. For the *Yeshibah 'Eṣ Ḥayyim* ['Tree of Life'] see Pieterse, *De Barrios*, pp. 97 f., and, for d'Aguilar's activity, p. 99. De Barrios, 'Hes Jaim Arbol de las vidas', *Triumpho*, Amsterdam, *EH* pressmark 20 E 61, ff. 589 f., 'los ojos sabe aclarar / a la estudiosa esperança / del Medras que antes alcança / Menasses Ben Israel'. See Kayserling, *De Barrios*, 1896, pp. 93 f.

[12] See Brugmans and Frank, p. 283; Pieterse, *De Barrios*, p. 77. In 1675, the year of the dedication of the great Portuguese-Jewish synagogue still standing in Amsterdam, d'Aguilar sat on the ecclesiastical court of the Congregation alongside Isaac Aboab and Mordecai de Castro. His annual salary was 450 fl., *plus* 100 baskets of peat and 60 pieces of unleavened bread (*maṣṣoth*) at passover, compared with Aboab's 950 fl., 200 baskets, and 40 *maṣṣoth*, and de Castro's 350 fl., 60 baskets, and 50 *maṣṣoth*; see Franco Mendes, *Memorias*, p. 79.

Doubt and Certainty

overshadowed by his senior colleague Isaac Aboab da Fonseca, many people—among them Isaac Orobio—looked to him as a religious guide and as their authority in matters of Halakhah on which they needed instruction.

Moses d'Aguilar was well suited to respond to Isaac Orobio's queries, for Isaac Aboab da Fonseca, the *Ḥakham*, or principal rabbi of the Congregation *Talmud Torah*, was engrossed in the world of the cabbala, making it difficult for Isaac Orobio, as a rationalist thinker, to find a common universe of discourse with him. As against Aboab, the disciple of Abraham Cohen Herrera whose cabbalistic works he translated from Spanish into Hebrew,[13] Orobio regarded d'Aguilar as a sage in whom Jewish and secular scholarship were synthesized. And indeed, a glance at d'Aguilar's literary productions at once reveals his many-sided interests and his authority both in Jewish sources and in the culture and philosophy of classical antiquity. Herein he was, without doubt, walking in the footsteps of his main teacher, Saul Levi Mortera, Aboab's opponent, who had come from Italy bringing with him a breath of the Renaissance.[14] D'Aguilar's writings addressed both

---

[13] Aboab's translation of Herrera's *Puerta del Cielo* and his *Libro de la Caza de la Divinidad* into Hebrew was printed in Amsterdam in 1655. See Scholem, 'Abraham kohen 'ereyra ba'al 'Sha'ar ha-Shamayim' — *ḥayyaw yeṣiratho we-hashpa'atho*, Jerusalem, 5738 [1978]; Altmann, p. 81. In his polemic about eternal punishment, printed in full by Altmann, Aboab wrote that the contents of Herrera's book had been communicated to him by the author himself. For the character of the translation see M. A. Anath [Perlmutter] in the *Scholem Festschrift* of 5718 [1958, = *Tarbiz* 27, ii–iii], 'Ha-Pereq Ha-ri'shon me-ha-Sepher ha-Shelishi shel sha'ar ha-Shamayim le-'abraham Herera', pp. 196–207, who points out that the translator was in fact concerned not merely to produce a Hebrew version of the Spanish original, but to modify it in such a way as to bring it into conformity with traditional Jewish orthodoxy as understood within his own circle.

[14] On Saul Levi Mortera see Kaplan, *Mortera*, pp. 9 f.; Altmann, p. 3. The structure and contents of his *Tratado da immortalidade* confirm the attraction that philosophical writing exercised upon Moses d'Aguilar. See M. de Jong's edn., Coimbra, 1935, pp. 8, 12, 13, 14. Further evidence of the link between d'Aguilar and Mortera is afforded by the former's tract on the eternal validity of the law of Moses which, as the author acknowledged, was based on Mortera's views: *Tratado de la divinidad y eternidad de la Ley de Mosseh coligido de la doctrina del Doctissimo Sr. H. H. R. Saul Levi Morteira*, MS Amsterdam, *EH* 48 A 11, ff. 755 f. Besides his Talmudic works *zekher rab* and *sepher ma'asim* written in Hebrew, d'Aguilar composed a long, and indeed exhaustive tract on rhetoric, in Spanish, based on Latin and Greek sources and intended, according to his own statement, for those ignorant of these languages; and as well as his homilies on the weekly lectionary he wrote a book on the study of logic, having been invited to do so (as he says) by 'learned members of the "Nation" who do not know any Latin'. He also wrote a Hebrew grammar (*Epitome da Grammatica hebrayca*, Leiden, 1660 and Amsterdam, 1661), and a book on the laws concerning Jewish slaughter-house practice (*Dinim de Seḥita y Bedica*, Amsterdam, 1681). Works by d'Aguilar surviving in manuscript deal with the immortality of the soul, the significance of the letters of the Hebrew alphabet, tracts

Judaism and general philosophy, and he was prepared to handle controversial issues in the Jewish–Christian argument of the seventeenth century. These qualities undoubtedly attracted the notice of Isaac Orobio, who was seeking answers to questions which had troubled him during the crypto-Jewish period of his life, and to which he had so far found no answer since his reintegration into the Jewish world.

Three of the problems that Isaac Orobio brought to Moses d'Aguilar concerned the christological exegesis of the apostate Pablo de Santa María of Burgos, alias Rabbi Solomon Ha-Levi, in his *Scrutinium Scripturarum*. Isaac wanted to learn from an authoritative Jewish scholar about rabbinic exposition of various biblical texts (Jeremiah 3: 14, Isaiah 8: 14–15, Psalms 72: 17). Christian exegetes claimed that these passages foretold the messiahship of Jesus and warned Israel of their coming rejection by God, that they were prophecies regarding the truth and ultimate triumph of the Christian religion.[15] Isaac had known Pablo de Santa María's book well when he was still in Spain, as he wrote in one of his works.[16] From the way in which his questions were formulated it is clear that over and above the confusion in face of anti-Jewish Christian exegesis that they evince, he was concerned to know how to prove that the Bishop of Burgos had distorted the text. That there was distortion in Pablo de Santa María's writings went without question for him. 'How can we demonstrate the distortions which this enemy of ours produces?' Orobio asks at the end of his first letter. 'I ask your reverence to do me the kindness to send me the true explanation of these verses, for the definitive refutation of this our adversary': so he asks in his second letter. In the third, he indicates his wish to know 'what answer can be given in this matter by way of defence of the truth in which we believe?'[17]

---

directed against the doctrine of Calvin and against the Jewish apostate Sixtus of Sienna, on the condition of Adam prior to and subsequent to his sin, and a rejoinder to the strictures of Uriel D'Acosta on the oral Law. D'Aguilar was in correspondence with Portuguese-Jewish circles in Antwerp and Bayonne, and in letters that he wrote to 'New Christians' of Jewish extraction who had settled there he endeavoured to convince them that they ought to return to Judaism. Most of his writings are included in the Amsterdam *collectaneum*, EH 48 A 11; see Kaplan, *d'Aguilar*, pp. 96 f. His rejoinder to d'Acosta was printed by Gebhardt, *Uriel da Costa*, pp. 195 f.

[15] See Paulus de Sancta Maria Burgensis, *Scrutinium Scripturarum* [Paris? c. 1520], ff. 2', 4', 49'.

[16] Orobio, *Cart. Apol.*, p. 879: 'En España ley con toda meditacion el Fortalitum Fidei ... despues el Burgense ...'

[17] MS Amsterdam, *EH* 48 A 11: 'Perguntase como se mostrara a falsidade que este adversario nosso pretende (f. 85); Suplico a Vms. me la haga en embiarme la verdadera

Doubt and Certainty 115

We may take it that it was not mere intellectual curiosity that led Isaac Orobio to address these questions to Moses d'Aguilar, but rather needs of a practical nature. It would seem that his appeal to the rabbi occurred just when he was beginning to meet Christian theologians in Holland and was engaging in dialogue with them, in the course of which they would adduce the exegesis of Pablo de Santa María as being professedly based upon rabbinic literature; and it was this that seemed so strange to Orobio.[18] At these symposia he felt in need of the expert support that d'Aguilar could provide. Furthermore, in his *Prevenciones Divinas* in which he records his answers to 'a certain distinguished person' after an encounter with some Carmelites, he devotes several chapters to the refutation of the author of the *Scrutinium*.[19] Amongst other things Isaac there wrestles with the comment of Pablo de Santa María on Jeremiah 3: 14, 'Come back to me, apostate children, says the Lord, for I am patient with you, and I will take you, one from a city and two from a clan, and bring you to Zion' (New English Bible), and everything that he says is based on the reply sent to him by Moses d'Aguilar.[20] We shall see below that there are grounds for assuming that Isaac Orobio's contacts with these

explicacion destos versos, para confuzion y conclusion deste adversario, y recibire favor (f. 109); preguntase que he o que se pode responder a isto em defença da verdade que profeçamos (f. 119).'

[18] See below, pp. 235 ff.
[19] See below, p. 246.
[20] Orobio, *Prev. Div.*, MS Amsterdam, *EH* 48 D 6, ff. 128ʳ f.: 'Esta interpretación de la Prophesia de Jeremias, califfican por n[uest]r[o]s mismos Doctores, en particular por el Doctissimo Rab Salomon, Libro Sanhedrin, Capitulo Helec ... y en el mismo capitulo Helec, uno de los antiguos Doctores Talmudicos dice, que como de seis sientos mil que salieron de Egipto, no entraron en la tierra de promision, sino dos, que fueron Kaleb y Jeosuah, assi sera tambien en el tiempo del Massiah ... Las palabras que alega el Burgense de R. Salomon en Perec helec tratado de Senedrin ... son falsamente citadas ... sigue el Talmud en el decurso del mismo capitulo, en donde se escrive que un Autor por nombre Reslaquis, queria, ò por lo menos dixo, que el verso alegado se podia entender literalmente, como suena, uno de cada ciudad, y dos de linage, mas luego repugna a este parecer Ruby Johanan gravissimo Doctor del Talmud ...' Cf. d'Aguilar, MS Amsterdam, *EH* 48 A 11, ff. 87 f: 'Mas o çerto he que não he tudo cegueira e ygnorancia mas pura malicia e dissimulação, como evidentemente se mostra no falso testimonio que levanta a nosso comentador Rassi ... segue o Talmud adiante no proprio cap. fol. 111 donde proponde hum Autor p[or] nome Res Laquis, que as palavras do dito verso, se podrão entender ככתבן assi como estão escritas; isto he como a primeira vista parece ser o sentido dellas ... lhe responde Ribi Yohanan gravissimo sabio, autor do Talmud Yerusalmitano לא ניחא ליה למרייהו דאמרתי לי הכי, não lhe agrada ao seu senhor em Perec helec que digas por elles isso ... Segue logo no proprio lugar outro Autor p[or] nome Ribi Simay explicando o verso do Exodo Cap. 7 v. 7 ... E diz compara a sua saida da terra de Egipto a sua entrada da terra santa; assi como sua entrada na terra; forão dous de seis centos mil (a saber, Jeossuah e Caleb) tambem os que sairão de Egipto forão 2 de seis centos mil.'

Carmelites took place in Brabant, so that it is not impossible that d'Aguilar's answers were forwarded to him from Amsterdam.[21] In one of his letters Orobio had requested d'Aguilar to have the goodness to send him the 'true explanation'—a request that would be surprising indeed if we were to assume that he was himself resident in Amsterdam at the time.

In his many meetings and discussions with Christian theologians of various denominations Orobio based his argument largely on d'Aguilar's answers and detailed explanations that were rooted in the Talmudic source-material and in medieval Jewish exegesis. Because he was himself so unfamiliar with Talmudic literature, his Christian controversialists more than once took him by surprise by quoting rabbinic passages which allegedly concurred with Christian claims. In reply to argumentation on those lines Isaac found a fundamental and unequivocal answer in the words of Rabbi Moses d'Aguilar:

The Burgos scholar ought, were he really delving after the truth, to have taken into account that all those whose comments on the said verse in Jeremiah [he adduces] . . . including Rabbi Solomon [i.e. Rashi] were excellent Jews, and not Christians—neither real Christians nor pretending to be Christians. It is obvious that being themselves Jews, they could never have asserted or taught that Scripture anywhere hints that it is essentially the Gentiles who will be saved by the Messiah and that but a few Jews will be associated with them [in salvation]; for their faith and opinions were quite to the contrary, as all Christians know perfectly well. In consequence, what advantage could possibly accrue to them in going round begging for crumbs that are at once jejune, conflicting, and indeed absurd, and in claiming that our sages, the pillars of our holy Torah, taught fabrications regarding our faith which they themselves saddle on to the biblical text—a thing that is utterly inconceivable so long as [the sages] were neither Christians themselves, nor out of their minds?[22]

The two other questions which Isaac put to d'Aguilar testify eloquently to his spiritual anguish during the period when he was taking his first steps in Judaism. The first of them is formulated as follows: 'a Jew, born and educated amongst Gentiles, and [thus] not obligated to observe the precepts of the holy Torah, who lives and dies in accordance with Gentile manners—will such a one be saved, or no?'[23] Having left behind him the sorry situation of the crypto-Jew, hopelessly entangled in the Christian world, Isaac—mindful of his

---

[21] See below, pp. 244 f.
[22] MS Amsterdam, *EH* 48 A 11, f. 92.
[23] Ibid., f. 131: 'Hum Israelita que naceo e se criou entre os gentios e não tem origem e obrigação da observança da Ley Divina, e assi viveo e morreo obrando como gentio perguntasse: se salvara ou não.' See Kaplan, *d'Aguilar*, pp. 101 f.

Doubt and Certainty 117

kinsfolk and friends who had lived and died as conforming Christians—could not come to terms with the notion that they must be condemned to eternal punishment.

D'Aguilar's attitude was that crypto-Jews do, indeed, have (in the traditional Jewish formulation) 'a portion in the world to come', provided always that their deeds and ethical conduct entitle them to it in virtue of their being descended from the ancestors of the chosen people. The crypto-Jew must, from a juridical point of view, be considered as in the same category as a '[Jewish] child taken captive amongst Gentiles and a self-declared proselyte in a Gentile environment' [neither of whom have opportunity of informing themselves of their Jewish responsibilities].[24] Just as these, in the opinion of the Talmudic sages Rab and Samuel, may atone for their sins by bringing a sin-offering, so crypto-Jews atone for their sins by fulfilling some penalty in lieu of the sin-offering that could be brought in the temple only. Alternatively, if one accepts the view of the earlier, tannaitic scholar Monabaz which was endorsed by Rabbi Yoḥanan and by Rabbi Simeon b. Laqish—a view which would exempt the child and proselyte in the aforementioned circumstances from any liability to bring a sin-offering—then crypto-Jews are absolved from any penalty whatsoever and are entitled, even without such, to a share in the world to come.[25]

In his other question Isaac sought to know 'whether Gentiles, in order to be saved [i.e. "have a portion in the world to come"], are obliged to observe the seven commandments of the sons of Noah[26] as being commandments that were enjoined upon Noah by God and were transmitted by our teacher Moses; or whether it suffices for them to observe them as commandments [or laws] that are dictated by natural reason, inasmuch as our understanding instructs us to conduct ourselves in accordance with them?'[27]

---

[24] Babylonian Talmud, *Shabbath*, 68a–b, Eng. trans. (Soncino Press, London, 1938), p. 327.   [25] MS Amsterdam, *EH* 48 A 11, ff. 131 f.

[26] [The notion of the 'Seven Commandments of the Sons of Noah', as originally ordained for Adam and re-promulgated (with the additional seventh) after the flood, is a rabbinic formula designed to take account of the existence of a civilized code of behaviour beyond the confines of Jewry; it is comparable, in some ways, with the Roman idea of *jus gentium*. See article 'Noachide Laws', *EJ* 12. 1189 f., and R. Loewe, 'Potentialities and Limitations of Universalism in the Halakhah', in *Studies in Rationalism Judaism & Universalism in Memory of Leon Roth*, ed. R. Loewe, London, 1966, pp. 115 f., 125 f. R.L.]

[27] Ibid. (see above, n. 25): 'Se pergunta, si para se salvar o gentio con a observança dos 7 preceitos de Noah, he forçoso que os observe como mandados por D[eu]s a Noah, e manifestados por nosso Mestre Mosseh? o si bastara que os guarde como dictados p[or] la razão natural, p[or] que assi lho ensina o entendim[en]to.' See Kaplan, *d'Aguilar*, pp. 102–3.

This question, which had occupied not a few Jewish thinkers in the Middle Ages, was a particularly worrisome one amongst the Sephardi Jews of Amsterdam in the seventeenth century, because of the historical situation in which they found themselves. The social and political atmosphere—relatively relaxed—amid which the Jews in Holland at this period could go about their daily lives forced them to formulate new terms of reference for relationships (as viewed from the Jewish angle) with Christians of the reformed churches who, in a spirit of toleration, had welcomed them with open arms. Some of those in the Portuguese community of Amsterdam who broke ranks during this period were able to seize upon extreme statements emanating from Jewish sages in order to point to the intolerance of Judaism, and the entirely negative attitude which it allegedly took towards even the most ethically regenerate of Gentiles. Spinoza inveighed against the pronouncement of Maimonides (*Mishneh Torah, Hilekhoth Melakhim* 8, 11) that the righteous amongst the Gentiles have a portion in the world to come if they observe the seven commandments of the sons of Noah as being ordained by the Torah: 'but' (wrote Spinoza), 'the view of the Jews is exactly the contrary, inasmuch as they declare that true attitudes and manner of life do not confer one whit of advantage in regard to happiness, so long as people see fit to adopt them purely in the light of reason, and not as being matters of Torah revealed to Moses through prophecy. Maimonides states this explicitly and emphatically, using the following language in his *Hilekhoth Melakhim* . . .'[28] (We shall have occasion to note (p. 357) the stumbling-block caused by a corruption in the text of Maimonides used by Spinoza and his contemporaries in this passage.) It would seem that Isaac Orobio turned to his rabbi with this problem whilst engaged in controversy with Juan de Prado—a subject to which we shall return.[29]

In his reply, d'Aguilar endeavoured to give a satisfactory explanation of words of Maimonides which, in the light of new historical circumstances, seemed to strike so trenchant a note:[30]

If we take these words [of Maimonides] at their face value, we [have to say] that what they constitute is an expression of his personal opinion, without support in the teachings of the earlier sages and indeed contrary to reason, as the commentators on his *Mishneh Torah* have indicated.[31] We must consequently

[28] [Spinoza], *Tractatus Theologico-Politicus*, chap. 5, end, Hamburg, 1670, p. 79, Eng. trans. (*Chief Works*) by R. H. M. Elwes, London, 1883, i, pp. 79 f.
[29] See below in this chapter, p. 154.   [30] MS Amsterdam, *EH* 48 A 11, ff. 132 f.
[31] See e.g. Joseph Caro's (16th-cent.) commentary (*Keseph Mishneh*) to *Hilekhoth melakhim* 8, 11, where he writes: 'when our teacher [Maimonides] declared that

find an explanation of them that accords with a [proper] understanding of the meaning that he really intended. For a gentile to achieve salvation, he is obligated to observe the said precepts as being something pleasing to God ... for what it is that essentially confers everlasting life on a human being is that his actions should be done from love of God, and as evincing honour and awe of Him.

D'Aguilar thus excludes from the category of 'the righteous among the Gentiles' those who follow Aristotle's view that good actions do not show any honour to God, and who stress the importance of ethical behaviour *qua* political philosophers. 'However,' (d'Aguilar continued) 'those who do not know that the said commandments were communicated to Noah and Moses by God, but none the less implement them as being a code dictated by natural reason, *in virtue of that very acknowledgement are* [implicitly] *serving God and satisfying his will*: and clearly Maimonides would not deny them their portion in the ever-lasting life of the world to come.'[32]

In quoting the relevant passage of Maimonides in the Hebrew original, d'Aguilar omitted (and clearly by no mere coincidence) the concluding words, '... nor [counted] amongst [the Gentiles'] scholars'. Modern research has shown that the *textus receptus* of Maimonides is corrupt, and instead of the reading in the crucial clause *we-lo me-ḥakhmeyhem*, 'nor amongst their scholars', the authentic text has *'ella me-hakhmeyhem*, '*but rather* amongst their scholars' (i.e. humanist Gentile moralists rank as philosophers rather than holy men). However, in the time of d'Aguilar and Spinoza the text had to be

[Gentiles qualify for the world to come] provided only that they accept [the Noachide laws as being toranically ordained], it appears to me that he so declares on the basis of his own opinion; but his conclusion is straightforward[ly plausible].' In other words, although—in Caro's opinion—Maimonides had no source, no inherent objection could be raised against his assertion. It is consistent with this that I have failed to discover amongst the medieval commentators on Maimonides a single one to argue that Maimonides' conclusion flies in the face of reason, and it would therefore seem that there is no basis in the tradition for d'Aguilar's contention (see the following quotation) that it does so. See Katz, *Mishp. 'apolog.*, p. 175, and his *Exclusiveness*, pp. 119, 174 f., 187; S. S. Schwarzschild, 'Do Noachites have to believe in Revelation?', *JQR* 52, 1962, p. 304.

[32] MS Amsterdam, *EH* 48 A 11, ff. 132 f. D'Aguilar's position is similar to the views expressed by Maimonides himself elsewhere—in his letter to Ḥisda'i b. Levi he adopted a more tolerant position than that under discussion here. 'The righteous among the Gentiles', he wrote, 'do have a portion in the world to come, so long as they have both attained such knowledge of God as is pertinent for them and also conduct themselves according to an exemplary moral code: and there is no doubt at all that whosoever conducts himself with moral propriety and with a proper intellectual approach to belief in the Creator, blessed be He, is certainly one who will find his place in the world to come.' *Qobeṣ teshuboth ha-ramba"m we-'iggerothaw*, Part 2, Leipzig, 5619 [1859], pp. 23 f.

understood in accordance with its current form, i.e. that a Gentile who observed the seven commandments of the sons of Noah 'out of intellectual conviction, is neither a proselyte nor an informal, virtual proselyte [*ger we-thoshab*], nor one of the righteous of the Gentiles, nor again one of their sages'.[33] Clearly, this last clause was too sharp for d'Aguilar, who possibly felt that to withhold the title of 'sage' from the greatest of the philosophers of Greece would not go down well with Orobio, who was perfectly at home in the world of ancient philosophy: and he therefore preferred to ignore the conclusion entirely.

How did Isaac Orobio react to d'Aguilar's answers? We have seen above that although he records that some of the answers of 'those friends who are expert in Scripture' satisfied him, there were others that did not satisfy him at all.[34] A specimen of such rabbinical answers as seemed to him satisfactory is to be found in Orobio's (albeit inexplicit) reference to d'Aguilar's remarks on Jeremiah 3:14. The same applies to d'Aguilar's reply regarding crypto-Jews who had not succeeded in returning to Judaism and observing the commandments of Jewish law. In a number of his writings Orobio touches on this question, and from what he says we learn that he was inclined to make no distinction of principle between Jews and crypto-Jews, whom he calls *israelitas*: for him they constituted an integral part of the Jewish people.[35] In one place he goes so far as to say that the victims of the Inquisition, those 'Jews' of Spain and Portugal who were being sent to the stake year in and year out, all that they wished to do [in accepting that fate] being to glorify God and to show their love for Him, attained the highest stage possible of loving God.[36]

But when it came to the question of 'whether the righteous amongst the Gentiles have a portion in the world to come', it would seem that Orobio's approach differed from that of d'Aguilar. He rejected, on principle, what d'Aguilar had to say about the great minds of pagan antiquity such as Aristotle, who had made such significant contributions to the elevation of ethical thinking among mankind. Although

---

[33] See Katz, *Mishp. 'apolog.*, p. 175; Schwarzschild (see above, n. 31), p. 302; and Spinoza, loc. cit. (n. 28), who cites Maimonides in the corrupt form of the *textus receptus*.

[34] See above, p. 110.

[35] See his remarks in the colloquy with Limborch in Limborch, *De Veritate Rel. Christ.*, p. 61.

[36] See *Resp. Pred. franc.*, MS Amsterdam, *EH* 48 D 6, f. 294ʳ: 'Este grado de amor han tenido y tienen muchos Hebreos que dan su vida, por la gloria de Dios y se dexan quemar bivos … y en España muchos Iudios todos los años en la Inquisicion de Portugal y España, a quien offresen la vida … y despreçian todas las cozas humanas por santificar el nombre de Dios en las llamas …' For Orobio's position *vis-à-vis* crypto-Judaism and its adherents see below, chap. 12, pp. 326 ff.

Doubt and Certainty

Orobio nowhere states explicitly that Aristotle was not destined for everlasting torment, what he has to say in this connection at any rate leaves the impression of a certain dissatisfaction with d'Aguilar's definitive pronouncement. In his *Respuesta Apologética* to Alonso de Zepeda he writes, 'had Aristotle lived in our own times, he too would be among the blessed, but he might be in Hell or anywhere else that God wishes, for God alone knows where he is, and where each and every individual ought to be'.[37]

There is still a long way to go from Isaac Orobio's approach to that of Moses Mendelssohn, who 150 years later wrote in a letter to Lavater that men such as Confucius and Solon have a portion in paradise: 'it is impossible that one who guides mankind in the path of justice in this world should find himself in Hell in the next'.[38] There is lacking in Orobio the rationalistic basis on which Mendelssohn established the concept of toleration, the principle of the humanity that is common to all. For Mendelssohn, that humanity was instrumental in the understanding which leads men to conduct their lives in accordance with natural law.[39] On the other hand, Orobio and d'Aguilar patently differed in their approaches to the relation, in principle, of Judaism to righteous Gentiles. D'Aguilar still feels himself fettered by Halakhic tradition, whilst the language Orobio uses, though he finds no clear-cut solution, nevertheless betrays a tendency towards the toleration that would characterize Mendelssohn and his followers, the devotees of *haskalah* (the Jewish equivalent of the Enlightenment).

It was not uncommon for refugees from the Inquisition, who on their reversion to Judaism encountered a world that was fundamentally strange to them, to ask rabbis to clarify both speculative matters and details of Jewish law. In some cases those approaching Jewish spiritual leaders expressed reservations regarding the Jewish tradition as it was conventionally understood, and indicated from the outset their opposition to its values and practices. Such was the attitude of Uriel d'Acosta, and his was not an isolated instance.[40] As against this, we know of many cases in which those making their enquiries did so in all humility, and

---

[37] *Resp. al Zep.*, MS Amsterdam, *EH* 48 A 12, f. 142ʳ: 'Y si fuera en nuestros tiempos, también fuera un bendito, con todo aunque esté en el infierno y adonde Dios quisiere, que el sólo sabe en donde esté y a de estar cada uno...'
[38] See M. Mendelssohn, *Gesammelte Schriften*, 7, ed. S. Rawidowicz, Berlin, 1930 (repr. 1974), pp. 11–12.
[39] See Katz, *Exclusiveness*, pp. 170 f.
[40] See Uriel d'Acosta's critique of Jewish tradition, in Gebhardt, *Uriel da Costa*, pp. 2–32, and cf. the questions addressed to d'Aguilar by crypto-Jews in Antwerp and in France, in Kaplan, *d'Aguilar*, pp. 98 f.

out of a desire to learn the principles of Judaism, its values, its precepts, and the detailed laws associated with them, from an acknowledged and generally accepted authority.[41] That was the way of Isaac Orobio, who was prepared, *ab initio*, to allow that Halakhic authority must have the last word. Even if one can detect in him an inclination to maintain an equilibrium between accepting the authority of Halakhah and the critical evaluation of issues in the light of reason (as evidenced by his inability to accept without demur all the answers propounded by recognized authority), nevertheless in the last resort, he bowed to Halakhah and rabbinic tradition.

ISAAC OROBIO AND JUAN DE PRADO: INTELLECTUAL FERMENT IN SEPHARDI AMSTERDAM

Isaac Orobio was involved with many people, and one of the distinctive threads running through the fabric of his life was provided by the character of Juan de Prado. Prado's life story was quite similar to Orobio's. Both were born into Portuguese crypto-Jewish families that settled in southern Spain. Each spent approximately half his life in Andalusia and studied medicine, philosophy, and theology at Alcalá de Henares. They both kept their Jewish connections secret, but assiduously and energetically disseminated belief in the law of Moses amongst the crypto-Jews of Spain. Members of both their families had been persecuted, arrested, and condemned by the Spanish Inquisition. Of the two of them, only Orobio had actually been held in confinement by the Holy Office, but this was merely because Prado had succeeded in sneaking out of Spain shortly before his friend's arrest. During the 1650s and 1660s his name frequently crops up in evidence given by crypto-Jews before the Spanish Inquisition, which for an extended period was trying to keep track of him. Both Orobio and Prado found refuge in Amsterdam and became absorbed in the Jewish community there. Prado did so in 1655 after a short stay in Hamburg (where he openly reverted to Judaism), and Orobio arrived in 1662. But it is at this point that their paths diverge: Prado was excommunicated by the Portuguese congregation because of his heretical attitude in regard to

[41] See e.g. the questions of Abraham Pereyra and his son Jacob in 5446/7 [1686/7], Amsterdam, AGA, PA 334 no. 139. The questions, and the replies that they elicited, were transcribed at the end of a catalogue of scrolls in private ownership deposited in the Portuguese-Jewish synagogue ('Registro dos Sepharim que estão na Esnoga pertenessentes a Particulares').

Doubt and Certainty

the major principles of Judaism, whereas Orobio, who had submissively accepted the yoke of the Torah, became the main exponent of the views of those faithful to Jewish teaching in the controversy that he conducted with his excommunicate friend.

We may suppose that Isaac Orobio was staggered, on arriving in Amsterdam, to learn that his boyhood companion Juan de Prado had been excommunicated by the *Ma'amad* (i.e. communal governing council) over four years previously. Echoes of the affair, which had let *inter alia* to the excommunication of Spinoza, were still sending shockwaves through the Portuguese congregation, where tempers had not yet died down. It is true that in his crypto-Jewish days in Spain, in 1643, Orobio had heard from Prado himself of his leanings towards deism when the two of them met in Lopera, but it must be doubted whether he ever imagined that his friend would go so far as to adopt an absolutely heretical standpoint in regard to the law of Moses and the immortality of the soul.[42] Prado, by now excommunicated, having heard about Orobio's arrival in Amsterdam, sent him a letter from Antwerp, where he had settled shortly before 1659. He apparently signed it with a pseudonym, in order not to complicate matters for his friend who had just become a member of the Jewish community. Orobio was in two minds about replying, since he hesitated to flout the prohibition of making contact with one who had been excommunicated; but personal concern for his former friend, and the hope of leading him back home from his heresy proved decisive.[43] His mind diligently focused and his zeal fired, Isaac composed a comprehensive and detailed treatise which he sent to Prado, apparently in the middle of 1663, thereby inaugurating a controversy with him that was to continue for the best part of a year.

Before, however, we attempt to understand the background to the quarrel which blew up between Prado and Orobio and the causes that led to the deep rift between them, it is appropriate to turn our attention to Prado's personal history. His family originated from Vila Flôr, a

---

[42] For the evidence for this encounter see above, p. 88.

[43] See Orobio, *Tratado contra la ympiedad de los deistas*, MS Amsterdam, *EH* 48 A 23, f. 109: 'Dexé de responder a una carta, quando llegué a esta Ciudad, aunque venia en nombre diferente, por entender que me era proibido [sic], siendo de sugeto apartado de la Congregasion Ystraelitica, y procurar, quanto en my fuese, no yncur[r]ir en esta espesie de culpa . . .' See also the continuation, in MS 48 D 6, f. 330ʳ: '. . . con todo diré lo que siento porque aunque no sea con acierto dezeo alentar los passos de su arepentimiento de que tengo noticias le trae al conocimiento de la verdad que antes observó y guardaron sus Padres.'

small Portuguese town in the region of Braganza. A document of 1614 tells us that of the 400 adult inhabitants of the town at that date the majority were 'New Christians' of Jewish origin who were observing Jewish customs in secret. Between 1583 and 1589 about twenty crypto-Jews amongst the local population had been condemned by the Portuguese Inquisition. As a consequence, many of the 'New Christians' of Vila Flôr had fled to Spain, the number amounting to seventy adults between 1600 and 1614.[44] The stream of emigrants included Francisco García de Prados and Felipa de Prados,[45] the parents of Juan de Prado. Together with them there went Luis García Zamora, brother of Francisco García de Prados, his wife Felipa Gómez, and her two brothers Francisco Gómez 'Romano' and Dr Gerónimo Gómez Pereda. In the manner customary amongst crypto-Jewish families that were concerned to preserve their Jewish identity, there had been much intermarriage of kin within this family. Francisco Gómez had married his sister's daughter, Gracia Gómez, and Juan de Prado at some unknown date married Gracia's sister Isabel Gómez, daughter of his paternal uncle Luis García.[46] The family settled in the little Andalusian town of Lopera in the region of Jaén, where Juan de Prado was born about 1612.[47]

[44] See Révah, *rupt. spin., nouvel examen*, 72, pp. 644 f.
[45] The family name was originally *Prados*, and it is difficult to determine when exactly it was changed to *Prado*. In documents up to and including the time of Juan's student days at Alcalá he still appears under the original form of the surname, but in inquisitional documents from the 1650s he is called Prado, which is the name that he bore for the remainder of his life.
[46] The genealogical tree is consequently as here shown:

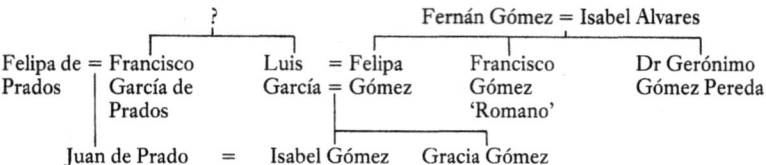

[47] In 1658 the Augustinian canon Tomás Solano y Robles estimated Prado's age at about 30, whence it would appear that he had been born *c*. 1628, but Fray Tomás' impression was totally mistaken; see below, n. 76. In two notarial deeds of Mar. and Apr. 1657, Prado's age is given as about 43 (See Amsterdam, AGA, Notariële Archieven no. 984, two medical certificates signed 'Daniel de Prado, aagé d'environ quarante trois ans . . .') He will consequently have been born *c*.1614. In the Alcalá matriculation registers he is listed in 1627 as being 14, in 1628 as 16, in 1629 as 17, in 1630 as 20, in 1632 still as 20, and in 1634 as 22; see Madrid, AHN, universities section, Alcalá 446F ff. 23ʳ, 30ʳ, 43ʳ; 447F ff. 48ʳ, 51ʳ, 56ʳ; 448F f. 56ʳ. Four of these registers, then, would make him

Doubt and Certainty 125

Juan de Prado was a student at Alcalá for nine years. From 1627 to 1629 he studied in the faculty of arts and philosophy under the direction of Dr Pedro Caballero, obtaining his BA.[48] In 1630 he was registered in the medical faculty in which he studied until 1635, simultaneously continuing in arts under Caballero until 1631, in which year he received his licentiate.[49] In 1633 he was admitted to Madre de Dios, one of the theological schools of the university: students of this college were elected by those of the main college of San Idelfonso, and Prado was elected in 1633, succeeding a certain Dr Cuevas.[50] During the academic year 1635/6 Orobio was likewise elected to the college of theology, and, as stated above, there are grounds for supposing that Juan de Prado, with whom he had apparently been acquainted for several years past, was one of those instrumental in securing his election.[51] The year during which they were fellow-students in the theological college was the time when close ties of friendship were forged between them. Prado left Alcalá in 1636, and thanks to the loss of one volume of the register of graduates of the university we are precluded from learning whether the degree that marked the conclusion of his medical studies was that of bachelor or the full licentiate.[52] On 22 August he was licensed as a physician by the quite undistinguished university of Toledo.[53] The following year he was living in Lopera. From evidence given by his wife's uncle, the above-mentioned Francisco Gómez 'Romano', before the inquisitional tribunal of Cuenca on 25 August 1654, we learn that in 1639 Prado had

born in 1612, two others in 1611, and the remaining one in 1613. Cf. Révah, *rupt. spin.*, *nouvel examen*, 71, p. 581, who states that according to 5 of the registers he was born in 1612. Lack of exactitude in regard to the year of birth was a common feature of the period. Juan Prado's father Francisco García de Prados is apparently identical with the shopkeeper of that name, resident in Lopera, who dealt in spices; he is mentioned in the Jaén district archives, Leg. 1386 ff. lxxxii^v-lxxxiii^r.

[48] See Madrid, AHN, universities section, Alcalá 492F, ff. 25^r, 27^r; 493F, f. 9^v (certificates of Prado's having passed examinations in logic, natural philosophy, and metaphysics); 447F, f. 88^r, list of Caballero's pupils graduating BA.

[49] On 21 Feb. 1630 Prado was first registered in the medical faculty: ibid., 447F, f. 48^r. On his being granted his degree in arts see ibid. f. 88^r. For certificates of his success in the medical examinations in 1631–4 see 493F, ff. 5^v, 33^v, 40^v; 494F, f. 12^v.

[50] On his election to Madre de Dios see 1045F, f. 69^r; Révah, *rupt. spin., nouvel examen*, 71, pp. 582 f. On his medical studies in 1633–4 see 448F, f. 56^r.

[51] See above, chap. 1, pp. 13 f.

[52] See Révah, op. cit., p. 581.

[53] The Colegio de Santa Catalina, founded in Toledo in 1485, was the kernel out of which the university of Toledo grew. Its corporate existence was acknowledged by the Pope in 1520 and by the King of Spain in 1529, and it survived until the end of the 19th cent.; *EUIEA* 45, pp. 1160 f.

convinced him that he must believe in the law of Moses and observe its precepts. From what Gómez said, it is to be understood that Prado had told him that he had arrived at his own conviction quite independently, after reading books and widening his intellectual horizon during his university studies. Prado was in the habit of translating various biblical texts for him from the Latin into Spanish, in order to persuade him that the law of Moses was the truth through which alone lay the road to salvation.[54]

In 1643 Prado and Orobio met again, this time in Lopera where Prado was living. At this encounter Orobio for the first time heard his fellow-student voice declarations bearing a markedly deistic character. Prado maintained that all men are entitled to redemption, each in virtue of his own religion—Jew, Muslim, and Christian are entitled to eternal happiness, because all three religions have political aims the source of which lies in natural law which, in Aristotle's philosophy, is styled *causa causarum*. At another meeting two days later Prado had expounded the view that all the said religions have the capacity to bring their adherents to salvation, all of them having the same object, namely to bring the believer to awareness of God. Nor was Prado unique in this attitude. His brother-in-law, Dr Duarte Diego Serrano, who was present at the latter meeting, expressed his agreement with Prado's deism.[55] In his *Epístola Invectiva* to Prado, Orobio stated that responsibility for Prado's conversion to deism lay with someone named Juan Pinheiro. He was a doctor, who apparently studied with Orobio and Prado at Alcalá, and died in Triana (Seville) around 1662.[56] At this

---

[54] See Révah, *rupt. spin., nouvel examen*, 72, p. 650.
[55] Ibid., pp. 650 f. His concurrence was reported by Orobio in his evidence before the Inquisition in Seville in 1656; see above, p. 88.
[56] See Orobio, *Epíst. Inv.*, MS Amsterdam, *EH* 48 D 6, f. 350ʳ: 'no es otro . . . rendir el antiguo y bien fundado dictamen a la impia persuasion de otro Hebreo de nacion, primero christiano, despues judio, despues ni judio ni xpiano, hombre de cortissimo juizio, poco Philosopho y menos medico, loco en sus discurrir, yntrepido en su hablar, amigo de novedades, solicitador de Paradoxas, y lo peor abominable en sus costumbres . . .' In the margin there is a note reading 'Don Juan Pinhero', and similarly in the other 3 copies of this work in the possession of the same library (48 C 4, f. 17ᵛ, 48 A 12, f. 17ʳ, 48 A 23, p. 153). In other copies I have not found Pinheiro's name noted in the margin to this section. On the MSS see below, Appendix E. Révah, op. cit. (above, n. 54), 70, p. 563, had noted the marginal reference to Pinheiro's name in 3 MSS only. Orobio knew him personally, and on one occasion borrowed from him a copy of Pablo de Santa María's *Scrutinium Scripturarum*: see *Cart. Apol.*, p. 879: '. . . despues el Burgense, que me le dio el maldito y detestable Pinheyro . . .'. It seems clear that there was no lack of students in Spain at the time who were attracted towards deistic ideas. Such was the case of Rodrigo Enríquez Fonseca, who was put on trial in the 1660s by the Inquisition of Lima, and who testified that whilst still a medical student at Alcalá he had known

Doubt and Certainty 127

stage of his life deism in no way alienated Prado from his connections with Judaism. Whether out of loyalty to his crypto-Jewish relatives and friends (some of whom had taken to Jewish observance because of him), or because he entertained the opinion that there was no incompatibility between a deistic outlook and his identification with one of the religions that rest on natural law, Prado still kept up his lively links with Judaism. In his home in Andújar (whither at this period he moved) he organized, in July 1649, a memorial celebration for Juana Gómez, a relative of his wife and herself wife of Pedro Marcos de Espinosa.[57] From the evidence of this last, who was held in Granada together with his brother Juan in 1650, we learn that Prado's wife was at that time also being held by the same Inquisition, along with her mother and two sisters. All these people, together with a group of some forty other crypto-Jews, fell victim to an informer, yet another crypto-Jew called Vasco Fernández de Valentín. Juan de Prado himself did not lose heart, and succeeded in smuggling a letter to Juan Marcos de Espinosa in which he encouraged the prisoners, being in a position to let them know that his wife's uncle Francisco Gómez 'Romano' had produced before the Council of the Inquisition in Madrid a long schedule of accusations against the informer Fernández de Valentín, which would have the effect of disqualifying his evidence against them and leading to their early release.[58] That is, in fact, exactly how it turned out. In 1651 they went free, and Juan de Prado and his wife Isabel went to live in Antequera.[59] That appears to have been his final staging-post in Spain. As a crypto-Jew with ample experience of being hounded by the Inquisition he had no difficulty in deciphering the ominous writing on the wall; and in a master-stroke of sagacity he succeeded in persuading Domingo Pimentel, the Archbishop of Seville who had in 1652 been nominated to the college of cardinals and was

---

Pinheiro; on proceeding to Valencia to continue his medical studies he had become a deist under the influence of a fellow-student from Majorca. See Révah, op. cit., 72, pp. 643 f.

[57] Révah assembled important material concerning Prado's history from records of inquisitional trials that were staged in the 1650s and 1660s in Cuenca, Seville, Granada, and Córdoba at which crypto-Jews who had had close acquaintance with Prado and knew of his Jewish links were arraigned. See Révah, op. cit., 72, pp. 650 f.

[58] Ibid. The circumstance that it was possible to smuggle letters into the inquisitional gaol is instructive of the conditions of confinement, and eloquent of the corruption prevalent within the organization.

[59] This emerges from the evidence given by the crypto-Jewish doctor Antonio de Fonseca at his two trials held in Córdoba in 1661 and 1665. It is implicit in his statement that Prado was continuing to observe Jewish practice in Antequera.

preparing to set off for Rome, to include him in his suite as his personal physician. Thus Prado managed to escape from the claws of the Inquisition together with his mother and his wife.[60]

Nothing is known of his sojourn in Rome. In 1654 he arrived in Hamburg, where he joined the congregation of Portuguese Jews and changed his name to *Daniel* de Prado. As testimony to his deep attachment to his Iberian roots stand the friendly relations that were cemented at this period between Prado and the Spanish Ambassador in Copenhagen, Conde Bernadino de Rebolledo. Prado wrote to him, and Rebolledo replied in a poem at the time when Queen Christina of Sweden had reached Hamburg after her abdication, and was lodging for a fortnight in the house of Abraham Teixeira.[61] The poem is both full of praise of Prado's literary abilities and replete with sarcastic digs at his Judaism, his observance of the dietary laws, and the enthusiasm by which the Jews of Hamburg were affected on the arrival there of Queen Christina ('the unhoped-for messiah of the female sex').[62] It is quite clear that Prado was at this time openly involved in Judaism, and there is nothing whatsoever during this Hamburg period to hint at the slightest reservations on his part in regard to the Jewish law, or links with deism. In his self-restraint during those days one can only see a stillness that heralded the great storm that was to come.

He reached Amsterdam in the middle of 1655. He joined the Congregation *Talmud Torah*, was admitted to the *Collegium Medicum* of

[60] Evidence of Francisco Gómez 'Romano' before the Cuenca Inquisition in 1654.

[61] For Rebolledo see Gigas; on his poem in honour of Prado, p. 198, cf. Kellenbenz, p. 346, Révah, *Spinoza et Prado*, pp. 155 f. This piece by Rebolledo was published as 'Romance lxiii' in his collected poems (*Ocios*, Antwerp, 1660, pp. 278–82). In the contents it is listed as 'Respondiendo al Doctor Daniel de Prado medico de Amburgo en ocasion que estaua alla la Serenisima Reyna Christina de Suecia alojada en casa de Abraham Texeira.' On Abraham (Diego) Teixeira and his connections with Queen Christina see Kellenbenz, pp. 282 f., and cf. M. Grunwald, 'Le Procès de L'Inquisition contre Diego et Manoël Teixeira', *REJ* 59, 1910, pp. 239–47.

[62] On Prado's literary accomplishments see Rebolledo's poem, p. 278: 'Ameno a las Musas Prado / en que tantas an cogido / hermosas fragantes flores, / de que coronar sus riços.' On his Judaism, see esp. p. 281: 'El no tener ni buscar / la noticia de los Libros, / me buelue a acordar aquello / de a troche moche judio. / El Gran Maestre vendra / segun el ultimo auiso / presto al Senur donde puedes / endereçar tu camino. / Si pasares por aqui / estaremos aduertidos / de que pase la comida / por todo tu catecismo. / Sin que aya en ella animal / que no pueda por lo linpio [sic] / parecer al Cenedrin / mas candido que un armiño. / Ariedro conejo y liebre, / con todos los prohibidos, / y aun por si eres Nazareno / reformaremos el vino.' On Queen Christina's arrival at Hamburg, see p. 279: 'Despechense los jamones, / enfurezcase el tocino, / indinense las salchichas, / y reuienten los choriços. / De colera de pensar / quan sin pensar a venido / el no esperado Mesias / en genero feminino.'

Doubt and Certainty 129

the city, and began to practise medicine.⁶³ His material situation was of the most abject. Throughout the years of his membership in the congregation he was not called upon to pay any *finta*, or congregational dues, and even the miserable sums that he occasionally offered for the synagogal charities he was never able to settle.⁶⁴ Quite the contrary: between 1 *Kislev* 5417 and 1 *Nisan* 5418 (December 1656–April 1658) his name appears in several lists of recipients of charity, and he was in fact being maintained at the congregation's direction.⁶⁵ His mother Felipa de Prado, who had changed her name to Leah on her integration into Judaism, needed a subsidy of thirty-six marks from the Hamburg congregation when she wished to join her son in Amsterdam.⁶⁶

To Prado's first Amsterdam period belong the two poems which he composed in honour of Jacob (Manuel) de Pina printed at the beginning of the collection of Pina's poems—a book that was proscribed by the *Ma'amad* of the congregation in 1656 on account of its allegedly immoral character.⁶⁷ The two poems by Prado hardly lend substance to the exaggerated compliments with which Rebolledo celebrated his literary gifts in his own poem mentioned above, but they do point to his

---

⁶³ See Amsterdam, AGA, Collegium Medicum, file no. 20. Two notarial documents are preserved containing evidence of Prado's medical practice in Amsterdam in 1657; see above, n. 47, and Révah, *Rupture Spinozienne*, pp. 389 f.

⁶⁴ Amsterdam, AGA, PA 334 no. 174. In the *Manual* of the Congregation *Talmud Torah* for 1653–76, p. 123, Daniel Prado is shown in a list dated 3 *Tishri* 5416 (2 Oct. 1655) as owing 3 fl. 18 stuivers (20 stuivers = 1 florin) for offerings declared by him in the synagogue over the previous 6 months: p. 150, he is similarly debited on 1 *Nisan* 5416 (25 Mar. 1656) 12 st. for the next half-year. On p. 178 he is mentioned amongst the Congregation's bad debts to the tune of 4 fl. 10 st., sc. the sum of the two half-yearly totals for offereings ('O KK de Talmutora debe ao Gabay Ishak Is[rael] Suasso fl. 3168:9 de que se da debito ao d[ito] K[ahal] por dibedas antigoas que se não poden cobrar').

⁶⁵ *Manual*, p. 192; Daniel de Prado received 10 fl. fuel grant for the winter 1656/7; on 1 *Nisan* 5417 (16 Mar. 1657) he received 7 fl. 10 st. (ibid., p. 200), and a similar sum a month later (p. 219); for the winter 1657/8 again 10 fl. for fuel (p. 243); and on 1 *Nisan* 5418 (3 Apr. 1658), i.e. a month after his excommunication, 7 fl. 10 st. were allotted to his wife, and when it became clear that she had deceased the *Ma'amad* cancelled the allowance (p. 253). Cf. Révah, *Rupture Spinozienne*, p. 385 f.

⁶⁶ See Cassuto, *Protokolb. Hamburg*, p. 160.

⁶⁷ *Chanças del ingenio y dislates de la Musa* [Amsterdam], 1656. The book was banned on 25 *'Ab* 5416 (15 Aug. 1656), 19 days after the excommunication of Spinoza, the sentence stating that the ban was imposed 'por causas das inormes deshonistidades q[ue] tem en si' (Ascamoth (see above, n. 8) of the Congregation *Talmud Torah*, Amsterdam, AGA, PA 334 no. 19, p. 407). The ban was lifted in 1665, only to be reimposed in 1669. See Révah, *Censure de la communauté*, pp. 74 f.

marked penchant for Spanish baroque poetry and its repertoire of simile and imagery.[68]

Shortly before the date when the *Ma'amad* placed de Pina's book under the ban they had, on the recommendation of their rabbis, excommunicated one destined for fame as one of the world's greatest philosophers—Barukh (Benedict) Spinoza. A scion of one of the most respected families of the Portuguese-Jewish community of Amsterdam, he was aged twenty-four when on 27 July 1656 (6 *'Ab* 5416) proclamation was made before the ark of the synagogue of his expulsion from the community. The edict of excommunication speaks in general terms of 'serious matters of heresy' that Spinoza had allegedly 'perpetrated and disseminated'. The *Ma'amad*, it is there stated, 'had attempted in various ways and with various assurances to bring him back from his paths of perversity', but all their endeavours had been in vain; Spinoza had refused to submit and to accept the authority of the leadership.[69]

As against this, the *Ma'amad* were successful, at precisely the same juncture, in reducing to submission another member of the community who had also been accused of heresy, but who agreed to read out the following declaration before the ark in the synagogue:

I, having in the past adhered to evil beliefs, and having evinced scant attachment to the service of God and the fulfilment of his holy Law, do hereby come before this ark, as enjoined so to do by the *Señores* of the *Ma'amad* [i.e. committee of lay management]: and of my own free will I hereby make confession before God, be He blessed, before his holy Law, and before all this holy Congregation, that I have sinned and trespassed, in word and in deed, against the Holy One, blessed be He, and his holy Law, and in so doing have caused scandal in the midst of this holy Congregation; for all of which I do now feel great remorse, and do humbly seek pardon from God and his holy Law and from all this holy Congregation for the scandal to which I have given rise: I am

---

[68] The following extracts exemplify the baroque style of Prado's two contributions to the book: '... La voz de Thrazia tu armonia acusa / ... Docto Marzial sus sales desalienta / ... No ay mas balor, mas asea / Pina, ni ingenio, que el tuyo, / Que en ti vive, à lo que arguyo, / Apolo, Marte, y Orpheo.'

[69] The formula of Spinoza's excommunication (PA 334 no. 19, p. 408) is cited in full in many biographies: see Vaz Dias, pp. 33–4; Révah, *Spinoza et Prado*, pp. 57–8. From its terms one learns of the manifold efforts fruitlessly devoted by the *Ma'amad* to the endeavour to convince Spinoza to recant and abandon his course of action. For the latest treatment see Biderman and Kasher; also Kasher and Biderman; on the wording of the decree see H. P. Salomon, 'La vraie excommunication de Spinoza', *Forum Litterarum: Miscelânea de Estudos Literários, Linguísticos e Históricos oferecida a J. J. van den Besselaar*, Amsterdam and Maarsen, 1984, pp. 181–99.

further obligated to be penitent in such manner as shall be imposed upon me by the *Señores Ḥakhamim* [rabbis], and do give my undertaking not to revert to the said sinful deeds or to anything similar to them; and I do hereby make request of your honours to support me in my asking the Lord of the universe for his forgiveness and for his pity on my offences. So may there be peace for Israel.

The person who made this declaration was none other than Juan de Prado.[70] Quite clearly there was some connection between the 'serious matters of heresy' of Spinoza and the 'evil beliefs' to which Prado had adhered. The text of his petition for pardon is entered in the congregational records before the text of the excommunication pronounced on Spinoza; and it is reasonable to conclude that not only were both of them accused of the same offences, but that the two of them were in fact hand in glove.

The first to draw attention to the evidence for a link between them was Gebhardt, followed in due course by Révah. Gebhardt assumed that it was Prado who impelled Spinoza into a negative position *vis-à-vis* Judaism as a religion: he was Spinoza's senior by some twenty years, and had already been acquainted with deism in Spain when he was a young man.[71] Révah further pointed out that in 1654–5 Spinoza was still taking an active part in synagogue life, as can be seen from the not insignificant sums that he was contributing when he received the honour of being called up for the reading from the pentateuchal portion, or of performing other ceremonial functions in the service. The amounts suddenly plummet during the second half of 1655, and they scarcely figure at all during the first half of 1656.[72] From this Révah deduced that immediately upon Prado's appearance, and as a direct result of it, Spinoza's links with the Jewish religion received a blow. One may doubt whether this was in fact the way things happened. It cannot be assumed that the intellectually circumspect, level-headed Spinoza would suddenly change his skin as a result of the influence of someone who, although (as all the evidence suggests) he was indeed a charismatic figure endowed with substantial gifts of persuasiveness, was as regards intellectual power Spinoza's inferior. It

---

[70] PA 334 no. 19, p. 407; cf. Gebhardt, *Prado*, pp. 273 f.; Révah, *Spinoza et Prado*, p. 57.

[71] Gebhardt, *Prado*, pp. 279 f.; Révah, *Spinoza et Prado*, p. 27.

[72] See Révah, *Rupture Spinozienne*, pp. 384 f. During the Jewish year 5415 (1654/5) Spinoza's contributions to the synagogue totalled 54½ fl.; in the first half of 5416 (beginning Sept. 1655) he offered 4 fl. 14 st., and during the second half-year a mere 12 st., which last sum he never paid: see the *Manual* (above, n. 64), pp. 63, 92, 122, 148, 178.

is hard to suppose that at the time of his encounter with Prado Spinoza's mind was a *tabula rasa*. What one can envisage is that their encounter gave Spinoza an opportunity to confront openly problems that had already been worrying him before then. This conjecture may be paired with another, of comparable plausibility, viz. that acquaintance with Spinoza reawakened in Prado the long-standing perplexities that had nagged at him ever since his crypto-Jewish days in Spain, when he had revealed the attraction that deistic attitudes had for him. In other words, as against Révah's view that the influence of Prado on the young Spinoza was both clear and incontestable, their encounter probably nourished doubts which had previously perturbed both men and heightened the tensions between their links with Judaism and their theological-philosophical endeavours.

Popkin, who was unaware of Prado's deistic past in Spain, held that the critical point in the development of the thinking of both Prado and Spinoza occurred as a consequence of the visit to Amsterdam of La Peyrère between the winter of 1654 and spring 1655, and the publication there in the latter year of at least three editions of his book entitled *Præadamitæ*. In that work La Peyrère contented, *inter alia*, that there is no proof of creation as described in the Bible, and that since the Chinese have a history of over 10,000 years, their origins must be anterior to those of the Jewish people itself.[73] These very assertions were at this period being voiced by Prado. Spinoza's opinions at the date of his excommunication are unknown to us, but in his *Tractatus Theologico-Politicus* he was to make use of La Peyrère's critique when developing his own principles of biblical criticism; one may assume that he had already adopted these views in the mid-1650s, and that he possibly published them in a lost tract that he composed after his excommunication. Certainly in the attacks on La Peyrère which appeared after 1656 there are occasional references to 'the preadamite sect of Amsterdam'.[74] The names of its adherents are never mentioned, but in Popkin's opinion there are grounds for thinking that

---

[73] On the dissemination of La Peyrère's ideas in Amsterdam, and their possible influence on Spinoza, see Popkin, *Men. b. I. and Peyrère*, p. 63. For the biblical criticism embodied in La Peyrère's *Præadamitæ* see Popkin, *Peyrère*, and his *Peyrère's Pre-Adamism*; for La Perèyre's influence on Spinoza, his *Scepticism Erasmus–Spinoza*, pp. 227 f.

[74] See Richard Simon's letter addressed to Z.S.: '... il est certain que le livre des Préadamites fit d'abord beaucoup de bruit dans le monde. Il s'éleva en Hollande une espèce de secte sous le nom de Préadamites ...' *Lettres choisies de Monsieur Simon*, Rotterdam, 1704, ii, p. 24).

Doubt and Certainty

the object of the attack was Spinoza and his friends who had been influenced by some of La Peyrère's ideas. It is difficult to substantiate Popkin's theory of a direct connection between La Peyrère and the views of Spinoza and Prado about Judaism, inasmuch as neither of them ever hinted at such a link; but it nevertheless commands a considerable measure of plausibility. At the end of his life, in his controversy with Limborch, Isaac Orobio pointed in unmistakable terms to the connection between 'pre-adamites', 'atheists', and 'theologico-politicians': 'Restat igitur liber Mosis ab omnibus sine controuersia receptus ... quidquid nostri seculi ethnici et scioli Præadamitæ, Athei, Theologi politici, Mosis librorum crisis, impie sed frustra oblatrauerint.'[75] As the champion of anti-Prado criticism twenty years before, it is possible that Orobio knew certain significant details regarding the source of his controversialist's ideas. It is probable that 'atheists' alludes to Prado, whilst 'theologico-politicians' incontestably points to Spinoza.

It is impossible to miss the clear connection between the excommunication of Spinoza and Prado's public recantation and request for pardon. The two events were consecutive, and even though there are no other documents dating from 1655–6 to point to any connection between the two men, there can be no doubt that they felt a mutual attraction. The Augustinian Fray Tomás Solano y Robles reported to the Madrid Inquisition that during his stay in Amsterdam between 18 August 1658 and 21 March 1659

> he had known Dr Prado, a physician, whose [first] name had been Juan, but he did not know what name he bore as a Jew, who had studied at Alcalá: he also knew someone whose family name was de Espinosa, of whom he had the impression that he had been born somewhere in Holland, who had studied at Leiden and was a good philosopher. Both had observed the law of Moses, but the Jewish synagogue had excommunicated and expelled them because they had become atheists. They themselves had told him that they had received circumcision and had observed the law of the Jews, but that they had changed their view after seeing that the said law was not true, that the soul does not outlive the body, and that God exists in a philosophical sense only; and they had consequently been expelled from the synagogue. Despite regretting the loss of the charity they had received from the synagogue, and the interruption of social relations with the remainder of the Jewish community, they were glad that they were inclined towards the perversions of atheism, inasmuch as they believed that God exists in a philosophical sense only, as he had declared, and

---

[75] Orobio, as quoted in Limborch, *De Veritate Rel. Christ.*, p. 148.

that there is no immortality of the soul, which, in consequence, stood in no need of faith . . .[76]

A further item of contemporary evidence can confirm the description given by the Augustinian canon and enlarges upon its detail. The reference is to a report to the Madrid inquisitional tribunal made by Captain Miguel Pérez de Maltranilla in evidence that he gave on the same day as Fray Tomás. He stated that

in Amsterdam at that time, until he left the city on 14 January of the present year [1659], he had known Dr Reynoso, a physician, born in Seville, and a certain de Spinosa of whose origins he was uninformed, and Dr Prado, also a physician, and one Pacheco of whom he had heard that he originated from Seville, who had been a confectioner and dealt in the manufacture of chocolate and tobacco. The aforesaid parties had been in the habit of visiting don Joseph Guerra, a *caballero* from the Canaries, who had come thither to get himself cured of the disease of leprosy. He himself had also visited there, being [Guerra's] friend and in correspondence with him. On the occasions when he saw [the aforementioned] there over a period of two months — many occasions, since they [sc. the doctors] regularly visited the said house to attend the said don Joseph Guerra, and to pass the time there — he had heard from the said Pacheco that they were Jews who observed their law; and though they had once been offered swine's flesh they refrained from eating it. He heard the said Dr Prado and Spinosa say that they had previously been Jews and had observed their law, but they had distanced themselves from it because it was not good, but a fabrication, and for that reason they had been excommunicated; they had investigated which was the best religion, in order that they might feel able to observe it, but to him [the witness] it seemed that they did not practise any religion at all.[77]

[76] See Madrid, AHN, Inquisition section, book 1123 (unpaginated). Fray Tomás' evidence includes a detailed description of Prado's outward appearance, mentioning *inter alia* his large nose: 'Dr. Juan de Prado es alto de cuerpo, delgado, narigon, moreno, cauello negro y ojos negros, de edad de treinta años, medico que estuo en Alcalá de Henares, no save quando y a que se fue a Abserdam [*sic*], y es descendiente de judios . . .' This description was furnished for purposes of identification in the course of investigations initiated by the Inquisition. Despite the circumstance that in 1658 Prado was 46, the Augustinian canon received the impression that he was but 30 years old. Apparently Prado retained his youthful looks — as is corroborated by a remark of Orobio in his *Cart. Apol.*, MS Paris (see above, n. 1), p. 900: '. . . no pienso que por pareçer moço se desquita del tiempo, no engaña la apariencia a la realidad . . .'. Of Spinoza Fray Tomás reported that he was 'of slight build, slim, and good-looking, of fair complexion, dark eyes and hair, being aged 24: without gainful employment, and of the Jewish nation' (the original is printed in full by Révah, *Spinoza et Prado*, pp. 61 f.).

[77] Madrid, AHN (see previous note). This testimony also is printed by Révah in full, *Spinoza et Prado*, pp. 66–8. It is of some interest to find reference here to proceeding to Holland for medical treatment: those doing so included regular clergy who had

Doubt and Certainty

These testimonies describe the friendship of Prado and Spinoza at the end of the 1650s, but there is no doubt that its foundation lay in earlier years. In 1658–9 there were further causes to reinforce it. Prado, who in 1656 had expressed his remorse in a public ceremony and had given an undertaking to mend his ways, did not abide by that undertaking. The *Ma'amad* of the Congregation *Talmud Torah* excommunicated him on 4 February 1658 (second day of *Rosh Ḥodesh* 1 *Adar*, 5418), after 'he had persevered in his evil and false opinions contrary to our holy Law, and through them had been instrumental in disaffecting a number of young students'. 'The *señores* of the *Ma'amad*, in association with their lordships the *Ḥakhamim* [rabbis], unanimously instructed that the said Daniel de Prado be excommunicated and excluded from the Nation, and under [threat of] the same penalties they prohibited any conversation with him.'[78] Prado was thus isolated, and it was natural that in his time of trouble he should find a friend in Spinoza. His situation was an extremely serious one. Unlike the young Spinoza who had been born in Amsterdam, knew the local vernacular, and had found a place for himself in non-Jewish circles that displayed an interest in his scholarship and in his views, Prado—more than half of whose life lay behind him—had no roots in Holland and only a very tenuous economic basis on which to eke out an existence. He had, indeed, good reason to regret—as the Augustinian canon had stated—the loss of material support from the charitable funds of the synagogue, on which he had had a claim prior to his excommunication.[79] The *señores* of the *Ma'amad* were very much alive to his predicament, and in

---

contracted scabies and other complaints. Prof. H. Beinart draws my attention to similar visits on the part of clergy from the Canary Islands, including that of an Augustinian canon from Tenerife named Joseph Franco who stayed in Amsterdam in 1656, likewise as the patient of Dr Reynoso: Madrid, AHN, file 1823 no. 14, ff. 15^{r-v} '... el qual se fue a curar de una grave enfermedad que padeçia que llaman epidemia de Laçaro y los medicos le aconsejaron, no teniendo otro remedio sino yrse de esta ysla a Francia que es la parte unica donde se halla remedio para este achaque ...' In his evidence he stated that he had been treated in Amsterdam, where the doctors had diagnosed his illness, 'que no era laçaro sino bubas y de mucho tiempo y como el se avia curado'. On the evidence given by Joseph Franco in the trial of Duarte Enríquez Alvares see Beinart, *Canary Islands*, p. 63 n. 122.

[78] *Ascamoth* (see above, n. 8), p. 427. Printed in full by Gebhardt, *Prado*, pp. 274 f., and Révah, *Spinoza et Prado*, pp. 58 f.

[79] See above, n. 76. Although Robles reported that both Prado and Spinoza regretted suspension of support from communal funds, it seems probable that it was Prado alone who gave expression to such regrets in his presence: unlike Prado, Spinoza was never dependent upon the charitable funds administered by the various organizations of the Congregation *Talmud Torah*.

their anxiety to remove him as far away from Amsterdam as possible in order to consign the whole chapter to oblivion, they actually proposed that he should leave the country and proceed overseas, in return for their promise of assistance on a generous scale.[80] The Portuguese congregation was particularly sensitive to the negative impression that was likely to be given to the Dutch public by the appearance of unbelievers in their midst, who, in casting aspersions on their own faith, were at the same time undermining the basis for belief in Christianity. At the beginning of the seventeenth century charges had already been made by certain Calvinist theologians, who bruited it around that the Portuguese-Jewish community was producing a large number of unbelievers.[81]

Prado rejected the offer of the *Ma'amad* and *per contra* attempted to get the instrument of excommunication revoked, claiming that he had never been recalcitrant in regard to his faith, and that the accusations which had been fastened upon him were without foundation. His son David Prado addressed a letter to the *señores* of the *Ma'amad*—apparently before the end of 1658—asking them to admit his father to conference with themselves, 'in order that he might definitively prove that the ban [*jerme (sic)* i.e. Hebrew *ḥerem*] which had been pronounced on him was contrary to justice and equity, since he had not offended in any matter against God's holy Law, which, indeed, he observed, and had not defended any unjustifiable proposition: and if in virtue of his human weakness he had perchance been in error, it was their bounden duty to admit him to conference in accordance with his request, that he might prove his loyal adhesion [to Judaism], and that it

---

[80] See the instrument of excommunication (n. 78 above): 'E praticando os Sres. do Mahamad algumas vezes sobre a gente de sua caza, dezejando atallar não cays[s]em em algum pres[s]epis[s]io, procurarão buscar meios para manda-la ultra mar a partes de jud[a]ismo, para o qual se deputarão dous Senhores Parnas[s]im que falarão com dito Prado, procurando persuadi-lo a que o quizes[s]e fazer, que o K[ahal] o ayudaria com [m]uita larg[u]eza, o qual não quis obedes[s]er, escuzando-se com rezoims de pouco fundam[en]to, antes pello contrario fazendo muita instansia a que se lle levantas[s]e o herem y se lle des[s]e a penitensia que mere[s]ia . . .' It is difficult to see what destination they could have had in mind for Prado. Since it is explicitly stated that they thought of sending him 'ultra mar a partes de judaismo', it is conceivable that they meant New Amsterdam which, until its capture by the English in 1664 and its consequent change of name to New York, had been a Dutch settlement. There had been a Sephardic community of Portuguese Jews there from the beginning of Sept. 1654. See M. U. Schappes (ed.), *A Documentary History of the Jews in the United States 1654–1875*, New York, 1950, pp. 1–15; J. R. Marcus, *Early American Jewry*, i, Philadelphia, 1951, pp. 24 ff.

[81] See Meijer, *Grotius*, p. 98; Teicher.

might be seen that he had not erred even in thought from the straight path of the truth of our holy Law, which same he did observe'.[82]

David Prado appealed to the damage to his family's reputation in order to urge that the case be referred back to a higher court of the congregation, 'which ought not adopt towards us the same attitude of hostility which his reverence *Ḥakham* Mortera had adopted towards him [sc. Daniel, alias Juan de Prado], whom he had insulted and attacked and whose [livelihood] he had destroyed: not by way of reproof, in order to reform him and bring him back to a better way, but, in order to treat him in the same way that he had treated others, as is well known to us. As a rabbi, he was under an obligation to teach him, should there be any necessity for such a thing, and not to say that he would not involve himself in argument with him.' A group of Dutch Christian scholars whom his father had succeeded in convincing that his views involved no denial of the fundamentals of Jewish faith probably stood behind David Prado's gambit. At their advice, Daniel (Juan) de Prado wrote a letter in Latin, in order to attract the attention of scholarly circles in the Dutch Republic, and procure their involvement in the affairs of the Portuguese congregation. According to his son David, Daniel de Prado submitted a draft of his letter to the *señores* of the *Ma'amad*, with the intention that they should append their observations and emend anything which they considered incorrect, so doing 'because [the Dutch scholars] have offered to have it printed thereafter, in order that the world may see, and the truth be placed on record for all', and in order that persecution of the Prado family might cease and the general contempt which had become their portion might be set aside.[83]

Daniel de Prado was at pains in his letter to stress his orthodoxy. He outlined his hatred for the Catholic religion and his own bonds with

[82] See Amsterdam, AGA, PA 334 no. 882, a file of documents concerning the investigation of Daniel de Prado and Daniel de Ribera (the letter was published in full by Révah, *Rupture Spinozienne*, pp. 397 f.).

[83] Amsterdam, AGA, ibid.: 'Y por q[uan]to el bulgo mal ynformado de quien dizen con dañada[s] entrañas se ha dejado creher que ay un judio que dezia no avia Dios y otras abominaciones que contra el ha formado la malisia, ynbidia y odio, por consejo y pareser de algunos hombres doctos y pios desta Republica ha escrito ese papel en lengua latina que suplica y encarga a Vms. manden se vea y que se corrija si tubiera [Révah: tuviera] algun defecto porque se le an ofresido darlo luego a la estampa p[ar]a que el mundo lo vea y conste a todos la verdad y ese [Révah: se] refrente el desafuero de traer a my y a my p[adr]e y todo n[uest]ra caza al retortero por placas y rincones maldiziendonos de dia y de noche en n[uest]ra cara y puerta a bozes [the two latter words omitted by Révah] por el d[ic]ho de dos muchachos . . .'

Judaism—which he had vindicated, beyond any shadow of a doubt, when he refused to assent to seductive offers put to him by the universities of Leiden, Utrecht, Brussels, and Antwerp, on condition that he would change his religion. He vehemently denied the accusations brought against him, impugning the credibility of the witnesses who had testified against him before the rabbinical court and who had misrepresented the essential point of his views. That court had not convicted him of any offence whatsoever against the precepts of the Torah; and, should it be the case that he had given expression to any unacceptable opinions, he had not done so in any spirit of defiance. He repeated his insistent plea that they should demonstrate to him the correct way, and that they should accept his statement of remorse in that same quality of mercy that they were accustomed to display towards crypto-Jews who had lived as Catholics in the Iberian peninsula, yet were none the less welcomed with open arms by the Jewish-Portuguese congregation of Amsterdam. Prado did not neglect to mention that when he acted as one of the panel appointed by the university of Leiden to examine the dissertation presented by Jacob de Paz (on 4 July 1658, i.e. after his excommunication), he had defended belief in creation, 'myself proceeding along the path of faith, and keeping myself aloof from the deviations into which the Philosopher [i.e. Aristotle] lets himself be carried'. He similarly denied that he had repudiated belief in reward and retribution in the hereafter: he had merely maintained that such an assertion was not patient of proof by reason or experience, and it must consequently be accepted purely as a matter of faith.[84]

But the *Ma'amad* of the Congregation *Talmud Torah* had been motivated by weighty considerations, and had had before them reliable proofs when they excommunicated Prado. In late January and early February 1658 a searching enquiry was instituted on the initiative of the *Ma'amad* into the actions and the attitudes of both Prado and a man named Daniel de Ribera. Révah's latest articles showed that Ribera, a person of purely Christian origin who had formerly been a member of one of the religious orders, apparently hailing from Catalonia, had originally borne the name of José Carreras y Coligo. From Spain he had gone to Italy and thence on to Brazil, and after a stay in Portugal he had arrived in Amsterdam between 1653 and 1655,

[84] Ibid., pp. 11–17. Printed in full by Révah, *Rupture Spinozienne*, pp. 398 f. On Jacob de Paz as a student at Leiden see Kaplan, *Studentim be-leiden*, pp. 68 f.

Doubt and Certainty 139

where he joined the Jewish community.[85] In 1656–7 he was employed as a teacher of secular subjects in a special school that had been started for the children of the poor, and it was at this time that he struck up a friendship with Prado, who was also engaged in schoolteaching— apparently in the same institution.[86] Rumours had reached the ears of the *Ma'amad* and the rabbinate about sundry items of serious heterodoxy that Prado and Ribera had mentioned in the hearing of their tender-aged pupils. The leadership of the Portuguese community was aghast: could it be that Prado had succeeded in pulling the wool over the eyes of the *Ma'amad* and the rabbis, and was continuing in his heretical ways even after he had expressed his regret for them *coram populo*? The task of conducting a rigorous and detailed enquiry into the veracity of the rumours had devolved upon Rabbi Saul Levi Mortera. Four youngsters from amongst Prado's pupils gave evidence against their master. Jacob Marchena, a sixteen-year-old, stated that he had heard Prado say in the house of Ribera that it was not a sin to comb one's hair on the sabbath, and that likewise one who touched fire or carried money on the sabbath was not guilty of any transgression. According to the boy, Prado had said 'these absurd Jews seem to want to set up an inquisition here, God help us! What needs to be done is to collect four or five fellows armed with swords, and go with them into the synagogue: and when any announcement is made about any congregational rulings against combing one's hair, or the observance of any laws whatsoever, they should start a mighty fracas in the synagogue building, in particular against the rabbis, to kill whom would be a most

---

[85] See Révah, *rupt. spin., nouvel examen*, 70, pp. 562 f. A collection of poems printed in Amsterdam *c.* 1655 in honour of the crypto-Jews Abraham Nuñez Bernal and Isaac d'Almeida, who had been burned in Spain by the Inquisition, contains 10 from the pen of Daniel de Ribera, 1 in Latin and the remainder in Spanish: *Elogios que zelozos dedicaron a la Felice memoria de Abraham Nuñez Bernal que fue quemado vivo santificando el nombre de su criador en Cordova 3 de Mayo 5415*, s.l.e.a., p. 12 f., 18, 40 f., 52 f., 128 f., 142 f. There can be no doubt that this Daniel de Ribera was identical with José Carreras y Coligo who, after leaving Amsterdam, acted as an *agent provocateur* in the interests of the Inquisition within the Sephardic community in London; see Beinart, *London*, p. 12, and cf. his *Canary Islands*, p. 56.

[86] See the *Manual* (n. 64 above), p. 194: 'Laus Deo Amsterdam a Jahacob Vaiz Rodriguez a 1° de Adar de 5417 a[n]os por ensinar moços pobres este ano se lhe pago f. 90; . . . A Daniel de Ribera e Izhack Ro[drigue]s seu companheiro, pello mesmo, se lhe pago f. 34:16.' Cf. Révah, *Rupture Spinozienne*, p. 387. From the evidence given by Jacob Monsanto (below, n. 91) against Prado in Jan. 1658, it seems clear that Prado was likewise engaged in schoolmastering, apparently in the same institution as that in which Ribera taught.

reasonable act.'[87] Marchena further stated that whenever he took issue with what Prado or Ribera said, 'it looked as though they would swallow me alive if they could, and so I was not so rash as to have very much to say. Prado said that it was a good idea to draw up a written statement, and to leave [copies of] it at Ḥakham Mortera's house and his *yeshibah* [rabbinic academy]', and between them they had set out a draft, 'full of matters so scandalous and so immoral (said Marchena) that I was constrained to tell them that I was the son of an honest man, and that I was not prepared to have any part in deeds of that kind'. He also said that Prado had spoken scornfully of the Jews for thinking 'that by maintaining the institution of circumcision, by attending synagogue three times [daily] and seeing how the scroll of the Law is elevated for view, they attain salvation'. According to him, Ribera once said that it would be good to take flight to other lands, 'where one could live in freedom, miles away from the "Inquisition" '.[88]

Another pupil, Samuel Nassi, gave evidence that on one occasion Prado had put to him four so-called questions about Jewish beliefs and law: (*a*) 'Why was it forbidden to carry a sharp needle on the sabbath, but permissible to carry a blunt one?' (*b*) 'In regard to matters of conscience, ought a man act in accordance with what others told him, or in the light of his own understanding, seeing that before the Law was given Cain and others already knew that it was a sin to have sexual relations with one's mother, or to commit murder? All that Moses had added thereto was sacrificial prescriptions, but before ever he spoke about them people had been in the habit of bringing offerings.' (*c*) That in order to prove the divine origin of the Law, the *señor Ḥakham* was wont to say that we are obliged to believe as much, in the same way 'as we believe that the Duke of Alba had once lived, for that is what history tells us: but that is no proof, for [St] Peter had once lived, and had claimed that God had converse with him. Prado had also mentioned the Notorious Personage [i.e. Jesus], and others.' (*d*) 'That since it is a fact that the Chinese people exist, and that they have a chronology in which they reckon ten thousand years since the creation, how could we say, in accordance with the Mosaic chronology, that the world is but something over 5000 years old? They [sc. the Chinese] could not be in error, since they raised a column for every year as it passed.' The

---

[87] See the file mentioned above (n. 82), p. 2; published by Révah, *Rupture Spinozienne*, pp. 391 f.

[88] File, p. 2; it is to be noted that it is the attitude of the *Ma'amad*, the executive body of the Sephardic congregation, that is here dubbed 'inquisitional'.

young Samuel Nassi was taken aback by Prado's sneering tone, and by the charge that he had laid at the door of *Ḥakham* Mortera: 'he said to me that *Ḥakham* Mortera and any other bearded sage would say that whoever is a philosopher is necessarily a sinner; but they themselves think that when they say "*yes* is *yes*, for *no* is *no*", they are speaking in a philosophical mode'.[89]

Isaac Pacheco presented a memorandum of heterodox statements that he had heard from Prado, in which he detailed the latter's critique of Judaism. (*a*) How could it come about that an omniscient God, in whose sight everything that exists is surveyed, created Adam knowing that he was going to sin? And, if He did create him, why did He embroil him with the tree of knowledge and the serpent? (*b*) How can there be regret on the part of the Deity, as the text states (Genesis 6: 6) 'the Lord was sorry that He had made man on earth...' (New English Bible) (*c*) The text of Deuteronomy 17: 10 'you shall act on the pronouncement which they make from the place which the Lord will choose: see that you carry out all their instructions...' is understood by us to refer to our sages the rabbis, but he [Prado] would have it apply to the Karaites as well, or indeed to any that he thinks fit, since that verse of the text is inexplicit about distinctions. (*d*) He professes astonishment, saying that whatever is exposed to chance is not to be regarded as perfect: the Law is exposed to chance, as e.g. in the case of the daughters of Zelophehad (Numbers 27), for had it not been for their casual predicament, it would not have been written [in the Law]: *ergo* it [the Law] is not to be regarded as perfect. (*e*) If God is beyond our comprehension, how can it be said of Him that He 'walked in the garden' (Genesis 3: 8)?[90]

In the light of the serious reports concerning Prado's doings and his views, Rabbi Mortera endeavoured to stop the young Jacob Monsanto from continuing to take Latin lessons with him. But when Monsanto countered by saying that he had never heard anything heterodox from his teacher, and gave an assurance that he would report any future act or expression of deviationist opinion that he might discern in Prado, Mortera agreed to let the young man continue his lessons with him. Not many days passed before Monsanto was compelled to recognize that suspicions regarding Prado were all too well founded. On 30 January 1658 (26 *Shebaṭ* 5418) he told Rabbi Mortera that 'three or four days ago, when Prado was giving his son a lesson, he asked the boy to go out of the room and the first thing that he said to me was, "why

[89] Ibid., pp. 3–4.   [90] Ibid., p. 19.

was I studying Latin"? I replied, "in order to become a doctor". Whereupon he retorted, "if so, what is the purpose of my learning Hebrew? It is neither of use nor advantage, but is one great mass of confusion, with no logic about anything written in it." I kept a poker-face as if I had not understood him, in order to draw him out. The next day in the evening, before our lesson, whilst he was chatting with me, he said, *inter alia*, "what cause have we to believe in the Law of Moses more than in the teachings of the various other sects? If we believe in Moses rather than in Muhammad there must be some cause for it; but it is all imaginative." Again, after he had asked me whether there is any such thing as reward and punishment, I replied, "how was it possible to prevaricate about the matter? Did he not realize that that was one of the thirteen principles of the Jewish faith"? To which he rejoined, haughtily, that up till now no one had ever come back from the other world to ask for our assistance ... In particular, he made fun of the statement by the sages [of Talmudic times] that the dead are rolled along underground [passages to Palestine for resurrection]. He said that that was impossible and irreconcilable with what the intellect dictates: and consequently nothing that is stated about the resurrection is true. He likewise proclaimed that the world is uncreated, but exists in eternity.'[91]

Similar accusations were brought by the board of enquiry against Daniel de Ribera. A dozen witnesses, mostly his pupils, adduced damaging proofs against him, including clear demonstration of the identity of his views with those of Prado. Isaac Pacheco, who had also testified against Prado, produced a bill of twelve indictments against the opinions and behaviour of Daniel de Ribera:

1. 'He admitted in my presence that in his opinion, Moses our Teacher was a great magician.'

2. 'That the soul dies together with the body.'

3. 'That the holy Law is false—perish the thought— like all the other systems of law which have become extinct.'

4. 'That in establishing all the precepts, Moses was acting in his own interest and that of his brother [Aaron]; e.g. [material] vows which men render to God, redemption [fees of first-born sons], sovereign authority [*principado*], priesthood, and similarly offices of authority in the nation carrying emoluments.'

---

[91] Ibid., p. 18. Averroistic notions of this kind were to be encountered amongst crypto-Jews in Spain already in the 15th cent.; see Baer, *History*, i, pp. 240, 291, and cf. Beinart, *on Trial*, p. 297.

Doubt and Certainty

5. 'That he consumes sausage-meat, cakes, and cheese of Gentile manufacture, which he has got his servant to buy for him, as the latter can testify.'

6. 'Had he arrived [in Amsterdam] during the [Maccabean festival of] *Hanukkah*, or on the days when the *Haggadah* [domestic narration of the exodus from Egypt] is read, he would never have converted to Judaism, for all these things are fictitious tales and fables.'

7. 'That the holy Law is a Law for children, because of the ceremonial institutions contained therein.'

8. 'He scoffed at the *dicta* of our sages, of blessed memory, and at their restrictive "hedges" [to protect Jewish commandments from infringement].'

9. 'He denied that God, blessed be He, exercises either individual or general providence.'

10. 'He made fun of us [Jews] for declaring that we are the children of God.'

11. 'He was uninhibitedly prepared to kindle fire on the sabbath, and that he similarly wrote that he handles money and combs his hair [on the sabbath].'

12. 'That there is no proof that the world had a beginning, as we assert that it had.'[92]

Jacob Marchena, to whom we have referred above, stated that at the time when Ribera lit the lights on *Hanukkah*, in place of reciting the appropriate benedictions he recited in its place the collect '*al ha-nissim* (the thanksgiving for the historical miracle); and when it was pointed out to him that that was not the benediction, he had said 'fustian twaddle!' (*calavernis, coques*).[93] He had likewise heard him say that he wanted to return to Portugal: and when he had pointed out to him the risks involved since he had been circumcised, Ribera had rejoined that in Portugal he would say that he had 'caught it from women, and if he sought absolution that would suffice, since he was a priest'. Prado, who

---

[92] File (n. 82 above), p. 11. The idea that Moses was a magician (see charge no. 1), who had learned sorcery from the Egyptians, is also to be found within the Hermetic tradition; see F. A. Yates, *Giordano Bruno and the Hermetic Tradition*, London, 1964, p. 353.

[93] [The occurrence here of this slang expression is worthy of note. *calavernis, coques-* = approximately 'skulls! polls!' (old Castilian *coco* = head). I have found it nowhere except in the *Diccionario de Autoridades* of 1776 (repr. Madrid, 1963), letter C, p. 60, where it is explained as sarcastic mockery of high-flown speech interlarded with Latin ('Latinismo bárbaro que usa el vulgo para reir, imitando à los que con impertinencia mezclan en la conversación algunos Latines.') No quotations are cited. R.L.]

had been present during the conversation, had concurred with his friend and had said, 'that is right'. In the presence of David Carrillo he had said 'God is powerless: if He had any power, He would save his people from the Inquisition; since He does not, it would seem that He is powerless.'[94]

Daniel Enríquez gave evidence that 'sometimes [Ribera] had sent him to get meat from a non-Jewish butcher. He had declined, and had fetched it from a *kasher* butcher only.' Ribera had told him that 'since "St Abraham" [*sic?*] was merely a miserable shepherd, it was impossible for God to have spoken with him: that it was only because he had numbers on his side that Moses killed those guilty in connection with the golden calf: and that for the past five years, since he had turned Jew, he had been at the mercy of devils.' He had also come upon him kindling fire and smoking on the sabbath.[95]

The poet Jacob de Pina, whom we have already encountered, also produced seven charges against Ribera:

1. He had heard Ribera expressing regret that he had been circumcised and that 'had he known how painful it would be, he would in no circumstances have had it done'.

2. During the plague, Ribera had expressed the wish to join his brother in Brussels. When it was pointed out to him that this would not be a good thing, since he would be forced to dissemble his Judaism and to eat swine's flesh, he had replied 'if [I travel away from here] for a mere four days, it is entirely unimportant to me if I eat it'.

3. He had been reluctant to construct a booth in honour of the festival of tabernacles, and when people had told him that 'it was an important duty, and that they all did so', he had replied, 'if so, I will build one—not because of the religious merit, but because everyone else is doing it'.

4. 'After he had shown us several of the psalms that he had translated into rhymed Spanish, I said to him—several other friends being present—that such action came within the sphere of what is prohibited, since he had intended the translation for use in church worship. However, he had taken no notice, and when the Preacher came in, he had handed [the translation] to him.'

5. On one occasion he had remonstrated with Ribera, whom he had found perusing the work which he [i.e. de Pina] had written and which had been proscribed by the *Ma'amad* in 1656, as noticed above. Ribera

[94] File, p. 6.   [95] Ibid.

Doubt and Certainty 145

had replied to him: 'the *Ma'amad* have no right to act as censors, for, from a philosophical point of view, two conditions must be fulfilled [for the ban to take effect]: first, there must be justifiable cause, and secondly those purporting to act as censors must be fit to act as such. In the instance concerned neither condition had been fulfilled; and consequently the deed could not in any way be reckoned a valid act of prescription.'

6. When *dicta* of the sages [of the Talmudic period] were cited to him, he made fun of them, saying 'what sages! what nonsense! If one were talking of the seventy translators [of the Hebrew bible into Greek] that was all very well, since they were regarded likewise by the Church as possessing authority: but as for those others, they were worthless.'

7. He had never said his prayers nor donned phylacteries [*tefillin*], nor had he attended worship in the synagogue 'until the [synagogal authorities] assigned him a seat to occupy on Mondays and Thursdays [when pentateuchal readings from the scroll took place], for on other days he did not go to prayers at all'.[96]

These proofs, so meticulously assembled by the *Ma'amad* and the rabbis, left no doubt in the minds of the leaders of the Portuguese community of Amsterdam as to the character of the activities of Ribera and Prado: and the complaints and self-exculpations of the latter bore no fruit. This time the leadership was not prepared to risk affording Prado a further opportunity of integrating himself once more into the congregation. Ribera, for his part, made no attempt to secure the *Ma'amad*'s pardon for his behaviour; but the congregational records contain no mention of his having been excommunicated. Clearly the *Ma'amad* did not want to stir up a scandal around a person who was neither of openly avowed nor of crypto-Jewish origin. It would seem that Ribera left Amsterdam about the time of the investigation that was instituted concerning him. Fray Tomás Solano y Robles and Captain Maltranilla, referred to above, made no mention of him in the evidence that they gave of meetings with Prado and Spinoza in 1658–9. Révah discovered that Ribera proceeded to England, where he once more changed his religious allegiance to become an Anglican until, in 1694, he left her shores with his two daughters in order to be united once again with the Church of Rome.[97]

An instructive example, to be sure, of an errant soul: one of the many such instances in the age of the crisis of faith that affected

---

[96] Ibid., p. 3.   [97] See Révah, *rupt. spin., nouvel examen*, 70, p. 563.

Europe in the seventeenth century. Was he a lost wanderer, unable to find a satisfactory answer to his doubts, constantly seeking a faith to satisfy his rationalistic demands? Or just an unstable adventurer, entirely lacking in faith or principles, who changed his religion as casually as a man changes his clothes?

As for Prado, on 1 June 1659 (10 *Sivan* 5419) he appealed to the *Ma'amád* of the Portuguese community in Hamburg and besought their intervention with the leadership of the Congregation *Talmud Torah* in Amsterdam with the object of getting his excommunication rescinded. However, the honorary officers at Hamburg rejected his request.[98] Echoes of the affair had reached their ears, and it would seem that they had been convinced that their opposite numbers in Amsterdam had watertight proof of the heretical position of one of their own erstwhile members. After 1659 there is no trace of him in Amsterdam, and when Orobio arrived there in 1662 Prado, writing from Antwerp, conducted an incisive polemic with him on the subject of those opinions which had led finally to his excommunication by the honorary officers of the Congregation *Talmud Torah*. In Antwerp Prado joined the local Portuguese community, most of whose members were 'New Christians' of Jewish origin who had found there both a refuge from the Inquisition and a developing economic centre which assured them a growing prosperity. Their links with Judaism became gradually stronger in the second half of the seventeenth century with the coming of some Portuguese Jews from Amsterdam itself, who took no pains to conceal their Judaism. Towards the end of the century the civic authorites gave *de facto* recognition to these 'Portuguese' to observe their Judaism openly; but at the time when Prado settled there, members of the Portuguese community were still considered as a separate enclave within the Catholic community.[99]

All that we have of the polemical correspondence between Prado and Orobio are the three pieces written by the latter. The contents of the letters that Prado wrote have to be deduced from Isaac Orobio's reactions to them, since nothing of the originals survives. One may surmise that Orobio lost no time in destroying them, in order to avoid any complications with the *señores* of the *Ma'amad* and the rabbis. They were aware of the correspondence, and were in fact summoned to

[98] See Cassuto, *Protokolb. Hamburg*, 8, p. 274.

[99] For the history of the 'New Christian' group in Antwerp up to the middle of the 17th cent. see H. Pohl, *Die Portugiesen in Antwerpen (1567–1648): Zur Geschichte einer Minderheit*, Wiesbaden, 1977; Baron, *Hist.*, 15, pp. 4 f.; and Denuce. On the link of these so-called 'New Christians' with Judaism see Révah, *'Nation Port.' à Anvers.*.

Doubt and Certainty

meet each time that Orobio wrote directly to the party who lay under their ban, since his doing so contravened the terms of the writ of excommunication which stated expressly that 'no member of this holy Congregation shall have any dealings with [Prado] or shall contact him, either by word of mouth or by means of written communication, neither within this city or outside its confines, but [any essential contacts should be made] with his family'.[100] The *Ma'amad* and the rabbinate were not opposed to Orobio's controversy itself, since they appreciated that Isaac was very well aware of Prado's views, and that he knew all about the vagaries of his speculative progress. In view of their concern about the possible influence of Prado's free-thinking attitudes on various groups within the congregation, and in particular on the youth,[101] they condoned the correspondence, and possibly even looked to some good coming out of it. Perhaps Orobio, in virtue of his natural talents and philosophical training, might succeed in winning back those devotees of Prado who were hovering near the threshold on their way out of Judaism. That consideration accounts for the great publicity that attended the controversy between the two, and it explains why at least one of Orobio's tracts was transcribed so frequently, copies being distributed in Amsterdam itself and elsewhere. In 1663 it was rumoured that Prado was prepared to recant and repent, and this in itself was sufficient to urge Isaac to take up his pen, ready to battle against his wayward friend's heterodoxies in trenchant language.[102] In a very detailed tract he entered into an examination of conscience with Prado that probed deep, endeavouring to investigate the roots of his repudiation of conventional Jewish thinking. The original title of the tract was *Tratado contra la ympiedad de los deístas que niegan la sacra escriptura*, with the subtitle *Respuesta a un Philósopho hebreo que pide fundamentos de Razón para persuadirse al crédito del Sacro Texto* (to be compared with the later title, below, p. 431 f.).[103]

[100] The *Ascamoth* (see above, n. 8) of the Congregation *Talmud Torah*, Amsterdam, AGA, PA 334 no. 19, p. 427, reads 'que ninhum jahid deste K[ahal] K[ados] lle fale de palavra neim por escrito, nesta sidade nem fora dela, salvo a gente de sua caza . . .'

[101] Evidence of Prado's considerable influence in certain circles in Amsterdam, and in particular on the youth, is to be found in De Barrios', *Coro*, p. 357: 'Quitó a muchos el juizio, / y de ello dio testimonio, / tan boticario del vicio, / que los llevó a su servicio, / con la ayuda del Demonio. / Los niños de erudición / echó de su engaño al Nilo / . . .' similarly Orobio, *Epíst. Inv.*, p. 687.: '. . . y lo peor es que consiguen esta opinion entre algunos que, o por sus pocos años o por su mal natural presumen de discretos'.

[102] See *Epíst. Inv.*, p. 693: '. . . deseo alentar los pasos de su arrepentimiento, de que tengo esperanza que le traera al conocimiento de la verdad', and note the textual variant in MS Amsterdam, *EH* 48 D 6, 'de que *tengo noticia le trae* al conocimiento . . .'

[103] Révah discovered the original text in MS Amsterdam, *EH* 48 A 23, and published the introduction in his *Rupture Spinozienne*, pp. 427 f.

From the introduction it would seem that Prado, having received no answer to his first letter to Isaac Orobio, had written again, remonstrating with him for hesitating to correspond with him out of concern at possible reactions on the part of the *Ma'amad*. It is clear that Prado had brought up Orobio's crypto-Jewish past, apparently arguing that it ill became such a one as he, who had himself set aside the precepts of the Torah whilst in Spain, to play the pietist in an exaggerated degree: and that it would be better were he to break his silence and respond to his questions.[104] Prado also wished to warn his friend about rumours circulating within the Portuguese congregation in Amsterdam in regard to his activities and his views: scandal-mongering which, he claimed, misrepresented the essence of his beliefs and intentions. In his reply Orobio refrained from brushing Prado's warning aside, indicating that 'some [of the rumours] I attributed to the shallowness of the understanding of those who picked them up, and some to the wickedness of a number of [your] adversaries'. Nevertheless, Prado's letter had convinced him that some of the gossip was well-founded, and that the cause was to be sought in 'failure to exercise adequate rigour of thinking on the part of the person who gave expression to unorthodox ideas' (i.e. Prado himself), and the 'insufficient circumspection of someone who knew neither how to practise the virtue of humility nor to keep his thoughts to himself', and who 'instead of voiding himself of them, preferred to air them in public'.[105]

In all copies of the tract but one, this recension of the introduction is omitted, as are also any sentences or even words in the body of the tract that pointed to direct dealings between the two participants.[106] It looks as if the *Ma'amad* had taken a hand, and possibly had rebuked Isaac Orobio for ignoring the provisions (cited above) of the instrument of excommunication. The honorary officers may also have been annoyed with Orobio for using language that might seem to imply that

---

[104] MS Amsterdam, *EH* 48 A 23, f. 109: 'ni motivó my silencio, como se dize, razón política dirigida a my conservasion, que, aunque no me abor[r]esco, no soy tan amigo de mi mismo que no me atreva a posponer mis conveniensias alguna vez por las de otros, como sean de calidad, que, ni aun yndirectamente, se opongan a lo sagrado de la Ley que profeso ... Dame Vmd. en rostro con los delitos cometidos en España contra la observansia de la Ley Santa; oxalá fuera para reprenderlos, y no para calificarlos.'

[105] Ibid., f. 110.

[106] e.g. the original text (n. 103 above), f. 114, reads 'las dudas que Vmd. tenía ...' as against the later version in MS 48 D 6, f. 329ʳ, 'las dudas que *uno* tenía'; original, f. 114, 'Ni me admiro que esta duda ...', where the later text (f. 329ʳ) has 'Ni me admiro que *diga este uno que* esta duda ...'. There are many other examples.

Doubt and Certainty 149

had only Prado had the sense to keep his thoughts to himself, he might have been in order. Such a background would make it possible to understand the second recension of the introduction, in which all reference to direct correspondence between the author and Prado has been suppressed, and there is to be noticed an extreme disassociation from Prado and from all his ways.[107] In this second version Orobio proposes an explanation of the roots of heterodoxy which had betrayed its presence amongst some of the crypto-Jews who had reverted to open Judaism in Amsterdam. Among those who had rejected paganism in its Christian form and had made their way to the security of Holland's shores where they were assured of religious freedom, Orobio claimed to distinguish two categories:[108] (*a*) First, those who fulfilled the holy Law with all their soul and all their might, striving to learn all that it was requisite to know in order to fulfil the precepts, their detailed Halakhic regulations, and traditional customs. 'These people arrived in a state of sickness—theirs was the disease of ignorance: but since they were not affected by the disease of pride as well, they recovered easily, and derived benefit from that health-restorative, holy medication which the devotion of their brethren made available for them: for, from the greatest of the sages to the least of the common folk, all alike strain every nerve to teach them, so that they may not stumble in observing the holy Law.' (*b*) The others were those who had come to Judaism after being submerged in paganism in its Christian form, where 'they had learned sundry secular sciences, such as logic, philosophy, metaphysics, and medicine. Their ignorance of God's Law was no less than that of the others, but they reeked of pride, superciliousness, and arrogance, being convinced of their own expertise in every subject under the sun, and that they knew all that there is to be known.' The problem of these was compounded by the fact that their 'pride and arrogance' prevented their learning about the Law and emerging from their ignorance, and 'they fancy that by setting forth sophistic propositions that lack all foundation they are seen to be wise, scholarly men, with razor-sharp minds. But worst of all is the success that they achieve amongst those whose tender years or natural proclivity to ill makes them put on understanding looks, and who, although

---

[107] Révah published a substantial portion of *Epíst. Inv.* from the second recension, as found in MS Paris, BN Fonds éspagnoles 40-1, a copy of Orobio's writings dated 1731: see Révah, *Spinoza et Prado*, pp. 86–129, and esp. Orobio's introd. to this recension, pp. 89–90: see the collation below, Appendix F.

[108] MS Amsterdam, *EH* 48 D 6, ff. 326ʳ–327ʳ.

they lack the capacity to understand a single word of what the foolish philosopher urges against God's Law, behave as though they knew ... It is these who cause the arrogance of the vain sophist to become even greater, and their own arrogance (and together with it their denial of fundamentals) to become dominant. After a few experiments they sink into the slough of heterodoxy and heresy—like the foolish philosopher himself, and those who sympathize with his views.'

Did Isaac really think that the roots of Prado's antinomianism lay in his university-nurtured sophistication, and that it was studies in medicine and philosophy that had engendered his intellectual arrogance? And, if he did, how did he account for the difference between his own attitudes and those of Prado, seeing that as former students of philosophy and medicine at the university of Alcalá, their intellectual background was one and the same?

Révah concluded from the difference between the two recensions of the introduction that what Isaac wrote about Prado was not aimed at all those with university training who had reverted to Judaism, but explicitly at Prado's own case: he was the 'foolish philosopher', and all those—including Spinoza—who were following his lead were here lumped together with him.[109] Although this could be right, it does nothing to explain why Isaac wrote in general terms, and spoke of 'those who had learned secular sciences' rather than singling out *some* of them. It seems to me that Isaac's choice of words was not casual: but that it rather derives from a desire to shut the door on his university past. His purpose might have been to reject the Christian element in his philosophical and theological studies in Spain, or it might have been apologetic: in order to disassociate himself unequivocally from the cabal of the 'philosophers'. They spoke of Jewish tradition in disparaging terms, whereas he, on the contrary, was prepared to learn about the holy Law from 'the least of the common folk'. He further castigates himself for his devotion to the subjects that he was constrained to study whilst living as a crypto-Jew. If, in consequence of his correspondence with Prado, the seeds of suspicion had been implanted in any minds that he, too, was affected with 'philosophical arrogance', the explicit terms in which he wrote would dispel all doubts as to his own loyalties, and his willingness to accept in humility whatever the rabbis might have to say.

One passage, especially, near the end of the introduction to the second recension, has attracted the attention of scholars. 'The origins

[109] Révah, *Rupture Spinozienne*, p. 381.

Doubt and Certainty 151

of this wretched degeneration [wrote Orobio] lie in the ignorance of the student or physician whose own arrogance will not permit him to take the holy antidote of the doctrine of our sages and scholars, both those of the earlier period and their present successors. And since a certain one [*uno*] who has caused great scandal in our nation has, by this road, descended to the bottomless pit, carrying others (themselves outside Judaism) along with him to believe in him and in his foolish sophisms, it has seemed to me urgent, and the proper due of those who fear heaven, to expose to public gaze the opinions which, in his impiety, he wishes to advance amongst simple folk, and to provide an answer to the principles which, under the veil of scepticism, he proposed to establish.'[110]

Gebhardt surmised that the one who had 'descended by this road to the bottomless pit' was none other than Spinoza. Révah was inclined to accept his view, until he realized that the passage appears in the first recension in a slightly different form. Instead of the unspecific 'one' (*y porque uno*) of the second recension, we find 'since this man' (*y porque este*): i.e. the reference is to Prado himself, and not to his friend and disciple.[111] One must doubt whether in 1663 the thinking of Spinoza still concerned the Portuguese congregation, and it is difficult to assume that by then Isaac Orobio even knew about it. Spinoza, who had left Amsterdam in 1660 and had settled in Rijnsburg near Leiden, published his *Renati des Cartes Principia Philosophiæ* in Amsterdam in 1663, and it can hardly be supposed that Isaac had had opportunity to peruse it before composing his tract against Prado,[112] wherein he certainly touched neither on Spinoza's book itself nor on the appendix (*Cogitata Metaphysica*) which foreshadows Spinoza's *Ethics* in many respects.[113] Once he had been excommunicated, Spinoza ceased to engage the interest of the Portuguese congregation, which had come to terms with his departure and was in no mood to rake up the embers of the story. Even in 1684, when Isaac Orobio wrote his *Certamen Philosophicum* against Spinoza, he did so (as we shall see below) at the instance of Bredenburg, who had found himself caught up in confusion about matters of theology and politics, and had appealed to him for help. And even then, Isaac did not advert to Spinoza's Jewish

[110] MS Paris (see above, n. 107), p. 688.
[111] See Gebhardt, *Prado*, pp. 299 f., and Révah, *Spinoza et Prado*, p. 22, and *rupt. spin., nouvel examen*, 70, p. 564; the variant reading, which is that of *EH* 48 D 6, f. 327ʳ, has 'y por que este con grande escándalo...'.
[112] Cf. S. Hampshire, *Spinoza*, London and Tonbridge, 1967, pp. 230 f.
[113] See L. Roth, *Spinoza*, pp. 24 f.

origins, but dealt with his views on metaphysics as these find general expression in the *Ethics*.[114]

Orobio's first letter against Prado was, in point of fact, not merely an endeavour to demolish the unorthodox pretensions which he had been disseminating on various occasions since he had first joined the Jewish community of Amsterdam; it was also a counterattack on a collectivity of heterodox assertions that had been noised within various different circles of Sephardi Jewry in western Europe during the seventeenth century. The tract is divided into four parts. In the first (*a*) Orobio claims to prove that the written Law (i.e. the Pentateuch) is divine, and that it is consistent with natural reason. Here his main contention is that to deny the written Law is to deny the existence of God. (*b*) In the second part Orobio defends the notion of the oral Law (the Rabbinic tradition as reflected in the Mishnah and the Talmud), which is likewise of divine origin, and without which the written Law could not be properly implemented. (*c*) The third part explains the necessity for protective 'hedges' introduced round the Law by the sages in the course of generations, whilst in the fourth (*d*) he attacks the false calumnies saddled on to the Talmud by its anti-Jewish critics.[115]

The tract, which was frequently copied in the last third of the seventeenth century and at the beginning of the eighteenth, carried in its final form the title *A Letter inveighing against Prado, Philosopher and Physician, who doubts or does not accept the verity of divine Scripture and affects to dissemble his Evil by a purported assertion of Belief in God and in the Law of Nature*.[116]

Prado seems to have bitterly resented Orobio's closely argued tract and the provocative tone in which it was couched. He sent him a reply to Amsterdam, repudiating the allegation that he had denied the immortality of the soul, and justifying his belief in exclusively natural religion.

---

[114] See below, chap. 10, pp. 263 ff.

[115] The first part, which contains 11 chaps., is entitled 'Contra la impiedad de quien duda la verdad infalible de la sagrada escriptura y pretende ocultar la malicia, con la affectada confesion de Dios y Ley de naturaleza'; the second (3 chaps.) 'Defiende la Ley mental o Tradicion Divina'; the third (6 chaps.) 'En que se defienden los Vallados que los antiguos Sabios y Doctores de Israel instituyeron para la mas perfecta observancia de la Ley'; and the fourth (9 chaps.) 'Defiendese la pureza y sinceridad del Talmud contra las inventadas y maliciosas calumnias.'

[116] Révah (*rupt. spin., nouvel examen*, 70, p. 563) stated that he had located 9 copies. I have, so far, collated 15, and it may be assumed that further copies will be identified. On the various MSS containing *Epíst. Inv.*, see below, Appendix E. The title given to the tract in the final recension was 'Epístola Invectíva contra Prado un Philosopho Médico que dudava o no creia la verdad de la divina Escritura y pretendió encubrir su malicia con la àffecta confessión de Dios y ley de Naturaleza.'

Doubt and Certainty

So much can be deduced from Orobio's second letter to Prado, the one entitled *Carta Apologética*.[117] From the way it is written, one can sense Isaac's mixed emotions regarding his controversy with Prado, one part of him drawn by love for his close friend of former years, and the other by his loyalty to the religion of Israel. He was quite clear in his own mind that the latter took precedence over all personal feelings, but all the same it went hard with him to join the chorus of those who were pointing the finger of scorn at Prado, ignoring his personal fate and accepting with equanimity his severing of his connections with Judaism.[118] Although Orobio did his best to observe the formal conditions of the writ of excommunication and to refrain from any direct address to Prado, the way in which his *Carta Apologética* is formulated shows that he did not always succeed in doing so. At the beginning of the letter he does not address him personally, but refers to him for the most part in the third person, as 'Doctor Prado', 'el Señor Doctor', or 'el Doctor',[119] in what follows he slips into the second person,[120] and towards the end of the letter, the walls of his own reserve having been breached, he actually goes so far as to excuse himself for his hectoring tone: 'I know well enough that I am human, yet give thanks that I am not unduly human [in my attitude] towards you; for I am striving to bring you to the recognition of truth, in a spirit of sadness the bitterness of which is far greater than duty requires, greater indeed than [all other] human duties. And in truth, I make no effort at all as I write to suppress this my duty, and your love for me is well known to me; yet I can repay it in no coin more precious than by my constant endeavours to persuade you of the truth.'[121]

[117] The full title in the original Spanish reads 'Carta Apologética del Doctor Ishack Orobio de Castro al Doctor Prado'. Révah printed it in full from the Paris MS (see above, n. 107), 2nd vol. (41), pp. 875–901; see his *Spinoza et Prado*, pp. 130–42.

[118] Ibid., p. 876: 'Como yo no he recivido algunos agravios del Doctor Prado, sino repetidas y continuadas experiencias de su buena voluntad y deseo de mis medras, sin olvidar los favores y assistencias en los primeros años de mi juventud, no pudiera, sin torpe nota de ingratitud, aborrecer su persona; mas tampoco pudiera, sin grandissima ofensa de la Divina Majestad, dejar de abominar sus desordenados dictamenes ... en nada me veo que mi silencio sea un dever y en nada lo estimaria quien no save tenerle antes mucha complacencia en que aya muchos noticiosos de las travesuras de su ingenio ...'

[119] Ibid., 'no he recivido algunos agravios del Doctor Prado ...'; p. 877, 'diga aora el Señor Doctor que lo cree ...'; p. 878, 'Esto le pareció al Doctor contradictorio y lo prueva con un syllogismo que, aunque no tiene modo ni el Señor Doctor le pudo comunicar mejor figura ...'

[120] Ibid., p. 894, 'Yo no sé de adonde saca Vmd. que tengo la fe de a paleta para creer los milagros que refieren algunos Sabios ... '; p. 895, 'Pésame de que solo Escoto le persuada a Vmd. la immortalidad del alma.' There are other examples of the same unconcious tendency. [121] Ibid., p. 889.

This letter is one of the most important autobiographical documents preserved from Isaac Orobio's pen, containing as it does not a few allusions to his life in Spain and France.[122] It has come down to us in a single copy, showing that those concerned may have refrained from putting it into circulation, either because Isaac himself kept it from the eyes of the *Ma'amad* on account of its personal tone, or because the *Ma'amah* regarded it as a serious infringement of the provisions of the excommunication promulgated against Prado.[123]

Isaac Orobio's third letter against Prado took the form of an epistle addressed to Prado's son. Isaac prefaced it as follows:

Sir,
Seeing that I am forbidden to write to Dr Prado, but my zeal for truth will not suffer me to refrain from providing an answer to his points of doubt (in so far as my meagre understanding makes such a thing possible), I have resolved to write this letter to yourself, in order that he may come to know about this written statement through the mediacy of one of those gentlemen who are not inhibited from coming into contact with him. Should he wish to reply to it, he can do so, provided that he does not send his answer direct to me; for it is permissible for me to hear what he says to others.[124]

Such caution on Isaac's part shows that the Portuguese congregation had withheld approval from the manner in which, up to this point, he had been conducting his disputation with Prado. He consequently decided to continue his correspondence through the medium of the excommunicate's son David:[125] to forgo its continuation altogether was something that he was not prepared to consider.

Prior to this Prado had apparently sent Orobio, by the hand of his son, three questions expressing criticism of conventional Jewish views: (*a*) regarding the differences of view between individuals, although their souls all consist of the same substance and are of the same nature; (*b*) regarding the right of the individual to decide by his private judgement, and not in accordance with the view of the majority; and (*c*) regarding the innocence of transgressors (meaning thereby the various pagan peoples) from whom knowledge of truth is precluded.[126]

---

[122] See above, pp. 103 f.
[123] See above, n. 117. It ought to be borne in mind that the one surviving copy is a late one, dated 1731, and it is to be supposed that errors and corruptions have crept into it.
[124] MS Paris, BN Fonds éspagnoles 41, p. 902.
[125] On David Prado see above, pp. 136 f.
[126] MS Paris, p. 905: 'Pregunta: Porque [sic] a unos les parece bien una cosa y assienten a una proposicion, y a otros mal y dissienten della, . . . siendo las almas de una misma substancia y naturaleza'; p. 908: ' . . . si ay dos Legisladores o mas, y cada uno intima y

Doubt and Certainty

Three copies of this letter of Orobio have been preserved, and the differences between them are of exceptional importance. Two of them bear indications of the place and date of its composition. On the Paris manuscript there is a note that it was composed in Weycke on 12 August 5424 (1664). On MS Amsterdam, '*Eṣ Ḥayyim* 48 A 21 the date is given, with the year expressed in the conventional Christian era, but the place of origin is stated to be Utreque (Utrecht).[127] Although MS Paris is the latest, it seems reasonable to regard it as the most faithful to the lost holograph, for it has far fewer errors than the other two, into which there have crept so many corruptions that frequently make it difficult to understand the sense.[128] Furthermore, in the two Amsterdam copies the author's anti-Christian attitudes have been deliberately tampered with, since they must have sounded too dangerous for dissemination. For example, in summarizing his views on those who are destined for life in the future world, Orobio writes (MS Paris, p. 921) that included among those condemned to eternal damnation are 'mainly the Christians'; because although they believe in the true doctrine, 'yet they practise what is contrary to what it teaches, and they believe in dogmas that contradict natural reason'. That pronouncement, like others of a similar character, has been omitted from the two other manuscripts.[129] Between the latter some variants are to be found, and one of them is occasionally close to MS Paris—a fact that shows that the two Amsterdam codices are not mutually interdependent.[130] One must assume that the original text of the letter was subjected to meticulous criticism at the hand of the *señores* of the *Ma'amad*. The subsequent copies were made from a censored archetype, and, as is normally the case, corruptions and errors have occurred in them and additions have been made by copyists, out of a desire to clarify or

promulga ley contraria, con titulo de divina, qual ha de seguir el entendimiento, la que le parece mal porque le aconsejan otros que es buena, o la que ... le parece bien aunque otros le digan que es mala?'; p. 919: 'Que por esso el niño innocente no peca, aunque haga acto que fuera pecado en el adulto: porque no conoce la malicia de aquel acto. Luego, los hombres que yerran el verdadero camino, no conociendo que yerran, tampoco deven ser tenidos por pecadores, pues ellos piensan que aciertan.'

[127] The letter was published in full by Révah from MS Paris, pp. 902–23; there are two further copies, both in Amsterdam, *EH* 48 A 21, ff. 239–51, and 48 A 23, ff. 310–31. Neither is included in Fuks-M., *EH*. For comparison between their texts, see below, Appendix F.

[128] MS Paris, p. 903, 'el ayre le recive', as compared with *EH* 48 A 23, f. 311, 'les resiste' (48 A 21 'le resiste'); MS Paris, p. 918, '... quieren no entender lo que creen ...', codd., pp. 326, 248, '... quieren no entender lo que no entienden ...'. For other examples see Appendix F.

[129] See Appendix F. [130] See p. 447.

amplify.[131] The scribe of the Paris text was lucky enough to find a copy of the original text. In 1731, when he approached his task, it would seem that the *señores* of the *Ma'amad* were not concerned about variants between the recensions. The Prado story had become a fading memory, and the leadership of the Amsterdam Portuguese congregation was not worried about checking this copy. We have to thank their lack of care for the fact that a copy of the original recension has reached us.

From the foregoing it seems probable that the place of origin of the letter is that indicated in MS Paris, i.e. Weycke. Probably one of the later copyists erroneously read *Utreque* instead of *Weycke* (Wijk), which seems to be the little town Wijk-aan-Zee situated in North-Holland on the coast, west of Beverwijk, not far from Amsterdam itself.[132]

This town was used by the Portuguese Jews as a place of refuge during epidemics, like Maarsen and Naarden. In 1664 an extremely severe plague epidemic broke out in Amsterdam, claiming many victims among the city's Jews, and it seems that several members of the *Talmud Torah* Congregation moved to Wijk, maintaining a prayer quorum of their own there. Isaac Orobio was apparently one of those who fled the grave dangers of the plague and took refuge in this town on the coast of the North Sea. He sent his letters to Prado from there, perhaps with David Prado, his son.[133]

We must suppose that this letter marked the close of the disputation of these two former friends who had each gone his separate way. Isaac repeated the arguments which he had put forward in his earlier letters, and devoted extended space to consideration of the problem of reward and punishment in the hereafter. The question that he addressed to Rabbi Moses d'Aguilar, on the subject of heavenly reward for righte-

---

[131] See pp. 445, 448 f.

[132] See A. G. van der Aa, *Aardrijkskundig Woordenboek der Nederlanden*, xii, Gorinchem, 1849, pp. 411 f. I am grateful to Mrs Tirtsah Levie for making me aware of the identity of this place and supplying the bibliographical references.

[133] On the plague of that year see C. Commelin, *Beschryving der Stadt Amsterdam*, Amsterdam, 1693, p. 1181. On the prayer quorum maintained by the Portuguese Jews in Wijk at that time see the *Livro Grande* of the *Talmud Torah* Congregation, Amsterdam, AGA, PA 334, no. 240, ff. 174ʻ, 192ʳ; as early as 1655 a special prayer quorum was maintained there, see ibid., f. 37ʳ. The contributions collected at prayers were generally sent to the 'Mother' congregation in Amsterdam. On these small communites outside Amsterdam see Brugmans and Frank, p. 396. Nevertheless, it could be that 'Weycke' refers to the little town of Wijk in the north of Bradant, north-west of s'Hertogenbosch. We may suppose that Isaac Orobio wanted to meet Prado face to face, and so decided to proceed to Antwerp. Perhaps he went there secretly, and as a precaution dated his letter from Wijk, which had been a staging-post on his journey.

Doubt and Certainty 157

ous Gentiles who observe the seven commandments of the sons of Noah, seems to have been sent at this period, as a result of the discussions with Prado.[134]

From the end of the letter it is clear that Isaac had come to the conclusion that it was beyond his power to shift his controversialist from his position. 'In a subject [he wrote] that so far transcends reason, I am unable to go further in discussion than my meagre reasoning can attain . . .'[135] So ended the last attempt by a member of the Portuguese community of Amsterdam to win back its recalcitrant son to the bosom of Judaism. Thereafter Prado lost all contact with the Jewish religion, and floundered ever deeper into his denial of its essentials.

In 1666 Prado's name figured in a list of members of 'the Portuguese nation' permanently resident in Antwerp.[136] At this stage he was still maintaining links with some of the members of his former congregation in Amsterdam, as is shown by a sonnet printed at the beginning of Miguel de Barrios' collected poems that were printed in Brussels in 1665: the sonnet is dedicated to the author. Nothing in this, however, implies any positive links with Judaism; the sonnet itself contains nothing to point to anything of the sort, and in any case, the leaders of the Amsterdam congregation inspected de Barrios' manuscript and pronounced it unfit to be published.[137] The book even contains a barbed poem which de Barrios wrote in criticism of Prado, containing some acid references to his shortcomings as a poet and his lack of literary talent—a judgement that did not, however, dissuade de Barrios from printing Prado's sonnet in praise of himself.[138] From de Barrios' piece we learn that Prado had approached one of de Barrios' own patrons, don Antonio de Córdoba, with a request for assistance in publishing his own poems, but that de Córdoba had dismissed them on account of their poor quality. He also hinted subtly at Prado's association with free-thinkers, which had led to his explusion from the

---

[134] See above, p. 117.

[135] MS Paris, p. 923: 'En materia tan sobre la razon, no puedo discurrir mas que hasta donde alcança la poquedad de mi discurso . . .'

[136] Antwerp, St., PK 1074, 'Relación de las casas, o familias Portuguezas, que al presente ay en la Villa de Amberes, las que tienen domicilio—sujetas a la Naçion de Portugal—y que gozan los Privilegios que la dicha Nacion tiene.' Dr Prado appears nineteenth on this list, which was published by Révah, 'Nation Port.' à Anvers, pp. 145–7.

[137] On the banning of the book see Révah, *Censure de la communauté*, pp. 83 f.

[138] See De Barrios, *Flor*, pp. 186–90: 'Correys en pies de versos las hispanas / Nimphas, que temerosas de fracassos / como de oro no arrojays mançanas. / En campos damasquillos mas que rassos, no abejas liban vuestras muchas flores / por que andays tras su miel en malos passos.'

Amsterdam congregation in 1658 ('place thyself ever beside good folk, as do I, nor keep on resorting with the evil').[139] Prado's material position did not improve in Antwerp: de Barrios styles him in his poem an 'impoverished physician' (*vos médico pobre*) and also casts doubt on his medical skill.[140] But even worse was his psychological plight: a lonely outcast, far from friends, bereft of roots, and with a surfeit of disappointments and fiascos trailing behind him, Prado resolved on a desperate and paradoxical attempt to put the clock back. In a letter written from Antwerp on 22 June 1667 he expressed grief about his lack-lustre origins as a Jew, and requested support from the Spanish Inquisition to return to Spain and the bosom of the Church without incurring any personal penalty or the confiscation of his property.[141] His request was turned down, and he spent his last years in Antwerp. In this final period he became enmeshed in amatory adventures; in a poem of de Barrios published in 1672, after Prado's death, one may read plenty of satire on his libertinism and moral degeneracy.

> A famous doctor, love is now the skill
> That he professes from the chair of joy:
> Though for the girls a gentleman, his will
> Makes clear to ladies he is but a boy.[142]

After the death of his wife his lust became unbridled; chasing women and devoting himself to a life of wanton extravagance financed by the generosity of others.[143]

---

[139] Ibid: 'La inquisicion de *Cordova* en aprieto / los puso, ventilando su cultura, / y sin duda temio cada terceto. / Tener en sus cenizas sepoltura'; and with a hint at Prado's free-thinking: 'arrimaos como yo siempre a los buenos, / y no andeys de continuo con los malos . . .'

[140] Ibid: 'Que las curas que hazeys son menos ciertas: / lo que a mi me remonta por las cumbres / á vos medico pobre os trae por puertas.' Documents held in Antwerp, St., do not include Prado's name amongst those of physicians practising in the city in the 17th cent.: see A. F. C. van Schevensteen, 'Naamlijsten van Antwerpsche Geneesheeren, Chirurgijns, enz. opgemaakt uit de voornaamste fondsen van het Stadsarchief', *AA* 7, 1932, pp. 122–160. De Barrios reprinted the poem, with certain changes, in 1672, in his *Coro*, pp. 588–92.

[141] Révah discovered the letter and published a French translation of part of it in *rupt. spin., nouvel examen*, pp. 578–9, without indicating where he had found it. Despite a search both in Madrid, AHN, and elsewhere, I have not succeeded in tracing it.

[142] *Coro*, pp. 355–61: 'Con fama de gran Doctor / en la cathedra del gozo, / enseñó el arte de Amor: / para las moças Señor, / para las Señoras moço.'

[143] Ibid.: 'La muerte de su muger, / le hizo de bastardas bodas / can, de modo bachiller, / que por darse a conocer, / se descubria con todas / . . . empeçó a vivir de renta, / con los immundos regalos / que de los buenos afrenta, / . . .'

Doubt and Certainty

Confirmation of what is said about him in some lines of de Barrios comes from a document in the municipal archives of Antwerp. In the same poem de Barrios says that after Prado's wife had died, 'he barked [for joy], being free of his collar; and, like the fierce dog that he was, he proceeded to throw himself upon a she-wolf [*loba*]'.[144] The word *loba* was printed by de Barrios with a capital *L*, which is itself enough of an indication that he was referring to the surname of some woman with whom Prado had apparently had an affair. And sure enough, in the baptismal register of the parish of St James in Antwerp it is recorded that on 6 July 1669 the bastard daughter of Juan de Prado and Eleonora Francisca de Lobo was christened Joanna Francisca:

> Joanna Francisca, illeg[itima]
> Ex p[a]re[n]ti[bu]s D[on] Joannes de Prado
> Do[n]cella Eleonora Francisca Lobo
> D[on] Joannes Mendes Blandon
> [Do]ncella Josepha Maria Lobo.[145]

At the beginning of his poem de Barrios says that Prado 'had promised to marry a certain she-wolf [*fulana loba*] and had lived with her in sin, but married another'. Providence requited his conduct: whilst he was crossing a bridge on horseback, a waggon collided with him and knocked him and his mount over the parapet into the waters of the river, into which he sank and so met his end.[146]

Such was the abrupt close of Prado's tragic life-story a rich combination of incompatibilities. He was one of the most colourful characters

---

[144] Ibid.: '. . . ladrava, suelto en su encierro: / donde como era gran perro osó embestir a una Loba'.

[145] Antwerp, St., PR 53, p. 132; Kaplan, *Prado*, pp. 159–63.

[146] *Coro*: 'Castiga la Divina justicia al Doctor Juan de Prado, maestro de falsos dogmas, que no tenia mas religion que la que convenia a su cuerpo, ni mas almas en su opinion que de cavallo; y dando palabra de casamiento a una Fulana Loba, la desfloró, y yendose á casar con otra ordenó la Suprema justicia que, por un carro que se le atravessó en una puente, cayesse della con su cavallo en un rio, donde le imitó en la muerte como en la vida.' In the parish church of St Philip in Antwerp one *Johannes* de Prado married María Marcelina on 4 Apr. 1669. If this refers to Juan = Daniel de Prado, it would confirm de Barrios' statement as to a marriage contracted by Prado at the end of his life: but for the problems regarding such identification see Kaplan, *Prado*, pp. 162 f. It is difficult to establish the date of Prado's death exactly, because the bills of mortality for the Antwerp churches at this period have disappeared. Lists from 1680 only survive of the church of Our Lady (Onze Lieve Vrouw); there is a gap in those of Onze Lieve Vrouw Zuid for 1636–1748, and in those of Onze Lieve Vrouw Noord for 1636–1709; likewise for the parishes of St James for 1654–81, St Andrew for 1636–1703, and St George (Joris) for 1636–1702.

in the history of the intellectual ferment within the western Sephardi diaspora in the seventeenth century. Prado's stormy life stands in complete contrast to the magnificent isolation and self-disciplined way of life of Spinoza. Whereas Spinoza had accepted excommunication by the congregation in a stoical spirit, and went his own way to lead a life of contemplative reflection, Prado had tortuously endeavoured to find his way back into the fold of his people; when he failed, he became progressively more alienated from the faith of Israel. The ways of Prado and Spinoza parted, and shortly after their separation Spinoza considered the possibility of attaining a 'new mode of living'. His consideration of men's life and actions convinced him that 'the things that they regard as the supreme good ... wealth, honour, pleasures of the flesh', were not merely not the 'assured, certain good' towards which he was striving, but that 'they constitute a stumbling-block, so long as they are pursued for their own sake, and not as means to other ends'. 'Compared to this, love of the perpetual and infinite drenches the soul with nought but joy, and takes away all pain.'[147] While Spinoza was putting these reflections into writing, Prado was being swept away on the waves of libertinism that came to be his whole life. Spinoza busied himself in formulating his own approach to metaphysics, in the consciousness that he was 'thinking on the true philosophy'.[148] Prado was endeavouring to excuse his actions to the Spanish Inquisition, and confessing his defeat and the failure of his search for a religion that should be founded upon natural law, and on 'faith in God in an exclusively philosophical sense'.

One of the most prominent features of the history of Judaism in the seventeenth century are the objections voiced by individuals in the Sephardi diaspora of western Europe against some of the principle articles of faith in Judaism. In particular they challenged rabbinic Halakhah, the legalistic elaboration and extension of biblical commandments. Very little has come down to us of the writings of these representatives of heterodox opinion, and we learn about them for the most part from critical reactions of their opponents, who were the rabbis and intellectual leaders of their congregations. The thinking of the critics is generally characterized by the following traits: (*a*) will to erode the authority of the religious leadership; (*b*) denial of the oral Law and rabbinic tradition; (*c*) rejection of belief in the survival of the

---

[147] *Tractatus de Intellectus Emendatione, Op. Post.* [Amsterdam], 1677, pp. 359 f.
[148] *Epistolae, Op. Post.* p. 612 (no. 76, to Albert Burgh), Eng. trans., A. Wolf, *The Correspondence of Spinoza Translated* ..., London, 1928, p. 352.

Doubt and Certainty 161

soul and a future world; (*d*) a negative attitude towards providence; (*e*) a shaking off of the yoke of the commandments; and sometimes also (*f*) negation of the uniqueness of Israel as God's elect.

Rivkin has claimed to see in these heterodox modes of thought the direct product of economic changes that were taking place in the West, as segments of society which were gaining strength began to rebel against the religious and ideological notions conventionally accepted in the Middle Ages. In his view, rejectionism was the active expression of the struggle of the new capitalist class against a traditional world-view according to which everything was subject to the arbitrary will of the Deity, whilst this social element was looking for a world governed by the orderly forces of reason that left no room for arbitrariness. God, too, must consequently be subdued so as to conform to the laws of nature, and religious faith must be made to bow the knee before human reason. According to Rivkin, such a reaction was no less characteristic of western Jewish communities; and it was that situation which prepared the ground for the rise of heterodox attitudes amongst them.[149] A major objection to Rivkin's simplistic explanation is that there is nothing to point to any connection between radical attitudes that were blossoming at this period within the Jewish community and individuals typifying the social forces which were supposedly the standard-bearers of changed economic conditions. Battles fought out between the heterodox and those of uncompromised Jewish traditionalism over matters speculative and ideological betray no sign of social difference, or of any clash of economic interests between the two opposing sides. In what way did the social background of Uriel d'Acosta, Juan de Prado, and Barukh Spinoza differ from that of Samuel da Silva, Rabbi Saul Levi Mortera, Rabbi Moses d'Aguilar, and Orobio de Castro?

I. Sonne, on the other hand, interpreted the expressions of heterodoxy within the western Sephardi diaspora as the battle of rationalism against a religious establishment that was allegedly under the complete control of mystics.[150] Such an explanation, so far from clarifying the root of the problem, obscures its whole nature. The vehement opponents of Uriel d'Acosta, Prado, and Spinoza were securely anchored in the tradition of Jewish religious rationalism, and the most prominent amongst them, such as Rabbi Mortera, were amongst the most distinguished opponents of cabbalistic tradition.[151]

---

[149] See Rivkin, pp. 1–17, esp. 3–4.   [150] See Sonne, *Da Costa*.
[151] See Altmann, pp. 3 f.

Gebhardt thought that the phenomenon of rejectionism amongst the Sephardim of western Europe was the result of the psychological dichotomy that affected crypto-Jews when, on reversion to Judaism, they were called upon to sever themselves from a deeply rooted Christian mindset.[152] Gebhardt was the first to take account of the impact of the religious confusion which was the heritage of crypto-Jews returning to Judaism, in which he identified the key to the understanding of the intellectual ferment amongst Sephardi communities in the seventeenth century. Nevertheless, Gebhardt's distinctions are too general. He was correct in pointing to the Christian education received by crypto-Jews, but he paid no attention to the content of the form of Christianity with which these crypto-Jews were familiar. His analysis likewise affords no help in understanding how it was that most crypto-Jews who left Spain and Portugal nevertheless succeeded in integrating themselves into Jewish communities regardless of the Christian notions that they had brought with them, traces of which remain recognizable in their religious productions after their return to Judaism. Above all, Gebhardt's approach goes nowhere towards supplying a satisfactory explanation of why it was that the criticisms which most of the heterodox Jewish figures advanced against Judaism did not attract them back towards Christianity; and that, on the contrary, their views led them far from the basic principles upon which all the monotheistic religions are founded, leading most of them into a universalistic deism and a minority into atheism and free-thinking.

Révah detected in these representatives of heterodoxy a new embodiment of the averroism and scepticism that had been spreading amongst the Jews of Spain even before the expulsion of 1492 and which were adopted by many a 'New Christian' in the sixteenth and seventeenth centuries.[153] He adduces writings composed in Spain and Portugal against the heresy of the 'New Christians accused of denying some of the cardinal principles of the Christian faith, as proof that attitudes of this kind were prevalent amongst crypto-Jews still

---

[152] Gebhardt, *Uriel da Costa*, introd., esp. p. xxii, on the situation in which the crypto-Jew found himself: 'Er stand zwischen den Welten. In seinem Bewusstsein war Katholicismus und Judentum, unvereint und unvereinbar, und in diesem inneren Kampfe war sein Bewusstsein gespalten.' At the same time, Gebhardt did appreciate that the religious establishment of the Portuguese Jews in Amsterdam was effectively controlled by devotees of the Cabbala, and it was this circumstance, in his view, that awoke the opposition of other forces within the community which were consequently branded as heterodox. Ibid., pp. xxv f.

[153] See Révah, *Spinoza et Prado*, pp. 13 f.; also his *Spinoza*, p. 177, and *Hérésie Marrane*, pp. 327–37.

resident in the Iberian peninsula after the official eradication of Judaism. Révah discovered an instructive example in a piece entitled *Ropicapnefma* dating from 1532 by the Portuguese writer João de Barros, in which he attacked those 'New Christians' who did not believe in the survival of the soul, or in reward and punishment in the hereafter.[154] In these attitudes Révah saw the roots of the deism characteristic of heterodox thinkers within Sephardi communities in the seventeenth century. He claims that certain principles lie behind that deism, viz. (*a*) the autonomy of the understanding in matters speculative and ethical; (*b*) repudiation of the conventional forms in which divine revelation was conceived; (*c*) insistence on the immutability of the natural order since creation, its laws having been determined by God in perpetuity; and (*d*) belief in a natural law, common to humanity from its outset, and having a moral rather than a religious quality.

Révah made an important contribution to the subject in drawing attention to the continuity of deistic speculation amongst crypto-Jewish circles in Spain and Portugal. But his explanation is weakened by its neglect both of the concrete historical situation of crypto-Jews in the Iberian peninsula at the period of Spain's imperial decline, and of the doctrinal struggles that were taking place there in the period under review. Moreover, Révah failed to see the connection between conflicts of ideas within western Sephardi communities and similar phenomena affecting the intellectual climate of Europe in general at the time.

It seems to me that the polemic of Isaac Orobio with Prado throws light on to this absorbing yet complex problem, and that it can serve to open a window into the intellectual world of crypto-Jews who were returning to the Jewish fold in the seventeenth century.

Since Orobio's three tracts (in particular the first, i.e. the *Epístola Invectiva*) were intended to controvert not only Prado's ideas but also unorthodox opinions that had gained currency both in European society generally and also within the Jewish community, it is sometimes difficult to distinguish, amongst matter that is adduced merely to dismiss it, between the views of Prado himself and those of other heterodox figures. In his anxiety to forewarn his one-time friend of the hidden dangers in his thinking, Orobio went out of his way to stress that such notions must, in practice, lead to outright denial of God. The

[154] See Révah's edn. of de Barros, *Ropicapnefma*.

result is to blur the distinction in his writings between Prado's personal views and what Orobio saw as their logical conclusion. In spite of this, it is possible to identify Prado's ideas, if only incompletely, from Orobio's three tracts.

The very structure of the *Epístola Invectiva*, its section-division, and its constantly reiterated emphases, all indicate that Prado denied the sacred quality and the reliability of both the written and the oral Law, and that he cast aspersions on the authority, and on the value, of rabbinic opinion on the import of scriptural narrative, prophecy, and ordinance. Scripture itself, according to Prado, was not the product of revelation, but rather a collection of late compositions, its description of events that purported to be prophetic statements being in fact *ex post facto* retrojections.[155] Revelation to Israel at Sinai was not, for Prado, a unique occurrence vouchsafed by God to the Jews, since other peoples, too, had been beneficiaries of similar favours, as their own historical traditions proved. It followed that the election of Israel as God's only, chosen people must be cast into doubt.[156]

Prado's rejection of the authority of the oral Law is based on attitudes similar to those to which, in the foregoing period, expression had been given by Uriel d'Acosta; and they may be brought into sharp focus by concentrating on three basic questions: (*a*) why was the content of the oral Law not included in the written Law? (*b*) if the oral Law has the same binding force as has the written, why was it necessary to encode the latter in written form? (*c*) why is the written Law not sufficiently clear in itself to exclude the possibility of error in its implementation?[157]

[155] See *Cart. Apol.*, part i, chaps. 3–6, 8, MS Paris (see above, n. 124), p. 735.
[156] Ibid., pp. 738 f.
[157] Ibid., p. 764: 'Y si preguntare el relaxado: Por que Nuestro Señor no puso por escrito quanto contiene la Explicacion Oral y Legal Tradición . . .'; p. 766: 'Puede replicar le contumacia que destas razones se colige que ni era tampoco necessario el escrivir los preceptos divinos, sino imprimirlos en la memoria de los Israelitas para que, por continuada tradicion, se continuasse y se communicasse a la posteridad, pues no son menos obligatorios los decretos de la Tradicion que los escritos . . .'; p. 767: 'Porfia mas el animo obstinado: Por que no dio Dios la Ley con tal clareza (y los demas preceptos) que no necessitasse communicasse a todos, pues, assi, no avria ocasion de errar ni dudar en su exercicio?' C.f. Uriel d'Acosta's critique of the basic principle of the oral Law, Question 7, in Gebhardt, *Uriel da Costa*, pp. 7 f., German trans., pp. 18 f.: 'To assert that we have to pronounce the law of the Torah in accordance with tradition, and to believe in it as the very Torah vouchsafed to Moses, is in itself sufficient to invalidate the whole notion of Torah; since the truth is that this procedure virtually amounts to change, with the newly emergent Torah being in contradiction to the original, genuine Torah. It cannot be contended that there exists an oral law apart from the written, for the following reasons. (*a*) In the [written] Torah there is to be found no reference to any other, or to

Doubt and Certainty 165

In marshalling the arguments that had induced him to reject rabbinic tradition and its protective hedge of safeguards, Prado (so we must gather) contended that those safeguards are so numerous that it becomes difficult to implement the whole institution, so that rather than aiding the one who wishes to observe it to avoid transgression, they lead, on the contrary, to his stumbling in the process, since by piling up a mass of legalistic minutiae they jeopardize prospects of avoiding sin.[158]

It is not so clear whether or not Prado really denied that the world is created, and that providence guides individual lives, since Orobio's remarks in this connection are directed against atheists and deists in general, and it is not necessarily the case that in this respect he lumped Prado together with them.[159] We have seen above[160] from Prado's letter

any explanation of the Torah itself ... (*b*) From the Torah itself it is apparent that there is no other, and that it is in accordance with its own statement of the law that one has to proceed ... Granted, then, that we have demonstrated that there is neither any other Torah or any explanation of the original Torah emanating from the Deity, it follows that what the commentaries referred to above and others like them call "tradition" is but a human enterprise, to which rejoinder is possible—to say nothing of the enormity of affording mankind the occasion of deviating from the Torah as promulgated by Moses, by means of explanations involving modification; and the presumptuousness of publishing merely human commentary in place of the divine. *Ergo*, if it is seen that this is but a system contrived by man, it is a monstrous denial of God to set it alongside that laid down by God, and to declare that we are in duty bound to observe all the laws of the Talmud as themselves being the Torah vouchsafed to Moses ...'

[158] See *Epíst. Inv.*, pp. 812 f.: 'Los que fundaron las demonstraciones de su agudeza en la ingeniosa censura de las cosas pias y religioso culto, procuran hacer absurdos los Vallados y Estatutos de los antiguos Doctores, provando su racionalidad por la Justicia con que se gradua su transgression ... mas es poner tropiezos a las almas para caer frequentemente que prevenirlas para que no lleguen al pecado, en quanto les proponen y mandan guardar mas decretos, que es lo mismo que mas lazos en que caer ...' Cf. Uriel d'Acosta's critique, Question 10, in Gebhardt, *Uriel da Costa*, p. 9, German trans., p. 21: 'Those elaborative regulations that they term a "fence" for the Torah are decidely counter-productive, inasmuch as they all too easily induce people to commit intentional offence, which is the very essence of sin, since they believe that in transgressing that fence they are thereby acting sinfully. Such institutions as are ordained as a precautionary measure to prevent a person from sinning ought explicitly be declared to be precautionary, and not represented as being divine commandments in their very essence: nor ought there to be erected upon the Torah a superstructure consisting of another Torah, more stringent that the first, and one which is virtually impossible of fulfilment ...'

[159] See *Epíst. Inv.*, pp. 714 f.: 'Para evadirse desta luz y seguir las tinieblas, responde la impiedad, con el acostumbrado pretexto de ingeniosa, que no es su animo negar la existencia del Criador ni limitarle su potencia, que Dios puede todo lo que no repugna, mas que asi mismo no hizo todo quanto puede ... Asi suele justificarse o paliar sus errores la perversa politica de los Deistas ...'

[160] See above, p. 138.

to the officers of the Congregation *Talmud Torah* after his excommunication that he claimed not to have advanced these heterodox views, although the accusations which his pupils laid against him with Rabbi Mortera certainly alleged that he had denied the survival of the soul after death. The substance of Orobio's objection to him in this connection was merely that Prado claimed that the only basis that he could find for such belief was in the writings of Duns Scotus.[161]

Between the views of Prado and the deistic opinions that were so widespread in the seventeenth century there is undoubtedly a clear link. Hence Prado denied the uniqueness of Judaism, which would preclude Israel's acceptance of a religious system based upon a purely intellectual understanding, and hence also his opposition to the notion of the election of Israel, which would run counter to his own ideas of universalist religion.

What is so astonishing in Isaac Orobio's rejoinder is his own complete adherence to the religion of Israel as understood in rabbinic tradition. Although he was writing immediately upon his own return to the Jewish fold, he flaunts at his erstwhile friend an absolute identification with Jewish tradition in all its detail: for him, there is no contradiction between Scripture and natural reason, there is no more lofty religious teaching than that of Judaism, nor any way of life more ethically sublime; every single precept is binding, every custom justified: the oral Law, the whole complex of Halakhic ordinance, the protective screen of supernumerary prohibitions, the rulings reached by the rabbis on specific issues—all these constitute a single, coherent system, the parts of which were not patient of being dismantled.[162] The interesting thing is that close scrutiny of his arguments shows that it was not only Prado's views that found a base in concepts that had crystallized out in certain streams of contemporary European thought. In refuting these Orobio, too, drew heavily on the teachings of Christian thinkers of the time who were making valiant efforts to make good the ever-increasing number of breeches made in the walls of faith—inroads that were robbing some of the best theological minds in reformed Christianity of their sleep. In order to justify this assertion, let us focus our attention on one of the central issues in the Orobio-Prado polemic, namely the sanctity and the authority of the Scriptures.

The scientific revolution which set in during the seventeenth

---

[161] See *Cart. Apol.*, p. 877.

[162] For Orobio's attitude towards Judaism and Jewish tradition in general, see below, chap. 12, pp. 343 ff.

Doubt and Certainty   167

century did not, in itself, bring about a clash between faith and science. Those who were its progenitors did not intend to introduce anything new into the sphere of theology. Quite to the contrary. Most of them found that mechanistic science, even in its most materialistic and deterministic manifestations, could be reconciled with Christian faith.[163] Descartes, the Jansenists, and Malebranche did not stand aside from Christian dogma: others, such as Gassendi, Mersenne, and the 'fideistic sceptics', found a golden mean that could reconcile scepticism in regard to any possibility of metaphysical knowledge with submissive acceptance of the directives of faith.[164] Nevertheless, from the moment that philosophers and theologians attempted to make use of the new scientific concepts that were being developed by Copernican astronomy and the mechanistic approach, in order to apply these to biblical criticism and a reconsideration of theological truth, a bitter conflict developed between science and religion. Fierce debates were aroused by questions as to the attitude to be taken towards miracles and the mysteries of religion, and towards the explanation of central episodes in biblical history, e.g. the duration of the process of creation or of Noah's flood. There were also discoveries of hitherto unknown peoples and cultures in far-flung quarters of the world, which stimulated a most animated discussion of the origin of the human species, produced masses of problems in regard to accepting the biblical chronology, and impugned the idea of the election of Israel and of the uniqueness of the tradition of religion and moral action which was the common property of Judaism and Christianity.[165]

Attempts to meet the challenge of the new-found radicalism were not slow in coming. 'Fideistic sceptics', Cartesians, the Jansenists of Port-Royal, as well as others, all braced themselves to defend the integrity of the orthodox faith; the common platform which united them being awareness that 'religious certainty' is not identical with 'scientific certainty', but belongs on a different plane. It was Pascal who laid it down that 'it is in the heart, not in the mind, that awareness of God occurs . . . we recognize truth not only by means of the intelligence, but also in the heart. In this last way we learn how to appreciate first principles; and intellectual consideration, which has no part to play in this, endeavours in vain to declare war on them.'[166] Against

[163] See Popkin, *Scientific Revolution*, pp. 8 f.   [164] Ibid., p. 12.
[165] Ibid., pp. 17 f.; Willey, pp. 58 f.
[166] See Pascal, nos. 278, 282. Cf. Willey, p. 59: 'It was one of the privileges of the seventeenth century to be able to believe, without any effort or striving, that "truth" was not all of one order.'

those who demanded proofs based on reason for everything—including matters of faith—Pascal insisted that 'there is nothing worth in such a procedure, and it is just as absurd for the mind to require the heart to produce proofs for all its first principles in order that it might find it convenient to assent to them, as it would be absurd for the heart to demand of the reason capacity to feel the correctness of all the conclusions at which it arrives, in order for the heart to find it convenient to assent to them'.[167] Where faith is concerned Pascal attributes no power to intellectual speculation, since (according to his theory) the intelligence can 'misdirect everything'. Hence it follows that one must accept the truth of religion on the basis of Scripture, the source of which lies in God.[168]

The Jansenist Antoine Arnauld, Pascal's teacher at Port-Royal des Champs, formulated his own view of the relationship between faith and understanding in a more systematic manner in his book *La Logique, ou l'Art de Penser*. A special chapter in it is devoted to discussion of 'whether that which we know by faith is human or divine'.[169] Arnauld follows in the footsteps of St Augustine: 'quod scimus, debemus rationi: quod credimus, auctoritati'. Faith, for him, is sustained by the power of authority, whereas human authority, unlike divine authority, is liable to err. Further, all faith has to be anchored in understanding: 'we would not be equipped to believe in anything that goes beyond our intelligence, did not our very intelligence convince us that there are certain things in which it is good to believe, even though we are not equipped to understand them'. In his view, this axiom holds good for everything that is bound up with belief in God, for 'true intelligence teaches us that since God is the quintessence of truth, He will not mislead us in whatsoever He reveals to us of his nature and his mysteries'.[170] This leads Arnauld to enunciate a second principle, viz. that 'of necessity, belief in God must exercise greater influence on our soul than does our understanding'. Understanding requires that we should always prefer the more certain to the less certain; 'and it is more certain that what God says is true than that what our understanding tells us is true, since God is less capable of leading us astray than our understanding is capable of avoiding stumbling'.[171]

---

[167] Pascal, ibid.   [168] Ibid., p. 561.
[169] Arnauld wrote the book in collaboration with his colleague Pierre Nicole; it was popularly known as 'Logique de Port-Royal' (*La Logique, ou l'Art de Penser, contenant, outre les règles communes, plusieurs observations nouvelles, propres à former le jugement*). See part iv, chap. 12, Amsterdam, edn. 1775, pp. 407 f.
[170] Arnauld, op. cit., pp. 408 f.   [171] Ibid., p. 410.

Doubt and Certainty 169

It must be doubted whether Isaac Orobio was familiar with the thought of Arnauld and Pascal. Pascal died in 1662, before completing his *Pensées*, which were first published in 1670. Arnauld's book first appeared in 1662, the year Orobio left France, and it cannot be assumed that he had already seen it. It is possible that whilst he was at Toulouse Orobio was introduced to the ideas current in Port-Royal, even though there is nothing in the sources to say so. Nevertheless there is an astonishing similarity between the opinions of the Jansenists, who were his contemporaries, and the arguments he uses to defend belief in God, founded in Scripture, against Prado's views. It is plausible that rather than any direct influence, we have here parallel reactions on the part of thinkers educated within the same theological-philosophical traditions and using the same sources against streams of thought that threatened the integrity of religious faith, be it Christian or Jewish. Like Arnauld, Orobio maintained there were two conditions for something to be worthy of belief: (*a*) it must not contradict the understanding, and (*b*) it must be backed by reliable authority.[172] He taunts Prado with his attempt to judge everything on the basis of intellectual principles, even regarding matters which, of their very nature, are not susceptible to intellectual proof:

It is true that acceptance or belief in a proposition is not a free action; however, it is true that one can deny or reject something, when, according to certain principles, the human intellect becomes convinced of its contrary. That general rule, however, does not apply when the matter under discussion, and the truth thereof, depend not on the understanding, but on the very fact that it exists. No one, by dint of intellectual proofs, can convince another that he was born in France, or that he is the son of his parents: and whoever would deny that assertion, will not be convinced by intellectual means. No one will be so bold as to deny it on the strength of the assertion that he cannot believe it, unless he has grounds for suspicion that he who asserts it is making false representations with evil intent for reasons of his own.[173]

Orobio's construction of the argument here is identical with that of Arnauld, who distinguishes two classes of truths: (*a*) truths which concern 'the nature and unchangeable essence of things, independently of their existence', and (*b*) truths which concern 'existing things, in particular contingent events in the life of man, which may or may not

---

[172] See *Epíst. Inv.*, MS Paris (see above n. 124), p. 696: 'Necesita lo creyble de dos circunstancias que, faltando qualquiera dellas, dexará de serlo. La primera, que no repugne al entendimiento sano y bien informado. La segunda, que aya authoridad competente de parte del que propone o persuade.' [173] Ibid., pp. 689 f.

transpire in so far as the present is concerned, and which could [or could not] have happened in the past'.[174] As far as (*a*) is concerned, 'nothing is true unless it is universally true', and consequently the judgement of reason is determinative. As regards (*b*), the determinative factor is the evidence, in so far as it is reliable and acceptable.[175] It is on the basis of this proposition that Orobio asserts that Israel's faith is true, since it is based upon dependable sources that have their own source in the Deity—than whom, in matters concerning faith, no authority can be higher.[176]

For Orobio, the faith of Israel does not conflict with the understanding: everything that it commands is compatible with reason, and even though it includes items which are beyond our comprehension, one has to take into account that 'belief in the invisible is not the same thing as belief in what contradicts the visible'.[177] Miracles do not run counter to reason, since they constitute demonstrative proof of the untrammelled power of God. Whoever withholds belief in them denies the infinite power of the Creator of the cosmos; and such denial itself conflicts with reason.[178]

Orobio sets out to demolish the theoretical possibility that one could believe in a God whose unity is uniquity, whilst not acknowledging the authority of the Hebrew Bible or accepting its sacred quality. There is, he says, not the slightest possibility of recognizing the existence of a

[174] See Arnauld, op cit. (n. 169 above), p. 412: 'La première réflexion est qu'il faut mettre une extrême différence entre deux sortes de vérités, les unes qui regardent seulement la nature des choses et leur essence immuable indépendamment de leur existence, et les autres qui regardent les choses existantes, et sur-tout les événemens humains et contingens, qui peuvent être et n'être pas quand il s'agit de l'avenir, et qui pouvoient n'avoir pas été quand il s'agit du passé.'

[175] Ibid.: 'Dans la première sorte de vérités, comme tout y est nécessaire rien n'est vrai qu'il ne soit universellement vrai: et ainsi nous devons conclure qu'une chose est fausse, si elle est fausse en un seul cas. Mais si on pense se servir des mêmes règles dans la croyance des événemens humains, on n'en jugera jamais que faussement . . . Que si on demande quelle preuve on a qu'un tel Roi ait regné quelque temps avec son père, il faut avouer qu'on n'en a point de positive; mais il suffit que ce soit une chose possible, et qui est arrivée assez souvent en d'autres rencontres, pour avoir droit de la supposer comme une circonstance nécessaire pour allier des histoires d'ailleurs très certains.'

[176] See *Epíst. Inv.*, esp. part i, chap. 5, 'Pruevase por sus decretos la Divinidad de la Sagrada Escritura.'

[177] Ibid., MS Paris, p. 710: 'Ni és lo mismo creer lo que no se vee que creer contra lo que se vee . . .'

[178] Ibid., p. 731: 'Todo es digno de la Providencia del Criador, todo conforme a razon natural y prudente govierno, y, consiguientemente, digno de absoluta credulidad y de que, en su confirmacion, hiziese Dios los milagros y portentos que refiere, aunque a nuestro juizio sean dificiles; y seria barbaridad y contra toda philosophia aprehenderlos por impossibles . . . No puede imaginarse cosa mas irracional ni dictamen tan opuesto al sano discurso ni tan sacrilego sentir de la Sabiduria y Omnipotencia Divina.'

creator-god on the basis of rational proof.[179] He reaches the same conclusion as that reached by Pascal in the *Pensées*, that one cannot know that God exists and acts except by means of Scripture: 'all those who, in the past, have so believed, as well as those who do so now, even though they may give grounds for their belief in other religious systems, in fact received [their faith] from what is recounted in the sacred writings'.[180]

A crucial issue which constituted a bone of contention for Orobio and Prado was the question of the election of Israel by God. Prado found insuperable difficulties in coming to terms with the belief that Israel is God's chosen people, and that God did not vouchsafe knowledge of his unity to mankind as a whole.[181] Orobio's choice of language gives us to understand that Prado held that Israel's Torah is not, from the point of view of the Deity, unique, or any better than the religious teachings of other peoples, since

> God granted similar revelations to various peoples who lived and continued to practise pagan rites. Sublime prophecies were communicated to the people of Rome, foretelling future events with an accuracy that deserves respect. Amongst the savages of New Spain, in particular in the [royal] court of Mexico, there was an ancient tradition telling how white men with beards would one day come, bringing with them utter destruction. Montezuma, the last emperor of the said kingdom, had dreams in which he saw the approaching end of his sovereign rule with a circumstantiality corresponding exactly to his own subsequent factual experience, and he consequently strove to ward off [destruction] by the inhuman offering of human sacrifices in order to appease his false gods. All this happened long before the Spaniards had reached those seas, and before they even knew anything of the landfalls which they had never imagined existed. That is why the people of Israel are no less entitled to the same providential care on the part of the Creator, but without implication of any superiority, and without the divine sanctity which they attribute to their Law and which Scripture attributes to them.[182]

As against this critique advanced by Prado, it is precisely in the election of Israel that Orobio finds God's justice demonstrated. That

---

[179] Ibid., part i, chap. 11, and esp. p. 751: 'Luego, dando este credito absoluto ynfallible a los hombres, se da necessariamente a la Sagrada Escritura que fue el unico medio para el cierto conocimiento desta verdad...'

[180] Ibid.: '...y quantos la han creydo y creen, aunque sea con pretexto de varias religiones, lo han recivido por las noticias que ha dado el Sacro Texto...'

[181] Ibid., p. 721: 'Pregunta la vana curiosidad de los impios por que el Criador no comunico a todos los hombres del Universo el conocimiento de su Unidad, evitando los errores y falsas opiniones a que se persuadió la fragilidad del humano juicio?'

[182] Ibid., pp. 738 f.

election is not sheer arbitrary favouritism; had God done otherwise than grant knowledge of his unity exclusively to the Jews, his own attribute of justice would have been impaired, since the Jews alone had been found fit, in virtue of their actions and their way of life, for that act of grace. 'God granted Abraham the supernatural merit of recognizing his uniqueness, and assured him of the transmission of such recognition to his descendants as a consequence of [Abraham's] merits.'[183] The Creator of the cosmos did not withhold from other peoples knowledge of the miracles which He had performed for Israel: but those peoples did not infer God's unity from those miracles, since 'in their blindness they believed in a plurality of gods'.[184] It was Israel alone that had behind it the merits of the patriarchs, and it was to them alone that God revealed himself without any intermediate agency. It was 'the people of Israel alone, who [already] in remote antiquity [when they were sunk deep] in ignorance, accepted a Law so holy, so intelligible, so well and perfectly matched with reason, so capable of subduing the evil impulse and blind ignorance'.[185] Israel, and no other people, merited 'this crown of perfection and supreme happiness'.[186]

The trend of Orobio's argument—throwing into relief the sublimity of Israel, and emphasizing on its superiority over other peoples—can also be sensed in the writings of Orobio's Sephardi contemporaries. The idea of Israel as the chosen people is of course as old as Israel itself, but a careful study of this literature will reveal expressions, a *façon de parler*, and a realm of ideas amazingly similar to what is found in Spanish literature of the same period. Let us take a few examples. Imperialist Spain, which had brought Christianity to the distant quarters of the globe, the power famed for its fight against heresy at home and abroad, saw in itself the heir of the chosen people of biblical times.[187] Her decline in the seventeenth century, so far from weakening this sense of superiority, actually intensified in various Spanish circles faith in the mission that was theirs by birth, to constitute the standard bearers of Catholic Christianity.[188] '[God] gave a promise to

---

[183] Ibid., pp. 722 f.

[184] Ibid., p. 723: 'No se ocultaron a las gentes de aquellas edades los portentos executados en favor del Pueblo Hebreo ni los desconocian de sobrenaturales, antes los confessavan efectos de un Dios poderoso; mas no inferian destas prodigiosas señales la Unidad de Dios, porque estavan en la ciega intelligencia de la multiplicidad de deidades...'

[185] Ibid., p. 755.   [186] Ibid., p. 745.

[187] See A. Castro, *Aspectos*, pp. 21 f.   [188] See Méchoulan, *Alterité juive*, pp. 50 f.

Doubt and Certainty

his chosen people in the written law; their successors in the matter of grace are the Spanish people.' So a Spanish author, writing in 1619, who endeavours to prove 'the almost total parallel between the two peoples'.[189] The idea was a common one in Spain, very much so at the period of acute crisis that marked the reign of Philip IV. A number of books written during those years carry titles such as 'the outstanding qualities [*excelencias*] of the Spanish kingdom', or 'Spain's outstanding qualities', and are stamped with a missionary spirit of national purpose expressed in terms of the Spaniard's heritage as God's elect.[190] And just so, when in 1679 Isaac Cardoso—Isaac Orobio's contemporary, and, like him, a crypto-Jew from the Iberian peninsula who had reverted to Judaism and settled in Verona—published a volume consisting entirely of an encomium of Israel as the chosen people, the title that he gave to it was *Las Excelencias de los Hebreos*. The similarity between Cardoso's book and the books devoted to Spanish *excelencias*—similarities of both concept and content— leaps to the eye.[191]

Another example is most instructive. The Spain with which we are dealing was surrounded by a fiery wall of messianism and religious purpose; and in this context the question of unsullied Christian descent became a social issue of the first importance. Such an origin meant, of course, membership of a Christian family of long standing, including neither in its pedigree nor in its living representatives the slightest hint of the presence of 'New Christians' of Jewish origin. The scions of the original chosen people came to be held of low account, and indeed in contempt, by the self-styled successors to their elected status—those Spaniards of uncompromised Christian descent who were carrying the Christian gospel to the world at large. By his own links with Judaism, the 'New Christian', or 'Portuguese', the descendant of Jews forced into crypto-Judaism, endangered the Christian integrity of Spanish society, an integrity which was held to be an indispensable condition of its messianic mission. Thus it comes about that

---

[189] See Juan de Salazar, *Política española*, Logroño, 1619, p. 79: 'Promessa hecha a su pueblo escogido en la ley escrita; cuyo sucessor es el Español pueblo, en la de gracia . . .'; and p. 82: 'Y con este pie entraré a probar mi intento, que es mostrar la similitud casi total de estos dos pueblos . . .'

[190] See G. López Madera, *Excelencias de la Monarquía y Reino de España*, Madrid, 1625; Fray Benito de Peñalosa y Mondragón, *Libro de las cinco excelencias del español*, etc. Pamplona, 1629.

[191] See Yerushalmi, *Isaac Cardoso*, pp. 352 f., and (pp. 357 f.) the comparison of Cardoso's book with the Spanish works mentioned in the previous note.

in the sixteenth and seventeenth centuries the category of 'purity of blood' (*pureza de sangre*) becomes a principle yardstick in establishing a 'good name' (*honra*); and efforts to prove title to such purity are one of the most prominent sociological features of Spanish society of the period.[192] Menasseh ben Israel knew, from his ancestors' experience, the importance of 'purity of blood' in the assessment by the indigenous population of every country of a nation alien to itself, and in his *Humble Address* to Oliver Cromwell in 1655 he wrote: 'Three things ... there are that make a strange nation well-beloved amongst the natives of a land where they dwell ... Profit ... Fidelity ... and the Nobleness and purity of their blood ...' At the end of his letter he again emphasizes that the 'nobility' of the Jews 'is well known amongst all Christians'.[193] Isaac Cardoso, in his book referred to above, likewise indicates that 'the Hebrews are, in point of stock, noble in a particular degree.'[194] There is no doubt that the language of Menasseh ben Israel, Cardoso, and others who write in a similar vein was directed at controverting claims which, during their life as crypto-Jews, they had heard being advanced in the Iberian peninsula. As against the *excelencias* of the Spanish and their mission they emphasized the *excelencias* of the Jews, and their divinely ordained purpose; and as against the 'purity of Christian blood' they brought to the fore the nobility of Israel's lineage.

This is the background against which Orobio's zeal in advocating the idea of the election of Israel must be understood. Like Cardoso and other Sephardim who had observed, during their crypto-Jewish period, how their persecutors were usurping the privilege of being God's elect, Orobio set himself to restore the crown to its pristine state, and the title to election to those who had originally borne it.

It will now be clear that Prado's antipathy to the notion of Israel's election had its basis in his crypto-Jewish past, its roots lying hidden in the historical situation of Spain in the days of her decline. Her loss of standing as a great power caused surprise and self-questioning in some of the best Spanish minds. These thinkers opposed the messianism and fiery mysticism that had become an encumbrance on Iberian society, and regarded them, along with discrimination against 'New Christians', as the main cause of the decline of their country. In contrast to those who were descanting on the *excelencias* of Spain and

---

[192] See A. Castro, *Edad Confl.*, pp. 55 f.
[193] Menasseh b. Israel, *Addr.*, ff. 1, 23.
[194] Cardoso, *Excel.*, p. 364.

Doubt and Certainty 175

her people, these thinkers were arguing for the 'triumph of disillusionment' (*desengaño*).[195] In their view, it was not the descendants of Jews that had brought about Spain's degeneration, nor was it they who imperilled her future. The roots of Spain's decline were intertwined with her very reluctance to let herself assimilate the Jews or the Moors, and in repugnance for any profession or type of work that carried a Jewish or Moorish identity-tag.[196] It was this standoffishness that had turned Spain into a nation of lounge-lizards, or, in the words of the *licenciado* Martín González de Cellorigo (one of the most important of those calling for economic reform at the beginning of the seventeenth century), into a 'republic of the bewitched, living outside reality'.[197] For these writers 'disillusionment' signified the exposure of Spanish delusions of grandeur and the shaking off of xenophobia. 'In all the world there are but two realms: the land of the good, and the land of the evil. All good people, be they Jews, Moors, pagans, Christians, or members of any other sect, belong to the realm of the good, sharing one house and one blood: and *mutatis mutandis* the evil.'[198]

Obviously this criticism found a sympathetic ear in many 'New Christians', who sometimes added their own voice to that of those calling for *desengaño*. Naturally enough, their demands (which meant, *inter alia*, a call for a new attitude towards descendants of crypto-Jewish families) gave expression to the yearnings of many of the 'New Christians' themselves, who hoped for a cancellation of the ordinances regarding purity of blood. Some of these, on leaving the Iberian peninsula and joining up with the Jewish community, found difficulty in accepting a belief in Israel as the chosen people—something which, for them, contradicted completely the spirit of *desengaño*. Such was the case with Prado. For him, the notion of the election of Israel smacked of that Spanish self-aggrandizement of whose zeal he had himself been a victim. And when he fell foul of the congregational leadership which marched out to do battle with him and his opinions, he did not hesitate to compare their behaviour to the Inquisition in Spain, even saying

---

[195] *Triunfo del desengaño* was the title of the book by P. Matute printed in Naples in 1632. On *desengaño* as a theme in Spanish literature see P. E. Russell, 'Spanish Literature (1494–1681)', in Russell, pp. 312 f., 335. Cf. Méchoulan, *Alterité juive*, part 2, pp. 189 f.

[196] See A. Castro, *Edad Confl.*, esp. pp. 153 f.

[197] See M. Gonzáles de Cellorigo, *Memorial de la política necesaria y útil restauración a la república de España*, Valladolid, 1660, f. 25: 'Una república de hombres encantados que viven fuera del orden natural' and cf. Révah, *M. González de Cellorigo*, pp. 279–398.

[198] F. Furió Ceriol, *Concejo y consejeros del Príncipe*, Antwerp, 1559, f. 41ʳ.

(whether ironically or in a fit of pique) 'these Jews seem to want to run an inquisition'.[199]

In the disavowal of the notion of election, Prado's rejectionism once again meshes in with the thinking of Spinoza, whose *Tractatus Theologico-Politicus* includes a special chapter entitled 'concerning the election of the Hebrews; and whether the gift of prophecy was unique to them'.[200] There Spinoza maintains that 'the Hebrew people was not chosen by God above the remainder of the peoples from an intellectual point of view, nor from the point of view of spiritual contentment: but rather from the point of view of society, and of that chance whereby it achieved its sovereignty and maintained it over the course of many years'.[201] For him, 'the Hebrews, despite frequent warnings, were not chosen by God over all other peoples for a life of truth and for sublimity of thought',[202] but 'for temporal prosperity of the body, for freedom, and for dominion'.[203] God's providential care of Israel, and his involvement in their history, were due to negative causes only: 'Moses having recognized his people's character and their stubborn spirit, clearly saw that they would not ever be able to complete what they had begun to do, without portents and especial help, of an extraneous kind, from God, and that without such help they would indeed perish.'[204] And election in even this limited sense was of temporary validity only. 'God did not choose the Hebrew people absolutely, nor in perpetuity.'[205] Consistently with his claim that the election of Israel 'related to nothing save dominion and physical advantage ... whereas from the point of view of the intellect or of true perfection no one people is different from another',[206] Spinoza declares that 'there is no doubt that the other peoples, too, had their prophets, just as the Jews had, who prophesied both to them and to the Jews'.[207] Although he had been born in Amsterdam, Spinoza had intimate knowledge of the tribulations and experiences of those members of his congregation who had been the victims of the Spanish Inquisition's fiery zeal. His chapter 'On the election of the Jews' closes with examples taken from Iberian history of his own time. When he comes to prove that it is anti-Semitism which is responsible for maintaining Jewry in existence, he

[199] See above, p. 139.
[200] Hamburg edn., chap. 3, 1670, pp. 30–43; Eng. trans. by R. H. M. Elwes (*Chief Works*), London, 1883, i, pp. 43 f.   [201] Ibid.; Eng. trans. p. 46.
[202] Ibid., p. 34; Eng. trans. p. 44   [203] Ibid., p. 37; Eng. trans. p. 48.
[204] Ibid., p. 40; Eng. trans. p. 52.   [205] Ibid., p. 42; Eng. trans. p. 55.
[206] Ibid., p. 43; Eng. trans. p. 56.   [207] Ibid., p. 38; Eng. trans. p. 50.

finds it apposite to contrast the fate of Spanish crypto-Jews who had (so he says) assimilated in Spanish society thanks to the liberal attitude shown towards them by the government, with that of the crypto-Jews of Portugal, 'who have always lived cut off from others, the king having disallowed their eligibility for any position of honour'.[208] Without entering into the correctness of this comparison, which will not stand up to an examination of the historical facts, what is important for us is Spinoza's laying down as a matter of principle that open attitudes and tolerance have the power to bring about a fraternal intermingling of separate social groups, whereas exclusiveness and ideas of grandeur that disqualify individuals and groups from 'all positions of honour' sow the seeds of divisiveness, and cause the triumph of alienation. What Spinoza has to say is in harmony with the spirit of what the Spanish political thinker Fernández de Navarrete wrote in 1621: '... I am convinced that were we to search out ways to furnish [Jews and *moriscos*] with some part of the positions of honour before they conclude that things are hopeless and turn to evil devices, instead of compelling them to wear the badge of shame, it is possible that they would enter through the portal of honour into the palace of good qualitites, and into the society of those loyal to the Catholic Church.'[209]

To sum up. The contrasting positions of Juan de Prado and of Isaac Orobio in regard to the election of Israel are no more than the diverging reactions of two ex-crypto-Jews to that Spanish ideology which had led Spain to confer on herself the position of the nation chosen by superior providence to lead the world towards that redemption for

[208] Ibid., p. 43; Eng. trans. p. 56.
[209] Fernández Navarrete, *Conservación de Monarquías*, Madrid, 1626, p. 72. Similar views were already being expressed in the 15th cent. by Alonso de Cartagena, son of the apostate Pablo de Santa María, Bishop of Burgos, alias Rabbi Solomon Ha-levi; see Beinart, *Inquisición*, pp. 16 f. The 'cult' of *desengaño* is to be linked with the revival of Stoic thought in the 16th and 17th cents., and the growing interest in the writings of Seneca both in Spain and in Europe generally; see Gay, pp. 295–304. Cf. Orobio's remarks, addressed to Prado in *Cart. Apol.*, MS Paris (see above n. 107), p. 900: 'Los Senecas, los Plinios, los Tacitos, y muchos de esta clase, son mis amigos para algunas noticias ... como no se gaste mal el tiempo, ay tiempo para todo y mas para mi; que, aunque no soy moroso ni melancholico, me distraen muy poco o ningun tiempo ...' The irony in this rejoinder was intended to taunt Prado who had, apparently, embraced these writers all too enthusiastically, and was not backward in citing from them. See David Prado's letter to the lay leadership of the Portuguese community (see above, n. 82), p. 10, '... diziendo con Séneca ...' (Révah failed to recognize this name, and in his *Rupture Spinozienne*, p. 398, he printed Semea(?)). See also the continuation, '... que no se ensoberbeció en las prosperidades ny se desmayó en los trabajos comformandose con todo con la boluntad del altiss[i]mo ...'

which it was yearning. This ideology legitimized, as it were, the persecution of 'New Christians' and their descendants in the Iberian peninsula, leading to discrimination against them and to their being burned at the stake. Prado reacted by rejecting absolutely the very notion of election, as introducing discrimination between peoples. In this he was undoubtedly falling in behind the standard-bearers of *desengaño* in contemporary Spain. Orobio's reaction was the opposite. Against the braggartly pretensions of Spanish messianism, which regarded the Spanish people as the heirs of the Hebrew people of antiquity, Orobio inscribed his banner with the device of the election of Israel, the force of which had never dissipated, since 'in order for [that election] to be preserved in perpetuity [God] gave them the Law'.[210] In Orobio's view it was those who fulfilled the holy Law who preserved the covenant which God made with Abraham, who have the title—in perpetuity—to the status of the elect.[211]

[210] *Epíst. Inv.*, MS Paris, p. 722.
[211] Ibid., p. 725: 'Solo se entendio este misericordioso privilegio, sin lesion de la justicia, con los que perseverassen como Abraham en el credito de la Unidad de Dios ... Estos merecen ser mantenidos de la Divina Providencia ...'

7
Philosopher, Communal Leader, Physician

RAYMOND LULL'S PHILOSOPHY DEBATED

In 1663, just when Isaac Orobio was completely absorbed in his disputation with Juan de Prado, there reached him in Amsterdam a book that had been published in Brussels in the same year. This was a Spanish translation of the *Arbor Scientiæ* (or, in the original Catalan, *Arbre de ciencia*) of the Franciscan theologian Raymond Lull (1232?–1316).[1] The translator was don Alonso de Zepeda,[2] a Spanish officer with a reputation as a military engineer, who resided in Flanders as *gobernador* of the Tolhuis. Zepeda was a distinguished follower of Lull's religious philosophy, which was much talked about at that period in intellectual circles in Brussels. There, in 1661, Pedro de Guevara's two books had been reprinted, giving a Spanish summary of Lull's *summa* as set forth in his *Ars Magna* and *Arbor Scientiæ*.[3] Raymond Lull's writings, which had been proscribed in the fourteenth century by Emeric, the Grand Inquisitor of the kingdom of Aragon, enjoyed a rehabilitation in the reign of the Catholic Sovereigns, who

---

[1] On Lull see Platzeck, and J. Sáiz Barbera, *Raimundo Lulio, genio de la Filosofía y mística española*, Madrid, 1963. On the possible link between his mystical system and the cabbala as developed by the Jews of Spain see J. M. Millás Vallicrosa, 'The Doctrine of the Lullian Dignities and the *Sephiroth*', *I. F. Baer Jubilee Volume*, Jerusalem, 5721 (1961), pp. 186–90 (Hebrew: Eng. summary, p. xv). Such connection is denied absolutely in a review by R. J. Z. Werblowsky, who is inclined to see a common background of the two in Neoplatonism, *Tarbiz*, 32, 5723 (1963), pp. 207–11.

[2] See Ramón Lull, *Arbol de la Ciencia de el Iluminado Maestro Raymundo Lulio*, Nuevamente traducido y explicado por el Teniente de Maestro de Campo General Don Alonzo de Zepeda y Adrada, Governador de el Thol-huys, etc., Brussels, 1663. Another edition, with a modified title-page, appeared in 1664. The work is exceedingly rare, but I have located a copy in the Royal Library at Brussels: see Peeters-Fontainas, pp. 400 f. In 1660 Zepeda held the office of Ayudante de Sargento General de Batalla, and in that same year he published proposals for the improvement of the Ostend docks (*Sobre el Remedio de el Puerto de Ostende*). He was promoted Teniente de Maestro de Campo General as early as 1669, the year in which there appeared his manual on up-to-date military engineering (*Epítome de la Fortificación Moderna*). See Peeters-Fontainas, pp. 714 f.

[3] See Rogent and Durán, pp. 202 f. De Guevara's books, *Arte general para todas las ciencias, en dos instrumentos*, and *Breve y sumaria declaración de la arte general*, both first appeared in Madrid in 1584.

not only tolerated but actively encouraged the study of his works in Spanish universities.[4] This process of rehabilitation reached its zenith at the time of Philip III and Philip IV, who likewise lent support to the proposal of P. Virgilio to secure the canonization of the Majorcan-born thinker.[5] The causes of the revival of Lull's theological and philosophical heritage are still insufficiently clear. Possibly the missionary spirit that pervaded the manifold branches of Lull's many-sided writings had cast their spell on many Spaniards, who were also attracted by the esotericism of mystical communion that they contain. It should, however, be noted that opposition to Lull's views continued, even at the time of this reawakened interest. Dominicus Báñez, a Dominican (1528–1604), and the Jesuits Gabriel Vásquez (1549–1604) and Francisco Suárez (1548–1617)—both of whom taught at Alcalá, where Orobio himself was a student in the 1630s—exposed the inadmissability of important parts of Lull's system, which could not be harmonized with certain concepts stressed in the Thomistic scholasticism that still dominated most of the universities of Spain.[6]

There is no doubt that don Alonso de Zepeda was the leading light amongst those in Flanders in the second half of the seventeenth century who, stirred by interest in Lull, were responsible for the revival. In a supplement to his translation of the *Arbor Scientiæ* to which he added explanatory notes of his own, he also included a Spanish translation of the *Liber Conceptionis Virginalis*: and there are grounds for supposing that it was on his initiative that Guevara's books mentioned above were republished.[7]

In the year of the publication of the translation of the *Arbor Scientiæ* Zepeda met Alonso Escudero in Brussels. Escudero was a Spanish actor who had converted to Judaism in Amsterdam and had adopted the name of Abraham Israel. He had been invited to the Flemish capital at the time of the festivities for the marriage of the Emperor Leopold and Margarita María, daughter of Philip IV and Marianne of Austria.[8] It seems likely that Zepeda exploited the opportunity to try to

[4] On Emeric's opposition to Lullianism see Madre, pp. 71 f., 107 f.; for the view adopted by Ferdinand and Isabella see *Dictionnaire de Théologie Catholique*, ix, Paris, 1926, col. 1138.
[5] Ibid., col. 1134.
[6] Madre, pp. 85 f., 109 f.
[7] R. Lull, *Libro de la Concepción Virginal, etc.* y traducido en Español por ... Don Alonzo de Zepeda, Brussels, 1664. The book appeared in the same year at Palma (Majorca) as well, but the title-page of that edition makes reference to the Brussels press from which the other was issued ('Brusselas, En casa de Balthazar Vivien'). See Peeters-Fontainas, pp. 400 f.
[8] See Kaplan, *Escudero*.

persuade Escudero to return to the bosom of the Church, and also lent him, with this object in view, a copy of his new translation, hoping that a study of it might influence him. Escudero had not sufficient interest in the things of the mind, nor indeed was he of adequate intellectual calibre for the task that had been set him. Lull's complex terminology was beyond him, but the actor from Seville, being aware of his own shortcomings, did not lose his head. He made clear, with pride, that within his congregation at Amsterdam there was someone completely capable of refuting Zepeda's claims and Lull's teaching. Zepeda, having heard of Escudero's challenge, had him bring a copy of his translation to Amsterdam; this reached Isaaac Orobio, the potential controversialist whom Escudero had in mind.[9]

At Alcalá Orobio had received an education founded upon medieval scholasticism, doubtless absorbing the critical attitude towards Lull that prevailed within its walls. Thus he was quite unlikely to be enthusiastic about a Lullian revival.[10] Having read Zepeda's version he composed a short tract entitled *Respuesta a una persona que dudava si el Libro de Raymundo Lulio nuevamente traducido y comentado era intelligible, y si concluyan sus discursos*.[11] In this treatise, which is couched in the form of a letter addressed personally to Escudero, Orobio did not set out to deal with Lull's theology in full. Rather, he chose to rain shattering blows on the way in which Lull had attempted, in accordance with his overall system, to prove the existence of the holy trinity, also questioning the methodological structure on which Lull's philosophy was in general based. Isaac was at pains to avoid involving himself in a theological disputation with Christianity about the trinity. 'It is not [he wrote] my intention to pillory the religious beliefs of others, or by any means to deny them; but merely to indicate the defects in the arguments that drop like windfalls from the Lullian *Tree*, taking it for granted that other classical scholars had different arguments [for the verity of the trinity] which they found convincing.'[12] The style in which Isaac's letter is written is provocative and satirical. He pokes fun at Lull's terminology, and at the obscure abstractions, which he himself regards as superfluous and unhelpful, to be found in the *Arbor Scientiæ*.

[9] Ibid.
[10] For Orobio's attitude towards scholastic philosophy see above, chap. 1, pp. 12 f., and below, chap. 11, pp. 313 f.
[11] Regarding copies of this see below, Appendix E. It was printed in full by Zepeda in his *Defensa de los términos y doctrina de S. Raymundo Lullio*, Brussels, 1666, pp. 2–77, and quotations below are taken thence.
[12] Ibid., p. 15.

'To teach does not mean the concealment of concepts, but the revealing of them to the understanding of others, and this by use of the *mot juste* to give expression to the concept in each case.'[13]

In the same way, Orobio dismisses the practical value of the translation: 'from the circumstance of its being written in Spanish it is to be understood that the book is meant for those who have no Latin, and who will consequently also be without expertise in most of the liberal arts ... Alas! Could there be found such a man as, himself knowing no Latin, logic, physics, or metaphysics, would still be equipped to understand three lines of this book?'[14] Even the translation itself was, in Isaac's eyes, defective: 'for anyone who knows Latin it is written in execrable Spanish, and for those whose knowledge is restricted to Spanish it passes for good Latin'.[15]

In Isaac Orobio's opinion Lull's teaching had been worth nothing even at the time when he put it together, and there was consequently no point in reawakening interest in it. However, 'in the world in which we live the custom has become widespread of publishing books in which certain *soi-disant* presenters of new discoveries scrutinize things written long ago in order to blow the dust off them, and then proceed to fill page after page in which the only thing that is new is [the quality of] the paper'.[16] In contrast to the writings of Origen, Tertullian, Augustine, Jerome, Ambrose, Thomas Aquinas, Duns Scotus, Durand de St Pourçain, Suárez, Vásquez, 'and all the others who achieved fame in the past and whose hold on mortals' attention still keeps their memory green as able teachers who could ease the path of learning for others', there was absolutely nothing worth having in Lull's philosophy.[17] Anyone examining his works 'would find in them many assertions—some of them untenable, others proving nothing except for the long-suffering patience of the reader'.[18]

In his tract Orobio endeavoured to refute the thesis by which Lull claimed to have proved the existence of the holy trinity, and for this purpose he drew attention to the contradictions which, in his view, were to be found in Lull's scheme; this confounded the three persons of the trinity, representing them as attributes of one sole God, existing from eternity and infinite. 'Even if the three attributes of the trinity are identical with the essence of the Godhead (as theologians say that they are) and constitute a single substance, they are not one attribute: it is

[13] Ibid., p. 7. [14] Ibid., p. 9.
[15] Ibid., p. 11. [16] Ibid.
[17] Ibid., p. 13. [18] Ibid., p. 15.

impossible that sonship should be identical with fatherhood, even if the essence of the first [person] is identical with that of the second . . . he ought therefore to have stated that the three persons or attributes of the trinity are of a single divine essence but not a single attribute . . . that, if I am not mistaken, is the position adopted by Christian scholars; nor, indeed, am I mistaken, since all the scholastics [would] assert that what I say is correct.'[19] The terminological confusion in Lull's claim that 'there is plurality in the Godhead' has about it something of the odour of paganism.[20]

Isaac Orobio likewise dismisses Lull's attempt at clarifying all wisdom—including divine wisdom—on the basis of a single, unitary scheme. Divine wisdom is of a discrete quality, and all the characteristics that we, using our human concepts, attribute to the deity by way of analogy are of a quality that is entirely distinct, and not patient of being conceived of by man.[21] Earlier Christian thinkers had not attempted any intellectual proof of the existence of the holy trinity, 'but were content that it should remain an article of faith . . . since it is not derived from the laws of nature, nor has it any consequences from which, by working back *ex post facto*, it might be grasped by our intellect'.[22] He similarly challenges the Lullian doctrine of parallel principles, according to which every concept can be explained as an interconnected triad—the active and passive parties and the action itself; it is these which, in Lull's view, articulate the relationship between God, his creative action, and the content of that action, and within the Godhead itself this triangularity finds expression in the three persons of the trinity—father, son, and holy ghost.[23]

Despite his severe criticism, Isaac found it possible to pay the translator a few compliments—'a great expert, of acute understanding and a

---

[19] Ibid., p. 21.

[20] Ibid., p. 27: '. . . y esta hoja del arbol debiera secarse, pues habla a secas de pluralidad en Dios, haziendo un titulo bueno para aquel tiempo de las muchas deidades, no para el presente de un solo Dios todopoderoso.'

[21] Ibid., p. 29: 'Es asi que a Dios se atribuye el saber por la sabiduria, querer por la voluntad, entender por el entendimiento, ser uno por su unidad; no por que en Dios haya sabiduria, voluntad, entendimiento, unidad, fuera de su divino ser, si, por que discurrimos con Analogia a lo que vemos en las creaturas; por que en Dios su entender, su entendimiento, su voluntad, su querer, y ser, son una misma cosa realmente.'

[22] Ibid., pp. 53 f.

[23] Criticism of the Lullian doctrine permeates the whole tract: see e.g. pp. 17 f., 33 f., 37 f., 49 f., 55 f., 61 f., 67 f. Orobio directed his major criticism at the eighth chapter (in particular at the second part) of the *Arbol de la Ciencia* ('Del Arbre Apostolical'), which Lull completed in Rome in Apr. 1296; see Platzeck, ii. p. 29, and, in Zepeda's trans. (n. 2 above), p. 172.

fine student of metaphysics, who had produced an elegant version'.²⁴ But if it was Zepeda's intention to follow in Lull's missionary footsteps and to win converts for Christianity, he had failed in the task that he had set himself, since 'this teaching [of his] will not give any reader even a moderately competent understanding of the fields of interest of which it treats; nor, as a result of having read it, will any Jew turn Christian or any heretic turn Catholic.'²⁵ Lull's undertaking had been extremely ambitious: 'it has never been possible to compress so many departments of knowledge into so small an amount of paper . . . in fine, it was the *Tree* in paradise alone that could teach [the difference between] good and evil, whereas Lull's teaches neither'.²⁶ Isaac concludes his brief tract with some words of apology: 'may I be pardoned for [any] errors I have committed, having taken upon myself the role of theologian, although being but a mere layman in cloak and sword'.²⁷

In a piece written by the poet Daniel Levi (Miguel) de Barrios there is a hint that it was he who translated into Spanish a book against Zepeda, written by Isaac Orobio himself in Latin.²⁸ It seems probable that the reference is to this tract, which excited considerable interest in Amsterdam and Brussels amongst circles concerned with philosophical topics.²⁹ Isaac had been opposed to sending what he had written to the Flemish capital because of its satirical style, but his opposition was of no avail. Some four months later it came into Zepeda's hands, apparently via Lorenzo Escudero, who himself added a short letter thereto.³⁰ Zepeda, who composed a rejoinder forthwith, addressed his

²⁴ See Zepeda's *Defensa* (n. 11 above), p. 75.
²⁵ Ibid.: ' . . . mas la doctrina a ninguno hara, aun mediocremente noticioso de las materias que promete, ni de judio christiano, ni de Herege Catholico . . .' For Lull's missionary activity see Baer, *History*, pp. 185, 417 f., and Werblowsky (see above, n. 1). See Millás Vallicrosa's introd. to the edition of Lull's *Liber prædicationis contra Judæos*, Madrid and Barcelona, 1957.
²⁶ As printed in Zepeda's *Defensa*, pp. 75 f.
²⁷ Ibid., p. 77: ' . . . y supla los desaciertos, que me entremeti a Theólogo, siendo un mero lego de capa y espada'.
²⁸ De Barrios, *Desembozos de Verdad*, p. 8: 'Algunos presumen no hize esta octava, que traygo en principio de mi Harmonia del Mundo: porque no tuve los estudios que el Doctor Orovio a quien la atribuyen. Nacio esta presuncion de trasladarle yo un libro que hizo contra D. Alonso de Cepeda . . .'
²⁹ See Orobio, *Resp. al Zep.*, MS Amsterdam, EH 48 A 12, f. 111ʳ: 'Este papelejo anduvo por ai algunas semanas y curiosos le leian por entretenimiento'.
³⁰ Ibid.: ' . . . pidi que no fuese a Bruselas porque estava algo satirico, despues io no se quando se remitio, pesome y olvidelo'. Cf. Zepeda's own statement in his introd., *Defensa* (unpaginated): 'y haviendosse passado casi quatro meses, me escribio la carta, y embió los escritos subgeto deste libro'.

long and detailed response (dated 28 July 1663) to Escudero, and had it delivered to him through the good offices of don Esteban de Gamarra, the Spanish Ambassador at The Hague.[31] It comprised a sharp attack on Orobio and on the attitude that he had adopted towards Lull's achievements. Although Zepeda conceded that Isaac 'showed himself to be a competent philosopher and familiar with the doctrine taught in Catholic schools, in regard to Raymond Lull he understood not one word'.[32] He repeatedly stigmatizes Isaac's composition as being a mere sheet of paper (*papelejo*), and complains that despite his declared intention to avoid the scoring of points against any religious system, he nevertheless does inveigh against the Christian religion:[33]

If he cannot understand the *Tree*, is it I, don Lorenzo, who am at fault? Moreover, despite being himself a scholar, he goes along with those empty-heads who insist that [the study of] the sciences cannot be prosecuted, nor can they be expounded, save in Latin. But, I ask, if Latin had been the language in which such scholarly studies were conducted in the distant past, there might have been some logical foundation for his claim. It is, however, well known that the sciences came to the Egyptians from the Chaldeans, from the Egyptians to the Greeks, and from the Greeks to the Latins, each of which translated them into their mother-tongue. In this day all the peoples of Europe do likewise, and methinks that we men of Spain are entitled to enjoy this same privilege.[34]

Zepeda proceeded to describe the chain of events in regard to the view taken of Lull's works in Europe after their condemnation, in order to prove that scholars of international stature and not a few crowned heads had regarded them with respect and had indeed promoted their study.[35] He further endeavoured to show that Lull's teaching does not

---

[31] *Resp. al Zep.* (see above, n. 29): 'A que respondi con la brevedad que pude. Y por medio del Excelentissimo Señor Don Estevan de Gamarra, Embajador de su Magestad a las Provincias Unidas, procure se entregase en mano propia de la tal persona . . .'

[32] Ibid., pp. 79 f.; 'Respuesta de D. Alonzo de Zepeda a las cartas y questiones susodichas que le remitio el dicho Lorenço Escudero y otros de la Synagoga, a quienes la remitio el Autor'; p. 81: 'no obstante que en el modo de proponer descubre ser Philosopho y versado en la doctrina de las escuelas Catholicas: pero en la de Raymundo Lulio . . . no entiende palabra'; p. 297: '. . . que aun que el Respondiente es gran Philosopho, Theologo y Metaphisico, que no entiende ny una sola hoja de el Arbol de Raymundo Lullio . . .'

[33] Ibid., p. 83: '. . . y esse Cavallero, que en el suyo supone no ser su intento impugnar religion alguna, quando sus obras y escritos dicen lo contrario . . .' Throughout his treatise Zepeda refrains from mentioning Orobio by name, referring to him as *el Respondiente*: see pp. 85, 91, 101, etc.

[34] Ibid., p. 105.

[35] Ibid., pp. 107 f.

essentially diverge from classical philosophy, but that few only had plumbed its meaning.[36] As against this, Zepeda was at pains to substantiate his own assertions by appeal to the positive stance towards Lull taken by philosophers of the hermetic school.[37] The book ends with an emotional address to Lorenzo Escudero, in which Zepeda expressed the hope that his response would lead him back from the edge of the abyss towards which he was hurtling, into the bosom of the Church.[38]

Isaac Orobio did not rush to reply. It is possible that the *Ma'amad* of the Congregation *Talmud Torah* persuaded him to discontinue the debate which, in their view, was liable to take on the form of a Jewish–Christian disputation—something with which they would have been out of sympathy. Or Isaac may himself have reached the conclusion that there was no point in getting involved in battle royal over the religious philosophy of Lull, which he had never in his life taken very seriously. But Zepeda construed Orobio's silence otherwise. When two years had elapsed without his having received a reply he decided to reopen the polemic spontaneously, suspecting that the Jews of Amsterdam might have prevented the circulation of his rejoinder to Orobio, and might be preening themselves that the latter's tract had been allowed to go unanswered from the Catholic side.[39] He consequently resolved to publish all the constituent parts of the disputation, and in 1666 there appeared in Brussels his *Propugnatio Terminorum et Doctrinæ Illuminati Doctoris Beati Raymundo Lullii . . .*[40] Orobio's short tract is consequently included, as is also Zepeda's response sent to Amsterdam, preceded by a dedication to the holy trinity and an introduction, in which he sets out a detailed account of the development of

---

[36] Ibid., pp. 113 f., 291 f.

[37] Ibid., pp. 137 f., 291 f., 295 f.

[38] Ibid., pp. 297 f.: 'Dichoso vuestra M. si sabe aprovecharse de la ocasion: y reconociendo la seguridad y certeza de nuestra Fée, retrocede de el precipicio, a que va corriendo por sus pasos voluntarios . . .'

[39] Ibid., introd. (see above, n. 30): '. . . se han passado dos años sin que me hayan respondido, y que pueden ocultando mi respuesta divulgar entre los de su gremio, que los Catholicos no havemos podido responder a sus errores, ny yo defender la doctrina de Raymundo Lullio.'

[40] See above, n. 11, for the Spanish title; Peeters-Fontainas, pp. 715 f.; Rogent and Durán, pp. 213 f. Copies of the book, which is rare, are to be found in Paris BN, Madrid BN, in the library of the Benedictines at Monserrat (Catalonia), and the private library of J. Peeters-Fontainas in Louvain. I have been unable to inspect copies located in Majorca. An engraved portrait of Zepeda appears at the beginning (missing in the Paris copy), regarding which see below, Appendix A. Sáiz Barbera (n. 1 above), p. 863, attributes the book in its entirety to Alonso Escudero.

Philosopher, Communal Leader, Physician 187

the polemic; a letter of apology addressed to the Marqués de Carracena, whom Zepeda had consulted at various stages; and the letter of Lorenzo Escudero mentioned above. Each item, including Isaac Orobio's tract, was printed by Zepeda in Spanish with an accompanying Latin translation,[41] presumably by way of rebutting Isaac's claim that Zepeda possessed inadequate control of the language.

On reading the book and discovering that Zepeda accused him of failing to understand Lull's system and of having slithered out of continuing the discussion, Orobio wrote a treatise in which he repeated, with enlarged detail, his charge-sheet of criticisms levelled at the *Arbor Scientiæ*, and replied to the counter-objections which had been advanced by Zepeda. The title of his piece is *Respuesta Apologética al libro que escrivió Don Alonso de Zepeda que intituló Defensa de los términos y doctrina de Raymundo Lulio*: it was never printed, although a number of copies were circulated in manuscript,[42] and it met with a positive reception in certain Christian circles in Brussels and Antwerp, where it won for Orobio quite a reputation.[43] The provocative tone has not disappeared. 'Some months having passed [sc. since the first letter had been dispatched to Brussels], there reached me a lengthy screed [*papelón*][44] directed against my short paper [*papelito*] ... which [Zepeda] did me the kindness to print, I venture to hope that he will do likewise with this treatise of mine, seeing that my superiors will not authorize me [to publish] it...'[45]

The treatise is divided into eight investigations (*escrutinios*), each containing a number of separate articles. As in his previous contribution, Orobio forbore from attacking the principles of Christianity and contented himself with invalidating the line of argument by which Lull and Zepeda had attempted to prove the essential reality of the holy trinity.

A nominalist cast of mind, such as that possessed by Isaac, was

---

[41] It is not clear whether the Latin text is Orobio's own original, which was put into Spanish by de Barrios (see p. 227), or whether it is a re-translation into Latin, by Zepeda himself, from the Spanish version.

[42] For a census of the codices see below, Appendix E.

[43] See MS Amsterdam, *EH* 48 D 6 f. 325ᵛ: '... fue aplaudido en Brusselas y Amberes de los jesuytas y muchos hombres Doctos ...'

[44] Orobio refers to Zepeda's tract as a *papelón*—a term with pejorative overtones—in allusion to Zepeda's own use of the diminutive *papelejo* (used disparagingly) to describe Orobio's own letter to Escudero.

[45] MS Amsterdam, *EH* 48 A 12, f. 111ᵛ: 'Pasados algunos meses vino un gran papelon contra el papelito ... pues me hiço caridad de imprimirlo y lo mismo espero que haga con este pues aca mis maiores no me dieron lisencia para ello ...'

unable to entertain the esoteric metaphysical construction and the complicated methodological system devised by Lull. He therefore launched himself into an attack on Lullian science, endeavouring to demonstrate that 'it is neither art nor science, as he claims that it is' (part i, art. 1),[46] and that his attempt to find support for it in Aristotle is fundamentally faulted (part ii, art. 2).[47] It is once again the discussion of the essential meaning of the holy trinity in Lull's thought that occupies pride of place in the treatise. Orobio denies the christological exegesis which Zepeda had adduced for various biblical texts (part iv, arts. 1–4),[48] and holds up to scorn the analogies which Lull and Zepeda purported to find between God and man (part v).[49] Zepeda's attachment to the stream of hermetic tradition likewise invites disassociation on the part of Isaac, who in the final article (part viii, art. 3) castigates blind faith in the utility attributed to chemical processes.[50]

One of the latest transcripts of this treatise, copied by Abraham Machorro in Amsterdam in 1707, contains a supplement bearing the title *Discurso sobre la Trinidad*.[51] This piece comprises an onslaught on Christian trinitarianism of unparalleled ferocity of language. Analysis of both content and style of this supplement leave me in no doubt that it is the product of Orobio's pen. Isaac had been careful to avoid attacking the principles of Christianity in his two treatises against Zepeda, which were aimed (at least in part) at a Christian public. But he felt obliged to clarify his position on the subject to the Jewish community.[52] His scholarship, and his considerable expertise in the more esoteric aspects of Christian theology, must have made its impact

[46] 'Escrutinio Primero, Discurso primero: Trata como la arte de Lulio no es arte y sciencia como pretende.'
[47] 'Escrutinio Segundo, Discurso segundo: Examinase dos Lugares de Aristoteles en que funda el comentador la defensa de su doctrina.'
[48] 'Escrutinio cuarto que examina los lugares de la sagrada escriptura que alega el comentador para prouar la fecundidad de Dios.'
[49] 'Escrutinio quinto que trata la Analogía entre Dios y las criaturas.'
[50] 'Escrutinio octavo, discurso ultimo: Censurase la grande fee que tiene el Comentador con las operaciones chimicas.' See also below, chap. 11, pp. 319 f., where Orobio's position *vis-à-vis* 'fideistic scepticism' is discussed.
[51] MS Amsterdam, *EH* 48 B 12, pp. 175–90, Fuks–M., *EH*, no. 238, pp. 123 f. The editors, who refer to this section of the MS as 'epilogue', overlooked the fact that it constitutes an independent item.
[52] The connection between this *discurso* and the controversy with Zepeda is palpable from the manner in which it is formulated. Zepeda is in fact mentioned, being referred to anonymously as *el comentador*—the same term by which he is referred to in Orobio's other writing. The *discurso* was not transcribed in the other manuscripts of his *Resp. al Zep.*, no doubt because of sensitivity lest its contents arouse resentment on the part of any Christian reader.

Philosopher, Communal Leader, Physician

on the members of his own community, who had doubtless already come to appreciate his intellectual stature.

COMMUNAL ACTIVITY WITHIN THE PORTUGUESE CONGREGATION

The speed with which Isaac Orobio integrated himself into the Portuguese-Jewish community is eloquent not only of the extent to which the congregation had attuned itself to the social and spiritual absorption of crypto-Jews reverting to Judaism, but also of Isaac's own readiness to play an active part in the communal life of its membership. He did not content himself with activities on the scholarly and spiritual planes alone, but indeed evinced a close interest in everything that went on in the Portuguese community of Amsterdam. The intense energy which, during his first years there, he devoted to theological and philosophical disputation did not get in the way of his involving himself in mundane communal matters. In virtue of his standing in the community as a scholar with a reputation, he was elected to a number of offices in the various ancillary communal institutions, and served as one of the honorary officers of the *Ma'amad* of the Congregation *Talmud Torah*—i.e. the united Portuguese congregation that had been formed from the merger of smaller units in 1639. It appears that the years of his first decade in Amsterdam were the fullest as regards communal activity within the congregation.

The first organization within which Dr Isaac Orobio found a niche for service to the community was the society *Biqqur Ḥolim* which, as its Hebrew name indicates, existed for the visitation of the sick. It had been established on 20 December 1609 (24 *Kislev* 5370) by the first Portuguese congregation in Amsterdam, known as *Beth Jacob*. Its functions included carrying out the religious injunction to visit the sick amongst members without means, the watching over the dead prior to their burial, and the making of funeral arrangements.[53] On 3 April 1639 (28 2 *'Adar* 5399) the three existing congregations (i.e. *Beth Jacob* already referred to, *Neveh Shalom*, and *Beth Israel*) united to form the Congregation *Talmud Torah*, and this involved changes in the constitution of the society: new statutes of 22 May (18 *'Iyyar*) of the same year laid down its executive structure and its functions. Six *parnasim* (officeholders), to be chosen annually on the sabbath in *Ḥanukkah* (during

---

[53] See Silva Rosa, *Geschiedenis*, pp. 22 f., Pieterse, *De Barrios*, pp. 95 f.

December), stood at its head, each of whom directed the society's business for two months. The last *parnas* on the list acted as *parnas da vestiarya*, i.e. he was appointed to supervise the provision of clothing for the congregational poor, this charity falling within the purview of the Society *Biqqur Ḥolim*.[54]

The six *parnasim* elected to preside over the society on 19 December 1664 (2nd day of *Rosh Ḥodesh Ṭebeth* 5425) included Isaac Orobio. Since his name appears second on the list of those newly elected, it may be deduced that his tour of duty as chairman fell in the months of *'Adar* and *Nisan* (March–April);[55] and in fact evidence of his activity during these months is to be found in the congregational ledgers for that year. On 3 March (16 *'Adar*) it was recorded that he owed the congregation 174 florins, this being the total of the offertory money on the foregoing sabbath *Mi kamokha* (or *Zakhor*) preceding the festival of *Purim*.[56] In the society's statutes of 1639 it is laid down that every year on that particular sabbath the offerings should be in aid of this society, the *parnas* whose rota of duty it was holding in his own house the chest (*caixa da despença*) for the dispensing of grants.[57] Although it was for the purposes of the society that the sum offered was collected, Isaac was obliged to hand over the money to the *Ma'amad* of the Congregation

---

[54] See the *Ascamoth (Acta)* of the congregation, Amsterdam, AGA, PA 334 no. 19, pp. 102–4. The bylaws of the confraternity were published by Pieterse, *De Barrios*, App. 25, pp. 175 f. The turn of the last *parnas* on the list to occupy the chair covered the two months *Marḥeshvan–Kislev* (Oct.–Dec.), and that is possibly the reason why he was put in charge of the provision of clothing, in view of the need to make adequate arrangements for the poor during the coming winter.

[55] PA 334 no. 19, p. 544: '5425. Termo de Eleissão de seys Parnasim da Hebra de Bikur [*sic*] Holiym. En 1° de ttebett se juntarão os ss^res do Mahamad con os ss^res Parnasim da Hebra de Bikur Holiym para elexerem outros novos que ajão de servir ditta Hebra este ano seguinte athe Hanuca q[ue] en Hora Boa de 5426 conforme as escamot de ditta Hebra e despoys de aver pratticado sobre as pessoas benemeritas para dita misva sayeeram eleitos por Bussolo e balas os ss^res abaixo nomeados q[ue] lles seja Besimantt[ov]: O S^er Abraham Franco Mendez, Ishac Orobio de Castro dottor, Mosse de Mesquitta, Jacob Semah Fero, Mosse Curiel, Isch. Israel Suasso ttss° da Biestiaria.' See also nos. 155, p. 31; 157, p. 136; 158; p. 153; and MS Amsterdam, *EH* 48 D 36, p. 119. For the two-month term of chairmanship by rota in accordance with an order predetermined by lot, see the constitution referred to in the previous note, Pieterse, *De Barrios*, p. 176: 'É feita a eleyção se meterão os nomes dos 6 ellejtos em hum vaso donde os tirarão por sortes para hirem servindo cada hum 2 mezes successivamente e o ultimo sera o parnas da vestiarya.'

[56] See *Livro Grande*, PA 334 no. 240, f. 191: 'Ishack Orovio de Castro, Parnas da hebra deve em 16 de Adar f. 174 q[u]e rendeo a nedava de o Sabath micamocha p[ar]a a despeza.' See G. Nahon, 'Amsterdam metropoli occidentale dei Sefarditi nel xvii° seculo', *RMI* 49, 1983, p. 178.   [57] See the bylaws, Pieterse, *De Barrios*, p. 178.

Talmud Torah, that body being responsible for the financial administration of all the congregation's ancillary societies. Accordingly on 9 March (22 *'Adar*) David Judah León, the treasurer, received from Orobio the aforesaid sum.[58] In *'Iyyar* (April–May) of that year Isaac received from the treasurer 361 florins and five stuivers.[59] Presumably this corresponds to Isaac's total disbursements in the discharge of his office, on completion of his tour of duty in which he was being reimbursed.[60]

There is no doubt that the foregoing responsibilities gave Isaac the opportunity of getting to know the life of the Portuguese-Jewish community of Amsterdam and its problems from the inside. Daily meetings with those in need, both the indigent and the sick, the arrangement of loans and the visitation of those housebound during the week of mourning, gave him an understanding of the straitened circumstances and the pain afflicting those members of his community who were not beneficiaries of Amsterdam's economic boom. And it would seem that the number of those in this category was by no means small.[61]

His duties in *Biqqur Ḥolim* terminated on 4 December 1665 (26 Kislev 5426), on which date he participated, as an outgoing *parnas* of the society, in the election of six new *parnasim*.[62] Within three years of completing his service as an officer of *Biqqur Ḥolim* he was called to undertake fresh responsibility when on 5 May 1668 (5 *Sivan* 5428) he was elected along with five other members of the congregation a *parnas* for one year of *'Eṣ Ḥayyim* ('the Tree of Life'), i.e. the society concerned with the supervision of religious education (*Talmud*

[58] *Livro Longo*, PA 334 no. 215, p. 99.
[59] Ibid., p. 141.
[60] See the bylaws of 1639, Pieterse, *De Barrios*, pp. 176 f.: 'E no fim de dittos 2 mezes dara sua conta ão gabay da sedaca com todas as recejtas o quel lhe satisfara tudo e que conforme a estas ashamot [sic] ouver despendido. E dara debito na conta da sedaca em huma verba de somma que foor.'
[61] The relevant clauses of the constitution set out in detail the duties of the *parnasim* for the time being; ibid.: 'O parnas que servir desprendera nos seus dous mezes o que for necessario para a cura dos enfermos pobres ... Falecendo algum pobre dos admittidos ão rol da sedaca em Roshodes o provera o parnas que servir de mortalha de pano ... E fara todos os mais custos de seu enterro que serão por conta desta santa hebra ... O parnas que serve assistira em todas as misvot para dar a ordem necesaria atte as meterem no barco e aly tomara conta dos yrmãos que sahyrão e vão ou outrem por ellos para nottar a pena aos que faltarem como fica ditto. Levara a custa desta santa companhia a casa de qualquer abel de nossa nação a primejra comjda despendendo de 4, 5, te 6 florins conforme a famjlia for e mais nada ...'
[62] *Ascamoth (Acta)*, PA 334, no. 19, p. 556.

Torah).⁶³ For someone like Isaac a responsibility of this kind was a real challenge. At last he had the opportunity of meeting those at the spiritual hub of the Portuguese community without the intermediacy of any third party, since the duties of his office involved contact with the rabbis of the congregation, its learned members and its paid teachers, as well as keeping a paternal eye on the youthful pupils, promoting their welfare and monitoring their academic progress. Once a week he had to visit all the classes in order to inspect the lessons which went on until evening. At times of prayer he had to take his place in the synagogue on the teachers' bench to watch the boys and see that they were all sitting in their proper place and paying due attention to the prayers. On sabbaths the *parnas* whose rota it was had to organize study of the week's portion of the Pentateuch, and on the first day of every month in the Jewish calendar the whole college of *parnasim* examined the pupils, noting in a record-book their impressions of each one's progress; when necessary, they would decide collectively about moving a pupil into a different class.⁶⁴

The election of Isaac Orobio as *parnas* of '*Eṣ Ḥayyim* before six full years had elapsed since his arrival in Amsterdam and reversion to Judaism is incontestable evidence of the complete confidence which the *señores* of the *Ma'amad* reposed in his ability, and of their assessment of his standard of Jewish knowledge. The very description of the tasks involved leaves no doubt at all that only someone perfectly at home in the world of Judaism, its rules, and its sense of values would be equipped to discharge them. It follows that in the view of the

⁶³ Ibid., p. 592: '5428. Em 5 de Sivan em conformidade do capitulo 21 dos acordos da Nação se juntarão os ss^{res} do Mahamad com os ss^{res} Parnassim de Talmud thora que servirão este ano pera elegerem em bora [= boa hora], e dispois de aver praticado e votado por busulo e bulas sahirão eleitos os ss^{res} abaixo nomeados que lhes seya Besiman tob, os ss^{res} Mosseh de Chaves, Eliau Bueno Henriques, Ishak Orobio de Castro, David Gabai Faro, Mosseh Curiel, Selomoh Salom tezouro.' The parallel text in the minutes of the Society *Talmud Torah we-'Eṣ Ḥayyim*, PA 334 no. 1051, f. 47ᵛ, states that those here named were elected 'after discussion of their qualifications' ('havendose descursado sobre as pesoas que pareserão benemeritas'). Cf. MS Amsterdam, *EH* 48 D 36, p. 91; Bibl. Rosen., no. 97, p. 89; AGA, PA 334 no. 155, p. 21; no. 157, p. 38; no. 158, p. 125. For the history of the congregation's Talmudic academy from the beginning of the 17th cent., and of the Society of '*Eṣ Ḥayyim* that was founded on 18 July 1637, see M. C. Paraira and J. S. Da Silva Rosa, *Gedenkschrift uitgegeven ter gelegenheid van het 300–jarig bestaan der onderwijsinrichtingen Talmud Tora en Ets Haïm*, Amsterdam, 1916. This pamphlet was reprinted as an appendix in Meijer, *Enc.*, ii, pp. 65 f.; see Silva Rosa, *Geschiedenis*, pp. 20 f.; Pieterse, *De Barrios*, pp. 97 f.

⁶⁴ See the bylaws of the Society of '*Eṣ Ḥayyim* after the union of the three congregations in 1639, in the Society's *Ascamoth*, PA 334 no. 1052, ff. 23ᵛ f., and resolutions, ibid., passed in 1651.

Philosopher, Communal Leader, Physician 193

congregational leadership Isaac Orobio was already by then considered fit for the function of guiding the young by watching over their education in Judaism.

On 4 June 1669 (5 *Sivan* 5429) Isaac completed service as *parnas* of *'Eṣ Ḥayyim*,[65] and on 25 September (29 *Elul* 5429) of the same year he was elected as one of the *parnasim* responsible for guiding the fortunes of the entire Portuguese congregation of *Talmud Torah*.[66] The statutes of 1639 laid down that the six members of the *Ma'amad*, *plus* the treasurer (*gabbai*) should hold office for a year, three of them and the treasurer to be elected on the sabbath preceding passover (March–April) and the other three before new year (August–September). This scheme ensured that in all cases there should be at the helm of the congregation men of some experience, who knew how to cope with the manifold problems in the life of the community.[67]

The assertion made by I. S. Emmanuel that it was the moneyed class alone that enjoyed the right to elect some of their own number to preside over the affairs of the community is too extreme.[68] Wealth did, it is true, afford an important criterion for determining the status of a member within the congregation, but it was by no means the sole criterion. The only restrictions upon eligibility for office in the articles of union of the three earlier congregations into the Congregation *Talmud Torah* in 1639 merely lay down that no one could be elected to the *Ma'amad* within three years of his reversion to Judaism, and that after holding office one might not be re-elected until three years had elapsed from vacating it.[69] It was subsequently enacted that close relatives might not serve on the same *Ma'amad*, i.e. father and son, brothers, grandfather and grandson, uncle and nephew, father-in-law and son-in-law, cousins, or brothers-in-law.[70] Not only is every

---

[65] On this date the 5 new *parnasim* of *'Eṣ Ḥayyim* were elected. The minutes of the proceedings for the election of the new board bear Isaac Orobio's signature, see PA 334 no. 1051, f. 48ᵛ, and similarly the congregational *Acta*, PA 334 no. 19, p. 605.

[66] Ibid., p. 609; see also PA 334 no. 157, p. 138; no. 158, pp. 18, 57; no. 1323, p. 7; Amsterdam, Bibl. Rosen., no. 97, p. 20; and *EH*, 48 D 36, p. 16.

[67] See clause 8 of the constitution of the Congregation as from 1639 in Pieterse, *De Barrios*, p. 157. It should be noted that in the instance with which we are here concerned an assistant treasurer was elected — contrary to the established custom — at the election preceding the new year (Sept.). On this constitution see Wiznitzer, *Merger Agreement*.

[68] Emmanuel, *Yedi'oth*, p. 166.

[69] Pieterse, *De Barrios*, p. 158.

[70] See *Livro de Elejçoëns do K. K.*, Amsterdam, AGA, PA 334 no. 158, p. 10.

[71] It is clear from the congregational dues paid by Jacob Ergas Henríquez (elected 5430/1670), Jacob Jessurun Henríquez (5432/1672), David Henríquez Faro (5439/1679), and Dr Daniel Semah (5455/1695) that none of them was amongst the wealthier

property qualification conspicuously absent here, but the lists of the office-holders from the date of the unification onwards indicate that not a few persons were elected to the Ma'amad who were very far indeed from enjoying easy material circumstances.[71] The very fact of Isaac Orobio's having been elected is enough to invalidate Emmanuel's far-reaching assertion, for Orobio was by no means a wealthy man. Certain it is that his election as *parnas* owed nothing to economic considerations, but that other thinking lay behind it. At the date when he was chosen for this particular office he was already well known in Amsterdam amongst Jews and Gentiles alike as being a considerable scholar. Edward Browne, an English traveller who visited Amsterdam in the 1660s, did not fail to mention him in the list (taking the city as a whole) of those who had made the most impression upon him.[72] There can be no doubt that Orobio's reputation, and the general assessment of his personal qualities, were the main factors in bringing about his election to this most prestigious office. The leadership of the congregation appreciated that it would confer lustre on the 'Portuguese nation' if a figure so well known as Orobio were to represent it *vis-à-vis* the municipal authority of Amsterdam and the various other civic institutions.

Congregational records inform us of the resolutions adopted by the *Ma'amad* during the period of Isaac's service on it. On 5 January 1670

---

members of the congregation. Nor is their case without parallel. It would seem that the sentiments expressed by Menasseh B. Israel in the dedication of his Spanish version of the Pentateuch (Amsterdam, 5415[1655]) to Conrad van Beuningen fairly summarize the attitude of the Portuguese-Jewish congregation towards social status and public regard, viz. that four considerations are relevant to securing approbation: personal qualities, as expressed in the 'four cardinal virtues' of prudence, justice, self-control, and courage; ancestral distinction; distinguished public service; and, in the fourth place only, wealth. 'Quatro son las cosas que a mi parecer, ha de tener un hombre para poder llamarse con razon honrado. La primera y principal, es el valor de la propia persona, en Prudencia, Justicia, Temperança y Fortaleza . . . La segunda es la nobleza, y antiguidad de sus passados, ser de preclara [sic] linage, y progenie famosa . . . La tercera es, tener dignidad y officio honrado en la Republica . . . La quarta es ser hazendado y rico.')

[72] Edward Browne, M.D., *An Account of Several Travels throught a Great Part of Germany*, London, 1677, quoted from Ranum, p. 162: 'I saw one Moses di Pas, a learned young man, and Orobio, a physician of note. And I was sorry to see divers here to profess themselves publickly jews, who had lived at least reputed christians, for a long time in other places: One who had been a Franciscan frier thirty years; and another who had been professour some years at Thoulouze (Toulouse), and before that a physician to the King of Spain.' Browne (for whom see *Dictionary of National Biography*, 7, London, 1886, pp. 42–3) was the son of the well-known English writer Sir Thomas Browne; see the Dutch edn. of Browne's work, *Naukerige en Gedenkwaardige Reysen*, Amsterdam, 1682 p. 24.

(13 Ṭebeth 5430) there was read out from the reading-desk in the synagogue the decision of the *Ma'amad* that the by-law of 7 February 1656 (12 *Shebaṭ* 5416) was to be re-enacted and extended. It had originally prohibited, under threat of excommunication, the purchase of meat from any source but the congregational butcher's shop.[73] That penalty was in fact imposed on Abraham Bueno de Aragão on 12 August 1670 (26 *'Ab* 5430), because he had bought meat from the butcher of the Ashkenazi (German-Jewish) community.[74]

Again it was decided on 10 February 1670 (20 *Shebaṭ* 5430) that all the members of the *Ma'amad* together with the *parnasim* of *'Eṣ Ḥayyim* and *Biqqur Ḥolim* must jointly take part in funerals to which communal representatives were invited by the municipal authorities.[75] On 6 March 1670 (14 *'Adar* 5430) it was resolved that as of the first day of the next ensuing month of *Nisan* the contributions of the charitable confraternity known as *'Abodath Ḥesed* ('Service of Mercy') should be distributed solely amongst the poor of the 'Portuguese nation'. Henceforth that society no longer worked on behalf of the poor Ashkenazis *(tudescos)*, as it had done since its establishment in 1642. The members of the *Ma'amad* of the Portuguese community claimed that the financial situation of the Ashkenazis had improved beyond measure, and thus they were no longer in need of the assistance of the *Talmud Torah* community.[76] In fact the economic conditions of the Ashkenazis had not changed at all; but from the moment that their numbers in the city increased and they became an independent community, the Portuguese community revised its policy of assisting them. As we shall see below, other things happened that year which heightened the tension between the two communites.

All three of these measures carry the signature of Isaac Orobio

---

[73] See the congregational *Ascamoth* (*Acta*), PA 334 no. 19, p. 611.

[74] See MS Amsterdam, *EH* 48 E 64, *Livro de Memorias donde se deixa notisia de alguas cozas*, f. 23ʳ: 'em 26 de Ab se pos em herem na Teba a Ab. Bueno de Aragão p[or] haver comprado carne na carnesaria dos Tudescos'. His sentence of excommunication was rescinded two days later, ibid.

[75] See *Ascamoth* (n. 73 above), p. 612.

[76] Ibid., p. 613. For *'Abodath Ḥesed* see Meijer, *Enc.*, i, p. 14. See also Pieterse, *De Barrios*, p. 132 n. 2, where it is erroneously stated that the decision to restrict the dispensing of charity to the Sephardi poor was with effect from 7 *Nisan*. On that date Jacob Franco da Silva was elected treasurer of the guild, but the restriction referred to had been resolved upon in the middle of the foregoing month of *'Adar*, as stated above; cf. Y. Kaplan, 'The Attitude of the Portuguese Jewish Community in the 17th Century towards the Ashkenazi Jews in Amsterdam', *Proceedings of the Ninth World Congress of Jewish Studies*, Jerusalem, 1986, pp. 159–64 (Hebrew).

together with those of his fellow *parnasim* of the Congregation *Talmud Torah*.[77]

On 21 July 1670 all the members of the community signed a series of regulations which were intended to define the authority of the *Ma'amad* in managing the community's affairs. These regulations were intended only to ratify those of 1639, but their wording implies a clear tendency to strengthen the authority of the *parnasim* and increase the rabbis' dependence upon them.

It is difficult to surmise what were the immediate causes for the above-mentioned decisions, nothing germane thereto being noted in the congregational records.[78] Conceivably they are to be connected with the wrangle which occurred early in 1670 between the *Ma'amad* and the heirs of Jacob del Soto regarding the latter's estate: and it may be that the vehemence of the tone in which the decision was formulated betrays the concern of the congregational leadership to impose its own will and to crush any possible opposition. Jacob del Soto, alias del Monte, was one of the richest members of the community and one of the most significant contributors to the funds of its ancillary societies. On his death in 1670 (5430) the *parnasim* of the congregation, being interested to know about any bequests that the deceased might have left, required of the heirs that they produce a copy of his will. What, of

---

[77] It is not clear from what date in *Tishri* (which began at the new year festival, falling on 14 Sept. 1669) Orobio began to discharge administrative functions. The date is missing from the record of the swearing-in of the 3 new *parnasim; Ascamoth* (n. 73 above), p. 609. His signature appears beneath all the routine decisions of the *Ma'amad* (in no fixed order of precedence), e.g. the election of *parnasim* for the charitable societies of *Biqqur Holim* and *'Eṣ Ḥayyim*, and the distribution of charitable funds for Palestine (pp. 609 f.) On 27 *Ṭebeth* 5430 (9 Jan. 1670), together with his fellow-*parnasim*, he signed the resolution of the *Ma'amad* authorizing the printing of Jacob Judah León's annotated translation of the Psalms into Spanish (*Las Alabanças de Santidad*), which appeared in Amsterdam in 5431 (1671). Amongst the various testimonials which the author printed was one by Orobio ('Aprobación del Muy Noble y Sabio Señor, Doctor Ishak Orobio de Castro, Philosopho Médico').

[78] See Amsterdam, AGA, PA 334 no. 119A, *Varios papeis de pleitos findados e outros mais que podem servir nas ocasioes que se ofreser*, pp. 754 f. The resolution is headed: 'Declarasão do modo e forma que se observa no governo da sinagoga e nação Ebrea portugueza en Amsterdam.' In regard to the subordination of the rabbis to the lay officers of the *Ma'amad* it is there stated that 'Os Hahamins, ou Predicantes são asalareados por os ditos Parnasim, e pello conseguinte estão sujeitos a ditos Parnases e a suas ordeins em tudo.' The procedure for dealing with problems potentially fraught with disturbance of the congregational peace is likewise laid down: 'Coando se ofreze algum caso grave que parese aos ditos Parnazes comunicar, mandarão chamar algumas pesoas as que lhes parese couvein [sic] seu parecer, na materia que se trata, e dipois tomarão a rezolução nela ditos Parnasim como superiores da nação em tudo com sinco votos dos sette como sempre...'

Philosopher, Communal Leader, Physician

course, they had in mind was mainly the offerings and regular contributions which del Soto had promised to the congregation and its various institutions. The heirs persistently refused to comply, and further defied the authority of the community by arranging for a private quorum of ten men to meet for congregational worship in the house of the deceased, in direct contradiction of the statutes of the congregation. The ban of excommunication was consequently imposed upon them on 27 August 1670 (11 'Elul 5430).[79] That extreme step was the culmination of a series of other measures which the *parnasim* had adopted, including the threat of excommunication promulgated on 1 April 1670 (11 *Nisan* 5430) on any member of the congregation who, being privy to the contents of a will, failed to come forward and inform the *Ma'amad* about them.[80]

It seems likely that Isaac Orobio played a central role in this chapter of events, not merely as being one of the *parnasim* engaged in the dispute with the del Soto family, but also as one of the principal witnesses who came forward with a declaration regarding offerings promised by the deceased. A record of the *Ma'amad*'s business on 3 June 1670 states that some five months previous, when discussion about building a new synagogue began, the late Jacob del Soto had told Isaac Orobio that he was interested in advancing capital of 100,000 florins to the congregation towards a building fund in return for interest at 3 per cent.[81] That piece of evidence in itself shows that the proposal to build the new synagogue (i.e. the one still standing) went back to 1670, at which date Isaac was in office as a *parnas* of the Congregation *Talmud Torah*.[82]

---

[79] See Pieterse, *De Barrios*, p. 86. Emmanuel, *Yedi'oth*, p. 164 gives a general summary of the episode, the documents concerning which are in the synagogal archives, Amsterdam, AGA, PA 334 no. 520A, ff. 69 f. including the instrument of excommunication (f. 80); cf. the text as recorded in the *Livro de Memorias* (n. 74 above), ff. 23ʳ f., where it is stated that first cousins and more distant relatives of the excommunicated persons were exempted from its effect; cf. D. M. Swetschinski, 'Kinship and Commerce: The Foundations of Portuguese Jewish Life in Seventeenth Century Holland', *SR*, 15, 1981, pp. 70–3.

[80] PA 334 no. 524A, f. 74.

[81] Ibid., p. 69: 'Nos os abaixo firmados, declaramos, que avera çinco meses pouco mais o menos, ofresendose em nosa nasão, o tratar de fabricar nova signagoga [sic], os ssʳᵉˢ Parnases que naquelle tempo serviam chamaram, para o milhor resolver a nos declarantes e outras pesoas, entre os quais foy chamado, Jacob del Soto, que Deus tem, e quando, chego a ves de falar, o Douctor [sic] Ishack Orobio de Castro, dixe, que o Sʳ Jacob del Soto, que presente estava, lhe avia dito que elle somaria ate cento mill florins para a dita fabrica, con pagarlhe a tres por cento de ynteresse . . .'

[82] Hitherto prevalent opinion has held that the proposal was advanced by Isaac Aboab on 3 *Kislev* 5731 (16 Nov. 1670) in the form of a petition to the *Ma'amad*, signed by a

198 *Philosopher, Communal Leader, Physician*

The complications about Jacob del Soto's estate caused a rift in the congregation that went as far as to involve the civic authorities of Amsterdam. The *Ma'amad* requested the city council to interdict the testamentary dispositions of the deceased, and that request was upheld. The heirs, being now excommunicate, but desirous of securing their future burial alongside their father, purchased a piece of ground at Ouderkerk adjoining the Portuguese cemetery, thereby attempting to circumvent the authority of the *Ma'amad*. In that endeavour they received a limited measure of support from the Ashkenazi community; and it is possible that the by-laws referred to above—inhibiting the purchase of meat save from the Portuguese congregation's own butcher's shop, and abrogating charitable support of the Ashkenazi poor from the funds of *'Abodath Ḥesed*—would not have been enacted had it not been for the dispute which had broken out between the two communities.[83]

L'affaire del Soto was not concluded during Isaac Orobio's period of office as *parnas* of the congregation. It was not until 7 October 1671 that a concordat was reached between the *Ma'amad* and the heirs, by which the latter paid the Portuguese congregation 6,000 florins, and accepted an obligation to pay a further 40,000, and transferred three-quarters of their parcel of land at Ouderkerk to the ownership of the trustees of the cemetery of the Portuguese community.[84]

It seems almost certain that Isaac Orobio occupied the chair of the *Ma'amad* as *parnas presidente* in the months of August–September 1670 (*'Ab–'Elul* 5430) in accordance with the convention, established at the time of the 1639 merger, that each *parnas*, in rotation, should preside for two months.[85] The ledgers record that, acting as *parnas*, during these two months he allocated money for various purposes, this being

---

majority of the members of the congregation, requesting that steps be taken to enlarge the synagogue building; see Silva Rosa, *Geschiedenis*, p. 89, and his article 'Over de oudste Potugeesche Synagoges te Amsterdam', *Chronicon Spinozanum*, I, 1921, p. 272; D. H. De Castro, *De Synagoge der Portugees-Israelitiesche Gemeente te Amsterdam*, 1950, pp. 29 f., and similarly Pieterse, *De Barrios*, App. 22, pp. 172 f. It would seem, however, that the idea had already been born early in 1670, and that it was only at the end of that year that the first practical steps were taken to implement it.

[83] On the del Soto plot in the Portuguese-Jewish cemetery see Pieterse, *De Barrios*, p. 86. Members of the family had been in correspondence with the Ashkenazi community, which accepted their overtures with marked signs of respect. Despite its endeavours, the *Ma'amad* did not succeed in securing the support of the Ashkenazim. See Emmanuel, *Yedi'oth*, pp. 164 f.

[84] See PA 334 no. 524A, f. 156, and cf. *Livro dos testamentos*, PA 334 no. 518, pp. 13 f.

[85] See clause 7 of the 1639 constitution, Pieterse, *De Barrios*, p. 157.

Philosopher, Communal Leader, Physician   199

part of the responsibilities for which the *parnas presidente* had authority.⁸⁶ If this is correct, it will follow that the pronouncement of the excommunication of the del Soto family must have been made public whilst he was in the chair, which would mean that Orobio had a decisive voice in having it publicly proclaimed. The members of the excommunicate family appealed to the city fathers and, as a result of their intervention, succeeded in getting the full rigour of the ban modified; but by the terms of the new concordat they were thenceforth precluded from maintaining a private quorum for congregational worship in their own house.⁸⁷

These, then, were days of feverish activity for the *señores* of the *Ma'amad*, and particularly for each successive *parnas presidente*, since it rested with them to insist with all their vigour on the right of the congregation to assert its authority over the membership of the Portuguese community, and also to defend that right before the civic authorities.

At the beginning of *Tishri* 5371 (August–September 1670) Isaac Orobio completed his service as *parnas* of the congregation, after which he never again held office in any of its ancillary institutions. It would seem that in the ensuing years he concentrated on activities within the field of medicine. A number of his polemical pieces were composed, as we shall see below, during this last period of his life, between his departure from the *banco* of the *Ma'amad* and his death. But despite his retirement from official functions in the Portuguese congregation, Orobio continued to show an interest in congregational problems. The community records show that in the early 1680s he frequently bestirred himself on behalf of members of his community who were in need. The number of occasions when his intervention met with success indicates that right up to the end of his life his voice continued to carry considerable weight in the chambers of the *Ma'amad*.⁸⁸

---

⁸⁶ See *Livro Grande*, PA 334 no. 240, f. 191: '5430. Ab 11: F. 707:9 cobrados do Parnas D^or Ishac Orobio; pelos 2 meses da carnis[eri]a 707:9.' Cf. *Livro Longo*, PA 334 no. 216, p.55; ibid., 'en 21 Ilul Asign[ação] de Ishack Orobio de Castro f. 25:14'.

⁸⁷ See *Livro de Memorias* (n. 74 above), f. 24ʳ.

⁸⁸ See *Livro Longo*, PA 334 no. 217, f. 265. On 9 May 1681, amongst those listed who had applied for subvention of their house-rental, there is included the name of Rachel de Paiba who at the instance of Isaac Orobio was granted 3 fl. Ibid., p. 419, on 6 *Tammuz* 5443 (30 June 1683) Orobio guaranteed a loan to the widow of Abraham Rois Carion of London. Ibid., 16 *'Ab* of the same year (8 Aug.) the *Ma'amad* paid over to Orobio 9 fl. 9 st. as a gift to 'someone [too] embarrassed [to make his own approach]'.

MEDICAL PRACTICE IN AMSTERDAM

Medicine continued to occupy Isaac Orobio—and to provide him with an income—after his settlement in Amsterdam. It is very difficult to tell, from the records of the local *Collegium Medicum*,[89] just when he was first registered there, since the dates listed are not those of registration, but of the conferring of the university licentiate by which medical qualification had been obtained. The entry for Isaac Orobio records that he originated from Seville and was licensed at Toulouse on 9 September 1660,[90] but we have already seen that Isaac in fact held no degree from the university of Toulouse. It is quite clear that what he presented to the authorities of the Amsterdam *Collegium* was the confirmation, received by him whilst in France, of a diploma from Alcalá, and this, as noted, appears to have been a forgery.[91] Unlike most of the Jewish doctors registered by the *Collegium* in the seventeenth century, Isaac Orobio is listed without any indication of his being Jewish.[92] Does such omission permit us to infer that he became registered shortly after his arrival in Amsterdam, before his Jewishness was generally known? One might suppose so; however the same volume of the records also contains a chronological list indicating the names of the physicians licensed in each year, and in that list it is explicitly stated that Orobio was Jewish.[93] Moreover, a similar omission was later to occur in the case of Isaac's son Moses on receipt of his licence from Leiden in 1678 and on his becoming a registered member of the *Collegium*, although his Jewish identity was, at the time, a matter of common knowledge.[94] Since it is difficult to believe that both these omissions were due to slackness on the part of the registrar, a satisfactory explanation is not forthcoming.

Despite the absence of documentary evidence for the date of Isaac's

[89] By the *Collegium* is meant the professional guild of local physicians, which maintained specific conditions as the qualification for admission and excluded non-members from practice.

[90] See Amsterdam, AGA, Collegium Medicum, file no. 20 (unpaginated), *Series Nominum Doctorum Medicinae, ab anno 1641*, 'Tolosa, Balthazar de Orobio Castelo hispalensi 1660 9 September'. [91] See above, chap. 5, pp. 101 f.

[92] Some of the names of the Jewish doctors have the description *Hebraeus* appended, others *Judaeus*; David [Sarfati] de Pina is labelled *Jood*, and Georges Brunt Ambona *Judeus Orientalis*.

[93] Ibid. (n. 90 above), after the aforementioned list, A° 1660 'Tolosae Balthasar de Orobio Castelo Hebr[aeus] 9 Sept.'

[94] The names of the other Jewish doctors left without indication of their being Jews are Abrahamus Israel Frois, Aron Mendez da Almansa, Moyses Salom Azevedo de Pas.

Philosopher, Communal Leader, Physician

registration with the *Collegium*, it seems probable that it took place immediately after his settlement in Amsterdam. In August 1662 he was still in Toulouse, so that his joining the *Collegium* cannot be placed earlier than the September of that year.[95] On the other hand, of the twelve doctors registered after Orobio, none had completed his medical course requirements later than 1662,[96] and it will not be straining the evidence to suppose that at least some of them were registered immediately on graduation. This would mean that Isaac was registered with the *Collegium* no later than 1663 and possibly in the last months of 1662.

It is worth taking a look at the institution with which he obtained professional registration as a medical practitioner. The *Collegium Medicum* of Amsterdam had been founded in 1638, and its statutes of 28 January 1641 confirmed the procedure that had hitherto required applicants for admission to produce a diploma of their licentiate from a university of repute. They likewise prohibited anyone who was not a citizen of Amsterdam from practising medicine there.[97] That regulation would, on the face of it, have largely shut the door of the *Collegium* to Jewish physicians, inasmuch as a Jew could obtain *poorterschap* (citizenship) in return for payment only, and even then but in exceptional circumstances—the reference being here to leading merchants engaged in foreign trade or in wholesale business. For Jews, moreover, *poorterschap* was not something heritable, and the sons of *poorters* who wished to retain the privileges of their fathers' status were constrained to acquire it afresh.[98] The bulk of the Jews in Amsterdam were classified as resident aliens, and so prohibited by a statute going back to 1465 from engaging in any trade or craft controlled by the guilds.[99] This statute had been re-enacted in 1632 as a result of intense pressure by the guilds, which were prepared to fight to the death in

---

[95] The name preceding Orobio's in the list is that of Aaron Mendez da Almansa (see previous note), whose Leiden degree was granted on 15 Dec. 1661, so that his admission to the *Collegium* must necessarily have been at a later date.

[96] Ibid. (n. 90 above).

[97] For the foundation of the Amsterdam *Collegium Medicum*, and its subsequent history, see Haver Droeze, pp. 3 f. Its statutes of 1641 were confirmed in 1654; see Amsterdam, AGA, Collegium Medicum, file no. 12, *Privilegien, Willekeuren en Ordonnantien, Betreffende het Collegium Medicum Amstelaedamense*, Amsterdam, 1728, pp. 18 f., and cf. D. E. Cohen, pp. 3 f.

[98] On the legal status of Jews in Amsterdam at this period see C. Reijnders, *Van 'Joodsche Natiën' tot Joodse Nederlanders*, Amsterdam, 1969, pp. 23 f., and cf. Bloom, pp. 22 f.

[99] Bloom, p. 23.

defence of their entrenched privileges against the powerful development of capitalist and industrialist activity which Amsterdam was then experiencing: but on this occasion the formulation of the statute made it absolutely clear that it was directed against Jews.[100] Even when the rights of aliens were extended in 1668, it was unequivocally stated that as regards Jewish aliens, no changes would be effected. There is no doubt that the Calvinists and Arminians, who still considered the Jews as a dangerous threat to Christianity, played a decisive role in this discriminatory action.[101] Despite this, Jewish economic activity in Amsterdam accelerated in the seventeenth century for various reasons. First, some industries were not organized or controlled by the guilds; foreign business and wholesale trade were open to residents who did not possess *poorterschap*; and the stringent regulations of the guilds were in any case frequently set aside.[102]

A glance at the roll of physicians of the *Collegium Medicum* from 1641 to the end of the century reveals that almost thirty Jews were registered with it, of whom three alone enjoyed the privileges of citizenship;[103] not one of the remainder is listed in the roll of *poorters*. It is quite clear that the *Collegium* was not in fact requiring that Jewish applicants for registration be in possession of *poorterschap*. The same situation held good as regards the Jewish surgeons and apothecaries.[104] Thus, although the *Collegium* never explicitly approved the acceptance of Jews, we find that they were nevertheless permitted to practise medicine. Many of the Jewish physicians had made their name before coming to Holland: in addition, the poor sanitary conditions prevailing in Amsterdam at the time constituted a powerful factor in inducing the heads of the *Collegium* to exercise their discretion as far as Jewish

---

[100] On the power of the Amsterdam guilds at this period, and their place within the economic structure of the city, see Barbour, p. 71. For the statute of 1632, see Bloom, p. 23.   [101] Bloom, p. 24.

[102] See Barbour, p. 16 n. 9. For the right of Jews to engage in wholesale trade, and in a limited number of other trades and artisan callings (e.g. in printing, tobacco-curing, dealing in oil products, acting as middlemen, etc.) although they were subjects rather than citizens, see Bloom, pp. 23 f.

[103] i.e. Ephraim and Aaron Bueno and Isaac de Rocamora: however, it is the last two only who are described as *civis* in the *Series Nominum* of the *Collegium* (see above, n. 90). Ephraim Bueno acquired his poorterschap on 24 Feb. 1651, apparently subsequent to his admission to the *Collegium*; hence the lack of reference in the list to his status as citizen. D. E. Cohen, p. 4, is wrong in asserting that Ephraim Bueno was the only one of the Jewish doctors to acquire *poorterschap* between 1641 and 1796.

[104] See D. E. Cohen, p. 4, and Bloom, p. 23. For surgeons see esp. D. E. Cohen, 'De Amsterdamsche Joodsche Chirurgijns', *Nederl. Tijdschrift voor Geneeskunde*, 74, no. 18, 1930; for Jewish apothecaries see Haver Droeze, p. 164 and Apps., p. viii.

Philosopher, Communal Leader, Physician

doctors were concerned.[105] None the less, their status within the College of Physicians was inferior to that of their Christian confrères: they could not, for example, attain the rank of inspector. On the other hand, no restrictions were placed on their treating Christian patients.[106]

Orobio's reputation in Amsterdam as a doctor is attested by a number of dissertations defended by Jewish medical students before the faculty at Leiden in which there are included not only laudatory remarks about him but also examples of his own clinical practice. It seems likely that Isaac Orobio directed the medical studies of his own son Moses and of David de Pina, his son-in-law, prior to their respective presentations of a dissertation to the senate of Leiden university.[107]

Some details of his work as a physician are brought into incidental focus by sundry notarial documents. It would appear that whilst a significant proportion of his practice was amongst the membership of the Portuguese community, Christian patients also turned to him for attention. That much may be learned from an authorization which Orobio gave in 1671, using the notarial services of Pieter Padthuysen, to Isaac Rodríguez Monsanto, to collect on his behalf the sum of thirty-two florins from the heirs of the merchant Hendrik Nesplet in respect of thirty-two 'special visits' paid to him by Orobio whilst attending him during his sickness. That document gives us a glimpse of what Orobio's medical income might have been. The fee of about one florin seems to have been what he would charge for a professional visit to such of his patients as were comfortably off.[108]

In 1679 Ernest Augustus, Duke of Calenberg and Hanover (father of the future George I of England) happened to fall ill whilst a guest in the house of Jerónimo Nunes da Costa (alias Moses Curiel), one of the wealthiest members of the Amsterdam Jewish community of the time.

---

[105] On the state of hygiene in 17th-cent. Amsterdam see Zumthor, pp. 148 f., Murray, p. 5.

[106] See D. E. Cohen, p. 5. Jewish apothecaries were prohibited from selling *materia medica* to Christians from 3 Feb. 1667; Amsterdam, AGA, Collegium Medicum, file no. 12 (see above, n. 97), pp. 22 f.

[107] See Kaplan, *Studentim be-leiden*, pp. 72 f.

[108] Amsterdam, AGA, *Notariële Archieven*, file 2904 (July–Dec. 1671), p. 387: '... de somm van twee en dartigh f. ... over twee en dartigh extraordinaire visiten die hij compt aan de selve Nesplet heeft gedaan in de ziekte daaraan de gesejde Nesplet is gestorven.' As à notary Pieter Padthuysen had numerous Jewish clients: on him see Bloom, p. xvii. It would seem that Nesplet was a well-to-do merchant. At this period, the fee chargeable for a doctor's home visit varied between 4 st. for petty traders to 1 fl. for substantial businessmen: see Zumthor, pp. 154 f.

It was Isaac Orobio who attended him and effected his cure.[109] Nevertheless, as stated above, it seems that most of his practice was within the Portuguese community. As a doctor of recognized standing he was sometimes called upon to provide the authorities with a doctor's certificate for Portuguese Jews who, having been summoned to appear before a court or governmental office in The Hague or elsewhere, were unable for reasons of their health to leave Amsterdam. Thus we find his signature alongside that of Dr Jacob Moreno[110] on a document dated 20 May 1677 certifying the inability of David Gutierres to travel to The Hague on account of his precarious state of health. Gutierres had lodged an appeal with the department of revenue regarding the inordinate sum which, on 1 February 1667, he had been ordered to pay as '*200ste Penning*' tax, and in accordance with the usual custom he was obliged to appear before the council in The Hague to justify his objections.[111] A similar document signed by Orobio and Dr Miguel Reynoso[112] on 19 July 1673 certified that Mrs Sarah de Pinto was not fit to leave Amsterdam in order to respond to a summons (likewise concerning fiscal affairs) served on her from Rotterdam.[113]

Isaac Orobio continued working as a doctor until the end of his life. His name appears in the list of those physicians who, in 1684–5, paid their annual subscription of five guilders to the Amsterdam *Hortus*

---

[109] For Jerónimo Nunes da Costa see below, Appendix D, and the bibliography there given. We are informed of Orobio's professional treatment of the Duke of Hanover from a letter written by the Duchess Sophia to her brother in the same year. See E. Bodemann, *Kurfurstin Sophie van Hannover, Briefwechsel mit ihren Bruder*, Leipzig, 1889 p. 369, and cf. L. Poliakov, *The History of Anti-Semitism from Voltaire to Wagner*, Littman Library, London, 1975, pp. 13 ff. I am grateful to Professor R. Popkin for drawing my attention to this source.

[110] Moreno graduated from Leiden on 15 Mar. 1658, see Kaplan *Ṣṭudenṭim be-leiden*, pp. 68 f.

[111] On the nature of this impost, and its significance for assessing the wealth of those who paid it, see below, p. 206 and n. 118. David Gutierres received a demand for 500 fl., from which it would appear that he was one of the wealthiest members of the Portuguese-Jewish community. His demand-note has been preserved (Amsterdam, AGA, *Archief Burg* no. 683, 46), alongside the medical certificate signed by Orobio and Moreno affirming that Guttieres was both elderly and unwell ('indien hij eenige voijage quaeme te doen soo soude hij met meerder sieckte bevangen worden'). On difficulties experienced by Jews in meeting their demands under this tax, and the individual case of Gutierres, see Pieterse, *Joodsche Natie*, p. 177. Despite what is there written, inspection of the documents makes it clear that Gutierres' fiscal appeal took place in 1667, and not in 1668.

[112] On Reynoso see above, chap. 6, p. 134.

[113] Amsterdam, AGA, *Notariële Archieven*, file 2097A, p. 855 (P. Padthuysen notary, see above, n. 108); Orobio here signs with his Spanish name of Baltazar. Cf. another document, of 4 July 1673, ibid., p. 931.

Medicus, curatorship of which was assigned to members of the *Collegium Medicum*.[114] And, as will be seen below, shortly before his death Orobio agreed to become the medical officer of health retained by the Portuguese community.[115]

PERSONAL STANDING AND MATERIAL CIRCUMSTANCES

During his own lifetime Isaac Orobio was reckoned to belong to the most highly regarded élite of the Amsterdam community. At the dedication of the present synagogue, which was celebrated by the congregation with eight days of most elaborate festivities and pomp in 1675, sermons were delivered each day. These were subsequently published in the same year by David de Castro Tartas in a single volume, each being preceded by a dedication to one of the *parnasim*, the magnates, or one of the particularly respected members of the congregation: and the seventh of these dedications was to Isaac Orobio.[116] He was assigned a seat in the synagogue near to the *banco* of the *Ma'amad*—seat no. 7 of the first row, where he was flanked by the men of property: Isaac de Pinto, Jacob Bueno de Mesquita, Joseph Jessurun, Daniel Jessurun Espinosa, and Abraham de Judah Touro.[117] All of these enjoyed seats of honour in virtue of their great wealth: Isaac, on the other hand, was allotted his because of his spiritual

[114] Amsterdam, AGA, Collegium Medicum, file no. 20 (unpaginated). This list comprises the names of 79 physicians, including 6 Jews—Salomon Rocamora, [David de] Pinna, Moses Orobio, Abrahamus Guttierres, Abrahamus Israel Frois, Balthasar de Orobio. Since it includes Abraham Gutierres who qualified at Harderwijk in May 1684, it cannot be any earlier than that. See ibid., file no. 29 (unpaginated): on 30 Nov. 1685 Orobio paid his subscription for that year. His name does not appear separately for the years 1686–7, but that is because the lists for these two years are not itemized. For the ordinances of the civic authorities of Amsterdam enacted on 18 Dec. 1683 in regard to the obligation of the physicians to provide for the upkeep of this garden, see ibid., file no. 9, p. 26, and file no. 12, pp. 25 f. [115] See below, chap. 10, p. 304.

[116] See *Sermoes que pregaraõ os Doctos Ingenios do K. K. de Talmud Torah, desta Cidade de Amsterdam, no alegre Estreamento e Publica celebridade da Fabrica que se consagrou a Deos, para Caza de Oração cuja entrada se festejou em Sabath Nahamu Anno 5435*, Amsterdam, 5435 [1675]. The addresses were delivered by Rabbi Isaac Aboab (pp. 1–14), Rabbi Selomoh de Oliveira (pp. 17–36), Rabbi Isaac Saruco (pp. 39–56), Isaac Netto (pp. 59–74), Elijah Lopes (pp. 77–98), Isaac Vellozino (pp. 101–29), and David Sarfati de Pina (pp. 133–55). They were dedicated, respectively, to the then *parnasim* of the Congregation, to the members of the building committee, to Isaac Penso, Isaac Gabay Henríquez, Jacob de Pinto, Jacob Telles da Costa, and (the last of them) to Isaac Orobio.

[117] See Amsterdam, AGA, PA 334, no. 338, 'Memoria dos Lugares que sederão os Senhores do Mahamad', p. 23, (Bancos entre as colunas grandes da Banda dos Senhores do Mahamad).

leadership and his intellectual attainments. His own economic position was, to say the least, no more than average.

In 1674 the city authorities of Amsterdam assessed Dr Isaac Orobio's income at 1,000 florins, and consequently when collecting the '*200ste Penning*' impost their demand from him was for 5 florins only,[118] whereas large assessments were levied the wealthy occupants of the synagogue seats adjoining—Isaac de Pinto 625 florins, Jacob Bueno de Mesquita 165, Joseph Jessurun 235, Daniel Jessurun Espinosa 95, and Abraham de Judah Touro, who in 1675 purchased the old synagogue building, had to pay 35 florins.[119] The '*200ste Penning*' was a tax imposed on all residents, whether indigenous or not, whose income was assessed at 1,000 florins or more: in 1674, 264 Jews were so taxed, out of whom 225 paid higher sums than the one demanded from Orobio.[120] Thus we may conclude that Isaac belonged to the lower middle class in his own community. Examination of the accounts of the Congregation *Talmud Torah* confirms the picture. Between 1663 and 1674 his annual dues (*finta*) were 8 florins per annum, from 1675 to 1677 16 florins, and from 1678 to 1687 12.[121] Such sums were characteristic of the middle financial stratum of the congregation, made up of small traders, pedlars, doctors, etc. The additional sums that Isaac contributed to the synagogue voluntarily are eloquent of his great involvement in congregational life, but they also indicate that his financial resources were quite limited.[122]

The economic circumstances of his brother Jacob, who in 1673 married their niece Rebecca Monsanto, daughter of their sister

---

[118] On the '*200ste Penning*' tax (i.e. 0.5 per cent) see Vrankrijker, pp. 27 f. It was raised principally in order to offset the heavy military expenditure incurred by Holland as a result of the wars with England and France. An interesting description of the impact of these wars on the economic situation of the Jews will be found in the introduction to the inaugural sermons (see above, n. 116) by David de Castro Tartas. See municipal archives, Amsterdam, AGA, 1674 'Quohier van de 200ste Penning', f. 579ʳ, 'Dr Isack Orobio — 5 [fl.]'.

[119] Municipal archives, ibid., ff. 569ʳ, 578ᵛ, 580ᵛ, 589ʳ.

[120] Those paying only 5 fl. included Isaac Pinheiro (f. 573ʳ), Gabriel Alvarez (ibid.), Dr Daniel Semah (f. 576ʳ), Isaac Monsanto (f. 577ᵛ), Jacob de Chaves (f. 578ʳ), and Jacob Jessurun (f. 582ʳ). The list includes only 10 Ashkenazim—Nethanel Cohen, 20 fl. (f. 571ʳ), Reuben Gompertz, 15 fl. (f. 576ᵛ), Levi Abrahams, 5 fl. (f. 578ˢ), Joseph Salomons, 7½ fl., Alexander Pollak, 5 fl., Joel Levi, 5 fl. (f. 589ᵛ), Aaron Joseph, 5 fl., Solomon Cobirin, 5 fl., Isaac Cohen 5 fl. (f. 590ᵛ), and Solomon Isaac, 12½ fl. (f. 592ʳ).

[121] See AGA, PA 334 no. 174, pp. 598, 667, 688, 714, 745, 759, 779, 795, 814, 831, 853, 869, 882, 899, 918, 936, 951, 970, 987, 1001, 1019, 1039, 1060, 1092, 1130, 1160, 1179; no. 175, pp. 12, 29, 47, 63, 83, 105, 122, 140, 159, 174, 190, 208, 229, 246, 268, 284, 310, 328, 351, 368, 388, 412.

[122] Ibid.

Leonor,[123] were less firm. In the early seventies he was engaged in import, and in 1673 he actually paid the *imposta* imposed by the congregation on profits from the import and export trade;[124] but he clearly did not do very well in business, and by the beginning of the eighties he was going down in the world.[125] It would seem that the circumstances of their sister Rachel, who had married Moses Barukh Pérez, merchant, of Middelburg, were similar to those of Jacob.[126]

Isaac Orobio's own children married in Amsterdam and in Hamburg, and raised families in both places. Moses Orobio followed in his father's footsteps not only professionally as a physician, but also in respect of close involvement in the life of the Portuguese community.[127] On 30 October 1686 (12 *Marḥeshvan* 5447) he married Sarah, daughter of Jacob Abbas in Hamburg, but continued to reside in Amsterdam.[128] Hannah was married on 17 January 1680 (16 *Shebaṭ* 5440) to David Sarfati de Pina, physician and preacher in the congregation, who was one of Isaac Orobio's own best pupils.[129] Rebecca was

[123] Amsterdam, AGA, DTB no. 689, p. 104. The marriage was registered on 12 Aug. 1673; see the transcript of the *kethubbah* (Aramaic marriage contract), PA 334 no. 382, vol. 4, p. 4.

[124] See PA 334 no. 174, p. 1019; at that date he paid 2 fl. 2 st. For his business affairs and his involvement with the firm of Isaac de Prado and Jacob and Solomon Lima see Amsterdam, AGA, *Notariële Archieven* no. 2907B, documents dated 2 and 30 June 1673, and ibid., no. 4077.

[125] In the years 1675–7 he paid 12 fl. in dues to the congregation; in 1678–80 his contribution was reduced to 8 fl., and in 1681 to 4: see PA 334 no. 174, pp. 1002, 1019, 1039, 1062, 1094, 1133, 1161, 1180, and no. 175, pp. 14, 49, 65, 84, 106, 125, 141, 160. On 15 *'Adar* (23 Feb. 1681) he was registered as being indebted to the congregation for 8 fl. 4 st., which he was unable to settle (ibid., p. 169). He died on 3 *Tammuz* 5442 (9 July 1682); see De Castro, p. 353.

[126] Such is the impression given by the amount of the synagogue dues paid by her husband; see PA 334 no. 174, pp. 816, 836, 856, 872, 884, 904, 920, 940, 975, 989, 1004, 1021. Moses Barukh Pérez died on 13 *Tishri* 5434 (23 Sept. 1673), and his wife Rachel on 5 *Kislev* 5447 (21 Nov. 1686); see De Castro, p. 94; PA 334 no. 916, p. 55.

[127] For Moses Orobio's medical studies at Leiden see Kaplan, *Sṭudenṭim be-leiden*, pp. 70 f. He served as *parnas* of the congregation in 5462 (1701/2) and 5467 (1706/7); in 5456 (1695/6) and 5465 (1704/5) as *parnas* of the Society of *'Eṣ Ḥayyim*, and in 5459 (1698/9) and 5464 (1703/4) as *parnas* of the Society of *Biqqur Ḥolim:* see PA 334 no. 155, pp. 10, 25, 36. He was a member of the academy of *Temimey Derekh* ('Integrity in Behaviour'), and one of the founders of the charitable fellowship of *Maskil 'el Dal* ('Regard for the Poor'). See Pieterse, *De Barrios*, pp. 123, 126, 186.

[128] The original marriage-document (*kethubbah*) is preserved in the collection of Professor M. Benayahu in Jerusalem, to whom I am grateful for opportunity to inspect it. See the poem specially composed for his wedding by de Barrios in his *Alegrías*, pp. 113 f. He died on 15 *Marḥeshvan* 5469 (29 Oct. 1708).

[129] On his Leiden studies and his gaining clinical experience as assistant to Isaac Orobio see Kaplan, *Sṭudenṭim be-leiden*, pp. 70 f., and also Amsterdam, AGA, DTB no. 692, p. 35, and the copy of his marriage-document (*kethubbah*) in the congregational transcripts, PA 334 no. 382, vol. 2, p. 171.

married in Amsterdam on 2 April 1686 (8 *Nisan* 5446) to Isaac Milano, a well-to-do merchant of Hamburg, where she settled.[130] Sarah was married on 2 March 1686 (6 *'Adar* 5446) to the widower Joseph Vieira, an Amsterdam merchant.[131] Abraham Orobio, who used also the name Alonso de Velasco, married Esther de León of Toulouse on 22 July 1695 (10 *'Ab* 5455) and settled in Hamburg, where as a merchant he distinguished himself by his success in business.[132]

Many descendants of the Orobio de Castro family struck root in Amsterdam, where they became an integral part of the Portuguese scene. In congregational documents of the eighteenth and nineteenth centuries the family names of Orobio de Castro Machorro, Orobio Furtado, Orobio de Castro Teixeira d'Andrade, Orobio de Castro Teixeira de Mattos frequently figure.[133] They lost their ancestors' Spanish and Portuguese vernacular, but continued to take pride in the origins and in the distinction of their lineage as descendants of one of those who had shaped the spiritual character of their community.

---

[130] See DTB no. 695, p. 136, and the congregational transcripts, PA 334 no. 382, vol. 2, p. 364. For Isaac Milano's activities in Hamburg see Kellenbenz, pp. 476 f. De Barrios composed two poems for his marriage to Rebecca; see his *Alegrías*, pp. 95 f.

[131] See Amsterdam, AGA, DTB no. 696, p. 437, and the congregational transcripts (see above, n. 129), p. 176. In his youth Joseph Vieira had been a pupil in the *'Eṣ Ḥayyim* academy and a member of *Temimey Derekh* (see above, n. 127). See Pieterse, *De Barrios*, pp. 104, 123, 186.

[132] See Amsterdam, AGA, DTB no. 699, p. 106; being absent from the city, Abraham authorized his brother Moses to register his marriage with the civil registrar.

[133] See *Libro das Ascaboth* (i.e. calendar of annual commemoration), MS Amsterdam, EH, 49 B 24, ff. 29ʳ, 43ʳ, 64ʳ, 67ʳ, 158r, 164ʳ, 165ʳ, 166ʳ.

8
Isaac Orobio and Sabbateanism

The great stir raised in Amsterdam by the Sabbatean movement occurred in the third year of Isaac Orobio's residence there. The majority of the local Jewish population, Sephardim and Ashkenazim alike, were caught up in the ferment of messianic enthusiasm which was sweeping through the Jewish world. News about Sabbatai Ṣevi, the self-declared messiah, was received with tremendous emotion by all segments of the Jewish people: as Scholem observed, 'there is no evidence of tension between prudent leadership, on the one hand, and mass enthusiasm, on the other. Their almost unanimous shouts of triumph were audible far and wide.'[1]

The longing for news of Israel's redemption on the part of those who had escaped from the Inquisition and of the survivors of the Chmielnicki massacres of 1648–9 had prepared the ground for the great excitement by which the Jews of Amsterdam were carried away in the years 1665–6. The relatively free conditions enjoyed by the Jews of the city enabled them to exhibit their enthusiasm quite openly. Rabbi Jacob Sasportas, the sworn enemy of Sabbateanism who held rabbinical office in Hamburg, kept up a correspondence with the rabbis and *parnasim* of the Portuguese community in Amsterdam, and in his anti-Sabbatean book *Ṣiṣath Novel Ṣevi* ('Beauty is a Fading Flower', a punning title drawn from Isaiah 28: 1 that plays on the *double entendre* of *ṣevi* ('beauty', also 'hart') used as a personal name Ṣevi) he gives a most graphic description of what was going on there. 'The whole of Amsterdam was agog—enough to put the wind up any God-fearer: in their excess of joy they were dancing in the streets and squares to the music of timbrels, reeling and cavorting in the synagogue, with all the scrolls taken out and carried round dressed in finery—no one caring a rap about hostile reaction and possible jealousy amongst the non-Jews. On the contrary, they kept advertising every bit of news that came their way to make sure that the non-Jews got to know about it.'[2]

Amidst all this euphoria, the tiny group within the Portuguese

---

[1] Scholem, *Sabbatai Ṣevi*, pp. 518–45, esp. p. 519; Benayahu, *Yedi'oth*, pp. 109–205; Silva Rosa, *Sabbatai Tsebi*, pp. 5–6; Kaplan, *Shabbetha'uth*.
[2] Sasportas, *Ṣiṣ. N. Ṣ.*, p. 17.

community of Amsterdam led by Abraham de Souza, who publicly opposed Sabbatai Ṣevi and his followers, was reduced to silence. Two forces converged to stifle their voice: the weighty authority of the *Maʿamad*, and the frenzied joy of the main body of the community, which breathed out threats against all who were opposed to Sabbatai Ṣevi.[3]

Just where, in this alignment of forces, did Isaac Orobio stand in relation to Sabbateanism? Did he join the throng of 'believers', or was he numbered amongst the small minority of 'non-believers'?

David Franco Mendes, in his *Chronicle* of the history of the Amsterdam community from its beginnings up to 1772, mentions a letter of Isaac Orobio in which he refuted the theory of Abraham Michael Cardoso regarding the supposed inevitability of the messiah's apostasy.[4] This repudiation by Orobio is confirmed by two letters written in Spanish by Abraham Michael Cardoso, in which he violently

---

[3] Scholem, op. cit., pp. 519–20. For Abraham de Souza see Sasportas, op. cit., p. 260: 'From the beginning of the affair to its end he lent no credence [to Sabbatai Ṣevi's claims] — on the contrary, he put himself at risk from the populace, who regarded him and all his household with loathing and with utter contempt: but none the less he remained steadfast in his beliefs [as to messianism], and maintained a private correspondence with me ... what he had to put with by way of insult and revilement cannot be imagined ... and but for the protective mercy of heaven, they would have set about him physically and would have killed him — in point of fact, they actually lay in ambush for him often enough, and but for God's help [they would have done for him].' For the stringency of the *Maʿamad* in its dealings with 'non-believers' the terms of the sentence of excommunication dated 28 *Nisan* 5426 (3 May 1666) are significant. This was pronounced upon all 'those who composed, or who were accessory to the composing of a certain statement that was printed at the instance of those lacking in faith ... in opposition to hopes regarding the coming of our Messiah'; MS Amsterdam AGA, PA 334 no. 24a (formerly in *EH* 48 E 64), f. 13ʳ; Kaplan, *Shabbethaʿuth*, pp. 200–3.

[4] See Franco Mendes, *Memorias*, pp. 68 f. Franco Mendes, who for some time acted as honorary secretary of the Portuguese Congregation, knew his way around the documents in its possession, and in compiling his chronicle he made good use of them; but for the events of 1665–6 he offers no new material, what he writes being based on Sasportas and Basnage's *Histoire des Juifs*. On the other hand he does include notes and cites hitherto untapped sources for the period following on Sabbatai Ṣevi's apostasy, and *inter alia* he states that 'O Doutor orobio de Verona escreveo hum discurso tão Elegante como falso, donde torsendo textos e sonhando misterios, disse que o messias devia renegar e o D[outo]r Is[hac] Orobio lhe respondeo renegando de tal sujeito e de todos seus Estud[o]s.' 'Dr Orobio of Verona' is, of course, an error for Dr A. M. Cardoso, who in correspondence from Tripoli as a Sabbataean protagonist engaged in controversy with his brother Dr Isaac Cardoso, as is well known. Franco Mendes not only confused the two brothers, of whom it was Isaac only who resided in Verona (the editors wrongly state, p. 162 n. 150, that A. M. Cardoso's correspondence emanated from Verona), but he compounded his confusion by giving Isaac's surname as Orobio instead of Cardoso. Nevertheless, there is clear evidence here of Isaac Orobio's having addressed an anti-Sabbataean letter to Abraham Cardoso. Cf. Kaplan, *Shabbethaʿuth*, pp. 212 f., App.

assailed the Amsterdam philosopher. The implication of these letters is that Orobio denied the messianic claims of Sabbatai Ṣevi.[5]

However, first we must ascertain at what point in time Isaac Orobio openly expressed his opposition to Sabbateanism. It is clear that A. M. Cardoso's letter reflects Isaac's views as they were after Sabbatai Ṣevi had apostatized to Islam. If, prior to the date of his apostasy, Isaac had done anything at all to indicate his own disapproval of the 'believers', it is not to be supposed that Sasportas would have ignored his stance in his *Ṣiṣath Novel Ṣevi*. But in marked contrast to the praises which Sasportas showers on Isaac Cardoso of Verona, he makes no reference at all to Orobio throughout the book.

Isaac Cardoso had, it is true, for a limited period swallowed Sabbatai Ṣevi's messianic evangelism. This emerges from one of the first letters that A. M. Cardoso wrote to his brother Isaac from Tripoli, in which he said: 'I have received your letter, and since you believed that what I sent you regarding our messiah is true, I will fully answer your questions in regard to [the information] which you lack.'[6] However, Isaac Cardoso changed from being a 'believer' to a 'non-believer' after Sabbatai Ṣevi's apostasy, and the controversy between the two brothers ensued between 1666 and 1668. Sasportas saw fit to close his eyes to Isaac Cardoso's initial flirtation with Sabbateanism, and described him as having been 'of the non-believers: when he heard the blatherings of his brother who wrote to him from Tripoli, he replied pouring scorn on him and his dreams, etc.'.[7]

Had Isaac Orobio travelled the same path, and was he, like his colleague in Verona, carried away by the wave of general enthusiasm which swept through the Jewish world in the years 1665–6? It is known that during this time he was very much under the influence of Rabbi Moses Raphael d'Aguilar, about whom Sasportas wrote in bitter tone that 'when talking to me, he represented himself as a non-believer in order to get me to show my hand, adducing wondrous problems and matters, and considering himself wiser than the proverbial Daniel;[8] to

---

[5] MS Bodl., Opp. Add. 4° 150, Neubauer, *Bodl. Cat.* no. 2481. Yerushalmi, *Isaac Cardoso*, pp. 320–49, gives a detailed analysis of these letters. Cf. Scholem, *Shabbetha-'uth be-kithvey Cardozo*, and his *Gilguley Shabbetha'uth*, pp. 274–97, esp. p. 290 n. 46; *Sabbatai Ṣevi*, pp. 4 n. 1, 645 f., 762, 797, 805, 860, 893 f.

[6] Sasportas, *Ṣiṣ. N. Ṣ.*, p. 289.

[7] Ibid., p. 270. Yerushalmi, *Isaac Cardoso*, pp. 314 f., had taken account of Isaac Cardoso's change of attitude towards Sabbateanism, and of the fact that Sasportas saw fit to ignore his earlier, pro-Sabbatean stance.

[8] Ezek. 28: 3.

[non-⁹]believers, he professed himself as believing in what could be very soon to come to pass—in such manner keeping a foot in both camps'.¹⁰ It is virtually certain that Isaac behaved similarly during the heady days before Sabbatai Ṣevi's apostasy. His experience as a crypto-Jew in Spain had taught him how to keep his thoughts to himself, knowing that to expose but the merest glimpse of them could put his whole position in jeopardy.

Isaac Orobio's letter referred to in David Franco Mendes' *Chronicle* has not survived. Franco Mendes gave but the briefest summary of it, from which all that can be gathered is that in it Isaac opposed the teaching of Abraham Michael Cardoso in regard to the alleged messiah's apostasy.¹¹ Nor do A. M. Cardoso's two letters, written in 1668 and containing an attack on Orobio, make it possible to reconstruct Orobio's position. The bulk of what the Tripoli doctor wrote consisted of an outpouring of fury against his brother Isaac Cardoso, in berating whom he does not mention any details of his opposition to Sabbateanism either. The essence of the offence of Isaac Cardoso and Isaac Orobio was seen by Abraham Michael Cardoso in their refusal to believe in the messiah who had (as he claimed) been revealed in their own time, and in their closing their eyes to the words of the prophets and the biblical exegesis of the sages, which were realized, according to him, in the personality and activities of Sabbatai Ṣevi. The ideological content of these two letters of A. M. Cardoso resembles that of his letter to the *dayyanim*, or rabbinical judges, of Smyrna written in May–June 1669 (*Sivan* 5429).¹² Central to his contention was his 'crypto-Jewish' attitude towards the character of the messiah, based on his own exegesis of Isaiah 53: 5, 'but he was pierced for our transgressions, tortured for our iniquities; the chastisement he bore is health for us and by his scourging we are healed' (New English Bible). He understood this verse to mean that the messiah would be constrained against his will not to fulfil the prescriptions of the Torah, and that in virtue of this punishment inflicted upon him atonement would be effected for the whole of Israel.¹³ In one of his first letters to his brother Isaac, quoted by Sasportas, he had already asserted with great emphasis that

---

⁹ In Tishby's view, the negative *u-[le-vilti-]ma'aminim* has to be omitted, as an error; see Sasportas, *Ṣiṣ. N. Ṣ.*, p. 74 n. 7.

¹⁰ Sasportas, ibid.; see Kaplan, *d'Aguilar*, pp. 95 f. For d'Aguilar's influence on Orobio see Kaplan, *d'Aguilar*, pp. 101–3, and above, chap. 6, pp. 110 f.

¹¹ Franco Mendes, *Memorias*, p. 68.

¹² See Scholem, *'Iggereth A. M. Cardozo*.

¹³ See Scholem, *Gilguley Shabbetha'uth*, pp. 306 f.

'two years ago now I had already been informed that King Messiah was destined to wear prison garb, which would prevent the Jews from recognizing his identity: to be short, he would become a crypto-Jew, just as I [used to be]'.[14] In the same letter he linked the fate of Sabbatai Sevi with that of the crypto-Jews in the Iberian peninsula, thereby conferring on the Christian conformity of the latter a religious and messianic significance:

The essential feature of the mystery is that we are all of us obliged by the Torah to have become crypto-Jews before we may go forth from exile, for it states in the Torah [Deuteronomy 4: 28] 'There you will worship gods made by human hands out of wood and stone' [New English Bible]. It is all measure for measure: we profaned the Torah, voluntarily practised idolatry, and brought about the desecration of God's Name, for his Name was profaned among the Gentiles because of our sins. It is therefore logical, and indeed is so explicitly decreed in the Torah, that we should willy-nilly have to become idolaters and to profane the Torah amongst the nations: and thus it comes about that we have ourselves been desecrated and wounded, forced into crypto-Judaism, and, being in that situation, we cry out to God, blessed be He.[15]

That is the position to which Abraham Michael Cardoso adheres in his two Spanish letters, without moving an inch. With much intensity of feeling, and full of the zealot's fire for what he believes in, he fulminates against those who reject his own messianic interpretations which are, he claims, based upon correct understanding both of what the prophets foretold and of rabbinic exegesis. It is not he himself who had deviated from the tradition handed down by those whose Jewish faith is intact, but rather his brother Isaac and Isaac Orobio, who in their self-esteem place themselves on a higher plane than some of the greatest sages in Israel.[16] His own interpretations, he claims, tally exactly with the words of the prophets and of the sages; he is not interested in dealing with the kind of messiah 'whom Dr Cardoso and Dr Orobio have conjured out of their imagination or about whom they have written'.[17]

[14] Sasportas, Ṣiṣ. N. Ṣ., p. 291.   [15] Ibid., p. 293.
[16] MS Bodl. (see above, n. 5), f. 11ʳ: 'No se contentara el senhor Dotor Ishack Cardozo de ser un Dotor Rabeno Moseh Bar Nahman, y el Doctor Orobio de ser un dotor Rabenu Mosseh de Egipto, sino que se consiguen guente y son nefilim, y el uno se queda caido, y el otro se aparta orbo.' In one passage (f. 3ʳ) Cardoso refers to Orobio as 'el Doctor Orobio y Silva', evidently by a *lapsus calami*.
[17] Ibid., f. 12ᵛ: '... que yo no trato del masiah escripto o ymaguinado del Doctor Cardozo ny del Doctor Orobio, ny de otro alguno; sino del masiah de Israel comforme sabios y prophetas de verdad.'

As in his letter to the *dayyanim* of Smyrna, so also in these letters A. M. Cardoso insists on the absolute obligation to believe in Sabbatai Ṣevi's messiahship because he fulfilled the criteria to which the Talmudic rabbis had pointed. Even were faith in him to prove illusory, those who had so believed would have fulfilled their duty; whereas the sceptics would have been sapping Jewish morale, and would have enticed the people away from the path of repentance. 'Whosoever will not entertain the belief that Sabbatai Ṣevi could be the messiah, even if [it should ultimately] transpire that he is not, entertains no belief in the messiah of Israel. Whoever derides him, transgresses the words of the sages and mocks the prophets: because even if Sabbatai Ṣevi himself should prove not to have been the messiah, the one who is to be the messiah would then come hard on his tracks.'[18] Belief in the messiah inspires men to good works and to repent of their sins, 'and in places where they met with disappointment, they turned away from penitence'.[19]

A. M. Cardoso holds up to ridicule the 'credulity' of his brother Isaac and the band of his 'perverted associates': their pictured messiah is 'neither Christian nor Jew, but a figment of the imagination. He [is supposed to] come hurling lightning and thunderbolts [?], all of a sudden in a trice to gather in the lost tribes, separate the wheat from the chaff, whilst hovering on an icing-sugar cloud, his body all butter and attired in raiment of fresh bread.'[20] They purported to find authoritative support for their views in Maimonides, but were in point of fact not competent to understand him.[21]

There can be no doubt that Isaac Cardoso and Isaac Orobio had pointed out to him the clear link between his own conception of messianism and the Christian version. A. M. Cardoso was not put out by the comparison. 'If', he wrote, 'the Christians, too, take that view, what harm can come to us from the truth? They [i.e. the Christians, must] have received the notion from the sages of Israel . . . Are we to

---

[18] Ibid., f. 7ʳ.
[19] Ibid., f. 7ᵛ: 'y donde desperaron del cazo, dexaron la penitencia'. In the continuation Cardoso avers that both in Tripoli, where he himself was living, and in the island of Djerba belief in Sabbatai Ṣevi had not been impaired, and that the Jews there were fasting from 3 to 6 days out of each week.
[20] Ibid., f. 14ʳ: ' . . . no es xtiano, ny Judio mas es ymaguinario[.] a de uenir tirando Rayos y estopones, luego de golpe en un santiamen, a de recoger los tribus los trigos en las pajas a de venir sobre una nuve de asucarcande su cuerpo de mantegillas [sic] su vestido de pan tierno.' [*estopón* means 'rough tow', as used for making sacking. Dr A. M. García suggests to me that since tow was also used for torches, it is here introduced in order to suggest 'lightning-effects contrived by mere theatrical devices.' R.L.]
[21] Ibid.

reject truth out of fear of what is false? . . . Or is it better, in order to avoid putting a weapon into their hands, to resort to pure imagination in order to describe a messiah who is not that whom the prophets foretold?'[22]

Of particular importance for our concern is the attempt of A. M. Cardoso to describe the attachment to Judaism encountered amongst those crypto-Jews who had left Spain and had become re-united with Jewry. Cardoso classified them in three groups.[23] (*a*) First, the philosophers and scientists. Many amongst these, Cardoso claimed, whenever they stumbled on anything in rabbinic literature for which, in their view, no philosophical proof was forthcoming, would pass negative judgements on the items concerned, rejecting them without making any attempt at understanding them. Since the Law cannot be expounded except as the sages have interpreted it, whereas this class of person is radically opposed to the sages, it follows that they are 'bad Jews, and yet not Christians'. Others within this category are prepared to submit to the yoke of the Law and its precepts, and turn into intellectuals of a religiously speaking disciplined type. Others again—still within this same first group—are philosophers of the kind known as 'naturalists' (i.e. deists),[24] who in terms of what they believe are neither Christians nor Jews. Writing of these elsewhere, Cardoso declares that 'there are, in our age, many of our own people—intellectuals, many of them indeed scholars of ability—who deny the assertions of our sages, some of them entertaining doubts as to the truth of Law, and others frankly disbelieving it: their arguments are powerful ones, and the objections which they raise are rooted in the very axioms of logically articulated thinking.'[25] (*b*) A second are those naturally wise and the arrogant bachelors (i.e. in possession of the lowest rank of university degree); for everything they seek a basis in Scripture, which, in their opinion, none of the sages of Israel either understood or were able to subject to proper exegesis. The only proper way to understand Scripture is, in their view, their own. That holds good for their approach to matters concerning the messiah; but 'these things are not explicitly detailed in the Scripture, every verse in which may bear a different meaning [from that conventionally accepted] as seen through the eyes

[22] Ibid., f. 4^r.
[23] Ibid., ff. 12^r f.
[24] *Naturalistas* was the term used at this period for deists, as denying that those religions which evince positive institutions involve any supernatural revelation; Scholem, *Shabbetha'uth be-kithvey Cardozo*, p. 290 n. 46.
[25] A. M. Cardoso, *Sod ha-'elohuth*, MS Adler (Jewish Theological Seminary, New York) 2432, ff. 140^v f., cited by Scholem, loc. cit.

of those who reject the corpus of rabbinic teaching'. (*c*) The third group consists of those former crypto-Jews who 'adhere loyally to every single item in the dicta of the rabbis, making no pretensions to being scholars themselves'.

Y. H. Yerushalmi has drawn attention to the interesting parallelism between this language of A. M. Cardoso and that used by Isaac Orobio himself in his *Epístola Invectiva* against Prado, where he attempts to classify those returning to the Jewish fold on the basis of similar criteria.[26] Yerushalmi maintains that A. M. Cardoso located his brother and Isaac Orobio within the same bracket in which Orobio included Spinoza and Juan de Prado, viz. the group comprising 'philosophers, naturalists, and atheists'. It seems to me, however, that in making this judgement Yerushalmi is not quite on target. A. M. Cardoso did not, in point of fact, lump his brother and Orobio together with those in the category of philosophers and scholars. He does not identify them with those philosophers who demand rational and demonstrative proof for what the sages said (see (*a*) above). He introduces the names of his two opponents when discussing category (*b*), i.e. 'those naturally wise and some bachelors, arrogant people, seeking a scriptural source for everything as if they were wiser than the sages of Israel'.[27] The gibe is unmistakable: Orobio is not, for A. M. Cardoso, a philosopher, nor indeed even a doctor in possession of the licentiate, but just a 'bachelor' (this term being used here with the disparaging nuance sometime injected into *sophomore*); and it may be surmised that his intention here was to hint at the circumstance that Orobio had not obtained his diploma in the orthodox manner, but by means of an act of forgery perpetrated by him whilst in Toulouse.[28] The matter becomes clear from the charges that he proceeds forthwith to bring

---

[26] On this tract see above, chap. 6, pp. 153 f.; Yerushalmi, *Isaac Cardoso*, p. 326. In two passages of this work Orobio attempted to classify the crypto-Jews reverting to Judaism on leaving Spain. See *Epíst. Inv.*, MS Paris, BN Fonds espagnoles 40-1, pp. 775 f.: 'Dividense en tres clases los sequaces de la impiedad, opugnadores de la virtud, amigos de su propio entender: Los primeros y de peor calidad son los infaudos Atheistas que osaron negar la Sagrada Escritura, aunque mas se excusen con confesar la Primera Causa; los segundos son Israelitas, creen en Dios, assienten al Sagrado Texto, y abominan la explicacion que el mismo Dios, con summa providencia, concedio a la Ley . . . resta la tercera en que se constituyen los que son verdaderos observantes de la Ley de Moseh . . . mas descaecen miserablemente en la observancia de los sagrados preceptos, juzgando la mayor imperfección por excusable . . .' See Révah, *Spinoza et Prado*, p. 126.

[27] MS Bodl. (see above n. 5), f. 12ʳ⁻ᵛ: 'otros naturalmente sabios y algunos Bachileres . . . gente soberbia y a todo piden su lugar de escritura la qual no ha sido hasta oy para con ellos de ningun sabio de Israel bien entendida y explicada.'

[28] See above, chap. 5, pp. 101 f.

against Isaac Orobio and Isaac Cardoso in the two letters referred to: they are suspect not because of their inclination towards philosophy and their delving after rational proof, but because of their presumptuousness in rejecting rabbinic statements and because of their ingenuous and unorthodox exegesis of Scripture. According to Abraham Michael Cardoso, it was not he who had strayed from the highway of perfection but rather his brother in Verona and the latter's colleague in Amsterdam. Unlike them, he had remained faithful to the tradition of the sages of Israel.[29]

As stated above, the letters addressed to A. M. Cardoso by Isaac Cardoso and Isaac Orobio have not survived. Yerushalmi has nevertheless succeeded in reconstructing Isaac Cardoso's attitudes to Sabbateanism by using, *inter alia*, passages from his philosphical *magnum opus* entitled *Philosophia Libera*, published in Venice in 1673, which deal explicitly with Sabbatai Ṣevi and the latter's 'prophet' Nathan of Gaza.[30] The task is more difficult in regard to Orobio de Castro, since in the whole of his prolific literary output there is no single direct reference to the Sabbatean movement, nor does he ever mention Sabbatai Ṣevi by name. However, examination of a number of his statements concerning messiansim, and of his approach to rabbinic tradition, makes it possible to learn what his attitude was towards a number of the subjects ventilated by A. M. Cardoso in his two letters.

Commenting on Genesis 49: 10, 'the sceptre shall not pass from Judah, nor the staff [or, lawgiver] from his descendants' (New English Bible), Orobio writes:

Those referred to here are the exponents of the holy Law [who will not cease] until the messiah comes. Although there was no sceptre in the hands of Judah in the Babylonian captivity, right up to the present day there has not failed a lawgiver from between his feet, these being the scholars of the Law who instruct and teach them [i.e. Israel] incessantly regarding the exact mode of fulfilling the holy commandments ... They are the judges of the people, [wielding] absolute [authority] not only in matters relative to bibical law, custom, and the precepts but also in regard to civil and criminal law: it is they who give decisions according to the Law and their ancestral tradition.[31]

In his *Carta Apologética* against Prado Orobio does, indeed, concede

---
[29] MS Bodl., ff. 2ʳ–3ʳ, in particular the passage beginning '... todo el que niega los Sabios de Israel, su tradicion, sabiduría y doctrina no cree en la Ley ny en los prophetas y sy la cree es por yerro ...'
[30] *Philos.*, ff. 641–2; Yerushalmi, *Isaac Cardoso*, pp. 328 f., 343 f.
[31] *Prev. Div.*, MS Amsterdam, *EH* 48 D 6, ff. 175ʳ f.

that 'there are certain customs, *responsa*, and rabbinical decisions' about which he is uncomfortable and against which his understanding protests. But since hesitations about such things do not inhibit him from implementing God's Law, he is not unduly worried by them.[32] He is very far from that arrogance which Abraham Michael Cardoso had imputed to him when accusing him of disrespect for his rabbinic heritage. True enough, he was not prepared to accord a blind belief to 'the miraculous feats with which certain of the rabbis were credited'. Clearly those miracles that were referred to in Scripture were true, since their source was divine, and as such 'had been accepted, by general agreement, amongst the peoples of the world'. Moreover, miraculous events adduced in rabbinic literature were plausible as well, in the light of the fact that 'they are adduced in order to confirm what is true doctrine'. On the other hand, 'the history of the rabbis themselves is not canonical Scripture, so that no one is obliged to believe in its certainty without reservations'. Even though there was no reason to impugn the reliability of the sages who recorded these matters, there might be grounds for suspecting that some of the anecdotes about the rabbis had been introduced by over-enthusiastic disciples, who had invented them with the object of presenting their teachers to the public as exemplary characters, whom it was one's duty to emulate.[33]

It may be supposed that Orobio expressed himself in similar terms when dismissing the messianic claims of Sabbatai Ṣevi. There was nothing in the proofs adduced by A. M. Cardoso from Jewish lore and legendary elaboration of the biblical text to convince him that the so-called prophecies of Nathan of Gaza were in fact true. Legend and lore were, for Orobio, deserving of credence so long—and only so long—as a Jew might find in them support for the implementation of the holy Law. But from the moment that Sabbatai Ṣevi strayed from the prescriptions of Israel's Torah, there was no longer occasion to rely upon pronouncements of the sages in order to authenticate his messianic pretensions. The primary aim of the sages had been to reinforce popular observance of Jewish precepts, whereas the shocking behaviour of Sabbatai Ṣevi as a prisoner in Gallipoli had the effect of distancing the Jewish public from that aim. On this point there is no

---

[32] *Cart. Apol.*, MS Paris (see above, n. 26), pp. 893 f.: 'En la verdad muchas costumbres, respuestas y conclusiones que no tocan a la misma Ley de Dios, no se ajustan a mi entendimiento y las repugna. No obstante, como no me obstan a guardar la Ley de Dios, no me embaraçan ni fuera razon inquietar de los otros con semejantes dudas.'   [33] Ibid., pp. 894 f.

Isaac Orobio and Sabbateanism

difference between Isaac's views and those of Isaac Cardoso of Verona.[34] Regarding A. M. Cardoso's allegation of the 'ingenuousness' of his brother and Isaac Orobio, who supposedly had a mental image of the messiah as some sort of superior being, a superman who would set aside the laws of nature, it does not tally with Orobio's own explicit statement on the subject:

> The messiah will be as humble as was Moses, as holy as his ancestors Abraham, Isaac, and Jacob, of meek temperament ... He will come to Jerusalem, to Mount Zion, to the place where dwells the glory of the Lord God of Hosts: not like some Antiochus or Pompey, or the other impure kings, but as the servant of the Lord, being himself the acme of humility, and will prove to Israel and the Gentiles alike that he enters Jerusalem as the Prince of Peace ... He will reign from sea to sea, and the whole of humanity will recognize him as their liege-Lord.[35]

It is now clear that even if Isaac Orobio's position *vis-à-vis* Sabbateanism prior to Sabbatai Ṣevi's apostasy is not as clear as one would wish, once it was known in Amsterdam that the supposed messiah had turned Muslim, he went on record publicly against the 'believers'. In this he was acting no differently from the Amsterdam Portuguese leadership, which already on 12 December 1666 (15 *Kislev* 5427) had taken its stand against the 'believers' and adopted various measures to prevent the spread of Sabbatean propaganda within the congregation.[36] Despite this, a cell of 'believers' still remained active in the Portuguese community of Amsterdam into the early seventies, customarily meeting under the leadership of the congregational cantor (*ḥazzan*) Emanuel Benattar (Abiatar) in his own house. Scholem surmised that they 'seem to have been unmolested by the Jewish authorities, possibly because they had the very pious and very wealthy Abraham Israel Pereyra among their members'.[37] The Sabbatean affiliation of Abraham Pereyra is of great importance, and is able to

---

[34] Cf. Isaac Cardoso, *Excel.*, p. 142, and Yerushalmi, *Isaac Cardoso*, pp. 333 f.

[35] See Orobio's *Resp. Pred. franc.*, MS Amsterdam, EH 48 D 6 f. 296ᵛ (*bis*); furthermore, the redemption for which Israel yearns is not, essentially, material redemption but a spiritual one, ibid., f. 296ʳ (*bis*): 'no espera Israel riqueza, ni potençia carnal ni los viçios y comodidades que lisonjean nuestra materialidad, sino un santo reposo en la Patria exerciendo libre de la Captividad de las gentes el divino culto, que recibio en Sinay, medio que el S[enho]r le dio p[ar]a alcançar la gloria eterna.'

[36] See Kaplan, *Shabbetha'uth*, pp. 203 f. News of Sabbatai Ṣevi's apostasy reached Amsterdam in *Kislev* 5427, and on 15th of that month (12 Dec. 1666) Moses Abudiente's Sabbatean work entitled *Fin de los Dias* was proscribed, 'seeing that the subject-matter of the said book conflicts with truth as set forth in our holy Law', MS Amsterdam, AGA, PA 334 no. 24a, f. 15ʳ.

[37] Scholem, *Sabbatai Ṣevi*, p. 893, ibid., p. 755.

throw light on a number of aspects of this whole chapter of events. It will therefore be useful to examine it afresh here.

It is known that Abraham Israel Pereyra was a crypto-Jew originating from Madrid. Having escaped from Spain to Venice, he made his way to Amsterdam where he reverted to Judaism. Already by the 1640s he was occupying a central role in the leadership of the Portuguese community. He contributed substantial sums to charitable institutions, and in 1659 he established a fund for the foundation of a rabbinical academy (*yeshibah*) in Palestine at Hebron, named out of courtesy to him *Ḥesed le-'Abraham* ('lovingkindness to Abraham', from Micah 7: 20). At the time when Sabbatai Ṣevi made his appearance Pereyra became an enthusiastic 'believer' under the influence of the Hebron rabbis and in particular Rabbi Me'ir b. Ḥiyya Rophe'. Before passover in the spring of 1666 he had already set off for Palestine accompanied by Dr Isaac Nahar, to pay his respects to the 'messiah', but the project was not accomplished and he was compelled to remain in Venice. Before leaving Amsterdam he had published a moral tract in Spanish entitled *La Certeza del Camino*. Although there is no direct reference in the book either to Sabbatai Ṣevi or to the messianic excitement which developed in the wake of his appearance, there is no doubt that Pereyra's object was the winning of converts to the pietistic penitential movement which followed on the heels of the intense messianic expectancy.[38] In 1671 Abraham Israel Pereyra published in Amsterdam another Spanish moralistic tract entitled this time *Espejo de la vanidad del mundo* ('mirror of the world's vanity').[39] Surprisingly, at the beginning of the book one finds the approbations of the three rabbis: Isaac

---

[38] Ibid., pp. 529 f.; Amzalak, *Pereyra;* Yaari; Scholem's critique of sundry conclusions in which should be noted (Scholem, op. cit., p. 529 n. 148). On Pereyra's activity within the Amsterdam congregation see C. Roth, *Men. b. I.*, pp. 62 f. For the continued support of the Hebron academy by his son Jacob Pereyra see Emmanuel, *Siyyu'an shel 'Amst.*, p. 403, and G. Nahon, 'Yeshivot hierosolymites du XVIII⁰ siècle', in G. Dahan (ed.), *Le Juif au miroire de l'histoire: Mélanges en l'honneur de Bernhard Blumenkranz*, Paris, 1985, pp. 301–26, esp. pp. 313 f., 319 f. For the liberal support afforded by Abraham Pereyra to the Amsterdam Congregation *Talmud Torah*, see *Livro Grande de Legados de Abraham & Sara Pereira (sic)*, Amsterdam, AGA, PA 334 no. 783 (1659–1746), esp. p. 1.

[39] A letter written by Pereyra to Isaac López de Quirós on 13 'Elul 5431 (19 Aug. 1671) indicates that at that date Pereyra was out of Amsterdam. It is difficult to decipher the name of the place from which he wrote (*Ala*[. . .]*a*), but it clearly lay beyond the Dutch frontier ('e como eu me acho remoto nesta parte'): see PA 334 no. 1152, p. 182. Is the implication that in that year Pereyra had not returned to Amsterdam, and that he arranged to have the book printed there in his absence, or is some brief journey abroad all that is meant? Our present state of knowledge does not make a definite conclusion possible.

Aboab da Fonseca, Moses Raphael d'Aguilar, and Josiah Pardo. All three had not only repudiated the Sabbatean movement in 1666, but they had also given vent to their chagrin at the 'believers', adding their own voices to those antagonistic towards them.[40] Moreover, following the rabbinic approbations one finds other commendatory remarks about the tract and its author from the pen of Isaac Orobio de Castro.[41] Was, then, Pereyra's influence in the Amsterdam community so great, and his standing so unshakeable, that the good fathers of the congregation shut their eyes to his being a Sabbatean and, so far from inhibiting the appearance of his book, actually added their approbations to it? As regards Isaac Orobio, he had publicly disavowed Sabbatai Ṣevi in his letter to A. M. Cardoso; what, then, was it that induced him to praise the literary production of an author who was numbered amongst the Sabbateans?

Inspection of Pereyra's work has made it apparent to me that these questions can be answered. Not only is his book absolutely devoid of Sabbatean content, but there are in it distinct indications of the author's own retraction of his Sabbatean beliefs, and of his deep sense of disappointment at the denouement.

Here is what Pereyra had to say about his messianic faith:

Let us pray to God that He may bring us to that blessed time, and send us the true redeemer [*el verdadero Redemptor*], the time of that most happy King who, being descended from David, must stand at the people's head: more learned than Solomon in his wisdom, and almost as great a prophet as Moses.[42]

When he comes to the passage in which he describes his journey from Amsterdam to Italy as a result of the feverish messianic interest that had been aroused, he prefaces it with the words 'there is no ill [*mal*] that does not turn out to be for the best',[43] and there can be no doubt

---

[40] See Kaplan, *Shabbetha'uth*, p. 206; Benayahu, *Yedi'oth*, pp. 203 f.; Scholem, *Sabbatai Ṣevi*, p. 755.

[41] Orobio's commendation, which is in Spanish ('Elogio de Ishak Orobio de Castro'), is followed by a sonnet in praise of Pereyra and of his book by Daniel Levi de Barrios, reprinted in the latter's *Coro*, p. 380. See below, n. 60.

[42] *Espejo*, p. 550: 'Pidamos a Dios nos llegue a esse feliz tiempo embiandonos el verdadero Redemptor, cuyo dichoso Rey, que de la descendencia de David ha de ser cabeça del Pueblo, sera mas docto que el sapientissimo Salomon, y casi tan gran Propheta como Moysen.'

[43] Ibid., p. 437: 'No hay mal que por bien no venga; bien lo experimientó [*sic*] Abraham Pereyra el año cinco mil quatro cientos y veinte y seis, que navegando con el antiguo desseo, de ir a recrearse, en la sombra del arbol, que Dios por su misericordia, le concedió plantar en Hebron.'

that by *mal* he is alluding to his previous belief in Sabbatai Ṣevi which had impelled him to set out together with Isaac Nahar. It is clear that, contrary to Scholem's opinion, by 1671 Pereyra had become disenchanted with the Sabbatean movement; and that as a consequence, the congregational rabbis (and, together with them, Isaac Orobio) were not able to find anything untoward in the book or in its author. Quite the contrary is the case. Still recognizable in the work are traces of the penitential movement of the years 1665–6 brought on in Amsterdam by messianic anticipations, and this feature made the book a potential instrument for rallying the morale of a community that had been bowled over by stupefaction at the news of Sabbatai Ṣevi's apostasy. It could underscore the message that disillusionment with Sabbatai Ṣevi did not have to turn his erstwhile devotees from the paths of penitence. The self-declared messiah might have met with failure, Sabbatai Ṣevi might have proved a disappointment: yet repentance still remained the way that was pleasing to God and the means of hastening the redemption, which would transpire once the people had achieved a penitence that was complete, and had severed themselves absolutely from their crooked paths.[44] The contribution by Isaac Orobio, printed at the beginning of the book, is redolent of the same spirit:

If [the reader] looks into the mirror of divine Law and sound morals, he will forthwith descry therein his own physiognomy so marred, so estranged from spiritual beauty, that he will be abashed that the image should be his own . . . the acknowledgement of which will lead to revulsion at his own actions, to his coming to abominate his own vanity, to the emending of what is corrupt, and the pursuit of what is holy and upright, wherein his entire happiness consists.[45]

All of this throws into question the alleged presence of Abraham Pereyra in the Sabbatean cell that used to foregather in the house of Emanuel Benattar. None the less, there is no room for doubt regarding the participation in that circle of the poet Daniel Levi (Miguel) de Barrios, who was himself numbered among Isaac Orobio's intimates. De Barrios had reached Amsterdam in 1662, the same year that Isaac

[44] *Inter alia*, Pereyra attributes the delay in messianic deliverance to the proclivity of Jews to engaging in games of chance; ibid., p. 320: 'Quando no huviera en la miseria de nuestro cautiverio mayores pecados, que los que causa este vicio; eran bastantes para suspender nuestra esperada Redención.'

[45] Orobio's *elogio*: 'Mas si se mirare al Espejo de la divina Ley y recta moralidad, verá luego su propia imagen tan desfigurada y agena de la hermosura espiritual, que se avergonçará que sea suya . . . de cuyo conocimiento resultará el aborrecer sus mismas acciones como feas, la detestación de su vanidad, la enmienda de lo vicioso y la prosecución de lo santo, de lo honesto, en que consiste toda su felicidad.'

Isaac Orobio and Sabbateanism

Orobio settled there, and from then on bonds of friendship developed between them.[46] It is therefore appropriate to examine that friendship here, in order to decide if, and how, their relations were influenced by de Barrios' Sabbateanism.

Daniel Levi de Barrios (who, whilst still a conforming Christian, bore the forename Miguel) had been born into a 'New Christian' family in Montilla, a little town in Andalusia.[47] In 1660 he moved to Italy, was circumcised in Leghorn (Livorno), and reverted to the open profession of Judaism under the influence of his aunt, Rachel Cohen de Soza. Whilst there he married Deborah Vaez, who died somewhat later in the isle of Tobago on their ill-fated journey to the American continent. Nothing is known about his return to Europe, but on 30 August 1662 he married Abigail de Pina in Amsterdam, where he devoted himself to writing poetry and also, in 1667, together with his brother-in-law Samuel Rosa, founded a theatrical company.

De Barrios was soon to fall foul of the *parnasim* of the congregation, who disapproved of the pagan elements and sensuous motifs of which de Barrios made frequent use. It was for this reason that his two books *Flor de Apolo* and *Coro de las Musas* were printed not in Amsterdam but in Brussels, in 1665 and 1672 respectively.[48] It would appear that for a

---

[46] On de Barrios see Scholberg, *Poesía de M. de Barrios*, also his *De Barrios and Amsterdam*; Glaser, *De Barrios*; Révah, *Censure de la communauté*. A list of de Barrios' writings is given by Kayserling, *Biblioteca*, pp. 16 f.

[47] He was baptized in the church of Santiago apóstol on 3 Nov. 1635; see Scholberg, *Poesía*, p. 3; Pieterse, *De Barrios*, p. 15.

[48] Documents throwing light upon the congregation's prohibition of the printing of these books were published by Révah, *Censure de la communauté*, pp. 82 f. The manuscript of de Barrios' *Flor de Apolo* was handed by the *Ma'amad* to Dr Isaac Nahar to peruse, as a result of which de Barrios was told on 13 'Adar 5423 (20 Feb. 1663) that he was being denied authorization to print it in Holland ('con orden expressa para q[ue] o não faça imprimir em nenhuma p[ar]te desta Provincia'; Amsterdam, AGA, PA 334 no. 24, unpaginated). In reporting on the book's contents Nahar had stated that '. . . ser todos versos amorosos e lascivos, pouco liçitos a nenhum judeu sacar a luz reparej nos lugares aqui nottados que: huno, p[or] se invocar Deidades gentilicas e attribuirlhes Deidade . . . julgo se não deve consentir q[ue] por burlas se digão palavras que, dittas de veras, são tão criminaes . . .' (ibid.) On Nahar's recommendation de Barrios was invited by the *Ma'amad* to emend those passages which had been marked as being incompatible with Jewish tradition, and this he agreed to do; but even the revised version of his poems was unacceptable to the Portuguese-Jewish leadership, which on 10 'Iyyar of the same year (17 May 1663) resolved to reaffirm its interdiction of publication. De Barrios consequently decided to get it printed in Brussels, at the press of Balthazar Vivien, whence it appeared in 1665; and in 1672 he published his *Coro de las Musas* with the same house. When the first copies reached Amsterdam, the *Ma'amad* handed them over for investigation to Isaac Aboab, Moses Raphael d'Aguilar, and Abraham Cohen Pimentel, who submitted a detailed report on the book's contents in which they drew

limited term de Barrios served as a captain in the Spanish army: and the current view amongst students of his biography has been that he served in that capacity up till 1674, support for this assertion being allegedly forthcoming from a number of his compositions.[49] But Révah and Pieterse have proved that de Barrios was a member of the Congregation *Talmud Torah* from at least 1663, and it is difficult to reconcile this detail with service in the Spanish army in Brussels.[50] True, de Barrios did stay for several extended periods between 1662 and 1674 in Brussels. The leadership of the Portuguese community reacted strenuously to this, and on 18 September 1665, standing before the ark in the synagogue, de Barrios sought pardon for having contravened the congregational prohibition of 1644 by having resided in Catholic countries where Judaism was prohibited (*terras de ydolatria*).[51] Whilst in Flanders, which was under Spanish rule, de Barrios succeeded in a surprising way in entering into close relationships with the local aristocracy—diplomats, army officers, writers, and poets—from many of whom he also received generous financial support: nor can there be any doubt that for the majority of them his Jewishness was not a secret kept from them.[52] He took advantage of his residence in Brussels to print his books of which the publication had been interdicted in Amsterdam.

---

attention to passages that ran counter to the spirit of Judaism; and they also pointed to the panegyrics showered by de Barrios on various Christian personalities who had themselves been the sworn enemies of Jewry (Amsterdam, AGA, PA 334 no. 66). In the congregational records I have succeeded in tracing the decision of the *Ma'amad* consequent upon the recommendation of the rabbinical commission of three, which was to prohibit sale in Amsterdam and to direct that copies already distributed should be recalled: '5432 . . . En 9 de sivan se ordeno a Daniel de Barios [*sic*] que el libro Coro de las Musas que venia ynpreso en Bruselas que no lo venda en esta ciudad de Amst[erd]am y lo que avia distribuido los bolbiese a recoxer por no convenir que no coriese [*sic*] en esta nacion . . .' (MS Amsterdam, AGA, PA 334 no. 24a f. 27ᵛ.) It is thus clear that distribution of the book was expressly interdicted: but for all that, in the very same year a second edition appeared, printed this time within the city of Amsterdam itself by Juan Luis de Pas. See Révah, *Censure de la communauté*, p. 84 n. 14.

[49] See Scholberg, *Poesía de M. de Barrios*, pp. 10 f.

[50] Révah, *Censure de la communauté*, pp. 79 f.; cf. Pieterse, *De Barrios*, pp. 19 f.

[51] As was usual in such cases, de Barrios' declaration was recorded in the *Ascamoth* (*Acta*) of the Congregation *Talmud Torah* (Amsterdam, AGA, PA 334 no. 19, p. 554). Révah published the record *Censure de la communauté*, pp. 81 f.; cf. Pieterse, *De Barrios*, pp. 19 f. The congregational ordinance of 1644 in regard to members residing *in partibus gentium* is registered in the *Ascamoth*, ibid., p. 172; see Y. Kaplan, 'The Travels of Portuguese Jews from Amsterdam to the "Lands of Idolatry" (1644–1724)', in Y. Kaplan (ed.), *Jews and Conversos*, Jerusalem, 1985, pp. 197–224.

[52] See Scholberg, *Poesía de M. de Barrios*, pp. 15 f. On Gentile relations with Portuguese Jews in Brussels at this period see above, chap. 7, pp. 180 f.

Isaac Orobio and Sabbateanism 225

In those two books Daniel Levi de Barrios paid lip service with a vengeance in return for the material aid and the social acceptance that he had met with in Brussels. They contain poems in praise of Spain as the land of the poet's birth, its landscapes, its kings, and its history. In the gallery of historical figures whom he celebrates, the reader will encounter arch-enemies of Israel such as Titus, 'the brave commander' 'who punished the rebellious [Jews] for their crime';[53] Reccared and Sisebut, the Visigothic kings, of whom the first is here celebrated because he 'oppressed the Jews', and the second because he 'unleashed against the Israelites the armoury of faith';[54] Ferdinand the Catholic, 'champion of the faith', who 'in his zeal founded [*sic*] the Holy Inquisition' and 'expelled more than 800,000 Jews';[55] and Nebuchadnezzar, who allegedly first brought to Spain the people of Jerusalem who 'in their exile drag the shackles of their errors'.[56] Nevertheless, the books are saturated with Jewish motifs, and the reader will notice in a number of the poems not a little of the author's pride in his Jewishness. *Sepharad*, the biblical place-name reapplied by medieval Jewry to indicate Spain, is alleged by him (absurdly) to derive from the Hebrew stem *SPR*, whence *sepher* = 'book', *sipper* and *sippur* = 'to recount, story'.[57] 'Poetry', implies de Barrios, 'was the invention of the Hebrews...'[58] Nor are there lacking pieces in which

---

[53] *Coro*, p. 81: 'Fue bravo Capitán de diez legiones / quando à Jerusalem destruyó Tito: / y Emperador, con fuertes esquadrones / de los rebeldes castigó el delito.' Cf. ibid., p. 80, on Vespasian and Titus.

[54] Ibid., p. 96: 'El Catholico Flavio Recaredo / dezimo octavo Rey del noble Hispano / con raro triumpho puso à Francia miedo, / al judio oprimió, y al Arriano / ... Sisebuto, tan fuerte en la campaña / ... Arco embió de paz el receloso / Heraclio à Sisebuto, que à su ruego / contra los Israelitas riguroso, / la [*sic*] armas de la Fé desnudó luego.'

[55] Ibid., p. 119: 'Fundó la Santa Inquisición, zelante / Campeon de la Fe, con los desseos / que del Imperio que alcançó triumphante, / echó más de ochocientos mil Hebreos.'

[56] Ibid., p. 70: 'Nabucodonosor, Rey Babilonio, / trajo à España el Ierusalemitano, / que en la dura prision de los destierros / arrastra las cadenas de sus yerros.'

[57] Ibid., p. 62: Sepharad se nombró del verbo Hebreo / Sepher, que es libro, relatar y cuenta.' On the medieval identification of *Sepharad*, a place mentioned in Obadiah verse 20 (? = *S[a]parda*, in Lydia or Phrygia, or possibly the south-western area of Media) with Spain, see S. Krauss, '*Ha-Shemoth 'ashkenaz u-sepharad*', *Tarbiz*, 3, 5692 [1932], pp. 423-35, with J. N. Epstein's editorial note, p. 435; *EJ* 14, 1164. The *paronomasia* adduced by de Barrios is not without interest, despite its wrong-headedness.

[58] *Coro*, introd. '... y la Sagrada Escritura lo verifica, donde dize Entonces cantó Moyses: porque hasta entonces la Poesía no se havia cantado al son de la lyra que inventó Moyses.' According to him, Moses went under the name Mercurius in the Gentile world, 'como pruevo en el tercer Canto de mi Harmonia del Mundo', and the name *Moses* is itself derived from *musa*: 'Con que parece que procedio de Moyses el celebrado nombre de las Musas, deribado del verbo Musa que en su lengua significa

the poet expresses his regret at the way that his life had taken him in his youth—clearly referring here to his crypto-Jewish period;[59] there are also poems about Tomé Pereyra (identical with the Abraham Israel Pereyra discussed above) 'who in his old age retreated to live a life of piety [*a buen vivir*] and composed a book called the *Mirror of the World's Vanity*'.[60] It may be doubted whether such marked dualism of attitude could be found in the writings of any other former crypto-Jew.

De Barrios frequently mentions individuals known to us as members of the Portuguese community in Amsterdam, without of course adverting either to their reversion to Judaism or to their new domicile. They are always referred to by the Spanish names which they had borne before fleeing from the Iberian peninsula.[61] Most surprisingly, he even refers to his own play *Contra la verdad no hay fuerça*, which was printed in Amsterdam in 1665 and was dedicated to the memory of three crypto-Jews who had been martyred by the Inquisition at Córdoba.[62] All of this comes in for mention in his *Coro de las Musas* which was published in 1672 in Brussels, where de Barrios himself was exposed to the watchful eyes of the Spanish Inquisition and within its cruel reach.

In each of his two books—printed, it must again be stressed, in Flanders—there is a sonnet in honour of Isaac Orobio: the two texts are almost identical.[63] Isaac is referred to by his Spanish name, don Baltazar, and it is stated that he is a doctor, professor, poet, and

---

Sacado.' [It is scarcely necessary to point out that all this is pure fantasy. *Sacado* alludes to the (Hebrew) etymology for the name Moses given in Exodus 2: 10, which is itself *ex post facto: mes[w]* in Egyptian means 'son'. R.L.]

[59] See his *Flor de Apolo*, p. 168: 'De un pecador arrepentido, . . . Ciego (mi Dios) te ofendi, / y oy que miro en ti mi bien / piadoso te aclamo, ten / misericordia de mi.' There is another poem on the same subject, and with identical title on p. 203; it is also printed in his *Coro*, p. 521.

[60] *Coro*, pp. 253, 380: 'A Tomé Pereyra que retirandose en su vejez a buen vivir, compuso un libro que intituló Espejo de la Vanidad del Mundo.'

[61] Thus e.g. he mentions (*Coro*, p. 226), 'Sargento Mayor Don Nicolas de Olivier y Fullana, grande Astrólogo y erudito escritor', who had by then settled in Amsterdam, reverted to Judaism, and adopted the name of Daniel Judah; on him see Kayserling, *Biblioteca*, p. 79. What de Barrios writes constitutes an important contributory source to knowledge of the outwardly Christian past of some of the crypto-Jews who returned to the faith of Judaism.

[62] *Coro*, p. 225: 'A Don Joseph Phelix en agradecimiento de haver satisfecho la dedicatoria que le hizo en una Comedia intitulada, Contra la verdad no hay fuerça.' The book itself was dedicated to the three martyrs Abraham Athias, Jacob Rodríguez Cáseres, and Rachel Núñez Fernández; see C. Roth, *A. Núñez Bernal*, pp. 38–51, and cf. Scholberg, *Poesía de M. de Barrios*, p. 21.

[63] *Flor*, p. 254; *Coro*, p. 513.

counsellor of the King of France—'greater than Galen' and 'more sublime than Virgil'. And, as if these encomiums were inadequate, de Barrios continues 'nor Homer in Greece, nor Tasso in Italy, merit a crown so much as thee'. But there is not the ghost of a hint at his having returned to the Jewish fold, or at his domicile in Amsterdam. It is obvious that panegyric reference to such matters could not be set down in writing about someone who had fled Spain and integrated himself into Jewry, so that de Barrios' silence about this chapter of Orobio's life is both understandable and, in the circumstances, logical. However, it is hard to understand how it came about that what he did write about Orobio evaded the notice of the Brussels censor. Orobio had been known about there since the early sixties, in consequence of his disputation with Zepeda, and the disputation itself had been printed there in 1666.[64] And apart from all this, is it really to be supposed that de Barrios' patrons in Flanders were ignorant of his life in Amsterdam and of his connections with the Portuguese-Jewish community there? We must assume that they were well aware of them. If, then, that is the case, it seems plausible that they preferred to shut their eyes to that part of de Barrios' story, and to play their parts according to his scenario; particularly since this arrangement made it possible for them to enjoy the panegyrics and the poetry which, with so open a hand, de Barrios lavished upon them.

It may be that the beginnings of Isaac's friendship with Daniel date from the year 1663–4, when the latter (as it seems) translated one of Isaac's tracts against Zepeda from Latin into Spanish.[65] But in 1675 there occurred a grave crisis in their mutual relations which ended in a bitter quarrel that is recorded in detail in one of de Barrios' compositions.

For de Barrios' attitudes and deviationism at this period of his life our evidence comes from Rabbi Jacob Sasportas, who wrote (in Hebrew) as follows:

One of the 'believers' in Amsterdam was Emanuel Benattar, cantor [*ḥazzan*] of the congregation, in whose house they all met to hold their confabulations: him they took as their gang-leader. One of them was a man named Daniel de Barrios, a vernacular bard—what they call *poeta*. He wrote a lot of books of poetry, including a verse translation of the Pentateuch to which he gave the title *Harmonía del Mundo*, divided into twelve parts. Each part he dedicated to a person of noble quality—the Duke of Leghorn, to the Prince of Holland, and to Portugal, Spain, and England. Each agreed to give him an appropriate

[64] See above, chap. 6, pp. 179 ff. [65] See above, p. 184.

reward, and to send him for reproduction in print his own portrait, crest, arms, and ancestral titles, and they sent him money to print and publish the work. This Daniel de Barrios became so ardent in his 'belief' that he cast all these books away, and gave his mind over to the rumours and written reports that were coming in. His imagination, working away through day and night, developed such intensity that he was all but claiming to be a prophet and to be fulfilling what Nathan [of Gaza] and Cardoso had said.[66]

It is not clear whether de Barrios was involved in Sabbateanism prior to 1674; at any rate there is no evidence to that effect in his writings. It is conceivable that he became tied up in belief in Sabbatai Ṣevi in the early seventies, perhaps under the influence of A. M. Cardoso's letters and the crypto-Jewish notions which he had developed in regard to both the character and prognostications of the messiah. There is some support for suspecting such influence in what has been quoted above from Sasportas. At the time, Daniel was passing through a tremendous psychological upheaval which led him to acts of self-mortification and a divorce from the world of reality. It is astonishing that of all people it was Sasportas—the doughty opponent of Sabbateanism, who had in 1673 settled in Amsterdam—who kept up friendly relations with the poet de Barrios at the very time when the leadership of the Congregation *Talmud Torah* was regarding him with suspicion and a majority amongst the congregational rabbis had inhibited the publication of his literary productions, and declared illicit the reading of what he had already published in Brussels.[67] No less surprising is the patience which Sasportas evinced in his dealings with de Barrios during the latter's deluded ramblings:

On the first day of passover of this year, his wife and father-in-law came to me and induced me to go to their house and talk to the said Daniel, since for four days and nights he had been behaving like a fool in all matters. When I got there, I found him physically unable to speak. I tried to persuade him to eat, but got nowhere with him, because, as he said, in the vision which he had had it had been thus decreed concerning him. He was uttering wild exaggerations and phantasmagorical nonsense, how that while he was fully awake [certain voices] spoke with him, telling him of signs in connection with himself that did in fact materialize: telling him that prior to the coming fast of 9 'Ab indications of the coming [messianic] deliverance would be revealed, and on the next [Jewish] New Year's Day for the first time the messiah, Sabbatai Ṣevi, would come ... I said to him, 'it would have been better if your informant had replied

---

[66] Sasportas, *Ṣiṣ. N. Ṣ.*, pp. 363 f. On *Harmonía del Mundo* see below, n. 70.
[67] See Scholem, *Sabbatai Ṣevi*, pp. 893 f.

giving you the information in Hebrew, since the angels know all languages; and so long as they have neglected to teach you Hebrew, the whole thing is ridiculous. Your power of imagination, and your self-isolation have got the better of you, so that it almost seems to you that you are having waking visions of [voices] communicating with you' . . . I warned him, and enjoined him to give consideration to the [likely] privations of his wife and family, and that if he became obsessed with the figments of his own imagination, and gave that imagination free rein, he would shortly die or go out of his mind, and his children would be left with none to spare a thought for them. If he wanted to believe that Sabbatai Ṣevi was the messiah, let him do so; but he must not give up taking care about providing for his children as he had previously done, or from continuing to write the books of poetry that he had begun.[68]

It was at this period that a quarrel led to a breach between Daniel de Barrios and Isaac Orobio, the cause being de Barrios' book *Imperio de Dios en la Harmonía del Mundo*. In dealing with this work Sasportas stated that it was a book containing 'a poetic version of the Pentateuch'.[69] Apparently de Barrios intended to produce a rhymed version and explication of the Pentateuch in Spanish: but as it has reached us—in two editions—it is no more than a metaphysical poem on the nature of God. There are certain variants between the two texts, in neither of which the date of publication is given.[70] However, in the records of the Congregation *Talmud Torah* I have found a note dated 23 April 1673 (7 'Iyyar 5433) indicating that the *Ma'amad* gave permission for the publication of the book, the manuscript having first been scrutinized by the rabbis Isaac Aboab, Benjamin Musaphia, and Josiah Pardo. It follows that the book first appeared in 1673.[71] From

---

[68] Sasportas, *Ṣiṣ. N. Ṣ.*, pp. 363 f.   [69] See above, p. 227.

[70] See Scholberg, *Poesía de M. de Barrios*, pp. 98 f., and cf. Pieterse, *De Barrios*, pp. 20 f. The first edition, of which copies are to be found in the British Library and in the library of the Hebrew University of Jerusalem, contains 125 stanzas; the second has 2 additional ones (following stanza 63), and there are modifications to the text in stanzas 2, 4, 63, and 64–78. In the additional stanza the poet attacks Spinoza's notion of the world being but a single, absolutely eternal substance, all existence being comprised within the Godhead; see 1st additional stanza following stanza 63, p. 17: '. . . Mas el ser de sustancia, es divisible, / y de todas distinta cada cosa: / todo es el Mundo, efecto de una Essencia, / que es diferente del, sin diferencia.' Similarly stanza 68, p. 18: 'Luego el Mundo no es Dios, ni una sustancia, / que figuras por si da accidentales, / sino materia por Divina instancia, / con diferentes formas essenciales.' Copies of this (second) edition are to be found in various libraries, including Amsterdam, *EH*, and that of the Hispanic Society of America in New York.

[71] Amsterdam, AGA, PA 334 no. 24a, '5433. Em 7 de hijar a pedimento de Daniel Levy de Barios [*sic*] em rezão de hum Livro intitulado Armonia del Mundo de que os s[enho]res Hahamim Ishack Aboab, Benjamin Musaphia e Iosiao Pardo comesarão a esaminarlo avendo de novo feitto petição se lhe ordenou o seg[uin]te: O Caderno ou

another work by de Barrios, entitled *Desembozos de la verdad contra las máscaras del mundo* ('Truth Unmasked against the Masks of the World') we gather what the causes were that led to the quarrel between himself and Orobio. This book, like the others, lacks an indication of the date of its appearance: but from the fact that on 15 August 1675 (23 *'Ab* 5435) the *Ma'amad* gave orders for it to be impounded one may take it that it had been published in that year.[72] From this work it becomes clear that de Barrios had asked Isaac Orobio to give his opinion regarding the first stanza of the poem *Imperio de Dios*, in which he had expressed the idea that God is the archetype of all creation.[73] Daniel claimed that what he was saying was based on what Orobio had allegedly written (in his controversy with Zepeda) that 'all creatures exist in the idea of God from eternity'.[74] Isaac had criticized de Barrios' exposition, writing that 'although the things which the Godhead contains, and is capable of creating, constitute a plurality, this does not

---

coadernos de mão escritto visto pelos ditos H[a]h[amim] se poderão ynprimir estando rupricados e sera obrigado o autor de dar a dittos s[enho]res as pr[imer]as folhas ynprensas que sairem da ynprença pera que as enxaminem se condizem com as originais rupricadas por dittos s[enho]res H[a]h[amim] vesalom. Samuel de Elisa Abravanel gabay de sedaca.' This decision indicates the close interest of the *Ma'amad* in what this literary product contained, and suggests that they may even have directed that certain stanzas be suppressed—hence, perhaps, their insistence that the quires of the manuscript be serially marked and that the first sheets off the press should be resubmitted for further scrutiny. The implication is that it was printed not in Brussels (as Scholberg and Pieterse surmise), but in Amsterdam; see Scholberg, *Poesía de M. de Barrios*, pp. 89 f.; Pieterse, *De Barrios*, p. 20. The 2nd edn. appeared *c.*1700; see Scholberg, op. cit., p. 103. It is quite clear that de Barrios intended to publish the sequel, as his letter of 1 Aug. 1679 to Duarte Ribeiro Macedo shows: '... pero nada anhelo en esta vida sino sacar quatro libros a luz dos en prosa y dos en octava rima intitulados Imperio de d[io]s en la Harmonia del Mundo.' The letter was published by Glaser, *De Barrios*, p. 206.

[72] I have located a copy in the British Library, pressmark 4033 a 37(12) (a convolute of items written by de Barrios). On *Desembozos* see Scholberg, *Poesía de M. de Barrios*, p. 98, *De Barrios and Amsterdam*, pp. 147 f. I have traced a reference to the impounding of copies of the book in the congregational annals (*Memorial de Advertencias*), Amsterdam, AGA, PA 334, no. 24a f. 33ᵛ: 'En 23 de Menahem 5435. Por quanto o S[enhor] Daniel Levy De barrios imprimiu hum libro que intitula desenbosos de la berdad [*sic*] contra las mascaraz [*sic*] del mundo, o qual mandaram rever os ss[enho]res do mahamad y ordenão dittos ss[enho]res que todos os que o tiveram os tragão a Camara do Mahamad dentro de 3 diaz [*sic*] sem ficarense con ninhuma copias. Abraham Zagache. Gabay.'

[73] The first stanza runs as follows: 'Antes de lo criado no huvo antes, / sino Dios que ve siempre lo que huvo, / notando quantas cosas emanantes / tuvieron el principio que no tuvo: / dentro de su atencion todas distantes, / sin tiempo hasta su tiempo las detuvo, / haziendolas de nada quando quiso, / prototypo de todas indiviso.' For de Barrios' address to Orobio requesting the expression of his opinion, see his *Desembozos*, p. 8.

[74] Ibid., preface, 'Todas las Criaturas estan en la idea de Dios ab eterno.'

mean that there is a plurality of things in God; seeing that his existence is infinitely simple, being uncompounded and without plurality. Consequently the plurality of creation within the Godhead does not compromise its simplicity, inasmuch as created things exist in God without themselves being patient of division.'[75]

Isaac's observations had riled Daniel, who alleged that it flatly contradicted what Isaac himself had written in his reply to Zepeda: 'had there been a plurality of concepts within the Godhead, it would not have been a unity of essence, since they are the same as the essence'.[76]

Countering the remarks of Isaac Orobio, de Barrios rejoined by defending his notion of the divine archetype. 'God created existing things *ex nihilo*, forming them outside Himself.' 'Everything that is not God is subject to change . . . and consequently could not have existed within the Godhead before it was created.'[77] There is no doubt that in the heat of the altercation, and thanks to his disturbed psychological state, de Barrios was fastening onto Orobio's words a significance other than their own. He was making his controversialist out to be one who asserted that there is a plurality in the Godhead, and he went so far as to hint at the similarity between what Isaac had said and the Christian dogma of the trinity. So it came about that the very writer who had uttered such forcible criticism of the notion of *tres in uno* became, in de Barrios' disturbed mind, suspected of maintaining a link with the central mystery of Christianity.[78]

Despite the absence from de Barrios' book of any hint at friction between the two of them arising out of the author's belief in Sabbatai Ṣevi, there is no doubt that his Sabbatean leanings have left their traces in the arguments that he advanced against Orobio. The critical remarks in which he taunts Isaac are reminiscent, both in their content

---

[75] De Barrios, (ibid., p. 8) quotes Orobio thus: 'Escrivio: "Aunque las cosas que contiene en si y puede produzir son muchas, no por esso hay pluralidad de cosas en Dios, porque es su ser infinitamente simplisissimo, sin compusicion [*sic*] ni pluralidad: y assi la pluralidad de las criaturas en Dios no obstan su simplicidad, porque estan en Dios indivisiblemente." '

[76] Ibid.

[77] Ibid., p. 6; similarly p. 21: 'Todo lo que no es Dios es mudable, o en el crecimiento de la edad, o en los passos de la sucesion; y no pudo estar en Dios por la mudança antes de ser obrado.'

[78] Ibid., p. 18: 'Aunque soy muy niño en la estudiada Philosophia, no ha de bolverme a engañar la Carantamaula de la Idolatria, diziendome como se usa en España a los niños "Mira el Tres", porque bien distingo que el tres no es uno, y el uno no es tres.'

and in their formulation, of what A. M. Cardoso had written in his two Spanish letters. For example, his attack on philosophers 'who study philosophy in opposition to the holy Law and mislead many Jewish people', and his claim as to the superiority of prophecy to philosophy — 'as between philosopher and prophet the prophet is of greater significance'.[79] Undoubtedly de Barrios had read A. M. Cardoso's letters, and his altercation with Orobio gave him the opportunity to trumpet abroad a repeated warning against the danger constituted by philosophers who allegedly ranked their own intellectual undertakings higher than the sanctity of the Torah.

So much for the speculative aspect of the dispute. But from what Daniel writes, it transpires that an additional factor was involved in the quarrel which grew up between him and Isaac. Certain people alleged that the opening stanza of the *Imperio de Dios* was a literary plagiarism, and that its true author was none other than Orobio. Daniel allowed that he had been influenced by Orobio, from whom he had learned much when translating his tract against Zepeda into Spanish; but, he claimed, the very differences regarding the question of plurality within the Godhead furnished abundant evidence that his own line of thought was not that of Orobio. What de Barrios wrote about literary plagiarism is expressed with great passion; he complains, *inter alia*, that Orobio had joined the chorus of those who were casting aspersions on his own mental clarity.[80]

From what has been said, one might have expected that an absolute and final breach between the two men would have taken place, but in the event matters developed quite differently. In 1677, two years after their bitter quarrel, another creation of de Barrios' pen was printed in Amsterdam, entitled *Respuesta panegírica a la carta que escribió el muy ilustre R. José Penso Vega al Sapiente Doctor Ishac Orobio*. The work was dedicated to the *Academia de los Sitibundos* in Leghorn, which was a literary association founded by Sephardi Jews including Joseph Penso.[81] De Barrios printed his *Respuesta* in full, and appended thereto

[79] Ibid., pp. 5 f.
[80] Ibid., pp. 8 f.: 'Algunos presumen no hize esta octava, que traygo en principio de mi Harmonia del Mundo, porque no tuve los estudios que el Doctor Orovio a quien la atribuyen ... Dispuso la inmensa Misericordia de Dios, que la primera proposicion fuesse la de la pluralidad para que se vea por su contradicion, y mi defensa ...'
[81] A copy is included in the British Library convolute (see above, n. 72), and there is another in a *collectaneum* in Amsterdam, *EH* 2 G 35, ff. 79 f. On the Leghorn *Academia* and that founded in imitation of it and with the same name in Amsterdam in 1676, see

Isaac Orobio and Sabbateanism

another piece consisting entirely of praises of Orobio's character and genius, as if his hectoring complaints against him had been consigned to oblivion. Neither Orobio's modesty, he said, nor the effectiveness of his thinking needed any commendations from himself. His greatness had found expression in his capacity to meet the great philosophers in combat.[82] To the same period belong two sonnets, two octets, two ten-line stanzas, and two *romanzas* composed by de Barrios in honour of his old friend. These poems are unpublished, but were transcribed at the beginning of several of the manuscripts of Orobio's *Prevenciones Divinas*. All of them throw into relief Orobio's achievements, and his triumphs in theological disputation and controversial writings against Christianity.[83]

What brought about this new turn in the relationship of Isaac and Daniel? Was it Daniel's shaking Sabbateanism out of his system that led to their reconciliation? Although it is known that in 1685 de Barrios publicly expressed his disillusionment in Sabbatai Ṣevi,[84] there is no proof that by 1677 he had already distanced himself from Sabbateanism. The contrary is the case. In his *Respuesta panegírica* Daniel published two Spanish quatrains of A. M. Cardoso which he himself worked up into a sonnet—and this at a date when the writings of Cardoso had been proscribed by the Ma'amad. Certainly this particular incident is not compatible with any real renunciation of Sabbateanism.[85]

Conceivably the psychological crisis by which de Barrios was affected in 1674–5 passed, and after he had recovered his equilibrium

---

Kayserling, *De Barrios*, 18, pp. 276 f., and Scholberg, *De Barrios and Amsterdam*, pp. 141 f.; also below, pp. 286 f.

[82] *Respuesta*, p. 5: '. . . No necessita de mi alabança ni el aliñado Penso con su realçado estilo: ni el modesto Orobio con su eficaz doctrina, quando uno ingenioso sabe luzir entre agudos Academicos y otro scientifico sabe campear entre grandes Philosophos.'

[83] The text will be found at the beginning of the British Library's manuscript *collectaneum* of works by Orobio, Harley 3430; Paris, BN Fonds éspagnoles 40; and Amsterdam, *EH* 48 D 6. One of the sonnets was printed by Pieterse, *De Barrios*, p. 148. See also de Barrios' *Eternidad de la Ley de Mosseh*, in his *Triumpho*, of which there is a copy in Amsterdam, Bibl. Rosen. (19 G 11), p. 73: 'Como instrue el sapiente Medico Professor Don Baltasar Orobio.'

[84] In his *Realze de la Prophezia y caida del Atheismo (Metros*, pp. 239 f.), also ibid., p. 243: 'ya con el abuso de tener la mayor parte del judaismo a Sabatay Sebi por Messias.' See Kaplan, *Shabbetha'uth*, p. 210.

[85] See *Respuesta*, p. 19, 'Assi lo exprime el Doctor Abraham Michael Cardoso en los quartetos deste soneto que acabé . . .'; cf. Kayserling, *Geschichte*, p. 304, and *De Barrios*, 18, p. 286, 32, p. 88.

he abjured the things that he had said when he was suffering from disorder. But whatever the reason for his reconciliation, their renewed friendship lasted until Orobio's death. It found expression in a number of de Barrios' later poems, and in their collaboration when, in 1685, they were together establishing the literary Academia de los Floridos.[86]

[86] Orobio is frequently referred to in de Barrios' *Alegrías*, which is a collection of poems composed to celebrate the weddings of a number of the most exalted and affluent members of the Portuguese congregation in Amsterdam. It includes pieces in honour of the marriage of Orobio's own daughter Rebecca to Isaac Milano (pp. 95 f.) and that of his son Moses to Sarah Abbas (pp. 113 f.). For the *Academia de los Floridos* and the collaboration of Orobio and Daniel de Barrios in connection therewith, see below, chap. 10, pp. 286 f.

9
Facing Calvinists and Catholics

When, in the seventeenth century, the Portuguese Jews of Amsterdam began to engage in disputations with Christian thinkers in regard to the fundamental principles of religion, and to reply to the Christian critique of Judaism, they had at their disposal a rich cargo of information about Christian theological literature and its sectarian and other divisions. Most of the Jewish participants in the debate had come from the Christian world: they had received their education in universities, abbeys, seminaries, and other Catholic educational institutions, and so had had opportunity of getting to know Christianity in its Catholic form at first hand. On reaching Calvinist Amsterdam they discovered a multi-coloured Christian world, whose confessional divisions and contradictions kept it in a constant ferment, for Amsterdam was, at the time, a refuge for exiles belonging to various sects from many lands. Their own historical experience furnished them with unique understanding of the differences among the various confessional streams within Christendom, and this, combined with the circumstance that so many of them had left Christianity to rejoin Judaism, provided the spur to investigation of the points of divergence between the two religions—the object being to throw into relief the superiority of Judaism, which they saw as the one and only valid implementation of the divine Law.

Isaac Orobio is an outstanding example of this phenomenon. He had arrived in Amsterdam with a mass of knowledge regarding Christian theology, christological exegesis of the Old Testament, and the various schools of Christian philosophy. In his *Carta Apologética* against Prado he gave the following testimony regarding his own reading:

> The Scriptures, in their Vulgate Latin translation, have never been out of my hands since my childhood. Later on, there came my way [the Latin versions of] Sanctes Pagninus and Arias Montano, and my favourite enjoyment still comes from searching out the inconsistencies between the various translations . . . In

---

[1] The *Fortalitium Fidei* was written by the Franciscan Alonso de Espina, himself in all probability either an apostate from Judaism or the son of converts, who was father confessor to Enrique IV of Castile. His work was completed at the end of the 1450s, and

Spain, I read the *Fortalitium Fidei*[1] with great care... later on, the [writings of] the man of Burgos[2]... and the *Bibliotheca* [*Sancta*] of Sixtus of Sienna[3]... I studied [the works of] Thomas [Aquinas] much, and Duns Scotus even more ... and for this purpose I acquired ancient tomes, including the complete corpus of the works of Aquinas. I have read everything that John Calvin wrote ... I have examined Luther, the writings of the revived anabaptists, the new sect of Mennists [*sic*],[4] the Socinians, significant disputations for which there has been occasion in these Provinces... [5]

Throughout all his writings Isaac shows marked expertise in early Christian literature as contained in the writings of the church fathers. The following are authors referred to by him: Justin Martyr,[6] Tertullian,[7] Eusebius,[8] Athanasius,[9] Hilary of Poitiers,[10] Epiphanius,[11] Augustine,[12] Damascius (one of the last Neoplatonists),[13] and Deodatus of St Blois,[14] and he is familiar with the writings of Isidore of Seville.[15] In the vast ocean which constitutes medieval Christian philosophy he was a strong swimmer, being very well informed about the writings of Thomas Aquinas;[16] towards Duns Scotus,[17] and the

---

it contains the earliest proposals to be made regarding the vigorous combatting of crypto-Judaism through the apparatus of the investigation of heresy. On him see Baer, *History*, ii, pp. 283 f.; Beinart, *on Trial*, pp. 9–20; also B. Netanyahu, 'Alonso de Espina: was he a New Christian?', *PAAJR* 43, 1976, pp. 107–65. Netanyahu endeavours to prove from Espina's book that he was not of Jewish extraction since, in his view, what he knows about Judaism is taken from Raymund Martini, etc.

[2] This somewhat disparaging form of description refers of course to Pablo de Santa María, alias Rabbi Solomon Ha-Levi, Bishop of Burgos, author of the *Scrutinium scripturarum*. On him see Baer, *History*, ii, index, pp. 531, 535; F. Cantera, *La conversión del célebre talmudista Solomon Levi*, Santander, 1933; P. Luciano Serrano, *Los conversos Pablo de Santa María y Alfonso de Cartagena*, Madrid, 1942.

[3] On the apostate Jew Sixtus of Sienna and his work, see C. Roth, *History of the Jews of Italy*, Philadelphia, 1946, pp. 302 f.; and Yerushalmi, *Isaac Cardoso*, pp. 282 f.

[4] Presumably the reference is to the Mennonites, i.e. disciples of Menno Simons, 1496–1561; on their place in 17th-cent. Holland see Zilverberg, pp. 8, 11, 20, 65; and cf. E. Troeltsch, *The Social Teaching of the Christian Church*, Eng. trans. by O. Wyon, New York and Evanston, 1960, ii, pp. 705 f. For general bibliography see F. L. Cross (ed.), *The Oxford Dictionary of the Christian Church*[2], Oxford, 1974, pp. 902 f.

[5] Orobio, *Cart. Apol.*, pp. 879 f.
[6] *Apud* Limborch, *De Veritate Rel. Christ.*, p. 65.
[7] Ibid., p. 110.
[8] Ibid., pp. 145, 146, and *Prev. Div.*, MS Amsterdam, *EH* 48 B 13, p. 230.
[9] *Resp. al Zep.*, MS Amsterdam, *EH* 48 A 12, f. 203^r.
[10] *Apud* Limborch (n. 6 above), p. 146.   [11] Ibid., p. 145.
[12] Ibid., pp. 93, 145; Orobio, *Cert. Phil.*, p. 41.
[13] *Resp. al Zep.* (n. 9 above), f. 203^r.
[14] 'Deodoto': *Prev. Div.* (n. 8 above), p. 229.   [15] *Resp. al Zep.* (n. 9 above), f. 178^v.
[16] *Apud* Limborch (n. 6 above), p. 110; *Resp. al Zep.* (n. 9 above), ff. 148^r, 175^r, 198^{r-v}.
[17] *Apud* Limborch (n. 6 above), *Resp. al Zep.* (n. 9 above), f. 176^r.

Facing Calvinists and Catholics 237

fourteenth-century French scholastic Durand de St Pourçain,[18] he evinces great respect. He frequently considers the biblical exegesis of Nicholas de Lyre,[19] and he polemizes zestfully with the apostate Jews Pablo de Santa María of Burgos and Sixtus of Sienna.[20] He was a considerable expert on Spanish theology of the fifteenth and sixteenth centuries: he deals with Alonso Tostado's commentary on the historical books of the Bible,[21] he refers to the *Monarquía Eclesiástica* of the Franciscan Juan de Pineda,[22] and he enters into a sharp polemic with Fray Luis de Granada.[23] He frequently adduces the biblical comments of Arias Montano, to whom he accords an appreciative respect.[24] Other works mentioned in his writings are the *Metaphysica* of the Jesuit jurist Francisco Suárez,[25] the Dominicans Gonzalo de Arriaga[26] and Pedro

---

[18] Died 1332. See e.g. Orobio's *Trin.*, MS Amsterdam, *EH* 48 B 12, p. 178: 'nótese el de Durando, autor gravissimo de cuya Doctrina hay cátedra particular en las mayores Universidades de Europa.' The Durand chair in the university of Salamanca was for a time filled by Luis de León; see *EUIEA* 18, p. 2578.

[19] He is mainly concerned with Lyre's *Tractatus de differentia nostrae translationis ab Hebraica Veritate* (completed 1333); see *Prev. Div.* (n. 8 above), pp. 104, 194; *apud* Limborch (n. 6 above), p. 78; *Resp. al Zep.* (n. 9 above), f. 157; and *Expl. Is. 53*, MS Amsterdam, *EH* 48 D 16, pp. 125, 127, 163. It was via Nicholas de Lyre that Orobio could have gained some knowledge of Rashi's biblical exegesis; see Beryl Smalley, *The Study of the Bible in the Middle Ages*², Oxford, 1952, and H. Hailperin, *Rashi and the Christian Scholars*, Pittsburgh, 1963, pp. 137–246; for printed editions of the *Tractatus differentiarum* (2, both prior to 1500) see Hailperin, pp. 283 f., n. 21.

[20] For his criticism of Pablo de Santa María (Paul of Burgos) see his *Expl. Is. 53* p. 125; *Prev. Div.*, pp. 104, 153, 165; and cf. above, chap. 6, p. 114. Several members of the Portuguese congregation in Amsterdam wrote controversially against Sixtus (see above, n. 3), in particular Rabbi Saul Levi Mortera, *Resp. obj. al Tamud*, MS Amsterdam, *EH* 48 D 9.

[21] He calls Tostado (1400–55) *el Abulense* from his birthplace (Avila); see *Resp. al Zep.* (n. 9 above), f. 157ʳ.

[22] Also known as *Historia universal del mundo desde su creación*, it was first printed in 1588, at Salamanca. See *Resp. al Zep.*, f. 157ʳ; *Prev. Div.* (n. 8 above), p. 95.

[23] He dubs him an 'outrageous idolater' ('miente sin duda el desbocado idólatra'), *Prev. Div.*, p. 79.

[24] Ibid., p. 171, 'el Doctissimo Hebraico'. Orobio frequently refers to the royal (polyglot) Bible which was printed at Antwerp in 1569–72 under Arias Montano's editorship. See *Expl. Is. 53* (n. 19 above), pp. 88, 134, 148; *apud* Limborch (n. 6 above), p. 7; *Resp. al Zep.*, f. 170ʳ. On f. 156ʳ he calls him 'insigne interprete de toda la biblia y testamento'. For Arias Montano see most recently B. Rekers, *Benito Arias Montano* (Eng. trans., London and Leiden, 1972; also Spanish, by Angel Alcalá, Madrid, 1973).

[25] 1548–1617. The full title of the work is *Disputationes metaphysicae*, Salamanca, 1597. For him see E. Gómez Arboleya, *Francisco Suárez*, Granada, 1946, pp. 83 f.; further bibliography in the *Oxford Dictionary of the Christian Church* (n. 4 above), p. 1318. See Orobio *apud* Limborch, p. 108.

[26] 1593–1657, author of a work on the life of Thomas Aquinas. See *Trin.* (n. 18 above), p. 180.

238   *Facing Calvinists and Catholics*

de Tapia,[27] and the Franciscan Francisco Félix.[28] He was at home with the various branches of Protestant theological writing: he had not only examined the works of Luther and Calvin, but he had read Cocceius,[29] Vossius,[30] and the *Encyclopaedia* of Johann Heinrich Alsted.[31] He was very familiar with the Protestant Latin versions of the Bible by the Italian Jewish apostate Emanuel Tremelluis and the Huguenot François du Jon (Junius),[32] that by the Dominican Sanctes Pagninus,[33] and the Spanish Protestant version of Cipriano de Valera which appeared in Amsterdam in 1602.[34]

Isaac Orobio was able to exploit his wide reading in Christian sources of different periods in debates with various Christian theologians in Holland; and on more than one occasion he tore their arguments to shreds by turning Christian sources to good use, and by making the divisions and disputations current within the Christian world serve his own purpose. In his debate with Zepeda about the teaching of Raymund Lull he based himself on the writings of Durand, Duns Scotus, and the lectures of Francisco Félix at the university of Alcalá;[35] in his *Prevenciones Divinas*, arguing against the Carmelites, he adduced proofs from the exegesis of Arias Montano;[36] and in order to trounce an anonymous Huguenot preacher with whom he disputed, he appealed to the commentaries of Jerome and Augustine.[37]

During the early 1670s Isaac was called upon to face up to Christian theologians of differing schools, and to wrangle with them over the points at issue in the Jewish–Christian debate. It seems likely that in

---

[27] 1582–1642, lecturer in theology at the university of Alcalá from 1623. There are grounds for supposing that Orobio knew him personally, since he belonged to the circle of the Duke of Medinaceli whose physician Orobio was during some part of his Andalusian period (see above, chap. 3, p. 65). Orobio refers to him warmly in his *Epíst. Inv.*, MS Paris, BN Fonds éspagnoles 40, p. 694.

[28] Orobio calls him padre Felix Franciscano. Felix was one of those in Spain devoted to the philosophy of Duns Scotus. He lectured at Alcalá, where Orobio could possibly have been one of his pupils. See his *Trin.* (n. 18 above), p. 178, 'y lo prueva unanimemente el Padre Felix Franciscano en su Curso Theológico Complutense'. The reference is to his *Tentativa complutensis*, 2 vols., Alcalá, 1642–5.

[29] See his *Expl. Is. 53* (n. 19 above), pp. 144, 148.

[30] *Apud* Limborch (n. 6 above), p. 146.

[31] i.e. *Cursus philosophici encyclopaedia*, 27 vols., 1620; see *Prev. Div.* (n. 8 above), p. 229.

[32] Orobio calls them 'Tremulo' (sometimes Tremelio) and Junio; *apud* Limborch, pp. 82, 93, *Prev. Div.*, p. 229. [*Trémulo* is presumably a disparaging glance at Tremellius' apostasy. RL]

[33] See *Resp. al Zep.* (n.9 above), ff. 156ʳ, 170ʳ; *Prev. Div.*, p. 204; *Expl. Is 53*, pp. 111.

[34] *Expl. Is. 53*, pp. 88 f.   [35] See his *Trin.* (n. 18 above), p. 178.

[36] *Prev. Div.* (n. 8 above), p. 150.

[37] See *Resp. Pred. franc.*, MS Amsterdam, EH 48 B 6, f. 309ʳ.

Facing Calvinists and Catholics 239

consequence of the reputation which he had won for himself in various Christian circles, he was regarded by many as the outstanding intellectual amongst the Portuguese Jews, so that to debate with him came to be a challenge of the first order. Two pieces of his polemical writing dating from this period have come down to us, throwing light on the intellectual atmosphere in which the Jewish–Christian argument was conducted in Amsterdam, as well as on the attitude of Isaac himself towards the religion in which he had been educated in his youth.

DEBATE WITH A HUGUENOT ON SALVATION

Around 1670 Isaac Orobio wrote a tract against the strictures raised by a French preacher against the religion of Israel. The preacher, who appears to have been a Huguenot, had placed before Orobio a polemical piece in which he assailed the adherence of the Jews to the law of Moses, and their continued observance of its commandments. Orobio's response generally goes under the title *Respuesta a un escrito que un predicante francés prezentó al D^{or} Orobio contra la observancia de la Divina Ley de Mosseh*.[38]

Isaac gives no indication about the circumstances in which he met his controversialist, of whose identity we are ignorant. According to one recension of the tract which appears in several surviving manuscript copies, it appears that the French preacher put his criticisms into Orobio's hands secretly. That item of information occasions surprise. If it is assumed that the author was one of the Huguenot exiles who found refuge in Holland in the last quarter of the seventeenth century, and that Isaac met him in Amsterdam, it is impossible to understand why he was so anxious to preserve secrecy, since his views were in no way out of step with the conventional position in Calvinist circles in the Netherlands.[39] Or does this note hint at the Huguenot's criticisms having been delivered to Isaac not in Amsterdam, but rather at some

---

[38] Amzalak published this, under the title *La Observancia de la Divina Ley de Mosseh*, with an introduction on Orobio's life and works (Coimbra, 1925). Numerous manuscript copies (*c.* 14 listed below, Appendix E) have survived, most of them dating from the 17th to the early 18th cents. There are no textual variants other than insignificant orthographical ones, but the title is given in different forms: see Appendix E.

[39] On the exodus of Huguenots to Holland as refugees see R. L. Poole, *A History of the Huguenots of the Dispersion at the recall of the Edict of Nantes*, London, 1880, pp. 34 f. Although it was the revocation of the edict in 1685 that gave great impetus to the flight of the Huguenots from France, many had already been reaching Holland in 1681, as part of the first wave of French refugees from the hardening policy of Louis XIV. See Yardeni, pp. 163 f., and Haley, pp. 170 f.

place where it was dangerous to express Calvinist views publicly? In other words, perhaps the pamphlet was given to him back in Toulouse, at the time when he held a position in the local university.[40] Orobio does state, in his *Carta Apologética* against Prado, that whilst in France he took part in a number of debates with some of the leading scholars there.[41] As against this, it is hard to imagine that Isaac Orobio dared to reveal his Judaism whilst he was residing in Toulouse even to his intimate friends there, and *a fortiori* it must be assumed that he would not have risked putting his views on to paper. Furthermore, a number of verbal expressions in his tract reveal his familiarity with what was going on in Amsterdam and the religious situation there. We must, then, assume that Isaac wrote the tract in Amsterdam;[42] but if so, how to account for the excessive secrecy of the French preacher? Isaac's rejoinder might have been written in Amsterdam in response to a pamphlet that had been given him by an anonymous Huguenot whilst he was still in France: but we cannot know for certain.

The disputation between the French preacher and Isaac Orobio centred essentially round two points: the problem of original sin, and that of the function of the messiah in the Jewish religion as opposed to his function in Christian belief. The anonymous Huguenot took as the basis of his faith the sin committed by Adam which, in his view, was the sin of the whole human race. For him, the souls of all men ever to be born were convoluted as part and parcel of Adam's soul; and as a consequence of the flaw in his soul and his resultant loss of freedom to choose good, all mankind are bent on evil. Adam's sin in itself rendered all his descendants enemies of God, condemned to eternal perdition. Jesus through his death redeemed from everlasting punishment all those who, believing in him, follow his way, and restored them to the bosom of God.[43]

---

[40] See above, chap. 5, pp. 97 f.

[41] Cf. MS Paris, BN Fonds éspagnoles 41, p. 888: '... y dispute en quantos actos publicos se hizieron en mi tiempo en Toloza [sic] ...', and cf. Révah, *Spinoza et Prado*, p. 136.

[42] See MS Amsterdam, *EH* 48 D 6, particularly f. 312ʳ: 'y si el christianismo idolátrico, y si el arriano y los demas heréticos no son Israel espiritual, ved Sr. que pequeño es el que queda reduzido a quatro provincias del norte en las quales aun una grande parte es de los herejes y idólatras ...'

[43] Ibid., f. 288ʲ: 'El principal fundamento que vos proponeis para vuestra Doctrina consiste en el peccado de Adam en el qual vos creeys a peccado todo el genero humano que estava contenido en Adam como en su unico principio, que la naturaleza humana desde la posteridad de Adam siempre estuvo corrompida, y que nunca pudo uzar de la Libertad que Adam perdio (de eligir el bien) mas por causa de la corrupcion toda su

Facing Calvinists and Catholics 241

From Isaac's treatment of the Huguenot's arguments we are able to reconstruct the remaining assertions in his lost pamphlet. Israel had always, from its very first beginnings, sinned against God, and it was for this cause that God rejected them in perpetuity.[44] God abrogated the covenant which He had made with the patriarchs because of the sins of the Jews from the time of their leaving Egypt right up to the age of the prophets.[45] Punishments inflicted on the world are due to Jewish rejection of the good news proclaimed by Jesus.[46] The hidden significance behind the surface meaning of the scriptural prophets was 'mystical, allegorical, and metaphorical'—a sense of Scripture which Jews were not equipped to understand, being 'blind, deaf, and devoid of knowledge'.[47] Jews believe in a swashbuckling messiah like Alexander the Great, who, they suppose, will conquer the world and subdue all nations.[48] All sects and streams within Christianity form part of the true Israel, inasmuch as they all believe in Jesus.[49] He adduced a series of christological interpretations of a number of biblical texts, and he appears to have asked thirteen questions about the meaning of a number of verses which had for generations been a bone of contention in the Jewish–Christian debate.[50]

inclinacion tira a la prevaricacion.' The influence of Calvin on the formulations employed by the Huguenot writer is not in doubt; cf. the first chapter of Calvin's *Institutio Christianae Religionis*, Geneva edn., 1585, ff. 69ᵛ f.

[44] *Resp. Pred. franc.* (n. 42 above), f. 297ᵛ: 'Dexando esta materia, disputais contra la aliança de Dios con Israel, y dezis que Israel fue siempre criminal contra el Señor su Dios, y por esso deshizo la aliança que havia entre Dios y su pueblo, y le abandonó para siempre . . .' There is no doubt that the guarded standpoint of the French preacher towards the Jews differs, to a significant degree, from that normal in Huguenot refugee circles in Amsterdam; see Yardeni, pp. 170 f., 178 f. This would explain Orobio's expostulations regarding his controversialist's hostile attitude, and his assertion that the latter's imputations of 'heresy' to Jewry were unprecedented: '. . . grande es el odio y la abominacion que este Señor tiene al pueblo de Dios, pues siegamente por blasfemar de Israel dize semejante herejia, que ningun christiano à dicho ni imaginado por que todos confiessan que Israel fue verdadera iglesia de Dios hasta la muerte de Christo.' Orobio's claim is of course exaggerated: not only had expression been given to similar notions by Christians—including Calvinists—but they are implicit in the doctrine of Calvin himself. See e.g. his comment on 2 Sam. 22, in Johannes Calvin, *Predigten über das 2. Buch Samuelis*, ed. H. Rückert, Neukirchen, 1961 p. 679, and Calvin's remarks on Mic. 2, in Jean Calvin, *Sermons sur le Livre de Michée*, ed. J. D. Benoît, Neukirchen–Vluyn, 1964, p. 174. On Calvin's attitude to Jews see Baron, *Calvin*, and his *Hist.* xiii, pp. 279 f.

[45] *Resp. Pred. franc* (n. 42 above), f. 298ʳ: 'dezis pues Monsieur muy contra la verdad en este escrito que Dios por los muchos peccados del pueblo repudio a la Iglesia de Israel, y deshizo la aliança que havia hecho con los Padres, lo qual provais alegando todos los delitos del pueblo desde que salió de Egipto hasta el tiempo de los Prophetas . . .'   [46] Ibid., f. 290ʳ (*bis*).

[47] Ibid., f. 293ʳ (*bis*).   [48] Ibid., f. 295ʳ (*bis*).   [49] Ibid., f. 312ʳ.

[50] Ibid., ff. 294ʳ (*bis*) f., 297ᵛ (*bis*) f., 309ʳ f., etc.

Isaac's answers are formulated in a somewhat acid tone, and occasionally more than a soupçon of sarcasm can be sensed in them. 'Monsieur' (he writes) 'these things [which you write] are quite good enough for Christian people, but Jews will not concede them ... regarding the miracles in the gospel to which you refer, the Jews will in no way entertain belief in them, since they are not Christians. Should it occur that a Jew were to turn Christian he would believe all of them, but as matters stand, not a man [of them] will want to believe them ...'[51] In several places Isaac makes direct allusion to the weak position of the Calvinists within Christendom, by far the greatest part of which lay under the 'pagan' thrall of the papacy: 'reformed Christians' with difficulty maintain their authority over 'four northern districts, and even within these the number of heretics and pagans is high'. 'Your [Protestant] religion', he writes, 'teaches that the popish religion is not that of the true church, and the popish religion time and again teaches that your religion is not the true one. The Jew, believing everything that all Christians on both sides say against each other, will persevere in his knowledge that the church founded by God at Sinai with the children of Israel more than three thousand years ago is God's church, and all the peoples know this to be the truth ...'[52]

Isaac does not hesitate to point out that (as he claimed) Jews do not in fact believe that Jesus ever existed. 'Rather, at that time, under the rule of Felix, Festus, and Pilate, certain Jews were executed by the Romans because they had claimed that they were prophets, and stirred up revolt amongst the people, as Josephus records; and it seems to them [i.e. the Jews] that those individuals could have been the beginning of something that in course of time grew ...'[53]

Orobio's critique does not distinguish between the various streams and divisions within Christendom. Precisely because the debate was being conducted with a Calvinist he is concerned to obscure the differences between Catholicism and the reformed churches, in order to prove that even reformed Christianity, which had on the whole met with a more sympathetic attitude on the part of Jews, was very far from

---

[51] Ibid., f. 288ᵛ: 'Monsieur, estas cosas son bastantemente buenas para los christianos, mas los judios no las admiten...' [52] Ibid., f. 313. Cf. above, n. 42.

[53] Ibid., f. 300ᵛ: '... yo os digo de verdad que aun no creen que ubo tal persona que decis, sino que en esse tiempo, governando Felix y Festo, y Pilatos fueron muertos por los Romanos algunos hombres que quenta Josepho porque se haçían Prophetas, y hacían rebueltas en el pueblo y les pareçe que destos personajes pudo tener principio lo que despues creció con el tiempo...' This was a view already commonly entertained by crypto-Jews in the 15th cent.; cf. Beinart, *on Trial*, pp. 286 f.

being the true faith—title to which was the exclusive heritage of Israel.[54]

'DIVINE FOREWARNING' AGAINST CATHOLIC 'IDOLATRY'

It was in his *Prevenciones Divinas contra la vana Idolatría de las Gentes* that Isaac Orobio let fly his razor-sharp arrows against Catholicism. This tract also had its origin in a disputation which actually took place, as is attested by Isaac's own language in the introduction: 'my sole intention is to accede to the request of a number of friends that I should make available the response that I made to a distinguished person when I met some Carmelite friars—learned men, with much expertise in Christian theology—and conducted discussions with them: in the course of which (according to my modest understanding) I laid their idolatry open for all to see. They had invited me to meet before the aforementioned signor in order to confront me with a major difficulty . . .'[55] A problem at once reveals itself in connection with this passage: could a meeting with members of a Catholic religious order really have taken place in Amsterdam? At the period under discussion Catholic worship was officially not tolerated in the city; but some twenty per cent of the Amsterdam population being Catholics, it was not possible to prevent the establishment of conventicles, or 'shelter-churches' (*schuilkerken*) as they were called, in attics or other places of concealment.[56] That, however, is a far cry from the untrammelled activity of members of religious orders. From evidence given by the Augustinian Fray Tomás Solano y Robles before the Madrid Inquisition we learn that an Irish Franciscan was living in Amsterdam and engaging in clandestine activity there.[57] But what Isaac Orobio has to

[54] Ibid., ff. 298ʳ, 303ʳ, 308ᵛ.

[55] See MS Amsterdam, *EH* 48 D 6, introd. From what Orobio writes elsewhere in this tract it is possible to see that the question raised by way of challenge by the Carmelite (in the passage concerned it is clear that it was but a single friar) was why God had not warned Israel in the Scriptures about the impending threat of Christianity. See f. 287ʳ: '. . . con que a mi veer queda bastantemente respondido a la duda o argumento del Carmelita, por que Dios no previno à Israel contra la secta Christiana . . .'

[56] See Haley, pp. 91 f. The church of 'Ons Lieve Heer op Solder' ('*Our Lord in the Garret*') which was established in Amsterdam in 1663 and turned into a museum in 1888, gives a good idea of the form and style of conventicles which grew up in secret in the 17th cent.

[57] Madrid, AHN, Inquisition section, libro 1123 (unpaginated): '. . . y posando en casa de Yambrune, donde se dezían todos los dias dos misas, que la una decía este y la otra Fray Carlos de Santa María, Yrlandés de la orden de San Francisco, que asistía allí

say in describing his meetings with the Carmelites does not leave the impression that the latter were situated in any danger, or that they were operating in a hole-and-corner fashion. Quite the opposite. From what he says, it would appear that it was they who took the initiative in arranging the meetings and in staging disputations in the presence of a personage of high degree.

A further consideration is the fact that during the seventeenth century no Carmelite house whatsoever existed in the Calvinist Lowlands.[58] If, then, it is difficult to assume that Isaac held his conversations with Carmelites in Amsterdam, where could they have taken place? It is out of the question that this polemical enterprise could have been undertaken whilst Isaac was resident in Spain or in France. The Carmelite order in the seventeenth century was in a flourishing state in both countries; but in either one of them such open expression of anti-Christian sentiments would have placed Isaac's life in jeopardy.[59]

Perhaps Orobio stayed in Brabant for a short time while disputing with Prado and trying to draw him back to Judaism. He may even have proceeded as far south as Antwerp, where Prado was living. There were Carmelite houses scattered over the southern Netherlands, in Bruges, Ghent, Valenciennes, Ypres, and other towns, so that it is conceivable that Orobio's interviews with the friars took place somewhere in Brabant at the time when he was engaged in disputation with Prado.[60] This can be no more than speculation: like many other details in Isaac Orobio's life, what is certain is greatly exceeded by what remains unknown. But if we cannot nail down the date of the disputation, there is no doubt that it was written after 1668 and it cannot have been written later than 1675. Isaac himself indicates as much, as do dates mentioned in several of the surviving copies.[61]

---

por misionario . . .' His evidence, deposed on 8 Aug. 1659, was printed by Révah, *Sopinoza et Prado*, pp. 60 f.

[58] See *Carmel, its History, Spirit and Saints*, New York, 1927, pp. 65 f., also P. W. Janssen, *Les Origines de la reforme des Carmes en France au XVIIe siècle*, The Hague, 1963, p. 2.

[59] On the growth of the Carmelite order in Spain and France during the period, see *Carmel* (n. 58 above); Janssen (n. 58 above), esp. pp. 114 f.

[60] See above, chap. 6, p. 156 n. 133.

[61] In a number of passages Orobio stated that the exile had already lasted more than 1,600 years, i.e. since Jerusalem was destroyed in 70 CE, he had to be writing after 1670; see *Prev. Div.* (n. 55 above), f. 50^r: '. . . y que este tan horrible castigo aya durado, no veynte ni quarenta, ni setenta años como antes padecían por la nefanda ydolatria sino mas de mil y seis cientos años.' See also f. 94^r. The earliest manuscript known to us containing *Prev. Div.* dates from 1677/8 (see below, Appendix E); but account must be taken of the separate copies of the chapters on the prophecy of Daniel and on Isaiah 53, which were made in 1674/5. See below in this chapter, pp. 249 f.

E. de Ochoa's assertion that the work was printed in Amsterdam in 1674 is without foundation. A book with so sharp an anti-Christian tone had not the slightest hope of receiving an imprimatur from the censor: and clearly the Portuguese-Jewish congregation would itself not have sanctioned the publication of a book liable to give rise to difficulties and problems for the community as a whole.[62] Although this tract, like the majority of Orobio's other writings, never itself saw print, it became one of the most widely diffused pieces of apologetic writing within the Sephardi Jewry of western Europe, as is attested by the number of extant manuscript copies of it.[63]

The work is divided into two books. In the first, containing twenty-nine chapters, Isaac sets out to prove that as early as the Pentateuch God had warned his people Israel against what Christianity was destined to fabricate against the Law of Moses, in order that, 'being forewarned, they should be incapable of concurring with those fallacies'.[64] Isaac discusses the dogmatic beliefs of Christianity forthrightly, indicating that in the Torah Israel had not only been already forewarned against idolatry but also against belief in the trinity (chap. 1), against belief in the incarnation (*personificación*) (chap. 2), and against the Christian conception of messianism (chap. 5). The author does not content himself with refuting the essence of Christianity's critique of Judaism and the Jewish people, but he also endeavours to prove that its commandments did not lapse with the appearance of Jesus, and that Israel's age-long exile was not a punishment for his crucifixion (especially chaps. 10 and 16). It would be difficult in the remaining writings of Isaac Orobio to find such outspoken language levelled at Jesus and his disciples as is to be found, in plentiful measure, in the present treatise.[65] He also disputes, on grounds of

---

[62] See Eugenio de Ochoa, *Catálogo razonado de los manuscritos españoles existentes en la Biblioteca Real de París*, Paris, 1844, p. 634; Menéndez y Pelayo, *Heterodoxos*, v, pp. 279 f., likewise assumes that the book was put into print at some time. It was, however, clear to Orobio himself at the time of writing that the work would not be printed: see f. 125ʳ: 'y es más de nuestro intento impugnar las respuestas últimas de los Christianos, que cumular textos contra ellos, y por la doctrina con que deshazemos su intento en uno o dos versos se infiere con facilidad la aplicación en todos los más que opusiezemos, para desbaratar sus vanas respuestas, y lo contrario pedía un grande volumen, que no pudiendo ser impreso sería muy diffisil [sic] reduzirlo a copias por la pluma.'

[63] See below, Appendix E.

[64] So, explicitly, in the subtitle to the first book: 'Pruevase que todo quanto se avia de inventar en el christianismo, previno Dios a Israel en los cinco Libros de la Ley, para que advertido no pudiesse admitir tales errorres'.

[65] See *Prev. Div.* (n. 55 above), f. 5ʳ; the earliest Christians were corrupt or gullible Jews ('unos segun se vee por sus escritos, mas prevertidores [sic] que ignorantes de las Sagradas Letras, otros idiotas, que les dieron entero crédito'); it was the bounden duty of

general principle, the Christian method of biblical exegesis, which disregards the plain meaning and invents mystical meanings allegedly borne by the scriptural text (chap. 12); there are also two chapters (14 and 25) specifically devoted to proving the unreliability of the gospels as a historical source. In direct contrast to this exposé of Christianity, Isaac finds occasion to express the basic principles of his own philosophy of the Jewish *galuth* (exile), the character of Israel's future redemption (chaps. 13, 16–20), and the nature of immortality (chaps. 28–9).

In the second book, containing twenty-seven chapters,[66] Isaac takes the field 'against the false mysteries of the Gentiles, about which Israel had been warned in the prophetical books'. Here the question of the messiah occupies the centre of the stage. The author rejects absolutely the christological significance which Christian exegesis had read into the prophetic canon, and he directs his heaviest fire on the apostate Pablo de Santa María, alias Rabbi Solomon Ha-levi, of Burgos.[67] In his introduction to this part Isaac indicates that whilst the Christians had found themselves unable to produce any support for their beliefs from the Pentateuch, the language of which is unequivocal, they purported to have found substantiation for their idolatry in the prophets, Psalms, and Proverbs because of the particular difficulties occasioned by the exegesis of these books. The essence of his charge is that Christian exegetes of the various denominations had torn verses, or fragments of verses, out of their context and deliberately distorted their meaning, whereas 'the most exact interpretation of every single piece of the holy Scriptures is that which takes into consideration the context in which it occurs; since the exclusive author of the Hebrew Bible is God, and it is a necessary consequence of his authorship that all parts should prove to be absolutely coherent between each other'.[68]

---

the Jewish sages, for which they should be given credit, to secure the capital conviction of Jesus, f. 20ᵛ, 'a quien tocava por derecho la decisión de aquella duda y la determinación de aquella muerte'. There are also outspoken expressions of hostility against Christianity, such as f. 135ᵛ, 'el vano edifficio de su Idolátrica secta; la bárbara máquina que inventaron'; f. 278ᵛ, 'el último y mas detestable crimen que fue la invención de la secta Christiana'; f. 281ʳ, 'el riguroso castigo que padecerán los impios que con pretexto desta hipochresia Christiana afligieron à Israel en tantas hedades'.

[66] In several MSS there is a variant chapter-division. *EH* 48 B 6 divides chap. 21 into two, but as against this it does not separate chap. 25 off from its predecessor. Similarly *EH* 48 C 42, 48 C 12, British Library MS Harley 3430, Madrid, BN MS 18249, Paris, BN Fonds éspagnoles 40, and London, Jews' College, Montefiore MS 525; but these last 6 MSS divide chap. 23 into two, resulting in a total of 28 chapters.

[67] See above, p. 114.   [68] See *Prev. Div.* (n. 55 above), ff. 113ᵛ f., 176ᵛ.

Chapters 20–2 (21–3 in some manuscripts)⁶⁹ deal with Daniel's prophecy of the seventy weeks (Daniel 9: 20–7). Isaac rejects the conventional Christian interpretation which finds reference to the crucifixion and the destruction of Jerusalem and the temple by the Romans in verse 26: 'after the sixty-two weeks, one who is anointed shall be removed with no one to take his part; and the horde of an invading prince shall work havoc on city and sanctuary' (New English Bible). As against both the Christian interpretation and the various Jewish ones Isaac proffers his own, claiming that verses 25 and 26 do not concern the same messiah. When Daniel says (v. 25) 'from the time that the word went forth that Jerusalem should be restored and rebuilt . . . till the appearance of one anointed, a prince', he is referring to the high priest Eliashib in the period of Nehemiah (Nehemiah 3: 1). When, on the other hand, he says (v. 26) 'one who is anointed shall be removed with no one to take his part', he is referring to the high priest Ḥanan ben Ḥanan who was murdered by the zealots John and Simon the Idumean (sic).⁷⁰ Once again Isaac reverts to his major theme, viz. that God knew that in course of time Christianity would wrongfully seize upon this prophecy and use it as confirmation of the veracity of its claims: and for that very reason He forbore to add thereto a single word that might hint at grace, justification, or the forgiveness of sins which, Christianity alleges, would be the consequence of the death of Jesus. That was not the import of the prophetic words 'the horde of an invading prince shall work havoc on city and sanctuary. The end of it shall be a deluge, inevitable war with all its horrors . . .' (New English Bible); on the contrary, there is here (according to Orobio) a clear indication of the spread of the Christian 'abomination' (NEB 'horror') through the Gentile world.⁷¹

⁶⁹ See n. 66.
⁷⁰ *Prev. Div.* (n. 55 above), f. 212ʳ: 'fue Judea república libre que tubo luego Príncipe que la governasse feudatario à los Reyes de Persia, que este Principe fue el summo Pontifice Eliasib, que primero en compañía de Nehemias, y despues sólo, exerció ambas juridiciones de ungido en Sacerdote grande y governador del pueblo.' So also continuation, f. 215ʳ: '. . . aora para tratar de la última ruina de la misma república empieça por la muerte violenta del ungido ò Sacerdote, que sería el último, con una muerte espiraría todo el ser de república, la ciudad y Santo Templo; y assi aconteció como predixo el Angel, porque despues de sitiada Jerusalem, los zelotes Joannes y Simon Jdumeo mataron cruelmente al summo sacerdote Anano varón Sanctissimo.' On the various interpretations of this prophecy within Judaism, see J. Sarachek, *The Doctrine of the Messiah in Medieval Jewish Literature*, New York, 1932, pp. 36 f., 56 f., 120, 258.
⁷¹ *Prev. Div.* (n. 55 above), f. 221ʳ: 'Vio el Señor que los gentiles del Christianismo havían de abusar de esta divina revelación, diciendo que en ella se prometía la redemción eterna de Israel, y de todo el género humano por la muerte del ungido que en ella se

In chaps. 23–5 (in some manuscripts 24–5 or 25–6)[72] Isaac offers a similar interpretation of Isaiah 53. Here, too, his aim is to shatter Christian exegesis which recognizes Jesus in the 'servant of the Lord', and in the servant's fate as 'despised, he shrank from the sight of men', and 'smitten by God, struck down by disease and misery' (vv. 3, 4) the fate of the saviour who allegedly came into the world to atone by his suffering for the sins of humanity. Whilst pointing to the gaps in the Christian interpretation Isaac exposes the fallacy of the whole Christian concept of original sin and its infinite gravity, making atonement for it impossible.[73] As against current Christian expositions, Isaac throws into relief the opinion of the Jewish exegetes who understand the prophecy as referring to the people of Israel collectively. In the same way he controverts the christological interpretation of Isaiah 65, Genesis 49: 10, Ezekiel 37, etc.[74]

Amzalak wrongly assumed that Philip van Limborch's *De Veritate Religionis Christianæ* was the reply of that Remonstrant theologian to Orobio's *Prevenciones Divinas*.[75] Comparison between what Isaac asserts in that tract and the questions critically raised in Limborch's book does indeed reveal certain parallels, but the differences stand out, quite apart from the fact that the two treatises differ from each other entirely in structure. What is contained in Limborch's book was expressed—as is explicitly stated—in the presence of a Christian personage, and Isaac assented to its being put into print; whereas the contents of the *Prevenciones Divinas* were put together primarily (if not, indeed, exclusively) for a Jewish readership, with the result that the formulation there is combative in the highest degree. If, in his debate with Limborch, Orobio reveals a more positive attitude towards Protestantism than towards Catholic Christianity, the critique in his *Prevenciones* in no way distinguishes between the various sects and

---

refiere, y previno el Señor a Israel contra tan horrible absurdo, no permitiendo una sola palabra que fuesse de consolación al pueblo de Israel ... sin algo que aluda à gracia, a justificación y a expiación de pecados, como pretenden que havía de seguirse à la muerte de aquel hombre, lo qual no fue assi, ni Dios dixo que sería, sino que muerto el ungido, y destruído el sacro Templo avría estendimiento de abominación, que es sin duda la secta Christiana que después en breve se estendió por la gentilidad ...'

[72] See above, n. 66. [73] *Prev. Div.*, f. 22ᵛ.
[74] Ibid., ff. 163ʳ f., 166ᵛ f., 283ᵛ f.
[75] See Orobio, *Resp. Pred. franc.*, ed. Amzalak, p. xxiii. Sokolow was likewise imprecise when he wrote that *Prev. Div.* includes a chapter 'entitled *Epístola Invectiva* in which [Orobio] levels accusations against Dr Prado, ...'. There is, of course, no connection between the two works. See Sokolow, p. 167. On the disputation with Limborch see below, chap. 10, pp. 270 f.

Facing Calvinists and Catholics 249

denominations within Christendom. 'Those who *carry* their *wooden idol* [Isaiah 45: 20] are the papists, and those who *pray to a god that cannot save* are the reformers who, although they have repudiated the externalities of idolatry, offer prayer to a dead man as if he were God—one who could not save himself, let alone save them.'[76]

At the conclusion of this book, Isaac wrote that he proposed to devote a special work to proving the falsehood of Christianity on the basis of natural reason, corresponding to his proofs of its falsehood from the text of the Pentateuch and of the prophets. No such work has come down to us, and it is doubtful whether Isaac ever managed to realize his intention of writing it.[77]

TRACTS ON THE 'SEVENTY WEEKS' AND THE 'SUFFERING SERVANT'

A unique manuscript preserved in the Bodleian Library contains a work by Isaac Orobio entitled *Tratado en que se explica la prophecía de las 70 semanas*.[78] Inspection reveals that the text is identical with the chapters dealing with the same subject in his *Prevenciones Divinas* (II, chaps. 20–2). Apart from minor differences in punctuation, orthography, and the division into four chapters instead of the three in the *Prevenciones*, there is nothing to distinguish this copy from the corresponding passages in Isaac's comprehensive work.[79]

On the title-page of the separate tract on the 'Seventy Weeks' there is a note stating that it was written in Amsterdam on 6 February 1675,

---

[76] *Prev. Div.* (n. 55 above), ff. 121ʳ f.

[77] Ibid., f. 287ʳ: '... en el libro de la razón natural en que seguiremos el mismo intento'. Some have endeavoured to identify this (supposed) third part with his *Resp. Pred. franc.*: see below, Appendix E.

[78] MS Opp. Add. 4° 51, Neubauer, *Bodl. Cat.* p. 878, no. 2475; *Resp. Pred. franc.*, ed. Amzalak, pp. xxvii f.; Kayserling, *Biblioteca*, p. 82. It contains 82 pages, and bears the ownership mark of a certain Jacob Guer—clearly a proselyte to the Sephardic community of purely Christian stock.

[79] At the end of the MS there is lacking the conclusion to the corresponding chapters in *Prev. Div.*, where Orobio emphasizes that this prophecy was not adduced in the Gospels naturally enough, he claims, since it did not refer to the coming of Jesus. Apparently the copyist found it inappropriate to support the refutation of Christian exegesis by appeal to the New Testament itself. The relevant passage in *Prev. Div.* begins (MS Amsterdam, *EH* 48 C 12, ff. 257ʳ f.) 'Mas lo que es digno de notar y de oponer a los christianos siempre que quisieran provar su intención con este capº de las 70 semanas que ni los Evangelistas, ni los Apóstoles en todos sus escritos alguno de sus versos, etc.'

and it would seem that the date here given refers not to composition, but to the transcription of this copy. This gives rise to the question of priority: did Isaac compose his commentary on the prophecy of Daniel before he wrote the *Prevenciones*, or is this Bodleian manuscript merely a separate copy of the three chapters excerpted from the major work? Although all the known manuscripts of the *Prevenciones Divinas* are later than 1675, this latter alternative seems the more plausible one.

There have also survived three manuscripts of a tract by Orobio on Isaiah 53.[80] Some scholars have advanced the hypothesis that this is a chapter of the *Prevenciones*, others that it is an abbreviated recension of the relevant part of that work.[81] Examination of the relevant manuscripts shows that although the essence of the separate piece is the same as that of the three chapters on the significance of this prophecy in Isaac's longer work, he prefaced them in the independent piece with five new chapters, which render the work an independent tract.[82] Of the three manuscripts in which it is preserved one is written in Spanish and the other two in Portuguese; but there is no doubt that the Spanish is the original. Isaac, educated in Spain on the basis of Spanish culture and its language, probably lacked sufficient command of Portuguese to be able to write a complete treatise in it.

Like the other tracts, it is difficult to fix the exact date when this one was written: but the Spanish original was clearly completed before *Tishri* 5435 (September–October 1674), since in one of the two surviving Portuguese texts that month is recorded. It can also be shown that it was written after the completion of the *Prevenciones Divinas*. In MS Amsterdam, 'Eṣ Ḥayyim 48 D 16, against chap. 6 (i.e. the first after the five prefixed introductory chapters) the number 25 is marked, and similarly 26 against chap. 7. It would seem that once the new introduc-

---

[80] MS Amsterdam, *EH* 48 D 16, *Explicación Paraphrástica del Capítulo 53 del Propheta Isaias*, containing 92 folios (the title appears on f. 5, after the introduction. The title-page itself reads simply 'Deplicação do Jes. 53', clearly the addition of some later cataloguer). The MS itself is not in a calligraphic hand, and appears to date from the 17th cent. Of this work two other copies have survived, in Portuguese: see below, Appendix E.

[81] See Sokolow, p. 167, and so Neubauer and Driver, ii, p. xx. These editors published 3 chaps. of this work (i, pp. 21–118, Eng. trans. ii, pp. 451–531) taken from *Prev. Div.*, without mentioning the existence of the first 5 chaps., here under discussion. See *Resp. Pred. franc.*, ed. Amzalak, pp. xxv f.

[82] The contents of these 5 new chaps. are as follows: 1, The difference between the pentateuchal canon and that of the prophetic books. 2, Description of Israel's redemption as foretold in the Pentateuch and by the prophets. 3, Christian exegesis of prophetic texts that concern Israel. 4, Christian rejoinder to those prophecies that foretell the redemption of Israel. 5, The true messiah and his future actions, both within Israel and amongst the Gentiles.

Facing Calvinists and Catholics

tory chapters were completed the author appended to them the chapters of interpretation which he already had at his disposal from his own comprehensive work, and noted at the head of each the corresponding chapter-number in the original work.

Elijah Montalto, Rabbi Menasseh ben Israel, and Rabbi Moses Raphael d'Aguilar were among the scholars of the Sephardi Jewry of western Europe in the seventeenth century who wrote polemically against the Christian interpretation of Isaiah 53.[83] Isaac Orobio likewise found it a matter of urgent necessity to make his own contribution towards the clarification of this most vexed passage which was forever cropping up in Jewish–Christian debates of this period. Of particular interest is what he has to say about the causes which impelled him to write this work:

> These chapters concerning Isaiah 53 have been written at the request of a number of individuals living outside Jewry, whom others strive to alienate from the fulfilment of the holy Law ... for which purposes [the latter] make use of sundry verses in this chapter ... And seeing that those who have not been educated within [any of] the Jewish communities are used to hearing these doctrines [sc. of Christianity] without intermission, and find that they [apparently] coincide with what is written in this chapter, there are amongst them some who because of their own weakness flounder in confusion, and others, because of their ignorance, are deceived. Many there are who are moved by much good will and zeal for the holy Law who wish to get to know the true interpretation, for the sake of their own spiritual peace of mind and in order to have at their hand a rejoinder to their opponents.[84]

We thus see that this separate tract was intended for crypto-Jews and was prepared at their request. From what Orobio writes here it may be concluded that his settlement in Amsterdam had not attenuated his feeling of solidarity with the crypto-Jewish community from which he himself had sprung; and this itself constitutes additional evidence for the double-sided character of the bonds between Jews and crypto-Jews which, at the end of the seventeenth century, had not lost any of their vitality.

Attention to Isaac Orobio's treatise on Isaiah 53 was revived in the eighteenth and nineteenth centuries when, for completely different reasons, Jews in England and Italy, the English deists, and the French encyclopaedists evinced interest in it. To this we shall have to return below, when discussing the translations of Orobio's works.[85]

[83] Neubauer and Driver, ii, pp. xix f.   [84] MS Amsterdam, *EH* 48 D 16, p. 1.
[85] See below, Appendix G.

JUDAISM VIS-À-VIS CHRISTIANITY

In the plethora of denominations and streams of tradition within Christendom and in their mutual rivalries Isaac Orobio saw distinct evidence of the weakness of Christianity. 'Do you really want the unfortunate Jews' (so he taunts the Huguenot preacher) 'to have to be such good scholars and such experts in understanding the New Testament, that they may be qualified to decide the major disputes and matters of doubt that obtain between yourselves and the romanists, Socinians, Arminians, and the many other sects, in order that they may thus be able to choose the true [faith] — something about which your own councils, doctors, writers, and learned folk have themselves not succeeded in reaching decisions . . .?'[86] Christianity might have come to bring unity, but it had in fact introduced divisiveness.[87] That objection was frequently voiced amongst the Portuguese Jews of Amsterdam, and it figures in many of the polemical tracts produced by Sephardi Jews in the seventeenth century. Rabbi Moses Raphael d'Aguilar drew attention to the fragmentation that prevailed throughout Christendom and the disputatiousness between its sects, 'for example Catholics, Lutherans, Calvinists, Anabaptists, Arminians, Socinians, and many others, between whom differences of belief are so important that they regard each other as heretics'.[88] When contrasting the vigour of Judaism with the debility of Christianity, Daniel Levi (Miguel) de Barrios pointed out that despite the Jews being 'oppressed and dispersed across diverse regions and languages, they are solidly united in the understanding of the Mosaic precepts and the implementation thereof', whereas the Christians are split up into 'Arians, Papists, Socinians, Lutherans, Quakers, Calvinists, and members of many other sects, who fail to understand that whatsoever is liable to alteration and shifting is neither permanent nor divine'.[89]

Study of Orobio's writings shows that his late declaration in the

[86] *Resp. Pred. franc.*, MS Amsterdam, *EH* 48 D 6, f. 303ʳ

[87] *Apud* Limborch, *De Veritate Rel. Christ.*, pp. 90 f: 'Sed quod hoc jam vestro Messia advento contigerit, nequaquam videmus, neque videtis. Cum major pars hominum nec vobiscum, neque cum Israele, in unum populum coalescat; potius tota Africa, tota Asia, magna Europae pars, tota America, vestram nec nostram fidem admiserint . . . sed neque caeterae gentes cum Christianismo praeter paucas, easque in mille sectas divisas, quae eidem fidei, in plurimis, maxime contrartiantur, et à multis seculis parum ultra religionis initium, quae sit vera Christi ecclesia penitus ignoretur.'

[88] D'Aguilar, *Preguntas de Anveres*, MS Amsterdam, *EH* 48 A 11, ff. 13 f.

[89] De Barrios, *Triumpho* (Amsterdam copy, Bibl. Rosen. 19 G 11), pp. 72 f.

Facing Calvinists and Catholics 253

course of his debate with van Limborch to the effect that it is only Jews and Christians who are suited to engage in discussion of the fundamental principles of their respective faiths in a spirit of amity, since they alone have a common denominator, is said entirely apologetically.[90] His attitude towards Islam is incomparably more positive than his attitude towards Christianity. Even though in his view Islam is swamped with impurities and abominable features, it is not to be regarded as a barbarous faith. The source of Muhammad's teaching is divine, although for Orobio the confusion in the Koran is evidence that the book is a purely human product.[91] In disputing with Zepeda he uses biting sarcasm because of Raymund Lull's resort to childish parables in order to convince Jews and Muslims of the truth of Christianity: from childhood onwards both Jews and Muslims believe in one, sole God, and that is why they recoil from Christians—'for they are convinced that the latter seek to win them to a belief in plurality in God'.[92]

For Orobio, all the ingredients of idolatry are present in Christianity. It demands belief in a God-man figure who died, and was buried: belief in feigned deities—one of them an older god, like Saturn, the father of the Roman pantheon, another youthful, the son, corresponding to Jupiter; and faith in sculpted and other images of the dead, arising out of a religious veneration of their remains.[93] Israel, he says, were not explicitly commanded in Scripture to be circumspect in regard to this particular form of idolatry, but no more does Scripture refer to the gods of Greece and Rome, because in the Torah God had taught Israel about his unity: and that teaching was in itself sufficient utterly to impugn Christianity.[94]

The personality of Jesus, and the character of the earliest Christians, are central matters of consideration in Isaac's theological disputation. In those of his polemical treatises which were not intended for publication in print he characterizes Jesus as a 'deviant Jew', 'a blasphemer, worthy of death', no different from all the other charlatans who made

---

[90] *Apud* Limborch (n. 87 above), p. 137.
[91] See *Epíst. Inv.*, MS Paris, BN Fonds éspagnoles 40–1, p. 697: 'Resta la secta Mahometana, grande en todo el Orbe, y en la opinion de muchos bárbara; mas en la verdad, aunque lo scan sus costumbres, no lo es su creencia. Componese su Alcoran de un grand [sic] numero de capítulos, de una continuada repetición sin orden ni methodo de varios fragmentos de la Divina Escritura ... La doctrina es divina, conforme al entendimiento humano; nada es repugnante a la razón y digna de la aceptacion de las gentes. Mas la obra es evidentemente humana, como se vee por su desorden...'
[92] *Resp. al Zep.*, MS Amsterdam, *EH* 48 A 12, f. 185ʳ.
[93] *Prev. Div.*, *EH* 48 B 13, p. 3.   [94] Ibid., pp. 10 f.

themselves out to be redeemers of Israel and led the masses into revolt.[95] 'He perpetrated numerous outrages against the Law of Moses, the prescriptions of which, like any other Jew, he was in duty bound to fulfil; he said things that experience shows to be false, and he desecrated the holy Law by violating the sabbath rest, together with his disciples.'[96] The miracles which Jesus allegedly performed were nothing other than sleight of hand, the proof being that they were carried out in remote localities where he could not be apprehended in the course of his chicanery.[97] A contemporary of Isaac Orobio, Dr Isaac Nahar, wrote in similar vein about the miracles of Jesus, and stressed that 'the tradition which those of his own people, country, and age left behind them, and which has been continuously passed down until our own day, shows just the opposite; in the senate [i.e. *Sanhedrin*] where his case was investigated he was condemned to death as a deceiver and sorcerer. If, then, that is so, whom are we to believe? Those [who denied his claims], or the few who, together with him, were his accessories in misrepresentation and deceit, by means of which they endeavoured to mislead the masses whom it is all too easy to dupe . . .?'[98]

In his *Prevenciones Divinas* Isaac justified the decision of the court of 'judges and priests' which convicted Jesus, nor did he deny the exclusive responsibility of the Jews for carrying out his execution. The court

---

[95] Ibid., pp. 17 f., 25.

[96] Ibid., *EH* 48 D 6, ff. 232ʳ f.: '. . . hizo muchas contra la Ley de Moseh, à que estava obligado como hombre judio, dixo otras que falsificó la experiencia, prevaricó la divina Ley, quebrantando el reposo del Sabath el y sus discípulos . . .' What Orobio and his contemporaries have to say about Jesus and the beginnings of Christianity undoubtedly reflects opinions already current in the 15th cent. amongst crypto-Jews in Spain, who had inherited them as part of the whole approach with which Judaism confronted the Christian world: see Beinart, *on Trial*, pp. 286 f. On the attitude in the older Jewish sources towards Jesus see J. Klausner, *Jesus of Nazareth*, Eng. trans. by H. Danby, London, 1925, pp. 18 f.; J. Parkes, *The Conflict of the Church and the Synagogue*, Philadelphia, 1961, pp. 106–15. On medieval Jewish attitudes see Schoeps, *Jewish Christian Argument*, pp. 53 f. For the reformation period see H. H. Ben-Sasson, 'The Reformation in Contemporary Jewish Eyes', *Proceedings of the Israel Academy of Sciences and Humanities*, 4, Jerusalem, 1969/70, pp. 239–326.

[97] *Prev. Div.*, *EH* 48 B 13, pp. 29 f. In his discussions with Limborch to be considered below (chap. 10, pp. 270 f.) which were intended for publication, Orobio views Jesus as an upright and righteous person who healed the sick and generally acted in a virtuous manner, being free of sin ('viro justo et innocente'), who in his preaching combatted sin and hypocrisy in the same way 'as the Jewish sages who nowadays receive a salary for such service' (*apud* Limborch, *De Veritate Rel. Christ.*, p. 63, '. . . peccata, et hypocrisim magnatibus urgeret, quod tunc Rabbini, et nunc etiam nostri singulis Sabbatis concionantur . . . neque ideo populus . . . eos . . . odio prosequuntur, sed annualia largiuntur stipendia . . .').

[98] MS Amsterdam, *EH* 48 C 24 (Nahar, *Discurso*), p. 13.

1. Alleged portrait of Isaac Orobio. Artist unknown

2. Title-page of G. de la Torre's Spanish translation of Orobio's *Certamen Philosophicum*, copied in The Hague in 1741. MS 'Es Hayyim-Montezinos 48 C 16

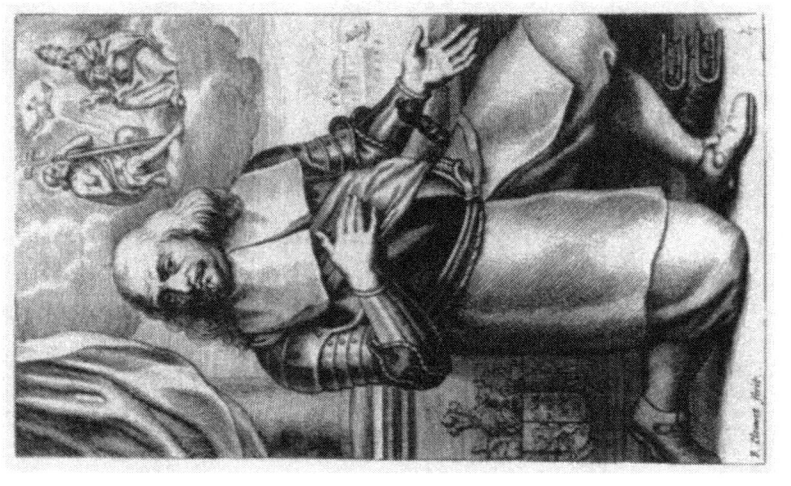

4. Portrait of Alonso de Zepeda

3. J. Groenwolt's portrait, wrongly described as that of Isaac Orobio

5. Gravestones of Isaac and Esther Orobio, at Ouderkerk, The Netherlands (*see* pp. 305 f.)

6. Title-page of Orobio's *Respuesta a un Predicante Francés*, copied by Jacob Guedelha (Gadella). MS '*Eṣ Ḥayyim*-Montezinos 49 A 16

7. Page of Orobio's *Respuesta Apologética* against Zepeda, apparently corrected (and perhaps entirely written) in his own hand. MS '*Es Hayyim*-Montezinos 48 E 42

8. Title-page of Orobio's *Respuesta Apologética* against Zepeda, copied by Abraham Machorro in 1707. MS '*Es Hayyim*-Montezinos 48 B 12²

Facing Calvinists and Catholics 255

which convicted him had fully constituted authority to do so, and the sentence which it passed must be regarded as if it had emanated from God Himself.[99] On the other hand in his disputation with the Huguenot preacher Isaac denied absolutely the whole account of the trial and death of Jesus, because 'the Jews do not know how all this could have taken place in Jerusalem, since they have never given credence to the account in the gospels . . . But in those days, under the rule of Felix, Festus, and Pilate a few men were put to death by the Romans as Josephus records, because they purported to be prophets and stirred up the people to revolt . . .'[100] Christianity was born in the Land of Israel and those who fashioned it were Jews—some of them deliberately setting out to corrupt, others merely foolish; they disseminated its doctrines to begin with in Judaea, thereafter in Samaria, and finally, when its number of adherents had increased, amongst other peoples of the West.[101] Christianity is a form of idolatry created by Jews: and in this circumstance is concealed the difference between it and earlier idolatrous systems invented by Gentiles. This point is important, indeed central to Isaac Orobio's apologetic argument, since in his view it sufficed to prove that during the period of the second temple and even after its destruction idolatry persisted, without inter-

---

[99] *Prev. Div.* (n. 97 above), pp. 29 f.

[100] *Resp. Pred. franc.* (n. 86 above), f. 330ʳ. In that tract Orobio invalidates Christian appeal to the evidence of the well-known passage in Josephus (*Antiquities*, XVIII, iii, 3), maintaining that Josephus himself 'never intended or wrote' that chapter; ibid., ff. 311ʳ f. On the alleged forgery of this chapter of Josephus see Klausner (n. 96), Eng. trans., pp. 55 f., who regarded the core as genuine, with interpolated accretions; F. C. Burkitt, 'Josephus and Christ', *Theologisch Tijdschrift*, 1912, pp. 135–44, argued for its authenticity but interpreted it in a non-Christian sense. [R.] B. Motzo, *Saggi di Storia e Letteratura giudeo-ellenistica*, Contributi alla Scienza dell' Antichita, v, Florence, 1924, part i, chap. 6, 'per il testo di Flavio Giuseppe', pp. 152 f., regarded it as a Christian interpolation and listed scholarly discussion up to 1913; for a recent survey see A.-M. Dubarle, 'Le Témoignage de Josèphe sur Jésus d'apres des publications récentes', *Revue Biblique*, *84, 1977*, pp. 38–58.

[101] *Prev. Div.*, MS Amsterdam, *EH* 48 D 6, f. 5ʳ: 'En esta tierra segun los Evangelistas, y los autores romanos de aquellos tiempos, como es el Tacito, y otros, y aun en el generalisimo sentir de todo el Pueblo judaico, se invento y tubo su origen el cristianismo, y esto por hombres Israelitas, unos segun se vee por sus escritos, mas pervertidores que ignorantes de las Sagradas Letras, otros idiotas, que les dieron credito, y estos en grande numero, cuia malicia y ceguedad, poco a poco fue creciendo y introdusiendose en los animos de muchos, en toda Judea, y con mayor larguza en la Provinsia de Samaria, cuyos habitadores, aunque de extraño origen, estauan ya de largos siglos, debaxo del iugo de la Ley, y obligados a su observancia, que presto corrompieron, con la novedad de la inventada Secta. Despues siendo ya grande el numero de los sequaces, revozó de Judea a las demas naciones de su Occidente, como Grecia, Italia, y las demas regiones de la Europa.'

ruption, in Israel; and it was because of this, and not because of the crucifixion of Jesus, as Christians allege, that the Jews were punished by God who scattered them amongst the nations.[102]

The apostles are pictured by Orobio as having been mere opportunists in search of notoriety and prestige, whose preaching served them as means of securing an easy livelihood. They never put their lives at risk, since the Greeks and Romans were not concerned about people adopting new gods and made no difficulties as to their admission to their pantheon. He casts doubt on the Christian tradition which would represent them as saints and martyrs, put to death because of their steadfast devotion to Christianity and their efforts to spread it amongst the Gentiles: everything that had been written about them was utterly impregnated with falsehood and inane beliefs.[103] The early Christians, members of Jesus' circle who were direct recipients of his teaching, were no more than simple folk, or drawn from the underworld.[104] Mary Magdalene, the prime witness for his resurrection, was a prostitute, and 'the others with whom he ate and who thronged about him were not merely men of the common horde, but criminal types, and addicted to unsavoury habits'.[105]

The way in which Isaac Orobio disassociates himself from the sort of society in which the disciples of Jesus lived tells us not a little about his own social and political philosophy. Where, he asks, is there a state that would acquiesce in having its fate settled by the judgement of the mob? The holy Torah had warned Israel not to accede to decisions made by the masses, but to conduct themselves in accordance with what the judges and priests should direct. In this way the door was blocked against the schemings of sorcerers, fishermen, and harlots who wanted to sap popular loyalty to Jewish law.[106] He does not merely invalidate dependence upon the judgement of the riff-raff, but he also goes on to the offensive against the egalitarian notions adduced by the gospels. The Christian claim that the source of holiness lies in poverty and indigence is no more than empty hypocrisy: the increase of wealth

---

[102] Ibid.: 'Bien se vee de este breue periodo, quan interesado fue Israel, en la nueva idolatria, pues en su corte y tierra se invento por sus mismos judios, entre si la formaron, la aumentaron, y como falsos Prophetas la llevaron hasta las gentes, con gran differencia de las otras antiguas supersticiones que inventaron gentiles entre si, y con ellas contagiavan al Pueblo Israelitico.'
[103] *Apud* Limborch, *De Veritate Rel. Christ.*, pp. 133 f.
[104] *Prev. Div.*, *EH* 48 B 13, pp. 13 f.
[105] Ibid., p. 24: 'Los demas con quien comía y le acompañavan, no solo eran vulgares, sino facinerosos y de infames costumbres.' [106] Ibid.

Facing Calvinists and Catholics 257

is a divine blessing, and the squandering of property invites divine judgement.[107] Nor is Isaac Orobio content to emphasize the value of material wealth as a reward conferred by God on those who deserve it, but he points to the importance of inequality in the distribution of wealth, but for which men would refuse to work in order to make money, with the result that nobody would be prepared to take on those menial tasks which are essential for the maintenance and the self-preservation of the human race. It follows that the doctrine of egalitarianism is incapable of being put into practice. Were Christians to live according to the precepts of the gospels they could be no more than an exiguous and dwindling groups of mendicants.[108] However, he adds sarcastically, there is no danger of that happening, since Christians are far from practising the values which they inscribe on their banners.[109]

In his disputation with Prado Isaac had addressed himself to the question of the reliability of the Hebrew Scriptures, concluding that the fact that they may be relied on points to the divine origin of Judaism.[110] As regards the gospels, he throws doubt upon their reliability because of the contrariness of their descriptions, so that the whole edifice of Christianity is built upon rickety foundations.[111]

In contrast to the meticulous care with which the Jews had preserved their own holy Scriptures, Christians could not even agree amongst themselves about the canonicity of certain gospels accepted by some of them and rejected by others.[112] After pointing his finger at the distortions in the gospels, Isaac pillories Christian dependence upon the 'mystical, tropological and spiritual senses' which they attribute to Scripture, 'converting earth into heaven, Jerusalem and Zion into the Church, Israel and Judah into Gentiles and the Gentiles into Israel', asserting that they introduce confusion by 'casting these shadows over the light of holy Scripture'.[113] In Isaac Orobio's opinion the Christian

---

[107] Ibid., pp. 88 f.
[108] *Expl. Is. 53*, EH 48 D 16, p. 93: 'Esta era doctrina repugnante al govierno del genero humano por que sin diferencia de los bienes temporales ninguno querria travajar para adquirirlos y siendo todos yguales ningunos se ocuparian en los ofizios serviles de que necesita la humanidad para su conservacion y no seria otra cosa que abrir la puerta a la ociosidad, madre de todos los vizios.'
[109] *Apud* Limborch, *De Veritate Rel. Christ.*, pp. 67 f. [110] See above, chap. 6, p. 170.
[111] *Apud* Limborch, pp. 144 f. [112] Ibid., esp. p. 146.
[113] *Prev. Div.*, EH 48 D 6, f. 184ʳ. Rabbi Isaac Nahar attributes the distortion allegedly inherent in Christian biblical exegesis to the veil of ignorance ('aquel obscuro velo de la ignorancia que costumbran llamar fe, les cubre los ojos, no les dexa ver la razon'). See *Discurso* (n. 98 above), p. 20. By this means Nahar throws back at Christianity the flaw

versions of the Bible are fundamentally faulty: in particular he accuses the 'impure [Latin] Vulgate which, in its manifold wickedness, shamelessly distorts the words of God...'[114]

On the ethical teaching of Christianity he vents his anger in full measure. On the one hand Jesus had nothing new to contribute in this regard, all ethical statements in his gospel having been transmitted before his time by the prophets of Israel.[115] And on the other, it was only in the first generations that Christians actually practised what the gospels teach, and with the establishment of the Church and the wide dissemination of its doctrines it changed its complexion.[116] Christians can be grouped as idolaters, sectarians, and infidels; 'and such they have ever been, from the beginnings of the Church until our own days, along with all the sins of commission and omission to which human wickedness renders the Church prone'.[117]

Isaac frequently crosses swords with the principles of Christianity and attacks its dogmas. Extended treatment is devoted, in his *Prevenciones Divinas*, to the belief in original sin, the actuality of which Isaac denies absolutely. Adam's sin did not alter human nature, nor did God punish his descendants for it. Admittedly the human race has not been privileged to enjoy all the advantages which were granted to Adam in the Garden of Eden, but 'that does not mean that God punished humanity for the sin of Adam, but rather that He withheld from them that which grace had given Adam and which, in the course of justice, he forfeited'.[118]

He similarly invalidates the role of Jesus as 'mediating Messiah':

Christian doctrine determines that the everlasting Father, being the judge in this case, sent his Son, and by the instrumentality of that third person whom they title the [Holy] Spirit, turned him into a man: the sole object being, that he should be condemned to that death [by means of which he would atone] for all mankind. They thereby convert the eternal Father and that other person into iniquitous judges who did not merely acquiesce in this in defiance of

---

which it had attributed to Judaism since St Paul (cf. Rom. 11: 25), viz. that the synagogue stood blinded by its own perverseness in face of the enlightenment of the church.

[114] *Prev. Div.*, f. 149ʳ.
[115] *Apud* Limborch, *De Veritate Rel. Christ.*, pp. 145 f.
[116] Ibid.
[117] *Resp. Pred. franc., EH* 48 D 6, f. 297ʳ.
[118] *Prev. Div.*, f. 227ʳ: 'esto no es castigar Dios a los hombres por el pecado de Adam, sino no dar Dios a los hombres lo que de gracia dio a Adam y despues le quito de justicia...'

natural justice, but actually pronounced the sentence and determined upon the means of its execution.[119]

In their attempts to reconcile the incompatibility of belief in the trinity with belief in monotheism Christians have tied themselves in knots, with hazy concepts and definitions that explain nothing, and which have no foundation either in the Hebrew Bible or in the gospels; but, 'being unwilling to see themselves worsted in debate, they make play with their [idiosyncratic] metaphysics, contrary to metaphysical truth...'[120]

Rebutting the claim that the political power of Christianity is testimony to its truth, Isaac rejoins that the wealth and power possessed by many peoples that have not accepted Christianity is immeasurably greater than what the Christians command. Most peoples of Africa never accepted Jesus' gospel and are still immersed in idolatry, and most parts of the world are subject to the dominion of Islam.[121] He does not deny the successes of Christianity amongst pagan peoples, but the inescapable fact is that Christianity took from paganism, no less than what the pagan world received from it. It has converted pagan temples into churches, slightly modifying the names of the pagan gods and goddesses, and has itself established a cult no less pagan, like that acceptable to and practised by the Catholics.[122]

The literature of anti-Christian polemic produced by Sephardim in western Europe recognized the positive continuation of the idolatry of antiquity in Catholic Christianity. Outspoken expression of this approach is to be found in Elijah Montalto's polemical interpretation of Isaiah 53: 'the truth is that you [Catholics] are the heirs of those who held Jupiter to be the supreme god'.[123] Following him Rabbi Saul Levi Mortera asserted that of all the forms of idolatry devised by the evil

---

[119] Ibid., f. 227ʳ. Cf. Elijah Montalto on Isa. 53, MS Amsterdam, *EH* 49 A 1, p. 58: 'Finalmente se vinha para morrer necessariamente crusificado, e dessa morte pendia a Salvação ... rezão tendes de agradeçer muyto a os judeus tal obra, è não de lamentar continuamente que vos matarão vosso Deus...'

[120] *Trin.*, *EH* 48 B 12, pp. 179 f.: '... por no darse por vencidos en las Disputas usaron de essas Methaphísicas, contra le verdadera Methaphísica'.

[121] *Resp. Pred. franc.*, ed. Amzalak (from MS Gans, see Appendix E), pp. 42, 72, and cf. Nahar (n. 98 above), pp. 17 f.

[122] *Apud* Limborch, p. 68: 'Paulo post vel statim a christianismi exordio paucis labentibus annis eadem gentium idolatria perstitit, divorum nominibus, atque dearum, dumtaxat mutatis, quibus eadem antiqua templa fuere dicata, et in quibus non minus idolatricus cultus celebratur, et adhuc pro majori parte in Christianismo consistit...'

[123] Montalto (see above, n. 119): 'A verdade he que sois heredeiros de aquelles que tendo a Jupiter por seu Supremo Deus...'

genius of man Catholicism was the worst.[124] In the collection of poems in honour of the memory of Abraham Núñez Bernal, who died at the stake at the hand of the Córdoba Inquisition on 3 May 1655, there are to be found many examples of this, emanating from the pens of poets in the Portuguese community of Amsterdam: 'Your false idols I abominate, their poison coated in gold and silver . . .',[125] 'Barbarians be ye, though styled Christians, your superstitions the proof that the way that ye follow is the pagans' way . . .',[126] 'Uncircumcized, inhuman successors of perverted Edom [i.e. Rome]',[127] 'Baal's satanic servants'.[128] Isaac's own language is not in any way more temperate. In the Catholic religion he sees 'abominable idolatry' and 'false worship', and he dubs its dogmas 'the vain construction of their idolatrous sect'.[129] The pagan world of antiquity knew no cult so abominable, so contrary to natural reason: worship of consecrated bread, and of the two sticks that make a cross, worship of a multiplicity of the dead, of images and the likeness of animals—such as St Agnes' lamb, the cock of St Nicholas, St Anthony's pig, and the ox of St Mark.[130] He renders thanks to God that reformed Christianity had at least restored to Scripture its true signification, and if at base it still clung to its belief in spiritual idolatry, it had at any rate torn itself away from the toils of material idol-worship. 'May our Lord God sustain these [United Dutch] Provinces and confer upon them a plethora of divine blessings, so that in the purity of their righteousness no man may be constrained

---

[124] *Resp. obj. al Talmud*, MS Amsterdam, *EH* 48 C 5, introd. (unpaginated), '. . . me dexé algunos años engolfar en aquel piélago de mizerias y idolatria, la mayor de quantas inventó el mundo'. Other outbursts against Christianity are found in his *Obstáculos*, *EH* 48 D 38; Kaplan, *Mortera*, pp. 15 f. Almost identical sentiments and language are to be found in Orobio's *Prev. Div., EH* 48 B 13, p. 6: 'esta abominable creencia y sacrilega idolatria . . . la mayor que pudo inventar la humana malicia, la mas injuriosa a la Divinidad de el criador . . .'

[125] *Elogios a la memoria de Abraham Núñez Bernal*, p. 91, (anonymous): 'Vuestros idolos falsos abomino / cuyo veneno cubre plata y oro . . .'

[126] Ibid., 'Barbaros sois, con nombre de christianos / vuestras supersticiones son la prueva, / que el camino seguis de los paganos . . .'

[127] Ibid., p. 3, introd. (by Elijah Núñez Bernal): 'Los incircuncisos, los inhumanos succesores del protervo Edom . . .'

[128] Ibid., p. 139: 'satánicos siervos de Baal' (a poem signed I. Ab. (? = Isaac Aboab).

[129] *Prev. Div., EH* 48 D 6, ff. 115ʳ, 135ᵛ, 136ʳ, 277ᵛ, 278ᵛ.

[130] See *Resp. Pred. franc.*, ed. Amzalak, pp. 67 f. On Sephardic Jewish equation of Catholicism with idolatry see Glaser, 'Auto da fe sermons', pp. 337 f. Similarly harsh expressions are to be found scattered all over the writings of Portuguese Jews in Holland, right up to the 18th cent.; cf. Pizarro, MS Amsterdam, *EH* 48 D 31, p. 44: 'Imágenes que pinta Hedom en las quales funda su ydolatría, creyendo que el Dios en quien adoran nació de una muger . . . ceguedad, y deslumbramiento abominable de todos los que creen en la torpeça, y ygnorancia de esta setta.'

Facing Calvinists and Catholics 261

to render to sticks and stones which our [remote] ancestors knew that worship which it is proper to reserve to the one, everlasting God, Creator of heaven and earth.'[131]

Nevertheless, assessment of reformed Christianity (and in particular of Calvinism) as standing on a higher plane than Catholicism did not hinder Isaac Orobio and some of his fellow-members of the west European Sephardi diaspora from polemizing against the fundamental teaching of Calvin and other Protestant sects. The treatment of predestination, and the question of the reward of the righteous in the polemical literature of the Sephardi 'Portuguese', must be accorded especial attention. On several occasions Isaac attacks Calvin for disallowing any possibility that man can attain salvation by his works: 'we maintain the contrary opinion to Calvin's, for he denies [the possibility of] man's being purified ... and declares that man remains forever devoid of grace in the eyes of God ... Wherein he errs, for, as we have already proved, man does become righteous and acceptable in the sight of the Creator through fulfilment of the divine precepts.'[132] Isaac similarly criticizes Calvin's assertion that the privilege of participating in the perpetual praise of God, i.e. life in the world to come, depends exclusively on God's grace. As against this Isaac maintains that the righteous man who keeps God's commandments attains a spiritual perfection which entitles him not only to material reward here and now, but also to that participation in the perpetual praise of God which God Himself, in his grace, makes available to him.[133] Like Isaac Orobio, Rabbi Moses Raphael d'Aguilar also exposed the shortcomings of Calvinist predestinarianism in his own *Breve discurso contra a doutrina de Calvino*, raising his protest against the 'pseudo-doctrine' which asserted that mankind is incapable of performing good works because of 'the corruption of their nature consequent upon the sin of Adam'.[134] On the contrary, declares d'Aguilar, man is capable of attaining the love of God with all his heart, all his soul, and all his might, proof for this being in his view forthcoming from the impressive number of Jews who had died as martyrs in vindication of God's holy name.[135]

Isaac Orobio styles the Protestants 'sectarians', this being the label current in most of the polemical literature of the Portuguese Jews of

[131] *Resp. Pred. franc.*, ed. Amzalak, pp. 70 f.
[132] *Prev. Div., EH* 48 D 6, ff. 106ʳ f.
[133] Ibid.
[134] *EH* 48 A 11, pp. 140 f.
[135] Ibid., pp. 141 f., esp. p. 143.

Amsterdam in the seventeenth century.[136] Despite the recognition of some superiority of the various streams of Protestantism over popish Christianity, he views Christianity as a whole as being an utter travesty of the divine Law: the terms 'Catholic' and 'reform' are both alike applied, in his thinking, as variant titles for one and the same idolatrous system. Belief in Jesus, which is the common heritage of Christendom, is disposed of as being demonstrably deceptive; his mission had brought about not the slightest amelioration in human conduct, for 'in the present sinfulness in which mankind is voluntarily immersed, no spiritual perfection is to be discerned'.[137] And, he ironically adds, 'to sum up, the number of those condemned to hell [since Christianity began] is like the number condemned before the passion and death [of Jesus], and indeed higher: inasmuch as before then, Israel could achieve salvation through fulfilment of the holy Law of Moses, and the Gentiles through fulfilment of natural law, but since his death no one [in the Christian view] can achieve salvation except those who believe in him and in his opaque mysteries . . .'[138]

When Isaac Orobio and his compeers came to consider where they stood *vis-à-vis* Christianity, they were ever mindful of the long record of persecution which they had endured whilst they were still residing in Christian (i.e. Catholic) countries. Their memory of the cruelty of the Inquisition had increased the sense of alienation which they felt in regard to the whole concept of Christianity and its principles, adding an extra revulsion from its beliefs and its symbols. Even the relative degree of toleration which they enjoyed in Calvinist Amsterdam could not easily dispel their antipathy. Unlike certain medieval Jewish sages and some seventeenth-century Jewish thinkers in central and eastern Europe, the Sephardi Jews of Amsterdam did not detach Christianity from paganism.[139] They felt the urge actively to pillory Christianity as being 'the meanest form of idolatry that the wickedness of man had ever devised'.

---

[136] Occasionally also *cismáticos: Resp. Pred. franc., EH* 48 D 6, f. 297ʳ. Cf. a letter from Elijah Montalto dated 28 Feb. 1612, to Dr Pedro Rodríguez and Isabel da Fonseca his wife, '. . . e assy caluinista, ou lutherano, ou sectador de qualquer outra ydolatria . . .', C. Roth, 'Quatre Lettres d'Elie Montalto', *REJ* 87, 1929, p. 153; see also de Barrios, *Libre Alvedrio y Harmonia del Cuerpo*, Brussels, 1680, p. 7: 'Esfuerço Harmonico, Descrive, defiende, y prueva la verdad del libre Alvedrio . . . Juzga el astuto Sectario . . .'

[137] *EH* 48 D 6, f. 231ᵛ.   [138] Ibid.

[139] Katz, *Exclusiveness*, pp. 115 f., 162 f.

10
Philosophers, Theologians, and Poets

SPINOZA AND METAPHYSICS: MEETING THE CHALLENGE

In 1684 Isaac Orobio published in Amsterdam his *Certamen Philosophicum, Propugnatae Veritatis Divinae ac Naturalis adversus Joh. Bredenburg*.[1] This work was received with marked respect in philosophical circles in Holland and abroad, and it constituted Orobio one of the leaders of the campaign against Spinoza's philosophy. Basically, his book is a rejoinder to the postulates of Bredenburg. Bredenburg was a retail cloth-dealer in Rotterdam, an active member of the Collegiants there, who having begun as an opponent of Spinoza found himself converted to his ideas *malgré soi*, becoming instead one of his devoted followers.

Very little is known about Bredenburg. In 1675 he wrote a tract against Spinoza's *Tractatus Theologico-Politicus*, and according to P. Bayle no one else had succeeded in pointing out with greater clarity the seeds of contradiction contained in that work.[2] Apart from his criticism

[1] See Carmoly, i, p. 177, *EUIEA* 40, p. 623. The statement that Orobio's *Cert. Phil.* was first printed in 1681 is incorrect; it was a rejoinder to Bredenburg, whose piece was itself published in 1684 only. *Per contra* Amzalak (Orobio, *Resp. Pred. franc.*, pp. xxviii f.), followed by A. Herzberg, *The French Enlightenment and the Jews*, New York and London, 1968, p. 44, maintained that it was not published until 1689. Although I know of no edition prior to that which appeared in 1703, it seems reasonable to suppose that the work first appeared in 1684, i.e. in the same year as Bredenburg's *Mathematica Demonstratio*, since Orobio would surely have appreciated the importance of getting what he had written into print. It was in 1684 that there also appeared the tracts of Aubert de Versé and Lemmerman (see below, p. 264), who likewise produced refutations of Bredenburg, so that Orobio will most probably have written his own rejoinder and got it published at the height of the controversy which was causing such a tumult in philosophical circles. See Carvalho, pp. 114 f., and A. van del Linde, *Benedictus Spinoza, Bibliografie*, Niewkoop, 1965, pp. 33 f.

[2] The full title of Bredenburg's work runs *Enervatio Tractatus Theologico Politici, una cum Demonstratione, geometrico ordine disposita, Naturam non esse Deum, cujus effati contrario praedictus Tractatur unice innititur*. For Bredenburg himself, see M. Francès, *Spinoza dans les Pays Neerlandais de la seconde moitié du XVII siècle*, Paris, 1937, p. 68; Carvalho, pp. 107 f., and Kolakowski, pp. 250–92. Such knowledge as we possess of him is fragmentary. The main primary source upon which scholars have relied is Bayle's article on Spinoza. Bayle himself was much impressed by Bredenburg's work, and by the circumstance that it was the product of one of but mediocre philosophical understanding; see Bayle, *Dictionnaire historique*[5], iv, 1740, p. 258: 'C'etoit un Bourgeois de Rotterdam . . . fut

of the principles underlying the thinking in the *Tractatus* Bredenburg demonstrated by application of Spinoza's own geometric method that, contrary to Spinoza's philosophy, the notions of Deity and nature are incommensurable. After he had published his book he reached a fresh conclusion: the principle *Deus sive Natura* which he had been opposing could be proved geometrically. Having completed a treatise in which he proved this, Bredenburg in his perplexity endeavoured to refute his own proof and to demolish its structure by whatever means he could, but his attempts came to nothing.[3] At this stage Bredenburg appealed to some of his learned friends, amongst them Isaac Orobio, asking for their help in extricating himself from his entanglement and in smashing his geometrical proof of Spinoza's system. In turning to them, he withheld authority for the publication of his own proof, with the intention of avoiding public scandal; however, one of his correspondents, Frans Kuyper (Cuyper, Cuperus), apparently disregarded his request, and in the rejoinder to him which he wrote in Dutch he placed Bredenburg's new proof in the public domain.[4] The book caused a great stir in philosophical circles, many people being dumbfounded when it became clear to them that the author of the critique of the *Tractatus Theologico-Politicus* had changed his spots and had become, so to say, a devotee of Spinoza.

Several speculative writers quickly came out against Bredenburg, accusing him of atheism. At the same time as Orobio de Castro's *Certamen Philosophicum* there appeared tracts by Noel Aubert de Versé and Abraham Lemmermann, both of whom wrote contraverting the learned shopkeeper of Rotterdam, and in 1686 there was published

---

surpris de voir qu'un homme qui ne faisoit point profession des Lettres, et qui n'avoit que fort peu d'etude eût pu pénétrer si subtilement tous les principes de Spinoza et les renverser heureusement.' Cf. Bayle, *Selections*, pp. 295 f.

[3] Bayle, *Dictionnaire*, ibid.: '... On m'a raconté que cet Auteur aiant réfléchi une infinité de fois su sa Réponse, et sur le Principe de son Adversaire, trouva enfin qu'on pouvait réduire ce Principe en Démonstration. Il entreprit donc de prouver qu'il n'y a point d'autre cause de toutes choses qu'une Nature qui existe nécessairement, et qui agit par une nécessité immuable, inévitable et irrévocable. Il observa toute la méthode des Géometres, et après avoir bâti sa Demonstration, il l'examina de tous le côtes imaginables; il tâcha d'en trouver le foible, et ne put jamais inventer aucun moien de la détruire, ni même de l'affoiblir.'

[4] '... et il prioit les plus habiles de ses amis de la secourir, dans la recherche du défaut de cette Démonstration. Néanmois il n'en laissoit point tirer de copies ...' In what follows Bayle states that Kuyper acted as he did out of jealousy of Bredenburg, whose own anti-Spinozan tract of 1675 had been so much more successful than his own: 'Cet homme rempli peut-être de la jalousie d'Auteur car il avoit travaillé contre Spinoza avec beaucoup moins de succès que Jean Bredenbourg se servit quelque tems après de cette copie pour l'accuser d'être Atheé' (ibid.).

Philosophers, Theologians, and Poets

correspondence on the same subject between Bredenburg himself and Philip van Limborch, who had likewise launched a fierce attack on Spinoza.[5]

The fact that Bredenburg regarded Orobio as an authority and thought it right to approach him about the questions raised by his critique of Spinoza, indicates at once both Orobio's standing in Dutch philosophical circles and the close links which he maintained with non-Jewish thinkers and scholars in the Netherlands. No doubt friendly relations already existing between Orobio and Bredenburg justified the confidence which the latter felt in the Jewish doctor, and but for such assumed friendship it must be doubtful whether he would have approached him with a problem of such refined intellectual subtlety, or would have laid his private thoughts bare before him. For our purposes the significance of the Orobio–Bredenburg disputation lies in what it tells us about Orobio's attitude towards Spinoza's philosophy, particularly since, so far as is known, his book is the one and only systematic consideration of the Spinozan system written by a Jewish contemporary of the author of the *Ethics*.[6]

Some scholars previously identified Isaac Orobio as the physician to whom on 24 January 1671 Descartes' pupil Lambert de Velthuysen

---

[5] See Carvalho, pp. 114 f. Bayle indicates that in the wake of Bredenburg's geometric *Demonstratio* there appeared numerous writings, both *pro* and *con*, mainly in Dutch; *Dictionnaire*, 'il parut plusieurs Ecritures de part et d'autre que je n'ai point lues, car je n'entens point le Flamand'. Cf. van del Linde (n. 1 above), pp. 60 f.

[6] It is pertinent to observe here that members of the Portuguese-Jewish congregation of Amsterdam which had excommunicated Spinoza and expelled him from the Jewish community completely, scarcely engaged in any direct controversy with him at all. De Barrios attacked him sharply in the early 1680s in his *Eternidad de la Ley de Mosseh*: 'Benedito Espinosa, echado del Iudaismo Amstelodamo por sus malas oppinones (*sic*) hizo un libro que al parecer es vaso de oro, pero con el ponçoñoso licor de que los Iudios no tienen obligación de observar la Ley Mosayca en quanto no tienen imperio: y sino la huvieran observado en la esclavitud no se distinguieran entre las demas naciones como no se distinguen los Moabitas, Amonitas, Idumeos, Phenices, y otras naciones, con la perdida de sus Reynos y leyes' *(Triumpho*, p. 85, copy in Amsterdam, Bibl. Rosen., 19 G 11). Similarly in his *Corona de Ley*, p. 2: '*Espinos* son los que en *Prados* de impiedad, dessean luzir con el fuego que los consume.' Dismissive judgements of this type are scattered over the corpus of de Barrios' works, but in none of them is there any systematic consideration of the axioms of Spinozan philosophy. For the most part the references consist of extremist animadversions aimed at rebutting Spinoza's critique of Judaism. It may be assumed that Jacob de Andrade's *Theologo Religioso contra o Theologo Politico de Bento Espinosa, que de Judeo se fez Atheista*, likewise confined itself to dealing with Spinoza's criticism of Judaism, and did not touch on his views as to metaphysics; I have not myself succeeded in locating a copy of it. Of Andrade and his work little is known. He was born in Pernambuco in the middle of the 17th cent., and was a doctor who lived for a time in The Hague and in Antwerp. See Kayserling, *Biblioteca*, p. 12, and Carvalho, p. 84. The book was printed in Amsterdam (date unknown).

addressed a letter embodying a vigorous attack on the *Tractatus Theologico-Politicus*, in which he accused Spinoza of atheism. Since the addressee of that letter was mentioned in it by the initials *J.O.* only, it was possible to claim that behind them lurked the name of Isaac Orobio.[7] And, starting from that assumption, it could be supposed that during the 1670s Orobio and Spinoza were on friendly terms.[8] However, in 1896 Meinsma proved that *J.O.* stood for Jacob Ostens, a Rotterdam physician who directed a group of the *Collegianten* sect there,[9] so that nothing can be learned about any personal relationships that may have obtained between Orobio and Spinoza. Although one cannot exclude completely the possibility of their acquaintanceship, it would seem probable that they did not know each other. On the other hand we need have no doubt that Orobio's approach to Spinoza's thought remained fundamentally unchanged throughout the years that he resided in Amsterdam. His book against Bredenburg was not the outcome of a speculative development which had led him from a 'sympathy with pantheism' to 'an absolute disavowal of the concept of *Deus sive Natura*', as certain historians have supposed (see above, n. 8). Scrutiny of Orobio's polemical writings against Prado has shown that in the early sixties Isaac had already been denying utterly what was then known of Spinoza's philosophy.[10]

Orobio's *Certamen Philosophicum* uses the same principles as those employed by Spinoza and Bredenburg, i.e. the method of geometric proof. Using arguments drawn from rationalist and scholastic philosophy, Isaac endeavoured to dismantle the whole structure upon which was founded the philosophical system of Spinoza and his followers. At

---

[7] Spinoza's reply was likewise addressed to the doctor as 'J. O.'. See the *editio princeps*, 'Epistolae Doctorum quorundam Virorum ad B. d. S. et auctoris Responsiones, in B[enedictus] d[e] S[pinoza]', *Opera Posthuma* [Amsterdam], 1677, pp. 541 f. Lambert de Velthuysen's name is similarly abbreviated to 'L. de V. M D'' (*Opera*, ii, pp. 157 f.).

[8] Graetz, *Geschichte*, x, Leipzig, 1896, pp. 415 f., indulged in some extravagance of language, maintaining that Orobio was reluctant to pass judgement on Spinoza's book until he had heard de Velthuysen's opinion, whence, allegedly, his appeal to him. (In the Eng. trans. of Graetz this is apparently watered down, it being merely stated that Orobio 'associated with Spinoza' (v, p. 117), and (p. 167) that he 'attempted a serious refutation of Spinoza's views. Though his intention was good, he was too weak to break through the close meshes of Spinoza's system.' See C. Michaelis de Vasconcellos, *Uriel da Costa, Notas relativas à sua vida e as suas obras*, Coimbra, 1922, p. 79, who states that Orobio originally adhered to Spinoza's pantheism. Cf. Kayserling, *Biblioteca*, p. 82, and Schoeps, *Jewish Christian Argument*, p. 189.

[9] See Meinsma, pp. 413 f., Carvalho, pp. 58, 106. Ostens, who stood close to Spinoza, encountered respect from de Velthuysen on account of his intellectual honesty.

[10] See above, chap. 6, pp. 146 f.

the beginning of the book he gives a sketch of the reasons which impelled him to write it. Some years previously he had read what 'the impious Spinoza' had written, and even then he had realized that Spinoza had not merely blazed the trail towards atheism, but that he had made it possible for atheism to strike sturdy roots. All the same, he had not felt it to be a matter of urgent necessity to write controversially against Spinoza, the reason being that he took it for granted that the common folk did not understand his teaching, and that the learned would be dismissing it outright. But then there had come into his hands two tracts which jerked him out of his complacency and caused him to revise his estimate of the dangers concealed in Spinoza's views. The first of these had been written by a scholar who claimed that despite his being a follower of Spinoza, he was a good Christian; the second was that of Bredenburg, 'a scholar and a man firm in his faith', who had approached him with the request for his opinion on the principles of Spinoza's philosophy. These two tracts had, he wrote, alerted him to the danger of Spinoza's teaching becoming widely known, and of its winning many adherents. It was consciousness of this that had persuaded him to put pen to paper.[11]

At the outset of his treatment of the subject Isaac set down the Spinozan definitions as quoted in Bredenburg's tract: that God is the indwelling and not the transient cause of all things; that besides God there can be no substance that is nothing in itself external to God; that of necessity in divine action; and that no existent is created *ex nihilo*.[12] As against these definitions Isaac tabulates thirteen propositions alternative to them, which he himself postulates as a negation of the axiomatic definition that 'everything is produced by an inexorable necessity'. The existent whose being is the necessity of existence (i.e. the Deity) can create existents *ex nihilo*, his actions not being involuntary ones but all of them originating in his free will.[13]

---

[11] See *Cert. Phil.*, introd., pp. 3 f., 9; cf. Kolakowski, pp. 267 f.

[12] *Cert. Phil.*, introd., pp. 10 f. See Spinoza's *Ethics, Op. Post.*, part i, *de Deo*, pp. 1 f.

[13] At the end of the book he cites the mathematical *Demonstratio* by Bredenburg which had given rise to the whole controversy, as also Bredenburg's rejoinder to Orobio's objections ('Authoris Defensio suae Demonstrationis adversus ejusdem Refutationem N. N.'). Bredenburg had proposed the following distinction. *Belief* and *intellectual comprehension* have to be kept apart from each other: and even though the intellect may be able to undermine, or even to demonstrate the utter impossibility of belief, maintenance of such belief is nevertheless justifiable, first, because the human intellect is limited and incapable of adducing grounds for complete certainty, and secondly because the individual prefers to attend to his own innermost feelings or the prompting of the word of God rather than to subscribe to any metaphysical proof.

Attention should be drawn to the fact that in Isaac Orobio's treatise the reader will find not the slightest hint at the circumstance that he was a Jew: he does not, in this book, take any account of the fact. Moreover, Isaac bases his contentions upon St Augustine, although for the object that he had in view he could perfectly well have relied upon medieval Jewish philosophers. Maimonides, in whom he could have found authoritative support, is not mentioned, whereas St Augustine — towards whom he evinces an undisguised respect — comes in for exaggerated praise.[14] Unquestionably this is not due to lack of expertise in Jewish sources. In 1684, when the book appeared, Isaac had behind him a long series of apologetic and polemical tracts in which he had evinced a most respectable degree of knowledge of Jewish philosophy and biblical exegesis. The deliberate neglect of these sources consequently occasions not a little astonishment.

It may be that Isaac was deliberately giving preference to the Christian sources because, when addressing himself to a Christian philosopher who was making a parade of his loyalty to his own religion, he wanted to emphasize the contrast of Spinoza's teaching to the classical literature of Christian philosophy, and to underscore the mutual incompatability of the two. There is, however, another possibility. The philosopher in him found it problematic to fuse the concepts which he acquired from study of Catholic texts in Christian universities with the Jewish values and ideas which he advocated in his theological disputations and anti-Christian controversial writing. Comparison of Isaac Orobio's *Certamen Philosophicum* with the philosophical encyclopaedia of Isaac Cardoso entitled *Philosophia Libera* which appeared in Venice in 1673, clearly shows that Orobio the philosopher and Orobio the Jew did not inhabit the same universe of discourse. Each of these two Jewish philosophers was writing approximately twenty years after his reversion to Judaism, one in Amsterdam and the other in Venice. Cardoso, although his intellect was formed by training in Christian sources, knew how to synthesize the speculative techniques he had acquired in his youth with those Jewish values,

---

Bredenburg's intention was thereby to emphasize that geometric demonstration of the validity of the principles of Spinoza's thinking had not distanced him from a perfect faith in Christianity. Bayle accepted Bredenburg's arguments as a sincere declaration of faith, and doubtless he found it similar to his own sceptical doctrine of the limits of the intellect. Cf. Bayle, *Selections*, p. 298, and Popkin, *Bayle and Scepticism*, pp. 1–19.

[14] See *Cert. Phil.*, p. 41: 'Profecto talem modum philosophandi de Deo, no ego excogitavi, sed mirabilis Augistini intellectus, cap. 29 Medit . . . Ecce sapientissimus iste Doctor . . .'

Philosophers, Theologians, and Poets 269

new to him, which he had internalized on his return to Judaism. However, unlike him, his fellow-philosopher seems to have failed in this particular.[15]

As against Cardoso's book which was consigned to almost complete oblivion, Orobio's *Certamen Philosophicum* received considerable acclaim, being reprinted in several editions and also translated from the Latin into both Spanish and French. Its examination led Bayle to characterize Orobio, in his *Dictionnaire historique et critique*, as being 'a most talented Jewish physician'.[16] In 1703, six years after the appearance of Bayle's *editio princeps*, a second edition of the *Certamen Philosophicum* appeared in Amsterdam; and in 1731 Orobio's tract was printed in full in an anti-Spinozan *collectaneum* printed in Brussels under the editorship of Lenglet Dufresnoy, entitled *Réfutation des Erreurs de Benoit de Spinosa*.[17] Conjoined with treatises by M. de Fénelon, Archbishop of Cambrai, François Lamy, of the Benedictines of St Maur, and Charles Boullainvilliers,[18] there is printed that of Orobio, of whom the editor writes in a special preface that 'his teaching is known as being that of the most scholarly of the Jews of contemporary Amsterdam', although 'there are few in France who have read his writings'.[19]

As indicated, Orobio's book was translated into Spanish and French.[20] The Spanish translator, G. de la Torre, who appears to have lived in The Hague, did his work both with fidelity to the original Latin and with great clarity.[21] From the personal dedications inscribed by de

---

[15] A detailed analysis of Cardoso's book will be found in Yerushalmi, *Isaac Cardoso*, pp. 216 f.

[16] Bayle, *Dictionnaire historique*⁵, iv, 1740, p. 258: '... Orobio Médecin Juif fort habile ...', and see n. 83 *in loco citato*.

[17] There is no basis for the conjecture *(EUIEA* 40, p. 623) that the tract was included in Limborch's *De Veritate Rel. Christ.*, which was published in 1687.

[18] See Fénelon, introd. Boullainvilliers' tract is closely sympathetic to Spinoza's teaching; on the question as to how it came to be included in this collection see Wade, pp. 97 f.

[19] Fénelon, p. 388: '... Nemo est inter Eruditos cui non fuerit cognita et perspecta Doctissimi inter hodiernos Amstelodamenses Hebraeos Ishak orobio doctrina; pauci tamen in Belgio, at multo pauciores sunt in Gallia qui ejus scripta legerint ... Hinc fiet apertum Hebraeis non satis fuisse justo anathemate impium Spinosam percutere; ipsis etiam cordi fluit acque ac christianis, ejus sophismata revellere ...'

[20] See Popkin's *Selections* of Bayle, p. 297. Popkin argued, without foundation, that Orobio's tract was originally composed in Spanish. His statement, ibid., that it was translated into Dutch derives from Bayle, ibid., 'il est en Latin et en Flamand'. I have not been able to substantiate whether any Dutch recension of *Cert. Phil.* ever in fact existed.

[21] The Spanish title reads *Certamen Philosophico, Defiende la verdad Divina y Natural, contra los Principios de Juan Bredemburg*. See below, Appendix E.

la Torre in two of the manuscript copies, it would seem that the book continued to attract interest amongst both a Jewish and a Christian public in the first half of the eighteenth century.[22]

A 'FRIENDLY CONVERSATION': ISAAC OROBIO AND PHILIP VAN LIMBORCH

During the seventeenth century differences began to appear in the attitude of Christians in western Europe towards Jews and Judaism. It was a time when principles of religious toleration were just beginning to crystallize out, and considerations of the economic advantage that Jews could contribute to the state were being weighed: and, in the post-Reformation world, Gentile Hebrew studies were beginning to take root. All of these factors paved the way for a fresh examination of the place of Jews in Christian society and the meaning of their survival from the point of view of Christian theology.[23] Although the traditional Christian attitude of guarded hostility remained dominant, the voice of Christian theologians and thinkers who stood aside from the age-long negative stance of Christianity towards the Jews was gradually making itself heard more loudly. That is of course not to say that any serious attempt was made to confer legitimacy on the Jewish faith or to recognize its existence alongside Christianity. The aim of the writers and thinkers concerned went no further than to point to the need to discover ways of approach by which Jews might be attracted to the Christian faith.

In the seventeenth-century Netherlands conversations and correspondence of theologians and other Christian scholars with rabbis and

[22] In the dedication to the Spanish Agent (MS Amsterdam, *EH* 48 C 16, *init.*) the translator wrote: 'El mérito y estima que los escritos deste grande hombre han exitado en my, me han movido a hacer esta traducción, y passarla a las manos de Vmd., de quien tantos favores recivo cada dia.' In the dedication to Solomon de Medina (MS Paris, BN Fonds éspagnoles 41, pp. 258, *init.*) it is stated that Medina and Orobio were friends ('Presento a Vmd. su antiguo/amigo el Doctor Ishack Orobio de Castro', and 'Este es aquel célebre combate que adquirio tantos laureles y elogios a su autor . . . La estimacion extraordinaria que he concebido al autor aviendo leydo sus Escritos; el summo deseo y cuidado con que Vmd. ha procurado y procura juntarlos sin consideración alguna a los grandes gastos y fatigas que por conseguirlo han sido necessarios; y las muchas obligaciones que toda mi vida confessaré dever a Vmd. me han como forzado, a hacer esta traducción y dedicarla a Vmd., que conserva tan viva la memoria de su amigo . . .'

[23] See Ettinger, *Change*, pp. 196 f., and his *De'istim*, p. 182.

Philosophers, Theologians, and Poets

other Jewish scholars became a significant feature of the scene.[24] Although a sizeable proportion of these Jewish–Christian interchanges resulted from the interest taken by Protestant professors belonging to various denominations in the Hebrew language, in Jewish biblical exegesis, in Talmudic and other rabbinic literature, in the *cabbala* etc., not infrequently they developed into religious debates that got down to the fundamental differences of principle separating Christianity from Judaism. Such was the origin of the discussions of Jan Pieterszoon Beelthouwer, the preacher of Enkhuizen, and several Portuguese Jews in Amsterdam in 1644–5,[25] and it was in the same manner that a bitter polemic was started between Jacob Alting, professor of theology at Groningen, and Abraham Senior Coronel.[26] The background was the same for the correspondence which developed at this period between Antonius Hulsius and Jacob Abendana.[27]

Millenarians and others concerned with eschatology, who were attracting much attention in Amsterdam at this period, stressed in their writings that the second coming of the messiah could not occur until the Jews had accepted Christianity. In 1686 there appeared in Rotterdam P. Jurieu's *L'Accomplissement des Prophéties*, in which he set out to prove that under the 'Fifth Monarchy' the entire Jewish people would turn Christian and would become leaders of the world.[28] Conrad van Beuningen gave expression to similar ideas in the letter which he addressed on 2 January 1689 to David de Pina, the son-in-law of Isaac Orobio.[29]

[24] See C. Roth, *Men. b. I.*, pp. 140 f; Cardozo de Bethencourt, 'Lettres de Menasseh Ben Israel à Isaac Vossius (1651–1655)', *REJ* 49, 1904, pp. 98–109.

[25] See van den Berg, p. 38. The first theological discussion between Jews and Christians in Amsterdam took place at the beginning of the 17th cent., between David Farrar and the English divine Hugh Broughton, who was resident in Amsterdam from 1605 to 1608. In 1606 Broughton had published, in Hebrew with a Latin translation, his conversionist *Responsum ad Epistolam Judaei sitienter expetentis cognitionem fidei Christianorum*. The book was addressed to 'Judaeus Byzantiacus' (i.e. Abraham Reuben), and its appearance sparked off the debate with Farrar. Broughton's book is prodigiously rare, but a copy of the Hebrew–Latin edition is in the British Library (pressmark T. 812 (9)). On Broughton's works published during his residence in Amsterdam, see L. Fuks and R. G. Fuks-Mansfeld, *Hebrew Typography in the Northern Netherlands, 1585–1815*, I, Leiden, 1984, pp. 94–9.

[26] Their correspondence (which was conducted in Hebrew) was printed at the end of Alting's *Fundamenta punctuationis linguae Sanctae*, Frankfurt am Main, 1746; see Silva Rosa, *Joden en niet Joden*, p. 24.

[27] See van den Berg, p. 12.

[28] See Yardeni, pp. 170 f., and cf. van den Berg, pp. 33 f.

[29] See C. v. B[euningen], *Sendbrief van de H' C. v. B. aan de Heer David Pina*, [Amsterdam, 1688]), pp. 3 f. Van Beuningen was an interesting character, who served several

The inducement of the Jews to change their religious allegiance was one of the central aims which many of the Dutch theologians of the period set themselves. At the Calvinist synod held at Dordrecht in 1676 the representatives of Gouda proposed a practically formulated plan of action, both comprehensive and thoroughgoing, for the dissemination of Christianity among the Jews.[30] One year later, at the synod held in Delft, many of the participants exposed the effect on Jews of Catholicism, with its vain beliefs and pagan rituals, since it induced in them a hatred for all things Christian. Members of the assembly resolved to use their best endeavours to eliminate those corruptions which adhered to Christianity that not only distorted the original good tidings proclaimed by Jesus, but also prevented the conversion of the Jews to Christianity. They likewise resolved to invite rabbis and other Jewish scholars to take part in 'friendly conversations' regarding the significance of Mosaic Law and the message of the prophets, the differences between what Christians styled the 'Old' Testament and the 'New', the function of the commandments, the personality and mission of the messiah, etc. The synod also recommended that preachers should devote time daily to the study of Hebrew, and should examine the Jewish case against Christianity presented in Jewish disputational literature.[31]

The resolutions opened the door to conversations and disputations between Christians and Jews, and it would appear that some of the latter threw off all self-restraint and in fiery defence of their own faith did not refrain from publicly assailing the principles of the Christian religion. The reaction of the Leiden preachers to this behaviour was to lay a complaint before the States General of Holland, demanding that steps be taken against those who were blaspheming Christianity.[32] The leadership of the Portuguese congregation accordingly resolved on 28 August 1677 (1 *'Elul* 5437) to forbid its membership engaging in discussions with Christians concerning matters of faith, enjoining

---

terms as burgomaster of Amsterdam and was thus at the centre of the affairs in the Netherlands after the mid-17th cent. On him see C. W. Roldanus, *Coenraad van Beuningen, Staatsman en Libertijn*, The Hague, 1931.

[30] See Silva Rosa, *Joden en niet Joden*, pp. 19 f.   [31] Ibid.

[32] See the Portuguese-Jewish community's *Ascamoth (Acta)*, Amsterdam, AGA, PA 334 no. 19, p. 769, resolution of the Ma'amad dated 1 *'Elul* 5437: '... pois ão sido novamente advertidos os Senhores do Mahamad de hua pessoa de consideração e authoridade, de que os Pregadores da Academia de Leyde, havião feito grandes queixas a os Senhores Estados de Holanda na Junta delles, dizendo que os Judeos muy libres e escandalosamente falavão mal da Religião Cristãa, e disputando publicamente contra ella tanto de palavras, como por escripto ...'

them to 'refrain from the practice of such disputation both in public and in private, since such things are prejudicial to the preservation of our safety, stirring up as they do the ill will of the Gentiles among whom we live: and whosoever shall act contrariwise, is to be put outside the Congregation, nor re-admitted until he shall have paid twenty florins . . . to the congregational charity . . .'[33]

The urgency of the *señores* of the *Ma'amad* was of no avail, and despite their prohibition conversations and debates on religious topics between Christians and Portuguese Jews continued. It seems quite clear that at any rate some of the Christian participants made no remonstrances when their partners in these 'friendly conversations' spoke without restraint about their refusal to come anywhere near Christianity, and vigorously exposed its fallacies. These learned Christians were sincerely convinced that the obduracy of the Jews would gradually lessen under the influence of the 'friendly conversations', through which they would progressively learn about the basic principles of Christianity and, in consequence, change their negative approach to the gospel proclaimed by Jesus.

It is against this backdrop that we have to view the debate which took place in Amsterdam in approximately 1684 between Isaac Orobio and Philip van Limborch. In the climate of the period such a debate was not an exceptional event: and, in its course, no new theological position on the Christian side in regard to Jews and Judaism was revealed.[34] The importance of the disputation inheres not so much in its content as in the intellectual weight of the two opponents, their position of seniority in learned circles of Amsterdam, and in the many echoes to which it gave rise after its publication.

Philip van Limborch (1633–1712) was in his time reckoned to be one of the leading Christian theologians in western Europe.[35] When

---

[33] Ibid.: '. . . pelo que resolverão os Senhores do Mahamad fazer saber a Vms. o referido, pedindolhes com todo encaresimento, sejão servidos de absterse de semelhantes praticas e disputas, tanto em publico como em segreto, pois são tão pernisiosas, e danosas a nossa conservação fazendonos odiar por ellas das gentes adonde abitamos, e quem o contrario fizer, serà apartado da congregação e não admitido a ella té pagar vinte lyvras de grosos para a Sedacá . . .'

[34] Cf. Schoeps, *Jewish Christian Argument*, pp. 78 f.

[35] For Limborch see van der Hoeven; A. J. van der Aa, *Biographisch Woordenboek der Nederlanden*, 12, Haarlem, 1865, pp. 451–5; *Biographisch Woordenboek van Protestantsche Godgeleerden in Nederland*, 6, The Hague, 1949, pp. 41–7; *Nieuw Nederlandsch Biografisch Woordenboek*, ed. P. C. Molhuysen and K. H. Kossmann, ix, Leiden, 1933, pp. 608 f. (F. S. Knipscheer). The short note in *Encyclopaedia Britannica"*, xvi, Cambridge, 1911, p. 691, includes a bibliography of Limborch's works; see the dissertation presented to the University of Groningen by P. J. Barnow, *Phillipus van Limborch*, The Hague, 1963.

his conversations with Orobio took place he was head of the Dutch Remonstrants, better known as Arminians after Jacob Arminius (1560–1609). Arminius was preacher in Amsterdam and professor of theology in Leiden; he dissented from Calvin's extreme position regarding predestination, and insisted on the freedom of the individual to accept or to reject divine grace at his own volition.[36] His pupils developed his theological thought under the influence of the teaching of unitarian and Socinian theologians with whom they were in close contact in Amsterdam, engaging in discussions with them regarding matters of faith.[37] The Remonstrants kept repeating time and again that Jesus was a prophet, sent by God, and that he was subject to his will; he was the messiah, but he was not part of the Godhead itself. Le Clerc, one of Limborch's good friends and himself close to Remonstrant circles, summarized the principles of remonstrantism in one of his articles in *Bibliothèque Choisie* as follows: 'The Remonstrants require nothing from any man save that he should acknowledge the Scriptures as the exclusive code on which his faith is based: that he should live a Christian life: that no vestige of idolatry should adhere to him, and that he should not persecute any man [because of his faith]. They do not hold up to scorn those who do not agree with them in matters that are subject to opinion, but believe that it is their own duty to live according to the light that directs their souls.'[38]

Limborch was born in Amsterdam at the period when persecution of the Remonstrants ceased.[39] His maternal grandfather was the brother of Simon Episcopius (1583–1643), one of the most important Remonstrant theologians after the death of Arminius.[40] Philip studied theology at Utrecht and in the Remonstrants' seminary in Amsterdam. From 1657 to 1667 he held the office of preacher to the Arminian congregation of Gouda, a small town which at the end of the sixteenth century was known as a place of refuge for dissenters and members of persecuted sects.[41] It was there that in 1661 he published his book against Jacob Sceperus in which he maintained that his personal beliefs were not true in any absolute sense, and that acceptance of

---

[36] On Arminius and his doctrine see Harrison. Haley, pp. 102 f., gives a summary outline of the controversy between him and Franciscus Gomarus.
[37] See Ollion and De Boer, pp. 150 f.
[38] Le Clerc, *Bibl. Choisie*, xix, p. 383.
[39] On the persecution of Remonstrants at the beginning of the 17th cent. see Haley, pp. 104 f.
[40] Ollion and De Boer, p. 152.
[41] See Zilverberg, p. 14; Ollion and De Boer, p. 153.

Philosophers, Theologians, and Poets 275

them was not an indispensability for salvation of the soul. In this work he gave expression to his heartfelt wish for the unification of all Christian sects beneath the exclusive authority of Scripture.[42]

After he had published the second volume of the theological writings of Episcopius in 1665 Limborch's name became widely known in scholary circles. He had long been in touch with theologians and thinkers outside the Netherlands, and in particular he was in frequent correspondence with Peter Gunning, Ralph Cudworth, Henry More, Oliver Doiley, and Henry Jenkes, the most distinguished names amongst the rationalist theologians of Cambridge: these saw in the Dutch Remonstrants their closest allies.[43] From 1667 he held the office of preacher to the Remonstrant congregation of Amsterdam, and one year later he was appointed professor of theology in the Arminians' seminary. He continued to fill that post for the remainder of his life.[44]

In 1684 he met the philosopher John Locke, then in exile from England, at Amsterdam, and between the two of them deep bonds of friendship developed.[45] They founded a circle for the clarification of philosophical and scientific problems, members of which included Le Clerc and the well-known Amsterdam physician Pieter Guenellon. Limborch revealed that his views and those of Locke shared a common denominator: both of them were searching after means by which there might crystallize out a theology at once rational and Christian, and for Christian unity which should be based upon belief in the messiahship of Jesus. Both yearned for the fusion of the various Protestant sects and they were of one mind in their negative attitude towards Catholic Christianity which, for them, was a pagan religion.[46]

Limborch was a competent Hebraist, and he evinced great interest in Jews and Judaism. In his extensive library were to be found the works of Maimonides, the *Semaḥ David* of David Gans, the works of Menasseh ben Israel, Jacob Judah León Templo's book on the design of Solomon's temple, Samuel da Silva on the survival of the soul, Isaac Aboab da Fonseca's commentary on the Pentateuch, and books concerning Hebrew grammar, Talmudic literature, and Jewish customs.[47] He was also interested in the history of the Portuguese Jews

---

[42] The book's title is *Korte wederlegginge van 't boecken onlangs uytgegeven bij Jacobus Sceperus*.
[43] For the rationalistic theology of Cambridge philosophers of the period, see Willey, pp. 123 f.
[44] Ollion and De Boer, p. 155.
[45] Ibid., pp. 149 f.; cf. P. King, Locke, p. 159.
[46] Ollion and De Boer, p. 158.
[47] Limborch, *Cat., Folio*, nos. 10, 16, 19, 73–6, 87, 304, 374–5, 464–5; 12mo, nos. 110, 544; *Miscellanei in 8vo*, no. 582.

in the Iberian peninsula at the period when, suffering persecution for their steadfastness to the Mosaic Law, they were constrained to practise it in secret; and he had read a lot about the history of the Inquisition and its procedures. The subject was one that engaged his sympathy, and he wrote a book about it which was published in 1692.[48]

He watched with close interest what went on in the Portuguese congregation, and in a letter which he sent on 12 March 1662 to his friend Theodor Graswinckel he castigated its behaviour in excommunicating Uriel d'Acosta for having rejected 'Mosaic Law and aligning himself with natural deism'. In that letter Limborch maintained that although the Jews were entitled to exercise their freedom and enjoy their rights, they ought to be prevented from exploiting them in order to force their views and their faith on others. According to him, by dint of exercise of the weapon of excommunication the Jews were bringing about an intolerable state of affairs—'a republic within a republic'—and were arrogating to themselves a right which belonged to the state itself alone.[49] Despite the presence here of a slight anti-Jewish tone, the letter is essentially concerned to enunciate Limborch's religious and political views, according to which a religious community had no right to impose its beliefs on the individual. In 1696, when a law was passed in the Netherlands rendering it a punishable offence to deny, whether in speech or in print, the divinity of Jesus, Limborch sharply attacked those responsible for getting the measure carried, and declared that 'books ought not to be written against those on whom the infliction of penalties is meditated, likewise those against whom the authors were writing ought not to be punished'.[50]

It is not clear when Orobio got to know Limborch. Possibly his

[48] His library contained numerous books about the Inquisition, including Ludovicus a Paramo, *De origine et progressu Sanctae Inquisitionis*, Madrid, 1598; Nicolas Eymeric, *Directorium Inquisitorum*, Venice, 1605; *Histoire de l'Inquisition*, Cologne, 1693 (? J. Marsollier), etc., *Cat.*, Folio, nos. 131-3, 262; *8ᵛᵒ*, 229. For Limborch's own work on the Inquisition see above, chap. 4, p. 79.

[49] See the letter of Limborch in MS Amsterdam, Univ., III D 17, ff. 88ʳ–89ʳ. Parts of it were printed by Meinsma, pp. 521 f; Michaelis de Vasconcellos, op. cit. (see above, n. 8), pp. 102–4. On the allegation that the Jews constituted a 'state within a state' see J. Katz, 'A State within a State: the History of an Anti-Semitic Slogan', *Proceedings of the Israel Academy of Sciences and Humanities*, 4, Jerusalem, 1969, pp. 29–58.

[50] See Bonno, pp. 80, 108 n. 239. There is no doubt that Limborch's opposition was due to his viewing the enactment as a direct attack on the Remonstrants, who recognized in Jesus merely the messiah: but at the same time he regarded it as improper, since it ran counter to his own principles of individual freedom in matters of faith.

Philosophers, Theologians, and Poets

Certamen Philosophicum against Bredenburg, in which the religious challenge of the metaphysics of Spinoza was trenchantly exposed, may have won Limborch's approval. Ever since the appearance of the *Tractatus Theologico-Politicus* in 1670 he had regarded Spinoza as a dangerous atheist who was undermining the foundations of religious belief.[51]

Orobio's scholarship and intellectualism certainly attracted the attention of the leader of the Remonstrants, who in his book on the Inquisition recorded his impressions of the character of the Jewish doctor, and his sufferings in the dungeon of the Inquisition whilst he was still living as a crypto-Jew.[52] The prevailing opinion is that the 'friendly conversation' of Orobio and Limborch took place in 1686. But John Locke's letter to Limborch of 8 February 1685 shows that the English philosopher had been able to read a manuscript report of the debate before then. Thus the proceedings evidently took place no later than 1684.[53]

It seems likely that Orobio and Limborch initially met merely to hold verbal discussions, and that only at a late stage did they decide to put their respective positions into writing. In the introduction to the printed version, which came out in Gouda in 1687, Limborch wrote: 'this disputation was not born out of any intention to make it public property so that all and sundry might give their views upon it, but out of the desire to hold a friendly, personal conversation regarding the

---

[51] See the German trans. of his letter to Oliver Doiley, dated 23 June 1671, Altkirch, p. 30. Doiley (cf. above, p. 275) (d. 1693) was vice-provost of King's College, Cambridge. Limborch's library contained most of Spinoza's works, *Cat.*, p. 80.

[52] See above, chap. 4, p. 87.

[53] The dating of the conversation to 1686 goes back to 1730; Niceron, *Mém.*, xi, p. 47; Philippe de Limborch, *Memoires pour servir à l'histoire des Hommes Illustres*, xi, Paris, 1730, p. 47: '... Limborch eut avec lui une conference en 1686.' See Schoeps, *Jewish Christian Argument*, p. 78. Locke's letter is included in MS Amsterdam, Univ., Ba 255a; in it Locke asks Limborch to afford him a second look at the manuscript account of the conversations ('... rogo ut scripta illa Tua et Don Balthasaris quae olim mihi accomodasti, jam denuo mihi perlegenda permitteres'), cf. Ollion and De Boer, p. 163. The English translator of Uriel d'Acosta's autobiography (*The Remarkable Life of Uriel Acosta*, London, 1740, p. 6) picked up an interesting echo of the occasion which led to the discussion between the two of them: '... happening to fall into a Discourse about Religion with Egbert Veene, a celebrated Phisician, and Friend of Limborch's, who much commended Limborch's Learning, Orobio desired to have a Conference with him; which was held at Dr. Veene's House, carried on in a regular and scholarlike Manner, and was afterwards reduced to Writing and published by Limborch.' Cf. Sokolow, p. 168, who however in his Hebrew trans. modifies the sense of the passage quoted.

truth of religion, between a Jew and a Christian.'⁵⁴ It would seem Limborch was motivated to publish it as a book by the echoes to which it gave rise amongst theologians and scholars, the encouraging reactions of Locke and Le Clerc who had read it in manuscript, and Limborch's own feeling that he had as he thought, succeeded in demolishing Orobio's objections to Christianity.

Orobio himself was not enthusiastic about publicizing the debate, and opposed its being printed.⁵⁵ On the one hand, he was apprehensive of the reactions of the Christian public to his forthright language attacking Christianity; and on the other, he did not wish to find himself at odds with the leadership of his congregation, which had stringently prohibited Portuguese Jews from engaging in disputations with Christians regarding matters of faith. The *Ma'amad* might be able to shut its eyes to a 'friendly conversation', in virtue of the unique status enjoyed by Isaac, so long as it was not made public: but Isaac appreciated that as from the moment of publication the leadership would be unable to condone his action, and would have no choice but to adopt serious measures to bring him to book.

In the event, the clash with the congregation about which the by now elderly Orobio had been so apprehensive was averted since the book appeared at the beginning of November 1687, about a week before Orobio's death. Isaac had been able to see the proof-sheets, as Limborch testified in his letter to Spencer of 20 June 1688,⁵⁶ but the book did not come to the hands of the *Ma'amad* until after Isaac was already dead and out of respect for his memory they refrained from reacting to it.

As an appendix to his disputation with Orobio Limborch printed the hitherto unpublished autobiography of Uriel d'Acosta, *Exemplar Humanæ Vitæ*. The publication of this piece, so alien both in spirit and in content to the disputation itself, gives rise to much puzzlement.

---

⁵⁴ Limborch, *De Veritate Rel. Christ.*, introd.: 'Disputatio haec neutiquam fuit inchoata eo consilio, ut publicam lucem adspiceret, totiusque mundi judicium subiret, verum ut privatim inter Judaeum et Christianum amica de religionis veritate disquito institueretur . . .'

⁵⁵ We learn as much from Locke's letter of 23 Sept. 1687 (Ba 255s, see above, n. 53): 'Istud Synagogae decretum satis ut mihi videtur a Judaeis astute promulgatum, ut eorum hic Hyperaspistes aliquid habeat quod alijs dicat.' It would seem that Orobio represented to Limborch that an ordinance of the Amsterdam synagogue precluded his engaging in religious discussions with Christians, and that he consequently urged him not to publish their conversation.

⁵⁶ Amsterdam, Univ., MS III D 16, f. 115ʳ: '. . . paucis vero post editam nostram collationem, quam tamen legit, hebdomadis obiit . . .'

Philosophers, Theologians, and Poets 279

Conceivably the Remonstrant theologian intended to make use of the deeply penetrating criticisms in Uriel d'Acosta's confession in order to castigate the Jews for the cruel manner in which they had treated one who had disassociated himself from their religion, and to represent them in the same negative light as that in which their own ostracized brother had painted them.[57]

Limborch took the title for his book, *De Veritate Religionis Christianae*, from the well-known work of his own teacher, Hugo Grotius, which had first appeared in Leiden in 1622. Undoubtedly he was influenced by many of the views of the founding father of international law, himself a member of the Remonstrant sect.[58] He opened it with an 'introduction to the reader', and then gave successively the three parts of the debate. In each section he first presents Orobio's objections, followed by his own rejoinders to them. These replies are about twice as long as Isaac's contributions, and there is no doubt that this inequality affects the balance of the book and conveys the impression that the opinions of the Arminian theologian are better supported by reasoned argument than are those of the Jewish scholar.[59]

Isaac opened the first session by posing four fundamental questions to Limborch. (*a*) What is the authority in the [Hebrew] Scriptures for the assertion that belief in the messiah is an indispensable requirement for man's salvation? (*b*) Where in Scripture is it stated that the one and only means of Israel's salvation, and of their restoration to divine grace, is belief in a messiah who has already come? (*c*) Where in Scripture is it stated that God warned Israel that on account of their lack of belief in the messiah they would be punished, and would cease to be the chosen people? (*d*) Where in Scripture is it stated that the precepts of Mosaic Law (other than those of an ethical content) are merely a shadow, or type, of what is destined to transpire when the messiah comes?[60]

In his reply Limborch maintained that revelation is not a single

---

[57] It is quite certain that into d'Acosta's autobiography as published by Limborch whole sentences have been introduced by an anonymous hand, with the object of besmirching the Portuguese-Jewish congregation. Conceivably Limborch himself worked over the original, in order to make it serve his own purposes. Cf. Meijer, *Enc.*, i, pp. 165 f., where a bibliographical summary of d'Acosta's self-account will be found. It is, however, possible that the whole autobiography is nothing more than a forgery; see R. H. Popkin, 'Spinoza and La Peyrèyre', *The Southwestern Journal of Philosophy*, 8, 1977, pp. 177 f., 191 n. 2.

[58] On Grotius' attitude towards Judaism see Knight, pp. 254 f., and cf. Baron, *Hist.*, xv, pp. 27 f., 390 f. nn. 30–6, which provided an up-to-date bibliography of the subject.

[59] Orobio's statements occupy pp. 1–2, 6–16, 49–148; Limborch's, pp. 3–5, 17–48, 149–340.   [60] *De Veritate Rel. Christ.*, pp. 1 f.

event once and for all, but rather a gradual process. Scripture merely hints that the messiah will come: once he had come, that hint was rendered palpable, and Jesus revealed the significance of his own role as redeemer and saviour. After his revelation, belief in him became a prerequisite for salvation of the soul: the 'religion of externalities' had forfeited God's grace, God having substituted for it a better and more sublime faith. Limborch concluded his answer with a question by means of which he endeavoured to widen the scope of the disputation: on what principle did the Jews accept Moses as prophet and law-giver and did not, on the same principle, accept the gospel of Jesus?[61]

Orobio rejected all Limborch's contentions. Divine revelation must necessarily be clear and unequivocal, and Israel's belief keeps faith with the divine will as it was given expression at the theophany at Sinai.[62] The scriptural prophecies that describe redemption are both clear and extremely specific, nor are extra levels of meaning to be superimposed upon them.[63] The messiah whom the prophets foretold will be king, judge, and leader; never in their prophecies did they refer to the additional qualities and significance which Christianity has attached to him. And if indeed those qualities and significance are of such importance as Christians assert, so that salvation of the soul is contingent upon acceptance of belief in them, why did not God reveal them explicitly to his chosen people?[64]

The binding force of the commandments had in no way atrophied. Since God had detailed them with much circumstantiality, and had commanded that they be meticulously and completely observed, it was not to be imagined that they had been given to Israel for a limited period only, viz. until the redeemer should come.[65] Israel would be

[61] Ibid., p. 4: 'Sufficit, deum dixisse, se Messiam missurum; et postea per Messiam, quando in mundum venerit, voluntatem suam plene declarasse ... Sufficit enim, postquam Messias jam in mundum venit, Deum per Messiam declarare, unicum medium ad salutem Israelis et restitutionis in divinam gratiam esse fidem in Messiam, que jam advenit ...', p. 5: '... Ea enim ratione satis evidenter ostendit, sibi cultum illum externum non amplius placere; sed meliori et perfectiori, per Messiam instituto, tanquam umbram corpori, cedere debere ...'

[62] Ibid., p. 7.

[63] Ibid.: 'Verum quidem est, Deum per Prophetas Israeli Messiam liberatorem promisisse, idque non obscure, sed satis clare et aperte; ideo non fuit necessarium aliud praeceptum ...'

[64] Ibid., p. 8: 'Futurus erat Rex, Judex, Pastor ... De Regno spirituali in coelo, de Judice in coelo praeter Deum, de Pastore in coelo nunquam a Deo admonitus ... Ad non est credibile Deum noluisse, cum summe bonus fit, qui omnia ad salutem revelavit Israeli ea claritate, quam sufficere praescivit, ut effectus sequeretur, nisi hominis malitia obstiterit.' [65] Ibid.

restored to divine grace by means of those methods for demonstrating true penitence described in detail in the Scriptures, which nowhere mention the obligation of belief in a 'meditating messiah'.[66] As for Limborch's question as to how it comes about that Israel believe in the Mosaic Law but reject the gospel proclaimed by Jesus, Isaac rejoined that the Sinaitic revelation was transparently clear, leaving no room for hesitations regarding the reliability of the account of it. Unlike the traditions of other faiths, including Christianity, Israel's tradition had not been passed from one people to another, but had been preserved as a national asset; whence it followed that no distortions or corruptions had been introduced into it.[67] The divine origin of the prophecies of Moses was vindicated by their realization in historical events.[68]

In his second article Limborch elaborated his teaching on the subject of the graduality of divine revelation, setting out to prove the superiority of Christianity over Judaism. In his view, Israel rejected the good tidings of the gospels because of their essentially material and carnal attitude of mind, and their incapacity to lift their thinking on to a heavenly plane.[69] Most of the prophecies of the Old Testament were fulfilled in the period of the second temple, and those still outstanding would ultimately be realized when Israel returned from their deviant path.[70] The commandments were not matters of urgent necessity for Gentiles who had accepted the evangelistic message of Christianity, they having achieved spiritual perfection through their faith in Jesus.[71] The long-continued, latter-day exile which is the condition of Jewish existence is indeed a punishment, but not a punishment for idolatry—which, as Isaac himself conceded, had never been eliminated from Israel, but for their rejection of Jesus and their responsibility for his crucifixion.[72] According to Limborch, God chose Israel and distinguished them from the Gentiles in order that the world might know the origins of the messiah; once Jesus had come, the Jews ceased to be the

---

[66] Ibid., p. 10.
[67] Ibid., p. 14: 'Non enim est haec traditio ab hominibus alicuius nationis, et sic de una in alteram per varias orbis partes propagata . . .'
[68] Ibid., p. 15.
[69] Ibid., p. 22: 'Sed carnalis quidam affectus, quod Israel terrae ita sit affixus, ut animum ad caelum et caelestia minime attollere velit.'
[70] Ibid., p. 23.   [71] Ibid., p. 24.
[72] Ibid., p. 29: 'Non ab idololatriam . . . Post reditum autem e captivitate Babylonica, gravissima illa afflictione melius edocti, nunquam leguntur in idolatriam relapsi judaei, sed alia quidem crimina et peccata commisisse . . . Si enim judaei jure Dominum nostrum Jesum Christum rejecerint, soli sunt hodie in terra veri gloriae ac veritatis divinae assertores ac patroni.'

chosen people and the value of the commandments lapsed.[73] The miracles of Jesus were incomparably greater than those that took place in Moses' time.[74] Christian tradition was more reliable than Jewish, since the evangelists had themselves witnessed the events which they described; and since they were common folk, and uneducated, there was no suspicion of their having fabricated the New Testament Scriptures.[75] Furthermore, the gospels had not suffered corruption as a result of the spread of Christianity, the original text of the New Testament having been preserved intact, unlike the original of the Old Testament, which had become flawed as a result of its many vicissitudes.[76]

In the third stage of the debate the contestants adduced no new arguments, but contented themselves with clarifying their respective basic claims by adding comment and illustration. Isaac rejected Limborch's statement regarding the cause of the Jews' long exile, claiming that not only had idolatry never been eliminated in Israel but that Jews practising Christianity were the worst kind of idolaters that Judaism had ever known.[77] He likewise dismissed the allegation that Israel was incapable of rising to the plane of a spiritual gospel. Had God given Israel the good tidings of a kingdom of heaven in the Christian sense, Israel would not have rejected them, and would, indeed, have made far less difficulty about bearing their cross than Christians, since Jewish experience of suffering and persecution was without equal.[78] The plethora of sects within Christendom proved, according to Orobio, that the Christian gospel so far from clarifying what allegedly needed clarification in the Hebrew Scriptures had in fact left confusion worse confounded.[79] In point of fact, the Christian sects were in agreement on one single thing only—that with the coming of Jesus the mandatory force of the commandments was abolished.[80] The Christian gospel had introduced no ethical innovations; all the ethical

---

[73] Ibid., p. 33: 'Ideoque et populo suo ritus praescripsit, ut plurimum contrarios gentium ritibus; ut ita populus ille esset peculiaris, ab omnibus distinctus: voluitque id populorum discrimen ad tempora usque Messiae religiose servari: uta toti: mundo constaret, Messiam ex familia et gente cui promissum erat, vere originem suam ducere . . .' See also p. 34.

[74] Ibid., p. 42: 'Verum hisce Jesus noster Mose multo est illustrior, neque Mosis miracula ulla ratione cum Jesu Christi miraculis comparari possunt . . .'

[75] Ibid., p. 43.   [76] Ibid., p. 46.

[77] Ibid., p. 79: 'Maxine postea plurimi in Christianismum ingressi pristina idolatria infecti fuere, et adhuc inficiuntur, originis et patriae legis penitus obliti. Hi sunt Dii alieni quos majores non cognoverant . . .'

[78] Ibid., p. 56.   [79] Ibid., p. 57.   [80] Ibid., p. 58.

Philosophers, Theologians, and Poets

values which Christianity inscribed on its banner—values which Christians in any case failed to implement—were already to be found in Mosaic Law.[81] Nor were the Jews to be charged with carnality—a quality to be met with more frequently amongst Christians.[82]

In this part of the discussion Isaac reiterated his explanation of the cardinal difference between the Jewish conception of the messiah and the Christian one. Israel had never looked for a messiah who would bring them salvation (in the Christian sense of the word) as individuals, but for a redeemer who would re-establish their political situation in its pristine state.[83] When eventually the true messiah appears, he will have to prove that he does not contradict the Law: then—and then only—will the Jews have no doubts to cast on his authenticity, any more than it occurs to anyone to doubt the legitimacy of the sovereigns of France or Spain.[84] The messiah will be merely God's agent: anyone declaring himself to be God must be a false messiah.[85]

Time and again Isaac emphasizes the unreliability of the gospels. Unlike Limborch, he did not regard their authors as being simple-minded people: but there were, he claimed, grounds to question their ethical ingenuousness. What they wanted was vainglory, and they looked on their preaching principally as a means of livelihood.[86] The spread of Christianity by no means attested its veracity or its sacred quality, since the victories and successes of Islam were incomparably more impressive.[87] Unlike Christendom's tendency towards fragmentation, Israel maintained its unity thanks to the oral Law, which trained Israel to fulfil the *Torah* as a single people, loyal to their God.[88]

In his lengthy response Limborch once again denied the divine source of the oral Law.[89] He held up to ridicule the messianic belief of the Jews and the deluded hopes which they had reposed in Sabbatai Ṣevi, that recent 'laughable messiah'.[90] The notion of Israel's return to their own land Limborch defined as being a utopian dream, since to

---

[81] Ibid., p. 67. [82] Ibid., p. 68. [83] Ibid., pp. 70 f. [84] Ibid., pp. 96 f.
[85] Ibid., p. 108. [86] Ibid., pp. 133 f. [87] Ibid., pp. 136 f.
[88] Ibid., pp. 141 f. Cf. Orobio's arguments against the Christian position in his other controversialist writings, chap. 9, pp. 252 f.

[89] Ibid., p. 176: 'Et haec traditiones a posterioris aevi Rabbinis collectae constituunt legem illam oralem, non vero mandata Dei, Mosi, ut judaei volunt, in monte dierum quadraginte spatio data, et per Mosem postae coram Aarone, ejus filiis, septuaginta senioribus, ac tandem populo, enuntiata, et per varias traditiones conservata, donec tandem circa annum post eversum templum septuagesimum in Thalmud sunt congesta.'

[90] Ibid., p. 163: 'Et similis omnium impostorum, quos in initio Judaei apertis ulnis avide exceperunt, exitus fuit, etiam nuperi ridiculi Messiae Sabetha Sevi.'

realize it the Jews would require an army the size of which had never been seen.⁹¹ The wretched state of Israel proved that God had withdrawn his grace from them, and the wealth of a few individual Jews could not offset the miserable condition of the generality.⁹²

Limborch had declared in his introduction that his intention was to present Christianity in general and not any particular denomination or stream within it; and he repeated that intention in a number of letters which he wrote both whilst the disputation was in progress and afterwards.⁹³ Despite his declared purpose, he in fact presents Christianity as seen through Arminian spectacles, both in establishing the pattern of life reflected in the gospels as being the ideal, and in his emphasis on the approach of Episcopius to the question of divine grace and free will.⁹⁴ Isaac turned Limborch's professed intention to present Christianity in its entirety to his own advantage, and he did not restrain himself from sharply attacking the Catholic form, despite his knowing that his opponent held it at arm's length and regarded it as a pagan cult.⁹⁵ *Per contra*, Limborch did not hesitate to cast in Isaac's teeth his Catholic education in Spain, and his adherence to concepts drawn from the theology of popery and its universe of discourse.⁹⁶

Contrary to current opinion, this 'friendly conversation' of Orobio and Limborch is not to be seen as a historical watershed in Judaeo-Christian relations, nor even as a phenomenon heralding changes in

---

⁹¹ Ibid., p. 265.

⁹² Ibid., p. 281: '... verum illa est privatorum faelicitas; set populus ut corpus unum consideratus est extorris ubique, proprio non gaudens regimine, sed alieno imperio subjectus, sine potestate, sine autoritate, et tanquam peregrinus dispersus et oberrans per totum terrarum orbem.'

⁹³ Cf. introd.: 'Hic autem ita me gessi, ut nullius peculiaris inter Christianos controversi dogmatis, sed solius Evangelii, patrocinium susceperim...' See his letter to Tillotson dated 15 Sept. 1687 (see collection above, n. 56), f. 114', 'Nullius inter Christianos controversi dogmatis prejudico gravari volui...' and ibid., a letter of the same date to Pierce.

⁹⁴ See *De Veritate Rel. Christ.*, introd., where Limborch refers to Grotius and Vossius, both of them Remonstrants, and indicates that he follows their lead; also ibid., pp. 242 f., 318 f.   ⁹⁵ Ibid., pp. 79, 118, 145.

⁹⁶ Ibid., pp. 221, 307, 324. To the assertion of Orobio (ibid., p. 212) that the general populace is not equipped to distinguish the work of God from that of the devil, or between true and false prophecy, and that in order to pronounce upon such issues it is requisite to have some assembly invested with authority ('Quod vero hoc judicium erat infallibile...'), Limborch rejoins 'Satis apparet Virum Doct. in Hispania inter Pontificios enutritum.' Cf. what Limborch wrote to Pierce about Orobio (see above, n. 93), f. 152': 'Quoniam itaque inter pontificios educatus est, in Academia doctrinis Jesuitarum imbutus, seapius totum Christianismum ex Papatu affirmat neque placita jesuitica ita penitus inurere potuit, quin aliquod ejus in disputatione sua reliquias hic illic offendat...'

their mutual relationship.⁹⁷ The disputation reflects the social and cultural climate of seventeenth-century Amsterdam. In his attitude towards Jews and Judaism Limborch remains faithful to the position established by Grotius in the *Remonstrantie* of 1615: (*a*) although the Jews rejected Jesus, hopes of their conversion to Christianity are not forlorn. (*b*) Their conversion will not transpire if direct contact with Christians is denied them. (*c*) Jews are less of a threat to reformed Christianity than is papism, precisely because in faith they stand further from it. (*d*) Contact with Jews is likely to prove beneficial to Christians, both in regard to learning Hebrew and in order to understand the Scriptures. (*e*) Judaism is belief in the true God, albeit belief compromised by lack of faith.⁹⁸

The spirit of these five principles shimmers between the lines of Limborch's writing against Orobio. It would seem that the Arminian theologian regarded the disputation as the beginning of the bridge which reformed Christians were in duty bound to build, in order to lead the Jews into the bosom of Christianity. He hoped that by vanquishing the 'learned Jew' he would demoralize the Jewish congregation, and that as a result many of them would convert. From his correspondence with his circles of friends and intimates between 1686 and 1688 it appears clear that he himself thought that he had won the debate.⁹⁹

Orobio's own impressions have not come down to us: but it must be doubted whether there were any new arguments at all put forward by the leader of the Remonstrants which he had not encountered in his earlier disputations with Christian theologians. According to one source, he concluded the debate by saying that 'everyone ought to continue in his own religion, since it was much easier to attack another man's than to prove one's own'.¹⁰⁰ If that sentence is indeed an authentic utterance of Orobio, then it has to be acknowledged that at the end of his life his own conception of religious toleration was far bolder and much further-reaching than that of Limborch and his fellow Remonstrants.

⁹⁷ Cf. Schoeps, *Jewish Christian Argument*, p. 78.
⁹⁸ See Meijer, *Grotius*.
⁹⁹ See his letter to Graevius, 25 Nov. 1687, in the same collection (see above, n. 56), f. 112ᵛ, and also to Locke, 24 Nov. 1686: 'Judaeum sub praelo sudare gaudeo, sed credo puls sudabit quando praelum in apertum illum emiseriet nec facile reperiet in sua metaphysica refrigerium . . .' Cf. Ollion and De Boer, p. 169.
¹⁰⁰ See the Eng. version of Uriel d'Acosta's autobiography (n. 53 above), translator's introd.

POETS, POETASTERS, AND PATRONS: THE *ACADEMIA DE LOS FLORIDOS*

In 1685 a number of writers, poets, and lovers of poetry and art in the Portuguese-Jewish community of Amsterdam founded a literary society with the name of *La Academia de los Floridos* — apparently injecting into *florido* the nuance of 'touched with grace', or 'gifted'.[101] Isaac Orobio, now in his sixty-eighth year, was a founder-member and one of the regular participants in its proceedings.

This was not the only society of this kind in the Sephardi diaspora of western Europe at this period. At least two others preceded it, one in Amsterdam and the other in Leghorn (Livorno), both founded in 1676, and both bearing the name of *Academia de los Sitibundos* — indicating their members' thirst for culture.[102]

In aim and in organization these societies largely resembled the literary academies that were established in Spain in the sixteenth and seventeenth centuries, particularly under Philip III. Some of them were no more than one-off gatherings for the sake of staging some literary competition, held on certain festive occasions. Those of them that enjoyed a widespread fame were permanent affairs, held at the mansions of members of the nobility, or occasionally in the royal court itself. The aristocracy afforded their patronage to poets and artists who were accustomed to gather in their palatial houses on fixed occasions, according to a constitution agreed in advance. At each session the writers would read some of their own work, present dramas or masques, and there would be singing, and discussion of a wide spectrum of topics, such as medicine and natural science, magic and astrology, art and literature, political theory and philosophy.[103] There is no doubt that the founders of the Spanish *academias* had it in mind to emulate the academies that had begun to flourish in Italy from the period of the Renaissance, although it must be doubted whether they

---

[101] The Spanish *florido* has some nuances that do not attach themselves to the English *florid*. For another possible factor in the choice of the name, see below, n. 116.

[102] For the Amsterdam *Sitibundos* see de Barrios, *Triumpho*, pp. 458 f.: 'Relación de los Poetas y escritores españoles de la nacion judadayca [sic] amstelodama' (copy in Amsterdam, *EH* 9 E 43). On the Leghorn *Sitibundos* see de Barrios' *Respuesta*, and Kayserling, *De Barrios*, 18, p. 289; J. M. Hillesum, *Vereenigingen bij de Portugeesche en Spaansche Joden te Amsterdam in de 17ᵈᵉ en 18ᵈᵉ eeuw*, Amsterdam, 1902, p. 171; Scholberg, *De Barrios and Amsterdam*, pp. 141 f.

[103] On the *academias* in Spain during the period see Sánchez, W. F. King, and Deleito, *Pueblo*, pp. 164 f., *Rey*, pp. 144 f., and Valbuena Prat, p. 248.

Philosophers, Theologians, and Poets 287

ever succeeded in producing anything to compare with the achievements of the well-known academies of Florence, Rome, and Naples.[104] Of the Iberian academies that attained any reputation one must mention that set up under the auspices of the Conde de Saldaña, that of the *Generosos* of Lisbon, and the *Ociosos* and *Anhelantes*, both at Saragossa. Philip IV set up a literary academy in his palace in which there participated at various periods poets and dramatists such as Vélez de Guevara, Quevedo, and Calderón de la Barca, who used to improvise poems and songs—for the most part burlesques in which there would sometimes be detectable a critical or even a mocking note directed at the religious establishment. At every meeting, in addition to the literary content of the programme, there would be interludes in which dancers, acrobats, and clowns, etc., would make their appearance.[105]

Not all the academies were linked to the royal palace or one of the ducal houses. Some of them were simply meetings held by societies composed of men of leisure and of common folk, who would get together in some back room or secreted upper chamber to improvise songs of a *risqué* character and to indulge in the recitation of ribald ballads.[106] But the literary *academias* of the period, which were to be found not only in Italy and Spain, but also in Germany and the Netherlands, were for the most part linked to the life of the nobility at court. Their social composition was multicoloured: alongside members of the aristocracy of the various degrees of precedence scholars and writers drawn from every social class took their place. At their head would be one of the senior members of the upper echelon, filling the position of a Maecenas. K. Mannheim has studied a number of the sociological traits characteristic of this type of academy. Despite the sharp differences in social origin of the membership, it was marked by an atmosphere of egalitarianism within its walls. And although its badge was the patronage afforded to it by members of the nobility, the values emphasized were distinctly bourgeois ones—equality, 'naturalness' of behaviour, objectivity, and tolerance.[107]

[104] The desire of those who staged the *academias* in Spain to emulate the Italian prototypes finds expression in Vélez de Guevara, *El Diablo Cojuelo*, Madrid, 1641, Tranco IX: '... pidiendo el Conde de la Torre a don Cleofás y al Cojuelo que honrasen aquella junta lo que estuviessen en Sevilla, y que dijessen los nombres supuestos con que habían de asistirla, como se usó en la Corusca y en la academia de Capua, de Nápoles, de Roma y de Florencia, en Italia' (Buenos Aires and Mexico edn., 1950, pp. 123 f.).   [105] Deleito, *Rey*, pp. 144 f.   [106] Deleito, *Pueblo*, pp. 164 f.
[107] See K. Mannheim, *Essays on the Sociology of Culture*, London, 1956, pp. 133 f.

Under Philip IV the quality of the *academias* patronized by members of the social élite progressively deteriorated. Political and social degeneration were reflected in the life of the culture of the court, and in the course of time these academies became lack-lustre literary platforms for poets and writers devoid of all talent.[108]

Amongst the Portuguese Jews of Amsterdam, too, as has been noted, such *academias* were set up. Alongside the Talmudical colleges and confraternities for the study of the Torah, they established literary coteries modelled on the Iberian type. Participation in such societies met several needs of which the membership was conscious. (*a*) It afforded the creative writers amongst them opportunities to present what they had produced to a select circle of the intelligentsia and lovers of literature. (*b*) It gave the magnates—some of whom bore titles of nobility conferred on them by kings and princes, in whose interest they occupied positions of political and economic importance—the opportunity to play patron to writers and poets, and thus to imitate the customs of the social élite in the lands from which they had sprung—a class to which they felt a longing to be compared in regard to outward trappings. (*c*) It provided participants with a social and cultural framework suitable for expressing their deeply felt links with the language of Spain, her values, and with concepts quintessentially Spanish.

It would seem that these *academias* were short-lived affairs. We hear nothing of the *Sitibundos* after 1677, and all that we know of the *Floridos* took place in 1685, the year of its foundation.

What could a man like Isaac Orobio, who understood the value of the written and the spoken word, find to interest him in the lightweight proceedings of the poets and rhymesters who constituted the circle of the *Floridos*? It seems clear that meeting with lovers of art and literature carried him back to the scenes of his youth and the literary contests of Andalusia—that baroque Spanish culture the memory of which was not dulled in him after twenty years and more residence in Amsterdam. This was not the first occasion on which he had evinced his attraction towards this type of cultural activity. When the *Academia de los Sitibundos* started in Leghorn, Joseph Penso de la Vega—one of its pioneers and founders—wrote to him from there on 14 December 1676, asking for his support for what they were doing, and also for a

[108] Deleito, *Pueblo*, p. 168.

Philosophers, Theologians, and Poets 289

letter of commendation for their literary activities.[109] This approach has to be viewed in the context of the literary connections which had been woven over the years between Isaac Orobio and the circle of writers and poets in Leghorn, of which Penso was one of the outstanding members. If one reads the commendation from Isaac Orobio's pen at the beginning of Joseph Penso's *Rumbos peligrosos*, which was published in Antwerp in 1683, it becomes patently obvious that the Amsterdam doctor followed with close and abiding interest the literary development of the gifted young writer, who for his part found in Orobio a faithful supporter.[110]

The *Academia de los Floridos* comprised thirty-nine members. From the account of the society which Daniel Levi (Miguel) de Barrios wrote, we learn that its organization corresponded to the regular pattern of the Spanish *academias* of the period. At its head stood the judges (*jueces*), who presided over the sessions and directed the order of proceedings. A number of members occupied the role of *mantenedores* (this here meaning prominent participants, *qua* contestants, rather than chairmen). In the literary competitions these presented items of their own creative work, or proposed subjects for the academy to debate—propositions, problems, or 'enigmas'. Another member acted as *secretario*, beside whom there sat the *fiscal* ('prosecutor', i.e. the challenger), whose part it was to raise difficulties about all notions or proposals that were advanced in the course of the proceedings.[111] It looks as if the life and soul of the *academia* was constituted by Joseph Penso, its secretary, and Daniel Levi de Barrios, who was one of the

[109] Printed in de Barrios, *Respuesta*, ff. 3ʳ–4ᵛ; see 4ʳ f.

[110] Penso, *Rumbos*. Amongst the encomiums printed at the beginning of the book there is to be found a contribution by Orobio: 'Digno Elogio del muy Ilustre Don Baltasar Orobio, Medico, Professor, y Consejero del Rey de Francia: . . . tocando apenas los primeros años de la adolocencia [*sic*] no solo dio admirables esperanças, sino tambien sazonados frutos de su ingenio: entendió con tanta perfección en la niñez, que fue admiracion y embidia, a los adultos mas advertidos. No podia contar tres lustros quando en actos publicos, y academicos congressos, ostento en propios discursos lo mas exacto de la oratoria, la retorica mas apurada, los mayores quilates de la eloquencia, y lo fecundo de la hermosa erudicion.' For Penso see further below, Appendix D. C. Roth stated that Orobio presided over the *Academia de los Floridos* in Amsterdam, but there is no foundation for his surmise ('Notes sur les marranes de Livourne', *REJ* 91, 1931, p. 3).

[111] De Barrios, *Metros*, pp. 253 f., 'Academia de los Floridos, Memoria plausible de sus juezes y Academicos'. This is the sole contemporary account of the activities and the membership of the *academia*. It was utilized in the 18th cent. by David Franco Mendes, who in his Portuguese *Memorias* included a general description of the *Floridos* into which a number of errors have crept. See *Memorias*, p. 93.

regular *mantenedores* and was himself responsible for proposing that the academy call itself *los Floridos*.[112] These two were the only ones to leave any written testimony about its proceedings, and from them we discover that a substantial proportion of the sessions were devoted to the public reading of de Barrios' own poems and riddles and of the discourses of Penso.[113] Both of them had previous experience of literary exercises of this kind: Penso had been one of the *señores presidentes* of the Livornese *Sitibundos*, and in 1676 de Barrios had been involved in the Amsterdam *Academia de los Sitibundos* alongside the poet Moses Rosa—like himself, a *mantenedor* in the *Floridos*—as well as in one-off literary occasions (dignified as *academias*), for the most part organized by himself.[114] His fellow-*mantenedores* in the *Floridos* included his own son Simon, Dr Abraham Gutierres, and don Manuel de Lara. Dr Moses Orobio, Isaac's son, acted as *fiscal*, and although there is no clear proof, it seems that Isaac Orobio himself was one of the permanent *jueces* at the proceedings.[115] As usual in such societies, the

[112] See Penso, *Floridos*, p. 17: '... Que Pluma puede dexar de hazerse lenguas, para offrecer a los sonores clarines de la Fama, las loas de un Barrios, que ponderando con tanto acierto, el título de los Floridos...' On the choice of the name see further below, n. 116.

[113] See ibid., and de Barrios' own *Alegrías*, pp. 63 f., 'Ansias de Epytalamio en Amstelodama Academia de los Floridos'.

[114] See de Barrios, *Respuesta*, where Joseph Penso is mentioned as being one of the 'señores presidentes' of the Leghorn *academia* alongside Raphael Díaz, Michael de Silva, and Moses Athias; see also 'Relación de los Poetas' (see above, n. 102) for de Barrios' own role in the *Academia de los Sitibundos* of Amsterdam: 'El mantenedor de la Justa Poetica fue yo y aventureros Abraham Henriques, Moseh Rosa, Moseh Dias y Abraham Gomes Silveyra.' For the one-off *'academias'* in which de Barrios participated see his *Triumpho*, p. 423 (copy in Amsterdam, EH 2 F 9): 'Sonoro Aplauso al muy Noble y discreto Manuel Levi, en ocasion de presidir en una Academia'. This cannot refer to the Amsterdam *Sitibundos*, in which Manuel Levi never took part, nor to the *Academia de los Floridos*, since the *Triumpho* was printed in 1683, two years before its foundation. See also de Barrios' *Metros*, p. 279, 'Énigma del Principio', which was presented at the festivities in honour of David Bueno de Mesquita who, as *ḥathan bere'shith*, had the honour to commence the annual cycle of readings from the Pentateuch in 5445 (1684). Although the word *academia* does not occur there, it is clear from the introductory description of the proceedings that they bore the character of one of these self-styled literary 'academies': 'Fueron Juezes en su explicación los inclitos señores Ishac Orobio de Castro médico, profesor y consejero del Rey de Francia, Don Manuel de Belmonte, Conde Palatino y Residente de su Magestad Catholica en los Países Baxos y Don Ioseph Athias; Explicáronlo los muy nobles y eruditos Señores Samuel Salom, Joseph Penso y Samuel de Leon. Compusolo Daniel Levi de Barrios.' I have to dissent from Scholberg's view (*De Barrios and Amsterdam*, p. 144) that the occasion was celebrated under the auspices of the *Floridos*.

[115] See de Barrios, 'Academia de los Floridos' (n. 111 above), p. 253. Franco Mendes, *Memorias* (n. 111 above), 'sendo Fiscal della o Afamado Doutor D[o]n Mosseh Orobio de Castro, alias Balthazar Orobio, etc.', where he has confused father and son (as observed by the editors of the critical edition, p. 164 n. 178).

Philosophers, Theologians, and Poets

academia had an *empresa*, i.e. emblem—an almond-tree in blossom, and beneath it the Latin taken from Psalm 1: 3, 'Fructum suum edet in tempore.'[116]

Before we turn to an examination of the character of the academy and an understanding of what its meetings comprised, it is appropriate to pass its membership in review, if only in brief. As in the case of other literary societies that were active at the period in the various countries of Europe, here also it is possible to distinguish a whole spread of colours across its social spectrum. Next to the financial magnates there were to be found those who, whilst still well-to-do, were but average

---

[116] See Penso, *Floridos*, p. 15, 'Discurso primero, hecho en la introduccion de la Academia de los Floridos cuya empresa es un Almendro Florido que tiene por Mote: Fructum suum edet in tempore suo.' [The following observations may throw light on the choice of the name *Floridos* for the *academia* (cf. above, n. 101).

(a) The motto *fructum suum edet in tempore* is taken from Ps. 1: 3, but it should be noted that both the Vulgate (i.e. Jerome's Gallican psalter) and his literal version (*Psalterium iuxta Hebraeos*) render the Hebrew *yitten* by *dabit*, as do also the 16th cent. versions of Pagninus, Felix Pratensis, and Arias Montano. It is conceivable that *edet* is a deliberate difference, in order to maintain the fiction that a 'Christian' version had not been adopted.

(b) Although horticultural allusions are scarcely surprising in names chosen for literary and scholarly academies, some circumstantiality in the present case invites explanation. The slightly later Savoy academy (founded in 1716) had as its crest an orange-tree in flower and fruit; its motto, *flores fructusque perennes* (not, apparently, a quotation from any of the classical poets) was taken over from the Florimontane Academy founded at Annecy by François de Sales (1567–1622). Possibly the *Floridos* deliberately chose as their motto a quotation which, whilst reminiscent of that of the Florimontane academy even as their own name echoed the other, should replace a pseudo-classical quotation by something taken from the Hebrew Bible in the Latin garb appropriate to a European literary *academia*.

(c) Why particularly an almond-tree? Ps. 1 does not specify any genus, and refers to a plantation beside a water-course—not the usual situation for almond-trees. There is a parallel text in Jer. 17: 8, but it omits the crucial phrase about fruit-bearing; and although the almond figures prominently in Jeremiah's inaugural vision (1: 11–12), the connection seems too tenuous to have prompted the choice of the almond-tree as the device borne by the *Academia de los Floridos*.

(d) It seems more likely that the choice was suggested by recollection on the part of one of the founder-members (perhaps de Barrios himself) of some lines by Calderón:

Bien como el florido almendro
Que por madrugar sus flores
Sin aviso y sin consejo
Al primer soplo se apagan.

This quotation is cited as illustrating the use of *florido* by Elías Zerolo (ed. Cl. Santos González, *Diccionario enciclopédico de la Lengua Castellana*, Paris, n.d., i, p. 1083), from Calderón, but without further specification. Although it has eluded search, it may be noted that the recent concordance, which covers the *autos sacramentales* only (*Konkordanz zu Calderon*, ed. H. Flasche and G. Hofman, 1–5, 'Autos sacramentales', Hildesheim, 1980) does not list it. I am obliged to Professor Flasche for his endeavours regarding the remainder of the corpus. It would be interesting to know whether the wider context had any bearing on the choice of the emblem. R.L.]

representatives of their financial class: also dealers in a smaller way of business, and those with university degrees, and the writers and artists. In addition to this, within the top financial grade there stood out the person of one of the patrons of the circle, himself the owner of a title of nobility, whose magnificent house afforded hospitality—just as might have been the case in Spain—for the meetings of the *academia*. This was don Manuel de Belmonte, known in the synagogue by the name of Isaac Nunes Belmonte, who had been the King of Spain's Agent-General in Amsterdam from 1664 and was also consul from 1674 until his death in 1705. In 1673 the Emperor Leopold III conferred upon him the title of Count Palatine, and in 1693 that of Baron. It was he who, in 1676, had set up the afore-mentioned *Academia de los Sitibundos*, the meetings of which had also taken place in his house. He himself experimented at writing Portuguese poetry, although his achievements in this field were not impressive. On the other hand he was a distinguished patron of writers and poets, whom he supported most generously.[117] His was not the only or the first instance at the time of a Jew of Spanish origins serving the crown of Spain. Joseph Jessurun Lobo, also a member of the *Floridos*, served as the Spanish consul in Zeeland. Another member of the *academia*, Jerónimo Nunes da Costa (whose Jewish name was Moses Curiel),[118] represented the Portuguese crown in Amsterdam, and he, together with Isaac Nunes Belmonte, was official representative of the congregation to the municipal authority. Until his death in 1697 he fulfilled cardinal functions in the congregation and several of its ancillary organizations.

Other members of the circle falling within the 'financier' class were don Nunes Marchena, otherwise known as Joseph Mocatta; also Manuel Levi, one of the Portuguese bankers of Amsterdam and a regular patron of the poet Daniel Levi de Barrios. Of the same financial standing were Moses Israel Pereyra (son of Abraham Israel Pereyra), Francisco de Lis (= Abraham López Berahel), Joseph Israel Alvarez, David Hamis Vaz, and Aaron (H)enríquez.

Amongst the multicoloured characters who took part in the meetings of the *academia* were numbered Moses Machado, *provéditeur* of the Dutch and English armies, one of the intimates of William III of

[117] On Belmonte and the other members of the *academia* see below, Appendix D.
[118] On Jerónimo Nunes da Costa see Jonathan Israel, 'The Diplomatic Career of Jerónimo Nunes da Costa: an Episode in Dutch–Portuguese Relations of the Seventeenth Century', *Bijdragen en Mededelingen betreffende de Geschiedenis der Nederlanden*, 98, 1983, pp. 167–90.

Philosophers, Theologians, and Poets

England on whose behalf he carried out several diplomatic missions; Joseph Raphael Athias, owner of the well-known Hebrew printing press; Abraham Penso, elder brother of the poet Joseph Penso, himself a well-to-do businessman and an active member of the congregation and its institutions; David Franco Mendes, grandfather of the eighteenth-century poet; Moses Mocatta, son of Joseph Nunes Mocatta mentioned above; Isaac Pessoa, Aaron Medina, and Moses b. Abraham Mocatta, who had been known whilst still a crypto-Jew as don Antonio Gabriel. All of these came from the wealthier echelon of the congregation.

Amongst the medium-scale merchants and smaller dealers who took part in the academy were Abraham Hai Lumbrozo, who arrived in Amsterdam from Venice in 1673; David Ximenes Cardozo from Bayonne, distinguished for his skill in the art of fencing, as was also Isaac Villegas; Jacob de Chaves, who was one of the pupils of Jacob Sasportas in the Talmudical college *Tiph'ereth Baḥurim;* also Jacob de Gama, Samuel Semah, Raphael del Castillo, Jacob Gabbay Isidro, Jacob Uzziel d'Avilar, Isaac Carrillo, and Gabriel Moreno.

Apart from the influential magnates and middle-range and smaller businessmen there participated in the *academia* a few scholarly persons, all of them physicians, who by virtue of their presence lent it a patina of intellectual and scientific pretension. Without doubt the outstanding figure amongst these was Isaac Orobio. Together with him, his son Moses was a member, as also Abraham Gutierres, and Abraham Frois from Lisbon, who in addition to being a qualified doctor also held a degree in law.

The roll of membership is concluded by the poets—Joseph Penso, Daniel Levi de Barrios, his son Simon, and Moses Rosa. Apart from Joseph Penso who was supported by his family (and principally, it would seem, by his brother mentioned above), the material situation of these artists was very poor indeed, and they were frequently obliged to accept assistance from the *Ma'amad* and the charitable institutions of the congregation.[119] Another active member of the *academia* was someone of the name of don Manuel de Lara, of whom all that is known is what the poet de Barrios tells us about him, viz. that he had 'led back to Judaism' more than 300 people;[120] and there was also

---

[119] De Barrios' own financial situation was particularly precarious: see Pieterse, *De Barrios*, pp. 144 f., and cf. above, chap. 8, p. 223 f.

[120] See de Barrios, *Triumpho* (copy in Amsterdam, *EH* 2 F 81), p. 63: 'A Manuel de Lara envidia de Narvays con la espada que tiene Escuela de Armas en Amsterdam

Duarte Blandon de Silva, whose identity is wholly obscure.[121] It is worth pointing out that of the thirty-nine members of the *academia*, at least eighteen were members of one or more of the various societies for study of the Torah that had been established amongst the Portuguese Jews of Amsterdam: and this circumstance shows that membership of the *Floridos* is not in itself an indication of preference for general cultural values rather than religious studies.[122] It is rather the case that those who participated in the literary proceedings of *los Floridos* did not look upon it as a forum that in any way competed with the associations for sacred study, but as an organization whose purpose was to cater for aesthetic needs and interests that did not find expression in the other groupings to which reference has been made.

The rabbis and quasi-professional Jewish scholars were not enrolled in the *academia*, although some of them possessed literary ability. There is no evidence at all of their opposition to its foundation, but the circumstance of their non-participation may point to their having entertained reservations about the literary activities of the *Floridos* which—from their point of view—implied more than a nod in the direction of the legitimacy of western, Greek-inspired culture.[123]

---

despues de que con gran valor en caminó [*sic*] al judaismo muchas personas de España como el Capitan Jorje [*sic*] Pimentel que oy vive en está [*sic*] Ciudad con nombre de David: Condugiste al Judaismo / mas de trecientas personas, / con las Mosaycas Coronas / que das honor al abismo. / Jorge quitó al Christianismo / setenta Almas, con gran zelo, / y los dos, sendas del Cielo, / guiays a la Religion, / uno de Armas Salomon / y otro de David modelo.' What de Barrios seems to mean is that Manuel de Lara assisted a number of crypto-Jews to get away from the Iberian peninsula and to make their way to Amsterdam.

[121] Possibly identical with the Abraham Blandon who married Simḥah Capadose in Amsterdam in 1684. See de Barrios, *Alegrías*, pp. 17 f.

[122] The *Torah 'Or* fellowship included Moses Curiel and Moses Pereyra. *'Abi Yethomim* (orphan aid society) numbered, in addition to these two, also Manuel Levi, David Franco Mendes, Moses b. Abraham Mocatta, Abraham Penso, Isaac Carrillo, Abraham Frois, David Ximenes Cardozo, David Hamis Vaz, and Aaron Medina. In *Maskil 'el Dal* (general charity) there participated Moses b. Joseph Mocatta, Jacob Gabbay Isidro, Isaac Carrillo, Gabriel Moreno, Abraham Frois, Simon Levi de Barrios, Samuel Semah, and Moses Orobio. *Temimey Derekh* ('perfect [in respect of their] way') had amongst its membership Abraham Penso, Isaac Carrillo, and Gabriel Moreno, and *Honen Dalim* (charity) Abraham Gutierres and Abraham Frois. *Kether Shem Ṭob* ('crown of a good name') included Simon Levi de Barrios, and *Tiph'ereth Bahurim* ('bachelors' guerdon') included Jacob Chaves. For these associations see de Barrios, *Triumpho* (see above, n. 120), pp. 61 f.

[123] The absence of the members of the Amsterdam rabbinate from the roll of the *Floridos* is emphasized by contrast to the situation in Leghorn, where the local rabbis played a part in the *Academia de los Sitibundos*. Of this we are informed by Joseph Penso's letter to Isaac Orobio (see above, n. 109): '... los Señores Hahamim noz hazen aqui favor de nombrarse Academicos para darnos aliento con tal proteccion...'

Daniel Levi de Barrios had even found it necessary, back in the days of the *Sitibundos*, to defend the use of the word '*academia*', the whole notion of which originated from the pagan world of Greece: 'there is nothing against our sacred law in entitling those whose discourse is in the sphere of divine instruction as *academics:* rather it is a happy blazoning of the triumph of Israel, it being the nature of a conqueror to take over the name of the vanquished.'[124] And indeed, in a flight of philological fancy Joseph Penso declared that the word *academia* was itself of Hebrew origin—from *qadem*, to 'take precedence', 'because of the spirit of competitiveness that prevailed in the earliest [Talmudic] "academies" of Pumpeditha and Maḥoza [in Babylonia/Iraq] amongst those of inquiring minds [*curiosos*], as they endeavoured to *gain precedence* over each other in keeping on the qui vive . . .'[125] Undoubtedly this 'etymological' derivation, far-fetched as it is, contains an apologetic element directed at the raised eyebrows of the congregational rabbinate, who had perhaps let their reservations about *los Floridos* and their criticisms of what went on there be noised abroad.

Although the rabbis did not give their blessing to the society and its undertakings, it is clear that it was not merely those on the congregational fringes that joined it, but that it included individuals at the centre of the life of the congregation and some of its most outstanding leaders and spokesmen. There is consequently nothing to be learned of the ideological hue of the *academia* itself on the one hand, or of the intellectual capacities of the congregation leadership on the other. Seventeen of *los Floridos* served for at least one year as officers of the congregation or of its Talmudical college '*Eṣ Ḥayyim*, twelve of them prior to 1685, the year of the foundation of the *academia;* and many of them filled positions of seniority in the congregation's ancillary associations and brotherhoods.[126]

As has been stated, all the social and financial groups in the

---

[124] De Barrios, *Respuesta*, p. 28: 'Aunque la Academia deriba [*sic*] el nombre de Academo: falso Dios entre otros de los Atenienses, no es contra la Sacra Ley intitularse Academicos los que discurren en la esphera de la divina enseñança: antes es feliz anuncio del triumpho Israelitico, por ser propio del Vencedor adquirir el nombre del vencido.'

[125] Penso, *Floridos*, p. 19: 'Los orígenes de las Academias, ponderé en la Academia de los Sitibundos, en Ytalia, donde prové que se derivava el nombre de Academia del gran philosopho Academo; o del verbo hebreo *Academ*, que significa *anticipar*, por la competencia con que procuravan en las primeras Academias de Pombadita y Measia [*sic*], anticiparse los curiosos en los desvelos . . .'

[126] For offices in the congregation and its affiliated organizations filled by members of the *academia*, see below, Appendix D.

congregation were represented in the *Floridos*; in 1685 four of its members each paid congregational dues of a hundred florins or over, whilst three others were not required to pay anything at all, because of their parlous material situation.[127] Twelve of the members were engaged in import and export, as we learn from the *imposta* paid by them—a tax levied by the *Ma'amad* on the income that members of the community made from that particular type of business. Outstanding in this field of entrepreneurial endeavour were Moses Curiel, Moses Pereyra, and Joseph Mocatta, each of whom paid on the average more than 200 florins per annum.[128]

To the air of intimacy which pervaded the *academia* one undoubted contributory factor was the circumstance that a number of the

---

[127] The following is a schedule of the assessed annual *finta* (i.e. community dues, not voluntary offerings) paid by members of the *academia* in 5445 (1684/5), i.e. the year of its foundation:

	florins		florins
Moses Curiel	200	Joseph Athias	24
Abraham López Berahel	130	Jacob d'Avilar	20
Joseph Mocatta	120	Isaac Pessoa	20
Moses Pereyra	100	Isaac Carrillo	16
Joseph Israel Alvarez	60	Jacob de Gama	15
David Hamis Vaz	60	Abraham Lumbrozo	12
Moses b. Abraham Mocatta	50	Dr Isaac Orobio	12
Jacob Chaves	50	David Ximenes Cardozo	10
Isaac Nunes Belmonte	50	Samuel Semah	8
Manuel Levi	50	Joseph Penso	8
Moses Machado	40	Gabriel Moreno	8
Abraham Penso	40	Joseph Jessurun Lobo	4
Moses b. Joseph Mocatta	40	Jacob Gabbay Isidro	4
David Franco Mendes	40	Dr Abraham Frois	3
Dr Abraham Gutierres	30		

Daniel Levi de Barrios and his son Simon never paid any *finta*; from 5441 (1680/1) Moses Rosa was no longer called on for a subscription, although he had hitherto paid (5435–7) (1674/5–76/7) at 4 fl. p.a., 5438–40 (1677/8–79/80) at 2 fl. p.a.; clearly the total discontinuation reflects his extremely reduced circumstances. Aaron Henríquez the younger began to pay at the rate of 60 fl. p.a. from 5446 (1685/6), Aaron Medina at 40 fl. from 5449 (1688/9), and Moses Orobio at 10 fl. p.a. from 5448 (1687/8). There is no evidence that *finta* was ever paid by Isaac Henríquez Villegas, Raphael del Castillo, Duarte Blandon, or Manuel de Lara. See the community *Manual*, Amsterdam, AGA, PA 334 no. 176, pp. 278 f.

[128] In the same year (1684/5) the amount paid by Moses Curiel as *imposta* was 500 fl.; by Moses Pereyra, 250 fl.; by Joseph Mocatta, 223 fl. 3 st. Others who were similarly taxed, and will therefore have been involved in import and export business, were Jacob de Gama (who in 1682/3 paid 200 fl.), Joseph Athias, Aaron Medina, David Hamis Vaz, Isaac Pessoa, Abraham Penso, Isaac Carrillo, and Gabriel Moreno. See *Manual* (n. 127 above), ibid.

members were linked by bonds of kinship. Membership included three whose sons were also members—Daniel and Simon de Barrios, Isaac and Moses Orobio, and Joseph and Moses Mocatta; there were also the brothers Abraham and Joseph Penso. Joseph Mocatta's daughter Rachel was married to David Franco Mendes mentioned above,[129] and the latter's own sister Rachel Franco Mendes was wife of Joseph Mocatta.[130] Joseph Israel Alvarez and Raphael del Castillo were brothers-in-law, as husbands of the sisters Gracia and Rachel del Soto.[131] Moses b. Abraham Mocatta was related to both the aforementioned Mocatta and Franco Mendes families.[132] Sarah, daughter of don Manuel Belmonte, was married to Aaron, brother of Moses Pereyra.[133] Rebecca, sister of Jacob Chaves, was the wife of Jacob de Gama.[134] Moses Rosa was brother to Samuel Rosa, himself the brother-in-law of Daniel de Barrios.[135] Although in each of the cases mentioned the marriage was between members of the same financial class, the extent of interrelationship certainly helped to cement the social solidarity of the *academia*.

The subjects that were debated in the proceedings of the *Academia de los Floridos* constituted another point in which it did not differ from the literary academies of Spain during the age of the baroque. A volume by Joseph Penso, entitled *Discursos Académicos, Morales, Rethóricos y Sagrados, que recitó en la florida Academia de los Floridos*, opens a window for us into the world of the society.[136] From what is said there it appears that at some of the meetings problems were propounded for discussion by one of the members, of which the following are a few examples. At one session don Manuel de Lara

---

[129] See below, Appendix D.
[130] See de Barrios, *Triumpho* (copy in Amsterdam, *EH* 2 F 9), pp. 373 f.
[131] See below, Appendix D.
[132] De Barrios, *Alegrías*, f. 80ʳᵛ, 'Silva Epitalamica en el feliz desposorio de los Ilustres Señores Mosseh de Abraham Mocata y Doña Esther Coen Camiña: ... Alegran su Hymeneo venturoso los de su sangre en harmoniosas venas, / Joseph Mocata, David Franco Mendes ...' Cf. Pieterse, *De Barrios*, p. 85, who asserts that there was no family connection between them.
[133] Cf. Amsterdam, AGA, DTB 685, p. 223. The marriage took place on 31 Oct. 1662. Cf. Pieterse, *De Barrios*, p. 87.
[134] Jacob Chaves himself married another Rebecca, daughter of Moses Machado, in 1691 (see below, p. 421). In 1687—two years after the establishment of the *academia*, by which time it was already defunct—Aaron Medina married Rachel, daughter of David Hamis Vaz (see below, p. 425).
[135] Pieterse, *De Barrios*, p. 143.
[136] Cf. above n. 112.

discussed the problem, formulated in a Spanish quatrain that may be rendered thus:

> The question that the wise address
> To loyal souls hangs in the scales:
> Which of the following prevails —
> Love's weight, or force of spitefulness?[137]

At another meeting the following question was posed:

> Two virtues show their difference,
> Of them the better please to show:
> Patience mid tribulation's woe,
> Or to stay meek, mid affluence?[138]

At one of the other sessions a debate was held on the subject of which of the senses is the most important: Joseph Penso represented the sense of smell, endeavouring to prove its superiority to the others.[139] Other problems discussed included:

> All human kind their life began
> Of women born: so make me see
> Why the first woman came to be
> Our mother, born herself of man?[140]

And again,

> Each sense we have its gift applies
> To sin, and make God's anger blaze;
> Why should the penalty always
> Be paid in tears, shed by the eyes?[141]

Likewise,

> Four senses are in balance hung,
> Each one in twofold organs placed:

---

[137] Penso, *Floridos*, p. 33: 'En igual balança; al Sabio / pregunta el Fiel, en rigor; / si pesa mas el Amor / que la fuerça del Agravio?'

[138] Ibid., p. 51: 'Por saber qual es mayor, / dos virtudes se distinguen, / la del paciente en lo adverso / la del prospero en lo humilde.'

[139] Ibid., p. 67: 'Sobre los Sentidos, hay / combate en el docto Circo; / paraque el Enigma humano / tenga oy su mejor sentido ...'

[140] Ibid., p. 87: 'Si del humano, es nacer / de muger; saber espero / porque del hombre primero / nació la primer muger?'

[141] Ibid., p. 107: 'Si pecando, dan enojos / a Dios, los demas Sentidos; porque en llanto convertidos, / lo pagan siempre los ojos? ...'

Philosophers, Theologians, and Poets

> Why, therefore, doth the sense of taste
> Have nought to ply save but the tongue?[142]

Also,

> Which of two vices is the worse—
> This learned house is called to say:
> Careless, to give one's all away,
> Or, as a miser, clutch one's purse?[143]

And,

> Misfortunes twain there be: I doubt
> Which is the uglier: in need
> Of all, yet to have sons to feed,
> Or rather to be rich, without?[144]

Did the sharp and penetrating mind of Isaac Orobio really find matter of interest to him in the discussion of subjects of such slight intellectual importance as these, and can one visualize him fitting in to the superficial atmosphere that pervaded the meetings of the *Floridos*? Joseph Penso records a problem being raised for discussion on the occasion of one of the meetings of the *academia* by a participant whom he dubs the 'Spanish Hippocrates' and the 'Andalusian Aristotle':

> The sage, all gravity, says: 'take
> Hypocrisy, the traitor's vice,
> And tell me if it be less nice
> Than is the frank, unbridled rake?[145]

There is no question but that the proposer of this problem for discussion by the *academia* must have been Isaac Orobio, the only one of its membership to have won laurels in both medicine and philosophy, and who, incidentally, had already in the past been accorded similar sobriquets amongst the compliments showered upon him by Daniel Levi de Barrios in his poems.[146] He had invested his best intellectual

---

[142] Ibid., p. 177: 'Si instrumentos duplicados / quatro Sentidos ostentan; / porque [sic] no tiene el del gusto, / sino solo el de la lengua?'

[143] Ibid., p. 201: 'Entre dos opuestos vicios, / propongo al Congresso Sabio; / qual es al hombre peor, / el del prodigo, o avaro?'

[144] Ibid., p. 271: 'Hay dos infelicidades, / y dudo qual es la mas fiera / si la pobreza con hijos, / o sin ellos la riqueza.'

[145] Ibid., p. 137: 'Pregunta el docto cuydado / qual en el vicio es peor; / si sobre el hipocrita traydor, / o el disoluto arrojado . . .' Cf. p. 139: 'un hipocrita y un disoluto, nos offrece oy el Problema, quien no teniendo nada de disoluto ni de hipocrita, tiene mucho de Hypocrates Español, y de Aristoteles Andaluz.'   [146] See above, chap. 8, p. 233.

powers in demolishing the philosophical system of Raymond Lull, and in the previous year he had shown that he knew how to bring to question the fundamental structure of the metaphysics of Spinoza: but, it would seem, he was able to find some psychological relaxation in these entertaining, albeit undemanding sessions amongst *aficionados* of the Spanish baroque.

Sometimes members of the *academia* would expound a scriptural verse, posing it as a problem or a riddle for discussion. At one meeting Joseph Penso held forth on the meanings of the phrase in Deuteronomy 20: 19, *ki ha-'adam 'eṣ ha-sadeh*, the context of which requires that it should be read interrogatively, 'is the tree of the field man?' although the Masoretic vocalization as *ha-'adam* (rather than *he-'adam*) directs one to read it as a statement.[147] But even in instances like these, the discussion was innocent of any specifically Jewish ingredient. The participants, who were in the habit of spicing their contributions from what Plato puts in Socrates' mouth, from Aristotle, Lipsius, Pliny, Zeno, Eusebius, etc., and who were by no means sparing in trotting out wise saws and proverbs from classical mythology, forbore from adducing the slightest allusion to rabbinic literature. They would, it is true, quote the occasional biblical tag, and in what de Barrios and Penso contributed there are to be found not a few puns based on the etymology of Hebrew words: but it is all without any connection with post-biblical Jewish sources. There is no doubt that the majority of those involved in the *academia* lacked the necessary competence, and the sketchy or quite defective Jewish education of some of them played a part in their ignoring the Talmudic and later Jewish sources. But that is neither the only nor the principal cause, since amongst the membership of the *Floridos* were some graduates of the rabbinic seminaries—Joseph Penso himself being one such—to whom the world of the Talmud was by no means strange. One must assume that their shutting of their eyes to Jewish source-material was a deliberate policy. Possibly the *Floridos* were intending to underscore the uniqueness, within the congregational context, of their *academia*, the interests of which were entirely comprised by secular subjects, as distinct from the other fellowships and associations for study—also

---

[147] Penso, *Floridos*, p. 251: 'Llama Dios Arbol del campo / al hombre, y saber la causa / solicito de raiz / para no andar por las ramas . . .' (For the point of Hebrew Grammar see *Gesenius' Hebrew Grammar*, ed. E. Kautzsch, Eng. trans. by A. E. Cowley, Oxford, 1980, pp. 296 §100n, 110, §35c.)

called *academias* in the popular parlance of the congregation—in which religious matters were studied.[148] Perhaps also they wished not to expose themselves to friction with the sages, or to antagonize them by making free use of rabbinic sources for purposes other than study or practical application.

As stated above, it was normal to close sessions of the *academia* with a performance of some kind of entertainment or other. We may assume that it was for one such *pièce de résistance* that Daniel Levi de Barrios intended his poem *Ansias de Epytalamio*[149] in honour of one of the members, Moses Nunes Marchena, on the eve of his marriage to Rebecca Núñez Enríquez. This is nothing more than a rhymed conversation-piece, into which snatches of song have been inserted, between Cupid, Hymen (the god of marriage), and Music. Probably three members of the *academia* presented the masque—presumably Daniel himself (who already in the sixties had tried his hand at acting on the stage), his son Simon, and Moses Rosa, brother of the actor Samuel Rosa who, on 1 September 1667, had founded a theatrical company in Amsterdam together with de Barrios.[150] Not all the performances were of this kind. Sometimes Isaac Villegas and David Ximenes, members of the academy praised in de Barrios' book about it for their talents in swordmanship, probably put on display fencing-matches.[151]

Had the 'Devil with a limp' (*Diablo Cojuelo*), or Cleofás—heroes of the well-known contemporary *novela* by the Spanish author Vélez de Guevara—happened to be present at one of the sessions of the *Academia de los Floridos* in the house of don Manuel Belmonte at Amsterdam, they would hardly have believed their own eyes. Exactly what they had seen in the *academia* of the Conde de la Torre—the same types of programme, the same protocol—would have been before them. They would have been able to hear the flowery style that was the product of the *culteranismo* of the Góngora school, familiar to them from the Seville *academia*, in the mansion of Manuel de Belmonte, Count Palatine. Their ears would have caught the timbre of the speech

---

[148] Cf. de Barrios, *Triumpho* (copy in Amsterdam, EH 2 F 9) pp. 61 f., who styles most of the rabbinical seminaries and other religious study-fellowships as *academias*. Thus the guild of *Kether Torah* ('Corona de la Ley') was, in his parlance, the 'academia primera', and *Torah 'Or* ('Torah is Light') the 'academia segunda'. Likewise 'Insigne Yesiba o Academia de los muy nobles señores Jacob y David Imanuel de Pinto', etc.

[149] Cf. above, n. 113. [150] See Pieterse, *De Barrios*, p. 18.
[151] See below, Appendix D.

of Andalusia, its peculiar flavour not forgotten by those who, like Isaac Orobio and Daniel de Barrios, came from southern Spain. In the creations of Penso and de Barrios they would have recognized the familiar literary forms; and it would have been the same enigmas and riddles that were conventional amongst the membership of the Spanish *academias* that they would have been called upon to solve.[152] Perhaps they might at once have sensed one obvious difference: in contrast to the Seville *academia* and others established in Spain at the same period, no women sat amongst the company of the *Floridos* to participate in its discussions. This circumstance elicited from Joseph Penso an exclamation of thanksgiving in one of his discourses; owing to their absence, he said, there was preserved the quiet atmosphere requisite for debate.[153] There was, too, another difference, and one of a fundamental qualitative importance, that our mythical visitors would not have detected so easily: all members of the *academia*, whether formerly crypto-Jews or the issue of crypto-Jews, were, in the fullest sense of the word, Jewish.

LAST DAYS

From the voluntary offerings and pledges (*promesas*) which Isaac Orobio gave to the synagogue in the years 1680–6, it is quite clear that during these years he attended services regularly in the magnificent Portuguese synagogue.[154] But in the second half of the Jewish year

---

[152] See *El Diablo Cojuelo* (n. 104 above), pp. 120 f.: 'Y el Cojuelo le dijo a don Cleofás: Esta es una academia de los mayores ingenios de Sevilla, que se juntan en esta casa a conferir cosas de la profesión y hacer versos a diferentes asumptos.' Of the constitution and office-holders of this *academia* Vélez de Guevara wrote: '. . . entraron muy severos en la dicha Academia, que apatrocinaba, con el agasajo que suele, el conde de la Torre, Ribera y Saavedra, y Guzmán, y cabeza y barón de los Riberas. El presidente era Antonio Ortiz Melgarejo, de la insignia de San Juan, ingenio eminente en la Música y en la Poesía, cuya casa fue siempre el museo de la Poesía y de la Música. Era secretario Alvaro de Cubillo, ingenio granadino que había venido a Sevilla a algunos negocios de su importancia, excelente cómico y grande versificador, con aquel fuego andaluz que todos los que nacen en aquel clima tienen, y Blas de las Casas era fiscal . . . Eran entre los demás académicos, conocidos Don Cristóbal de Rozas y don Diego de Rosas, ingenios peregrinos que han honrado el poema dramático, y don García de Coronel y Salzedo, fénix de las letras humanas . . .' For specimens of the poems recited, see pp. 122 f.

[153] Penso, *Floridos*, p. 89. For the most part, women were permitted to participate in the sessions of the Spanish *academias*; see Vélez de Guevara, ibid., p. 121.

[154] For Isaac Orobio's contribution to the congregation (by way of voluntary offerings, as distinct from regular dues) between 5440 and 5447 (1679/80–1686/7) see the

5447 (i.e. the summer months of 1687) there is a steep drop in the size of his contributions as compared with the relatively high sums that he had hitherto been accustomed to offer. Whereas between (approximately) October 1686 and April 1687 the total received from him (under this heading) was twelve florins and eighteen stuivers, in the following six months his contribution was reduced to a mere ten stuivers, or half of one florin.[155] And this was while there was no change at all in the regular dues that he was paying to the Congregation *Talmud Torah*, viz. the six florins for each half-year at which he had been assessed by the *Ma'amad* back in 1677, and which he continued to pay right until the end of his life.[156] It follows that an explanation for the marked diminution in his offerings during the six months in 1686–7 is not to be sought in his economic circumstances, which had apparently not altered. It would seem that Isaac, now on the threshold of his seventieth year, was prevented from attendance at synagogue because of failing health.

It looks as though there must have been some improvement during August–September of 1687, for the synagogal records contain a poignant entry that has something to tell us about the end of the journey which he had travelled for so long with the Portuguese congregation of Amsterdam:[157]

Manual, vol. 4, of the Congregation *Talmud Torah*, Amsterdam, AGA, PA 334 no. 175. They were as here set out:

		Florins	Stuivers	Manual
5440 [1679/80]	1st ½-year	11	10	p. 105
	2nd ½-year	4	2	p. 122
5441 [1680/1]	1st ½-year	9	1	p. 140
	2nd ½-year	5	4	p. 159
5442 [1681/2]	1st ½-year	7	2	p. 174
	2nd ½-year	12	12	p. 190
5443 [1682/3]	1st ½-year	2	8	p. 208
	2nd ½-year	9	12	p. 229
5444 [1683/4]	1st ½-year	8	15	p. 246
	2nd ½-year	6	8	p. 268
5445 [1684/5]	1st ½-year	7	16	p. 284
	2nd ½-year	4	—	p. 310
5446 [1685/6]	1st ½-year	4	6	p. 328
	2nd ½-year	13	—	—

[155] *Manual*, pp. 368, 388.

[156] On the regular dues paid by him see above, chap. 7, pp. 206.

[157] See the congregational *Ascamoth (Acta)*, MS Amsterdam, AGA PA 334 no. 20, p. 110: '5447—Em 8 de Ilul se presentou O S[enho]r d[ou]tor Ischack Orobio de Crasto [sic] para servyr a os Pobres Doentes da Hebra por Caridade em compagnhia do S[enho]r D[ou]tor David Serafattim seo yerno o que lhe foy consedido pelos ss[enhore]s do Mahamad ordenando se fissese este termo p[ara] membransa.' The decision is signed by the members of the *Ma'amad*.

On 8 'Elul 5447 [17 August 1687] Dr Isaac Orobio de Crasto [sic] presented himself, [offering], as a matter of charity, to attend the indigent patients of the Society [sc. *Biqqur Ḥolim*, for the Visitation of the Sick] alongside his son-in-law Dr David Sarfati [*Serafattim*] [de Pina];[158] a request which was considered by the señores of the *Maʻamad*, and so ordered . . .

The aged doctor, who had apparently by now given up all activity, felt that his own end could not be far off, and he wanted to fulfil one last deed of piety whilst life remained to him. So he volunteered to serve as physician to the congregational poor together with his son-in-law, who had been officially appointed to the Society *Biqqur Ḥolim* since the end of 1680.[159]

On 6 November 1687 (1 *Kislev* 5448) Isaac Orobio died: and so ended the engrossing life-story of a colourful personality, who was also one of the noblest spirits amongst the Sephardi Jewry of Amsterdam. His son, Dr Moses Orobio, anxious to remain faithful to his father's ideals, applied to the *señores* of the *Maʻamad* on 24 November 1687 (18 *Kislev* 5448, i.e. after the end of the seven days' full mourning period for his father), offering to take his place as doctor to the congregational poor.[160] Within a year of Isaac Orobio's death his sons Moses and Abraham between them donated 120 florins to the synagogue, in order that a 'memorial prayer (*hashkabah*) for their father might be recited annually on the sabbath preceding the anniversary of his death, on the first day of every [Jewish] month, and in the evening service at the entry of the day of atonement, in accordance with the usual custom'.[161]

---

[158] i.e. David de Pina Sarfati, for whom see above.

[159] For the appointment of David Sarfati to this office on 29 *Kislev* 5441 (20 Dec. 1680) see the *Ascamoth (Acta)*, p. 10. During the first 2 months of the Jewish year 5448 (commencing 7 Sept. 1687) Orobio was still able to offer altogether 43 fl. 6 st. to the congregation or its associated charities. These amounts would appear to be donations from his sick-bed. See *Manual* (n. 154 above), p. 412.

[160] *Ascamoth (Acta)*, p. 110: '5448—En 18 de Kislef foy pedido Por O S[enho]r D[out]or Moshe Orobio de Crasto, [sic] a los S[enhore]s do Mahamad para que fose admetido en lugar do S[enho]r seo pay Ishack Orobio de Crasto [sic] que D[eus] aiga para servyr os Pobres da Hebra com a mesma comformidad asina o que lhe foy consedido pelos S[enhores] do Mahamad.' Signed by the members of the *Maʻamad*.

[161] Ibid., f. 131ʳ: 'Termo de florins sento e vinte que fez Codez os s[enho]rez Mosseh e Abraham Orobio de Crasto [sic] p[ara] seu paaj [sic] o Douttor Ischaq Orobio de Crasto [sic] para se observar o seguinte: Em 3 de Elul estando juntos os s[enho]res Mosseh e Abraham Orobio de Crasto [sic] fossemo[s] servidos aceitar florins sento e vinte que fiserão codes com condisão que se haya deitar escaba au doutor Ischaq Orobio de Crasto [sic] aos sabatot que coinciden de aodia de seu falecimento e o mesmo em Roschodes e noutte de Kipur como ee estilho e lhes foy concedido p[or] os S[enho]res do Mahamat [sic] e o gabaij recebeo o d[it]to e se nottou nos libros do K. K.' See also *Manual* (n. 154

Philosophers, Theologians, and Poets

Prior to his decease Isaac Orobio had acquired graves for himself and his wife in the Portuguese-Jewish cemetery at Ouderkerk, in the ninth row—considered one of the more honorific parts of the ground.[162] His tombstone, together with that of his wife who outlived him by twenty-four years until 4 July 1712 (1 *Tammuz* 5472), is still preserved, although the ravages of time are evident on both. The visitor cannot fail to be impressed by the simple, clear-cut slab, bearing a memorial inscription in Hebrew and Portuguese:[163]

Translation

Isaac [still] lives in heaven[164]

מצבת קבורת איש חיל	[This] stone [marks] the grave of a
ואיש חי אשר האיר פני	man of worth, A man [still] living who
תבל בחכמתו שמו נודע	gave light to The world: For wisdom is
בכל פינה הלא הוא הרופא	his name famous in every corner [of
המובהק יצחק אורוביאו די	it]; namely, a skilled Physician, Isaac
קאסטרו אשר עלתה	Orobio de Castro, whose spirit Went
נשמתו למרום ביום א	up on high on the first day of the
לחודש כסלו שנת תמח	month of Kislev year [5]448
ת נ צ ב ה	M[ay] H[is soul be] B[ound up] I[n the bond of] L[ife]

[162] For the beginnings of the Portuguese-Jewish cemetery at Ouderkerk see Pieterse, *Livro de Bet Haim*, esp. introd. pp. xii f. Although the fixed charge per grave in this row was 50 fl., Orobio paid a compound charge of 70 fl. only for the graves of himself and his wife, by a special agreement approved by the *Ma'amad* on 6 Nov. 1687, i.e. on the day of his death: *Livro de Bet Haim* (Amsterdam, AGA, PA 334 no. 916), p. 58: 'em prim[er]o de Kislef (5448) Isaque Orobio de Crasto [*sic*] Bethaim novo c[areir]a 9: s[epultur]a n° 16 y n° 17 p[ar]a a mulher, pagou—f. 70 com parecer dos s[enho]res do Mahamad.' For the cost of plots in the Ouderkerk cemetery see PA 334 no. 930, and for the location of the graves of Orobio and his wife see no. 916, p. 32..

[163] The text of the inscription is given by De Castro in his article 'De Ned. Port. Israel. Begraafplaats te Ouderkerk a/d Amstel', *NIW* 3, no. 34 (20 Mar. 1868), where the heading (see next note) is omitted; also in his *Graafsteenen*, p. 23, which also gives the inscription on Orobio's wife's grave: also, most recently, by L. A. Vega, *Het Beth Haim van Ouderkerk*, Assen and Amsterdam, 1975, p. 39. Cf. also Amzalak's edn. of Orobio's *Resp. Pred. franc.*, p. xvi, and Kayserling, *De Barrios*, 32, 1896, p. 89.

[164] An ingenious re-application of the first words of Ps. 2: 4, where *yishaq* (spelled thus, abnormally, for *yiṣḥaq*) is not the name *Isaac*, but a verb—'He that dwells in heaven laughs [sc. at the boasting of the wicked]'.

S^A 165
DO BEMAVENTURADO
E YNSIGNE VARAO
DOUTOR YSHACK
OROBIO DE CASTRO
FALECIO EM 1 DE
KISLÊF
A° 5448[166]

In contrast with the elaborate carving that characterizes the surrounding slabs of glistening marble with their rich (and indeed somewhat exaggerated) decoration—the relics of an opulent and blooming Jewish community—the modesty of Isaac Orobio's memorial is particularly conspicuous. When one appreciates this contrast between simplicity and vainglory, one is inclined to recall the objection raised by the Dutch historian J. Huizinga to the description of the seventeenth century as constituting the Low Countries' 'golden age'. 'If [he wrote] our great age must perforce be given a name, let it be that of wood and steel, pitch and tar, colour and ink, pluck and piety, fire and imagination. The term "golden" applies far better to the eighteenth century when our coffers were stuffed with gold-pieces.'[167]

Such, then, was the life of Isaac b. Abraham Orobio de Castro, both in character and in deed a faithful representative figure of his period. His life's story encapsulates the fate of a whole community—its problems, its inner contradictions, its aspirations, and its dreams. Before us lies

---

[165] = Sepultura.

[166] The inscription over the grave of his wife is in Portuguese only: S^a [Sepultura] Da bemaventurada Ester mulher do Dr Ischak Orobio f° [faleceo] em 1 Tamus A° [Ano] 5472. S. A. G. D. G. [Sua Alma Goze Da Gloria]. The lettering on this side of the stone is partly worn away. The slab is ornamented by three figures in relief, viz. at the head to the left (Isaac Orobio's grave) a flower, probably a rose, in full bloom, and similarly right (Esther Orobio's grave); in the centre, a fleur-de-lis between the semicircles that surmount the beginnings of the two inscriptions. Floral motifs (intended to symbolize life) are not uncommon among the reliefs on the tombstones at Ouderkerk. They also figure in antiquity on Jewish ossuaries: see P. Figueras, 'Jewish and Christian Beliefs on Life after Death in the Light of the Ossuary Decoration' (Doctoral Thesis, Hebrew University, Jerusalem, 1974), pp. 20 f. On the other hand the fleur-de-lis does not appear anywhere else on the Ouderkerk gravestones; and possibly its function here is to point to the circumstance of Orobio's having allegedly held appointment as medical counsellor to Louis XIV at an earlier stage of his life (see above, chap. 5, p. 104).

[167] Huizinga, p. 104.

the portrait of a man re-created in all his sinews against the background of his period and his own society. His development illustrates the problematic elements of which were compounded the life of a congregation of former crypto-Jews who had reverted to the observance of their ancestral faith and had erected in Amsterdam a congregation of great distinction amid one of the most important cultural centres of the seventeenth century. Isaac Orobio became integrated into normative Judaism at the very time when men like Prado and Spinoza might so easily have precipitated a schism. Orobio's own spiritual and ideological exertions to justify his Jewish traditionalism and his constant disputations with deviationists from within, and with representatives of his Christian environment from without show us not merely his stature and the significance of the apologetic mission that he took upon himself, but also something about the vitality of his own Jewish community and its capacity to stand on its own feet. His was a unique community, which was summoned to prove its mettle and was tested through many an ordeal at a turning-point in history when the modern age of Jewry was just dawning.

11
The Intellectual World of Isaac Orobio de Castro

THE HISPANIC HERITAGE

The crypto-Jews of Spain and Portugal brought with them to Amsterdam a treasure-house of values and concepts derived from the Spanish culture in which they had been educated, and on which they continued to draw after they had left the Iberian peninsula and had become reintegrated into the Jewish community. In their new domicile their fostering of Spanish and Portuguese speech was maintained; and, so far from losing interest in everything that was going on in the artistic and intellectual life of their birthplace, they continued to take an active part in literary movements that pervaded its atmosphere such as *culteranismo* and *conceptismo*.[1] Their philosophical and scholarly thought was likewise bound up with the development of humane letters in the peninsula.

Nor was this link weakened for the children of those who had fled, whether born in Amsterdam or having arrived there in their infancy. Barukh Spinoza, himself a native of Amsterdam, had in his exiguous library the works of Quevedo, Saavedra Fajardo, Góngora, Pérez de Montalbán, and Gracián, all these being among the most prominent Spanish authors of the seventeenth century. Calvin he preferred to read in a Spanish translation, and the same applies to the *Dialoghi di amore* of Leone Ebreo, alias Judah Abravanel. Other Spanish books in his possession included Covarrubias, and the poem about Queen Esther by the crypto-Jewish Juan Pinto Delgado.[2] Menasseh ben

---

[1] *Culteranismo* is the name given to a literary style that became widely diffused amongst Spanish poets at the end of the 16th and the first half of the 17th cent. through the influence of Luis Argote de Góngora (1561–1627). It is marked by an exaggerated use of Latin vocabulary and of uncommon, not to say obscure expressions. *Conceptismo* insisted on clarity of conceptual thinking, and looked to Seneca as the appropriate model to emulate. At the head of this latter movement there stood Quevedo y Villegas (1580–1645). These two streams characterize the literary baroque of Spain, and despite the difference and indeed opposition between them, they are sometimes found lying cheek by jowl in the writings of many an author of the period. Amongst the many who have studied these phenomena see most recently P. E. Russell in Russell, pp. 316–28.

[2] See van Praag, p. 21.

Israel, who came to Amsterdam whilst still a child, also knew his way around in Iberian literature, and in his writings he frequently refers to Spanish and Portuguese authors.[3] Like Quevedo, he also translated Phocylides into Spanish;[4] and when quoting from the *Examen de los Ingenios* he found it unnecessary to state the name of the author, since he took it for granted that his Jewish readership would know that it was by Juan Huarte de San Juan—whose thinking would have been well known to every Portuguese-Jewish physician.[5]

For Jews like these, the bond with the cultural heritage of Spain found expression not only in their surprising familiarity with Spanish and Portuguese literature, but above all in their intense psychological attachment to the aesthetic types and conceptual content of the books that were being widely read in Spain and Portugal in the seventeenth century.

Daniel Levi (Miguel) de Barrios was not merely a great devotee of Luis de Góngora, to whose defence he sprang in a sonnet written in honour of Miguel de Silva,[6] but in a substantial proportion of his poetry and dramatical works he attempted to emulate the style of the father of *culteranismo* in Spanish.[7] The final act of his play *The Spaniard of Oran*—written in Spanish—is based entirely upon two *romanzas* of Góngora.[8] At the same time, there is no doubt that in his satirical poems he was influenced by Francisco de Quevedo, leader of the *conceptismo* school and himself one of Góngora's sharp critics.[9] He likewise held in high regard Camões, 'príncipe de los Poetas Lusitanos'.[10] The style of the Spanish baroque found expression not only in de Barrios' poetry, some of which, it could be claimed, was written primarily for a Spanish-speaking Christian readership, but also in what other poets in the Portuguese congregation of Amsterdam were writing. Abraham Gómez de Araujo and Abraham Israel Pizarro

[3] In his *Esperança de Israel* (Amsterdam, 1650) he quotes from Alonso de Ercilla, Francisco de Ribera, Garcilaso de la Vega, Pedro Hernandes de Quirós, etc.
[4] Quevedo's version appeared in Madrid in 1635: *Epicteto y Focílides en español*. Menasseh b. Israel's was never published, but it is mentioned in the list of his writings at the end of his *Piedra Gloriosa o de la Estatua de Nebuchadnesar*, Amsterdam, 1655. See Roth, *Men. b. I.*, p. 104.
[5] Menasseh b. Israel, *De la fragilidad humana*, Amsterdam, 1642, p. 77; see van Praag, p. 20, and, on Huarte de San Juan's book, see Méchoulan, *Alterité juive*, pp. 174 f.
[6] De Barrios, *Coro*, p. 222: 'Don Miguel de Silva, que escrivió contra los que dixeron mal de las Soledades de Don Luis de Góngora.'
[7] See Gates.
[8] Ibid., pp. 394 f.
[9] See e.g. his sonnet 'Postura de Fregona' printed in his *Coro*, p. 534, and 'Al Casamiento de un ciego y una muda,' ibid., pp. 583 f.
[10] Ibid., p. 221, Elogio XLV: 'Al Príncipe de los Poetas Lusitanos, Luis de Camões'.

did not hesitate to make use of similes drawn from the most familiar items in the pagan repertoire even in compositions written for the synagogue service in honour of those chosen for the distinction of concluding and recommencing the annual cycle of pentateuchal readings. These poems were declaimed at religious ceremonies held by the congregations of The Hague and Hamburg.[11]

Some pieces included in the works of Abraham Israel Pereyra were written under the influence of Fray Luis de León.[12] J. A. van Praag has proved beyond doubt that Pereyra was not simply influenced by Fray Luis de Granada, Fray Diego de Estrella, and Quevedo, but that whole sections of their writings are plagiarized in his own two works, without indication of the source and omitting the references to Christian writings that these had contained.[13]

A great respect for Seneca and for the Stoics of antiquity is to be felt in writings of Isaac Orobio and others of the Portuguese community. Its source lies quite certainly in the neo-Stoic revival in Spain at the end of the sixteenth century and the beginning of the seventeenth.[14] That revival did, of course, find expression in other countries of Europe as well; but members of the Amsterdam congregation swelled the ranks of this new veneration for Seneca under the impress of contemporary Spanish thought. In Spain Stoic notions were mobilized both with the object of attacking the orthodox Catholic establishment, and out of a feeling of dissatisfaction with the aims of the neo-scholasticism that was engrossing itself entirely in natural philosophy to the exclusion of existential human problems.[15] Just as Quevedo

[11] See Abraham Gómez de Araujo, *AEnigma*, En celebración de la Fiesta de los S^{res} Novios Mosseh Nuñez Henriquez, Hatan Thora y Isack Israel Bravo, Hatan Beresit, Hamburg, 5439 (copy in Amsterdam, Bibl. Rosen., Einbladsdrukken Ebl. C. 87): 'Al fin de las andanças de Neptuno / El que me ignora, experto norte llama.' On Gómez de Araujo see Kaplan, *Zion*, 39, 5734 [1974], p. 216 (in Hebrew). See also Pizarro, MS Amsterdam, *EH* 48 D 31, p. 3: '... Que passando de aquesta a mexor vida / a esclarecido el Mundo como Apollo.'

[12] Pereyra, *Espejo*, p. 181: 'No digo, que deven todos ir a los desiertos, sino, que deven todos, buscar la tranquilidad de la vida: la qual, aunque se peuda hallar en la ciudad, no tiene la excelencia de la que se passa en el campo.' Cf. the well-known poem of Luis de Leon, 'Qué: Vida Retirada descansada vida / la del que huye del mundanal ruido, /...'

[13] See van Praag, pp. 18 f.

[14] See Russell, pp. 334-7, who states that although the respect in which the echoing of Stoic ideas was held was extreme in 17th-cent. Spain, it is not to be exaggerated. Despite this, it seems to me to be beyond doubt that the influence of Seneca is easily recognizable in the writings of Quevedo and Gracián, as well (to some extent) as in the political thought of Spain during the same period. Cf. Méchoulan, *Alterité juive*, pp. 191 f. See also above, chap. 6, p. 177, for Prado's links with Seneca and the Stoics.

[15] Russell, ibid.

The Intellectual World of Isaac Orobio de Castro 311

endeavoured to show that Stoic and Christian values could prove congenial bed-fellows, the Portuguese Jews had no difficulty in finding within the thought of Seneca items that were compatible with Judaism.[16]

In the written form of their language, too, the Amsterdam Jews for the most part obeyed the canons of Spanish as spoken within the frontiers of Spain itself. The language of Daniel de Barrios, Isaac Orobio, Abraham Israel Pereyra, and Isaac Aboab is both rich and correct, even though one may sense a slight Portuguese influence in the positioning of the pronouns and the conjugation of the verbs.[17]

But over and over their attachment to the cultural content and aesthetic forms of the Iberian society of their own time, the Sephardi Jews felt a deep psychological kinship with the land of their origin, its past, its landscape, and its customs: the sweet memory of these things was not blurred in their consciousness, even after the humiliations and assaults of which they had had their fill whilst they lived as a minority subjected to discrimination and persecution.

> Farewell, Montilla, Thou land of my birth, and Spain
> Farewell: the Lion bears me midst his hurricane.[18]

Thus de Barrios wrote in a poem published in 1672, ten years after his arrival in Amsterdam; and in a sonnet dedicated to Montilla he hailed it as 'most noble and loyal city', 'the green star in the heavens of Córdoba', and he emphasized that it was the home of the descendants of Alonso, 'who died whilst laying low the hordes of Muhammad'.[19] In one of his later poems he even asserted that 'Spain, as a geographical unity, is called *Celtiberia*: this not being, as many suppose, a compound

---

[16] Thus Orobio, in his *Cart. Apol.*, MS Paris, BN Fonds éspagnoles 41, p. 900: 'Los Senecas los Plinios, los Tacitos y muchos de esta clase, son mis amigos para algunas noticias.' Cf. A. I. Pereyra, *Certeza*, pp. 89, 120, 127, 130, and *Espejo*, pp. 28, 114, 362, 368 f. See p. 263: 'Plugiera a Dios, lo obraramos los Iudios, como este Philosopho Gentilico lo aconseja.'

[17] See van Praag, p. 23.

[18] De Barrios, *Coro*, p. 245: 'a Dios Patria, Montilla, a Dios España / que me lleva el Leon en gran tormenta.'

[19] Ibid., p. 196. The full text of the poem runs as follows: A la muy Noble y leal Ciudad de Montilla / Mi gran patria Montilla, verde estrella / del Cielo Cordoves, agrado a Marte, / con las bellezas de la Diosa Marte / del fuego militar aurea centella. / San Francisco Solano es hijo della, / padre el Magno Pompeyo, lustre el arte, / por Baco y Ceres, del Elysio parte, / y por Phelipe el Grande Ciudad bella. / Corte de los famosos descendientes / del Alonso que en una del sol cumbre / murio matando Mahometanas gentes. / Da con su fama al Moro pesadumbre, / de hojas marciales, y Astros eloquentes / sombra a las Deas, y a las Musas lumbre.'

of *Celtas* and *Iberos*, but the name is derived from the [Hebrew] word *Celatot* [*sic:* read *Cela'oth*], meaning *ribs*, alluding to Genesis 2: 21, *God . . . took one of the ribs of the man*. For the site of Paradise was Spain.'[20]

The object of the community's chiefest pride was their Iberian origin. In Saul Levi Mortera's apologetic *Obstáculos y oposiciones de la Religión christiana* he makes the 'amigo' (i.e. friend, who is an ex-crypto-Jew) say, 'our Portuguese nation has the edge over the others'.[21] Jacob León Templo certainly had the Jews of Spain in mind when, commenting on Psalm 77: 16, 'with thy strong arm Thou didst redeem thy people, the sons of Jacob and Joseph' (New English Bible), he wrote 'it is possible that the reason why [the psalmist] refers to the sons of Joseph as a class apart was because they were the *hidalgos*, the stoutest-hearted of all the people; consequently they were reluctant to leave Egypt, and God [had to] take them all out together with his outstretched arm'.[22] A similar parallel between Israel's sojourn in Egypt and the stay of the Jews in Spain is to be found in Isaac Aboab's commentary to the Pentateuch: 'as further proof of Abraham's being God's elect, and furthermore to demonstrate to the world his merits and his steadfastness, divine Providence directed him to go down to Egypt, because it was there that the sciences were in a more flourishing state than anywhere else . . . He occupied a professorial chair in Egypt, and evinced his great competence in philosophy, astrology, and the other liberal arts . . .'[23] One can hardly miss here the attempt to justify, in some measure, the continuance of crypto-Jewish residence in Spain, where many of them held chairs in the Iberian universities, which were amongst the most distinguished on the continent of Europe.

Van Praag is so impressed by the deep pyschological bond of these Sephardi Jews with Spain and her culture that he goes so far as to dub them 'divided souls': and from the clash of individuals like Uriel d'Acosta, Juan de Prado, Barukh Spinoza, and others with Jewish traditionalism, he draws conclusions as to the ambivalent attitude of the whole group towards the world of Judaism. Van Praag's illuminating notes certainly stimulate us to trace out the multicoloured cultural

---

[20] De Barrios, *Imperio*, p. 40: 'Que toda España se nombro *Celtiberia*: y es (no por componerse este nombre de Celtas, y de Hiberos como muchos entienden) sino del verbo Celatot, que se traduze costillas donde dize el Genesis c. 2: *Hizo caer el Señor Dios, sueño sobre el hombre, y adormeciose y tomo una de sus costillas* porque en España fue el Parayso. . .'

[21] Mortera, *Obstáculos*, MS Amsterdam, *EH* 48 D 38, f. 1ʳ: '. . . nuestra Nacion Portugueza haze ventaja a todas . . .' See Kaplan, *Mortera*, pp. 23 f.

[22] See Jacob Judah Leon Templo, *Las Alabanças de Santidad*, Amsterdam, 1671, p. 209. [23] Aboab, *Pent.*, p. 33.

sources upon which the Portuguese Jews of Amsterdam drew, and to understand the stark dilemmas with which they were faced, when they stumbled upon incompatibilities between the Christian values that they had brought with them from the Iberian peninsula and those which they encountered upon becoming reintegrated into the world of Judaism.[24] However, the majority of these Jews did become absorbed into the life of Judaism, and they vociferously repudiated those amongst their own number who dared question the authority of Torah and the obligatory force of its precepts, showing that for the majority of them the dilemmas and contradictions were resolved. Thus, the sobriquet 'divided souls' cannot be applied to the community as a whole. Isaac Orobio never dissembled his own links with those cultural values which he had acquired in Spain; but he did not see them as something that had to enter into competition with his Jewish *Weltanschauung*. 'We', he wrote to Prado, 'are now too old to [seek consolation] in the poets. Read rather holy Scripture, and you will find divine consolations, not the petty conceits of all-too-human poetry.'[25] The cultural values of Spain contained nothing to seduce him from his fundamental attachment to Judaism: on the contrary, as we shall see below, he well understood how to make use of certain items taken from that culture in order to help crystallize his own conception of Judaism.

BETWEEN SCHOLASTICISM AND FIDEISTIC SCEPTICISM

During the sixteenth and seventeenth centuries scholastic philosophy was the object of a reawakened interest in western Europe, the centre of such interest being Spain. The thinkers who stood at the head of this revival were for the most part themselves Spanish, the most prominent amongst them being Francisco de Vittoria (1480–1546), Domingo de Soto (1494–1560), Melchor Cano (1509–60), and Domingo Báñez (1528–1604), all Dominicans; and the Jesuits Francisco Toletus (1528–1604), Pedro de Fonseca (1548–99), Gabriel Vásquez (1549–1604), Gregorio de Valencia (1551–1603), Francisco Suárez (1548–1617), and Juan de Lugo (1583–1660). A number of commentaries on Aristotelian philosophy were published at the university of Coimbra by a group of learned Jesuits who came to be known as

[24] See van Praag, p. 23.
[25] Orobio, *Cart. Apol.* (see above, n. 16), p. 897: '... estamos ya viejos para poetas. Lea la Santa Escritura y hallara consuelos divinos, y no conceptillos poeticos muy humanos ...'

the *Conimbricenses* under the leadership of Pedro de Fonseca. A parallel group of scholars was active at Alcalá under Gaspar Cardillo de Villalpando (1537–81), known as the *Complutenses*. The Carmelites at the latter university published in 1624 the *cursus artium* which was thenceforth to serve as the basis of philosophical studies for the students there; it was reissued in several revised editions. It is these neo-scholastics who must be recognized as being responsible for the gradual bifurcation which took place between theological and philosophical studies. Although for them Aristotle remained 'the Philosopher' and ultimate authority, and numerous commentaries on his works continued to be published, already at this period there is detectable a tendency to convert the philosophy courses in Spanish universities from lectures devoted exclusively to exegesis of Aristotelianism into systematic and methodologically self-conscious courses on the problems which philosophy has to consider.[26]

Those former crypto-Jews from Spain and Portugal who had attended Iberian universities in the sixteenth and seventeenth centuries had consequently drunk from the wells of neo-scholastic thought. Isaac Orobio, who had studied at Alcalá, absorbed the foundations of the system there from his Jesuit and Carmelite teachers; and even after his reversion to the open profession of Judaism in Amsterdam he continued to entertain a profound respect for St Thomas Aquinas — 'though not a Jew, yet like an angel' — whom he frequently quoted throughout his own works.[27]

Following in the footsteps of the Christian scholastics — who were on this point at one with the rationalists amongst Jewish and Muslim philosophers of the Middle Ages — Orobio took it as axiomatic that contradiction between natural reason and revealed religion was impossible.[28] In his *Respuesta Apologética* to Zepeda he wrote that 'even if we

---

[26] See F. Copleston, *A History of Philosophy*, iii, part 2, New York, 1963, pp. 153 f.

[27] See *Resp. al Zep.*, MS Amsterdam, *EH* 48 A 12, f. 197ʳ: '... y Thomas como un Angel sin ser Judio ...'

[28] *Epíst. Inv.*, MS Paris, BN Fonds éspagnoles 40, p. 704: 'No parece que se necessita de mas authoridad de parte del que propone que sea creyble lo propuesto, como sea ajustado al entendimiento y nada repugnante a la razon humana.' Cf. p. 719: 'Ademas que la cosa, para ser creyble, no necessita de ser scible [MS *EH* 48 D 6, p. 344ʳ: scible, o demostrable, sino que no se oponga, o repugne, a lo scible] en el modo que queda explicado, y esta es la fee digna de serlo en qualquier era buen entendimiento, fee racional, clara prudente; no fee repugnante a la razon, hija de la obsuridad, y acto confuso y tenebroso de entendimiento seducido [MS *EH* 48 D 6, loc. cit.: entendimientos seducidos] por sola la authoridad del que propone, negada a el examen del juizio humano.'

cannot conceive the Godhead, at any rate we do not believe anything about it which conflicts with our intellect'.²⁹ That was the reason, he claimed, why Jews rejected Gentile beliefs, and in particular the dogmas of Christianity, since they could not stand up to rational scrutiny.³⁰ In Orobio's view, if one was to keep faith with the system of scholasticism in its integrity, this meant to reject the Gentile religions and to embrace Judaism, and—by the same token—to break away from the theology of Artistotle.³¹ Faith is not sustained by the will alone: one is not entitled to believe in whatever one likes, but must believe that which one can believe: and one can believe in that only which, according to the understanding of one's own reason, is true.³² The Jew believes in what God had revealed of Himself in the holy Law, and in that revelation there is nothing that is incompatible with human reason.³³

Spanish neo-scholastics such as Vásquez and Suárez are mentioned in Orobio's works in the same breath as Thomas Aquinas and Durand de Saint Pourçain. In his disputation with Zepeda he relied, *inter alia*, on the *Cursus Philosophicus* of Gonzalo Arriaga printed in Antwerp in 1632, which immediately became one of the commonest philosophical text-books in the universities of Spain.³⁴

So much for the scholastic basis of Isaac Orobio's theology, which served him well both in his controversy with Prado and Spinoza, who had impugned the intelligibility of revealed religion, and in the anti-Christian writings in which he exposed the fallacy of the mysteries of Christianity that could not—for him—keep company with the principles of rationalist philosophy. But Orobio was, at base, an eclectic; and his own philosophical thought absorbed not a little from the influence of those trends of speculative thinking that were being

---

²⁹ *Resp. al Zep.* (n. 27 above), ff. 207ʳ f.

³⁰ Ibid.,: 'Por eso no creemos ni admitimos las leyes de los christianos, digo chinos, ni de griegos, ni romanos, ni moros, no porque a unos y a otros falten medios o de rason o de autoridad para persuadir sus dogmas, sino porque sus dogmas o muchos de ellos, son contrarios a la lumbre de la rason.'

³¹ Ibid.: 'ni por ser Aristoteles metaphisico fue buen religioso'.

³² See *Trin.*, MS Amsterdam, *EH* 48 B 12, p. 184: '. . . y todos los hombres quieren creer de Dios, solo lo que es verdad; y no todos pueden, aunque quieren. Siguese de esto, que la Fe es acto del entendimiento.'

³³ Ibid., p. 186: 'Y assi solo cree de Dios el Israelita lo que el mismo Dios revelo de Si, en la Sancta Ley. Y su Magestad Divina, nada revelo, que no fuesse muy proporcionado, al entendimiento humano.'

³⁴ See *Resp . . . Lul*, MS Amsterdam, *EH* 48 D 6, f. 315ʳ, where Thomas Aquinas, Scotus, Durand, Suárez, and Vásquez are mentioned in the same context. Cf. *Trin.* (n. 32 above), p. 180, where there is a reference to a passage of Arriaga.

developed in Europe outside the confines of scholasticism, and indeed in opposition to its purposes. While from scholasticism Orobio took the conceptual basis of his thinking, in a significant amount of what he wrote one may distinguish his openness to the critique of scepticism, and particularly of that 'fideistic scepticism' that had struck root in intellectual Catholic circles in western Europe, with France as its centre.[35] The axiomatic basis of this movement was the assertion that to attain religious truth lies beyond the power of the human intellect, and that it is the Catholic Church alone that is capable of furnishing the faithful with certainty. Such scepticism had played an important part in the struggle in which, from the Counter-Reformation onwards, the Catholic world had been engaged against the individualism of Protestantism, that proclaimed the ability of the individual Christian to attain certainty of knowledge in matters of faith. Scepticism afforded a means of justifying the uncompromised authority of the Church, since in the absence of any criterion of rational certitude by means of which the truth of religion could be tested, fideistic sceptics could point to the Catholic Church as being the sole factor in Christendom capable of forestalling the anarchy of pandemonium.[36]

In his various writings, and in particular in his 'friendly conversation' with Philip van Limborch, Orobio adduced arguments of the sceptics in regard to the possibilities of the individual's attaining knowledge of God and religious certainty by means of his own reason. It is his view that there is no possibility of demonstrating the existence of God to one who does not already believe, since it does not fall within the category of things susceptible of rational proof. It is belief in the prophetic inspiration of Moses, and that alone, which is able to put a person in possession of that knowledge.[37] In his *Epístola Invectiva* against Prado he wrote, 'our understanding cannot comprehend

[35] See Popkin, *Scepticism Erasmus–Descartes*, pp. 1–16.

[36] During the first half of the 17th cent. a working concordat was established between protagonists of the Counter-Reformation and the *Nouveaux Pyrrhoniens*. Writers such as François de Sales, Jacques du Perron, and Robert Bellarmine (the last two both cardinals), the Jesuits François Veron and Gontery were drawing, for the argumentation wherewith to support their case, on the school of fideistic scepticism that had been enjoying much success since the publication of the *Hypotyposes* of Sextus Empiricus in Paris in 1562; they were glad enough to lay such resources under contribution in their endeavour to combat the spread of Calvinism, which had struck strong roots in the soil of their country. See Popkin, ibid., pp. 67–88.

[37] *Apud* Limborch, *De Veritate Rel. Christ.*, p. 136: '... nulla demonstratione Mosis Prophetiam divinam esse, contra Ethnicum probare posse: quippe id demonstrabile non est. Sicuti si Deum ipsum negaverit ejus existentiam demonstrative convincere nec possem.'

The Intellectual World of Isaac Orobio de Castro

supernatural matters, attaining as it does to but a modest knowledge of matters natural: rather, it can but comprehend the possibility of their existence'.[38] Disputational dialogue is possible between Jews and Christians alone, since both accept the actuality of the Sinaitic event as a matter of faith. For either to engage in debate with a party that denies Moses' prophetic inspiration would, according to Orobio, be a pointless exercise; since in the absence of belief in prophecy, which is the one and only means designed and attuned to the revelation of religious truths, there is no possibility of obtaining knowledge of the Godhead.[39] In his *Academias Morales* the crypto-Jewish poet Antonio Enríquez Gómez wrote:

> Where, lacking knowledge, should I go, to seek
> What no one yet found clear before his eyes,
> Whilst doubting that I live, for all I speak,
> How wish that I could reach what sight denies?[40]

Man, in Isaac Orobio's view, has not the capacity to grasp by his reason the quality of the Godhead, nor can he understand the meaning of eternal life. Human reason being limited by its very nature, since it is embedded in man's physical materiality, it is not equipped through any potentialities of its own to achieve certain knowledge: and the only

---

[38] *Epíst. Inv.*, MS Amsterdam, *EH* 48 D 6, f. 339ʳ: 'Es asi que no puede nuestro entendimiento comprehender las cosas sobrenaturales, pues apenas consigue un mediocre conocimiento de las naturales, mas bien comprehende su posibilidad...'

[39] *Apud* Limborch (n. 37 above), p. 137. In his *Prev. Div.* (MS Amsterdam, *EH* 48 B 13, pp. 1 f.) Orobio goes so far as to say that since the cessation of prophecy in Israel the Jewish people have lost all certain knowledge of matters esoteric, and of the mystic quality of scripture: '... es infalible que desde que el Señor bolvio el rostro de nosotros, desde que suspendio la communicacion e influencia Profetica, falto juntamente, esta exacta noticia de lo abdito, de lo recondito, de lo misterioso de el Sacro Texto; aunque el desseo de saber aliente cada dia a los humanos entendimientos, para querer vencer esta dificultad, y conseguir lo que es inaccessible, tropeçando unos, y otros, cayendo en varias y vanas, que son el fruto de nuestra atrevida Naturaleza.'

[40] *Academias Morales*, p. 156 ('Albano a la incapacidad del juizio humano'): '... Adonde voy sin ciencia, procurando / lo que ninguno pudo hallar visible / si aun yo dudo si vivo, estando hablando / Capaz me quiero hacer de lo invisible?' The poem was first printed in Bordeaux in 1642. Its author was born into a crypto-Jewish family at Segovia c.1600. After prolonged service in the army, in the course of which he attained the rank of captain, he settled in France together with his son, Diego Enríquez Basurto, and it was there that he published the main part of his *œuvre*. He was condemned by the Inquisition, and, being beyond the confines of Spain, he was burned in effigy at the *auto-da-fé* celebrated at Seville on 13 Apr. 1660. There are grounds for supposing that he was subsequently arrested and that he died in an inquisitional prison-house in 1662—but this (if it is in fact the case) did not prevent the publication of his works in Spain in the 18th cent. See Révah, *Marranes*, pp. 50 f., 71 f.

cure for man's ignorance is the Torah.⁴¹ That function which for the fideistic sceptics within Catholicism was fulfilled by the Church, is for Orobio fulfilled by the oral Law and the additional prohibitions by which the rabbis 'fenced' the *written* Torah. There is no type of activity in which man is not prone to make mistakes; and since God is concerned that Israel should implement the precepts of the Law correctly, an oral explication necessarily had to be delivered together with the written text of the Law.⁴²

Isaac Orobio's axiomatic postulates tell us less about the universe of discourse from which they derive, or of any clearly crystallized, systematic philosophy of his own, than they do about his application of them as a weapon wherewith to attack his Calvinistic controversialists. This is particularly clear in his disputation with Limborch. Examination of what the latter has to say throws a spotlight on the differences between the two parties to the conversation. The Remonstrant theologian reveals his links with the Protestant approach that rejected any need to rely upon ecclesiastical authority, and replaced it by the responsibility that it laid upon the individual conscience. Limborch is not prepared to accept Orobio's view that it is impossible to prove the existence of God to non-believers; belief in the prophecy of Moses is not the primary precondition for recognizing the existence of God and attaining knowledge of Him, but rather the straightforward application of the intelligence (*recta ratio*) which is the common heritage of all humanity.⁴³

⁴¹ *Epíst. Inv.*, MS Paris (n. 28 above), p. 685: 'porque el alma racional, sumergida desde su origen en la grosera materialidad del cuerpo humano, no participo sciencia o noticias algunas de la poderosa mano de su Criador, ni puede conseguirlas hasta que, por extrinseca enseñança se le communiquen por los interiores y exteriores sentidos. Es pues, la Doctrina el unico remedio para que el intendimiento humano combalezca del ignominioso achaque de la ignorancia.'

⁴² Ibid., p. 769: '... digo que no era possible, sin variar y prevertir grandemente el orden de la naturaleza, poner Dios el Sagrado Texto en tal disposicion y clareza que no necessitasse de explicacion para su intelligencia y, consiguientemente, fue presiso [sic] conservar la tradicicion [sic] el desvelo de los estudiosos Sabios Isrraelitas en los passados siglos y en el presente ...'; p. 767: '... los Sabios ... con sus interpretaciones y recivida tradicion, han sido siempre firme muralla a la conservacion de la Ley de Moseh, en la mayor y mas dilatada dispersion que nunca previno el juicio humano ...'

⁴³ *Apud* Limborch (n. 37 above), p. 168: 'Et sicut Lex Christiano et Iudaeo est communis ita et recta ratio omnibus Christiano, Iudaeo et Ethnico, communis est ...' There can be no doubt that the predominant influence behind this assertion is what Descartes wrote at the beginning of his *Discours de la méthode* (1637): 'Good sense is of all things in the world the most equally distributed ... it seems ... to be evidence in support of the view that the power of forming a good judgment and of distinguishing the true from the false, which is properly speaking what is called Good sense or Reason, is

The Intellectual World of Isaac Orobio de Castro

It is obvious that some of Orobio's claims for scepticism are rooted in medieval Neoplatonic religious thought; and if the influence upon him of the *Nouveaux Pyrrhoniens* is to be observed, the impress of the Augustinian school may be felt more powerful still. But it should not be forgotten that amongst the factors that prepared the ground for the spread of fideistic scepticism in western Europe (and especially in France) Augustinianism was one.[44]

Orobio's scepticism was not limited to the question of obtaining certainty in the recognition of religious truth, but also involved certainty in science. The final chapter of his *Respuesta Apologética* against Zepeda is entitled 'Criticism of the excessive faith reposed by the Commentator [Zepeda] in the processes of Chemistry'. In it Isaac sharply attacks Zepeda's attachment to the hermetic tradition, whilst equally assailing belief in the unlimited power of chemical science. In his view, chemistry is not only incapable of solving questions regarding the nature of man, as those who believe in its power boast that it can: but it may actually occasion 'most serious damage and pitiful forms of death'. Chemistry likewise exercises a baneful influence on science in general, which because of it was, in his time, turning into 'an empiricism at once over-bold, false, and dangerous'.[45]

Orobio found an authority to support his line in Henricus Cornelius Agrippa von Nettesheim (1486?–1535), who in his *De incertitudine et vanitate scientiarum declamatio invectiva ex postrema authoris recognitione*

---

by nature equal in all men' (*Philosophical Works of Descartes*, trans. Elizabeth S. Haldane and G. R. T. Ross, Cambridge, 1911, i, p. 81). On Descartes as the 'conqueror of scepticism' see Popkin, *Scepticism Erasmus–Descartes*, pp. 175 f. Limborch, however, stresses that revelation is a *sine qua non* for the attainment of recognition of those things which human reason is not equipped to arrive at unaided; see his introd. (unpaginated): 'cum enim revelatio ad ea solum necessaria supponatur, quae ratio per se ex principiis mere naturalibus assequi non potest.'

[44] See Popkin, ibid., p. 68.

[45] The chapter is itself headed 'Censurase la grande fee que tiene el comentador con las operaciones chimicas' (*Resp. al Zep.*, MS Amsterdam, *EH* 48 A 12, ff. 208^r–210^r. See f. 208^v f: '. . . porque negar que de algunas separaciones sacamos remedios utiles y de que usa la Medicina fuera mentir, mas que ay alguno tan eficaz como prometen los chimicos, que haga admirables efectos y remedie toda indisposicion de nuestra afligida naturaleza es vanidad fabulosa; antes bien gravissimos daños y muertes lastimosas que causaron hombres arrastrados de la vana confiansa de sus remedios chimicos, que condenaron los doctores serios de nuestro tiempo, porque con essas casi diabolicas preparaciones a degenerado la sciencia en una atrebida, falsa y peligrosa empirica.' On the Hermetic stream in European thought in the 16th–17th cents. see Thomas, pp. 266 f., and cf. F. A. Yates, *Giordano Bruno and the Hermetic Tradition*, London, 1964; id., 'The Hermetic Tradition in Renaissance Science,' in C. S. Singleton, ed., *Art, Science and History in the Renaissance Science*, Baltimore, 1967, pp. 265–70.

was one of the earliest in the sixteenth century to disparage the capacity of man to attain knowledge. His book was an outspoken debunking of all scientific and other forms of intellectual endeavour which, in the author's view, represent no more than unreliable, human opinion. In the chapter to which we have referred Orobio praises the 'eloquent, penetrating' Cornelius Agrippa, and directs Zepeda's attention to the German sceptic's work.[46]

Similar scepticism in regard to the possibility of intellectual knowledge in general is to be found in the writings of both crypto-Jewish and Jewish Spanish and Portuguese authors of the seventeenth century. Antonio Enríquez Gómez vents his disillusionment with not only theological and philosophical speculation, but also with medical and astrological studies: 'having found that there are so many opinions regarding every science, my understanding bade me rather cleave to the good and forswear all discussion: and thus, through having come to feel that I was done for, I found my salvation in the higher wisdom'.[47] Isaac Cardoso, too, in his *Excelencias de los Hebreos*, exposes the fallacy of 'philosophy that lacks certainty, medicine of dubious efficacy, the deceitfulness of astrology, chemistry with its mass of delusions, and the mysteriousness of magic'.[48] Y. H. Yerushalmi finds it perplexing to reconcile the aged Cardoso's diatribe with his earlier professional activity as a practising physician and author of books on medicine and philosophy. The explanation which he proposes seems somewhat forced. He argues that, in his old age, Cardoso underwent a metamorphosis in which he exchanged the stance of Maimonides for that of Judah Ha-Levi.[49] But it may be surmised that the inner contradiction to which Yerushalmi points is based in the opposing tendencies that struggled for supremacy in Cardoso's eclectic mind and psychology, subjected as he was to the conflicting influences of traditional scholasticism on the one side and the processes of sceptical thought on the other.[50] Such oscillation in Cardoso, Orobio, and their

---

[46] *Resp. al Zep.* (n. 45 above), f. 209ʳ: 'mas tambien lo explica el agudissimo y eloquente Cornelio Agripa ... y hace de el candidamente el juicio que le parecio verdadero en el Libr. de Vanitate S.' For the place of Cornelius Agrippa in Renaissance thought see Nauert, pp. 116 f., and cf. Popkin, *Scepticism Erasmus–Descartes*, pp. 22 f.

[47] Enríquez Gómez (n. 40 above), p. 262.

[48] Isaac Cardoso, *Excel.*, p. 135.

[49] See Yerushalmi, *Isaac Cardoso*, p. 371.

[50] See my review-article on Yerushalmi's *Isaac Cardoso*, in *Kirjat Sefer*, 48, 5733 (1973), p. 673 (in Hebrew). Cardoso's links with believing scepticism are clearer than Orobio's; he was well enough acquainted with the works of Gassendi. See Cardoso's *Philos.*, pp. 18 f.

The Intellectual World of Isaac Orobio de Castro   321

compeers indicates a spiritual confusion which affected many intellectuals, both Christian and Sephardi Jewish, in western Europe. They found it difficult to effect a compromise between the conflicting conceptual endeavours that crowded the intellectual universe of the seventeenth century. Their openness to every newly minted idea that gained currency in the contemporary world of philosopy exceeded their capacity to decide in favour of one, unequivocal course, or to construct for themselves syntheses that would be simultaneously both consistent and crystal-clear in their design. That is the principal cause of the eclecticism that characterized the thinking of so many of them; and in this respect Orobio typifies the spiritual situation of a whole community.

To be sure, Orobio had been educated in the Spanish culture within whose heavens neo-scholasticism was the dominant star. But in Spain, too, in the words of Otis H. Green, scepticism had its small band of spiritual brethren. Thinkers such as the Jesuit José d'Acosta were advancing sceptical arguments as to the possibility of human reason attaining knowledge which were similar to those that were being aired by contemporary French sceptics.[51] Moreover, at least two of the outstanding sceptical thinkers in the sixteenth and seventeenth centuries were of Sephardi stock. Michel de Montaigne (1533–92) was the son of a Sephardi 'New Christian' mother belonging to the López family of Calatayud, many members of which had apostatized at the beginning of the sixteenth century.[52] The second, Francisco Sánchez, came of Portuguese 'New Christians' who had settled in Bordeaux from fear of persecution by the Inquisition.[53] This does not justify far-reaching conclusions as to links between the crypto-Jewish community and sceptical thought, but it does show that some of them at any rate found in scepticism a spiritual refuge from the conceptual constraints inherent in their situation. Sánchez, who was one of those that laid the foundations of the school, had taught in the medical school of the university of Toulouse from 1611 to 1621; and one may assume that when Orobio was teaching there from 1660 to 1662 he would have had the opportunity to get to know the writings of the fellow-countryman of his in whom the university took so much pride.[54] In Toulouse he could not only have had access to the work of one of the most important

---

[51] Green, ii, pp. 182–8.
[52] See C. Roth, *Michel de Montaigne*.
[53] Popkin, *Scepticism Erasmus–Descartes*, pp. 45 f.
[54] On Orobio's Toulouse period see above, chap. 5, pp. 97 f.

harbingers of fideistic scepticism, but he may quite possibly have met those who were carrying on the tradition. At all events, his own leanings towards scepticism may well have been crystallizing while he was living there.

POLITICAL AND SOCIAL ATTITUDES

The Portuguese Jews of Amsterdam also derived their political and social views from the contemporary Spanish thinkers whose books were found on the shelves of their libraries. Although these Portuguese Jews were not called upon in their communal life to address themselves to practical political problems (and apart from Spinoza, none of them produced an articulated theory of political philosophy), in their writings they did sometimes have resort to political and social concepts that derived from contemporary Spanish writing which dealt with the subject.

Abraham Israel Pereyra launched a bitter attack on the political philosophy of Machiavelli, whom he labels 'divisive', 'corrupt', 'accursed', 'despicable', etc.[55] In his two works Pereyra contrasts the 'divine, Jewish political system' with the 'satanic political system of Machiavelli'.[56] Machiavelli's disciples are, according to him, 'politicians (or rather plotters of impiety) who separate reasons of state from the most holy Law'.[57] If one reads the indictment which Pereyra brings to bear on the Florentine political philosopher with such outspokenness, one is bound to ask oneself what it was that prompted this well-to-do Amsterdam merchant to devote two books to stigmatizing a political system in the contents of which it is difficult to find any point of contact with the social realities in which the members of his own congregation found themselves. Who could the disciples of Machiavelli have been, on whom he was pouring out his accumulated fury?

In the passages cited Pereyra clearly intended to expose certain views and patterns of thought that were widely current within his own community. Those politicians who 'wear sheep's clothing, whilst sowing that venomous seed wherewith they slay and tear to pieces the

---

[55] Pereyra, *Certeza*, p. 81; *Espejo*, pp. 395 f., 408 f.
[56] *Certeza*, p. 81: '... por querernos acomodar la politica divina, y judayca, a la diabólica de Machiavelo ...'
[57] *Espejo*, p. 396: 'Y estos Políticos (por mejor dezir impios) apartan la razón de estado de la Ley Santíssima ...'

flock of the Lord like wolves'[58] are none other than those Jews who 'teach the art of government as if divine providence had nought to do with them, and as if the world governs itself at fortune's whim'.[59] Following Machiavelli, they 'deny the immortality of the soul, and reward and punishment'.[60]

There can be no doubt that Pereyra's language was aimed specifically at Spinoza and Prado. For all that the congregation had put them at arm's length, Pereyra was nevertheless sensitive in regard to the continuing influence of their ideas. His intention finds palpable expression in the following sentence: 'this world is but barren ground, a field full of thistles and thorns [*abrojos y espinos*], a green meadow [*prado*] full of poisonous serpents'.[61] By means of this wordplay Pereyra made it unequivocally obvious just who were the wolves that endangered the peace of the flock of God's pasturing, viz. those who were teaching that divine providence did not direct human behaviour or guide the destiny of history.

Pereyra derived his ideas from seventeenth-century Spanish political thought, one of the principal characteristics of which was the stubborn struggle against the machiavellianism which it viewed as the absolute negation of the idea of the Christian state, morally bound above all other aims to implement the religious values upon which it was based.[62] He transcribes whole passages from the writings of Pedro de Rivadeneyra and Claudio Clemente, removing from them the specifically Christian import and introducing in its place a Jewish content.[63]

Isaac Orobio behaved in a similar way. In his *Prevenciones Divinas* he indicated his own aloofness from the 'common herd', the 'rabble', and from the 'tempestuous notions of the vulgar, from which empty credence in legendary fancies has ever derived its origin and firm

---

[58] Ibid.: '. . . y vestidos de piel de oveja, siembran este tan inficionado veneno, conque matan y despedaçan como Lobos el ganado del Señor.'

[59] Ibid.: '. . . Y este el Iudaismo que observan, los que leen en su contagiosa doctrina enseñando a governar, como si Dios no tuviesse providencia con ellos, y el Mundo se governasse acaso . . .'

[60] Ibid.: '. . . negando la inmortalidad del Alma; el premio y el castigo . . .'

[61] *Certeza*, p. 29: 'Que es este mundo, sino tierra esteril, campo lleno de abrojos y espinos, prado verde lleno de serpientes venenosas.'

[62] See Maravall, *Teoría del estado*.

[63] P. Rivadeneyra, *Tratado de la Religión y virtudes que debe tener el Príncipe cristiano para gobernar y conservar sus Estados. Contra lo que Nicolás de Maquiavelo y los políticos de este tiempo enseñan*, Madrid, 1595; C. Clemente, *El Machiavelismo degollado por la Christiana sabiduria de España y Austria*, Alcalá de Henares, 1637. Cf. Pereyra, *Espejo*, pp. 408 f.

endorsement, the masses being an unbridled monster'.[64] These words occur in a disputation with a Catholic theologian; and Orobio's purpose here was to assail Christianity as being, in his view, a product of the 'rabble' that mutinied against the constitutional leadership of the sages, who had been entrusted by a heavenly providence with the authority to decide on action, and to pronounce judgement in matters of law.[65] This whole approach, and the concepts which it subsumes, is the corner-stone of Iberian political writing of the period, and there can be no doubt that Orobio was influenced by it.[66]

The same influence can be distinctly felt in the attitude of the membership of the Amsterdam Portuguese community towards the proselytes to Judaism who joined their congregation. The Portuguese community did not fall over itself to open wide its doors to strangers who expressed the wish to join it; and it would seem that on each separate occasion they instituted detailed and meticulous enquiries into the origin of the applicant and his motives. We should not forget that they were dealing with unknown parties arriving in the Netherlands and it was hardly an idle fancy to suspect that amongst such there might be potentially disruptive and even hostile elements. But most important of all was the ideological consideration that controlled the whole principle of their attitude towards converts. Since it was the case that the Jewish people had been qualitatively distinguished from the Gentiles, the process of conversion was not capable of effecting a qualitative change in the convert himself.[67] This notion had had its adherents amongst some medieval Jewish scholars, and it finds clear expression in the thought of Isaac Orobio: 'the covenant between God and the children of Israel, as being the seed of Abraham, Israel being not a spiritual entity but a people, for better or for worse . . .'[68] In another passage we find an even clearer expression of what constitutes the uniqueness of Israel and its special relationship to God, as compared with the unique character and relationship of converts to Judaism: 'neither in times past, nor today, are those who voluntarily

---

[64] *Prev. Div.* (MS Amsterdam, *EH* 48 D 6), f. 16ᵛ: '. . . las tumultuosas opiniones de los vulgares, entre quien tubieron siempre su origen . . . y su segura aprouacion las fabulosas superticiones, siendo el vulgo desenfrenado monstruo . . .'

[65] Ibid., also f. 22ʳ.

[66] See V. Mut, *El Príncipe en la guerra y en la paz*, Madrid, 1640, pp. 18 f.: 'Los facinerosos son los incentivos de discordias, creyendo asegurarse y ser temidos por aquel camino . . .' Cf. Maravall, *Teoría del estado*, pp. 358 f.

[6] On a similar approach amongst some of the medieval Jewish writers cf. Katz, *Exclusiveness*, pp. 146 f.

[68] See his *Resp. Pred. franc.*, MS Amsterdam, *EH* 48 D 6, f. 307ʳ.

The Intellectual World of Isaac Orobio de Castro 325

take upon themselves the fulfilment of the Mosaic Law called Israelites, but rather proselytes; and so the holy book styles them in bidding us behave towards them as brothers, without however conferring on them the honorable name [*honroso nombre*] of the "house of Israel" — until, that is, in the course of generations they have become utterly assimilated amongst the individual members of the people ...'[69] It is no accident that Isaac has resort here to the notion of *honour*, which he no doubt derived from the concepts which characterized the Spanish world from the fifteenth to the seventeenth centuries: a period in which, in Spain, *honra* and *hidalguía* came to be values of major cultural and social consequence.[70] These concepts came to be implicitly compounded with the categories of 'purity' and 'completeness' as descriptions of ancestral origin of exclusively 'old Christian' descent (*Christianos viejos*), as opposed to 'New Christian' forebears of Jewish or Islamic origin. It is one of the ironies of history that those who had escaped from the Inquisition, themselves victims of ordinances concerning *limpieza de sangre*, carried with them the outlook that prevailed in the land of their birth, and internalized within their own *Weltanschauung* the concepts of *honra* and *hidalguía*. In the writings of Isaac Cardoso of Verona, Orobio's contemporary who, like him, had escaped from Spain to revert openly to Judaism, we likewise find clear and unequivocal indication of this 'Spanish heritage':

> We seek to reach a clear understanding about the thinking which leaves Jews unconcerned to persuade the Gentiles to accept their Law: for why should they come to involve themselves in such an undertaking? Certainly not in order to acquire title to nobility or glory, for the Hebrews are the noblest stock of all, and their pedigree the most ancient ... because of their antiquity, their election, their purity, and their separateness, the Jews are the noblest nation on the face of the earth.[71]

Thus it was that the political and social thinking of Spain found its way into the writings of the Jews of Amsterdam, to become integrated as part and parcel of their heritage.

[69] See *Prev. Div.* (n. 64 above), f. 141ʳ.
[70] See above, chap. 6, pp. 173 f.
[71] Isaac Cardoso, *Excel.*, p. 364.

12
From Crypto-Judaism to Open Judaism

A NEW JEWISH PERSPECTIVE ON *CONVERSO* LIFE

The majority of the Portuguese congregation of Amsterdam in the seventeenth century had either themselves been crypto-Jews, or were the children of such, who had reverted to the open profession of Judaism and had subjected themselves to the discipline of the kingdom of heaven as Judaism understands it. It was consequently natural that the problem of crypto-Judaism loomed large at the very nerve-centre of their being, and unceasingly preoccupied their consciences. Many of them had personally experienced life as crypto-Jews in the Iberian peninsula, where they had been constrained to deny their faith and people, and in outward appearance to conform to the beliefs and practices of Christianity. After they had joined the Jewish community they continued to apply their minds to the phenomenon of forced conversion, its causes, effects, and influence, and to trace out its religious and historical significance.

The problem—a sensitive one, in all conscience—was intensified by the practicalities of the situation and its concrete issues. The very large crypto-Jewish community still remaining in Spain and Portugal throughout the seventeenth century included kinsfolk, both close and more distant, of those who had reverted to open Judaism elsewhere; the flight of crypto-Jews from the peninsula was a continuous one; and, on their escape thence, both they and the host community had to face the problems attendant upon their reversion to Judaism and absorption into the various communities of the Sephardi Jewish diaspora.

No one, of course, will dispute the assertion that crypto-Jews did not constitute a monolithic homogeneity. Immediately after the anti-Jewish outrages of 1391 Rabbi Isaac b. Shesheth Perfet, better known acronymically as *Ribash*, acknowledged the intensity of the impact of the crypto-Jewish problem in drawing up his own distinctions between different types. Some of them, he declared, 'after their enforced conversion to Christianity, despite the fact that they had originally acquiesced under duress, have subsequently thrown off all traditional links with the Torah and have repudiated the sovereignty of God, in that they voluntarily assimilate themselves into Gentile ways and transgress all the commandments of the Torah. Not even content with that, they actually harass those amongst their own number who have retained their Jewish loyalties, by denouncing them: in order to destroy Jewish peoplehood altogether, and to eliminate all vestiges of identity associated with the name of Israel. And as for those crypto-Jews who, clinging steadfastly to their faith, endeavour to get out of the land where they have suffered persecution—these miscreants betray them to the government.' As opposed to this type, said Isaac b. Shesheth, there were 'others who would give heart and soul to get themselves beyond the reach of persecution, but they are unable to do so since they have not the means to meet the very considerable expenses involved in getting their wives and families out with them . . .'[1]

This distinction by Isaac b. Shesheth clearly holds good for subsequent generations, even after the expulsion of 1492 and the decree of forced conversion enacted in Portugal in 1497, when the problem of the crypto-Jews became more intense as the numbers of those involved increased.

There survive a number of *responsa* dealing with points of Jewish law concerning the question of crypto-Jews in the Iberian peninsula. These legal opinions were drawn up by rabbis within Spain itself and, after the expulsion, in the Sephardi diaspora. There is much material of historical significance in them in regard to crypto-Jewish problems and the relations obtaining between *conversos* and Jews whose integrity was uncompromised by pro forma conversion. Rich, however, though this material is, it is not of its nature to give the whole picture of the attitude of both Sephardi rabbis and the lay leadership to the problem, let alone the approach adopted by their rank and file. All that the rabbis were concerned to do in their *responsa* was to define the status of crypto-Jews from the point of view of Halakhah, or Jewish canon law—not that the practical problems that they were called upon to deal with were not poignant ones: problems of widows, and grasswidows, integrating into the Jewish community whose residual matrimonial obligations towards those left behind in the peninsula had, if legally possible, to be severed, so as to permit them a reconstructed life in which they could begin a new page.[2]

---

[1] Isaac B. Shesheth, §11. On this *responsum* see Assaf, *'Anusey Sepharad*, pp. 53 f.; Zimmels, pp. 15, 22, 42, 45; Netanyahu, *Marranos*, pp. 29 f.

[2] For crypto-Jewish concerns dealt with in the *responsa* literature see the works cited in the previous note, and cf. Yerushalmi's critique of Netanyahu's working method in his

Seventeenth-century rabbinical *responsa*, too, refer to 'crypto-Jews by descent who have forsaken the Lord and have forgotten Him', alongside those 'whose spirit God had awakened' preventing their complete abandonment of the traditional precepts and prompting them actually to 'reveal some of those precepts to their children'.[3] Rabbi Saul Levi Mortera identified two categorically distinct types: (*a*) 'those resident in realms where they are not only precluded from observing the Law, but also prevented by frontier control from emigrating thence'; and (*b*) 'those resident in realms emigration from which is not precluded, but who can leave without let or hindrance and proceed whithersoever they want'. To these classes Rabbi Mortera added a third category, of those 'sons of the Jewish people who, though Christians at heart, acknowledge their Jewishness even though they are unlike Jews, out of terror or physical torture and risk of losing their life ... this being the effect of the sheer unpredictability of the inquisitional tribunal in which the blood of so many is shed: for they see clearly how [the whole machine] compels them, in violence of their conscience, to admit to being what they are in fact not.'[4]

Isaac Cardoso, pp. 24–31, and similarly A. A. Sicroff, 'The Marranos—Forced Converts or Apostates', *Midstream*, Oct. 1966, pp. 71–5; G. D. Cohen, *JSS* 29, 1967, pp. 178–84.

[3] See Mortera's *responsum* in the *collectaneum* of rabbinical *responsa* from Palestine, Turkey, the Levant, and Italy, MS Jerusalem, University Library, Heb. 8° 2001, f. 164ʳ f. On this *responsum* see F. Kupfer, *Przeglad Orientalistycny*, Warsaw, 1955, pp. 97–9, and Kaplan, *Mortera*, pp. 16 f. See also Sasportas, *Resp.*, §59, f. 64ᵛ, and Samuel Aboab, §45, f. 18ᵛ.

[4] See Mortera, *Clérigo de Ruan*, MS Amsterdam, *EH* 48 C 9 (unpaginated). Of the 3 categories of crypto-Jew here listed, it was (in Mortera's view) those in the first category only that would qualify for salvation, and this thanks solely to the divine mercy that takes into consideration human weakness and because God 'sees that their souls are predisposed to serve Him, as experience has caused many to note' ('... y todavia siendo el Señor misericordioso y luengo de furores, considerando la flaquesa humana y los grandes aprietos de estos persiguidos en aquellas tierras, mitiga su rigor y los favorese viendo sus animas dispuestas a servirlo como la esperiençia lo tiene mostrado a muchos'). H. P. Salomon was the first to deal with this item of Mortera's *œuvre*, using MS Amsterdam, *EH* 48 D 38, in his *Mortera*, pp. 135 f., but his conclusions as to its implications are entirely misconceived. It is not the case, as Salomon contended, that one may deduce from what Mortera wrote that 'crypto-Jews at the end of the 16th and beginning of the 17th centuries no longer had any links with Jewish religious obligations.' Accordingly, this disposes of Salomon's endevour to find support in Mortera for the theory of Saraiva, according to which the Portuguese Inquisition was nothing more than a charade, the object of which was not to wear down the 'Judaism' of the crypto-Jews, but merely to expropriate their possessions. Mortera expressly states that there are two categories of crypto-Jews who consider themselves held to Judaism by a bond, but that of these it is (in his opinion) those in the first category only who qualify for salvation, since it does not lie in their power to escape from 'the lands of idolatry'. The second category are condemned to eternal punishment—not because of any alienation from

The fear of the Inquisition was indeed real enough even amongst many who had themselves severed all connections with Judaism. They were regarded with suspicion by the authorities, for a systematic study of the many case records preserved in the files of the Spanish and the Portuguese Inquisitions, and an understanding of the processes by which thousands of crypto-Jews left both countries in the sixteenth and seventeenth centuries, leave no doubt that many *conversos* had secretly maintained a link with Judaism despite the severe dangers that lurked around them.[5]

Such information as we have from rabbinical sources regarding the emigration of crypto-Jews from the Iberian peninsula and their return to the bosom of Judaism can be materially supplemented from literary productions of the Portuguese community of Amsterdam in the seventeenth century, in particular from sources written in Spanish and Portuguese. These writings provide an insight into the spiritual world of Isaac Orobio, helping us establish his own position, and that of his contemporaries, on the crypto-Jewish problem. Because of the restricted character, indicated above, of the rabbinic sources, the intimate personal insights preserved in the literary writings of the lay membership of the congregations in the Sephardi diaspora acquire a historical importance of the first order. These glimpses can tell us something of their value-judgements and ideological approach to the various factors of which the crypto-Jewish problem was compounded, and can help us to understand the profound psychological conflicts occasioned by their close involvement in the problem.

In his *Carta Apologética* to Juan de Prado, Isaac Orobio described his own crypto-Jewish past, laying open his heart with great ingenuousness: '... in Spain I presented a Christian appearance, since life is sweet; but I was never very good at it, and so it came out that I was in fact a Jew. If, then, whilst I was there, confronted with the risk of [loss

---

Judaism on their part, but because of their remaining in their domicile despite the circumstance that nothing whatsoever precluded their leaving it. The importance of the third category is inflated by Salomon, who purports to represent it as being typical of the mass of crypto-Jews; but, from the citation given above, it is clear that that was not the drift of Mortera's argument. This is not an isolated instance of Salomon's endeavour to prove, at all costs, the essential aloofness of crypto-Jews in the Iberian peninsula in the 16th and 17th cents. from Judaism: see his prolegomenon to C. Roth's *Marranos*[4], pp. vii–xix, and his articles *Reply to Cranganore*, *Portuguese Inquisition*, and *De Pinto MS*.

[5] For the latent potentialities, in regard to Jewish history, of a systematic exploitation of the inquisitional records, see Beinart, *on Trial*; also the following other works by Beinart, *Te'udoth, 'Inq. ḥus. Sepharad, Ciudad Real*, pp. i–ii, *Conversos, Yeṣi'ath 'anusim*. Also Révah, *Marranes, Hérésie Marrane*.

of my] freedom, status, property, and indeed life itself, I was in reality a Jew and a Christian merely in outward appearance, common sense shows that in a domicile where providence from above affords me a life of freedom, a true Jew is what I shall be.'[6] And writing in his *Epístola Invectiva* of his own past and that of crypto-Jewish members of his circle of friends in Spain, he said: 'we dissembled our faith, and although the sin of one who conceals truth or denies it is unforgivable, not all of us were aware that it was in fact our duty to affirm it . . .'[7]

Return to Judaism was, in Orobio's case, to be sure, accompanied by remorse as to his 'Christian' past and the way of life that enforced conformity had imposed upon him, just as it was in the case of others who reverted to Judaism. A moving expression of the deep-felt sentiments of those returning to the Jewish fold at this period is to be found in a sonnet entitled *Words of a penitent Sinner*, of which the author was Daniel Levi (Miguel) de Barrios:

> Lord, not with tears shall I wash clean the stain
> That robs my soul of sunlight from thy face:
> I feel my errors more, the crass disgrace
> Of folly, if to plaints I give no rein,
> Thy liege at last, thy praises my refrain,
> Whilst, humbled now, salvation's road I chase:
> To fate's fell hand did I, blind, risk my case—
> Errant, seduced, in serfdom to remain.
>
> Contrite, in Thee I trust: yet all my mind
> Makes known before Thee how, mid Barbary
> Of sin, its galley-slave am I confined.
> Have mercy, Lord, for from myself I flee,
> Striving, self-ownership through grace resigned
> To gain the glory to belong to Thee.[8]

---

[6] *Cart. Apol.*, MS Paris, BN Fonds éspagnoles 41, p. 881.

[7] *Epíst. Inv.*, introd. (in MS Amsterdam, *EH* 48 A 23: '. . . Es assi que disimulabamos lo que creyamos y aun que ese crimen de selar la verdad, o negarla no admite escuza no todos sabiamos la obligacion de confessarla . . .'

[8] De Barrios, *Flor*, p. 203: 'No con llanto (Señor) la mancha labo / que al alma priva de tu Sol divino / por que mi error, mi grave desatino / lo siento mas si de llorar no acabo / Ya humilde, te obedezco, ya ta alabo / y de la salvacion busco el camino; / ciego me expuse el [*sic*] barbaro destino / del yerro que me yerra por su esclavo. / En este del pecado Argel impio, / me confieso ante ti captivo suyo; / mas que en mi contricion en ti confio. / Piedad (Señor) que de mi propio huyo, / procurando en tu gracia no ser mio / por merezer la gloria de ser tuyo.' The poem was reprinted, without change, in de Barrios' *Coro*, p. 521. For the anguish felt by crypto-Jews in regard to their continued residence in Christian (i.e. Catholic) lands, see also Joseph Ha-Kohen, *'Emeq Ha-B.*, p. 100, where Solomon Molcho is quoted as saying 'for the period during which I

From Crypto-Judaism to Open Judaism

While reproaching themselves for their outwardly Christian past, Isaac Orobio and others, who shared both his congregational membership and his earlier experiences, recognized those crypto-Jews still remaining in the Iberian peninsula as Jews. Therefore, in the fullest sense, their own people's past, its present hopes, and its ultimate aspirations still belonged to these crypto-Jews. Isaac invariably refers to them as 'Israel' (*Israelitas, hijos de Israel*) or as 'Jews' (*judíos*), and it is clear that he looked upon the crypto-Jewish community as an integral part of the house of Israel.[9] One of the questions (referred to in an earlier chapter) that he addressed to Rabbi Moses Raphael d'Aguilar reflects his concern for the situation of crypto-Jews as regards the hereafter. In that question, the crypto-Jew is defined as 'a Jew born and educated amongst Gentiles'.[10] As Orobio would have it, the gates of salvation are open to such a one: since those who do not in point of fact believe in the Torah, but maintain the semblance of such belief while implementing its commandments, are themselves more guilty than those who do believe but are precluded from implementation by their own human weakness. 'One who affirms [to himself] his belief, but, out of frailty, does not observe, deserves his Creator's wrath but is not excluded from his mercy.'[11] He goes further: the highest degree of the love of God is, for him, achieved by the victims of the Inquisition, the 'Jews' of Spain and Portugal who, year after year, submit to being sent to the stake, their entire will being to glorify God's name and to testify to their love of Him. The death of such he defines as martyrdom,[12] and this view of it was not unusual among his fellow-congregants in Amsterdam. In Daniel Levi de Barrios' play *No power against Truth*, when speaking of the crypto-Jews of Spain Truth is made to say: 'take for an example those who live constantly in the presence of God and die for their love of me'.[13] Jacob Abudiente, too,

---

conducted myself in conformity with that religion, my heart is beset with storms of bitter regret', indicating that this sentiment was already widespread in the 16th cent. See also Joseph Ha-Kohen, *Hist.*, ff. 95ᵛ–96ʳ.

[9] See e.g. his *Prev. Div.*, MS Amsterdam, *EH* 48 D 6, f. 70ʳ, and similarly *apud* Limborch, *De Veritate Rel. Christ.*, p. 61, and many other passages in Orobio's writings.

[10] See above, chap. 6, pp. 116 f.

[11] See *Epist. Inv.*, MS Paris, BN Fonds éspagnoles 41, p. 726: 'Mas el que la afirma, el que la cree y, por su fragilidad, no observa, digno es de la irra [*sic*] del Criador, mas no excluydo de su Misericordia.'

[12] See *Resp. Pred. franc.*, MS Amsterdam, *EH* 48 D 6, f. 294ʳ: 'Este grado de amor han tenido y tienen muchos Hebreos que dan su vida por la Gloria de Dios y se dexan quemar bivos ... y en España muchos Iudios todos los años en la Inquesicion [*sic*] de Portugal y España, a quien offresen la vida.'   [13] *Contra Verdad*, p. 54.

in his discourse in memory of Abraham Núñez Bernal and Isaac d'Almeida, burnt at the inquisitional stake in Córdoba in 1655, picks up the same theme: 'these men demonstrated that in their hearts there reigned the perfect love of God, in paying to Him the tribute of the greatest courtesy [*finesa*] of which men are capable, in offering their own lives for the honour of his holy name; by such an act, they have brought glory to their God and lustre to their stock, and have increased the treasury of merit of the chosen people'.[14]

Yet this intimate psychological bond with the plight of the crypto-Jews, and readiness to recognize them as constituting a limb of the body of the Jewish people, did not mean the turning of a blind eye to the serious religious implications of their day-to-day existence in which, through force of circumstances, they had to make obeisance before images of wood and stone and to present to the world a Christian front. An anonymous tribute to Abraham Núñez Bernal includes the following passage:

> Thy soul sinned not, for praise she did sustain
> Of one, sole God in secret: ne'er to kneel,
> Or turn to what is base, staunch, did she deign . . .
> Henceforth let no Jew think fond hopes are real
> That, though he worship idols deified,
> A blest hereafter waits for him to gain.
> Unless with mind steadfast on faith applied
> As thine was, he confesses God his Lord,
> From heaven far he lives, its bliss denied:
> Whoso salvation seeks from things adored
> As idols, reason's sovran law denies,
> From craven custom turning not aside . . .[15]

Isaac Orobio himself, for all that he considered crypto-Jews an integral element in his people's solidarity, did not close his eyes to the fact that

---

[14] *Elogios*, p. 169: '. . . mostraron reynar en ellos el perfecto amor de Dios, hasiendo por el, la mayor finesa que se puede considerar en los humanos, entregando sus propias vidas al sacrificio, por la honra de su sancto nombre, con cuya accion glorificaron su Dios, ilustraron su linage, multiplicaron el caudal de los merecimientos del pueblo electo . . .' For Bernal see C. Roth, *A. Núñez Bernal*, pp. 38–51.

[15] *Elogios*, p. 60: 'Tu alma no peccò, porque en lo oculto / Solo un Dios adorava, que tu zelo, / jamas se arrodillò, al turpe vulto / . . . No conciba de aqui vana esperança / Aquel Israelita idolatrante, / Que le aguarda la bienaventurança. / Que si con zelo y animo constante, / No confiessa a su Dios como tu hiziste, / Del cielo y de su bien vive distante. / A la razon legitima resiste, / El que salvarse quiere idolatrando, / Si del abito torpe no desiste . . .'

From Crypto-Judaism to Open Judaism 333

they were sunk in a form of idolatry the like of which, in his view, Jewish history had never seen.[16]

Abraham Israel Pereyra's approach is even sharper, in that he disallows any distinction between the innermost intention of the crypto-Jew and his outward behaviour. 'As for the delusive assumption', he writes, 'of those who imagine that a good heart and fair intention suffice—that is how the fiend effects his distortion, making sophists of them to their own hurt.'[17] In making that assertion he disqualified the opinion current among not a few crypto-Jews that 'whosoever keeps his inner self distinct from the face that he shows to the world, his real actions being kept within for fear of the Gentiles, is exempt from heavenly condemnation'.[18]

The seventeenth-century Amsterdam rabbis were divided in their views as to what punishment in the hereafter awaited those crypto-Jews who died without throwing off the mask of Christianity and openly reverting to their ancestral religion. Rabbi Isaac Aboab da Fonseca had been the disciple of the cabbalist Rabbi Abraham Cohen de Herrera, who had claimed that 'all Israel are a single body, their soul quarried from the very location of the divine unity—whence the old rabbinic dictum "all Israel are responsible for each other"'.[19] Aboab himself expounded the rabbinic principle that 'a Jew, even though he sins, remains a Jew'[20] as meaning that 'even though he sins, he will not for that reason be cut off from the tree in perpetuity: to be sure, he is a Jew, and although he may have exchanged his God for false gods of his own choice, yet will he come to be called by the name of Jew once more through a series of reincarnations and punishments, all this being in accord with justice, as we have explained'.[21]

As against Aboab's assertion that life in the hereafter is assured for

---

[16] See *Prev. Div.*, MS Amsterdam, *EH* 48 B 13, p. 6: '. . . esta abominable creencia y sacrilega idolatria . . . la mayor que pudo inventar le humana malicia . . .'

[17] Pereyra, *Espejo*, pp. 558 f.: 'Y en quanto a la falsa suposición que toman de que basta buen coraçon, y la buena intencion, es obra del atorcedor q' les constituye por sabios para su mal . . .'

[18] See Samuel Aboab, §45, f. 18ᵛ.

[19] Babylonian Talmud, *Shevu'oth* 39a *infra*, etc. See Isaac Aboab, *NH*, MS Manchester, John Rylands Library, Heb. 5; cited from Altmann's critical edition ('Eternal Punishment'), p. 81. Altmann deals in detail with the controversy between Isaac Aboab and Mortera on the subject of eternal punishment. For Isaac Aboab see Meijer, *Enc.*, i, pp. 11–14.

[20] Babylonian Talmud, *Sanhedrin* 44a. Regarding the vicissitudes of the Halakhic validity of this adage see Katz, *Yisra'el she-ḥaṭa*, pp. 203–17.

[21] Isaac Aboab, *NḤ* (n. 19 above), p. 88.

those crypto-Jews who had not, in this life, reverted to the practice of Judaism, after they had undergone a process of spiritual purgatory effected through punishment and reincarnation, Rabbi Saul Levi Mortera declared that 'it is a denial of God to believe that these very grave sinners will not be subjected to eternal punishment',[22] and that 'theirs is but a vain trust in salvation who say that, since they are of the stock of Israel, no absolute ill can touch them'.[23] In Mortera's view, the attitude of Aboab is not only contrary to the view of earlier and the more recent rabbinic juridical authorities, but it is liable to put a stumbling-block in the path of those crypto-Jews who, in biblical phraseology, ' "are settled on their lees"[24] in the lands of their enemies, day by day "sailing along like clouds, flying like doves to their dovecotes";[25] for should any such notion reach their ears, not one of them would leave his domicile, and things would go on as ever before—and alack for the one who would prove to have been instrumental in causing this . . .'[26]

In his poem *A Letter to one Following Tortuous Paths* addressed, beyond doubt, to a crypto-Jew who had not yet reverted to Judaism, de Barrios described the situation of crypto-Jews, cut off from a nourishing soil since lacking roots in both Jewish and Christian society:

> Thou by one folk unwanted must remain
> Since thou, from them, dost hold thyself apart:
> The other cannot meet in trust thy heart
> Since they have seen that thou art used to feign.[27]

For the poet, therefore, there is but one counsel to offer:

> As victor leave this world, and bear thy palm
> If, ere the peace of death, dost seek thy way
> Towards the sacred shores . . . this vain display
> Self-metamorphosed, leave behind, and calm

---

[22] Mortera's Hebrew *Proposition that whosoever bears the name of Jew will not suffer eternal punishment even though he has committed all the gravest possible sins* is included in the Manchester MS (n. 19), ff. 1ʳ–4ʳ; Altmann, p. 41.

[23] Ibid., ed. Altmann, p. 50.

[24] Jer. 48: 11.

[25] Isa. 60: 8.

[26] Mortera, ibid., ed. Altmann, p. 50, and cf. Mortera's reply to the Christian cleric of Rouen (n. 4 above). For d'Aguilar's views on the matter see above, p. 117.

[27] De Barrios, *Triumpho* (copy in Amsterdam, *EH* 20 E 61), pp. 409–12: 'Con un Pueblo estas mal quisto / por lo que te apartas del: / otro no te juzga fiel, / por lo que fingir te ha visto.'

Set thou thy course to where truth's light doth shine
From spheres in Hebrew heavens riding high . . .
Let love of God thy being sanctify,
Because thy face turns to his house divine.[28]

And indeed, the Portuguese Jews devoted much unremitting effort to the restoring of crypto-Jews to their rightful home in Jewry. In evidence before the Inquisitional tribunal in Madrid on 15 May 1635, Esteban de Arias de Fonseca gave a detailed description of the ways in which they had endeavoured to win him back to the Jewish religion:

In [Pamplona] he had met Miguel Fernandes de Fonseca, a Portuguese, who was at the time domiciled in Bordeaux, but of whom he had later heard that he was living within the kingdom of Spain, at Cádiz. He took him back with him to Bordeaux. On their journey, and also subsequently to their reaching that city, he convinced him that he should reject the religion of our Lord Jesus of Nazareth and transfer [his allegiance] to the religion of Moses, that being the true religion by which he might be saved. By means of these words, and influenced by others urged upon him by Dr Duarte Enríquez, deceased, his brother Miguel Gómez Bravo, the *licenciado* Diego Barbosa, Miguel Gómez Vittoria, and Manuel de Serra, brother of Fernando de Montesinos, all of them at the material time residents of Bordeaux, having become convinced that he was a Jew, he was about to return to Spain a second time. He requested some support from them for his journey, but this they refused to produce unless he would first proceed to Amsterdam in Holland, where he had kinsfolk: they told him that those there would subvent him, and that he would be able to proceed thence to [Spain], and might go as seemed best to him. By the influence that they brought to bear they convinced him that before making the journey he should be circumcised, since were he to perish at sea he would not qualify for salvation if he were not a Jew, and that it would be good to bear God's token on his person. It was thus that he came to embark, and had arrived at Amsterdam some nine or ten years previously, where he encountered a number of his kinsfolk, including Lope Ramírez, Francisco Ramírez Pina, Duarte Núñez da Costa . . . all being his kin. They received him with great joy, and told him that it was [part of] God's wondrous deeds that He led home to Judaism, along routes not to be imagined, those living amid the blindness of the Christian religion. Forthwith they began to address themselves to preparing him to become a Jew and to have him circumcised, since [they stated] that he had been born of a mother of Jewish descent. When he saw

[28] Ibid.: '. . . saldras del Mundo con palma / si antes de la mortal calma / buscas las sacras riberas / . . . dexa pomposas quimeras: / y assi con seguridad / daras luz de las [*sic*] verdad / en las judaycas espheras / . . . Torna a la Casa Divina / con amante coraçon . . .'

what was going on, he was unwilling to submit to circumcision or to become a Jew. They then introduced him to the group around a certain rabbi named Mortera, a preacher of the Law of Moses, in order that the latter might convince him to fulfil [the obligations of that religion]. After he had spent more than six months with him and they had realized that it lay beyond their power to convince him, they imposed the sentence of excommunication upon him in the synagogue, declaring that no Jew should be in contact with him or talk to him. When this state of affairs had lasted some fifteen or sixteen days, without anyone either conversing with him or giving him any assistance, he approached [them] and agreed to be circumcised. When the operation was performed they gave him the name David: the surgery had been carried out by Isaac Farhi, alias Antonio de Aguilar, whom the witness had seen eight days earlier in Madrid. The sole purpose of his coming there had been to carry out circumcisions both there and elsewhere in Spain, he being adept at performing the operation; and by engaging in that calling he was making a lot of money, since they paid him well . . .[29]

It is doubtful whether we can rely upon all the details in the foregoing testimony, since it is that of a crypto-Jew speaking after his voluntary return to Spain where he was seeking to purge himself, and to represent his Judaizing in Amsterdam as having been something forced upon him against his will. But there is, no doubt, enough in it to indicate the collective endeavour of the Portuguese community in Amsterdam—and likewise that of the still crypto-Jewish communities centred in the south of France—to bring back their errant brethren to the Torah of Moses. It is clear that the Portuguese Jewish community set great store by the circumcision of crypto-Jews, in which it saw, on the one hand, a symbol of the individual's strength of purpose in reverting to the Jewish religion, and, on the other, a means of deterring him from returning to 'the lands of idolatry' where exposure of the fact that he had been circumcised could put his life in jeopardy. There were even occasions when they sent Jewish surgeons into Spain itself in order there to initiate crypto-Jews into the Covenant of Abraham by circumcision, despite the risks attendant upon such an undertaking.[30]

---

[29] Madrid, AHN, Inquisition section, Toledo, 142 no. 6, ff. 39ʳ–42ᵛ, file of the investigation of Francisco Mendes Brito, son of Jorge Rodríguez da Costa, Canciller de la Santa Cruzada, resident in Madrid. The trial dragged on from 1653 to 1657, and in the course of it he was tortured and condemned to be burned.

[30] Cf. Beinart, *Ben saloniqi*, p. 195, recording how Isaac Benzemero, a Jew from Salonika, spent some time in Spain in the middle of the 17th cent., and possibly circumcised there sundry crypto-Jews who had so requested. There were also cases of crypto-Jews performing the operation on themselves. Such was the case of don Lope de Vera y Alarcón, born into an aristocratic family of old Christian stock, who, whilst confined in

A significant proportion of the literary output of the Amsterdam Jews was intended to serve this same communal endeavour of restoring crypto-Jews to Israel's Torah. Various apologetic tracts, designed to dispose of Christian contentions against Judaism, were composed with an eye to the crypto-Jewish community and in particular those of them who, having got away from Spain, preferred to remain in southern France or in Antwerp, far from the prying eyes of the Inquisition, and yet to go on living behind a mask of Catholic conformity.[31] In a moving plea to the crypto-Jews of Bayonne Rabbi Moses Raphael d'Aguilar wrote: 'flee away, flee away, haste you from this your Babylon, and come to find medicament that shall procure your salvation; for it is something that rests upon your own will, and it is within your power to achieve it'.[32]

As stated above, Isaac Orobio claimed that in Spain he had 'presented a Christian face to the world, because life is sweet'. As against this, Abraham Israel Pereyra declined to entertain any justification whatsoever for crypto-Jews remaining in the Iberian peninsula on grounds of economic or social convenience:

Let us not be so cruel [to our true selves] and, for the sake of anything involving mere transient, financial interest, or out of fearfulness for our loss of wealth, put at risk what is our own essential concern. A man is in duty bound to give up everything that he has for [the salvation of] his soul, even as the king of Sodom said—for all that he was but himself a worshipper of idols—'Give me the "soul" [in context it means, however, "persons"] and keep for thyself the [plundered] property' (Genesis 14: 21). But we are wont to invert this, and say to our enemies 'take ye the souls and give us the property'. The cause for the continued residence of those domiciled in such places springs not, as we know full well, from lack of will for what is good and true, but from lack of capacity to attain by use of reason to a proper appreciation of the grave responsibility which is cast upon them . . .[33]

His heart grieves for those of his community who, after having returned to the bosom of Israel and having been educated within

---

an inquisitional gaol, 'requested that he be brought some lamp chops, apparently for his dinner; but he threw away the meat, and whetted the bone on some stone. He then proceeded to tie a thread round his own prepuce, and circumcised himself.' See Isaac Cardoso, *Excel.*, p. 363.

[31] See Kaplan, *d'Aguilar*, pp. 98 f., and *Mortera*, pp. 30 f. In my opinion Isaac Cardoso's *Excel.* was inspired by the same motive.

[32] D'Aguilar, *Reposta e discurso sobre certas perguntas de Bayona*, MS Amsterdam, *EH* 48 A 11, ff. 425 f.

[33] Pereyra, *Espejo*, pp. 560 f.

Judaism, forsake secure shores and 'go forth to seek their fortune within the realm of idolatry'.[34] This phenomenon, which at various times reached sizeable proportions, engaged the concern of the leadership of the Portuguese community. In 1644 they enacted a measure that obliged any member who, having gone back to 'idolatrous parts', subsequently returned to Amsterdam, to go before the ark in the synagogue and formally to seek pardon *coram populo*. The measure likewise precluded them from occupying any congregational office during the first four years after their return.[35]

It is an inescapable fact that the attitude of the Portuguese Jews of Amsterdam towards crypto-Jews was an ambivalent one. On one hand, they entertained no doubts as to their belonging to the collective identity of Israel, and indeed they placed those who had died at the inquisitional stake on a par with the martyrs of Jewish history. On the other, they were not prepared to condone continued crypto-Jewish residence in the Iberian peninsula or in other places where they were not at liberty to revert to the open profession of Judaism; and they declined to manufacture any excuses at all that could justify the actions of those who, being domiciled in 'the lands of idolatry', continued the practice of a Christianity viewed as 'paganism'.

Even those who, having escaped from Spain and Portugal, had become integrated into the Jewish community, did not succeed in expunging from their conscience the stain on their past by means of a mere gesture in which it was acknowledged. 'It is only by means of the most profound remorse', wrote Abraham Israel Pereyra, 'that I may escape from the falsehood in which I was sunk. But alack! so deeply engrained is it in my being ... that it is with difficulty that I can emancipate myself from the corrupt opinions which had imposed themselves upon me.'[36] 'Use your intelligence and your will-power; and, if you have already succeeded in escaping from the hazards of the Inquisition and have come to worship the Lord, shake yourself free of weakness [of resolution]: for it will condemn you—not to four years' imprisonment [i.e. by the Inquisition], but to imprisonment for those hundreds of years of purgatorial torment, of which the most severe

---

[34] Pereyra, *Certeza*, p. 62: '... como experimentamos cada dia, que muchos nascidos y criados en judaismo, por falta desta confiança, buelvan las espaldas à Dios, yendo a buscar su remedio a tierra de ydolatria.'

[35] See the congregational *Ascamoth (Acta)*, Amsterdam, AGA, PA 334 no. 19, p. 172, and see above, p. 224, for the penalty imposed on de Barrios in 1665 for having disregarded the prohibition and having resided for extended periods in Brussels, then under Spanish rule. [36] *Espejo*, p. 10.

From Crypto-Judaism to Open Judaism   339

would be God's hiding his face from you.'[37] Penitence, however, could annul the divine decree; a crypto-Jew returning to the bosom of the Torah is called upon to achieve a state of sincere repentance, and to see in the attaining of it the primary object of his life. One may surmise that when, in 1665, a wave of penitential intensity swept through the Portuguese congregation of Amsterdam at the time of the Sabbatean awakening, its roots lay in the striving of ex-crypto-Jews to atone for the sins that they had committed earlier on, during the time when they had been living as Christians.[38]

The literary work of Isaac Orobio and of fellow-members of his community likewise reveals an attitude towards the place of crypto-Judaism in Jewish history, and the object that a philosophy of Jewish history might assign to it. In refuting Christian claims of the divine rejection of Israel because of their refusal to accept the gospel of Jesus, Orobio advances a counter-claim:

> It is possible that, on account of the great numbers of this people [of Israel] who have violated the covenant which they made with God, and have accepted popish Christianity, [the Jews] have to endure this long drawn out exile; since it is the case that in all generations countless Jewish families have joined the popish church, and there is not an abbey in Spain wherein those of Jewish origin are not to be found, and the same applies to the [secular] clergy, and even amongst the very inquisitors. All [*sic*] have their origin from this nation or are linked thereto; and similarly in the case of nearly all families in Portugal, many also in France, and numberless instances in Italy ... As long as so many sons of the Jewish people persevere in this form of paganism, the people will have to go on suffering the vicissitudes of exile. And since to this very day many indeed are those Jews who worship the abject and impure abominations of Christian paganism, and follow the forms of its reprehensible rites, who will make so bold as to maintain that this people does not deserve to bear all the weight of its sufferings, or that it is not responsible, in its entirety, for this protracted state of sinfulness?[39]

It is clear that Isaac's diatribe is aimed primarily at crypto-Jews in the Iberian peninsula: these constituted a symbol of the continued existence of idolatry within Jewry. Nor is he alone in maintaining this view. It is also to be found in the writings of a number of members of his community who, like him, saw in the phenomenon of crypto-Judaism the implementation of the dire warning (Deuteronomy 28: 26)

---
[37] Ibid., p. 435.
[38] See above, chap. 8, p. 209.
[39] *Resp. Pred. franc.*, MS Amsterdam, *EH* 48 D 6, ff. 304ʳ f.

'there you will worship other gods, gods of wood and stone' (New English Bible). When Isaac Aboab da Fonseca came to expound this verse, he wrote: ' "may the Lord give you up, you and the king whom you have appointed, to a nation neither you nor your fathers have known" — as happened at the [end of] the period of the first temple; "and there you will worship other gods, gods of wood and stone" — as experience has proved in the Spanish lands and in other places.'[40] Rabbi Isaac Nahar also touched on this forecast in the course of his exegesis of Isaiah 53: '. . . there are to be found today countless numbers of the seed of Israel in many a place beneath the rule of tyrannical princes who offer to idols that worship which ought to be the prerogative of God alone, thereby fulfilling [the prophecy (Deuteronomy 28: 64) "the Lord will scatter you] amongst all the peoples from one end of the earth to the other", "and there you will worship other gods, gods of wood and stone".'[41] On the link between this commination and crypto-Jewish existence in Spain de Barrios allows himself to be even more explicit:

In Deuteronomy 28: 64 f. is described the horrendous fate in which there have been caught up the Jews in the Spanish extremity of the [old] world, whence they have been driven into exile to many a region at differing periods of time, from the time of King Pirro [Pyrrhus] who led them captive to the city and district of Asta[42] (known today as Jerez) at the end of the earth. 'And the Lord

[40] Isaac Aboab, *Pent.*, p. 607.

[41] Nahar, *Muestrase como el capitulo 53 de Isaias no trata del Hombre que ellos tienen por Messias y se absuelven los argumentos q' el escritor propone contra la verdadera explicación*, MS Amsterdam, *EH* 48 C 24, p. 31: '. . . se hallan oy inumerables de la simiente de Israel en muchos lugares que estan baxo el tiranico imperio de los Principes atribuyendo a los Idolos el culto que solo se deve a D[io]s donde se cumple en todos los Pueblos de Cabo de la tierra y hasta cabo de la tierra, . . .' On Nahar see Brugmans and Frank, pp. 267, 283, 664, 671, 676; for his part in the Sabbatean ferment in Amsterdam see Scholem, *Sabbatai Ṣevi*, Eng. trans. pp. 465, 488, 522, 529, 532, 541, 577–9, 755, 760–1. For his medical studies at Leiden see Kaplan, *Studenṭim be-leiden*, pp. 68 f.

[42] The legend of the antiquity of Jewish settlement in Spain is to be found in Solomon ibn Verga, pp. 33 f. According to this, 'Pyrrhus', a Greek king, was son-in-law of king '<H>isp[i]anus', the eponymous ancestor of the Spaniards. Hispanus, as senior of Nebuchadnezzar's vassals, was assigned from the spoils of Jerusalem that area where members of the house of David lived. 'This Pyrrhus got together ships, and transported all these captives of Old Spain, i.e. Andalusia, and to the city of Toledo, whence they were dispersed—for there were many of them, too many for one [part of the] land to contain. Some of the seed royal proceeded to Seville, and thence also to Granada . . .' Asta was founded (or refounded) by the Romans: see *Diccionario Geográfico de España*, v, Madrid, 1958, p. 577. None of the non-Jewish Spanish chronicles that describe the beginnings of Jewish settlement in Spain mention a Jewish presence there in even late antiquity: see e.g. the *Refundición de la crónica de 1344*, or the *Historia de España* by the Jesuit Juan de Mariana. For the traditions regarding the first coming of the Jews to Spain see Beinart, *Cuándo llegaron*, pp. 5 f.

From Crypto-Judaism to Open Judaism

will scatter you among all the peoples, etc.' Despite the fact that to outward appearances they worship images, they for ever live in a state of panic, in terror of the cruel Inquisition . . .'[43]

Elsewhere he states:

The ones who acknowledge that they have gone to meet the Lord are they that feel remorse for [having compounded with] idolatry, proclaiming the unity of God and dying the death of martyrs. In Deuteronomy 28, 65 are foretold the frightful events, the occasions of terror and of scarifying panic that have affected those who have professed Judaism in the dread *autos* [*da fé*] in Castile and Portugal: 'among those nations you will find no peace, no rest for the sole of your foot. Then the Lord will give you an unquiet mind, dim eyes, and failing appetite. Your life will hang continually in suspense, fear will beset you night and day, and you will find no security all your life long. Every morning you will say, "Would God it were evening!", and every evening, "Would God it were morning!", for the fear that lives in your heart and the sights that you see' [vv. 65–7]. There, amidst the grim constables [*familiares*] [of the Inquisition], the terror-struck sons of Moses must needs make feigned show of ceremonious prostration in front of images, whilst in their abject misery seeking the God of truth who, with justice, inflicts upon them the penalty of enforced idolatry in a foreign land, because in their own land they had worshipped other idols of their own free will'[44] . . . ' "[gods of] wood and stone" refers to the cross' . . . ' "They sacrificed to foreign demons that are no gods, gods who were strangers to them; they took up with new gods from their neighbours, gods whom your fathers did not acknowledge" (Deuteronomy 32: 17): the *demons* are the *familiares*—this same word being applied to demons [*familiar*, as also in English, cf. *familiar spirit*]—who stab Jews in their very soul with the sword and olive-branch [i.e. the inquisitional emblem]; also meant are those who, having been cast into the frightful dungeons, make confession and so entrap others that they, too, may fall, as it says in the fourth [*sic*] book of the Pentateuch (Leviticus 26: 36–8), 'when a leaf flutters behind them in the wind, they shall run as if it were the sword behind them; they shall fall with no one in pursuit. Though no one pursues them they shall stumble over one another, as if the sword were behind them, and there shall be no stand made against the enemy. You shall meet your end among the heathen, and your enemies' land shall swallow you up.'[45]

In the sequel he expatiates on a point in this last verse:

Those who *perish* [New English Bible 'meet your end'] refers to none other than the ones who make semblance of following the laws of the Church, for *abad* [the Spanish word for *abbot*] means, in the holy language, *perish* [*'abad*].

---
[43] De Barrios, *Triumpho* (copy in Amsterdam, *EH* 2 F 81), p. 422.
[44] De Barrios, *Metros*, p. 242, 'Realse de la Prophezia y caida del Atheismo'.
[45] Ibid., p. 241.

Those 'perished' are the clergy; and the soil of Spain devours the Jews, since everyone who professes Judaism is called a sinful miscreant. 'New Christians' is the sobriquet given to those of the sons of Moses who remain in Portugal, who in the multitude of their afflictions 'confess their iniquity, their own and their fathers''; but it is all a feigned confession. For in their hearts they continue faithful to Judaism, and so it is that the holy King adjured them, 'those who are left shall pine away in an enemy land under their own iniquities; and with their fathers' iniquities upon them too, they shall pine away as they did. But though they confess their iniquity, their own and their fathers', their treachery, and even their defiance of Me, I shall defy them in my turn' (vv. 39–40).[46] 'Yet if then their stubborn spirit is broken . . . I will remember' (vv. 41 f.) . . . in the lands to which they go forth from Portugal they succeed in openly implementing the Law of Moses, the observance of which the cruel inquisitors dub 'sin'. That is the 'sin' for which, above all, the children have to give satisfaction, even as the prophecy in the book of Leviticus (26: 41) reads, 'they accept their punishment in full'.[47]

Confirmation of the view that the prophets of ancient Israel had in view the phenomenon of crypto-Judaism and the persecution of the Inquisition was discovered in Isaiah 53. Verse 7, 'he was afflicted, he submitted to be struck down, and did not open his mouth' (New English Bible), was expounded by Isaac Nahar as follows:

Our exposition will not seem in any way problematic to one who is familiar with the sorry state of the people which is not permitted to utter a single word in reply to its oppressors, in particular those of them who are to be found beneath the yoke of the Inquisition.[48]

On v. 9, 'he was assigned a grave with the wicked', Rabbi Moses Raphael d'Aguilar commented:

'The grave of the wicked' cannot be other than the graves of those who, over many generations, have been butchered by the inquisitional tribunal; for after their bodies have been reduced to ashes, they make public cry about them as though they were but carrion, devoid of rights, respect, and titles of dignity, condemned by ceremonious proclamation in the sight of the rabble that gather to hear it all, as having been heretics and infidels.[49]

We have noted above that Abraham Michael Cardoso formulated a theory of messianism according to which the messiah, against his own will, would be forced into a situation in which he could not fulfil the

---

[46] Ibid.   [47] Ibid., p. 246.   [48] Nahar (n. 41 above), p. 38.
[49] Moses d'Aguilar, *Explicasão do Cap. 53 de Yesaias, feita no Brazil*, MS Amsterdam, EH 48 A 11, f. 878.

Torah, and, through suffering that penalty, would atone for the sins of Israel's collective personality: and we have already observed that behind this assertion of his lay the wish to furnish crypto-Jewish life with a religious, and indeed a messianic significance.[50] It is beyond doubt that a similar intention is to be descried between the lines of the comments and discourses of the Amsterdam rabbis to whom we have here referred. But, unlike Cardoso, according to whose messianic theory 'the essence of the *mysterium* is that we are all obligated by the Torah to become crypto-Jews before we can go forth from exile',[51] these rabbis saw the crypto-Jews of the Iberian peninsula as embodying the realization of the biblical commination, in that in them was fulfilled the text 'there you will worship other gods, gods of wood and stone'. The crypto-Jews, willy-nilly, were turning out to be the fulfilment of a mission for the whole of the Jewish people—the mission of implementing a 'meritorious deed brought about by means of transgression' (*miṣwah ha-ba'ah ba-'averah*), in default of which redemption could not take place. It would appear that the return of the crypto-Jews to the Jewish fold was construed, in their consciousness as Jews, as symbolizing the beginning of the redemptive process. In those who were getting out of Spain and reintegrating themselves into the Jewish community, they were witnessing the fulfilment of Ezekiel (20: 39) 'in days to come you will never ... desecrate my name with your gifts and your idolatries' (New English Bible). Commenting upon that verse, Rabbi Isaac Nahar wrote:

Until there is fulfilled that which Ezekiel prophesied, viz. that not for any merit of ours, but rather for the sake of God's name that is profaned amongst the Gentiles; when, that is, that the time will come which was decreed by his divine judgement—and then shall we go forth from this protracted exile ...[52]

THE JEWISH WORLD: FROM DREAMS TO REALITY

In a valedictory discourse pronounced by Moses Zurreño in the Rotterdam synagogue in 1698 prior to his departure for Palestine, he rendered thanks to heavenly providence for his redemption from the idolatry in which he had been sunk in the Iberian peninsula, 'and for

---

[50] See above, chap. 8, pp. 212 f.   [51] See Sasportas, *Ṣiṣ. N. Ṣ.*, ed. Tishby, p. 293.
[52] Nahar (n. 41 above): 'Hasta que se cumpla lo que vaticina Ezequiel que no por nuestros merecim[ien]tos y mas por el nombre de Dios profanado entre las gentes quando llegare el tiempo decretado por su divino juizio entonces saldremos desta dilatada cautividad ...'

setting me amongst men of piety, righteous men . . . nor had I occasion to miss my parents' (he blithely proclaimed) 'for every Jew proved a father to me . . .'[53] Zurreño, a former crypto-Jew who had been absorbed into the Portuguese-Jewish community in Holland, regarded the fact of his return as constituting an absolute break with his whole Christian past. The poet Daniel Levi (Miguel) de Barrios, too, in a moving confession declared that ever since returning to Judaism he had felt himself to be a different person.[54] Details of some interest have been preserved for us concerning the circumstances of Abraham Israel Pereyra's return to Judaism, in what Rabbi Moses Raphael d'Aguilar wrote about him:

> This noble gentleman arrived from Spain, bringing with him but such over-simplified and clouded knowledge regarding the truth of our holy Law as those lands make it possible to attain. He came here, to a place where it is permitted to implement it and to teach it in sufficient freedom: but he was already of adult years, at which age the learning of the holy tongue proved for him an arduous and back-breaking task. However, piety being engrained in his innermost nature, he first of all began by taking his place, with sustained regularity, at sessions of the academies, listening with close attention to the words of the Law to which utterance was given there, and learning about our teaching from books on [the Jewish] faith. In this way he accumulated a valuable treasure-house of holy wisdom . . . but this gentleman, with all the generosity towards which he is inclined, was not satisfied in learning merely on his own account, but endeavoured to make others his partners in his devoted studies, for 'it is not good for man to be alone' . . . For this purpose he gave up all worldly concerns, forswearing common talk and devoting himself to an internal life of contemplation.[55]

In his own writing, Pereyra set out the programme which, in his opinion, the crypto-Jew aspiring to revert to Judaism was obliged to follow:

---

[53] See Amzalak, *Zurreño*, end (unpaginated): '. . . poniendome en las compañia de los pios y justos . . . no haviendo echado menos a mis padres, pues he tenido en cada Israelita un padre . . .' Amzalak, who prefaced his reprint of Zurreño's *Discurso* with biographical details of the author, did not draw attention to the circumstance, which a reading of the text clearly indicates, that Zurreño had been a crypto-Jew and that his parents had remained within the Iberian peninsula.

[54] De Barrios, *Triumpho* (copy in Amsterdam), Bibl. Rosen., 19 G 12, p. 81: 'No mires a mis inormes culpas, sino a tus puras misericordias; porque ya estoy tan mudado de mi passada vida, que apenas me conozco . . . y assí huyendo de mi mismo al Santuario de tu pura benignidad creo que tu recta justicia no ha de hallarme en aquello que fui, porque ya anhelandote estoy en otro convertido.'

[55] See d'Aguilar's approbation printed at the beginning of Pereyra's *Espejo*.

From Crypto-Judaism to Open Judaism

When you leave the synagogue and go home, you must take the Bible and read some of it . . . during the period of your study devote all your attention thereto, nor read anything else . . . Pause, endeavouring to understand every matter of difficulty, and ask concerning it: establish for yourself, with fixed regularity, an hour of attendance at one of the academies, for that is the true medicament, by means of which you will learn through stating those matters regarding which you are in doubt . . . listen to the answers given by the experts, and thus, in the aforesaid hour, you will bring healing to your soul . . . in this manner you will derive benefit from the dedication and attention that you bring to the study of the Bible and the investigation of other [religious] books. In was in this wise that I myself studied in the Academy of 'Light of Torah' [*Torah 'Or*] with our faithful pastor, the right noble and learned Rabbi Isaac Aboab; I derived much benefit from his learning and from the pleasurable company of the gentlemen and other participants.[56]

For all this, most of those reverting to Judaism could not so easily make the break with the burden of their past, and not all of them burned their bridges with the Catholic world of Spain on which they had turned their backs. In reality, things were far more complex than emerges from what the aforementioned writers had to say. The breach with the past was something involving stupendous efforts and demanding great sacrifice, for which not all of those who were coming home were prepared. Not a few of those returning to their ancestral religion faltered, and some of them actually collapsed under the yoke of the commandments. Uriel d'Acosta grumbled about the protective 'fences' for the Torah erected by the sages, which, according to him, 'were decidedly not a good thing, since they so easily cause people to sin by intent, which is the very essence of transgression'; in his view, the 'fences' had become a Torah in their own right, more demanding than that of Moses, 'and virtually impossible to fulfil'.[57]

Isaac Orobio viewed those crypto-Jews who 'forsake idolatry and emigrate to regions in which liberty is afforded to practise Judaism' as being 'sick with the disease of ignorance', the only appropriate cure for which — the 'holy medicament' — was contact with Judaism.[58] His friend Abraham Israel Pereyra gave a frank description of the psychological crises that he underwent after moving to Amsterdam and openly reverting to the practice of the Torah of Moses:

---

[56] See Pereyra, *Certeza*, p. 266.
[57] See d'Acosta's strictures (in Hebrew, with summary in Portuguese) on Jewish tradition, Gebhardt, *Uriel da Costa*, p. 9.
[58] See *Epíst. Inv.*, MS Amsterdam, *EH* 48 D 6, ff. 326^v f.: 'Los que se retiran de la Idolatria a las provincias donde se permite libertad al judaismo . . . estos vinieron enfermos de ignorancia . . . sanaron, goçando la saludable y Santa Medicina.'

It was with difficulty that I was able to liberate myself from the wry opinions with reference to which I had hitherto orientated myself, for it is a hard thing to cut oneself off from one's roots . . . having secured some competence in the wisdom of secular books, I regarded myself (how crassly!) as wiser than the sages of the Torah . . . when I spoke of them, I did so with scant respect; and my will being set on pleasure, I crammed my mouth full of arguments [whereby I set out] to confound what is blandly straightforward.[59]

As far as concerned any enlightened approach to traditional Judaism, the situation of crypto-Jews escaping from the Iberian peninsula was parlous in the extreme. What knowledge they had in this area was for the most part derived from secondary sources, some of them with a hostile bias, such as the anti-Jewish literature that enjoyed a considerable circulation in the peninsula in the sixteenth and seventeenth centuries. It was not only their restricted intellectual apprehension of things Jewish that rendered the process of their absorption into Jewish society difficult, but also the cultural baggage which they had brought with them from Spain and Portugal, and the Catholic concepts which, in the case of many of them, had been rendered second nature to them by their education in ecclesiastical institutions that were amongst the most fanatically conformist in the contemporary Catholic world.[60]

We have seen above how Isaac Orobio saw in rationalism derived from the universities, which was the cultural heritage of a proportion of ex-crypto-Jews, the principal barrier that deterred some of them from accepting the yoke of Torah and its commandments. A. M. Cardoso, too, came out vehemently against those whose philosophical and scientific education led them to reject the authority of the Talmudic rabbis and prodded them into denial of the truth of Torah.[61] It is quite clear that this generalization as formulated by the two of them is an overstatement, and therefore inaccurate. It was not all of those returning who, having received university education in Spain or Portugal, rejected the sovereign power of Judaism's Halakhic code, or endeavoured to undermine the authority of rabbinic leadership. Isaac Orobio's own case, educated as he had been in the theological school of the university of Alcalá, is eloquent testimony that education in a Catholic univeristy did not invariably impede reintegration into Judaism, identification with its *Weltanschauung*, and submission to the yoke of the commandments of Mosaic Law. At the same time, there is

[59] Pereyra, *Espejo*, p. 100.
[60] Regarding the intellectual comprehension of matters Jewish that was to be found amongst crypto-Jews in the Iberian peninsula, see Beinart, *Conversos*, pp. 465 f., Yerushalmi, *'Anusim ḥozerim*, pp. 201 f. [61] See above, chap. 8, pp. 215 f.

no doubt that Isaac did appreciate the hidden hazards of the scale of values, and other intellectual baggage brought with them by those crypto-Jews who had been introduced to the intellectual world at an academic level in the land of their birth. He understood that some part of Prado's critique of the Jewish religion and rabbinic tradition was rooted in his intellectual background; and possibly he sensed that the seeds of the very same rejectionism were hidden within himself, and that it accordingly rested with him to make great efforts in order to avoid stumbling in the same way that his own erstwhile friend had done. His writings open a window on the struggles with which he was faced, on being confronted in Amsterdam by the world of Judaism. 'To tell the truth', he wrote to Prado, 'with many of the customs, rabbinical *responsa* as to practicalities, and rulings, which do not inherently affect the law of God, my own understanding cannot come to terms, and it rebels at them.'[62] He was likewise aware that certain customs were prevalent within various segments of Jewry which had never been either authenticated by the sages of Israel, or accepted by the majority of Jewish communities. But Orobio, although he did not conceal his perplexity when confronted with the commandments and all their exigencies, found the solution to his difficulties in speculative concepts derived from the school of 'fideistic scepticism' that he had made his own during the time that he spent at the universitites of Alcalá and Toulouse; if, in matters of faith, the sole determinant was the divine categorical imperative, because the human intellect was limited by its very nature, it followed that such difficulties as the intellect might raise in regard to religious tradition were of no significance whatsoever.[63] 'What, then, does it matter if this or that protective "hedge" appears incompatible with the understanding? How important is it if, to us, the prohibition of eating dairy products with poultry does not seem to make sense? . . . Would it be right because of this [lack of understanding] to proceed to violate the sabbath, or stuff oneself with food on the Day of Atonement, or to consume blood?'[64] And, he continues, 'whoso loves [the Torah], whoso believes in it and fears God, will not go

[62] *Cart. Apol.*, pp. 893 f.: 'En la verdad muchas costumbres, respuestas y conclusiones, que no tocan a la misma Ley de Dios, no se ajustan a mi entendimiento y las repugna . . .'

[63] Ibid., p. 889: 'Que uno es lo que dijo Dios, y es lo summamente verdadero, como nacido de la Verdad infinita; y lo otro es hijo del entendimiento humano que puede errar . . .' On the links of Orobio with 'fideistic scepticism', see above, chap. 11, pp. 316 f.

[64] Ibid.: '. . . que importa que mi entendimiento aprehenda impertinente el uso de vno o otro vallado? que importa que se le proponga impropio no usar lacticinios con las aves? . . . Sera bueno yr por esso de carrera a quebrantar Sabat? a hartarse el dia de Kipur? a comer sangre?'

looking for straws of sophistication to justify rejecting it'.[65] The Torah contains no commands that conflict with natural law: it does not enjoin 'the eating of children, or murder, or robbery, but imposes on us some actions which are either both holy and urgently necessary in themselves, or which contain no particular significance', but which can promote obedience and humility in us.[66] For him, nothing amongst the inexplicable items in the Torah affords grounds for desecrating its precepts, 'nor is it a reasonable thing to unsettle other people's peace of mind with such doubts as these, and to induce in them a dubiety from which would ensue consequences of the gravest negative import for the holy Law'.[67] In matters of faith, human reason is inadequate to reach decisions: hence the vital need for some power commanding the ability and the authority to direct the community of the faithful. Isaac acknowledges the legal sanction behind the decisions of the rabbinical sages throughout Israel's history, 'for it is a matter of necessity that at all times the people should be instructed in the Law by sages who have gone deeply into its purport, just as was done in former days by the priests, judges, and prophets; for man is not born with legal expertise'.[68] Whoever maintains that the sages, whom providence has charged with the duty of giving the people instruction in doctrine, deceive or mislead the community, thereby casts aspersions on the Deity itself, since 'for untold centuries God has made use of no other instrument to expound his law and to transmit it, save the sages whose teaching the people follow as being true'.[69]

After refuting the accusations levelled at the Talmud by Christians, Isaac indicated that 'over and above the sublime doctrine and holy recommendations for conduct' that it contains, there are also to be found within it opinions which it is inappropriate to accept and which, indeed, had never been accepted by Israel as a whole.[70] The worth of

[65] Ibid.: 'quien la ama, quien la cree, quien teme a Dios, no anda buscando palillos para dejarla.'   [66] Ibid., p. 893.

[67] Ibid., p. 894; '... ni fuera razon inquietar los animos de los otros con semejantes dudas y persuadirles a que duden, en cuya consequencia se seguirian grandissimos inconvenientes contra la Ley Sagrada ...'

[68] See his *Epíst. Inv.* (n. 58 above), f. 397ʳ.

[69] Ibid.: '... y como fuera deffecto en Dios, que aquellos Prophetas en las passadas edades errasen en la enseñanza, lo fuera tambien en la nuestra, que los Doctores a quien pertenecia dar doctrina, fuesen falsos y superticiosos, pues no uso Dios de otro instrumento para la explicacion y tradicion de su Ley, en tantos siglos, sino solos de estos Sabios cuia doctrina sigue el Pueblo por verdadera ...'

[70] Ibid., f. 397ᵛ: 'Ni se embarace el entendimiento con las noticias de algunas acciones ympropias y dissonantes, que en algunas prouincias, asi septentrionales como de España y Berberia hacen los nuestros, por que estas no fueron jamas deliberadas por nuestros Doctores, ni universalemente recividas en la congregación Israelítica.'

the Talmud is not thereby impugned: *per se*, it is not God's Torah, or indeed God's literary creation, but the creation of mere humanity. And although it is the case that in everything where the holy precepts are involved, and the 'oral tradition received by the sages from their predecessors, ascending to Moses', the Talmud contains no errors, it does contain corruptions in some of its explanations and personal opinions. The Talmudic sages were liable to err, just as 'Plato, Aristotle, and other great philosophers of those centuries erred: Seneca uttered many a false statement, as did also Pliny and others of the outstanding figures among late classical writers. If that is so, why should the Talmudic sages not be equally exposed to error in formulating opinions concerning matters not fundamentally affecting law, but to do with conceptual thought, philosophy, or theology?'[71] Isaac might possibly feel unable to concur with this or that opinion cited in the Talmud or in the name of one or other of the sages, but all such things belong to the sphere of pure opinion, and there is nothing here to compromise the holiness of Torah or to invalidate the fulfilment of its prescriptive precepts. 'What does it matter if Rabbi Moses b. Naḥman, or fifty [Jonathan] b. Uzziels [to whom one of the Jewish Aramaic versions [*targumim*] of the Bible is ascribed] utter more extravagances [*desatinos*] than there are hours in the year?'[72]

It was during his early years of residence in Amsterdam that Isaac Orobio put these reflections and considerations on to paper, i.e. in the first years as a Jew living an open Jewish life within the framework of a full Jewish communal existence. It is natural to compare the foregoing citations with some of the criticisms formulated by Uriel d'Acosta in 1616, at the time when their author was likewise taking his first steps within the Jewish community. D'Acosta, too, took issue with opinions enjoying currency within Jewry that were, in his view, 'not appropriate to be held by anyone bearing the title of Jew, but fit for Gentiles—and not, indeed, any Gentiles, but to the silliest of their number'.[73] Like Orobio, who regarded the Greek philosophers as a prestigious intellectual class with which the sages of the Talmud might legitimately be compared, even so d'Acosta used the 'books of [other] peoples', and the

[71] Ibid., f. 422ʳ.
[72] See *Cart. Apol.*, MS Paris, BN Fonds éspagnoles 41, p. 892: 'Que importa que Arramban y cinquenta Ben Uzieles ayan dicho mas desatinos que oras tiene un año?' I have not noted any other contact with the works of Moses b. Naḥman in Orobio's writings: and it may be supposed that his adducing of Naḥmanides' name, and that of Jonathan b. Uzziel, is merely for general effect, his real object being to point his finger at this (allegedly negative) aspect of the spiritual tradition of rabbinic Judaism throughout its history.   [73] See d'Acosta's strictures (n. 57 above), p. 9.

'laws of the nations' to apply the argument *a fortiori*.[74] But whereas Orobio drew a distinction in Judaism between the realm of laws and commandments and that of ideas and opinions. Only the first of these was binding and not subject to appeal even if defects were discovered within the second. In contrast, d'Acosta found flaws and distortions of truth even in the realm of the Jewish precepts and laws, attributing them to wrong-headed opinions, the legacy of the rabbis and 'also contrary to the ethical good'.[75] Whilst d'Acosta declared invalid the authority of rabbinical leadership and called for reform in the manner of religious life and the observance of the commandments, Isaac demonstratively identified himself with the oral Law and with the authority of the rabbis to pronounce upon it. Unlike d'Acosta, Isaac regarded the 'fences' in a positive light: for him, their sole purpose was to render possible the most complete fulfilment of the precepts, and not, as d'Acosta would have it, 'to pile on top of the Torah another, more burdensome than the original'.[76] Such precautionary 'fences' had been instituted amongst other peoples also, their entire object being to deter men from immoral behaviour. As regards the contention that some of the 'fences' had no connection at all with the precepts of the Torah, but were supplementary injunctions arising out of historical events, such as certain festivals and fasts, Isaac rejoined that such things were 'not in fact "fences" at all, but holy usages and customs deserving of respect and applause, in honour of the Creator and in praise of Him.'[77] Judah Leone da Modena, in his response to the stric-

[74] Ibid., p. 7, Qu. vi, on the *lex talionis*, point no. 6: 'where the laws of the Gentiles involve retaliatory measures, they are not content with monetary penalties [sc. as is the case in rabbinic law], but they require physical ones, sometimes even the death penalty.' Similarly p. 4, Qui. ii, on circumcision: 'if it be claimed that it is justifiable on medical grounds, this is false, for it is not therapeutic, as any doctor of practical experience will confirm; and, if it had indeed been a practice conducive of hygiene, would it not have been publicized as such in Gentile [medical] works?'

[75] Ibid., p. 9.

[76] There are clear indications of d'Acosta's critical attitude towards rabbinic leadership, ibid., p. 8, 'when Solomon saw what a burden the administration of the law entailed, he requested of the Lord an understanding heart in order to judge his people in accordance with God's Torah: he did not judge them according to the oral Torah, but rather through the application of reason in all cases where serious matters were at stake. The public observed this, and were amazed at his wisdom. And since it is the case that the qualities requisite in a judge are the ones which Jethro detailed to Moses [Exodus 18: 21], that, and nothing else but that, constitutes the tradition appropriate to the implementation of the Torah.' For d'Acosta's negative standpoint in regard to precautionary measures, see ibid., p. 9.

[77] *Epíst. Inv.*, MS Amsterdam, *EH* 48 B 12, p. 42: 'De suponerse, para mayor inteligencia, que los Vallados, nunca en Israel se han observado, ni tenido por Decretos

tures of Uriel d'Acosta, insisted that 'the prime foundation in the intention of the divine Torah is that we should observe it in its every detail—each one of us in an identical manner, and not this way and that: otherwise, Israel would not be a single nation'.[78] And so we find Isaac Orobio, in the year 1663 a former crypto-Jewish neophyte in the Jewish community, advancing the same arguments as those which had been put forward by a Venetian rabbi. In his view, the 'republic' was obliged to be punctilious in ensuring that feasts and seasons of mourning common to the whole nation should not be observed by its citizens in a casually variable manner. This uniformity in fulfilment of religious precepts not only demonstrates the superiority of Judaism over a Christiantity fissiparously divided, but it also points, by implication, to God's providential care for his people. Anyone who repudiates a Halakhic ordinance, 'fence', or *ad hoc* enactment established by the sages, thereby imputes impropriety to God who, in his wisdom, had instigated the sages to bequeath the Torah to Israel as their heritage, and to ensure its observance in a uniform manner in all lands of their dispersion.[79]

It is evident that Isaac Orobio unreservedly accepted the rule of Halakhic ordinance and the authority of rabbinic leadership. Nevertheless, between the lines we catch glimpses of his perplexity in face of the world of Jewish beliefs and opinions. We have observed above how in every instance where he encountered any doubts, he referred his problem to the rabbis, 'friends learned in the text of Scripture'. In the same passage Orobio reveals to us that there were instances in which he found the rabbinical replies 'not in the least degree convincing'.[80] It is only reasonable to suppose that not all the beliefs and opinions of the Jewish world and rabbinic tradition would be able to come to terms with the philosophical and theological concepts which still constituted part of his internal world, even after his integration into the Jewish community. We cannot tell from his writings what 'mistaken opinions' of the rabbis of the Talmud aroused his opposition. It seems probable that this critical stance of his elicited

---

divinos; sino por instituciones de los Antiguos Doctores que de tal suerte apartassen al hombre de aquel acto, en que consiste la transgrecion de qualquier precepto . . .' Cf. ibid., p. 46: '. . . santas instituciones y loables costumbres en honra y gloria del criador.'

[78] See Modena, *Mag.*, f. 4ʳ.

[79] *Epíst. Inv.*, pp. 46 f.: '. . . lo qual en las acciones de la República, a que se obliga el concurso de todo el Pueblo; no permite, que se dexe, al arbitrio de cada individuo o particular, el modo de executar y obedecer aquel Decreto.' See also the continuation, pp. 56 f.   [80] See above, chap. 6, p. 110.

no objection or recrimination amongst the rabbinical leadership, which reacted to his criticisms in the same spirit as that displayed by Judah Leone da Modena when, writing from his Venetian domicile in the first quarter of the seventeenth century, he had come out in defence of Dr David Farrar—another crypto-Jew who reverted to Judaism in Amsterdam and was suspected of entertaining heretical views. 'And suppose', he wrote, 'that he does interpret figuratively one of the rabbinical dicta that are not intellectually tenable if taken literally, or if he explains the literal meaning of some biblical text in a way different from that of Rashi and the earlier commentators of blessed memory, is that not exactly what every student of the text and expositor does?'[81] It seems probable that criticisms of this kind were current amongst some of the intellectual strata of the Portuguese community of Amsterdam, such as Dr David Farrar at the beginning of the century and Dr Isaac Orobio during its second half. The rabbinical leadership did not take issue with them, and was happy to close its eyes to their criticisms so long as there was nothing in what they were saying that involved strictures on the implementation of the commandments. Dr David Farrar aroused the admiration of Judah Leone da Modena 'since his forehead was one on which phylacteries are set, and one who dons the fringed-prayer-shawl almost every day; he has refrained from drinking wine and spirits prepared by Gentiles ever since he came to seek refuge beneath God's protection; and he strictly observes rabbinical ordinances which many of those who were duly circumcised on their eighth day, and who teach the Torah in our dwelling places, treat casually or even disregard altogether'.[82] Although the Amsterdam rabbinical authorities have left us no similar indication regarding Isaac Orobio's manner of Jewish living, it may be presumed that his practical regimen was not very different from that of Farrar. Isaac emphasizes time and time again, in different connections, the importance in Judaism of practice, i.e. of fulfilment of the commandments 'to

---

[81] Modena, *Ziq. Yeh.*, §33, pp. 48 f. For David Farrar see Meijer, *Enc.*, ii, pp. 154 f. I. Sonne was of the opinion that Farrar and Uriel d'Acosta belonged to the same circle, and that they were invited to Venice to engage in debate there with Rabbi Emanuel Aboab on matters concerning faith. See Sonne, *Da Costa*, pp. 247 f., and *Leon de Modena*. This suggestion seems to be improbable. Leone da Modena knew both Farrar and d'Acosta well; and whereas towards the former he evinced obvious respect, and could find no flaw in his Jewish integrity, he was at the very same time pillorying the latter as 'an utter sectarian and heretic [*min we-'apiqoros gamur*], in that he has the effrontery to rail against the words of our sages, of blessed memory'. Cf. the terms in which Leone da Modena wrote to the Ma'amad of the Sephardic congregation of Hamburg, *apud* Gebhardt, *Uriel da Costa*, p. 150. [82] Modena, *Ziq. Yeh.*, ibid.

expound the Law with incisive insight, to draw neat parallels in matters of ethics, to refer to [the text] time after time as "holy writ" without fulfilling it, without acting consequentially on it, without observing [its ordinances] exactly according to the terms in which they are prescribed—to do all this is to behave in explicit contradiction to the will of the lawgiver, who did not command us to expound them, but to learn about them in order to fulfil them'.[83] It was in practice that Orobio saw the foundation of Judaism, and in its commandments he saw a superiority to Christianity which, for him, was distinguished as being a religion of mere dogmas and articles of faith.

To be sure, the Catholic-Spanish cultural background of a proportion of those crypto-Jews who had fled from the Iberian peninsula, did constitute a stumbling-block in the way of their integration into Judaism; and not a few of them shied away at a world governed by a round of Halakhic ordinances that represented itself to them as being 'virtually impossible to implement'. But it is just as true to say that another section—and it seems reasonable to conclude that they formed the majority—found in the values and other intellectual baggage that they brought with them from the conceptual world of the peninsula a support in submission to the rule of Halakhic ordinance and the authority of rabbinic Jewish leadership. The 'fideistic scepticism' of which they had made the acquaintance in the days of their residence in Catholic lands predisposed some of them to relate positively to congregational discipline and rabbinical leadership. For such crypto-Jews as these, Isaac Orobio among them, the Jewish way of life—thanks to its practical precepts—showed the way towards religious certainty in a world beset by a crisis of faith and spiritual values.

ISRAEL AND THE GENTILES

Throughout his theological and apologetic writings Isaac Orobio insists on the uniqueness of Israel as God's chosen people. As he saw it, Israel's status as God's elect derived neither from special favour, nor from any divine arbitrariness, but from justice, in that Israel alone had attained to recognition of the unity of the Creator.[84] Abraham was the

---

[83] Orobio, *Prev. Div.*, MS Amsterdam, *EH* 48 D 6, f. 36ᵛ.

[84] See *Epíst. Inv.*, MS Amsterdam, *EH* 48 D 6, ff. 345ʳ f.: 'A esta duda se responde que no era ymposible a la divina potencia introducir en los animos de todos los hombres este verdadero conocimiento de si mesmo, sin separacion de un pueblo, que solo gosase

first to believe in that unique quality, for which reason 'God extended to him his mercies, marked him out as the recipient of support that went beyond the natural, and reassured him with promises ... of which the primary one was the assurance that He would extend those same mercies to his posterity'.[85] Although the Gentiles had witnessed the miracles wrought by God for his people, and indeed had conceded that they emanated from an omnipotent Deity, 'they did not deduce from these wondrous signs the unity of God, since their belief in a plurality of gods blinded them ... and they maintained that every god naturally undertook especial exertions in the interest of those who believed in him and gave him worship'.[86] God fulfilled his promise to Abraham: the Hebrew shepherd-folk, for all their rustic lack of sophistication, were possessed of that same knowledge (peculiar to themselves) which even the sages amongst the Gentiles failed to attain. 'It was by means of divine revelation that they were guided, and it was the Creator Himself who, in his goodness, undertook the task of communicating to them knowledge of his unity in such manner that human reason might be able to conceive it, and that man's understanding might reach its apogee. Of all the inhabitants of the world, it was Israel that attained this blissful state in centuries long past, and it was to them alone that there was vouchsafed the certain knowledge of the existence of a Deity unique, eternal, and altogether infinite.'[87]

True, in those times the Israelites were but 'rude shepherds' as compared to the Greeks, who established 'far-famed academies': at Athens all the sciences were fostered and distinguished philosophers attained greatness whose teaching was still, in Orobio's age, held in high regard by the nations of the world, its validity being accepted by them. These thinkers of antiquity had been contemporaries and near-neighbours of the aforementioned Jews, and they applied their acute perception to investigating the origins of the world and the cause behind its existence; but their wisdom foundered without achieving any true, firmly-based knowledge of the divine unity. They continued in their misconceived attitudes, false teaching, and worship of a

---

esta gracia: mas para executar este universal beneficio, era forçoso que suffriese indignidad y violencia su infinita justitia [sic] y que sola obrase su misericordia, dando gratuitamente a todos lo que solo merecian algunos.' Cf. Orobio's controversy with Prado in regard to the election of Israel, above, chap. 6, pp. 171 f.

[85] Ibid., f. 345ᵛ: '... comunicole Dios sus favores, illustrole con auxilios sobre naturales, y alentole con promessas ... y la principal que continuaria en su posteridad las mesmas piedades ...'

[86] Ibid., f. 346ᵛ. [87] Ibid., f. 360ᵛ.

plethora of vain gods, and indeed human wisdom was so far from a monotheistic view that anyone who professed that belief was reckoned a believer in insubstantialities, fit to be put to death. Socrates was executed for disseminating the doctrine, which he had himself learned from the Jews; Plato, too, got it from the same source, but after taking two steps along its road he tottered, fell into the abyss of a low-grade pantheon, and adhered to a belief in polytheism. Similarly Aristotle arrived at the same truth and came to recognize the existence of an unmoved mover, 'yet instead of proving its uniqueness, he posited that ultimately all motion has its own cause in a mover not itself moved ... whence he reached the all-embracing idea of the absolute independence of each of the [Greek] gods, and failed to deduce the ineffable uniqueness of the Creator'.[88]

The distinction which Orobio draws is a clear and unequivocal one between Israel and the Gentiles. Israel alone recognized the unique quality of the Creator, and possessed that recognition not as a matter of grace or privilege, but out of natural justice. Amongst the Gentile world a few sages stood out as having approximated to such recognition. Socrates, who had got nearer to it than anyone else, did so thanks to the influence of his postulated Jewish teachers; but his experiment ended in disaster, because those amongst whom he lived utterly and completely rejected his teaching.[89]

An additional characteristic emphasized by Isaac as being the exclusive prerogative of the people of Israel is that of nobility of lineage,[90] which the vicissitudes of exile had in no way served to dim. 'God did not permit that Israel should be deceived, and so come to reckon the Gentile people[s] as being of noble stock—something to

---

[88] Ibid., f. 360ʳ.

[89] *Prev. Div.*, MS Amsterdam, *EH* 48 D 6, f. 67ʳ: 'Este dictamen fue y es generalissimo en todas las naciones del mundo exceptos algunos, que como Socrates con los estudios y naturales meditaciones alcansaron el dichoso conocimiento de la unidad de Dios ...' For the notion of a link between Plato and the prophet Jeremiah see Abravanel, *Bibl.*, on Jer. 1: 6: 'the Greek sages testify to the fact that Plato had discourse with him in Egypt.' Josephus, *contra Apionem*, i, 22 (176) reports the statement of Clearchus, the pupil of Aristotle, to the effect that his master met one of the sages of the Jews. Cf. Isaac Cardoso, *Excel.*, pp. 362 f. A succinct account of the whole topic and of its reflection in both Jewish and Christian literature, leading to the erroneous conclusion regarding Aristotle's conversion to Judaism, will be found in the Jerusalem Ph.D. thesis of A. David (in Hebrew) on historiography as reflected in the work of Gedaliah ibn Yahya, author of the *Shalsheleth ha-Qabbalah*, pp. 29 f., cf. also Yerushalmi, *Isaac Cardoso*, pp. 449 f., and the bibliography in his note 85.

[90] Cf. such expressions as ' ... la nobleza que heredo de sus Santos progenitores', *Prev. Div.*, f. 79ᵛ, and cf. above, chap. 6, pp. 174 f.

which Jews might easily have given credence through observance of [the Gentiles'] arrogant strength and their greatness.'[91] 'If,' he tauntingly writes in oblique address to Alonso de Zepeda, 'if we are to talk about origins and distinction of lineage, then it is a more glorious thing to be one of the descendants of Abraham, Isaac, and Jacob than of Julius Caesar—not, indeed, that all Spaniards are descended from Julius Caesar.'[92]

Isaac Orobio's written works include much treatment of the status enjoyed by the righteous amongst the Gentiles. We have noted above that one of the questions which he addressed to Rabbi Moses Raphael d'Aguilar concerned the implementation by Gentiles of the basic norms of civilized society which rabbinic Judaism categorizes as the 'Seven Commandments incumbent upon all Descendants of Noah'. Was Gentile obligation to fulfil these precepts a biblical ordinance to be identified in the text of the Pentateuch (*mi-de-'orayetha*), or was it binding upon them *qua* rabbinical deduction as to the import of Jewish law (*mi-de-rabbanan*)?[93] In this connection we may usefully take note of the definitions offered by Isaac in regard to the qualitative essence of the righteous amongst the Gentiles, their obligations, their rights, and their future status in messianic times. According to Isaac, the prescriptions of the Mosaic Law are not an obligation incumbent upon humanity at large. Following Maimonides, he asserts that Israel aside, all that humanity is obligated to do is 'to implement natural law, to express its recognition of the unity of God through fearing Him and worshipping Him out of a reverence internally sensed, by means of regular implementation of such acts as natural reason enjoins them to do'.[94] When, in the messianic age, Israel are redeemed, the righteous amongst the Gentiles—and no others of the Gentile peoples—will be delivered, 'the remainder being destroyed by divine justice'.[95] At the

[91] *Prev. Div.*, f. 81ʳ.
[92] See *Cart. Apol.*, MS Amsterdam, *EH* 48 A 12, ff. 111ᵛ f.
[93] See above, chap. 6, p. 117.
[94] *Epíst. Inv.*, MS Amsterdam, *EH* 48 D 6, f. 333ʳ. The complete passage runs as follows: 'Esta primeramente no predica generalidad; quiero dezir que no se haze obligatoria a todos los hombres como presumen las obras, antes deducido de sus principios, y particularidad con que fue encomendada a los Israelitas, asienta que todo el genero humano, menos los dichos esta excluido de esta obligacion solo debaxo de la Ley de la naturaleza, conociendo la unidad de Dios, adorandole, y reverenciandole con el ynterior culto obseruando la regularidad en las obras que la misma rason natural enseña . . .' On the vicissitudes, from the time of Maimonides onwards, of the rabbinic dictum that 'the righteous amongst the Gentiles have a portion in the world to come', see Katz, *Zion*, 23–4, 5718–19 [1958–9] (Hebrew), pp. 174 f.
[95] *Prev. Div.*, f. 122: 'Mas por que no entendiesen las gentes que todas ellas hauian de ser saluas, sino las que tuuiesen la dicha de conocer sin Idolatricas invenciones à su

same time he is careful not to blur the qualitative difference which, as he declares, distinguishes Israel from the righteous amongst the Gentiles—a distinction which not even in the messianic age will be obliterated. Redemption has been assured, first and foremost, to the Jewish people, and although those amongst the Gentiles who acknowledge God will be redeemed, 'the redemption of non-Jews is secondary and incidental'.[96] These Gentile saints will not be called 'the house of Jacob' or 'the house of Israel', and ought not to be so styled, but rather 'righteous ones amongst the Gentile nations':[97] 'and though it is correct to state that many nations will benefit from the advantages entailed in [Israel's] redemption, it is not correct to say that their own redemption is none other than that promised by God to Israel [sc. as Christianity maintains]: for it is Israel that will be redeemed, and the Gentile peoples will merely receive some part in their bliss'.[98]

Isaac certainly recognizes the privileges of the righteous amongst the Gentiles, i.e. those elect from within the Gentile peoples, granted only their acknowledgement of the unity of God and their implementation of the 'Seven Commandments of the Sons of Noah'. It seems probable that he was following the *responsum* of Rabbi Moses Raphael d'Aguilar, who diverged slightly from Maimonides in the matter of the duty of the righteous amongst the Gentiles to accept the Noachide precepts and to implement them 'because the Holy One, blessed be He, commanded them in the Torah, and informed us by Moses' agency that Noachides had already been commanded to observe them'. D'Aguilar modified Maimonides' formulation, stating in summary form that in order to be saved, the non-Jew is obligated to implement the aforementioned precepts 'as being something pleasing to God', and not through any explicit recognition of a link between them and the Jewish tradition of the Sinaitic origin of the Torah.[99] We have also noted above that in

---

Criador, que llamamos los Pios de las gentes, y que todo el resto sera destruido por la divina justicia.'

[96] Ibid., f. 154ᵛ.   [97] Ibid., f. 141ʳ.
[98] Ibid., ff. 130ᵛ f., and cf. ff. 152ᵛ f., where Orobio is concerned to contravert Pablo de Santa María, who had claimed that in messianic times Gentiles would carry out priestly functions which, in biblical law, are restricted to priests of levitical stock: 'No dice que seran Sacerdotes Legales, no conforme el rito que la diuina Ley dio a los hijos de Aharon, no que sacrifiquen en el Sagrado Templo, sino que seran Sacerdotes, y sacrificaran segun la Ley de la naturaleza ... Porque los que de las gentes creieron en el verdadero Dios y le amaren no siendo obligados a la Ley de Moseh, sino a la de naturalesa y preceptos de Noah, es forçoso que con señales exteriores y sensibles muestren su fee, y el amor y rendimiento que deuen a su criador, y esto sera con la oracion y el Sacrificio, quedando solo para Israel el sacerdocio legal que el Señor instituio en el Tribu de Levi ...'   [99] See above, chap. 6, pp. 118 f.

regard to such Greek figures as Aristotle Isaac evinced a more tolerant attitude than that of his teacher d'Aguilar.[100] As against this, one can detect in him a tendency to play down the rights and the privileges of the righteous amongst the Gentiles. They are obligated to implement natural law, and nothing else, whereas Israel have been summoned by precept to fulfil the Torah which, *qua* divine law, is superior to natural law even in regard to its ethical quality. One may infer from what he writes that what God demands of Israel is not merely that they should cleave to what is ethically good, but rather to what is perfect.[101]

Here we have to ask ourselves whether there is any distinction to be drawn between Isaac Orobio's approach to Christendom in general and his approach to the Christian society of Amsterdam that had afforded him and his fellow-fugitives from Spain and Portugal a secure place of refuge, in which they and their Jewish beliefs were treated with relative tolerance. Does his pillorying of Christianity as being 'the lowest form of idolatry that human wickedness has ever invented' mean that in his thinking the Christian nations stood on a lower plane than the peoples of paganism? Did the adherence of Christians to belief in the holy trinity signify that they could not be included amongst the righteous of the Gentiles from whom all that was required, in his view, was acknowledgement of the divine unity? And finally: was his severely negative attitude one adopted by him towards Christians in general, or did he draw a distinction in this respect between the Catholics for whom he entertained so bitter a hatred and Christians of the reformed churches—in particular, those of the northern Nether-

[100] Ibid.
[101] *Apud* Limborch, *De Veritate Rel. Christ.*, pp. 121 f. It should be noted that Limborch himself rejected Orobio's view absolutely, even though, as a disciple of Grotius, like his master he denied any identification of natural law with divine law. However, unlike Orobio, Limborch held that divine law merely gives expression to the will of God, without its necessarily embodying any particular moral dimension. Whereas natural law is common to all humanity and constitutes 'the directive of straightforward reason', divine law has been revealed to a specific community only: and the period of its validity within that community is—once again—dependent upon the divine will. For Limborch, the Mosaic Law is essentially a ceremonial law, and the prophets had already indicated that, at the appropriate time, the sanction behind its force would lapse. In the same way, the Christian gospel is not to be identified with natural law, and, in Limborch's view, it obligates those only who have received the evangelical message of Jesus. Those Gentile peoples whom that message did not reach, but who implement in their own lives the code of natural law, are assured of their place in the salvational scheme: for although belief in the messiahship of Jesus is a *sine qua non* for salvation, these Gentile peoples nevertheless have a right to a portion therein thanks to Jesus' own abounding love. See pp. 34 f, 199, 322. For Grotius' view, see Husik, pp. 381 f.; cf. Grotius, *Jure Belli*, i, chap. 1, and see Schwarzschild, 53, p. 52.

From Crypto-Judaism to Open Judaism 359

lands amongst whom (and indeed under whose protection) he had himself become reintegrated into the Jewish community and had reconstructed his own family's way of life?

In the letter which Orobio addressed to Juan de Prado's son he dealt at some length with the degree of culpable responsibility resting upon Gentiles—including Christians—for their deviationism from the dictates of natural law.[102] In that tract Isaac spoke of those peoples 'who invest all the means which their understanding could command in approaching the way of truth which, for the Jew, is the way to the Mosaic Law, and for the rest of humanity is the way of understanding directed towards the true God'.[103] He distinguished this category from those peoples that act in opposition to the dictates of natural reason: since 'in whatever concerns natural reason, no one can plead ignorance as a defence save one whom [mental sickness has] deprived of rational judgement'.[104] Following up this distinction, he comes to the conclusion that 'Christians are particularly blameworthy because of their distorted opinions, and are deserving of punishment, inasmuch as it is their wish to suppress their own understanding by believing in vain things that conflict with human intelligence . . .'[105] Whereas the punishment that overtakes pagan idolaters whose own ignorance inhibits their comprehending the notion of the divine unity is essentially 'negative punishment', viz. deprivation of the right to participate in the future life, Christians merit 'positive punishment', i.e. to be condemned to eternal perdition, because 'they do believe in the truth of the Law but conduct themselves contrariwise to what it teaches, and cling to belief in dogmas which contradict natural reason'.[106]

As Orobio saw it, Christians were not merely debarred from being reckoned amongst the righteous of the Gentiles, but in respect to their ethical code they were inferior to those pagans who, owing to their ignorance, had not attained to a recognition of the unity of God. So outspoken a formulation is unparalleled in Orobio's public anti-Christian polemical writings.[107] It clearly demonstrates that what he felt inhibited from saying explicity in his disputations with theologians

---

[102] See above, chap. 6, p. 155, and below, Appendix F.
[103] *Carta al hijo de Prado*, MS Paris, Fonds éspagnoles 41, p. 917.
[104] Ibid.: '. . . a todo lo que es de razon natural no puede el hombre escusarse por ignorancia, salvo si fuere privado de juizio . . .'
[105] Ibid., p. 918.   [106] Ibid., p. 921.
[107] The anti-Christian passages in the *Carta al hijo de Prado* appear in the Paris exemplar (see n. 103 above) only; in the other two copies, in Amsterdam, *EH*, they have been omitted. See below, Appendix F.

and other Christians of various denominations, because of a sensitivity towards their reactions and that of the general Christian environment, he did not hesitate to express quite unequivocally in a personal letter addressed to a member of his own community.

But we still must deal with the question which we have raised: did Isaac's extreme dismissiveness of Christianity apply equally to the Christian society in which he himself lived, and which had furnished him and his fellow-congregants with a refuge in which they could implement the Torah of Israel without let or hindrance?

In the writings of the Portuguese Jews of Amsterdam contemporary with Isaac the predominating tone is one of openly declared respect for the seven United Provinces whose foundation-deed had been the Union of Utrecht of 1579, for the Province of Holland, the city of Amsterdam, and its inhabitants. De Barrios draws attention to the fact that 'nowhere else in the world do [the Jews] have less to worry about than in Amsterdam, thanks both to the freedom of conscience that prevails in the seven United Provinces, and to the big-heartedness of her quick-witted inhabitants . . .'[108] 'Amsterdam,' he writes elsewhere, 'with its massive population, is a veritable Babylon in what concerns the sciences as they vie with one another, and an Athens of polyglot speech. Her crowning glory is that despite the differences of the nations that live in her midst, adhering to their various mutually opposed religions, she keeps the peace amongst them — and this with a paucity of governors and an amplitude of justice.'[109] Abraham Israel Pereyra wrote large upon his banner the generosity customary amongst the Dutch, 'in return for which they have been afforded divine support and an especial providence . . .'[110]

Isaac Orobio could not ignore the protection, and the specially favourable conditions, which the Jews of Holland enjoyed at a time when the situation of the Jews in most countries in a professedly Christian Europe was at its nadir. In his *Epístola Invectiva* against Juan de Prado, written earlier than his letter quoted above to Prado's son, Isaac had asserted that 'in the Talmud there are found sundry veiled passages, to expound the import of which even in these times would be an insensate act: because, in the period when the Talmud was written down, there were as yet no republics established, nor princes [such as] those under whose protection we live and for whose prosperity we daily

---

[108] De Barrios, *Triumpho*, p. 24, 'Triumpho del Govierno popular en la Casa de Jacob'.
[109] De Barrios, *Luna*, p. 3.   [110] Pereyra, *Espejo*, p. 225.

From Crypto-Judaism to Open Judaism

and uninterruptedly pray to God. And if the sages of antiquity wrote something that would seem to offend the present [enlightened] state of some areas in Europe and indeed to evince hostility, they are not to be reproached, inasmuch as there were [in their time] no Christian folk, nor had there come to the fore Christian princes for whom they might, in their writings, have expressed either praise or contemptuous disapproval. Hence it rests on Judaism in our day not to give offence, even in thought, to those commonwealths or kingdoms that make our existence possible [in a way that] never happened to them.'[111]

It could be argued that the foregoing is no more than flattery and ingratiation of the kind to be found both in medieval Jewish writing and in the apologetic literature of the western Sephardi diaspora of the seventeenth century.[112] But it is quite possible that there is not, in point of fact, any conceptual incompatability between Isaac's contradictory assertions. Indeed, in one place he is denying Christians any title to life in the hereafter because of the dogmas on which their faith rested; and in the other he stresses that Jews pray for the worldly happiness and success of those Christian princes and kingdoms who extend their protection to their Jewish citizens. And yet, there can be no doubt that he felt uncomfortable about his extreme position in regard to the essence of the Christians denying them a place in the hereafter. How could he fail to acknowledge the tolerant attitude of the Christian society in which he himself was living, which had opened its doors to him and to his fellow-members of the Jewish community? At any rate, Isaac did not find it appropriate ever again to revert in his *œuvre* to the question of the lot of Christians in the hereafter. He never modified or moderated the outspoken language which he had used in his letter to Prado's son. Nor did he attempt to reformulate his views in the spirit of the rabbinic *dictum* that 'Gentiles outside Palestine are not to be reckoned idolaters' (Babylonian Talmud, *Ḥullin* 13b), and of all that

---

[111] See *Epíst. Inv.*, MS Amsterdam, *EH* 48 B 12, p. 74.

[112] See the sentiments placed in the mouth of 'Tomás' in his debate with 'Al[f]onso', King of Spain, by Ibn Verga, p. 29: 'I had a discussion about this with a person belonging to the [Jewish] Aristocracy—one of the Abravanels, who had come from Seville, where he was born. He said that anyone with a knowledge of Hebrew would find no difficulty here. There is a difference in meaning between the terms "stranger" [*nokhri*], "Christian" [*noṣeri*], and "Gentile" [*goi*]. The *nokhri*, or stranger, is one who behaves as a stranger towards his Creator, not believing in the basic principles of all religious faith; the Christian, on the other hand, who does believe in creation, miracles, and divine providence, cannot be properly styled a *nokhri*.' See Isaac Cardoso, *Excel.*, pp. 350 f., and cf. Menasseh b. Israel, *Vind. Jud.* (quoted by L. Wolf, *Men. b. I. and Cromwell*, pp. 125 f.).

could be thought of as flowing from the position. At that time amongst the rabbis of central and eastern Europe there was a growing tendency to regard contemporary non-Jewish nations (and in particular the Christian nations) as faithful bearers of a tradition common to Judaism and Christianity. Yet the age-old polemical tone was maintained within the Portuguese community of Amsterdam, even though that same congregation was enjoying incomparably better political and social conditions than elsewhere in Europe.[113] Residence in Dutch Christian society did not obscure the memory of the injustice suffered under Christianity by the refugees from the Inquisition in the Iberian lands. Isaac Orobio's writings constitute an outstanding example of an attempt to write at an enlightened conceptual level about speculative matters and abstract values without breaching, even on this plane, the fence that must keep Christians and Jews apart.

THE JEWISH FATE: EXILE AND REDEMPTION

The trials and tribulations to which Portuguese-Jewish fugitives from the Inquisition had been exposed, and the transition from a crypto-Jewish life beneath a Christian mask in the Iberian peninsula where, for generations, they had been cut off from the Jewish community, to a full reintegration therein for the purpose of observing the Jewish religion in its pristine purity—all of this instigated them to ask some fundamental questions in regard to the fate of the Jewish people, and the meaning of *exile* and *redemption* as speculative concepts. These two themes are, so to speak, distinctive threads that can be seen running right through the fabric of their religiously orientated writings.

The unremitting necessity of facing the theological challenge of the Christian environment, and experience in countering plaintive criticism from heterodox circles within Jewry which denied the notion of Israel as the chosen people, led the Portuguese Jews in Amsterdam time and time again to insist on the uninterrupted validity of God's covenant with Abraham and his seed. 'Always', wrote Orobio, 'right up to the present day, Israel has held fast to the true knowledge of the Deity',[114] and according to his own philosophy of Judaism, Israel will

---

[113] On new approaches to this subject in eastern and central Europe in the 17th cent. see Katz' article (n. 94 above), pp. 186 f., also his *Tradition and Crisis*, pp. 37 f.

[114] *Epíst. Inv.*, MS Paris, BN Fonds espagnoles 40, p. 722: '... porque siempre hasta el presente dia perseveran los Israelitas [sic] en el verdadero conocimiento de la Deidad...'

From Crypto-Judaism to Open Judaism

continue to occupy its position as the elect of all nations so long as they remain faithful to that knowledge, and cleave to faith in a sole Creator-God. They might, indeed, be punished for their sins, but so long as those sins did not sweep them into complete loss of religious loyalty, or alienate them from belief, God would once more vouchsafe them his grace after their return to Him in penitence.[115] The pox of paganism had, it is true, infected the descendants of Abraham frequently enough, but it had never been the case that the entire Jewish people had bowed the knee to Baal. Had Israel as a whole ever chosen to adopt the pagan way. God would have had no option but to revoke his promises, since they in no way tied his hand: 'God could never promise to act with impropriety, or to maintain Abraham's seed *qua* the elect, should Israel through wickedness or lack of faith itself prefer to be a sinful nation.'[116]

Israel's long drawn out exile constitutes divine punishment for their sins; but, serious though these be, there is nothing in them that is adequate to alienate them from God's mercy. Yet it was only in the period of the second exile that had continued since the second temple's destruction that the indictments of the biblical prophets who threatened punishment had been fulfilled, in that in this second exile Israel had been found worshipping idols of wood and stone:

> Israel has undergone, and still undergoes—or at any rate a substantial segment of it suffers—this grave punishment. Terror compels many to desecrate the holy laws and to confer worship upon [the Gentiles'] idols, as has happened in the kingdom of Naples and in many other parts of Italy, in France, Spain, Germany, England, and Poland. At this very day many a family, having become mixed up with Gentiles and having forgotten their splendid lineage, is steeped in this evil: others, who do not disavow their salvation and their duty, are (in regard to their outward actions) placed in the same benighted situation, unfit for the efficacious operation of the Creator's salvation—and all this thanks to the transgressions of others . . .[117]

Who but God Himself could have envisaged and foretold a historical event like this, so contrary to the natural order of creation, that a people scattered over the world, *sans* commonwealth, *sans* king, *sans* land, *sans* government, should over the course of many centuries—thousands of years—preserve its identity, its name, and its actuality, being in its entirety discrete from all other peoples: should preserve its ancient language, its religion, its insitutions, and its customs, and all this whilst being confronted by the consensus of all nations,

---

[115] Ibid., p. 725.   [116] Ibid., pp. 724 f.
[117] See *Prev. Div.*, MS Amsterdam, *EH* 48 D 6, ff. 92ʳ f.

their aversion and hatred, in face of the hostility, dominion and power of the whole world, through so many an age and in the period of empires so mighty? ... Having announced publicly that his people Israel would survive in perpetuity, God had no wish to conceal the fact of their future preservation as an entity, as we ourselves in this day and age are witnesses — and that not by any natural means, such as our concentration in some region or other at a far distance from our own land, whilst from the point of view of all nations we became suddenly converted into friends. For if that had been the complexion of affairs, our preservation would not have excited any wonder amongst them.[118]

No, God had determined that Israel's preservation should be through means that ran contrary to the natural order of things, 'and He publicly proclaimed that He would disperse us and that we would be persecuted, and yet at the same time continue to be preserved'.[119] It was heavenly providence that both decided Israel's fate and guided its history. From this point of view, Jewish history differed from that of every other people, in that it was not determined by the natural order that directs human history. In this same way Abraham Israel Pereyra distinguishes the fate of Israel from that of the Gentile peoples: and when discussing Jeremiah 10: 2, 'do not fall into the ways of the nations, do not be awed by signs in the heavens', he calls in aid the well-known Talmudic adage 'Israel is not [astrologically dependent on] any zodiacal sign' (*'eyn mazzal le-yisra'el*, Babylonian Talmud, *Shabbath* 156a), and writes:

the people of Israel is not governed by the heavenly bodies, nor is it placed under the tutelage of the causes that move these — still less any ethereal prince: rather it is guided by divine and individual providence ... whence it emerges that all other nations are subject to astrological influences, but not Israel ...[120]

Rabbi Isaac Aboab da Fonseca saw in Israel's dispersion amongst the nations God's particular mercy being extended to his people, since 'in this way they might be the better preserved, and might weather the storms occasioned by waves of anger [being subject to] Gentile history

---

[118] Ibid., ff. 90ʳ f.

[119] Ibid., f. 91ᵛ: '... affirmando que nos esparsiria, y seriamos perseguidos y juntamente conseruados...'

[120] See Pereyra, *Espejo*, p. 496: '... el pueblo de Israel, no es governado por los cuerpos celestes, ni está baxo de la proteccion de sus movedores, ni menos de algun ethereo Principe, sino guiado de la particular y divina providencia.... De donde consta, que estan todas las demas naciones sujetas a los influxos de los Astros, ecepto Israel...' See Babylonian Talmud, *Shabbath* 156a, and cf. E. E. Urbach, *The Sages, their Concepts and Beliefs*, Eng. trans. by Israel Abrahams, Jerusalem, 1975, i, p. 277.

From Crypto-Judaism to Open Judaism

... and thus through [the Jews'] agency, the knowledge [of God] might be broadcast through the world'.[121] Pereyra also recognized an educational function in the vicissitudes of exile, the object being to protect the lofty ethical standards of the people and to induce in it the moral scrutiny of its every deed,

> for we have to assume that if we are beset by sickness, this can only be because God foresaw the evil to which we would be prone, were we in possession of sound health; therefore did he clip our wings, and by means of infirmity withheld [sin] from our reach, for it is better that we should be broken down by our sickness than that we should in health persevere in sin ... God in his mercy derives no pleasure from our sickness and pain, and if He inflicts them upon us, He does so in order to cause the growth of sound flesh, and to heal us of our sins ...[122]

From the foregoing it is clear that the philosophy of Jewish history of Orobio and of his fellow-members of the community was set within the framework of the traditional scheme that took shape in rabbinical attitudes of second temple times, or more particularly following on its destruction—terms of reference accepted with some modification, extension, and fresh exegesis, down the medieval generations of Jewish history.[123] Amos' words (3: 2) 'for you alone have I cared among all the nations of the world; therefore will I punish you for all your iniquities' (New English Bible) provided a formula by which to account for Israel's punitive sufferings through long generations as being cathartically motivated, in order to recondition them to their pristinely good state through purgatory.[124] Even thinkers like Isaac Abravanel and Solomon ibn Verga (particularly the latter), who adopted a critical and empirical approach and endeavoured to assess various phenomena of Jewish history according to the operation of the natural order, ultimately remained faithful to the traditional view, seeing the history

---

[121] Isaac Aboab, *Pent.*, p. 89, cf. also p. 610.

[122] Pereyra, *Certeza*, p. 69. Cf. also the sermon delivered by Hezekiah da Silva, one of the disciples of Moses Galante, on 18 *Marḥeshvan* 5451 (21 Oct. 1690), *Del fundamento de nuestra ley*, Amsterdam, 5451 (1690/1), p. 24: '... pues como se conocerá el poder de Dios? Yo lo diré; siendo general la redempsión. Derrámense pues los judíos; espárçanse por todos partes; de un cabo del mundo, hasta otro cabo; siendo este el fin, para que quando la suma bondad de Dios nos recojiere, se manifieste a ojos de todos su gloria, que es Señor Soberano del universo ...' Regarding the various ideas and approaches current in the Middle Ages towards the problem of the purpose of Israel's exile, see B.-Z. Dinur, *Yisra'el ba-Golah²*, i book 4, 5723 [1963], pp. 193 f., ii book 5, 5731 [1971], pp. 342 f., and cf. Ben-Sasson, *Galuth u-ge'ullah*, pp. 221 f.

[123] On this see Baer, *Galut*.

[124] Cf. Urbach (n. 120 above), i, p. 526.

of the Jewish nation as the expression of the bond connecting God and his people, in accordance with a predetermined plan. Even more so was the concept of history which Menasseh b. Israel made his own, impregnated as it was with the religious tensions attendant upon messianic expectancy.[125]

Isaac Orobio's understanding of Jewish history does not, in its essentials, diverge from this theological view. It would seem that he was familar with the work of Ibn Verga, for whom the interplay of 'where for this explosion of wrath?' (Deuteronomy 29: 23) with Amos' 'for you alone I have cared, . . .' constitutes a leitmotiv running through the whole. Isaac was influenced by the ideas put forward in the fictitious debate between a 'King Alfonso' of Spain and 'Thomas the wise' in the 'Seventh Catastrophe' of Ibn Verga's *Shevet Yehudah*. However, when considering concrete historical instances, and endeavouring to trace out their roots and their conformity to the laws of history, Orobio steps aside from the theological scheme and dissects them with the scalpel of rational criticism, explicitly correlating with the laws of nature and general principles by which societies may be seen to operate. Thus, for example, his explanation of anti-Semitism:

The fact of [the Jews] being hated corresponds to the natural order of things, inasmuch as they are everywhere foreigners, belonging nowhere, and wherever they do live an unmolested life it is only by the agreement and goodwill of others. Not having a prince of their own, they lack that protection which confers a respect that can strengthen the morale of the citizen body and can check the violence of strangers, just as has proved to be the case in Portugal. And precisely so, one of the writers of this kingdom has contended that whereas the Jews have been most cruelly persecuted, their children being torn from them and they themselves being made into abject slaves, the Moors have been allowed to depart in peace, without the slightest harrying or oppression, out of fear [of adverse reaction by] Muslim kings in Africa . . .[126]

---

[125] Even so sober a rationalist as Simone (Simḥah) Luzzatto (c. 1580–1663), who in analysing the Jewish situation of his own day made much use of statistical and economic evidence, did not swerve in any qualitative sense from the theological concept which, for him, explained the main lines of Jewish history. See his *Discurso circa il stato de gl'hebrei, Et in particolar dimoranti nell' inclita Città di Venezia*, Venice, 1638, Considerazione xviii, f. 89ʳ: 'e non è dubbio, che per se stessa [la hebrea natione] non hauerebbe hauuto tanto vigore di opponersi alla edacità del tempo, & esimersi dalli suoi fieri insulti per si lungo tratto di 1600. Anni in circa, ma ciò dipende dal volere della Diuina Maetsà, perseruandola a fini a lui manifesti . . .' Cf. Baer, *Galut*, pp. 60 f., 77 f., 83 f., 97 f.

[126] *Prev. Div.*, MS Amsterdam, *EH* 48 D 6, f. 62ᵛ. For treatment of the motif of the Amos citation (3: 2) by Ibn Verga, see the 7th Catastrophe, p. 37, and the 61st, pp. 127 f. Regarding the differing attitude adopted by Catholic rulers towards Jews and Moors, cf. Luzzatto, op. cit., *Considerazione* xvii, f. 87ᵛ: 'quelli Prencipi . . . fecero risolutione . . . più

It was the foreign status of the Jews, combined with their lack of an independent sovereign government that could 'confer respect' on them, that gave rise to Gentile hatred. Elsewhere he says:

> There is here a contrast. Slaves, and all types of captives who are placed in a situation of servitude or oppression amongst any given nation, but who (had they still been in their own country) would have had authority, government, and lordship, and freedom from contempt, do not—whilst being themselves subject to oppression or captivity—attract contempt, for they belong to a free nation and are thus placed in a situation from which they will, ultimately, be liberated: as for example is the case with the Turks, the Moors, and other peoples. On the other hand Israel is abominated the world over, because nowhere do they enjoy the authority that comes with self-government: and consequently they do not merit any respect whatsoever in the sight of any people, and every nation—seeing that they are universally held in contempt—similarly contemns them.[127]

Here we have a phenomenological analysis of anti-Semitism that makes no appeal at all to any religious deposit in the mixture, and which disregards completely the theological dimension as it had been enunciated both within Christendom and in the world of Islam.[128] For the hatred of the Jew there were, however, additional causes. 'Since divine law is in conflict with the laws of all the nations, it follows inevitably that the nations should hate those who implement it, particularly since the holy Law forbids [the Jews'] participation in all those means of promoting friendship and the sense of unity amongst men, prohibiting as it does intermarriage and inter-community conviviality.'[129]

Isaac Orobio, as it would seem, even goes so far as to offer a justification for the virulence of anti-Semitism. The Jewish people style

tosto bandire li Hebrei che li Mori, essendoli questi più necessarii a suoi Regni . . . oltre di ciò per non irritare quel Popolo, che ancora ritineua la sua primiera ferocità, e che haueua Capo potentissimo della sua propria Religione.'

[127] *Prev. Div.*, f. 250ʳ.

[128] Contrast, e.g., what Moses d'Aguilar had to say in his reply to crypto-Jews in Antwerp, MS Amsterdam, *EH* 48 A 11, f. 11: 'Mas dado cazo que todos fuesen malos e enganhadores (como parece lo supone el que pregunta). No es essa la cauza, cierto, por que sus inimigos tan crudamente los manijan, en la honra, en la hazienda y en la vida mas solamente por la religion y la Ley que profeçan, como por exemplo lo muestra la experiencia en las tierras de inquissicion.' D'Aguilar finds the principal cause of anti-Semitism in religious sentiment, economic and ethical allegations being, for him, mere pretexts for Gentile action against Jews.

[129] Cf. *Prev. Div.* (n. 126 above), f. 62ʳ; also the words ascribed to King Alfonso in Ibn Verga's 7th Catastrophe, p. 31: 'I also take into account a further argument, viz. [the Jews'] holding aloof from eating and drinking with Gentiles; for nothing brings together the hearts of those who stand apart so much as regular dining together . . .'

themselves 'God's people', and call others 'the nations of the [various] lands', so that it is hardly surprising if they all recoil from Israel inasmuch as 'this glorying [in being God's people] is a claim proceeding from a scattered nation without king or territory, without the slightest shadow of human power, and without there being anything about them to indicate that they are subject to God's especial providence'.[130] The intensity of Jew-hatred is such that 'even if [the Jews] join one of the [Gentile religious] denominations, there is not accorded to them the same respect that is enjoyed by those who have been of the religion concerned since birth. If a Turk or a Moor turns Christian, or if a Berber acknowledges the authority of the *Qor'an*, the [admitting religious group] show him respect and confer great marks of honour upon him, but the Jew who converts remains in the same situation of oppressed humiliation as before.'[131] Unquestionably this assertion by Isaac originates in his own historical experience in the Iberian peninsula, in which the divisions between 'Christians of purely Christian [i.e. Gentile] origin' and 'New Christians' were not abrogated even after ten or more generations of the persecution of the Jews; and the hostility which had previously been levelled at professing Jews was transferred to 'New Christians' whose conversion had not relieved them of the badge of shame that was constituted by their Jewish origins. There is, however, in this assertion of Isaac's an attempt, albeit a partial one only, to arrive at an understanding of Jewish–Gentile relations that transcends the traditional plane of theological account. This same critical-empirical approach finds expression in his attempts to explain the guiding factor in the Jewish relations of Gentile peoples and kings. According to Orobio, so long as Jews are urgently required to fill some political, economic, or social need, they are accorded respect and relations towards them are positively welcoming: but once they have discharged their function, and the surrounding society no longer needs their services, the governmental authorities change their spots, revise their policy, and subject the Jews to ill-tempered outbursts of persecution. If in time of war or other constraint Jews are necessary, because of the substantial support which they can bring to the royal administration, the return of peace and prosperity leads to their expulsion from the nation-states of their domicile. That is what happened in medieval France. So long as France was subject to the yoke of the English who occupied vast tracts of her territory, divided as it was into various principalities, the Jews were genially accepted

[130] *Prev. Div.*, ibid.   [131] Ibid., f. 247'.

From Crypto-Judaism to Open Judaism 369

because of royal dependence on their services. But once the English had evacuated the country, and the different regions became united under a crown that was increasing its authority and was enjoying peace and prosperity, the position of the Jews was changed: 'the shepherds, who were none other than the lords of France and her people, rose up against the Jews and butchered them throughout the kingdom until their innocent blood covered street and market-square alike, and those who could flee made their way as refugees to Poland, Germany, Hungary and Bohemia.'[132] Similarly in Spain:

When 'Spain' meant no more than a benighted nook enclosed between the mountains of Oviedo, León, and Old Castile, all the rest of the country being in the hands of a plethora of Moorish kings with whom [the Christians] were incessantly at war, the [Jewish] people was accepted and a fuss made of them, for their financial support was urgently needed for military expeditions. But once the Moors had been driven out and the various districts of the kingdom reconquered, including Granada, the last [Moorish-held] city to fall, the whole of Spain now being in the hands of a single monarch, viz. Ferdinand the Catholic—immediately on the fall of Granada that was the culmination of the battle which he had mounted against her, this king issued the edict requiring those same Jews who by the support of their wealth had made possible that victory, together with other conquests, to forswear the kingdom within a very short interval of time and to leave it as exiles. Some of them rejected God's Law for want of means [to get away], or lack of resolution to wander forth. Others left, to encounter whatever tribulations, humiliations, and forms of death awaited them in the world beyond. Spain flourished, expanded, and, amid conditions of peace, asserted her authority over all her constituent kingdoms: but the cost by which that peace was achieved fell punitively upon Israel.[133]

And history repeated itself in Portugal:

Twenty thousand families crossed the frontier into Portugal, to be received by the King, don João II, in return for a vast sum which he needed for his wars of conquest overseas. His successor, don Manoel, made many kingdoms in India subject to himself, enlarged the borders of his kingdom both by means of dynastic marriages and by treaties with Castile, and by dint of the treasure that reached him from the east: and he enjoyed peace and great prosperity. But the punitive price of that peace fell upon Israel, and, [don Manoel's] golden age once achieved, he expelled them most cruelly from his kingdoms.[134]

---

[132] See *Expl. Is. 53*, MS Amsterdam, *EH* 48 D 16, pp. 137 f.   [133] Ibid., pp. 138 f.

[134] *Prev. Div.* (n. 126 above), ff. 257ʳ f, and cf. *Expl. Is. 53*, p. 139, where, by the copyist's error, the number of households is given as 2,019 instead of 20,000, and João II is styled III. Orobio's figure tallies with the estimates given by Jewish chronographers

War, then, by bringing such kingdoms as are engaged in it to reduced straits, spells the rise of Jewish fortunes, and peace, bringing blessings and happiness in its train for Gentile lands, means Jewish impoverishment and indeed elimination.

One cannot be other than impressed by the sobriety of Isaac Orobio's endeavour to reach some intellectually defensible understanding of the historical laws governing the fate of Israel in the diaspora. One must contrast the ingenuous schematism of Solomon ibn Verga, who identifies the cause of the persecution of the Jews in the ignorance of the masses as opposed to royal appreciation of the facts of political life,[135] or of Menasseh b. Israel, who regards the failing fortunes and the fall of oppressive regimes as the direct result of their negative Jewish policy:[136] Orobio attempts rather to understand the oscillating, accident-prone situation of diaspora Jewry through a critical understanding of the position occupied by the Jews within the historical processes that affected the nationalities of Europe in general.

---

writing soon after the Spanish expulsion of 1492. For the number of Jewish exiles who proceeded to Portugal see A. Marx, 'The Expulsion of the Jews from Spain', *JQR* OS 20, 1908, pp. 251, 255; Marx printed a copy, made from a Parma Hebrew MS, in the Jewish Theological Seminary of New York (Sulzberger Collection), in which it is stated that 120,000 Jews entered Portugal, cf. also pp. 245 f. The same figure is given by Abraham Zacuto, *Sepher ha-Yuḥasin ha-Shalem*, ed. H. Filipowski, London and Edinburgh, 1857, p. 277: 'the bulk ['*iqqar*] of [the Jews of] Castile went into Portugal, since they could not enter (sc. depart by sea), . . . more than 120,000 persons.' Cf. Baer, *History*, ii. pp. 438, 510 f. For what he writes about Portugal Orobio relies on Gerónimo Osorio, bishop of Silves, author of *De rebus Emmanuelis regis Lusitanae*, which is itself an extended translation of the chronicle of Damião da Goes.

[135] Ibn Verga, p. 30, where 'Tomás' is represented as saying to the 'king', 'I never saw a person of intelligence possessed of hatred of the Jewish people—the only ones who hate them are the generality (*kileloth ha-'am*) . . .' See Baer's introd. p. 13, and cf. his *Galut*, p. 79.

[136] *Humble Addresses*, see Wolf, *Men. b. I. and Cromwell*, pp. 75 f.: '. . . All things being governed by Divine Providence, God dispensing rewards unto Vertues, and punishments unto Vices, according to his own good Will. This the Examples of great Monarchs make good; especially of such, who have afflicted the people of Israel: For none hath ever afflicted them, who hath not been by some ominous Exit, most heavily punished of God Almighty . . .' Contrast Simone Luzzatto's explicit rejection of the possibility of describing the fate of the Jewish people in its dispersion as if it constituted a single collectivity affected by one and the same fortune; *Discorso* (n. 125 above), ff. 86ʳ f., and *Considerazione* xi, f. 37ᵛ: 'e se cosi malageuole è il diffinire li costumi interni d'vn sol huomo, che sarà poi in volere terminare quelli d'vna intiera Natione? e massime dell' Hebrea, distratta per tutte le parte del mondo, ch'è impossibile il dirne cosa certa, e risoluta, essendo gl' Hebrei disseminati per l'vniuerso, & a guisa de fiume che scorre per lungo tratto di paese, che reciuono le sue acque impressione dalla qualità de diuersi terreni oue passono, cosi gl' Hebrei dall' altre nationi oue dimorano acquistano diuersi costumi, e per ciò tanto differenti sono le maniere dell' Hebreo Venetiano del Constantinopolitano, e questo dal Damaschino, e Cagliarino, e tutti essi da Tedeschi, e Polachi . . .' Cf. Baer, *Galut*, p. 87.

From Crypto-Judaism to Open Judaism

Following on the partial attempt at historical analysis, Isaac reverts to an over-arching theological view. He explains that anti-Semitism, the historical inevitability of which corresponds to the 'natural order of things',

> is one of the greatest mercies that God has conferred upon Israel; it being the one and only means by which we are preserved against that happy age for which we hope, as a people constituting an independent entity as evinced in our name, our ancient customs, our miraculous situation as a commonwealth scattered throughout the world, punished by forfeiture of our ancient power, bereft of the lustre of nobility that we once enjoyed and without continuance of prophetic inspiration, and yet possessed of that prophetic forecast—unbroken and certain—in regard to both our present state and that blessed age for which we hope.[137]

At the very time that Orobio was formulating the foregoing sentiments, Spinoza was writing that 'experience proves that it is anti-Semitism which preserves [the Jews]'.[138] Both saw in anti-Semitism the factor which preserved the Jews as a national, if fragmented and dispersed entity, but a qualitative difference which separates their attitudes is eloquent of the yawning gulf between their respective conceptions of Judaism and Jewry. Whereas Orobio saw anti-Semitism as being, in the last analysis, a means of the exercise of divine providence, Spinoza viewed it as a social and historical phenomenon devoid of any theological significance; and just as he repudiated the notion of Israel's election, so he denied the validity of any reading of the facts that would postulate a separate and especial link between divine providence and Jewish history.

The apologetic element is relatively circumscribed in the writings of Orobio, in comparison with the work of other authors who shared his environment and also entered upon disputation with Christianity, e.g. Menasseh b. Israel and Isaac Cardoso. But the apologetic motif is not entirely lacking. Similarly to Emanuel Aboab, he underscores the loyalty and the ethical and social uprightness of the Jew:[139] and like Cardoso, he too takes issue with those who would smear the Jews with

---

[137] *Prev. Div.* (n. 126 above), f. 63ᵛ.
[138] 'Quod autem nationum odium eos admodum conservet, id jam experientia docuit', *Tractatus Theologico-Politicus*, chap. iii, *Opera*, ii, p. 419. For the date of *Prev. Div.* see above, p. 244.
[139] *Expl. Is 53* (n. 132 above), pp. 163 f.: 'no le desprecian y abominan por ladron, traidor o homizida, etc. . . . .' So also p. 160: '. . . Considera despues a Israel respecto de las gentes nunca ubo engaño en su boca mas ellas siempre hizieron de el pésimo concepto de indigno de toda confiança . . .' Cf. Emanuel Aboab, *Nomologia*, chap. 26, and similarly S. Luzzatto (n. 125 above), ff. 113 f.

calumny. But Orobio's tone of altercation is by far the sharper.[140] In his Respuesta Apologética against Zepeda he casts the following rejoinder into the teeth of his controversialist:

> you nickname us 'pigs', although we neither eat their flesh nor can even bear the sight of it in a picture. You also say that we are dogs [canes], as if we were descended from the Gentile world, or the Canaanite [cananea], rather than from the sons of those from whose paternal board your own gospel scarce allows Gentiles the crumbs...[141]

It was apologetic considerations, too, that led him on some occasions to suppress his essential position in regard to the pitiful plight of Israel scattered amongst the Gentile peoples. In his 'friendly conversation' with Limborch, for example, he claims that Jews do not constitute the peril that Christians are accustomed to represent them as being. Almost all Christian sovereigns, he says, appoint Jews to their most important governmental posts, as also the Turkish sultans are accustomed to do, and the shahs of Persia as well; they do nothing at all without taking Jews into partnership. The whole world envies them their wealth, but also assesses their significance in respect of it. In

[140] Cf. Isaac Cardoso, *Excel.*, part ii, pp. 333–431, which is devoted to the refutation of ten calumnies commonly alleged by Gentiles against Jews.

[141] *Resp. al Zep.*, MS Amsterdam, *EH* 48 A 12, f. 111ᵛ: 'Llamanos puercos, siendo que no lo catamos, ni lo podemos ver pintado; dice tambien que somos canes, como si decendiesemos de la gentilidad, o de la cananea, y no de los hijos de cuya mesa apenas las migajas consede su evangelio a las gentes...' Cf. Ibn. Verga, 7th Catastrophe, p. 30 (words attributed to the 'king'): 'as regards love of one's fellow [raḥamanuth], a leading bishop was once preaching before me, and he said that it was a mistake to call Jews "dogs"—they ought rather be called "pigs", since it is not the dog's character but that of the pig that the Jew shares. We see from experience that if someone beats a dog, all the other dogs set on it, trying to bite, over and above the drubbing that it has had: but if you throw a stone at a pig and it grunts, then all the other pigs start grunting too. It is just the same with the Jews. Suppose that one of them gets into a church and steals the chalice [sc. and is later caught], all the rest of the Jews come hurrying along to secure his release. The [Jewish] tailor is off to see some officer that he knows, the goldsmith goes to the *duque*, and so on: some of them proffer financial inducements, others just give vent to pleas and petitions, and they do not give up until they have got their man out of his trouble. Now that ought to be reckoned one of those qualities commanding respect.' This is clear evidence that Jews in the Iberian peninsular were frequently given the sobriquet *dog* or *pig*. See also an amusing anecdote in Isaac Cardoso's *Excel.*, p. 349. A Christian was engaged in banter with a half crazy Jew, and called him 'dog', whereupon the Jew caught hold of a cur that happened to be passing and, yanking it up by its tail, bade the other observe that since the animal was uncircumcised, the resemblance lay elsewhere—thereby turning the joke on him. ('Gracioso fue un cuento de un Judio medio loco con un Christiano, que burlandose con el y llamandole perro, tomó un can que acaso passava entre ellos, y levantandole en alto por la cola le dixo que le mirasse que no estava circunciso, que mas se le asemejava à el, que assi, retornandole desta suerte la burla'.)

Amsterdam itself, he points out, there resided Jewish agents of the Kings of Spain, Portugal, and Denmark, the Duke of Hanover, and other princes as well.[142]

As against analysis and conceptual views of the situation of Israel amongst the nations, the yearning for redemption is woven into the very fibre of the religious literature produced by the Portuguese Jews of Amsterdam. From Spain and Portugal they had brought with them a princely cargo of hopes and expectations as to the realization of the prophetic visions of the end of days and Israel's deliverance.

In the course of generations of crypto-Jewish experience in the Iberian peninsula the concept of hope—*esperanza*—had come to be a messianic *terminus technicus*: and awareness of this circumstance was so widespread amongst Christians there that Spanish literature evinces many an example of its satirical and provocative application in order to characterize that feature which so obviously identified 'New Christians', viz. their living in a state of persistent hope and expectancy of redemption.[143] Once having reached Amsterdam, former crypto-Jews unbridled their tongues to give expression to those messianic yearnings which, over generations of residence in lands where persecution stalked abroad, had been checked or suppressed. Their aspirations took various forms, and found expression in differing ways of which the content and import were not always mutually compatible. Some of the poems of Daniel Levi (Miguel) de Barrios, whom we have already noticed as having been one of the most far-going enthusiasts for Sabbatai Ṣevi in Amsterdam, are stamped with the mark of ecstatic expectation of the arrival of the messiah; and his writings are, in general, imbued with a messianic orientation of a utopian and apocalyptic kind. Scarifying pictures of the 'end of days'—the 'war of Gog and Magog' developed by rabbinic eschatology from a hint in Ezekiel, the clash of the mighty rulers which he visualizes as being fought out between Rome and the Ottoman empire, the end of the world and the redemption of Israel which would rise out of its ruins—plenty of this is to be found in de Barrios' messianic writings.[144] The

---

[142] *Apud* Limborch, *De Veritate Rel. Christ.*, p. 103.

[143] Herrero García, pp. 629–35. See e.g. the poem by David Antunes printed in *Elogios . . . Bernal*, p. 42: 'En otra esperança hallamos / segun la presente accion, / Que esta nuestra redencion, / Propinqua con el Masias, / quiere Dios en nuestros dias / Restituirnos Sion . . .' and cf. *Prev. Div.* (n. 126 above), f. 2ʳ: 'en la esperança de nuestra redencion . . . y animarle a la esperansa de su redemcion . . .'

[144] See, *inter alia*, de Barrios' *Imperio de Dios—Piedra Derribadora de la Soñada Estatua, desde el Año de 1639 al de 1700*, Amsterdam, undated, but written after he had become

settlement of Jews in the smiling city of Amsterdam was for him a symbol pointing towards the coming dawn of redemption. He finds hints at this in fragments excerpted from prophetical texts, which he analyses for numerological cyphers or by resort to sometimes strange or far-fetched exegetical onomatopoeia.[145] In the encounter within a single city, i.e. Amsterdam, of Sephardi Jews with Ashkenazi, i.e. German and Polish Jews, de Barrios claimed to recognize a precondition for the fulfilment of the prophecy of Jeremiah (3: 18), 'in those days Judah shall join Israel, and together they shall come from a northern land into the land I gave their fathers as their patrimony' (New English Bible). 'Here we are,' he writes, 'two peoples, that of the Jews of Spain and that of the Jews of Germany and Poland, in Amsterdam today, as symbols of the house of Judah and the house of Israel.'[146] The circumstance that de Barrios was producing these prophetic and indeed apocalyptic items of exegesis during a period when he personally was affected by intense emotional disturbance does not lessen their significance as evidence of the immediacy of messianic sentiment and commitment that was the heritage of some, at least, of his fellow-congregants in Amsterdam. The items here referred to were printed in books to which lay leaders and rabbis of the congregation alike appended their commendations: and taken together, they are valid indicators of the predisposition of those who had escaped from the clutches of the Inquisition to recognize, in the distinct improvement in their situation marked by their settlement in Amsterdam, the beginnings of a process which would inexorably conduct them from the 'northern land' to the 'land of their fathers'.

There was another figure within the congregation in whose writings the motif of longing for redemption stands out in high relief, and he too had been one of the followers of Sabbatai Ṣevi during the great

disillusioned in Sabbatai Ṣevi (see above, chap. 8, p. 233). It is to be observed that already in the 15th cent. the idea of an imminent end to the world was widespread amongst crypto-Jews in Spain; see Beinart, *on Trial*, pp. 284 f., and *Ciudad Real*, i, p. 27 (evidence of Juan Morales, in the case of Sancho de Ciudad). Isaac Abravanel dealt with the subject in his *Miph'aloth 'elohim*, (Venice, 1592, part ii, chap. 4, p. 18), and Netanyahu (*Abravanel³*, pp. 132 f.) assumes that he took his eschatology from Origen, *de Principiis*, iii, 6 (J. P. Migne, *Patrologia Graeca*, 11, Paris, 1857, col. 333 f.): but the evidence is seriously overstrained.

[145] e.g. expatiating on Isa. 30: 17, 'like ... a signal post [Hebrew *nes*] on a hill', he detects a pointer to Nes, a village near Amsterdam; see his *Monte Herm.*, f. 15ʳ, similarly *Mediar*, p. 70, on the Ij at Amsterdam, p. 68, on the significance of the name Amstel and the hints with which it is supposedly pregnant.

[146] *Mediar*, p. 60: '... los dos Pueblos de los Judíos de España, y de Alemania con los de Polonia; somos mapas oy en Amsterdam de las Gentes de Juda, y de Israel ...'

From Crypto-Judaism to Open Judaism 375

upsurge of enthusiasm in 1666. Pereyra's messianism is of a different order from that of de Barrios, and it contains no apocalyptic or utopian ingredients: furthermore, his writings bear no trace at all of eschatological calculation of a messianic timetable or of purported explanations as to why such a timetable was in point of fact running late. Neither does he devote the slightest attention to the content of the vision of the end of days, or to the character of the messianic age. On the contrary, his work is entirely permeated by concern regarding the right path for the Jewish people to chose in order that redemption might be realizable. 'A feeling of repentance that is truly alive, a penitence that makes strict demands upon us—that is the way to secure God's mercy, and with it reconciliation to the divine grace.'[147] The object of his two books (referred to in an earlier chapter)[148] was to prepare the ground for a popular penitential movement that should induce the Jewish people to implement the precepts of the divine Law in a perfect manner and in utter self-dedication, since it was through divine Law that 'God demonstrated what is implied by the obligation of serving Him, whose service is the acme of happiness and the means of achieving salvation'.[149]

Isaac Orobio's approach is yet again different. On the one hand, he denies the propriety of would-be prognosticators of eschatological dates, and he takes his stand against the 'idle curiosity of some of our sages of antiquity, who professed to be able to pinpoint the stages of our redemption within a bracket of dates: when they had been proved wrong, and their prognostications a delusion—since the opposite of what they so confidently forecast transpired—this led to an increase in the arrogant disdain of the Gentiles for the holy words of truth regarding our ultimately assured bliss'.[150] On the other hand, he hints at his own rejection of the view that held redemption to be something contingent on Israel's own actions. 'When God says that He will deliver them from amongst the nations', he says, 'He does not make such deliverance conditional upon [the Jews'] will, but on the fact that such is the will of divine providence, so that his holy promise shall be fulfilled.'[151]

What Isaac has to say about redemption and Jewish messianic hopes all occurs within the context of his disputational writing directed at

---
[147] Pereyra, *Certeza*, p. 287: '... el vivo arrepentimiento, y estrecha penitencia, es el medio para conseguir esta misericordia, y con ella la reconciliacion a la divina gracia ...'
[148] See above, chap. 8, pp. 220 f.
[149] *Certeza*, p. 4: '... pues en ella les mostro qual sea la obligacion de servirle, que es la summa felicidad, y medio para adquirir la salvación ...'
[150] See *Prev. Div.* (n. 126 above), f. 51ʳ.   [151] Ibid., f. 73ᵛ.

Christian theologians. The latter had pointed the finger at the *naïveté* of those eschatological prognostications and self-proclaimed heralds of redemption who had risen from within Jewry over the generations, and whose hopes and blithe predictions had been proved false by events. They also maintained that part of the promises divinely vouchsafed to Israel had already been fulfilled, and some others had been conditional on Jewish behaviour; and that from the moment when Jews had gone off the rails and had spurned the ways of God, God Himself had annulled those promises. There is no doubt that Isaac's principal aim here was to dispose of these contentions completely, but what he says does make it possible to deduce that his basic position in regard to messianism was essentially a circumspect and conservative one. He understood well enough the dangers implicit in any messianic activism that stimulated ecstatic enthusiasm, nurtured exaggerated aspirations, and led in the end to disappointment and disillusion. During his early Amsterdam years he had been a witness of the Sabbatean excitement, and the overwhelming disappointment which followed in the wake of its débâcle reinforced his circumspection. What he has to say, addressed as it is to his Christian controversialists, is intended to expose the fallacy of the active and radical messianic self-orientation which was still prevalent amongst some members of the Amsterdam community to which he belonged.

Orobio's conservatism likewise finds expression in his description of the messianic age:

> The messiah is not going to come in order to effect miracles, nor did Isaiah declare that he would revive the dead or exorcize those possessed by demons, or anything else of the sort, but that he would make truth and justice prevail on earth, and would defend God's people . . .[152]

God had promised his people a redemption that was to be both physical and spiritual, the latter meaning 'the stripping away from their hearts of all human predilections, and of the evil inclination in its entirety, in order that, being purified, they may apply themselves to the love of their Creator and so attain divine grace'.[153] However, until physical redemption has taken place Israel's spiritual redemption will

---

[152] See *Resp. Pred. franc.*, ed. Amzalak, p. 58: 'El Massiah no ha de venir a hazer milagros, ni esso dixo Iesayas, que resucitaria muertos, ni livraria endemoniados, ni cozas semejantes, sino que haria verdad, y justicia en la tierra y protegaria [*sic*] al pueblo de Dios . . .'

[153] *Prev. Div.*, f. 74ʳ: 'Esta es la redemcion espiritual de Israel, que consiste en desnudar sus coraçones de los affectos humanos, y de toda mala inclinacion, para que puros se empleen en el amor de su Criador, y consigan su diuina gracia . . .'

not ensue, 'for so long as they are not gathered in from amongst the nations to the beloved land of their birth, Israel know that they cannot merit that spiritual redemption which God has promised them'.[154] In Orobio's view, redemption will enable Israel to achieve five things: (*a*) ingathering of the exiles to the Land of Israel, (*b*) liberation from domination by world-powers, (*c*) conversion to a holy and righteous people, (*d*) the attainment of perpetual peace, and (*e*) the subjugation of those enemies who had enslaved them during the period of their exile, and their elimination.[155]

The utopian basis is not, indeed, altogether lacking in Isaac's eschatology, but it is relegated to a purely secondary position. Typologically, his approach stands closer to a restorative messianic concept, longing for national renewal whilst idealizing the past, when Israel dwelt in their land and supposedly served God in humility and dedication.[156] In this regard, return to the land of the fathers occupies a central place in Orobio's thinking. Whilst still in exile, Israel is sunk in 'the barren desert of the nations, like a root in parched soil: but when his divine power lovingly redeems them, when they are in receipt of that irrigation which flows from his mercies, Israel will spring up like a verdant willow, like a sprig from earth that is dry, back in the land where, over so many centuries, they had struck root'.[157]

In Isaac Orobio's theology the vision is turned into a wistful dream that strengthens the morale of the people amid the darkness in which, during their exile, they are engulfed. But behind his fierce longing for Israel's liberation from subservience to the Gentiles, one can detect the warning accents of a sober and conservative rationalism, sensitive to any erosion of the continuous existence of an 'independent commonwealth' that is constituted by the Jewish people, for all that it is still in exile. 'And when once "he comes to Shiloh" [in accordance with the messianic interpretation of Genesis 49, 10 so beloved of Jewish tradition] — something that will take place at the time when divine providence shall determine — then "the sceptre will never [more] depart from Judah".'[158]

[154] Ibid., f. 75^r.
[155] Ibid., ff. 159^r f.
[156] See the typology of messianism propounded by Scholem, 'Towards an Understanding of the Messianic Idea in Judaism', *Messianic Idea*, pp. 3 f.
[157] *Prev. Div.*, ff. 246^v f: '... en el dicierto esteril de las naciones, esta como raiz en tierra seca, mas quando su divino poder le redima amoroso, quando reciba el riego de sus piedades, subira como verde sauce, como ramo de la seca tierra, en donde por tantos siglos echo sus raizes...'
[158] Ibid., f. 181^v.

Epilogue

The life and literary undertakings of Isaac Orobio de Castro are symbolic of the fate and fortunes of the Spanish and Portuguese Sephardi diaspora in seventeenth-century western Europe. His passage from Christianity to Judaism—the crucial watershed of his life—is a faithful mirror of the history of a whole community that succeeded in dropping the mask of a Christian conformity that had been forcibly imposed upon them by life in a society where the open profession of Judaism was proscribed, and in finding their bearings again within the Jewish community.

Their reversion to Judaism was the result of changes both subjective and objective. The cruelty of the Inquisition that spread its terror through the 'New Christian' population of the Iberian peninsula, and the ordinances regarding *limpieza de sangre*, made it impossible even for those who wished to do so to become indistinguishably integrated into Christian society. It was these factors which constituted the crypto-Jewish community as an isolated and persecuted social group. Flight from Spain and Portugal made it possible for them to be rid of the badge of shame which, over a couple of centuries, had been the heritage of the 'New Christian'. But in addition to this, the yearning of crypto-Jews to reintegrate openly into Judaism in lands where this was feasible was principally nurtured by their feeling of Jewish identity which, for many of them, generations of an enforced life of Christian conformity had not dulled. That sense of identity had both spiritual and ideological components, which had crystallized out during the generations that they had had to brace themselves to meet the experiences of persecution and of leading a double life. Despite severance of connections with the major centres of Jewish activity many of them managed to keep the commandments of Judaism by means of various subterfuges—organizing secret meetings for joint prayer and other ceremonies, and transmitting some knowledge of traditions, customs and basic principles of faith from one generation to its successor. The history of the Alvares de Orobio family offers an instructive example of this phenomenon—which, as an instance of human perseverance, captures the imagination and surely arrests attention.

Of course, not all members of the 'New Christian' community in Spain and Portugal were cast in the same mould. Not a few of them willingly accepted Catholic Christianity and made efforts to assimilate into it: but even these were subject to the influence of their origin and their status within Iberian society, *qua* members of an isolated minority regarded with suspicion on religious grounds, and this in itself rendered them particularly sensitive where matters of faith were concerned. The facts of life in the peninsula goaded many of them into investigating the differences between the various religions, and made them hesitant about swallowing whole the complex of attitudes maintained by the Catholic establishment that was itself responsible for imposing the constrictions to which they were subject: with the result that their ears were alertly tuned to pick up any criticism or strictures concerning the way that the Church conducted itself. This is the reason why so many 'New Christians' were attracted by the influence of Erasmus and by the spiritual movements that flourished in Spain in the sixteenth century. Some 'New Christians' came, in course of time, to be nihilists or sceptics; others of them inclined towards a philosophical, universalist faith of markedly deistic complexion.

Not dissimilar were the modes of thinking of those crypto-Jews who openly reverted to Judaism in the Sephardi communities of western Europe. Occasionally they attempted to introduce into Judaism reforms of a rationalist or spiritual variety analogous to those which their opposite numbers in Spain would have liked to introduce into Catholicism. It is in this light that we have to view the criticisms advanced by Uriel d'Acosta against the commandments whose sanction is the oral Law. Others proceeded so far as to deny the election of Israel and its unique character altogether, this being of a piece with their rejection of all forms of religious particularism in their heartfelt desire to achieve a faith that should be philosophical and rational. It was down that road that Spinoza and Prado went when, in 1656–8, they were excommunicated by the *Ma'amad* of the Portuguese community of Amsterdam.

The majority of former crypto-Jews, like Isaac Orobio, adapted themselves into Judaism, giving the seventeenth-century West European Sephardi diaspora its character. However, they also brought with them from the land of their birth a cultural and intellectual cargo of extraordinary richness: and it was a cargo which, as far as concerned Jewish values, was a strange one. Many of them had received their education in the leading universities of Spain and Portugal, in Dominican priories and Jesuit seminaries, and they were soaked in concepts from the sphere of Catholic theology, Iberian neo-scholasticism, and the Spanish baroque. Clearly, included amongst all this there would be fragile items, liable to fly into pieces on colliding with a normative Judaism, as distinct from the Judaism about which they knew from occasional, superficial glimpses derived from secondary sources. What, therefore, is surprising is the way in which so many of them succeeded in giving a new expression to those Christian values which, in their youth, they had made their own. Quite paradoxically, that same Christian (and specifically Catholic) cultural tradition which they had carried away from the Iberian peninsula sometimes permitted them to articulate their Jewish thinking. If one studies the literature produced in the academies of this Sephardi diaspora, it is sometimes difficult to accept what a careful investigation shows, namely that many of the arguments advanced in defence of the concept of the election of Israel and its unique quality, or to confirm the reliability of Scripture, have been borrowed from distinguished Christian writings produced in Spain and in Portugal. In controversy with the dissident proponents of heterodox views who arose in their own midst, the spokesmen of the congregation—both rabbinical and lay—advanced arguments drawn both from Christian scholasticism and from new lines of thought current during their own period in Catholic speculation and theology, in response to the criticism voiced by the Protestant camp.

Crypto-Jewish life in the Iberian peninsula brought about in many of those concerned a new address to the question of Jewish identity—an approach which is, to some extent, a harbinger of the contemporary difficulty in determining who, and what, is a Jew. Since, as crypto-Jews, they had been precluded from sharing a mode of life guided by Jewish Law, many of them came to feel that an interior, emotionally-felt identity with the Jewish heritage was more important than the actual implementation of the commandments. Many of those who escaped from the lands of the Inquisition and became reintegrated into the house of Israel did not lose this attitude. And, although it was declared invalid by the spiritual leadership of the various Sephardi congregations, the rabbis of which engaged in crusades against it, it left its stamp upon the ways in which the Sephardi diaspora of western Europe conceived its Judaism. In the same way that many of them were prepared, at the time of the Sabbatean bubble, to lap up its antinomian doctrines (which, for former crypto-Jews like Abraham Michael Cardoso, were recognized as being an integral element in the working out of the messianic process), so they evinced a readiness to absorb deistic and rationalist ideas. The writings of Isaac Orobio are consequently an accurate image of the reaction against ideas of this kind that had found a receptive audience amongst some sections of the Amsterdam community.

As heirs to two traditions, the Jewish and the European, they evolved a new understanding of what it was that constituted their Jewish heritage. This new conception was achieved by application of concepts and values brought from the Christian world in which they had been educated and acquired from the new Europe that was emerging around them. But it was precisely their own intimate acquaintance with the world of Christian concepts, and their considerable competence in the techniques of Christian theology, that impelled them to accentuate the differences between Judaism and Christianity, in their desire to have their own religious and spiritual identity emerge clearly as an entity that they could describe. In this sphere of activity, the contribution of Isaac Orobio is of great significance.

Characters like Orobio aroused the curiosity of Christian scholars in western Europe, who found matters of particular interest to them in their literary productions—written mainly in Spanish, Portuguese, or Latin. Correspondence and meetings between Christian and Sephardi Jewish men of learning came to be common. These 'friendly conversations' and disputations were nourished by a conceptual world based upon philosophy, theology, and general culture shared by both the Christians and the Jews who had been educated in Christian establishments. Such contacts contributed not a little to the great change in the relationship of Jews to the Christian environment which was to leave so clear a mark on seventeenth-century history.

Indeed, in many spheres these Sephardi Jews had realized the ideals of the *haskalah* ('enlightenment') movement of the central European Jewry that followed in the wake of the German *Aufklärung*, and they in fact anticipated German Jewry's cultural enlargement by at least a century. They created a rich literature in Spanish and Portuguese, and in the educational institutions which they established these languages were formally taught. Both by private teachers and by those in congregational employ, the youth were taught Latin and other European languages. Their schools were amongst the most modern in Europe both in regard to organization and pedagogical method. Particular emphasis was placed on learning the Hebrew language grammatically, and study of the Bible preceded study of the Talmud and other literature of Jewish Halakhic self-regulation. The economic activities of the members of the congregation and their social connections induced them to study the local vernacular literature, to cherish the cultural values of their environment, and to achieve a new appraisal of relations with the non-Jewish world, attempting to fit into its society successfully. But in contrast to the *haskalah* in Germany and to the movement that followed in its wake in eastern Europe, this seventeenth-century Sephardi type of Judaism had no ideology with a professed programme of 'enlightenment' intended to engineer changes in Jewish society. The syntheses that these Sephardi Jews fashioned grew up so to speak organically, as part and parcel of their unique form of Jewish social and spiritual life.

In studying the character, the life-history, the world of intellectual ideas and religious belief of Isaac Orobio de Castro, I have attempted to draw attention to the roots of the changes which came about amongst the membership of this remarkable Jewish community—brands plucked from the pyres of those 'exiles of Jerusalem in the land of Spain'—as they made their way from crypto-Judaism back into the Jewish fold, and as there took shape a cultural and spiritual type of which the house of Israel in its widest sense has known no parallel.

Appendices

APPENDIX A
The Iconography of Isaac Orobio

As far as is known, two portraits exist which are alleged to show the likeness of Isaac Orobio, both of them being copperplate engravings. The first,[1] by Jacobus Groenwolt, is dated 1727 (see Plate 3): the second (see Plate 1) is anonymous and undated. It has been claimed that the second of these represents the seventeenth-century Dutch-Jewish calligrapher Jacob Gadella (Guedelha) but Brugmans and Frank reproduce it as being that of Isaac Orobio, and this identification is accepted by Alfred Rubens.[2] The first is the better known of the two: in it Isaac appears as a military figure wearing a corselet and holding a baton in his right hand. In the background may be seen an edifice suggestive of a shore-line fort, with a man-o'-war standing off. The scrollwork beneath the portrait is surmounted by a coat of arms, dexter a lion rampant and sinister nine upward-pointed crescents arranged in descending rows of three, two, and one: the helm, a helmet with visor lowered. The impression conveyed is that these are the arms of Orobio.

The portrait excites surprise in view of the military dress in which Groenwolt saw fit to portray his subject. Since Orobio, the well-known Jewish physician and philosopher, never in his life served in the army, the style of portraiture has invited figurative interpretation—as if the artist was concerned to throw into relief the subject's character as a doughty fighter who took part in many a polemical encounter both with Christian theologians and heterodox Jews, offering a vigorous defence of his faith and religious views. Great, therefore, was my astonishment on discovering that this portrait is substantially identical with another (see Plate 4), which appeared in a book published in Brussels in 1666 as the likeness of Alonso de Zepeda, with whom Isaac Orobio engaged in controversy regarding the philosophy of Raymond Lull: it was, in fact, published in Zepeda's rejoinder to Orobio, entitled *Defensa de los términos y doctrina de S. Raymond Lullio*.[3] The similarity between the two portraits is amazing: the dress is identical, and the coat of arms figured on the left of the portrait of Zepeda is identical with that in Groenwolt's portrait of 'Orobio'. It is also understandable that Zepeda, as an offficer in the Spanish army, should be represented in military dress. Obviously Groenwolt omitted the specifically Christian symbolism which surmounts the portrait of Zepeda: but no one will

---

[1] See Rubens, *Iconography*, p. 94, no. 2036/7.
[2] The portrait forms part of the Solomons collection in the Jewish Theological Seminary of New York, where it is described as being the likeness of Jacob Gadella; see Rubens, ibid., and Brugmans and Frank, p. 657.
[3] On Zepeda's book, and his controversy with Orobio, see above, chap. 7, pp. 179 f.

doubt that he used the central figure as the basis of his own representation of Isaac Orobio.

It is difficult to account for Groenwolt's error. Could it have been that Zepeda's picture had become detached from a copy of his book, and, in the course of events to which it was subject, not only the fact of the disputation became forgotten, but meanwhile all living memory (or other evidence) of Orobio's physiognomy was lost? Or was there someone around in 1727 who recollected that the portrait was in some way or other linked to the Jewish doctor of Amsterdam? Such a conjecture cannot be substantiated, and indeed any explanation that is put forward must remain speculative. The one thing that is clear is that the portrait in Plate 1 is not that of Isaac Orobio, but that of Alonso de Zepeda, his controversialist.

As regards the likeness in Plate 1, we have no means of proving that it is, in fact, that of Isaac Orobio. Rubens,[4] who claims to be able to see a similarity between some of its facial features and those in the portrait in Plate 3, regards this as proof that Plate 1 does figure the likeness of Orobio. One may entertain doubts as to the supposed similarity, but, even if it is granted, it is now clear that this can do nothing to substantiate the claim that Plate 1 displays Orobio's portrait.

[4] Rubens, ibid.

APPENDIX B

Poetical Account of the Plague at Málaga, 1637, by Baltasar Alvares (Isaac Orobio de Castro)

(See pp. 15–24)

The only known copy of the original print (Málaga, 1637) is in the library of the Hispanic Society of America. It was reprinted by Y. Kaplan in *Helmantica* (Salamanca), 29, 1978, pp. 212–31.

Epilogo | de lo que | passo en la peste de | la ciudad de Malaga este año de | 1637.

Dedicado al insigne | Colegio de la Madre de Dios de los Teologos, | de la Universidad de Alcala.

Por el licenciado Don | Baltasar Alvarez de Orobio, Colegial | del mismo Colegio y natural | de Malaga.

Con licencia en Malaga, por Iuan Serrano | de Vargas y Urueña, Año de 1637.

[*1v*] Al Insigne Collegio [*sic*] de | la Madre de Dios de los Theologos | de la Universidad de Alcala.

Teatro illustre, archivo de la sciencia,   1
Tesoro de eloquencia,
A quien insigne, hasta la imbidia llama,
Materia dando al Canto de la fama
Atiende al son de un rustico instrumento,   5
que en lastimosas vozes divertidas,
Temiendo si del vulgo el vituperio
Ocaziona tristeza al pensamiento,
Perdidas tantas, descriviendo vidas,
Que es funesto terror à este emisferio.   10

No ambiciosos aplausos solicita
De mi ruda camena el tosco acento,
Vana esperança, no mi pluma mueve,
ni presuncion inadvertida incita:,

Appendix B

De propia obligacion de vido intento 15
Inculta Lyra à descrivir se atreve:
Atiende pues, o celebre liceo,
De la parca el mas tragico trofeo.

El lic. Don Balthasar Alvarez de Orobio

[2r] Breve Epilogo | de lo que passo en la | Peste de Malaga, Año de | 1637.

Concede (o Clio) a estancias lastimosas 1
sonoro el son, y tristes los acentos,
vozes no inspires, a mi lengua hermosas,
dignas de alegre canto, y mas alientos;
pues para cantar cosas tan penosas 5
retorica son claros sentimientos:
mueve mi pluma, a que funesta cante,
y tanto mueva, que su canto espante

Bellos matices renovaba el prado
pagandole al Abril tributo en flores: 10
de plantas odoriferas poblado,
beldades obstentava en sus verdores:
mas claro nunca de Faeton dorado
el sacro Padre comunicó ardores,
quando a Malaga tanto mal oprime, 15
que llora Telus y Neptuno gime.

[2v] La Causa inmensa, y Causa no causada, 1
por delitos humanos ofendida,
pretende a esta Ciudad, ya dessolada,
dar con justicia mas constante vida:
y en medio de sus gustos olvidada 5
de quien la busca, quando mas perdida;
rigorosa permite, que influencia
castigue tanto error con pestilencia.

Llega primero el mal, aunque encubierto
con sus claros efectos ofendiendo: 10
empieça a divulgarse con un cierto
rumor del Pueblo, que ya esta temiendo:
derriba algunos, sin bastar acierto
de arte Apolinea, que le va ocurriendo:
que quando llega del morir la suerte 15
no ay remedio eficiaz, y ay cierta muerte.

El gran castigo conocio la pleue
que ya por la Ciudad se dilatava,
cada qual mira lo que al Cielo deve,
y atiende a muchos, que ya el mal acaba: 20
el vulgo ciego, que a su Dios se atreve,
los precautorios, y clausura alaba,
sin mirar, que si esta Dios ofendido,
negocia mas humilde, que escondido.

[*3r*] Empieça otro rigor, que juntamente   1
al mas constante coraçon aflige:
faltan los alimentos a la gente
aunque el sacro Pastor tal mal corrige,
disponiendo piadoso, si prudente,   5
comun limosna, a cuyo fin ellige
noble un criado de piedad armado,
que en las armas mostro ser su criado.

La dura parca con su accion prosigue
joven hilo y adulto destroçando: 10
tanto el rigor de su tixera sigue,
que es el matar, el ir amenaçando,
y con tanta crueldad el mal persigue
que a quantos va ofendiendo, va matando,
ocasionando en timidos espantos   15
infaustas penas, lastimosos llantos.

El Marques diligente de la Rosa
cuya prudencia a Malaga sustenta,
ocurre a esta tragedia lastimosa
al uno ampara, quando al otro alienta,   20
su persona permite, que animosa
de todas partes el peligro sienta,
andando entre los muertos tan galante,
que es a la muerte afrenta, si arrogante.

[*3v*] Formase un Hospital, con advertencia   1
de escusar el contagio, que se enciende,
señala del Cabildo la prudencia
(que estorvar solo tanto mal pretende)
hombres cuyo cuidado, y assistencia   5
alivia el daño, a quien el mal ofende,
devido, sin faltar medicamento
sobrada cura, y prodigo alimento.

Divagan muchos hombres diligentes,
llevando al Hospital al que padece, 10
pues de los padres, hijos, y parientes
ninguno a verle, ni a assistir se ofrece,
cosas tan tristes, trances tan urgentes,
que huye el marido, y la muger perece,
dexa su alvergue apenas, y se ausenta, 15
quando el mismo rigor experimenta.

Prestos los cavalleros Regidores,
con noble zelo, con Christiano intento,
los medios mas seguros, y mejores
buscan, por dar en tanto mal aliento: 20
siendo tan a su cargo los dolores
de la Ciudad, y el justo sentimiento,
que era morir, en ocasion tan dura,
pena menor, que ver tal desventura.

[4r] La peste apenas con rigor derriba 1
hombre qualquiera, quando al punto llegan
unas andas, en quien del bien estriva
la mayor parte, porque en ellas llevan,
toda persona enferma, o ya no viva, 5
sin que ningunas escusarse puedan,
y assi aunque el mal se aumenta, y multiplica,
tan facilmente no se comunica.

Crece el numero tanto de los muertos,
que les falta sagrado al enterrarlos 10
recurre la piedad a los desiertos,
hazen carneros para sepultarlos,
donde con poca tierra, y cal cubiertos
apenas ay lugar adonde echarlos,
siendo en aquesta sin defensa guerra, 15
dulce lisonja siete pies de tierra.

Timido el Pueblo, hazia los campos huye,
ocupando los vientos sus gemidos:
choças el miedo, de arboles construye,
tristes dexando ya los patrios nidos, 20
crece el contagio, la Ciudad destruye
adonde buelven de la peste heridos:
todos pidiendo en tanto desconsuelo
remedio humano, si piedad al Cielo.

The Plague at Málaga, 1637

[4v] Llora Malaga sola, y despoblada,   1
solo de penas, y desdichas llena:
no ay casa en ella que no este cerrada,
siendo una general, y comun pena,
de cuerpos muertos (o, dolor!) sembrada   5
esta su selva, en otro tiempo amena:
en una casa ayer suspiros davan,
y oy salen muertos los que ayer lloravan.

Sucedio en la Ciudad un caso estraño,
muy digno de admirarse, y referirlo: 10
conociendo una Mora el desengaño
creyo el Baptismo, y quiso recebirlo,
y previniendo en la tardança el daño,
no cessando la Mora de pedirlo,
antes que el mal llegasse a desalmarla   15
un Religioso quiso Baptizarla.

Hallose à aquesta accion presente un Moro,
y sintiendo el desprecio de su seta,
por impedir a la alma tal tesoro
el braço al padre con furor aprieta,   20
Barbaro sin respeto, y sin decoro:
vozes da el Religioso, al vulgo inquieta,
que a voz de moros, y de Sacramento
dize, mueran los moros al memento.

[5r] Que era, se persuadio la turba loca,   1
el sacro Pan, de su altivez despojo;
la Fe le incita, y a vengar provoca,
si incierto agravio, su devido enojo:
mientras a guerra la campana toca,   5
al uno dexan muerto, al otro cojo;
donde huye el Moro, alli el peligro encuentra
y sale la alma, por do la alma le entra.

Otra sospecha incierta nacio luego,
que estando la ciudad inadvertida,   10
el Alarbe esquadron quiere con fuego,
que Malaga se atienda destruida:
impetuoso el vulgo, ardiente y ciego,
quita a los Moros con rigor la vida,
haziendo que aquel barbaro trofeo   15
vaya a pisar las ondas de Letheo.

A lastima movia el tierno llanto,
que forman en su mal los Sarracenos,
estavan todos con dolor y espanto,
viendo a sus hijos, y a los padres menos: 20
levantase una voz del vulgo, en tanto,
diziendo: Los Arabigos obcenos,
divino del Altar llevan sustento,
propicio el mar, y favorable el viento.

[5v] No queda mozo que atrevido y fuerte, 1
no quiera con sus armas embarcarse,
va un esquadron, espanto de la muerte,
a alcançar a los moros, y vengarse,
teniendo cada qual a buena suerte, 5
brazo robusto hallar donde emplearse;
temio Neptuno la animosa gente,
y le rindio su timido tridente.

Quando unos Lusitanos este dia,
por huir de la peste, con destino 10
de llegar a su patria, y alegria,
salen del puerto en diafano camino:
llegan los Castellanos, y a porfia,
alma se hazen del breado pino,
danles entrada con sencillo pecho, 15
y ellos intenan un inorme hecho.

Empiezan a robarles sus haziendas,
hiriendo al que procura la defensa,
no contentos de aver sus ricas prendas,
con heridas a tres hazen ofensa, 20
por robar, entre si tienen contiendas,
sin que de la razon el freno vença;
en rojo humor los dexan ya bañados,
y con alma, se buelven desalmados.

[6r] Supo el noble Marques desdicha tanta 1
y haziendo informacion justa primero,
haze que paguen dos con la garganta,
sin bastar ruegos, ni admitir tercero:
otros azotes, su justicia canta, 5
que es tanto como sabio justiciero:
luego patente se miro el engaño,
y se sintio de la morisma el daño.

The Plague at Málaga, 1637

En tanto, la ciudad sus males siente,
ya perdido el vigor, y sin aliento,
menos dolor tal daño no consiente,
pues en un dia mueren mas de ciento:
los Capuchinos, con amor ardiente,
por aliviar tan rigido tormento,
andando entre el peligro de los malos,
pobres reparten, providos regalos.

Luego su Magestad, que guarde el cielo,
en los lugares mas circunvezinos,
Alcaldes pone, que con noble zelo
den alimento, y guarden los caminos;
siendo en aquesto tanto su desuelo,
que humanos si, parecen ya divinos,
pues fue con abundancia su remedio
para vivir, en tanta muerte, el medio.

[6v] Quando los Reynos mas necessitados
de acudir a las guerras con dinero,
mirò su Magestad los desdichados,
que padecen miseria en mal tan fiero:
liberal libra treinta mil ducados,
que entriega el de millones Tesorero;
y assi celebra el pueblo, aunque no sano,
mano de un Rey, divinamente humano.

Muchas nocturnas se hazen Processiones,
a caños derramando el humor rojo,
todo son vozes, todo exclamaciones
al son de azote, y de delgado abrojo:
ya no rezan, si lloran, oraciones,
para aplacar de Dios el justo enojo,
ningunos llanto tan devido niegan,
lagrimas todas a la tierra entriegan.

Con fuertes sogas muchos van atados,
por desatar de su pecado el nudo,
otros van por la calle arrodillados,
siendo al demonio la rodilla escudo:
otros en las espadas van aspados,
el medio cuerpo palido desnudo;
los niños tiernos, en comun concordia,
piden llorando, a Dios misericordia.

[7r] Un juyzio final Malaga obstenta   1
en vozes tristes, llantos lastimosos:
remedio en vano el temeroso intenta,
pues a los de salud mas cuydadosos
la dura muerte, de matar hambrienta,   5
ocasiona desastres dolorosos,
hiriendo sea, al que en los montes solo,
dexa apenas llegar la luz de Apolo.

Ay en el hospital cuydado grande
de socorrer a tan tremendos males,   10
no ay corazon tan duro, a quien no ablande
el ver destrozos de la muerte iguales,
ni quien limosnas licitas no mande,
y viendo ya morir los oficiales,
su adversa teme, cada qual, ventura,   15
pues sobra el mal, y falta ya la cura.

Todo, el Obispo y el Marques, atienden,
que en valor ambos, y piedad, florecen,
valientes, tanto mal vencer pretenden,
cosas haziendo, donde convalecen   20
los que huyen a la muerte, y se defienden
de los rigores, que furiosos crecen,
con tal prisa, que llenos los primeros,
hazen para enterrar, otros carneros.

[7v] Confuso el hospital, es cosa estraña,   1
verlo que incluie, y espantoso encierra:
unos con frenesi, con rabia y saña
mueren, tascando de furor la tierra;
otros, a quien el juizio no se daña,   5
sienten el mal, que fuerte le haze guerra;
este gime, aquel llora, el otro muere,
y llegan otros, que la peste hiere.

En tanto que veloz, la parca fea,
desune almas de cuerpos animosos,   10
el boraz elemento al cielo humea,
quemando muchos bienes muy preciosos,
sin ser excesso, que al mirarle crea
qualquiera, viendo fuegos tan briosos,
(de ignea exalacion, si no esta ciego)   15
que baxo al suelo la region del fuego.

The Plague at Málaga, 1637

El Cabildo Eclesiastico resiste
a tanto daño, si animoso, estable,
mientras el mal al mas guardado embiste,
sin guardarse se muestra incontrastable,
en cuya generosa mano assiste
caridad liberal, piedad notable,
limosnas dando pues, dos Prebendados
andan a socorrer necessitados.

[8r] El Provisor, a cuyo pecho ilustre
le negocia el valor eternidades,
dando a su nombre el mas devido lustre
que admiró el mundo, y vieron las edades;
aunque la peste su salud deslustre,
propias negando ya comodidades,
sin observarse a tan molestos males,
visita con amor los hospitales.

El Alcalde Mayor, con fe gallarda,
lo que conviene a la ciudad ordena,
negociando el remedio, nada tarda,
por dar alivio grande a grande pena
su vida, liberal, tan poco guarda,
que a la parte que ve de enfermos llena
llega atrevido, con amor visita,
y dando alientos, desalientos quita.

El Pan divino, si vida del hombre,
executa piedad donde castiga,
que disfrazando el Pan su excelso nombre,
de tanto daño la crueldad mitiga,
no admite Palio, por tener renombre
de Capitan que a penitencia instiga,
pues dando vida aqui, y alli matando,
a los mismos que mata, va animando.

[8v] Mueren los Curas, otros sostituyen,
que con el Olio, y Dios Sacramentado,
el peligro buscando, el mal no huyen,
fe constante y solicito cuydado:
a mucha dicha todos atribuyen
aver a tiempo con su Dios llegado:
llama al Cura una casa desdichada,
y no ha llegado quando esta assolada.

Los Capuchinos a curar se ofrecen,
imbidia dando a aquella sierpe aleve, 10
entranse al hospital, donde parecen
exercito de Dios, que guerra mueve:
diez y ocho, curando, alli perecen,
y aunque a sus cuerpos tanto mal se atreve,
es su muerte una pena lisongera, 15
con que se passan a mejor esfera.

Los que nombre tomaron del Carmelo,
insigne Religion, lo mismo intentan,
procuran dar contra el rigor consuelo,
todas sus vidas con piedad presentan, 20
passando muchos deste suelo al cielo,
con otros Religiosos que se alientan,
qual el casto Ioseph, dexando santos,
la vidal al mundo, quando no los mantos.

[91] Algunos Cavalleros advertidos, 1
mirando los castigos que amenazan,
timidos, de su culpa arrepentidos
enfermos curan, con amor abrazan
a los que el fiero mal tiene rendidos, 5
con los frios cadaveres se enlazan,
apartando, divinamente altivos,
los ombres muertos, de los cuerpos vivos.

El sacro dia de San Juan Bautista,
a quien hasta los barbaros festejan, 10
dozientos y setenta en una lista
se escriven hombres, que la vida dexan,
sin otra muchedumbre, que no vista,
causa pavor a los que mas se alejan,
pues sin numero, en rusticos desiertos, 15
ay poblaciones de los cuerpos muertos.

No basta un hospital a tanto estrago,
diligente el Marques otro dispone,
porque prudentes curen con halago,
Medicos doctos a estos males pone: 20
la misma execucion es el amago;
con que la peste ya al viuir se opone,
pareciendo que casi en solo un punto
ay sano, cae enfermo y es difunto.

The Plague at Málaga, 1637

[9v] La Religion Serafica, animosa,
acredita el valor, desmiente el miedo,
sus efectos mostrando generosa,
que en tosco acento celebrar no puedo,
altiloca la fama venturosa
cante, pues mi thalia canta quedo,
mostrando, que sus rusticos sayales
tienen virtud para curar los males.

Passan por la ciudad mucho ganado,
para que humido el ayre purifique,
solo se atiende ya, y pone cuydado
en que el mal no se aumente y multiplique,
el hombre mas confuso y mas turbado,
su virtud hace que el enebro explique,
haziendo que movido a calor summo,
despida olores de su cuerpo en humo.

Una Iunta se haze, que compuesta
de ambos Cabildos, refrenar procura
daño, que tanto a los vivientes cuesta,
que es el morir descanso, sino cura:
dudase alli, y ofrece la respuesta,
el que discurre con mayor cordura,
proponiendo las cosas que convienen
a males tantos, como sobrevienen.

[10r] Muchos suspensos, con enfermo sueño,
con racionales almas animadas,
dando lugar pestifero beleño
fueron en los carneros sepultados,
y dispertando al ultimo despeño,
passaron plaza de resucitados,
y aunque de viva calla carne herida
se curaron, y gozan desta vida.

Una muger, mirando el trance estrecho,
en que solo ha de aver una mortaja,
con vivo brio, aunque con muerto pecho,
busca de lienço la mejor alaja,
y atendiendose sola, buelve al lecho,
donde su cuerpo, aun vivo, se amortaja;
despues la hallaron muerta con espanto,
humido el rostro de su tierno llanto.

En este tiempo se admiro una cosa,
que para el miedo fue bastante assunto;
alçando de una bobeda la losa
para enterrar dos hombres un difunto,   20
se exalo una sustancia vaporosa
de un cuerpo muerto que alli estava junto,
y en maligno va por ambos ahogados
quedaron por si mismos sepultados.

[10v] Querer dezir en metros numerosos,   1
lo que en confusa voz canta la Fama
Es querer de los astros luminosos
Obscurecer la luz, cegar la llama:
solo dire, dos niños lastimosos,   5
que muertos con su madre en una cama,
fueron de la piedad imagen cierta,
asidos ambos de la madre muerta.

No del alto tonante ardiente rayo,
con tanta furia a lo que encuentra hiere,   10
no causa en el viviente tal desmayo,
suelto el Leon, que ya matarle quiere:
es cualquier muerte de la muerte ensayo
viendo la gente, que de peste muere
con tanta brevedad, violencia tanta,   15
que aun a la muerte tanta muerte espanta.

Entre tanto temor, tantos azares,
nadie a la Madre de Piedad olvida,
devotos hazen por la calle Altares,
sin que el llanto comun al gozo impida: 20
pues al son de su nombre, los pesares
en lugar de dar pena causan vida,
que adonde está de todo el bien la fuente,
sobran las dichas, y no ay mal presente.

[11r] Dos en particular la calle Nueva   1
erige Altares, que fulgentes luzen,
de su constante amor bastante prueva;
preciosas piezas todos les conduzen:
no ay instrumento que la voz no mueva,   5
dulces concentos, musicos, produzen;
y parece, que son las negras horas,
si opuesto el Sol, mas candidas Auroras.

The Plague at Málaga, 1637

Aunque no crece el mal, esta constante,
ya no se estrañan los que fuerte mata,
del corazón humilde al mas gigante
teme el rigor con que la peste trata:
todo pecho, aunque sea de diamante,
en lagrimas copiosas se desata,
porque al mas duro llega ya ablandalle
ver olear los hombres por la calle.

El Santo, que del nectar dulcemente,
que a Dios alimento, bevio suave,
el gran Bernardo, que resplandeciente
su intercession, el mal haze que lave;
galante, haziendo en obras evidente,
que Dios le dio de la salud la llave,
mientras piadoso tanto estrago mira,
haze portentos, que la tierra admira.

[11v] Al glorioso Francisco un feliz dia,
fundador de los Minimos mayores,
como por experiencia se sabia,
que sus remedios eran los mejores,
acude el pueblo, con intencion pia,
para participar sus esplendores,
que es el gran Paula, Santo muy piadoso,
pues tiene por blason ser amoroso.

Sacanle en procession de la Vitoria,
al triste, de su luz rayos despide
con que convierte la tristeza en gloria,
al que en suspiros su favor le pide:
mas dilatada necessita historia,
el celebrar que su presencia impide
tanto mal, que en mirando su presencia,
haze salud la misma pestilencia.

Sus rayos el dorado Apolo buelve
por la vereda que dexo luziente,
ligeros sus cavallos ya rebuelve,
crepusculos dorando del Oriente,
quando viendo, que el mal, Francisco absuelve,
instrumento es de Dios clama la gente,
pues si ciento, el dia antes perecieron,
la mitad el siguiente no muerieron.

Appendix B

[*12r*] Llega el dichoso dia de Santa Ana
de cumplida salud dando esperança
permite ya, piadosa y soberana,
a pestifero mal dulce bonança,
rogando al nieto Dios en carne humana,
que diesse el premio a tanta confiança,
y el que el Orbe govierna, y todo puede,
dexa la espada, y la salud concede.

La gente ausente, a la ciudad se acoge,
que si timida fue, contenta viene,
ya no ay peste que aflija, mal que enoje,
casi nadie en el campo se detiene:
la gente del temor se desencoje,
y en dicha tanta como sobreviene,
unos sus males, lastimados, quentan,
y otros dichosos, al lloroso alientan.

El dia de la Madre inmaculada,
que el mes de Agosto, alegre ve la tierra,
dando gozo a la gente tan cansada,
el primero hospital la ciudad cierra;
y a los seis de Setiembre, libertada
del contagioso mal, que dava guerra,
cierra el otro hospital, quedando ufana,
si lastimada ya, del todo sana.

[*12v*] Los que en Malaga a peste fueron muertos
con diferencia en la ciudad se quentan,
de casas, hospitales y desiertos,
los que con mas verdad dezir intentan,
quince, o diez y seis mil descriven ciertos,
aunque muchos el numero acrecientan,
quantos dichosos viven, que enfermaron,
al contarlos los numeros faltaron.

El Obispo y Marques, que en propios hechos
materia dan con que el valor se assombre,
obran tan fuertes con piadosos pechos,
que cada qual se niega ya al ser hombre,
visitando los mas humildes lechos,
con que acrecientan a su nombre el nombre,
siendo impossible en su valor vencerles,
timido el mal, no se atrevio a ofenderles.

The Plague at Málaga, 1637

Ya el infausto de Malaga destrozo
en concursos alegres se convierte,
ya, gozando salud, es todo gozo,
ageno ya de tan violenta muerte; 20
suspenda ya mi pluma el alborozo
de tan feliz, en tanta pena, suerte,
porque funesta se oyga mi thalia,
desde el Septentrion al Mediodia.

APPENDIX C

Schedule of Moveable Property of Baltasar (Isaac) Orobio Sequestrated by the Inquisition at Cádiz, August 1654

(See pp. 75–8)

Source: Archivo Histórico Nacional, Madrid, Sección de Inquisición, Leg. 2067, no. 95.

Primero de Agosto 1654

Cadiz
Copia de el secreto que se hiço de los vienes de el Doctor Don Baltassar de Orovio Medico Veçino de Cadiz

Sevilla
Secrestadores Alonsso Gonzalez Barriga, Don Gutierre de Çetina y otros Ba el audiençia de Haçienda que con este presso se hiço en esta Inquisiçion Para el registro ba en 13 folios, Martin Carrascal de Prado

1r secreto de los vienes de el doctor don Baltasar de Orobio Medico
En la ziudad de Cadiz, sauado por la mañana en primero dia de el mes de agosto de mill seysçientos y zincuenta y quatro años, el Señor Liçençiado don Julio Cauallero de los Oliuos comisario de el Santo Ofiço de la ziudad de San Lucar de Varrameda y el Señor Liçençiado Don Julio de Zetina maestro escuela de la Santa Iglesia de esta ziudad de Cadiz y Comisario de el Santo Ofizio en ella, en presençia de mi, Seuastian Garçia Moreno Villacresess, familiar y notario de el Santo Ofiço en esta ziudad, con asistenzia de Alonso Gonzalez Barriga, familiar y teniente de reçeptor de el Santo Ofizio, le hiçieron secreto y encargo de los vienes de el Doctor don Baltasar Orobio, medico en esta ziudad, preso por el Santo Ofizio y allandosse el dicho Doctor presente deste secreto e ynuentario se hiso en la forma siguiente:
Entrose en la cassa, prinçipal quarto alto de las cassas de su morada, en que auia doze sillas de vaqueta de moscouia, con el clauaçon dorada—
—Vn quadro grande de lucha de Cacob [sic] y el anjel—
—Otro el anjel de Touias con el pez—
—Otro de el anjel San Miguel—
—Otro quadro de la Madalena—
—Otro quadro de el Anguel San Rafael—

—Otro quadro de San Joseph y el anguel—
—Otro de el niño Jessus y San Juan—
—Zinco cuadros pequeños de las siuilas—
—Onze fruteros pequeños—
—Vna lamina en piedra de el gloriosso Santo Thomas—
—Seis cuadritos pequeños de lauados—
—Vn bufete de caoua y sobre el vna sobremessa tapete cairelaio— //

1v
—Dos espejos de cristal, con guarnizion negra de pen[— —]
—y zinco laminitas pequeñas alrededor de ellas un [— —] y vn baulito de china y vn escritorito—
—Vn baulito pequeño de carei guarnezido de plata
—Vn cofreçito de vidros de Varçelona y una flasquerita pequeña de Phelpilla verde con galonzito de plata—
—Sobre un bufetillo de zedro, un escritorio de carea y auierto en una gaueta, se allo una peleta de plata y un pon[ ] de plata—
—En otra gaueta, un tocada de vidrio de muger y algunas siete varas de zintas de resplandor y un librito de color—
—En otra gaueta, seis valonas de muger de puntas de pitas blancas y dos pares de guantes con bueltas vordadas y vn auanillo—
—En otra gaueta, vn librito de color de granada y en vna cajetilla vnas pastillas de vlandurillas—
—En otra gaueta, dos jicaras negras ya viejas—
—en otro gaueta, tintas y flores de tocado de muger—
—y vna cajetila de plata con tres sortijas de oro, van de nueue dobletes y otra de nueue granates y otra de diez diamantes—
—Vnas arracadas grandes de perlas—
—Dos anillos de feligrana, vna con cuatro piedras de cristal y otra sin ellas—
—Vn rascador de caueza con vna sortija de diez y nueue esmeraldas—
—Vnas pulseras de perlas gruessas—
—Vn gorro de filigrana con su joya de pecho, guarnezido de //

2r
perlas guar [?] en vna lamina de Nuestra Señora de la Soledad de vna parte y de la otra vnos anjeles—
—Vn zerçillo de perlas y vnas flores de diferentes colores de seda para la caueza—
—Vn bolsillo de vadanilla guarnezido de oro y verde—
—Vna flor de oro con quarenta diamantes—
—en otra gaueta, dos valonas de golillas viejas—
—en otro gaueta no hauia nada

Otro escriptorio
— Abriosse otro escriptorio de carey ygual y conpañero de el referido, que estaua sobre vn bufetillo de zedro, y en vna jaueta auia como cossa de dos libras de vojias, y algunas ocho o diez varas de puntas vasias blancas en dos pedaços, y vn relox de bronze de muestra, y una peleta de piedra quebrada, y vnos pedaços de galon de oro viejos—
— En otra gaueta auia vna cartera de vadanilla guarnezida con vna puntilla de pita y un poco hilo alisado—
— En otra gaueta, vna caja con solo tres cuchillos de Yngalaterra y un poco de pita y un pedaço de olanda dos varas—
— En otra gaueta auia diez y nueue reales de plata y no tenia otra cossa—
— En otra gaueta, un par de guantes de Valenzia, vn pebete y vn caracol de nacar—
— En otra gaueta, vn rosario guarnezido de azero, con dos camandulas—
— En otra gaueta, vna pantalla pequeñita de plata y vn pedaço dee olanda e media vara, vn auanillo quebrado, vn peine y vnos listones viejos—

2v 327 Pessos
— Otra gaueta esta vazia—
— En otra gaueta auia trezientos y siete pessos de a ocho reales de plata y zinco doblones de a dos esqudos—
— Vn vaulito muy pequeño de guierro con su llaue—
— Vna estera de junco fino—
— En vna bentana, vna tinaja de agua y vna alcaraza de agua—
— Vn libro de Florum Sanctorum, segunda parte—
— Otro libro de el Priuado Cristiano—
— Otro libro de las obras de Zeneca en latin y otros libros pequeños por encuadernar, conpuestos por el Doctor don Baltasar Orobio y otro libro de el Doctor Alonsso Nuñez, que todo estaua sobre el bufete de la dicha sala—

aposento otro
— Entrosse en otro aposento, que dizen hera pieza de estrado, que sobre vna silla auia ocho cojines de terçiopelo y damasco carmesi y dos tapetes cairitinos y tres pedaços de corredores de tafetan carmesi y dos bufetillos lustrado [sic] de caire y marfil—
— Quatro colchones llenos de lana de lineo listado—
— Dos savanas y dos almuadas lizias y vna colcha vieja de seda color amarillo, con listas encarnadas—
— Vn cuadro de Jan Carlos Borromeo—
— Otro cuadrito pequeño de un santo Cristo de talla y pasta dorada—
— Vna esterilla de Juncos—

otra cuadra
—Entrose en otra cuadra a donde se allo vn tapete usado—
—Vna caja grande de nogal y en ella vn cubertor de cama colorada—
—Vna colgadura de cama de sarga de cochinilla //

3r
de seis cortinas y su zielo de lo mismo aforrado en lienço blanco—
—Vna presilla de gasa amarilla—
—Vna caja de vaieta—
—Vna caja de albornoz aforrada en vaieta negra—
—Vna capa de paño negro—
—Vna ropilla y calçones de vaieta negra—
—Vna ropilla de traço labrado—
—Vnas mangas de gorgaran negras vsadas—
—Vnas mangas de riço negras aprensadas nueuas—
—Vn couertor de sarga cochinilla—
—Vnos calçones de raço negro bordados—
—Vna caja con dos fundas de moros—
—Vn bestido de tauinegro, con dos pares de calçones ya traidos—
—Vna toalla blanca con dos millares de caino, poco mas o menos—
—Vn bufete de zedro de vara y media de largo y vna de ancho—
—Dos tauretes de vaqueta de moscouia con clauador de bronze dorado—
—Vna escouilla de limpiar ropa y otra de la caueça—
—Vn bufetillo de zedro de vna vara de largo y dos cuartas en ancho—
—Vna vatea de Indias—
—Vn cojin de damasquillo viejo de lana—
—Vna escrivania de Flandes—
—Otro vn escritorio con vnos papeles y cartas viejas—
—Vn guierro de adereçar valonas //

3v escriptorio
Abriosse un escriptorio de pino con su pies de lo mismo; hauia dentro seis cajas de chocolate de Nueua España de una libra—
—Mas otras seis de vna libra y media de chocolate de Guajana—
—Mas seis tortas de chocolate como de a media libra—
—Dos jicaras de coco—
—Mas vn bidrio grande en que pareçe auido dulçes—
—Dos medias cajas de chocolate—
—Mas otra jicara de coco—
—Mas vn vidrio con vnas pocas de guindas en almiuar—
—Mas vna jicara grande de calauaça—
—Siete paños paños (*sic*) vastos para tomar chocolate—
—Dos molinillas—

—Vna orca de Talauera vaçia, dorada—
—Vn plato de pleite vaçio—
—Quatro naranjas de dulçes rellenas—
—Seis cajas de chocolate de Nueua España de una libra y media—
—Vn plato grande de estaño y otro pequeño de lo mismo—
—Vn cuchillo viejo de cauo blanco
—En vn armario que estava en la dicha cuadra se allo un jicarillo de cairel con seis jicaras; dijo con seis gau[— —] de jicaras guarnezido de plata—
—Vna vaçia de estaño—
—Vn mostasero de lo mismo—
—Vnas tijeras de espauilar de plata—
—Siete vucaras de lamaya—
—Vn bidrio grande con vna poca de pimienta—
—dos vidrios grandes a modo de alcarraças—
—Vna taça de vidrio de olanda—//

4r
—Otro vidrio grande—
—otros dos vidrios usados—
—Vn bugel de estaño—
—Vn varrelillo viejo con vn poco de almiuar—
—Vn varrelillo de azeitunas y vna cuchara de plata con que se hiua sacando—
—Vnos manteles viejos rotos—
—Vna seruita usada—
—Vnos manteles vastos y dos seruilletas—
—otra seruilleta vieja—
—Vna uela de zera blanca a medio gastar—
—Vna selleta [sic] de paja
—Vn bufetillo vajo de tres quartas de largo y los pies forrados—
—Vna votija de vinagre—
—En otra quadra adentro estaua vn armadura de vna cathetre dessecho—
—Vna viguela de marfil y heuano con su funda—
—Vn capote de grana viejo y vna montera de alborroz—
—Vn cajonçillo con quatro arrouas de azucar—
—Vn espejo viejo dorado—
—Vna taquilla, dos taças y zinco platos de estaño, vna cuchara de plata y dos jicaras de coco con unas listicas de plata en las bocas—
—Vn cantarillo pequeño con sal—
—En otra taquilla dos votijas vazias y otra con vn poco de azeite—//

4v
—Vna votija media de vinagre—
—Vna camtimplora de vidrio pequeña con su corcho—

—Vn velonçillo de azofar con dos candeleros para velas—
—Vn velador de palo en que se pone el candil—
—Vna flasquera con siete flascos—
—dos flascos vaçios—
—Abriosse vn vaul aforrado en pellejo y dentro del estavan vnos calçones de tafetan carmessi con punticas de oro—
—Vn vestido de muger de razo negro con guarnizion negra, saya, jubon y ropa capona—
—Vn capotillo de grana de muger con puntas de plata—
—Vna pollera y almilla de lama verde, con puntas de plata, aforrado en tafetan anteado—
—Vn jubon de razo flor de romero, con guarnizion negra de seda—
—Vn rosario de pasta morado ensartado en oro y negro de seda—
—Vn bestido de mujer de taui platiado, vasquina, jubon y ropa lapona guarnezido de puntas negras de seda, afloreado de tafetan negro—
—Vna pollera de taui verde—
—Vn regalillo de martas ya traydo—
—Vnos guantes viejos—
—Vnas mangas de riso azules y blancas—
—Vn rosario de coral guarnezido en bronze—
—Avriose otro baul aforrado por de fuera de pellejo y por de dentro en lienço y en el se allaron vnos papeles sueltos que se a uerificado lo que sean—
—Vn jarro de plata quel doctor Don Baltasar Orouio dijo ser de un tauernero pintor de la Compañia de Jessus //

5r
y que se le enpeño en zien reales de plata—

200 Reales
—Dos esportillas que reconozidas consto tener cada vna a zien reales de moneda resellada—
—Diez varas de lama color zeleste labrada—
—Vna colgadura de cama de gassa encarnada y blanca, metida en vna talega y en ella vna colcha de taui encarnado y blanco todo guarnezido de listones destocados—
—Vn roda pie de cama guarnezido de galon de oro—
—Dos seruillitas nueuas alemanescas—
—Otras tres de el mismo genero ya viejas—
—Vna tabla de manteles fina alemanisca—
—Otras del mismo genero ya raidas—
—Vna sauana trayda—
—Diez seruilletas nueuas alemaniscas—
—Dos paños de manos con puntas de pita—

—Vna toalla con puntas blancas trayda—
—Vna toalla de olan con puntas de Flandes vlancas—
—Vn paño de manos—
—Vn rodapie de cama blanco con puntas y lauor—
—Vna camisa de manga con bara[   ]de pita—
—Vna sauana con puntas de lo mismo—
—Vna sauana trayda
—Vnas enaguas de muger con puntas blancas—
—Vnos manteles alemaniscos traydos—
—Vna sauana trayda—
—Vnos manteles traydos—
—Vna toalla de olan con puntas de Flandes—
—Vnos manteles alemaniscos—
—Dos almuadas traydas labradas de pita—//

5v
—Otra almuada de lo mismo—
—Vn paño de rostro traydo—
—Vn rodapiez de lienço labrado de azul—
—Otra toalla de olan labrada con puntas de Flandes—
—Otra almuada de lienço de pita—
—Dos toallas de lienço para hącer la uarba—
—Vn azerilo labrado de pita—
—Vna almuada llana—
—Vna toalla labrada de red—
—Vna camissa de onbre—
—Tres pares de calçones—
—Vn acafate labrado de palma—
—Vna faja de orillo de paño—
—Vn pedaçillo de taui anteado azul—
—Dos pares de calçetas—
—Tres panitos pequeños de tomar chocolate—

$3500+1250=4750+327=5077$
—Abriosse otro vaul de vaqueta colorada y en el se allo siete talegos pequeños y vno grande y reconozidos y contados, se allaron en los siete talegos pequeños a quinientos pessos cada vno y en el grande mill duçientos y zinquenta pessos, todo de moneda de plata mejicana y seuillana que el dicho Doctor dijo ser de su suegro Françisco Perez vezino de Puerto Real
—Iten vn peinador con su toalla para quitar la uarba—
—Vn auito de plumas viejo—
—En vn pazillo, al entrar de la cozina, estaua en vna talega como cosa de vna fanega de trigo—

—Entrose en vna cozina y allose en ella vna caldera mediana
—Vna vazinilla grande—
—Vn cuvo viejo de sacar agua—
—Vn perollillo de haçer almidon—
—Vna chocolatera de cobre—
—Vna vaçinita grande—
—Vn almires con su mano—
—Tres platos medianos de estaño y otro pequeñito—
—Vna tinaja que haçe como cosa de quatro votijas de agua—
—Otra vaçinilla vieja—
—Vnos treuedes de hierro—
—Vna freidera vieja y rota—
—Dos sedaçillos viejos—
—Vn canastello viejo—
—Vna caja de vn asero con su bazco—
—Dos frasadas vlancas traydas—
—Vn colchon viejo—
—Vna alfonbra vsada—
—Al bajar de vna escalera a vn patinejo que ba al pozo, esta vna tinaja y vna boteja y dos lebrillos grandes y vna mesa de pino para lauar en ella.
—Subiosse en vn palomar en que estauan dos palomas y dos pichonçillos criandose—
—En otro aposentillo junto al palomar estaua la armazon de vna cama—
—Entrose en otro aposentillo en que estauan tres fanegas de zeuada poco mas o menos—
—Vna caja de arpa muy vieja—
—Vn costal con vna poca de sal—//

6v
—Vnos estriuos de palo—
—Ocho arcos pequeños de guiero—
—Vna tabla vieja de lleuar pan al orno—
—Vnos correones de silla de manos—
—Bajose a vn zotanillo y en el se allo zincuenta cordouanos negros, y un cajo [*sic*] çerrado que auierto parezio ser con cajas de chocolate y tubo duzientas y nueue cajuelas de una libra marcadas con la mano de la marjen—
—Entro en vna libreria, digo estudio, adonde estaua vna libreria de libros de mediçina, en vn estante zinco hileras de libros grandes y pequeños; en la primera treinta y dos cuerpos de libros;
—en la segunda quarenta y seis:
—en la terçera zinquenta y dos;
—en la quarta quarenta y seis:

—en la postrera sesenta y zinco y sobre un banco grande çinco cuerpos de libros grandes;
—y sobre vn bufete grande otros tres grandes;
—y en vn papelero algunos papeles menudos y catorçe libros pequeños y en el suelo vn libro grande de tablillas—
—En el mismo escriptorio tres retratos pequeños de Galeno, Hiprocrates [sic] y Auicina y vn mapa en papel de la planta de Lisboa y tres sillas, dos de vaqueta viejas y otra nueua—
—Vna mesa de pino—
—En la entrada de este estudio estauan quatro cajones que el dicho Doctor Baltasar Orobio dijo ser de Tomas de Quintanilla, vezino de Zeuta, //

7r

y reconozido y auierto por el vno, parezio ser de cochinilla—
—Vna silla de manos viejas de vaqueta con tres palos, vn cuadro de papel con zinco paises de diferentes pinturas—
—Entrose en vna caualleriça adonde estaua vna mula ensillada y enfrenada y vn burrilo con su albason y aguaderas—
—En el patio de la dicha cassa estauan tres votijas vazias—
—Iten vna negra llamada Maria de la Encarnaçion de hedad de diez y ocho años—
—Iten otra negra llamada Maria Manuela de hedad de veinte y quatro años, el dicho doctor don Baltasar de Orouio declaro hauer comprado de la Almoneda de el Liçençido don Françiso Antonio Claros, alcalde mayor que fue de esta ziudad, ya difunto—
—Iten un moro corcouado color blanco, señales de hierro junto a la nariz, de edad de veinte años.
Con lo qual se acauo este dicho secresto he Inventario de vienes de el dicho Doctor Don Baltasar Orovio que se allo presente, deuajo de juramento que hiço, declaro que no tiene mas vienes ni haçienda que la referida, y que el dinero en talegos es de su suegro Don Françisco Perez, rejidor de la villa de Puerto Real, prozedido de vna partida de zera que le vendio a Damian Lopez, vezino de Cadiz, y los cajones de chochinella son de quenta de Thomas de Quentanilla, vezino de Zeuta, que se compraron con ynteruençion del dicho su suegro, y que no le deue ninguna persona en este ziudad ni fuera de ella, ningun dinero ni haçienda //

7v

ni dado la a guardar ni en caueza ajena y lo firmo y los Señores comisarios siendo testigos Alonso Gonzales Varriga, Julio de Armuñia, familiares, y Bartolome de Casares y Seuastian Dominguez Camacho, Vezino de Cadiz = Liçençiado don Julio de Zetina = Doctor don Baltasar Orouio = Liçençiado don Julio Cauallero de los Oliuos = ante mi Seuastian Garçia Moreno, notario de el Santo Ofiçio en dos de agosto del año de mill seysçientos y zinquenta y quatro, ante los señores comisarios y ante mi, el presente notario theniente de reçeptor y ministros, fue llamado Antonio Suares, platero contraste de esta ziudad, para apreçiar las joias ynventariadas y pesar la plata que se allo y se hiço en esta forma:

—Vna joia de pecho de oro con quarenta diamantes, vale ochoçientos reales plata 0800 R
—Vn rascador con veinte y quatro esmeraldas, vale veinte pessos 0160 R
—Vna sortija con diez diamantes, vale veinte y zinco pessos 0200 R
—Vn gorro de filigrana guarneçido de perlas, vale diez y seis pesos 0128 R
—Vnas arracadas de perlas netas, valen treçientos reales 0300 R
—Tres onças de perlas de a treçientos granos en onça, valen quinientos y veinte reales 0520 R
—Dos sortijas, vna de granates, otra de dobletes, valen treinta y dos reales 0032 R
—Dos sortijas de enrragado, valen quarenta y ocho reales 0048 R

8r
—por la de atras 20288 R
—Vn salsillo de azofar, vale treinta y dos reales 0032 R

Plata labrada que esta en este ynuentario 20320 R
—Vna palangana, quatro platillos, dos escudellas, quatro cucharas, vnas tijeras de espauilar, vn pomo de agua de olor, vna peleta de agua bendita, vn salero, dos candeleros, vna cajetila de plata, todo esto pessa veinte y dos Marcos 22 marcos

Plata labrada que se allo en vn pozo
En tres de agosto, antes de amaneçer, por auiso secreto dado por vna persona confidente al Señor comisario don Julio de Zetina, se fue a las cassas de el Doctor don Baltasar Orouio y en vn poço se allo y saco la plata siguiente:
—Vna fuente lissa, dos platones, quatro platillos, vna saluilla, otra saluilla aueda (?) con dos vinajeras, vn jarro, dos escudillas sin assas, dos candeles, vno grande y otro chico, anuos [*sic*] sin assas arriba y el dicho sin puntoalla, todo esto pesso quarenta y siete marcos y medio de plata 47½ marcos
Con lo qual se acauo todo este dicho ynuentario y de los vienes contenidos en el, saluo de los esclauos que quedan repartidos en terçeras

8v
personas, como // adelante se dira y de el cajon de chocolates y de quatro cajones de cochinella y de el dinero que se allo, asi de los treçientos y treinta y siete pessos y zinco doblones de a vna gaueta, y *357×4750=5107*

los quatro mill setezientos y zinquenta pessos en talegos, que esta queda depositado en poder del capitan don Gutierre de Zetina; de todo lo demas en este ynventario contenido fue encargado y puesto en deposito de el dicho Alonsso Gonzalez de Varriga, familiar y teniente de rezeptor de el dicho Santo Ofiçio, que yo el presente notario doy fee que conosco, el qual se constituyo por depositario de ello y se obligo de tener de manifiesto y de los dar y entregar cada y qual que los señores Inquisidores les sea mandado y a su fauero en esta zuidad, en pena de encurrir en las establezidas por derecho y por el su balor, a que obligo su persona y vienes con poder y su mision a los dichos señores Inquisidores del tribunal de el Santo Ofiçio de la Ynquisiçion de Seuilla en forma y lo firmo siendo testigos Julio de Armuña, familiar, Bartolome de Casares y Seuastian Dominguez Camacho, vezinos de Cadiz, Liçenciado don Julio de Zetina, don Julio Cauallero de los Olivos, Alonsso Gonzalez Varriga, ante mi Seuastian Garçia Moreno, notario de el Santo Ofiçio.

deposito de las cajones y dineros
En este mismo dia el cappitan don Gutierres de Zetina, rejidor de esta ziudad de Cadiz que yo el notario doy fee que conozco por elezion de

9r
los Señores comisarios y por persona confidente // y segura le entregaron y despositaron las cosas siguientes:
—El cajon de chocolate, ynuentariado de la marca de afuera, que auierto tubo duçientas y nueue cajuelas de vna libra—
—Iten los quatro cajones de cochinilla, marcados con la marca de la marjen, que auiertos y reconozidos tubo el pesso siguiente:
—Cajon numero çinco tubo seis arrouas con el saco y cordel   6a
—Cajon numero dos tubo siete arrouas con el saco y cordel   7a
—Cajon numero nueue tubo otras siete arrouas con el saco y cordel   7a
—Cajon numero tres tubo otras siete arrouas con el saco y cordel   7a
—Iten treçientos y treinta y siete pessos en reales y zinco doblones de a dos allados en vna gaueta de vn escriptorio haçen   357 pessos
—Iten siete talegos de a quinientos pessos y en vno grande e mill y duçientas y çinquenta pessos que por todos haçen   4750 pessos
De todo lo qual dinero y cajones el dicho cappitan don Gutierres de Zetina se dio por entregado porque lo rezeuio contado y pessado ante

9v
y en prezençia // de los señores comisarios y de mi, el presente notario, y testigos de que damos fee, y se obligo de los tener en deposito a ley de depositario y de los dar y entregar cada vez y quando que por los dichos

Señores Inquisidores de el tribunal de el Santo Ofiçio de la Inquisiçion, de la dicha çiudad de Seuilla, le sea mandado so las penas de los depositarios, y se pague su valor en esta ziudad de Cadiz y al fuero y juridiçion de los señores Ynquisidores, a que se obliga su persona y vienes, con clausula carentija en forma y lo firmo, siendo testigos Alonso Gonzalez Varriga y Julio de Armuña, familiares, y Bartolome de Caçarez, vezino de Cadiz, y lo firmaron assi mismo los dichos Señores comisarios don Julio Cauallero de los Oliuos, Liçienciado don Julio de Zetina, don Gutierres de Zetina, ante mi Seuastian Garçia Moreno, notario de el Santo Ofiçio.

deposito de Maria Manuela, negra

En Cadiz, en tres de agosto de este dicho año, los dichos señores comisarios entregaron y pusieron en deposito y en poder de don Alonso Gonzalez de Aluelda, cauallero de la orden de Santiago y familiar de el Santo Ofiçio, a Maria Manuela, negra de edad de veinte y cuatro años, y el susodicho la reçeuio y se dio de ella por entregado y se obligo de la tener de manifiesto y de la dar y entregar cada vez y quando que le sea mandado por los señores Ynquisidores de la Ynquisiçion de Seuilla y a su fuero y que a de pagar su balor y en lo que se tasare, aunque sea sin su çitaçion y en las penas en que fuese condenado, a

1or

que obligo su persona y vienes // y lo firmo, testigos Alonso Gonzales Varriga y Julio de Armuña, familiares, vezinos de Cadiz, e yo el presente notario, que conozco al otorgante don Alonso Gonzalez de Aluelda, ante mi Seuastian Garcia Moreno, notario de el Santo Ofiçio.

deposito de Maria de la Encarnaçion negra

En Cadiz, en este mesmo dia tres de agosto, los dichos Señores comisarios entregaron y pusieron en deposito y en poder de don Esteuan Chilton Fantoni, cauallero de la orden de Calatraua y rejidor de esta ziudad de Cadiz, a Maria de Encarnaçion, negra de hedad de diez y ocho años y susodicho la reçiuio y se dio della por entregado y se obligo de la tener de manifiesto y de la dar y entregar cada vez y quando que por los señores Inquisidores de la Inquisiçion de la Ziudad de Seuilla le sea mandado y a su fuero pena de pagar su valor en lo que se tasare, aunque sea sin su çitaçion, y en las penas en que fuere condenado, a que obligo su persona y vienes y lo firmo, testigos Alonso Gonzales Varriga y Julio de Armunia, familiares, y yo el presente notario que conosco al otorgante Don Esteuan Chilton Fantoni, ante mi Sevastian Garçia Moreno, notario de el Santo Ofiçio.

Costas

—En la çiudad de Cadiz, a quatro dias de el mes de agosto de mill seyscientos y zinquenta y quatro años, el Señor Liçençiado don Julio Cauallero, comisario de el Santo Ofiçio de la zuidad de San Lucar saco de poder de el capitan don Gutierres de Zetina, depositario de el dinero secresto al Doctor don Baltasar Orobio, las costas y gastos causados en su prision y remiçion, la cantidad seguiente:

10v

—De dos guardas que asistieron en cassa de el dicho doctor a guardar los vienes, mientras se acauaba el secresto y entregaua al depositario de tres dias, a pesso cada dia a cada guarda, son seis pessos   6 pessos

—De la comida y vna guarda que asistio a la vista de el dicho Doctor en su prission y el darle de comer al dicho preso, doçe pesos   12 pessos

—De remitirlo a Seuilla al dicho señor preso de flete de el varco que lo lleua y pagar a Julio Gil de Segovia, familiar, y a vn guarda en todo treinta pessos   30 pessos

—Al Señor Comisario don Julio Cauallero, de venir de San Lucar a la prision de el dicho doctor y su familiar a Cadiz y gastos de zinco dias con sus criados se tazo quarenta pessos   40 pessos

     88 pessos

Todo lo qual monto ochenta y ocho pessos de a ocho reales de plata que cobro y saco de poder de el dicho don Gutierrez de Zetina y para que conste lo firmo Seuastian Garçia Moreno, notario de el Santo Offiçio.

Doctor Orouio

—En la Inquisiçion de Seuilla, en catorçe dias de el mes de agosto de mill seysçientos y zinquenta y quatro años, estando en su audiençia de la mañana el Señor Inquisidor don Pedro Majarres de Credia, mando traer a ella vn onbre recluso en carçeles secretas, de el cual fue rezeuido

11r

juramento en forma // de derecho y auiendolo fecho prometio dezir verdad y fueron fechas las preguntas siguientes:

—Preguntando como de llama, de adonde es veçino y natural, que edad, estado y ofiçio tiene,

—Dijo que se llama el doctor Don Baltasar Orouio, de ofiçio medico, vezino de Cadiz y natural de la ziudad de Verganca, cassado con Ysauel Perez de la Peña y que es de hedad de treinta y seis años.

—Preguntando que haçienda tiene en vienes muebles, oro o plata, mercaderia, deudas que le deuen, asi en Cadiz como en otra parte, diga y declare la verdad.

—Dijo que los vienes muebles que se allaron en su cassa, al tiempo que fue

presso por don Julio Cauallero, comisario de la ziudad de San Lucar que no puede acordarse yndiuidualmente de todos son suyos, como algunas sillas de vaqueta de Moscouia, ocho nueuas y mas seys usadas; vna cama entera de vna madera que llaman chacaranda y esta con dos dos [sic] colgaduras, vna de senpiterna cochenilla con galon de oro y otra de verillo encarnado y blanco de Italia —
—Dos escritorios yguales de caire ebano y marfil —
—Diez o doçe cuadros de difentes [sic] pinturas y vno es el niño Jessus y San Juan, pintura de Flandes que es mejor pintura que los demas cuadros y tanvien otra pintura de Santo Thomas de Aquino, en lamina de piedra —
—Dos bufetes grandes, vno de nogal y otro de zedro, vn estrado de ocho

11v

cojines de terçiopelo y damasco // con galones de oro y sus vorlas pequeñas —
—Vna alfonbra de zinco varas de largo y tres de ancho, poco mas o menos, y esta buena por que no a que sirue mas de tres años —
—Vn escriptorio de China y vn cofrezillo de lo mismo pequeño —
—Tanvien tenia colchones y ropa blanca que no se acuerda la cantidad remitese al ynuentario que se aria —
—Tanvien declara tenia su muger algunos vestidos que no se acuerda lo que en esto abra y se remite al ynventario —
—Tanvien declara tiene su muger de otras algunas joyas de oro y se acuerda que vna de ellas es vna rosa con quarenta diamantes, no saue el balor que tenia; tanvien tenia vna sortija con çinco diamantes que esta se la dieron a este en el puerto y vnos çersillos con perlas y vnos vraçaletes de perlas, no saue la cantidad ni ualor, tanvien algunas sortijas de diferentes piedras, que la susodicha trujo de casa de su padre —
—Iten tiene dos esclauas negras, vna dellas de edad de diez y ocho años y otra de veinte y zinco años y le pareçe valdran seysçientos pessos —
—Iten vn esclavo moro corcouado de asta veinte años que valdra zien pessos —
—Tanvien vna mula negra zerada que valdra çien pessos —

12r Plata

—Iten declara tiene de plata labrada vna fuente blanca, no saue el peso, es mediana; vna palanga que le pareçe pesara ochenta pessas; vn velon que pesara otro ochenta pessos y otro mas pequeño de estrado que pesara diez y ocho o veinte pessos; diez platillos, dos platones, no saue el peso; vnas vinajeras con su saluilla a lo largo, que pesara todo treinta y zinco pessos; iten zinco escudellitas de plata, dos candeleros, vn jarro de pico, vn salero pequeño; vna saluilla y vernegal y algunas cucharas, no saue quantas, ni el pesso de las demas piezas de la plata que a declarado —

Dinero en Plata

—Iten declara tenia como trezientos y zinquenta pessos y estos son de este:
—Iten declara tenia en vn cofre ordinario, que estaua en vna quadra, auia siete talegos pequeños y vno grande de plata mejicana, todos no saue cantidad que auia en ellos por que no es esta haçienda suya sino de Thomass de Quintanilla, castellano de Zeuta que tiene correspondençia con Françisco Perez, suegro de este, que viue en Puerto Real, a el qual le remetio vna partida de çera para que la vendiesse como vendio a Damian Lopez, vezino de Cadiz, y por tan façion y paga de ella cobro su yerno de el dicho su suegro, que se llama Manuel de Espinossa, la moneda que estaua en dichos talegos y como cassa tam propia del dicho su suegro se pusso en poder de esta en la forma y presente que se allo no saue como tiene el dicho la cantidad que hera, remitesse a lo que costara por el ynuentario por que se conto en presençia deste.

12v
—Iten declara que tenia en su cassa tres o quatro cajas de cochinilla, las quales pertenezen al dicho Thomas de Quintanilla por el valor que resulto de vna partida de çera suya, que en su nombre vendio el dicho su suegro a el cual que fue en los vltimos galeones que es el conde de Portalegre, por que avn que le pago en doblones con ellos el dicho su suegro compro los dichos cajones de cochinilla que pesaron veinte y siete arrouas netas—
—Iten declaro tenia vn cajon de chocolate echo en cajas, no se acuerda quantas cajas heran, pero son suyas, labradas en su casa—
—Iten declara tenia vna libreria, sera de duçientos y zinquenta, quien por de libros de su profession y otros diferentes—
—Iten declara tenia vn jumentillo para el seruizio de su casa, no saue lo que baldra—
—Iten declara tiene vn rejimiento que hera de su suegro y esta en caueça de este por hauersele dado en confiança, con que es de su suegro de este—
—Iten declara no tiene mercaderias ni vienes algunos ni mas haçienda que la que a declarado, assi en Cadiz como en otras partes—
—Iten declara tiene por haçienda suya lo que pareçe deue a este Manuel Aluares, su padre, veçino de Cadiz, y no tiene de lo que les deudor

13r
papel ni escripto, mas constara en el libro de cuenta y razon // que tiene dicho su padre y reconoziendo la tenia, como a dicho en su libro, no tenia este en su papel razon ninguna y no tiene quentas con nadie ni le deuen otra cosa—
—Y preguntado que deudas deue este a que personas y en virtud de que ynstrumentos y por que raçon.
Dijo que este se casso tres años con doña Ysauel Perez de la Peña, y esta yja

de el dicho Françisco Perez, vezino de la villa de Puerto Real, con quien rezeuio de dote seys mill sueldos de vellon en dinero y joias, que se apreçio todo en costo y esta cantidad deue tan solamente, y a otra persona no deue cossa alguna y si se acordare de mas vienes que este tenga lo declarara; y la escriptura de dote la otorgo ante Phelipe de Heredia, escriuano publico de Cadiz y fue vn año poco mas o menos que se casso, pero escrito que antes de efectuarse el matrimonio, el dicho su suegro le auia prometido a dote y obligaçion, que hiço ante el dicho escrivano Phelipe de Eredia y no le dio todo el dicho dote asta que se hiço la carta de dote, sin enuargo que antes le tenia entregado la mitad o mas de el y aguadarda [*sic*] este a su suegro y la resta que le dio y porque al tiempo que deja dicho y declarado por darle mas tiempo para la salida de algunos efectos para su rafa[ ]do, con que lo hiço con mas comodidad, prinzipalmente por tener que pagar otro dote a otra yja que casso con el dicho Manuel de Espinossa la semana//

13v
misma que este se casso con la dicha Doña Ysauel—
—Iten declara que al tiempo que este se casso no tenia hazienda alguna, por que lo que ganaua que no hera mucho y las amistades que haçia si era poco y haçia mucho en sustentarsse y a sus padres y hermanos pobres con el [ ]miento que podia y que es la uerdad, so cargo el juramento que a fecho y lo firmo de su nonbre y el vezino Joseph Guerra que se allo presente leyosele el sussodicho y declarazion y dijo estaua vien escripta, Doctor Don Baltasar Orouio = Joseph Guerra, ante mi Martin Carrascal de Prado, notario, como pareçe de el secresto y audiençia de haçienda original que queda en mi offiçio a que me refiero en la Inquisiçion de Seuilla en veinte y çinco dias de el mes de Agosto de mill y seysçientos zinquenta y quatro años.

Martin Carrascal de Prado

APPENDIX D
Membership of the Academia de los Floridos

(See pp. 286–301)

Note. This alphabetical list omits the following members: Isaac and Moses Orobio, details regarding whom are to be found throughout the book; Daniel Levi (Miguel) de Barrios, for whom see chap. 8, pp. 222 ff.; and Manuel de Lara and Duarte Blandon de Silva, regarding whom biographical details could not be found.

For congregational offices, etc. filled by members of the *Academia* see pp. 428–430: for amounts paid by them as synagogal dues, p. 296.

The following abbreviations are used:

b.	born	*m.*	married
d.	daughter	*ob.*	died
i.	interred	*res.*	resident, resided (name of street in Amsterdam)
ket.	*kethubbah*, i.e. [copy of] marriage certificate	*s.*	son

Brief bibliographical indications of the sources referred to are given here for convenience, with reference to the section of the bibliography in which full particulars will be found.

Amst. Arch.	Archief der Gemeente Amsterdam	bibl. (1C)
DTB	Dopen, Trouwen, Begraven	
Not. Arch.	Notarial Archief	
PA	Particuliere Archieven	
	27 Collegium Medicum	
	334 Portuguese Community	
Bloom, *Economic*		
Activities	H. I. Bloom	bibl. (4)
De Barrios	Daniel Levi (Miguel) de Barrios	
Academia	*Metros–Nobles*	bibl. (3)
Alegrías	*Alegrías . . . de Hymeneo*	bibl. (3)
Triumpho	*Triumpho del Govierno Popular . . .*	bibl. (3)
De Castro,		
Ouderkerk	D. H. de Castro, *Grafsteenen . . . te Ouderkerk*	bibl. (4)
DTB	*see* Amst. Arch	
Eṣ Ḥayyim	L. Fuks and R. G. Fuks-Mansfeld, *Hebrew . . . Manuscripts in Amsterdam . . .* II, Ets Haim	bibl. (2D)

Membership of the Academia de los Floridos

Franco Mendes, Memorias	D. Franco Mendes, *Memorias... dos judeos portuguezes... de Amsterdam*	bibl. (3)
Gans, *Memorboek*	M. H. Gans, *Memorboek... der Joden in Nederland...*	bibl. (4)
Kaplan, *Studenţim*	Y. Kaplan, 'Jewish Students in seventeenth-century Leiden' (Hebrew)	bibl. (4)
Kayserling, *Biblioteca*	M. Kayserling, *Biblioteca española-portugueza judaica*	bibl. (4)
Meijer, *Enc.*	J. Meijer, *Encyclopaedia Sefardica Neerlandica*	bibl. (4)
Not. Arch.	*see* Amst. Arch.	
PA	*see* Amst. Arch.	

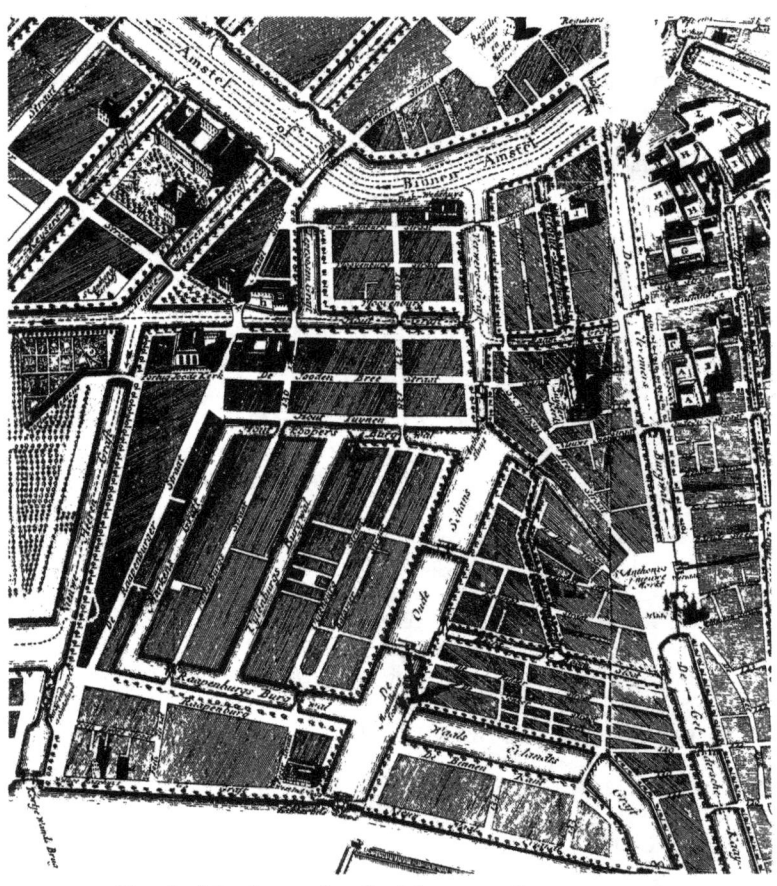

3. Detail of the Amsterdam Jewish quarter from a street-plan

Pieterse, *De Barrios*   W. Ch. Pieterse, 'Enige ... brieven van de Barrios' bibl. (4)

*Article in *Encyclopaedia Judaica*

*ATHIAS, JOSEPH RAPHAEL (1635–1700), Amsterdam printer, bookseller, and exporter. Originated from Lisbon, *s.* of Abraham A., burned at stake in Córdoba, 1665; opened printing-house, 1658; admitted member of local guild of booksellers, 1661. Granted by Council of States General exclusive right to print Old Testament in English and in Judaeo-German, and according to his own account printed more than one million English Bibles sold to England and Scotland. Acquired, 1681, the Elzevir type-foundry: this caused conflicts with the Guild, which had opposed the deal, leading to his incurring substantial loss, but with the financial help of Moses Machado (see below) he recovered. Friend of the well-known Dutch poet Justus van den Vondel, who used to show him his work prior to printing, *m.* 4 May 1663 Isabel Duarte; *res.* Binnen Amstel. *ob.* 3 May 1700 (15 *'Iyyar* 5460), *i.* Ouderkerk. Press thereafter managed by his son Immanuel A.

Amst. Arch. *DTB* No. 685, p. 297, *PA* 334 No. 916, p. 127; Bloom, *Economic Activities*, pp. 48 f.; J. F. M. Sterck, *Vondel en Joseph ben Abraham Athias*, s.l., 1916; J. S. da Silva Rosa, 'Jozef Athias (1635–1700)', *Vridagavond*, 4, 1927, pp. 534–7.

AVILAR, JACOB UZZIEL d', alias **d'AVILAR CARDOZO** (1654–1706). *b.* Antwerp, *m.* 7 May 1683 Rachel, *d.* of Benjamin d'Espinosa. In a poem celebrating his wedding de Barrios refers to him as *Noble Conde de Abilar*, but it is not clear whether he actually possessed a patent of nobility or whether the language is figurative. *ob.* 23 Apr. 1706 (9 *'Iyyar* 5466), *i.* Ouderkerk.

Amst. Arch. *DTB* No. 693, p. 355, ket. *PA* 334 No. 382f, ii. p. 264; De Barrios, *Alegrías*, pp. 33 f.; De Castro, *Ouderkerk*, 2, p. 265; Pieterse, *De Barrios*, pp. 85, 119.

BARRIOS, SIMON de (1665–88). *s.* of Daniel Levi de B. and Abigail de Pina; studied under Jacob Sasportas in *yeshibah* (religious academy) *'Eṣ Ḥayyim*. Two Spanish poems by him printed in Joseph Penso, *Rumbos peligrosos* (Antwerp, 1683), see above, chap. 10, n. 110. Acted as *mantenedor* (see above p. 289) in the *Academia. ob.* Barbados, 16 May 1688.

De Barrios, *Academia*, p. 253; Kayserling, *Biblioteca*, p. 26; Pieterse, *De Barrios*, pp. 105, 126, 129.

BELMONTE *see* **NUNES BELMONTE**
BENTIVOGLIO *see* **CURIEL**
BERAHEL *see* **LOPEZ BERAHEL**
CARDOZO *see* **AVILAR; XIMENES CARDOZO**
CARRILLO, ISAAC (1657–1707). Merchant. *b.* Amsterdam, *s.* of Samuel C.; involved in import and export trade, 1693. *m.* 12 Feb. 1689 Leah, *d.* of Jacob Tartas. *ob.* 20 Nov. 1707 (25 *Marḥeshwan* 5468), *i.* Ouderkerk.

Membership of the Academia de los Floridos

Amst. Arch. *DTB* No. 696, p. 256, *PA* 334 No. 176, p. 128, *ket.* No. 382f., iv, p. 156, No. 442, *sub nomine.*

CASTILLO, RAPHAEL del, alias **RAPHAEL** (or **GABRIEL) HEZEKIAH MONTEZINOS.** Amsterdam; *m.* (1) 7 May 1683 Gracia, *d.* of David del Soto, and (as widower) (2) Rebecca Montezinos. Apparently left for Surinam in 1689.

Amst. Arch. *DTB* No. 693, p. 356, *ket. PA* 334 No. 382f, ii, p. 268, *Not. Arch.* 3706, p. 553 (notarial power of attorney in favour of Abraham Lumbrozo (see below) prior to C's departure for Surinam).

CHAVES, JACOB de (1658–1709). *b.* Amsterdam, *s.* of Moses C. and Rachel Rodríguez de Mattos. Pupil of Rabbi Jacob Sasportas in *yeshibah* (religious academy) *Tiph'ereth Baḥurim. m.* 22 Nov. 1691 Rebecca Alvarez Machado, *d.* of Moses M. (see below). According to de Barrios, he must have been a calligrapher:

> Jacob de Chaves elegante de pluma
> joven de cuenta y de discretos suma.

ob. 24 Oct. 1709 (20 *Marḥeshwan* 5470), *i.* Ouderkerk.

Amst. Arch. *DTB* No. 697, p. 237, *ket. PA* 334, No. 382, i, p. 212, 422, *sub nomine;* De Barrios, *Academia,* p. 255: Franco Mendes, *Memorias,* p. 71.

CURIEL, MOSES, alias **JERÓNIMO NUNES da COSTA** or **GIULIO BENTIVOGLIO** (1619–97). One of the richest members of the Portuguese community of Amsterdam, some idea of whose wealth may be gained from his will, drawn up by him on 14 Feb. 1673. Representative in Amsterdam of the King of Portugal; contributed a quantity of jacaranda wood for the construction of the ark and reading-desk in the great Amsterdam synagogue, dedicated 1675. *m.* 5 Nov. 1654 Rebecca Abbas. The façade of his splendid mansion (now no. 49 Nieuwe Herengracht) illustrated in an etching by Romeyn de Hooghe. *ob.* 15 Feb. 1697, *i.* Ouderkerk.

Amst. Arch. *DTB* No. 682, p. 211, *Not. Arch.* 2907B, 1621f; Gans, *Memorboek,* p. 118; J. F. van Agt, *Synagogen in Amsterdam* (The Hague, 1974), p. 43; Meijer, *Enc.* 1, p. 178; D. Swetschinski, 'The Spanish Consul and the Jews of Amsterdam', in Fishbane and Flohr (eds.), *Texts and Responses: Studies presented to N. N. Glatzer,* p. 169; J. Israel, 'An Amsterdam Jewish Merchant of the Golden Age: Jeronimo Nunes da Costa (1620–1697), Agent of Portugal in the Dutch Republic', *Studia Rosenthaliana,* 18, 1984, pp. 21–40.

D'AVILAR *see* **AVILAR**
DE BARRIOS *see* **BARRIOS**
DIRKS *see* **FRANCO MENDES**
(H)ENRÍQUEZ, AARON, alias **A. NUNES ENRÍQUEZ** (1664–?). Merchant, originated from Rouen, where known as **MANUEL ENRÍQUEZ.** *m.* 15 Dec. 1685 in Amsterdam Sarah, *d.* of Aaron Alvarez. *res.* S. Antoniesbreestr.

Amst. Arch. *DTB* No. 695, p. 94, *ket. PA* 334, No. 382, p. 358; De Barrios, *Alegrías*, pp. 47 f., Epythalamio de los muy Ilustres señores Aaron Henriquez Nuñez y Doña Sara Albarez, año 1685.

FRANCO MENDES, DAVID alias **SIMON RODRÍGUEZ MENDES** or **SIMON DIRKS** (1645–94). Wealthy merchant. *b.* Amsterdam, descendant of Melchor Mendes Franco who on 27 Apr. 1598 reached Amsterdam with his two children, reverted to Judaism, and adopted the name Abraham. *m.* 3 Sept. 1677 Rachel, *d.* of Joseph Mocatta (see below) being then *res.* Houtgracht.

Amst. Arch. *DTB* No. 691, p. 56, *ket. PA* 334 No. 382, p. 98; Franco Mendes, *Memorias*, pp. 12 f.

FROIS, ABRAHAM (1636–1704). Physician and lawyer. Originated from Lisbon, and probably qualified in law in Portugal. Licensed as medical practitioner, university of Utrecht, 18 Mar. 1663. *m.* (1) at Amsterdam, 10 Apr. 1671, Rachel Carvalho, being then *res.* Vlooyenburg; she died 12 Apr. 1683 (28 *Nisan* 5444), *i.* Ouderkerk; (2) 5 Apr. 1691, Judith Carvalho, being then *res.* Zwanenburgerstr. *ob.* 1 Oct. 1704 (3 *Tishri* 5465), *i.* Ouderkerk.

Amst. Arch. *DTB* No. 688, p. 214, No. 695, p. 151; *ket.* (2) *PA* 334 No. 382f, ii, p. 365; No. 916, p. 43; *PA* 27, file 20.

GABBAY ISIDRO, JACOB (1661–1714). Merchant. Originated from Madrid. *m.* 19 Dec. 1682 Rachel de la Peña of Bayonne; *res.* S. Antoniesbreestr. *ob.* 3 May 1714 (18 *'Iyyar* 5474), *i.* Ouderkerk.

Amst. Arch. *DTB* No. 693, p. 272, *ket. PA* 334 No. 382f, ii, p. 214, No. 422 *sub nomine;* Pieterse, *De Barrios,* p. 127.

GABRIEL *see* **MOCATTA, MOSES** b. **ABRAHAM**

GAMA, JACOB de, alias **JACOB MENDEZ GAMA** (1654–1716). Merchant, *b.* Amsterdam, *s.* of Abraham G. *m.* 7 Nov. 1681 Rebecca *d.* of Moses Chaves Vaez; *res.* Zwanenburgerstr. *ob.* 26 July 1716 (7 *'Ab* 5476), *i.* Ouderkerk.

Amst. Arch. *DTB* No. 693, p. 22, *ket. PA* 334 No. 382f, ii, p. 217; No. 422 *sub nomine.*

GÓMEZ *see* **GUTIERRES GÓMEZ**

GUTIERRES (GÓMEZ), ABRAHAM (?–1691). Physician, qualified May 1684 at Harderwijk. Referred to by de Barrios as *mantenedor* (see above, p. 289) in the *Academia. ob.* 23 Feb. 1691 (24 *'Adar* 5451), *i.* Ouderkerk.

Amst. Arch. *PA* 27 file 20; De Barrios, *Academia,* p. 253; De Castro, *Ouderkerk,* i, p. 24; Kayserling, *Biblioteca,* p. 51.

HAMIS VAZ, DAVID (?–1697). Merchant. A congregational list of married men dated 1675 shows him married. From de Barrios we learn that his wife was named 'Esther'. *ob.* 23 Sept. 1697 (9 *Tishri* 5458), *i.* Ouderkerk.

'Eṣ Ḥayyim 48 D 43 (Fuks no. 358), f. 29ʳ, *Memoria de las Personas que ay en la Nacion cazadas, en 19 de Sivan 5435;* De Barrios, *Alegrías,* pp. 143 f.; Franco Mendes, *Memorias,* p. 93 gives his name as Ximenez Vaz.

HENRÍQUEZ *see* **ENRÍQUEZ**
ISIDRO *see* **GABBAY**

Membership of the Academia de los Floridos 423

JESSURUN LOBO, JOSEPH, alias **JOSEPH DE MEDINA LOBO**. Originated from Rouen. According to de Barrios, he was Spanish consul in Zeeland:

> Joseph Jesurum [*sic*] Lobo, al primor anda
> del Rey Hispano Consul en Zelanda.

After his first wife's death, *m.* 23 July 1684 in Amsterdam Rachel, widowed *d.* of Moses Levi, he being then *res.* Muidergracht. Together with his co-*parnasim* (lay officers) of Congregation *Talmud Torah*, was honoured in 1681 with the dedication of Isaac Aboab's *Commentary* on the Pentateuch.

Amst. Arch. *DTB* No. 694, p. 416, *ket. PA* 334 No. 382, p. 314; De Barrios, *Academia*, p. 255; Isaac Aboab da Fonseca, *Parafrasis comentada sobre el Pentateucho*, Amsterdam, 5441 (1681).

JIMENEZ *see* **XIMENES**

LEVI, MANUEL (1639–1713?). Merchant banker. *b.* Amsterdam, *m.* 26 Nov. 1668 Constancia Duarte. One of the regular patrons of de Barrios, who in a letter dated 17 Jan. 1698 solicited his help in publishing part ii of his *Flor de Apolo*. On death of his only granddaughter on 15 Dec. 1697, received a consolatory poem from de Barrios. Towards the end of the seventeenth century settled in Antwerp. Acted as banker for a number of members of the *Academia*.

Amst. Arch. *DTB* No. 684, p. 378; *PA* 334, No. 681 (the letter printed in full by Pieterse, together with another of 4 Jan. 1698, *De Barrios*, pp. 145, 147, 149). For his clientele, *PA* 334 No. 686 (Levi's *Bankboek* for 1675–96): Joseph and Abraham Penso (pp. 4–5, 9), Moses Pereyra (pp. 6, 8, 9, 13, 15, etc.), Joseph Nunes da Costa (pp. 12, 14, 16), Isaac Carrillo (pp. 13, 14, 17), David Ximenes Cardozo (p. 15), David Franco Mendes (p. 21), Joseph Athias (p. 43), David Hamis Vaz (p. 50), Raphael del Castillo (p. 53), Joseph Jessurun Lobo (p. 54), Abraham Lumbrozo (p. 69): see Pieterse, pp. 27 f., 39, 83. A Manuel Levi Duarte was buried at Ouderkerk died 2 Oct. 1713 (13 *Tishri* 5474), but since his wife was named *Deborah* identity cannot be established, although *Deborah* is possibly a Hebrew counterpart of *Constancia*; De Castro, Ouderkerk, i, p. 321.

LIS *see* **LÓPEZ BERAHEL**
LOBO *see* **JESSURUN LOBO**
LÓPEZ BERAHEL, ABRAHAM, alias **FRANCISCO de LIS** (1648–*c.*1725). Merchant. *b.* Amsterdam, *s.* of Jacob and Rachel B. *m.* 19 June 1667 at Amsterdam Rachel, *d.* of Isaac Israel Suasso y López, in which year he was *res.* in London (apparently until 1685). A sonnet dedicated to him by de Barrios shows clearly that he had assisted him and other poets. Himself a poet, he dedicated his own *Estrella de Jacob sobre flores de Lis*, Amsterdam, 1686, to his two children.

Amst. Arch. *DTB* No. 691, p. 30, *ket. PA* 334, No. 382, p. 95. The date of his settlement in Amsterdam is attested by the commencement of his dues paid to the Congregation *Talmud Torah* in 1685; No. 175, p. 305; De

Barrios, *Alegrías*, p. 94; Pieterse, *De Barrios*, p. 25: for date of his death Meijer, *Enc.* i, p. 185.

LÓPEZ ROSA *see* **ROSA**

LUMBROZO, ABRAHAM HAI (1651–?). Merchant. *b.* Venice, *s.* of Benjamin L. Reached Amsterdam in 1673 with Manuel da Vega, whom he had succeeded in ransoming from the Inquisition in Venice. *m.* 22 July 1678 Clara, *d.* of David de Soto, being then *res.* Vlooyenburg.

Amst. Arch. *DTB* No. 691, p. 143, *ket. PA* 334 No. 382f, ii, p. 131. For a vivid account of Lumbrozo's ransoming of da Vega in Italy and their journey to Amsterdam, see Franco Mendes, *Memorias*, pp. 88 f.

MACHADO, MOSES, alias **MOSES ALVAREZ MACHADO** (?–1706). Merchant and *Proveedor General* to Dutch and English armies; friend of William of Orange, later William III of England. In 1673, after the battle of Remmich between William and the forces of the Archbishop of Cologne, he saved approximately 120 Jewish inhabitants whose lives were at risk after William's sack of Remmich. Together with Jacob Pereyra, signed (1690) contract of supply to the Dutch forces, which led him into financial difficulties when the council of the United Provinces failed to pay a debt of 25,000 guilders. *ob.* 19 Dec. 1706 (14 Ṭebeth 5467), *i.* Ouderkerk.

Amst. Arch. *PA* 334, No. 42, *sub nomine*, and cf. L. A. Vega, *Het Beth Haim van Ouderkerk*, 1975, p. 44. J. S. da Silva Rosa, 'Twee Portugeesch Joodsche legerleveranciers van den Staat (1691)', *Vridagavond*, i, 1924, p. 44. De Barrios, *Triumpho*, p. 523 f., describes the Rijnbach incident as follows: '... y Mosseh Machado muy estimado de Guillermo de Nasao Principe de Orange, merece la alabança de la noble acción que manifestó su generoso animo: porque siendo Proveedor General del exercito de los Altos y Poderosos Señores Estados Generales de las Provincias Unidas en el Año de 1673, acontecio que en el mes de Noviembre marchando el Auriaco exercito, para juntarse con el de Alemania que acaudillava Montecuquili; no le quisieron dar entrada en la Cuidad de Rimbach, plaça del Obispo de Colonia. Ordenó el Principe de Orange que se ataquesse [*sic*] y no dar quartel a ningun morador. Suplicole el Proveedor Machado que ordenase a sus Soldados diessen buen cuartel a los judios que se hallassen dentro de la Ciudad: concediosselo el Principe: y el Proveedor prometió a los saqueadores treinta florines por cada Israelita. Hallaronse 18 judios de los quales rescató 37 y de los otros no consintieron los Officiales que tomassen dinero sus Soldados: y de este modo no perecio ningun judio.' [It should however be noticed that the circumstantial journal of Constantine Huygens the younger, who as William's secretary was with him at the sack of Remmich, records no such occurrence. (Just as de Barrios writes *Rimbach*, so Huygens who regularly uses the form *Remmich*, at the end of his account has *Rheinbach*.) Historisch Genootshap te Utrecht, *Werken*, N.S. 32, 1881, pp. 13–17. R.L.]

Membership of the Academia de los Floridos 425

MARCHENA see **MOCATTA, JOSEPH**

MEDINA, AARON, alias **JOSEPH ENRÍQUEZ MEDINA** (1657–1725). Merchant. *s.* of Gaspar and doña Isabel Rodríguez M. *m.* 3 June 1687 at Amsterdam Rachel, *d.* of David Hamis Vaz (see above), whilst *res.* Zwanenburgerstr. Testamentary dispositions drawn up 14 Sept. 1716, before Cornelis von Achehoven, Amsterdam notary; *ob.* 11 Mar. 1725 (26 *'Adar* 5485), *i.* Ouderkerk.

Amst. Arch. *DTB* No. 695, p. 409, *ket. PA* 334 No. 387f, ii, p. 400; will, No. 738, pp. 2–7; No. 422, *sub nomine.*

MEDINA LOBO see **JESSURUN LOBO**

MENDES see **FRANCO MENDES**

MOCATTA, JOSEPH, alias **JOSEPH NUNES MARCHENA.** Merchant. Originated from Bayonne, reaching Amsterdam *c.* 1673. One of the wealthiest members of the congregation, and one of the principal benefactors of the *Academia de los Floridos.* Recipient of the dedication of Joseph Penso Vega's *Discursos Académicos,* 1658 (see bibl. (3)); *m.* Rachel, sister of David Franco Mendes (see above).

Amst. Arch. *PA* 334, No. 174, p. 973 (payment of congregational dues begins 1673); cf. above, p. 296; De Barrios, *Triumpho,* Ms *Eṣ Ḥayyim* 2 F 9, pp. 373 f.

MOCATTA, MOSES, alias **MOSES NUNES MARCHENA** (1665–?). *s.* of Joseph M. (see previous entry). *b.* Bayonne, *m.* 1 Nov. 1685 in Amsterdam Rebecca, *d.* of Rodrigo Núñez Enríquez of London, being then *res.* Zwanenburgerstr.

Amst. Arch. *DTB* No. 695, p. 71; *ket. PA* 334, No. 382f, ii, p. 353 (the bridegroom's marriage settlement was 60,000 fl. and the bride's 50,000); Pieterse, *De Barrios,* p. 84.

MOCATTA, MOSES b. ABRAHAM, alias don **ANTONIO GABRIEL** (1659–?). Merchant. *b.* Peyrehorade, France; related (*contra* Pieterse) to Joseph M., and *m.* (*contra* Pieterse) 1 Sept. 1684 in Amsterdam Esther Cohen Camiña. Probably to be identified (rather than Moses b. Joseph M., then aged 8) with the 'young pupil Moses Mocati' (*sic*) the author of a Hebrew sonnet in honour of Joseph Penso printed in the latter's *'Asirey ha-Tiqwah* (Amsterdam, 1673), when Moses b. Abraham M. was 14.

Amst. Arch. *DTB* No. 694, p. 168, *ket. PA* 334 No. 382f, ii, p. 329. Pieterse, *De Barrios,* p. 85, whose assertion of M's bachelorhood depends on de Barrios, *Triumpho* (1683) (see *sub* Joseph M.), p. 424, *'Galan sin pension de Dama'.*

MONTEZINOS see **CASTILLO**

MORENO, GABRIEL. Apparently originated from Bayonne; related to Dr Jacob Moreno: listed, 1675, amongst married members of the congregation. His sister Beatriz Gómez M. *m.* Raphael Athias, 1684; a brother was named Abraham Shalom M.

'Eṣ Ḥayyim 48 D 43 (Fuks no. 358) f. 30ʻ; De Barrios, *Alegrías*, pp. 37 f.; Kayserling, *Biblioteca*, p. 74; Kaplan, *Studentim*, pp. 68 f.

*NUNES BELMONTE, ISAAC, alias **don MANUEL (de) BELMONTE** (?–1705). From 1664 acted as Agent-General of the King of Spain in Amsterdam, and from 1674 until his death as Consul. The Emperor Leopold III ennobled him as Count Palatine (1673) and he became a baron in 1693. One of the founders of the *Academia de los Sitibundos* in Amsterdam in 1676, meetings of which were held in his house, as also apparently those of the *Academia de los Floridos* (see above, p. 292). From 1700 until his death res. in the splendid mansion now no. 586 Herengracht. Recipient of dedication of de Barrios' *Bellomonte de Helicona* (Brussels, 1686). Two Portuguese poems by him printed in the *collectaneum* in memory of the crypto-Jew Abraham Núñez Bernal, burned at the stake in Córdoba 3 May 1655. ob. 18 Feb. 1705, *i*. Ouderkerk.

Amst. Arch. *PA* 334, No. 422, *sub nomine;* Meijer, *Enc.* i, p. 59; Gans, *Memorboek,* p. 116; Pieterse, *De Barrios,* p. 25; Roth, 'Abraham Núñez Bernal, etc.' (bibl. (4)): *Elogio que zelozos dedicaron a la Felice memoria de Abraham Nuñez Bernal que fue quemado vivo santificando el nombre de su criador en Cordova a 3 de Mayo 5415, s.l.e.a.,* pp. 46 f.

NUNES DA COSTA see **CURIEL**

PENSO, ABRAHAM (?–1710). Wealthy merchant, *s.* of Isaac Penso Felix and Esther de la Vega. His father after imprisonment by the Inquisition fled from Spain to Antwerp and thence to Middelburg, where he was circumcised. Subsequently settled in Amsterdam, where in 1643 he made his house available for use by the *yeshibah* (religious academy) *Kether Torah* founded by Rabbi Saul Levi Mortera. After death of Isaac P. on 24 Feb. 1683 (28 *Shebaṭ* 5443) Abraham P. kept up his father's tradition, and the best room in his house became the permanent home of the *yeshibah. m.* Rebecca Penso Alvarez. His will was drawn up on 28 May 1710. Without doubt one of the principal benefactors of the *Academia de los Floridos. ob.* 27 May 1710 (29 *'Iyyar* 5470), *i.* Ouderkerk.

Amst. Arch. *PA* 334, No. 695; Pieterse, *De Barrios,* p. 107; De Barrios, *Triumpho* ('Eṣ Ḥayyim 2 F 9), pp. 95 f: *Lamentación funebre en el Parnaso de Daniel Levi de Barrios, por el bienaventurado Ishak Penso, que fallecio de setenta y cinco años, en el de 5443 de la Universal Criación a 28 de Sebat;* and p. 70: *Abraham Penso, imitador de su gran Padre Ishac Penso en la Religion, y Caridad, y en franquear dos horas cada dia, el mejor quarto de su casa, al estudio de la Sagrada Doctrina.* De Castro, *Ouderkerk,* i, p. 18.

*PENSO, JOSEPH (1650–92). Younger brother of Abraham P. (see previous). Lived for some time in Leghorn (Livorno), where he founded the local *Academia de los Sitibundos* (see above, p. 290). One of the most prolific writers of the west-European Sephardi diaspora; his Hebrew play *'Asirey ha-Tiqwah* ('prisoners of hope') was published in Amsterdam, 1673. Apart from his *Rumbos peligrosos* (1683) he wrote, *inter alia, Triunfos del Aguila* (1683), and

Membership of the Academia de los Floridos

Retrato de la Prudencia (1690). Became widely known through his *Confusión de Confusiones* (1688), the first comprehensive treatise on the stock exchange. Secretary of the *Academia de los Floridos. ob.* 13 Nov. 1692 (4 *Kislev* 5453), *i.* Ouderkerk.

Amst. Arch. *PA* 334, No. 422, *sub nomine;* De Barrios, *Academia,* p. 253; Kayserling, *Biblioteca,* pp. 85 f.; Amzalak, *Joseph de la Vega* (bibl. (4)).

PEREYRA, MOSES ISRAEL (1635–1702). Wealthy merchant, one of the richest members of the Portuguese congregation of Amsterdam. *b.* Madrid, *s.* of Abraham Israel P., on whom see above, pp. 219 f. After the death of his niece and first wife Sarah, elder *d.* of his brother Isaac, *m.* 16 July 1666 in Amsterdam Esther de Souza, being then *res.* S. Antoniesbreestr. *ob.* 11 Dec. 1702 (21 *Kislev* 5463), *i.* Ouderkerk.

Amst. Arch. *DTB* No. 686, p. 363; De Castro, *Ouderkerk,* i, p. 16.

PESSOA, ISAAC (?–1707). Wealthy merchant in import and export trade. *m.* Sarah Paz. Of his sons, Abraham *m.* Hannah Cohen Camiña and Moses, Hannah Pessoa. *ob.* 9 Aug. 1707 (11 *'Ab* 5467), *i.* Ouderkerk.

Amst. Arch. *PA* 334, No. 422, *sub nomine;* De Barrios, *Alegrías,* f. 86ʳ.

RODRÍGUEZ MENDES see **FRANCO MENDES**

ROSA, MOSES, alias **DUARTE LÓPEZ ROSA** (?–1702). *b.* Beja, Portugal; lived for some time in Rome, whence he proceeded to Amsterdam and there reverted to Judaism; brother of Samuel R., the brother-in-law of Daniel Levi de Barrios. Participated in the Amsterdam *Academia de los Sitibundos* and as *mantenedor* (see above, p. 289) in that of the *Floridos.* Published several books of verse, including *Alientos de la Verdad, 1688,* also *Panegyrico sobre la restauración de Inglaterra en la coronación de las inclitas Magestades de Guillermo III Y Serᵗ. Maria por Reyes de la Bretaña,* Amsterdam, 1690, and *Luzes de la Idea y Académicos Discursos* (s.a.) *ob.* 15 July 1702 (20 *Tammuz* 5462), *i.* Ouderkerk.

Amst. Arch. *PA* 334, No. 442, *sub nomine;* Kayserling, *Biblioteca,* p. 95; Pieterse, *De Barrios,* p. 143. A sonnet by Rosa in honour of don Joseph Toledano, the special envoy of Muli 'Isma'il, Sultan of Morocco, who came to Amsterdam in 1684, *apud* D. Franco Mendes, *Memorias,* pp. 92 f.

SEMAH, SAMUEL (1653–?). Merchant. *b.* Verona, *s.* of Ḥakham (= Rabbi) Abraham S. *m.* 17 Nov. 1679 Jael, *d.* of Joseph Jessurun López.

Amst. Arch. *DTB* No. 691, p. 282, *ket. PA* 334, No. 382f, ii, p. 158.

VAZ see **HAMIS VAZ**

VILLEGAS, ISAAC. Nothing is known of him save that he was expert in swordsmanship, as de Barrios recorded:

> Ishac Villegas, con la espada y brio
> pasma al valiente y prende el alvedrio.

De Barrios, *Academia,* p. 255.

XIMENES CARDOZO, DAVID (1650–?). Merchant; originated from Bayonne. *m.* (1) 26 Feb. 1673 Rebecca, *d.* of Benjamin Aboab, being then *res.* Houtgracht; after her death (2) 27 Dec. 1685 Judith da Rocha, he being then *res.* Rapenburg; after her death (3) 10 Sept. 1698 Rachel de Medina Cardozo, he being then *res.* Muiderstr. He was a good swordsman, as appears from de Barrios' poem:

> David Ximenes, diestro por la espada
> al fuerte asombra, y al discreto agrada.

Amst. Arch. *DTB* No. 690, p. 270, No. 695, p. 97, No. 701, p. 52; *ket.* (1) *PA* 334, No. 382, p. 87, (2) ii, p. 359. (3) i, p. 12. His second wife, Judith, died 17 Sept. 1696 (20 *Elul* 5456). De Barrios, *Academia*, p. 255.

OFFICES HELD BY MEMBERS OF THE ACADEMY

The following list indicates the offices of the Congregation *Talmud Torah* and its ancillary organizations filled by members of the *Academia de los Floridos*, the relevant years being given:

Parnasim (i.e. lay executives of the Congregation):

Moses Curiel	5425 [1664/5], 5431 [1670/1], 5435 [1674/5], 5439 [1678/9], 5445 [1684/5]
Isaac Nunes Belmonte	5458 [1697/8], 5461–2 [1700–2], 5464 [1703/4]
Joseph Mocatta	5447 [1686/7], 5451 [1690/1], 5455 [1694/5], 5459 [1698/9]
Joseph Athias	5448 [1687/8], 5453 [1692/3]
Moses Pereyra	5435 [1674/5]
David Franco Mendes	5445 [1684/5], 5450 [1689/90], 5454 [1693/4]
Joseph Jessurun Lobo	5427 [1666/7], 5434 [1673/4]
Abraham Gutierres	5438 [1677/8], 5442 [1681/2], 5447 [1686/7]
Abraham Penso	5452 [1691/2], 5456 [1695/6], 5460 [1699/1700], 5468 [1707/8]
Isaac Orobio	5430 [1669/70]
Moses b. Joseph Mocatta	5472 [1711/12], 5476 [1715/16]
Moses b. Abraham Mocatta	5453 [1692/3]
Moses Orobio	5462 [1701/2], 5467 [1706/7]

Parnasim of *'Eṣ Ḥayyim* (i.e. education)

Moses Curiel	5428 [1667/8]; *tesoureiro* 5438 [1677/8] and 5448 [1687/8]
Isaac Nunes Belmonte	5436 [1675/6], 5441 [1680/1], 5446 [1685/6]

Membership of the Academia de los Floridos

Joseph Mocatta	5445 [1684/5], 5450 [1689/90]; *tesoureiro* 5457 [1696/7]
Joseph Athias	5446 [1685/6]
Moses Pereyra	5436 [1675/6], 5455 [1694/5]
David Franco Mendes	5447 [1686/7]
Joseph Jessurun Lobo	5429 [1668/9], 5439 [1678/9]
Abraham Gutierres	5435 [1674/5]
Abraham Penso	*tesoureiro* 5459 [1698/9], *parnas* 5464 [1703/4]
Isaac Orobio	5428 [1667/8]
Moses b. Joseph Mocatta	5466 [1705/6], 5473 [1712/13]
Moses b. Abraham Mocatta	5452 [1691/2]
Moses Orobio	5456 [1695/6], 5465 [1704/5]
Jacob Chaves	5458 [1697/8]
Isaac Pessoa	5433 [1672/3]
Abraham López Berahel (Francisco de Lis)	5451 [1690/1]

Parnasim of *Biqqur Ḥolim* (sick visitation)

Moses Curiel	5415 [1654/5], 5425 [1664/5], 5432 [1671/2]
Joseph Mocatta	5437 [1676/7], *tesoureiro* 5453 [1692/3]
Joseph Athias	5445 [1684/5], *tesoureiro* 5455 [1694/5]
Moses Pereyra	5429 [1668/9], *tesoureiro* 5438 [1677/8]
David Franco Mendes	5439 [1678/9]
Abraham Penso	5456 [1695/6]
Isaac Orobio	5425 [1664/5]
Moses b. Joseph Mocatta	5450 [1689/90], 5475 [1714/15]
Moses Orobio	5454 [1693/4]
Joseph Jessurun Lobo	5427 [1666/7], 5435 [1674/5]
Jacob Chaves	5457 [1696/7]
Isaac Pessoa	5430 [1669/70]
Moses Machado	5449 [1688/9]
Jacob de Gama	5456 [1695/6]

Parnasim of *'Abi Yethomim* (orphan care)

David Franco Mendes	5443 [1682/3]
David Hamis Vaz	5443 [1682/3]

Parnasim of *Maskil 'el Dal* (charity)

Gabriel Moreno	*tesoureiro*, 5441 [1680/1]
Isaac Carrillo	*tesoureiro*, 5444 [1683/4]
Jacob Gabbay Isidro	5444 [1683/4]

Appendix D

Parnasim of *Tierra Santa* (holy land charities)
    Moses b. Joseph Mocatta   (*gabbay*, i.e. treasurer, 5445 [1684/5])

Cautivos (i.e. ransom of galley-slaves from Barbary)
    Isaac Nunes Belmonte   (*gabbay*, 5438 [1677/8])

Dotar (i.e. dowry provision)
    Moses Pereyra   (supervisor, 5443 [1682/3])

Gemiluth Ḥasadim (charitable and loan fund)
    David Hamis Vaz   5434 [1673/4]
    Joseph Jessurun Lobo   5444 [1683/4]
    Jacob de Gama   5450 [1689/90]
    Gabriel Moreno   5449 [1688/9]

Temimey Derekh ('perfect way')
    Isaac Carrillo   ?5443 [1682/3]

Ouderkerk Cemetery
    Joseph Jessurun Lobo   *tesoureiro* 5444 [1683/4]

Vistiaria dos Talmidim (school clothing supervisors)
    Jacob de Gama   5444 [1683/4]
    Jacob Uzziel d'Avilar   5446 [1685/6]

See Amsterdam, AGA, *PA* 334 no. 158.

APPENDIX E
Manuscripts of Works by Isaac Orobio de Castro

I: CONTROVERSY WITH PRADO

A   Epístola Invectiva (15 MSS; published in part, see MSS 1, 15).
1. Amsterdam, 'Eṣ Ḥayyim-Montezinos 48 A 23, ff. 107 f.
    Date 1719 *Copyist* David Núñez Carvalho (?)
    Title Tratado contra la ympiedad de los deístas
    The original text; the introduction, which differs from that in all other MSS, was published by Révah in *REJ*, 123, 1964, pp. 427 f. [The title in this form, not found in any of the other MSS here listed, is given as that of a manuscript in the library of Aaron Colace of Bayonne in an inventory of 1783, Amsterdam, AGA, Archief Weerkamer, K 18; published by G. Nahon, *Les 'Nations' juives portugaises du sud-ouest de la France (1684–1791)*, Fontes Documentais Portuguesas xv, Paris, 1981, pp. 448 no. 209, 248, 251. Fuks-M., *EH*, does not include MS 48 A 23; inspection might indicate whether it is in fact A. Colace's copy. R.L.]
2. Amsterdam, 'Eṣ Ḥayyim-Montezinos 48 C 4 (Fuks-M., *EH*, no. 242, p. 126).
    Date 1668 *Copyist* Abraham Machorro
    Title Respuesta a un Filósofo Hebreo que pide fundamentos de razón para persuadirse al credito de el Sacro Texto
3. London, British Library, Harley 3430, pp. 165 f.
    Date 1679 *Copyists* Joseph and Samuel Israel Pereira
    Title Epístola Invectiva contra Prado, un Philósopho Médico que dudava o no creía la verdad de la divina escriptura y pretendió encubrir su malicia con la afectada confessión de Dios y Ley de Naturaleza
4. Amsterdam, 'Eṣ Ḥayyim-Montezinos 48 D 6, ff. 326^r–432^r (Fuks-M., *EH*, no. 196, p. 99).
    Date Late 17th cent.
    Title Lacking
5. Amsterdam *Eṣ Ḥayyim*-Montezinos 48 A 12, ff. 1^r–71^r (Fuks-M., *EH*, no. 244, p. 127).
    Date Late 17th cent.
    Title Epístola Invectiva contra un Philósopho Médico que dudava o no creía la verdad de la divina escriptura y pretendío, etc.

432 *Appendix E*

6. Amsterdam, *'Eṣ Ḥayyim*-Montezinos 48 C 12, ff. 382ʳ–503ᵛ (Fuks-M., *EH*, no. 194, p. 96).
   Date Late 17th cent.
   Title As 5
7. London, Jews' College, Montefiore 525, p. 347 f. (Hirschfeld, no. 298, p. 93).
   Date Late 17th cent.
   Title As 5
8. Madrid, Biblioteca Nacional, Gayangos 18249, ff. 340ᵛ f. (Roca, pp. 312 f.).
   Date Late 17th cent.
   Title As 5
9. Amsterdam, *'Eṣ Ḥayyim*-Montezinos 48 C 3, ff. 43ʳ–147ᵛ.
   Date Early 18th cent.
   Title As 5
   Part of vol. iii of the (3-vol.) *Works* of Isaac Orobio which had belonged to Jacob Nahar, donated to the *Eṣ Ḥayyim* Library by Jacob Mendes Chumaceiro, rabbi of the Curaçao congregation.
10. New York, Jewish Theological Seminary, Adler 2359³, ff. 41ᵛ–142ᵛ (Marx, no. 67, p. 264).
    Date Early 18th cent.
    Title As 5
11. Amsterdam, Universiteitsbibliotheek 1 H 13, ff. 124ᵛ–225ᵛ.
    Date Early 18th cent.
    Title As 5
12. Amsterdam, *'Eṣ Ḥayyim*-Montezinos 48 B 12, pp. 1–87 (Fuks-M., *EH*, no. 238, p. 123).
    Date 1705   *Copyist* Abraham Machorro
    Title Epístola Invectiva, contra la impiedad de quien duda la verdad infalible de la Sagrada Escritura y pretende ocultar la malicia, con la afectada confessión de Dios y Ley de Naturaleza. Respuesta a un Filósofo Hebreo
13. Amsterdam, Bibliotheca Rosenthaliana, Cassuto 631², pp. 1–79.
    Date 1712   *Copyist* Daniel López Quiros
    Title Ynvectiva contra un Philósopho Médico sobre la Verdad de la Divina Ley
14. Oxford, Bodleian, Opp. 4° 147c, pp. 63–214 (Neubauer, no. 2472, p. 878).
    Date 1724
    Title As 5
15. Paris, Bibliothèque Nationale, Fonds éspagnoles 40–1, pp. 875 f. (Morel-Fatio, nos. 33–4, pp. 8 f).
    Date 1731
    Title As 5

Révah published a substantial portion of this MS in his *Spinoza et Prado* (bibl. (3B)), pp. 86–129.

B **Carta Apologética** (1 MS; printed, see following).
   Paris, Bibliothèque Nationale, Fonds éspagnoles 41, p. 875 f. (Morel-Fatio, no. 34, pp. 8 f.).
   Date 1731
   Published by Révah in full in his *Spinoza et Prado*, pp. 130–42.

C **Letter to Prado's son** (3 MSS; printed, see below, 3). For collation of variant texts in the following three MSS, see below, Appendix F.
1. Amsterdam, 'Eṣ Ḥayyim-Montezinos 48 A 21, ff. 239–51.
   Date 1719   *Copyist* Abraham Machorro
   Title Carta del Doctor Ishac Orobio de Castro a un sujeto de Amberez, contra el Doctor Prado que vivía allí, siendo apartado de la Nación, y publicado en Herem, en la Synagoga de Amsterdam
2. Amsterdam, 'Eṣ Ḥayyim-Montezinos 48 A 23, ff. 310–31.
   Date 1719   *Copyist* David Núñez Carvalho(?)
   Title Respuesta del mismo autor a siertas preguntas del Doctor Prados que por segunda persona fueron dichas
3. Paris, Bibliothèque Nationale, Fonds éspagnoles 41, pp. 902 f. (Morel-Fatio, no. 34, pp. 8 f.).
   Date 1731
   Title Carta al hijo de el Doctor Prado
   Published by Révah in full in his *Spinoza et Prado*, pp. 143–53.

II: CONTROVERSY WITH ZEPEDA

A **Respuesta ... si ... Lulio ... era intelligible** (6 MSS; printed in Alonso de Zepeda, *Defensa de los Términos y Doctrina de Raymundo Lullio*, Brussels, 1666, pp. 2–77).
1. Amsterdam, 'Eṣ Ḥayyim-Montezinos 48 D 6, ff. 314ʳ–325ᵛ (Fuks-M., *EH*, no. 196, p. 99).
   Date Late 17th cent.
   Title Respuesta a una persona que dudava si el libro de Raymundo Lulio, nuevamente traducido y comentado por don Alonso de Zepeda era intelligible, y si concluyan sus discursos
2. Amsterdam, 'Eṣ Ḥayyim-Montezinos 48 A 12, ff. 100ʳ–110ʳ (Fuks-M., *EH*, no. 244, p. 128).
   Date Late 17th cent.
   Title As above
3. Amsterdam, 'Eṣ Ḥayyim-Montezinos 48 B 5, pp. 1–20.
   Date 1703   *Copyist* Abraham Machorro
   Title As above

Appendix E

4. Amsterdam, 'Eṣ Ḥayyim-Montezinos 48 B 12²
   Date 1707 *Copyist* Abraham Machorro
   Title As above
5. Amsterdam, Bibliotheca Rosenthaliana, Cassuto 631⁴, pp. 1–12
   Date 1712 *Copyist* David López Quiros
   Title As above
6. Paris, Bibliothèque Nationale, Fonds éspagnoles 41, pp. 115–27 (Morel-Fatio, no. 34, pp. 8 f.).
   Date 1731
   Title As above

B Respuesta Apologética al ... Zepeda (8 MSS; unpublished, apart from quotations above, pp. 187 f.).

1. Amsterdam, 'Eṣ Ḥayyim-Montezinos 48 E 42, pp. 104 (Fuks.-M., *EH*, no. 234, pp. 120 f.).
   Date 1670s
   Title Respuesta Apologética al libro que escrivió Don Alonso de Zepeda que intituló Defensa de los términos y doctrina de Raymundo Lulio
   Possibly Orobio's holograph; contains many erasures and corrections
2. Amsterdam, 'Eṣ Ḥayyim-Montezinos 48 D 6, ff. 433ʳ–548ʳ.
   Date Late 17th cent.
   Title As above
3. Amsterdam, 'Eṣ Ḥayyim-Montezinos 48 A 12, ff. 110ᵛ–210ʳ.
   Date Late 17th cent.
   Title As above
4. Amsterdam, Universiteitsbibliotheek 1 H 13, ff. 1ʳ–138.
   Date Early 18th cent.
   Title As above
5. Amsterdam, Eṣ Ḥayyim-Montezinos 48 B 5, pp. 211 (Fuks-M., *EH*, no. 237, pp. 112 f.).
   Date 17th–18th cent. *Copyist* Abraham Machorro
   Title As above
6. Amsterdam, 'Eṣ Ḥayyim-Montezinos 48 B 12², pp. 190 (Fuks-M., *EH*, no. 238, pp. 123 f.).
   Date 1707 *Copyist* Abraham Machorro
   Title As above
7. Amsterdam, Bibliotheca Rosenthaliana, Cassuto 631⁵, pp. 13–130.
   Date 1712 *Copyist* Daniel López Quiros
   Title As above
8. Paris, Bibliothèque Nationale, Fonds éspagnoles 41, pp. 128–257 (Morel-Fatio, no. 34, pp. 8 f.).
   Date 1731
   Title As above

Manuscripts of Works by Isaac Orobio de Castro 435
III: ON THE TRINITY (I MS; UNPUBLISHED APART FROM EXTRACTS CITED ABOVE, P. 188).

Amsterdam, 'Eṣ Ḥayyim-Montezinos 48 B 12, pp. 175–90
Date 1707   *Copyist* Abraham Machorro
Title Discurso sobre la Trinidad

IV: REJOINDER TO HUGUENOT REGARDING LAW (13 (14) MSS: PRINTED BY AMZALAK, *LA OBSERVANCIA DE LA DIVINA LEY DE MOSSEH*, 1925).

1. London, British Library, Harley 3430, pp. 147–64.
   Date 1679   *Copyists* Joseph and Samuel Pereira
   Title Respuesta a un escrito que prezentó un Predicante Francés a el Author contra la observancia de la Divina Ley de Mosseh
2. Amsterdam, 'Eṣ Ḥayyim-Montezinos 48 C 12, ff. 340ᵛ–381ᵛ (Fuks-M., *EH*, no. 194, pp. 96 f.).
   Date Late 17th cent.
   Title Respuesta a un escrito que un predicante francés prezentó al Dᵒʳ Orobio contra la observancia de la Divina Ley de Mosseh
3. Amsterdam, 'Eṣ Ḥayyim-Montezinos 48 A 12, ff. 71ʳ–100ʳ (Fuks-M., *EH*, no. 244, p. 128).
   Date Late 17th cent.
   Title Respuesta a un tratado que escrivió un docto Predicante de la religión reformada en que procurava probar que la esperança de Ysrael y observancia de la Divina Ley, no tenia fundamento y que la cristiana demostrava su verdad por los sagrados escriptos
4. Amsterdam, 'Eṣ Ḥayyim-Montezinos 48 D 6, ff. 288–313 (Fuks-M., *EH*, ii, no. 196, p. 99).
   Date Late 17th cent.
   Title Tratado o respuesta a un cavallero francés reformado doctísimo y estudioso en su religión que con el devido secreto propuso diferentes questiones para probarle y oponer a la Divina Ley con expecífica demonstrativa respuesta
5. Madrid, Biblioteca Nacional, Gayangos 18249, ff. 300ʳ–340ᵛ (Roca, pp. 312 f.).
   Date Late 17th cent.
   Title Respuesta a un escrito que prezentó un Predicante Francés a el Author contra la observancia de la Divina Ley de Mosseh
6. Amsterdam, Universiteitsbibliotheek 1 H 13, ff. 75–124.
   Date Early 18th cent.
   Title As 2

7. Amsterdam, 'Eṣ Ḥayyim-Montezinos 48 C 3, ff. 1ʳ–42ᵛ.
   Date Early 18th cent. (Fuks-M., *EH*, no. 220, p. 113).
   Title As 2
   The Nahar-Chumaceiro copy, see above, I A 9.
8. New York, Jewish Theological Seminary, Adler 2359³, ff. 1ʳ–41ᵛ (Marx, no. 7, p. 264).
   Date Early 18th cent.
   Title As 5
9. Amsterdam, private collection (M. H. Gans), pp. 138.
   Date 1712(?)
   Title Respuesta a un tratado que un Predicante Francés prezentó al Dᵒʳ Orobio, contra la observancia de la Divina Ley de Mosseh, al qual le respondio como sigue
   The first page contains a copper engraving by B. Picard dated 1712, and the copy may be assumed to be approximately contemporary.
   It is clear from the edition of the work by Amzalak, p. [ix], that he utilized this MS as the basis of his edition.
10. Amsterdam, Bibliotheca Rosenthaliana, Cassuto 631³, pp. 1–35.
    Date 1712   Copyist Daniel López Quiros
    Title As 4
11. Amsterdam, 'Eṣ Ḥayyim-Montezinos 48 A 21, ff. 195–236.
    Date 1712   Copyist Abraham Machorro
    Title As 4, except reading *con todo secreto* for *con el devido secreto*.
12. Oxford, Bodleian, Opp. Add. 4° 147c (Neubauer, no. 2472, p. 878).
    Date 1724
    Title As 5
13. Paris, Bibliothèque Nationale, Fonds éspagnoles 40, pp. 329ʳ–367ᵛ. (Morel-Fatio, no. 33, pp. 8 f.).
    Date 1731
    Title Respuesta a un escrito que presentó al autor un predicante francés contra la observancia de la Divina Ley
[14. Recorded by J. Fürst, *Bibliotheca Judaica* III, Leipzig, 1863, p. 54; untraced.
    Title Respuesta a un Predicante sobre la perpetua observancia de la Divina Ley]

V: BLANDISHMENTS OF IDOLATRY (21 MSS: UNPUBLISHED SAVE FOR EXTRACTS ABOVE, pp. 243 f.).

1. London, British Library, Harley 3430, pp. 1–146.
   Date 1679   Copyists Joseph and Samuel Pereira
   Title Prevenciones Divinas contra la vana Idolatría de las Gentes

Preceded by 8 poems of Daniel Levi de Barrios in honour of Isaac Orobio.
E. Carmoly, *Histoire des Médecins Juifs*, i, p. 179 mentions a MS dated 1677/8.

2. Amsterdam, '*Eş Ḥayyim*-Montezinos 48 B 6, pp. 109 + 174 (Fuks-M., *EH*, no. 195, pp. 97 f.).
   Date Late 17th cent.
   Title As 1
   The *collectaneum* begins with 2 of de Barrios' poems mentioned above (see 1).

3. Amsterdam, '*Eş Ḥayyim*-Montezinos 48 D 6, ff. 1ʳ–287ʳ. (Fuks-M., *EH*, no. 196, pp. 98 f.).
   Date Late 17th cent.
   Title As 1

4. London, Jews' College, Montefiore 525, pp. 1–305 (Hirschfeld, no. 298, p. 93).
   Date Late 17th cent.
   Title As 1

5. Madrid, Biblioteca Nacional, Gayangos 18249, pp. 300 (Roca, pp. 312 f.).
   Date Late 17th cent.
   Title As 1

6. Amsterdam, '*Eş Ḥayyim*-Montezinos 48 C 2, pp. 510 (Fuks-M., *EH*, no. 194, pp. 97 f.).
   Date Late 17th cent.
   Title As 1

7. Amsterdam, '*Eş Ḥayyim*-Montezinos 48 C 1/2
   Date Early 18th cent.
   Title As 1
   Contained in vols. i and ii of the Nahar-Chumaceiro MS of Orobio's *Works*, see above, I A 9.

8. Amsterdam, Universiteitsbibliotheek 1 H 12, ff. 1–248, and 1 H 13, ff. 1–75.
   Date Early 18th cent.
   Title As 1

9. London, Wellcome Historical Medical Library, no. 3722, pp. 194 (Moorat, ii, pp. 779 f.).
   Date Early 18th cent.
   Title As 1 (contains part i only)

10. Oxford, Bodleian, Opp. Add. fol. 29 (Neubauer, no. 2471, pp. 264).
    Date Early 18th cent.
    Title As 1
    The *collectaneum* begins with 2 of de Barrios' poems mentioned above (see 1).

Appendix E

11. Oxford, Bodleian, Opp. Add. 8° 7, pp. 185 (Neubauer, no. 2473, p. 878).
    Date Early 18th cent.
    Title As 1 (contains part i only)
12. New York, Jewish Theological Seminary, Adler 2359^1, pp. 1–154, 1–201 (Adler, p. 53, Marx, no. 67, p. 63).
    Date Early 18th cent.
    Title As 1
13. Amsterdam, 'Eṣ Ḥayyim-Montezinos 48 B 13, pp. 325 (Fuks-M., *EH*, no. 202, p. 102).
    Date 1704   *Copyist* Abraham Machorro
    Title Prevenciones contra la Idolatría de las Gentes
    The title-page includes ink drawings on biblical subjects, apparently by Jacob Guedelha (Gadella).
14. Amsterdam, Bibliotheca Rosenthaliana, Cassuto 631^1, pp. 125 + 199.
    Date 1712   *Copyist* Daniel López Quiros
    Title Prevenciones Divinas contra la vana Idolatría de las Gentes
15. Amsterdam, Bibliotheca Rosenthaliana, 459, pp. 446 (Fuks, *Ros.*, no. 282, p. 131).
    Date 1713   *Copyist* Michael López [Pinto]
    Title As 14
    A de luxe copy, including 60 aquatints.
16. Hamburg, Stadtsbibliothek, Cod. Hebr. 85a, pp. 66 + 104 (Steinschneider, no. 342, p. 166).
    Date 1713/14   *Copyist* Jacob Guedelha
    Title As 14
17. Hamburg, Stadtsbibliothek, Cod. Hebr. 240a, pp. 89 + 157 (Steinschneider, no. 343, p. 167).
    Date 1713/14
    Title [erroneously given as] Tratado o Repuesta a un Cavallero Reformado
18. Amsterdam, 'Eṣ Ḥayyim-Montezinos 49 a 16, ff. 5^r–38^v (cf. Fuks-M., *EH*, no. 207, pp. 104 f.).
    Date 1714   *Copyist* Jacob Guedelha
    Title erroneously, as 17
19. Oxford, Bodleian, Opp. Add. 4° 147 a–b, vol. i, pp. 189, vol. ii, pp. 296 (Neubauer, no. 2472, p. 878).
    Date 1724
    Title As 14
20. Paris, Bibliothèque Nationale, Fonds éspagnoles 40, pp. 1–656 (Morel-Fatio, no. 33, pp. 8 f.).
    Date 1731
    Title As 14

Manuscripts of Works by Isaac Orobio de Castro 439

21. New York, Jewish Theological Seminary, Sulzbacher Collection; pp. 246 (Marx, no. 66, p. 263).
    Date 1731   *Copyist* Michael López Pinto
    Title As 14

VI: BIBLICAL EXEGESIS

A   The Seventy Weeks of Daniel (1 MS; unpublished).
1. Oxford, Bodleian, Opp. Add. 4° 51, pp. 82 (Neubauer, no. 2475, p. 878).
    Date Late 17th cent.
    Title Tratado en que se explica la prophecía de las 70 semanas
    Belonged to Jacob Guer (Ger).

B   Isaiah Chap. 53 (3 MSS, + overlap with MSS of *Prevenciones Divinas* [see above, V]; printed from the latter (MS Oxford, Bodl. Opp. Add., fol. 29, see above, V 10) by A. Neubauer and S. R. Driver, *The Fifty-Third Chapter of Isaiah according to the Jewish Interpreters*, 1876 (repr. 1969), vol. i, second pagination, pp. 21–118, with an English translation, vol. ii, pp. 450–531, with reference to one of the 'Eṣ Ḥayyim-Montezinos MSS, see vol. ii, p. xx).
1. Amsterdam, 'Eṣ Ḥayyim-Montezinos 48 D 16, pp. 92 (Fuks-M., *EH*, no. 197, p. 99).
    Date Late 17th cent.
    Title Explicación Paraphrástica del Capítulo 53 del Propheta Isaias
2. London, British Library, Add. 40084.
    Date 1675
    Title Explicação paraphrastica sobre o capítulo 53 de profeta Izahias
    (Portuguese version).
3. Oxford, Bodleian, Opp. Add. 4° 148, f. 153 (Neubauer, no. 2474, p. 878).
    Date 1675
    Title As 2
    (Portuguese version).

VII: CONTROVERSY WITH BREDENBURG (3 MSS: PRINTED AMSTERDAM, 1703, *CERTAMEN PHILOSOPHICUM, PROPUGNATAE VERITATIS DIVINAE AC NATURALIS*).

1. Paris, Bibliothèque Nationale, Fonds éspagnoles 41, pp. 258 f. (Morel-Fatio, no. 34, pp. 8 f.).
    Date 1731

Title Certamen Philosophico, Defiende la verdad Divina y Natural, contra los Principios de Juan Bredemburg

Spanish version by G. de la Torre of 1721.

2. Amsterdam, 'Eṣ Ḥayyim-Montezinos 48 C 16, f. 150 (Fuks, ii, no. 245, pp. 128 f.).
   Date 1741
   Title As 1
3. London, Jews' College, Montefiore 532, f. 144 (Hirschfeld, no. 299, p. 93).
   Date Early 18th cent.
   Title As 1

APPENDIX F
Orobio's Letter to Prado's Son: A Textual Comparison

This letter was printed by Révah in his *Spinoza et Prado*, pp. 143–53, from MS Paris, Bibliothèque Nationale. Fonds éspagnoles 41 (see above, Appendix E). The two slightly earlier Amsterdam MSS offer significant variants, which are here set out in parallel to the Paris text. The sigla adopted are as follows:

P   MS Paris, Bibliothèque Nationale, Fonds éspagnoles 41, pp. 902–23, dated 1731

A2   MS 'Eṣ Ḥayyim-Montezinos 48 A 23, ff. 310–31, dated 1719

A1   MS 'Eṣ Ḥayyim-Montezinos 48 A 21, ff. 239–51, dated 1712

P	A2	A1
p. 902 Carta al hijo de el Doctor Prado	p. 310 Respuesta del mismo Autor a siertas preguntas del doctor Prados, que por segunda persona fueron dichas	p. 239 Carta del Doctor Ishac Orobio de Castro. Escrita a un Sujeto de Amberez, contra el Doctor Prado, que vivia alli, siendo apartado de la Nación, y publicado en Herem, en la Synagoga de Amsterdam.
p. 903 ... Antes, en esta confession reconozco mi poca de vanidad, porque aprehendo que tengo a todo el mundo por compañero. Y, si el Doctor no quiere serlo mio y de los otros en la cortedad del conocimiento en las cosas naturales ...	p. 311 ... antes, en esta confision reconosco my poca devanidad por que aprendo, que tengo a todo el mundo por compañero, y si Prados no quiere serlo mio, y de los otros en la cortedad de conosimiento de las cosas naturales	p. 240 Antes en esta confession, reconozco mi poca de vanidad; porque aprehendo que tengo a todo el mundo por compañero. Y si el Señor Doctor, no quiere serlo mio y de los otros, en la cortedad de conocimiento, en las cosas Naturales;
p. 903 Y no se vaya a las especies intencionales, porque el sonido es corporeo, y el ayre le recive, le divierte y aun del todo le embaraza. Tampoco se como se hace la vision, si es por extramision, si por idolos; ni	p. 311 ... Y no se vaia a las espesies Intencionales por que el sonido es corporeo y el aire les resiste, le devierte, y aun del todo le embarasa. Tampoco se como se haze la visión, si es por extramision; si por Idolos, ni entiendo aquello	p. 240 Y no se vaya a las Especies intencionales: porque el Sonido es corporeo, y el Ayre le resiste, le divierte, y aun del todo le embaraça. Tampoco se, somo se haze la vision, si es por extramission, si por idealos. Ni

Appendix F

P	A2	A1
entiendo aquello de venir las especies, per modum pyramidis, para que la pupila como una lanteja vea una montaña y quanta distancia y objetos ciñe el orizonte. Diga tambien por donde van las especies de la vista y los demas exteriores al organo de la imaginacion, si por venas, arterias, nervios, o si llevadas a cuestas por los espiritus animales?	de venir las espesias, por modum piramidis, para que la pupilla como una lentexa vea una montana, y quanta distansia y objetos /312/ ciñe el orisonte. Digan tambien por donde van las espesias, de la vista, y los demas exteriores al organo de la Imaginativa si por venas arterias, nervios, si llevados a cuestas por los espiritus animales...	entiendo aquello de venir las Especies, per modum piramidis; para que la Pupilla como una Lenteja, vea una Montaña, y quanta distancia, y objectos ciñe el Orizonte. Diga tambien por donde van las Especies de la Vista, y los demas exteriores, al organo de la imaginacion? Si por Venas, Arterias, Nervios, si llevadas a cuestas, por los espiritus animales?
p. 904 Haga el Señor Doctor por acordarse de quanto passo en el medio siglo de su santa vida y digame luego en donde tenía guardadas aquellas ideas, si estavan pintadas en el meollo o recogidas en algunos de sus sonos [sic] o alazenas?	p. 240 Haga el Sr. Doctor, por acordarse, de quanto passo en el medio siglo de su santa vida; y digame luego; en donde tenia guardadas aquellas Ideas? Si estavan pintadas, en la meollada, o recogidas, en alguno de sus cenos, o sus alacenas...	p. 312 Haga Prados por acordarse de quanto paso por el medio siglo de su sancta vida, y digame luego en donde tenia guardadas aquellas Ideas si estavan pintadas en la meollada, o rrecogidas en algunos de sus senos o sus alasenas.
p. 904 ... ni porque el utero se agrada de buenos olores, siendo el no muy limpio, y a comete adonde los halla como si tuviera narizes, como el Señor Doctor, para olerlos. (mas aqui encaxa...)	p. 240 Ni porque el vivo se agrada de buenos olores; siendo el /p. 241/ no muy limpio, y acomete a donde los halla, como si tuviera narizes, como el Señor Doctor, para olerlos. (mas aqui encaxa...)	p. 312 — — ni porque el utero se agrada de buenos olores siendo el no muy limpio y acomete donde los halla como si tubiera narizes para olerlos (mas aqui encaja...)
p. 905 Preguntesselo a Cardano, de Subtilit[ate], que ventilo este punto, y a Escaligero...	p. 241 Preguntesselo a Cardano de Subtilitate, que ventilo este punto en muchas lineas. Y a Escaligero...	p. 313 Preguntesso a Cardano de subtilitate que ventilo este punto en muchas lineas, y a Scaligero...
p. 905 Si no le satisface, lea a Seneca el Tragico, desde adonde dice el furioso Quaeque nascentem videt ora solem, y vera...	p. 241 Si no le satisfaze este Comico; lea a Seneca el Tragico, desde adonde dize el Furioso Que, q[uaeque] nascentem vidit ora Solem, que q[uaeque] ad occassum iacet ora ferum, y vera...	p. 313 Sino le satisfaze este comico lea a Seneca el tragico desde adonde dize el furioso, que q[uaeque] na sentem vidit ora solem, que q[uaque] ad occassum jacet ora ferum, y vera...

P	A2	A1
p. 905 ... y con cojerle algunos discursitos, se puede, repitiendolos, graduar de discreto entre los reciennacidos otro que no lo sea tan de verdad como el Señor Doctor	p. 241 ... y con cogerle algunos Discursitos; se puede, repitiendolos, graduar de Discreto; inter recentissime natos. Otro, que no lo sea tan de verdad, como el Sor. Doctor.	p. 314 ... y con cojerle algunos discursos se puede repitiendolos graduar de discreto. Inter resentisime natos otro que no lo sea tan de verdad como vmd.
p. 906 Ni le de pena que le arguya el Metaphisico y le pruebe que aquel grado de perfeccion substancial se predicaria essencialmente de muchas almas que tuviessen el mismo grado y assi seria predicado essencial de pluribus differentibus, numero in quale quod. Pues por el se differenciarán essencialmente de todas las que no lo tuvieren.	p. 242 Ni le de pena, que le arguya el Methaphisico, y le prueve, que aquel grado de Perfeccion substancial se predicaria essencialmente de muchas Almas que tuviessen el mismo grado. Y assi seria predicado essencial, de Pluribus diferentibus numero, ni quale quod, pues por el, se diferenciarian essencialmente de todas las que no lo tuviessen.	p. 314 ni le de pena que le arguian el metaphisico, y le pruebe que aquel grado de perfeccion substancial se predicaria essencialmente de muchas almas que tubiesen el mismo grado, y asi seria predicado esensialmente de todos los que no lo tubiesen.
p. 907 ... y assi el alma que tuviere mejores noticias, obrará con mas acierto ...	p. 242 Y assi el Alma, que tuviere mejores noticias, mejor informada, obrará con mas acierto ...	p. 315 ... y asi el alma, que tubiere mejores notisias, mejor informada, obrará con mas asierto, ...
p. 910 ... con la destemplanza? Dispongase el hombre ... que conoce lo interior de nuestros corazones ...	p. 318 ... con la destemplansa en todas las virtudes. Dispongase el hombre ... que conose lo intrinsico de nuestros corasones ...	p. 244 ... con la destemplança en todas las virtudes? Dispongase el hombre ... que conoce lo interior de nuestros coraçones
p. 911 ... que seria muy molesto ...	p. 320 ... que seria azas molesto ...	p. 244 ... que seria muy molesto ...
p. 911 ... Pregunto pues al Señor Doctor ...	p. 320 ... Pregunto al D[oct]or ...	p. 244 ... Pregunto pues, al S[eño]r Doctor
p. 911 ... porque no ay, ni ha avido legislador que diga que no sigue la Sagrada Escritura, ni que le enseñe o persuada a negar su Divinidad ...	p. 320 ... por que no ay ni à auido legislador que le diga que no siga la sacra scriptura, que le enseñe o persuada a negar su Divinidad ...	p. 244 Porque ni hay, ni ha havido Legislador, que le diga, que no siga la Sacra Escritura. Que le enseñe, o persuada a negar su Divinidad ...

Appendix F

P	A2	A1
p. 912 le pone leyes a que de muy buena gana se sugeta	p. 320 ... le pone Leyes a que el mismo muy bien se sujeta	p. 245 le pone leyes, a que de muy buena gana se sujeta
p. 912 ... que no ay mas cortesana politica que zelar su honrra y defenderla ...	p. 320 ... que no ay mas cortezana politica que zelar su honra, que defenderla ...	p. 245 que no hay mas cortezana Politica, que zelar su Honra, que defenderla.
p. 912 ... y passado algun tiempo a Abraham diferentes preceptos y ceremonias, en que quiso que consistiesse su verdadero culto y la mayor pureza de su adoracion.	p. 320 ... y pasado un tiempo a Abraham diferentes preceptos, que yntimo a los hijos de Israel Leyes, fueros y serimonias, en que quizo que consistiese su verdadero culto, y la maior pureza de su adorasión.	p. 245 ... y passado un tiempo a Abraham diferentes Preceptos. Que intimo a los hijos de Israel, Leyes, Fueros, y Ceremonias en que quiso, que consistiesse su verdadero Culto, y la mayor pureza de su Adoracion.
p. 912 En cuya confirmacion se refieren los prodigios que alli se cuentan, con tal concatenacion que no avra entendimiento que pueda entresacar del Sacro Volumen enarraciones que no tengan conexion con el Origen Isrraelitico, y sus progressos hasta la Ley, y despues a su observancia en Juezes y Reyes ...	p. 320 ... en cuia conformasion se refieren los prodigios que alli se cuentan con tal catenasion que no avera entendimiento que pueda entresacar del sacro volumen en errasiones que no tengan connexion con el origuen Israelitico, y sus progressos hasta la Ley y despues en horden a su observasion, en juezes y Reyes ...	p. 245 ... en cuya confirmacion, se refieren los prodigios que alli se cuentan, con tal concadenacion, que no havra entendimiento que pueda entresacar del Sacro Volumen, e narraciones, que no tengan conexion con el origen Israelitico y sus progressos hasta la Ley. Y despues en orden a su observancia, en juezes y Reyes ...
p. 912 Y aun la descripcion de la Creacion del Mundo principio la Escritura /913/ porque avia de ser articulo de fee en la Ley Divina, siempre celebrado con la eterna celebridad del dia septimo. No puede, pues, creer la Escritura y negar la Ley, porque la Ley es la misma Escritura y la Escritura dice la Divinidad de la Ley. Luego si cree que Dios la dió a sus padres Israelitas, que ellos la recivieron, ya cree que ay	p. 321 Y aun la descripcion de la criasion del mundo, prinsipió la escritura por que auia de ser articulo de fee en la devina Ley ni puede dezir que cree la escritura y no la Ley, por que la escriptura dize la divinidad de la ley, luego se cree que D[io]s la dio a sus Padres Ysraelitas, que ellos la resibieron, y no cree que ay Ley divina que obligava a su observansia ...	p. 245 Y aun la Discripcion de la Creacion del Mundo, principio la Escritura; porque havia de ser Articulo de Fe, en la Ley Divina, siempre celebrado, con la eterna celebridad, del Dia Septimo. No puede pues creer la Escritura y negar la Ley: porque la Ley, es la misma Escritura, y la Escritura, dize la Divinidad de la Ley. Luego si cree, que Dios la dio a sus Padres Israelitas, que ellos la recibieron, ya cree que hay Ley Divina que

P	A2	A1
Ley Divina que obligava a su observancia...		obligava a su observancia...
p. 913 ... que le tiran de lo cierto...	p. 321 ...... que le tiran del jarapo...	p. 245 ... que le tiran del jarapo...
p. 913 ... que de inquietudes? que de escrupulos...	p. 321 ... que de inquietudes escrupolosas...	p. 245 ... que de inquietudes, y escrupulos
p. 913 ... a Phylis o a Lisarda	p. 322 ... a filis o Alizarda...	p. 246 ... a Filis o a Lizarda...
p. 914 ... siempre afirma que solo se ha de regular lo creyble por el entendimiento...	p. 322 ... siempre afirma que solo se a de regular p[or] el entendimiento...	p. 246 ... siempre afirma, que solo se ha de regular lo creible por el entendimiento...
p. 914 ... una simulacion estadista...	p. 323 ... una estadista simulacion...	p. 246 ... una estadista simulacion...
p. 915 ... o en algun missionario jesuita...	p. 323 ... o en algun missionario de los Featinos...	p. 246 ... o en algun Missionario, de los Featinos...
p. 915 ... que se gasta en verlos...	p. 323 ... que se gasta en leerlos...	p. 246 ... que se gasta en verlos...
p. 915 ... otra alguna cosa que tenga indicios de racional, de opinable o de divina a un mediano entendimiento...	p. 324 ... alguna cosa que tenga indisios de divina, de Racional, o de opinable a un mediano entendimiento...	p. 247 ... otra alguna cosa, que tenga indicios de Divina, de Racional, o de opinable a un mediano entendimiento...
p. 916 Es forçoso responder ya a aquella consequencia que dejamos y era desta forma: Cada qual...	p. 324 Es forsoso responder ya aquella consequensia q[ue], dejamos y era en esta forma, (luego todos y qualquiera siguiendo). Cada uno...	p. 247 Es forçoso responder ya, a aquella consequencia, que dexamos, y era en esta forma. Cada uno...
p. 916 ... mas quien ninguna religion sigue...	p. 325 ... mas quien ninguna Religion tiene o sigue...	p. 247 ... mas quien ninguna Religion sigue...
p. 917 ... es materia muy recondita...	p. 325 ... es materia mas recondita...	p. 247 ... es materia muy recondita...
p. 917 ... para conseguir el verdadero camino...	p. 325 ... para conseguir el verdadero conosimiento...	p. 247 ... para conseguir el /248/ verdadero camino...

P	A2	A1
p. 917 ... la de la razon ...	p. 325 ... la de Razon ...	p. 247 ... la de Razon ...
p. 917 ... y alcançarian la verdad ...	p. 326 ... y alcansaran la verdad	p. 248 ... y alcançarian la verdad ...
p. 917 ... se imputara a pecado el yerro, porque en su modo ...	p. 326 ... se imputara a pecado el yerro de Religion por que en su modo ...	p. 248 ... se imputara a pecado, el yerro de Religion porque en su modo ...
p. 917 Mas esto creen los píos, no los políticos ...	p. 326 Maestro creeran los píos, no los políticos ...	p. 248 Mas esto creen los Pios, no los Politicos ...
p. 918 ... aceptan novedades y paradoxas, y assi se precipitan del verdadero camino, y como tales seran tratados por la Divina Justicia.	p. 326 ... affectando novedades y paradoras [sic] y asi se presepitan del Verdadero Camino.	p. 248 ... affectan novedades y paradoxas; y assi se precipitan de el verdadero camino ...
p. 918 Otros son los Christianos, los quales en su yerro son muy culpables y dignos de castigo, pues quieren vencer su propria racionalidad, creyendo desatinos indignos del juicio humano ...	p. 326 Otros quieren venser su propria Rasionalidad creiendo destanios indignos del juizio humano ...	p. 248 Otros quieren vencer su propria racionalidad, creyendo desatinos, indignos del juizio humano ...
p. 918 Todos estos yerran y, aun los primeros, no pueden ser bastantemente disculpados en no haver exami[na]do todos los cultos que ay para escojer el mejor, como hizo el Rey Cuzari. Los primeros, por su ignorancia invincible, se pueden piamente escusar de pecado, porque nadie esta obligado a hazer mas de lo que puede y estos se supone que hizieron quanto pudieron. Todos los demas tienen detestable malicia, cada uno en su genero : unos evidente, otros encubierta.	p. 326 Todos estos yerran y solos los primeros por su Ignorancia Invensible se pueden piamente escuzar de pecados por que nadie esta obligado a hazer mas de lo que puede, y estos se supone que hizieron quanto pudieron, todos los demas tienen detestable malisia cada uno en su genero unos evidente, otros encubierta.	p. 248 Todos estos yerran y solos los Primeros, por su ignorancia invencible, se pueden piam[en]te escusar de pecado: porque nadie esta obligado a hazer mas de lo que puede. Y estos, se supone, que hicieron quanto pudieron. Todos los demas, tienen detestable malicia, cada uno en su genero: unos evidente, otros encubierta.

P	A2	A1
p. 918 ... nacieron en el, siguieron culto divino a que nunca repugno la razón, porque el es ajustado a las leyes de la razon; y despues, sin fundamento /919/ seducidos o de algunos motivos humanos ...	p. 326 ... nasieron en el, criaronse en el, /327/ siguieron culto divino a que nunca repugno la Razón por q[ue] el es ajustado a las Leyes de la Razon, y despues sin fundamento, reduzidos o de algunos motivos humanos ...	p. 248 ... nacieron en el, criaronse en el, siguieron Culto divino a que nunca repugnó la Razon; porque el es ajustado a las leyes de la razon. Y despues sin fundamento, seduzidos, o de algunos motivos humanos ...
p. 919 ... dejaron el camino de la Verdad por andarse descaminados.	p. 327 ... dexan el camino de la verdad por andar descaminados ...	p. 248 ... dexaron el camino de la verdad, por andarse descaminados ...
p. 919 Estos son malditos, ignorantes, livianos, monstruos de la naturaleza ...	p. 327 Estos son malditos Ignorantes, mentirosos de la naturaleza ...	p. 248 Estos, son malditos, ignorantes, livianos, monstruos de la Naturaleza ...
p. 919 ... aunque haga acto que fuera pecado en el adulto ...	p. 327 ... aun que aga un acto que en el adulto fuera pecado ...	p. 248 ... aunque haga un acto que en el Adulto, fuera pecado ...
p. 920 ... quien no sabe que peca, no incurre en pecado. Solo un loco, falto de seso, o un niño puede ser excusado enteramente de pecado por la ignorancia. Esta obligado el hombre a saber en que peca ...	p. 328 ... quien no sabe que peca, no incurre en pecado: esta obligado el hombre a saber en que peca ...	p. 249 ... quien no sabe que peca, no incurre en pecado. Esta obligado el hombre, a saber en que peca ...
p. 920 ... quanto la Ley tiene de mas sobre naturalidad ...	p. 328 ... quanto la Ley tiene mas de sobre natural ...	p. 249 ... quanto la Ley tiene mas de sobre natural ...
p. 920 ... el que no pudo conocer que yva errado y siguio un culto en que creyó que acertava ...	p. 329 ... el que no conosio que errado y sigio un culto en que creio que asertava ...	p. 249 ... El que no conocio, qui iva errado, y siguio un culto, en que creyo que acertava ...
p. 920 ... no comete /921/ delito a que se deva pena positiva, mas tampoco acerto para que se le diesse el premio que Dios promete a los que le adoraren con verdadero culto: de modo que se dira que no se salvan, pero no se condenan. Que hara la Divina Magestad ...	p. 329 ... no comete delito a quien se deva pena positiva, mas tampoco aserto para que se le diese el premio que D[ios] promete a los que le adoran con verdadero culto. Que hara la Divina Magestad ...	p. 249 ... no comete delito, a quien se deva pena positiva: mas tampoco acerto, para que se le diesse el premio, que Dios promete, a los que le adoraren con verdadero Culto. Que hara la Divina Magestad ...

Appendix F

P	A2	A1
p. 921 Tendran estos forzosamente pena privativa, que es no darles aquel bien que pudieran merecer por el verdadero culto; y algunos avrá que la padezcan también afirmativa, segun fueron flojos y diminutos en las diligencias que devian poner para acertar, y principalmente los Christianos, porque tienen la Ley por verdadera y siguen lo contrario de lo que ella enseña, y siguen por fee dogmas contrarios a la razón natural	p. 329 Tendran estos forzosamente pena privativa, que es no darles aquel bien que pudieran merecer por el verdadero culto y en esto ninguna Injusticia se les haze...	p. 249 Tendran estos forçosamente pena privativa, que es, no darles que pudieron merecer, por el verdadero Culto. Y en esto ninguna injusticia se le haze...
p. 921 ... como si huviessen acertado. Si uno, queriendo hacer un servicio al Rey, lo hiziesse a quien por el tal incurriesse en crimen de lessa magestad, seria bueno que le pidiesse al Rey la paga de la buena /922/ intencion, quando en el acto fue un grande agravio el que le hizo? Pues lo mismo es el idolatra ignorante. Para yr a Dios dejo su Providencia un camino muy ancho y muy real...	p. 329 ... como si ubiesen asertado. Para yr a D[ios] dexo su providencia un camino muy amplio, muy Real...	p. 250 ... como si huviessen acertado. Para ir a Dios; dexo su Providencia un camino, muy amplio, muy real...
p. 922 ... que apenas puede errarse, sino por summa malicia o por un excesso extraordinario de sobervia ignorancia...	p. 329 ... que apenas puede errarse sino por suma malisia, o por sobrada Ignoransia...	p. 250 ... que apenas puede errarse, sino, o por suma malicia o por sobrada ignorancia...
p. 922 ... y los Isrraelitas no pudiessen errarlo. Por lo qual es muy mas culpable su apostasia y, aunque alegue[n] ignorancia, siguiendo su dictamen, no puede[n] dejar de conden-	p. 329 ... y los Israelitas / 330/ no pudiesen errarlo. Por esso los que van a D[ios] y sin culpa suia y por su ignoransia no asiertan, no meresen llegar a D[ios], ni que D[ios] los premie	p. 250 ... y los Israelitas, no pudiessen errarlo. Por esso, los que van a Dios, y sin culpa suya, y por su ignorancia no aciertan; no merecen llegar a Dios, ni que Dios los premie, como

P	A2	A1
arse. Por esso los que van a Dios y, sin culpa suya, y solo por su ignorancia, no aciertan el camino, no merecen llegar a Dios, ni que Dios los premie como a los que acertaron, ni que los castigue porque erraron; antes se deve creer en buena razon que su buena intencion y verdadero deseo de servir a Dios tendra el premio que corresponde a la bondad destos actos y de las virtudes que huvieren exercitado en este mundo, como enseñan los nuestros. Esto suponiendo siempre la ignorancia invincible y que el hombre hizo quanto pudo por no errar. Mas el que erro por malicia o por omissión y falta de aplicacion a saber lo bueno o por soberuia y propria presumpcion, este tendra los castigos que le corresponden y que correspondieren a su malicia, aunque nadie sabe hasta aora quantos ni quales ni adonde seran, ni es menester saberlo, pues Dios no quiso revelarlo...	como a los que asertaron, ni los castigue por q[ue] erraron antes se puede creer en buena razon que su buena yntension y verdadero dezeo de servir a D[ios], tendra el premio que corresponde a la bondad de sus actos, y de las virtudes q[ue] ubieren exercitado, esto siempre suponiendo la Ygnoransia Invensible y que el hombre hizo quanto pudo por no errar. Mas el que erro por malisia o por omission, y falta de aplicación, a saber lo bueno, o por sobervia, y propria presumsion este tendrá los castigos que le coresspondieren a su malisia como, y quantos, y adonde sean, nadie lo sabe ni es menester saberlo pues D[ios] no quizo revelarlo ...	a los que acertaron, ni que los castigue, porque erraron. Antes se puede creer en buena razon, que su buena intencion, y verdadero desseo de servir a Dios; tendrá el premio, que corresponde, a la bondad de estos actos, y de las virtudes, que huvieren executado. Esto siempre suponiendo la ignorancia invencible, y que el hombre hizo quanto pudo, por no errar. Mas el que erro por malicia, o por omission, y falta de aplicacion, a saber lo bueno, o por sobervio, y propia presumpcion; este tendra los castigos, que le correspondieren a su malicia. Como, y quantos, y adonde sean; nadie lo sabe; ni es menester saberlo, pues Dios no quiso revelarlo.
p. 923 Porque, como la Divina Misericordia me hizo ser Isrraelita [sic]...	p. 330 ... porque como por la divina mizericordia soy Israelita...	p. 250 ... porque como por la Divina Mizericordia, soy Israelita...
p. 923 ... segun mi fragilidad...	p. 330 ... conforme my fragilidad...	p. 250 ... conforme mi fragilidad...
p. 923 ... confiessan que guardan Ley Divina...	p. 330 ... confiesan que guardo Ley devina...	p. 250 ... confiessan, que guardo Ley Divina...
p. 923 ... y los philosophos, alumbra...	p. 331 ... y al Philosopho alumbra...	p. 250 ... y al Philosopho, alumbra

Appendix F

P	A2	A1
p. 923 Esto dijo el mismo Dios...	p. 331 Esto dixo el mismo D[ios]	p. 250 Esto me dixo el mismo Dios.
p. 923 En Weycke. Agosto 12 de 5424 años.	[date and place lacking]	Utreque a 12 Agosto 1664.

APPENDIX G

Translations of Orobio's Works in the Eighteenth and Nineteenth Centuries

A: FRENCH TRANSLATIONS

The interest which the works of Isaac Orobio attracted amongst thinkers of various classes, both Jewish and non-Jewish, proved the occasion of several of his works being translated into a few languages in the eighteenth and nineteenth centuries in France: England, and Italy. Those who reissued his writings—and they were motivated by varying and to some extent conflicting reasons—felt the need to lay some of his works before a reading public that had no access to them in their original language (for the most part Spanish).

In 1770 there appeared, in London, a French translation of a book by Orobio with the following title:

ISRAEL
VENGÉ.
OU
Exposition naturelle des Prophéties
Hébraiques que les Chrétiens
appliquent a JÉSUS, leur
prétendu Messie.
Par ISAAC OROBIO.

It is divided into two parts, the first (entitled *Israel Vengé*) consisting of seven chapters, the seventh being in point of fact an independent composition: the second (*Disseration sur le Messie*) consisting of eight chapters.[1]

In his introduction the editor explained that the book had been translated into French, from a hitherto unpublished manuscript, by a Jew named Henríquez, at the request of a man of letters living in Holland.[2] A number of scholars have ventured different opinions as to the book and its Spanish original. Some have claimed that it is simply a collection of Orobio's views culled from his various writings.[3] Sokolow assumed that it was a version of the work

---

[1] *Israel Vengé*, 1770, part i, pp. 1–186, part ii, pp. 187–243.

[2] Editor's introd.: 'Cet ouvrage a pour Auteur un Juif Espagnol nommé Isaac Orobio qui le composa dans sa langue; il a eté depuis traduit en françois par un juif appellé Henriquez sur le manuscrit de l'Auteur qui n'a jamais été publié, à la priere d'un homme de Lettres résidant en Hollande: celui-ci paroit avoir retouché ou corrigé la traduction.'

[3] See G. B. de Rossi, *Bibliotheca Judaica Anti-christiana*, Parma, 1800, p. 86, and *Dizionario Storico degli Autori Ebrei e delle loro opere*, Parma, 1802, ii, p. 84.

that Orobio set down following upon his discussion with Limborch,[4] and others have supposed that it was a selection of chapters taken from his *Prevenciones Divinas*.[5] Finally, a few scholars have drawn attention to the fact that the book is a translation of Orobio's *Explicación Paraphrástica* of Isaiah 53.[6] Whilst it is true that these two last opinions come closer to the truth, neither of them is absolutely accurate. It would seem that the first part is indeed a French version of Orobio's commentary on Isaiah 53, with the omission however of the introduction in which he explained the reasons that had induced him to write it. The translator also abridged the original in a number of places, and was at pains to moderate its tone lest the work appear too provocative. But in general what he offers is a faithful rendering of the original.[7]

The second part, entitled *Dissertation sur le Messie*, is in general terms similar to the early chapters of the first part of the *Prevenciones Divinas*. The introduction is of similar structure to that in the Spanish work, but it is much shorter. There is likewise a difference in the account given of the causes leading to its having beeen written. As stated above (p. 243) the *Prevenciones* tell of religious altercations with members of the Carmelite order, who come in for no mention at all in the French version. Instead, Orobio there speaks of other reasons for putting his work into writting: having once been in the house of a *grand Seigneur*, he had been constrained by him to make rejoinder to the claims of some Catholic theologians who were visiting him, the latter having assured their hosts that it would be impossible for Isaac to refute their argument.[8]

The first chapters of the *Dissertation sur le Messie* are similar both in title and content to the early chapters of the *Prevenciones*, and chapter 6 of the *Dissertation* corresponds with chapter 9 in the Spanish work. But the last two chapters of the *Dissertation* (chaps. 7 and 8) are original, having no parallel in the other works of Orobio.[9]

[4] Sokolow, p. 169.   [5] R. H. Popkin, art. Orobio de Castro, *EJ* 12, col. 1475f.

[6] The first to realize this was Carmoly, i, p. 177, followed by Neubauer [and Driver], ii, p. xx; L. Wogue, *Histoire de la Bible et de l'Exégèse Biblique*, Paris, 1881, p. 311.

[7] As an example of the tranbslator's softening of the tone, cf. MS Amsterdam, *EH*, 48 D 16, p. 183: 'Y se cumplirá lo que dixo el Sr. en el Cántico de Moshe cantad gentes su pueblo que sangre de sus siervos vengará y venganza tomará de sus angustiadores y perdonará la tierra por su pueblo.' with *Israel Vengé*, p. 186: 'Les prières de ce saint peuple ne seront point infructueses et le Seigneur daignera les exaucer et pardonner aux nations tous les maux qu'ils ont faits injustement souffrir aux véritables Israélites.'

[8] *Israel Vengé*, p. 190: 'Une autre raison encore m'a determiné à écrire cette dissertation: un grand Seigneur chez qui je me suis trouvé, m'a forcé de répondre à des theologiens catholiques que étoient chez lui, et qui l'assuroient qu'il me seroit impossible de refuter un argument qu'ils vouloient me proposer.'

[9] The following comparative table will illustrate matters.

Prev. Div.: Cap. 1 'Prueva que en los Cinco libros de la Ley, previno Dios a Israel, contra todas las idolatrías de las gentes'; Cap. 2 'Prevención a Israel, contra la encarnación de el Christianismo'; Cap. 3 'Prevención a Israel, contra la Idolatría de el Cristianismo'; Cap. 4 'Prevención a Israel, contra la multitud de las gentes Cristianas'; Cap. 5 'Prevención a Israel contra la necessidad de venir Dios al mundo, por el pecado de Adam y de los hombres'.

Dissertation sur le Messie (Israel Vengé, part i): Chap. 1 'Dans lequel on prouve que Dieu

Translations of Orobio's Works

Two possibilities lie before us. Either the *Dissertation sur le Messie* is an abridged reworking of selected chapters of the *Prevenciones Divinas*, or it is translated from a lost work in Spanish by Orobio, similar in general terms to the early chapters of the *Prevenciones*, but constituting an independent composition written as the result of another disputation conducted by Orobio with Catholic theologians. The second suggestion seems the more plausible: since the first part of *Israel Vengé* was translated by Henríquez from an original work, it seems reasonable to suggest that that the second part also rests upon an independent Spanish original.

The question as to who was behind the French book and planned its publication lay shrouded in secrecy until the French scholar P. Naville discovered that it was Baron d'Holbach and Jacques Naigeon who planned the printing, the former actually contributing the introduction. There is nothing surprising in this. Some years earlier d'Holbach had published *Le Christianisme devoilé*, and in Orobio's book he found objections to Christianity and argumentation which it suited his purpose excellently to exploit in his struggle against the Catholic Church. Orobio could serve him and the fellow-members of his circle as the symbol of a doughty fighter struggling to defend his faith and his opinions against the cruelty of the Inquisition.[10] Moreover, three years before the appearance of *Israel Vengé* Voltaire had written his *Letter concerning the Jews* as the ninth of his *Letters* to the Duke of Brunswick; and in it he had dealt at length with Orobio's critique of Christianity. When referring to Orobio, he is not sparing with his praise: he sees in him, as opposed to the fanaticism and obscurantism of the rabbis a 'rabbin . . . savant . . . profond', and a fair stylist.[11]

a fait connoître aux Israélites dans les cinq livres de la loi tout ce qu'il devoient faire pour ne point se laisser séduire par les nations et pour ne point abandonner la véritable religion pour suivre celle des chrétiens'; Chap. 2 'Où l'on prouve qu'Israël ne doit point ajouter foi à l'incarnation'; Chap. 3 'Où l'on fait voir à Israël l'idolatrie du christianisme a fin qu'il ne tombe pas dans le meme erreur'; Chap. 4 'Où l'on donne â Israël les moyens de ne point se laisser séduire par le christianisme'; Chap. 5 'Où l'on fait voir à Israël qu'il n'est point nécessaire que Dieu vienne au monde pour expier le peché d'Adam'. Chap. 6, 'Que les miracles ne suffisent pas pour confirmer les vérités Divines ni pour faire reconnaître les veritables Prophetes', corresponds to *Prev. Div.* 9, 'Prueva la falsedad de los milagros de aquel Hombre'. The headings of the two last chaps. in *Israel Vengé*, part ii, read as follows: Chap. 7 'Dieu a conduit les Israelites dans leur captivité avec les mêmes signaux dont il s'est servi pour les conduire dans le désert'; Chap. 8 'Que notre foi doit s'accomoder aux révélations Divines'.

[10] See Pierre Naville, *D'Holbach²*, [Paris], 1967, pp. 170 f.; A. Hertzberg, *The French Enlightenment and the Jews*, New York and London, 1968, pp. 44 f. J. Lough's bibliography of d'Holbach's publications makes no mention of the *Israel Vengé*: 'Essai de bibliographie critique des publications du Baron d'Holbach', *Revue d'histoire littéraire de la France*, 46, 1939, pp. 215–34, 47, 1947, pp. 314–18. On links between d'Holbach and Jacques André Naigeon see Naville, pp. 103 f., and Ch. Avezac-Lavigne, *Diderot et la Societé du Baron D'Holbach*, Geneva, 1970, p. 164 f.

[11] Voltaire, *Œuvres Complètes*, Paris, 1827, vol. 34, p. 340 f.: 'Orobio était un rabbin si savant qu'il n'avait donné dans aucune des rêveries qu'on reproche à tant d'autres rabbins; profond sans être obscur, possédant les belles lettres, homme d'un esprit agréable et d'un extreme politesse.' On Voltaire's attitude to Jews and Judaism see

Not surprisingly, Orobio's work was already known to Voltaire prior to the publication of *Israel Vengé*. The second edition of his disputation with Limborch, which appeared at Basle in 1740, had given rise to many echoes in France. In addition to this, during the first half of the eighteenth century Orobio's writings had already been in circulation there in French translation in numerous manuscript copies. The deists at the beginning of the century, and following them the *Encyclopédistes*, knew how to turn to their own account writing that was so to speak custom-built to assist their struggle against the Catholic Church and the French religious establishment. The strict censorship which prevailed in France in the first half of the eighteenth century precluded them from publishing matter that ran counter to conventionally accepted notions; but it was powerless to prevent the distribution of dozens of tracts, in manuscript copies running into hundreds, to propagate views that could not be expressed in print. More than a hundred such treatises are preserved in manuscript in the libraries of France, all of them in copies dating from the first half of the eighteenth century: and all of them are redolent of a critical approach to questions of religion, theology, ethics and political philosophy.[12] Amongst these pieces there are included three from the pen of Orobio de Castro, viz:

> *La Divinité de Jésus-Christ détruite, ou commentaire d'un rabbin sur le LIIIe chapitre d'Isaïe, qui sert de fondement à la religion chrétienne, pour faire voir le fausseté de la mission de J.C.*[13]
>
> *Explication du cinquante-troisième chapitre d'Isaïe*[14]
>
> *Dissertation sur le Messie où l'on prouve qu'il n'est pas encore venu, et que suivant les promesses des prophètes qui l'ont annoncé aux Israelites, ils l'attendent avec raison*[15]

Investigation of these tracts shows that they were the source for the book entitled *Israel Vengé*, published by d'Holbach and Naigeon. The first of them

---

H. Emmrich, *Das Judentum bei Voltaire*, Breslau, 1930, and with reference to Orobio in particular, pp. 224 f.

[12] On the underground dissemination at this period in France of philosophical notions unacceptable to the establishment, see I. O. Wade, *The Clandestine Organization and Diffusion of Philosophic Ideas in France from 1700 to 1750*, Princeton, 1938, including (pp. 10 f.) a list of such productions circulated in manuscript; cf. M. Cranston, *Philosophers and Pamphleteers: Political Theorists of the Enlightenment*, Oxford and New York, 1986.

[13] Two MS copies of this have survived, viz. Paris, BN Fonds français 14928, and Bibliothèque Mazarine 1190. The first of these contains all 3 of the works here listed. The title-page claims that the piece had been trans. from the Hebrew [sic] in London: 'Ouvrage traduit de l'hébreu, par un auteur désintéressé, à Londres ...' See Wade, p. 14, no. 49.

[14] MS Paris, BN Fonds français 14928, MSS Bibl. Mazarine 1178 and 1190. Wade, p. 13, no. 36.

[15] This piece was apparently the most widely distributed. Paris, BN, has 3 copies (13351, 14928, 24884), and there are further copies in Bibl. Mazarine (1194), and in the library of the Sorbonne (761). See Wade, p. 11 no. 16.

corresponds to the first part of *Israel Vengé*, the second to chapter 7 of that part, and the third to part ii of the book.[16]

From a letter of Jean Levesque de Burigny to Barthélemy Mercier we learn that at the beginning of the eighteenth century these tracts were well known amongst the school of writers known to be free-thinkers. On 23 March 1780, after the printed edition of *Israel Vengé* had come into his hands, de Burigny wrote:

Whilst I was living in Holland I became acquainted with a number of Jewish scholars, one of whom made in my presence the claim that there was a certain tract, in manuscript, by Orobio, the arguments in which Christians could not refute. I knew about Orobio, having seen his name referred to in Limborch's treatise against the Jews. I made a copy of Orobio's manuscript, which was an exposition of Isaiah 53 . . . it also included a well-written disquisition in which Orobio endeavoured to prove that the qualities attributed by the prophets to the messiah did not cohere with the characteristics of Jesus. Some years ago I passed this manuscript to one of my friends, shortly after which I received a copy of a book printed under the title of *Israel Vengé* . . .[17]

De Burigny was living in Holland in 1718. It was in that year that he first encountered the work of Orobio, with which the Huguenot exiles in Amsterdam were already familiar. Basnage makes reference to the existence of manuscript copies of his works in the second edition of his *Histoire des Juifs*, published in The Hague in 1716.[18]

The *Prevenciones Divinas* were also translated into French *in extenso*, but there is nothing in the sole surviving manuscript to point either to those who promoted the translation or to those who executed it.[19]

Amid the growing inefficiency of French censorship during the second half of the eighteenth century d'Holbach and his circle succeeded in publishing the

---

[16] Wade, pp. 229 f.

[17] The original of de Burigny's letter is attached to one of the exemplars of *Israel Vengé* in Paris, BN (Réserve D^2 5193). At its end is a remark in Mercier's hand: 'La Dissertation sur le Messie est très forte en preuves. C'est ce qu'il y a de plus curieux dans ce volume.' The letter was printed in full by Wade, pp. 229 f. For de Burigny's integration in the circle of free-thinkers see ibid., p. 266.

[18] Wade, p. 230. Basnage, *Histoire des Juifs*^{2}, I, i, p. 47: 'Les Manuscrits Espagnols d'Orobio, de Mortera, de Montalto, de R. Ménasseh, et de quelques autres célèbres juifs modernes, m'ont paru dignes d'être éxaminez d'autant plus qu'aiant vécu dans le dernier Siècle; aiant eu plus de Commerce avec les Chrétiens, et s'étant éloigné de l'ancienne Méthode Rabbinique, ils ont raisonné plus judicieusement que les autres . . .' For Basnage's attitude towards Judaism see Yardeni, pp. 178 f.

[19] The only known MS is in Bordeaux, Bibl. Municipale 347: 'Traité des preventions divines en faveur d'Israël, divisé en deux parties . . . , ouvrage composé par D. Isaac Orobio . . . traduit de l'espagnol en françois depuis la mort de l'auteur.' It numbers ff. 343, and its hand is certainly 18th-cent.; see C. Couderc, *Cataloque Géneral des Manuscrits des Bibliothèques Publiques de France—Départements*, xxiii, Bordeaux, Paris, 1894, p. 187.

book, but they saw fit to have it printed in London.[20] The work of the scholarly Jew proved no disappointment as a source of arguments to raise against Catholic Christianity which men like d'Holbach, Naigeon, Voltaire, and others could adduce indirectly, without exposing themselves to criticism from the establishment in their own country. Despite their own aloofness from Jews and Judaism, they did not hesitate to seize upon Orobio and to publicize what he had to say in the course of their own stubborn fight with the Catholic Church. They were not particular as to the means that they employed: and it was precisely the Jews—above all the 'enlightened Portuguese rabbis' of Amsterdam, at once faithful to their own Scriptures, expert in their exegesis, and determined in their refusal to acknowledge the New Testament—who proved a useful instrument by means of which to assault the foundations of the Church.[21] That is not to say that for these free-thinkers Judaism was any more enlightened than was the Christian religion. On the contrary: the Mosaic Law is generally presented by them in a negative light. But in this way the French free-thinkers could invalidate the foundations of Christianity since in their own writings the Law of Israel is described as being the basis of the teaching of Jesus. There was no innovation here. The writings of the English deists of the seventeenth and eighteenth centuries provided a torch to guide their path. Hence the great interest which the French free-thinkers evinced in having them translated into French.[22]

Israel Vengé was still attracting interest in nineteenth-century France: a second edition, identical with the first, was published in Paris in 1845.[23]

Orobio's *Certamen Philosophicum*, which constituted his rejoinder to

[20] For breaches of French censorship regulations from 1750 onwards see Wade, p. 264. A significant proportion of the books pub. by d'Holbach during these years were printed in London; for a list of works compiled or ed. by him see Naville (n. 10 above), pp. 421 f.

[21] See P. Gay, *Voltaire's Politics*, Princeton, 1959, p. 354.

[22] For the relationship of the deists to Judaism see Ettinger, *De'iṣtim*, pp. 182–207. For their influence on d'Holbach see Naville, *D'Holbach*, pp. 205 f. D'Holbach translated into French the works of John Toland, the sympathy of whose approach to Judaism was quite exceptional, and those of Collins: see Naville, p. 428. It may be noted in passing that Collins knew of Orobio's work, and discussed it in his *Discourse on the Grounds and Reasons of the Christian Religion*, London, 1724, p. 82; and during one of his visits to Holland he actually acquired 3 MSS of works by him. See J. O'Higgins, *Anthony Collins, The Man and his works*, The Hague, 1970, p. 239.

[23] See Z. Szajkowski, *Franco-Judaica*, New York, 1962, p. 128, no. 1543. I have located a copy of this edn. in Amsterdam, *EH*. There is also a MS copy in Paris, BN (Var. 282)—a late copy, apparently dating from the first half of the 19th cent. The title reads: נקמת ישראל / Israel Vengé / ecrit par mi [sc. par moi] / Le / Citoyen / Raphaël / Isaac Ione. This MS contains 372 pages. The copyist seems to have had the 1st edn. as his archetype, and in the margins he inserted the references to the biblical citations in Hebrew. I take him to have been an Italian Jew, since (e.g. on p. 127) he quotes from St Paul in Latin, adding in Italian *cosi il testo latino*. The Portuguese-Jewish Theological Institute *Ros Pina* translated *Israel Vengé* and published it in 2 separate booklets in Oporto in 1947: *Israel Vingado* and *Dissertação sobre o Messias*.

Bredenburg and which, as noted above (p. 269), ran into several editions, was also translated into French, but was never printed in that language; and only a single manuscript copy survives.[24]

B: HEBREW

Napoleon's vast expansion of the area subject to France at the turn of the eighteenth and nineteenth centuries opened up new markets for the writings of the French free-thinkers. Together with the French army, many a book reached the occupied territories which, in former times, could doubtfully have been even smuggled in. Italy was no exception, and proved ready enough to absorb ideas engendered by the French revolution.[25] Amongst the Jews, too, there was great enthusiasm for the victories of Bonaparte that had brought about Jewish political and social emancipation.[26]

The French occupation of Piedmont in 1796 fired the hearts of the local Jews, whose great sufferings under the oppressive rule of the Duke of Savoy went back to 1714.[27] Echoes of their enthusiasm can be heard in the words of one of their number written at Ivrea in August–September 1811; they are taken from a Hebrew poem devoted to celebration of the military successes of France:

> Ye captains, see, a hero—nonpareil,
> Who, humbling princes, leaves them breathless, cowed
> By sword and stratagem, all in dismay:
> God blazons forth his glory, telling loud
> How 'goodly' in his 'lot',[28] as heaven shows;
> Mere grasshopper they prove that are his foes,
> Warred down at sea: Fortune her future gives
> To him as heir: and our Redeemer lives.[29]

The author of this piece was Rabbi Elisha Ḥanan'el Pontremoli—rabbi, educator, exegete, homilist, poet, and translator who left behind him a plethora

---

[24] See above, chap. 10, p. 269. This MS, dating certainly from the 18th cent., is in Bordeaux, Bibl. Municipale (828): *Traduction de la pretendue démonstration proposée par Jean Bredembourg [sic] . . . Refutation par Isaac Orobio*. See Couderc (n. 19 above), p. 478.

[25] See R. R. Palmer, 'The Impact of the French Revolution: Recent Interpretations', in G. S. Metraux and F. Crouzet (eds.), *The Nineteenth Century World*, New York, 1963, p. 56.

[26] On the Jews of Italy at the time of Napoleon's conquests see C. Roth, *The History of The Jews of Italy*, Philadelphia, 1946, pp. 421–45; A. Milano, *Storia degli ebrei in Italia*, Turin, 1963, pp. 342–51.

[27] See G. Levi, 'Gli Ebrei in Piemonte nell ultimo decennio del secolo XVIII', *RMI* 9, 1943/5, pp. 511–34.   [28] A Hebrew pun (*ṭov ḥeleq*) on *buona parte*.

[29] MS Warsaw 221 (Jerusalem Microfilms Institute, Hebrew Univ. (JMI), 30669). The title-page, elaborated into a florid introduction, explains that the composition, styled *Ne'oth ha-Shalom* ('Meads of Peace'), was occasioned by the fact that Rabbi

of writings not one of which ever found its way into print. He had been born in Casale Monferrato in Piedmont late in the eighteenth century, and in the course of his life he migrated through various Jewish communities in the area including Ivrea and Chieri before finally settling in Nice, where he died in 1855.[30] The pseudonym behind which he concealed his identity, *'Aleph ze'ira* ('minuscule *'aLePh'*), the abbreviation of *'ELisha Pontremoli*, he took from the technical Aramaic terminology of rabbinic scrivenery.[31] His translations from

---

Elijah Ḥalfon ha-Levi of Fürth had written a rhymed ode that was sung by the Jews of Paris in 5562 (1801/2), and that in the month of *'Elul* (Aug.–Sept. 5571 [1811]) in Ivrea 'Aleph Ze'ira' (i.e. Elisha Pontremoli) had felt inspired to produce a metrical Hebrew version. Elijah Ḥalfon ha-Levi's original piece and Pontremoli's metricized recension appear in parallel; see stanza xxiii. The full text of Elijah Ḥalfon ha-Levi's original was pub. by Barukh Mevorah (ed.), *Napoleon u-thequphatho*, Jerusalem, 5728 (1968), pp. 59 f.

[30] Little has been written about Elisha Pontremoli,; see Samuel Ghirondi and H. (Graziadio) Neppi, *Toledoth gedoley yisra'el u-ge'oney 'iṭalia*, Trieste, 1853, p. 41, no. 13, where the account is much mangled. In the memorial notice for his son, Ezra Pontremoli—rabbi, educationist, and member of the editorial board of the Italian *Educatore Israelita*—which appeared in *Il Vessilio Israelitico*, 36, 1888, pp. 71 f., some details about the father's life were recorded. Evidence for his birth at Casale comes from the title to his collected sermons, *Pethaḥ tiqwah*, MS Cincinnati, Hebrew Union College, Acc. 436, Jerusalem Microfilms Institute (see n. 29), no. 31060. His own father's name was also Ezra, as proved by the colophon of his poetic treatise on immortality, *Sepher tiqwath yesharim u-she'erith ha-Nefesh*, MS Paris, BN, héb. 253 (Jerusalem Microfilms Institute no. 3280), p. 26. Indication of his residence in Ivrea, Chieri, and Nice comes from the colophons etc. of his numerous writings, e.g. the title-page of the aforementioned *Pethaḥ tiqwah* 'begun in Ivrea, home of my joy [*qiryath mesosi*] and completed in Chieri, land of my affliction [*'eres 'onyi*]'. For the Jewish community of Chieri see G. Tedesco, 'Il Ghetto di Chieri', *RMI* 27, 1961, pp. 63–6, 172–8. He apparently settled in Nice prior to 1837 (5597), that being the value of the chronogram in the title of his *Tiqwath yesharim*, which alludes to his being situated there; see *Vessilio Israelitico*, p. 71. His educational activities are attested in his *Sod baḥurim* (introd., end), MS New York, Jewish Theological Seminary of America, Mic. 1458 and Oxford, Bodleian 19332 (Jerusalem Microfilms Institute 28380 and 18866 respectively, signed in Nice, where he preached in the synagogue self-styled *Ḥevrath zerizim* (introd. to his *Pethaḥ tiqwah*). In Nice he held appointment as the congregational rabbi—see the title to his special prayer occasioned by the threat of cholera, MS Cincinnati, Hebrew Union College 432 (Jerusalem Microfilms Institute 18793). Other writings of Pontremoli's that may be mentioned are his alphabetic anthology of citations from Psalms (New York, J[ewish] T[heological] S[eminary of America] 460, J[erusalem] M[icrofilms] I[nstitute] 23735); a rhymed commentary to Ecclesiastes (Paris, BN, héb. 251, 3, JMI 3278); *Novellae* on the Bible (Cincinnati, H[ebrew] U[nion] C[ollege] 26, 1, JMI 17308); poems, mostly in Hebrew, some in Italian (New York, JTS Mic. 1457 JMI 28379); a composition (*'Elleh ha-Devarim*) on deliverance from an attack mounted in 5561 (1800/1) (New York, JTS Acc. 3667/2, p. 7, JMI 29472); a rhymed piece on the story of the Four Cups by Solomon Pappenheim (Paris, BN, héb. 252, JMI 3279); a commentary on the *haggadah* for Passover eve (New York, JTS, Mic. 4554, JMI 25457); and a book of amulets and charms (*Sod yesharim*) (Cincinnati, HUC 558/1, JMI 19483).

[31] See Saul Chajes' thesaurus of Hebrew pseudonyms (*'Oṣar beduyey ha-Shem*), Vienna, 1933, p. 38, no. 587.

French into Hebrew include Baron d'Holbach's *Le Christianisme devoilé*,[32] and from his introduction thereto one learns of the motives that impelled him to translate the French free-thinker's work into Hebrew:

I have entitled this little composition *mas[h]gi' la-goyim* ['misleader of the Gentiles', cf. Job 12: 23]; and if the truth be told, its conception and origin lay outside the sphere of holiness, for it proceeded from a member of their own faith who printed it anonymously in Amsterdam in 1767,[33] or 5573 [*sic*] according to the Jewish reckoning. Its Gentile author styled it a rigorously rational investigation of Jesus Christ, wherein he exposed the mysteries and inner contradictions to be found in the New Testament, by them called *Evangelium* [*'awen gillayon*, 'vain revelation' a well-known pejorative play on words] . . . The reader will understand that for all that falsity cannot ultimately withstand the truth, nevertheless because of *force majeure* truth is sometimes cast down to the ground: at which times he who is prudent will hold his tongue, and we are now in evil times because of the repressiveness with which Christendom sorely harries Israel. So we have had perforce to muzzle ourselves, lest we bring to light the shortcomings and falsity of their faith . . . But now, God, be He blessed, has so contrived matters that those who demolish and destroy their [religion] proceed from their own midst [cf. Isaiah 49: 17], bringing upon them chagrin by the arguments which they base upon straight reasoning: so that they can no more lift up their heads against truth, which ever rises superior to all . . .[34]

Pontremoli, who had personally experienced tribulation from the oppressive measures against Piedmontese Jewish communities enacted on the French evacuation of 1814, exploited the work of d'Holbach (referred to in his introduction as being 'a member of their faith') in order to dispose of the fundamental principles of Christianity at a period when, he says (echoing Isaiah 51: 13) the 'fury of the oppressor' made it impossible for Jews to advance their own arguments against the dominant religion. From the same introduction we discover something else of importance regarding Pontremoli's work as a translator:

. . . The advantage in reading this little composition is substantial; because when you look at the apologetic literature written by the sages of Israel [you find that the essence of their argument is that] the Christian [fallacy has come about] because they flourish at us misinterpretations of [Old Testament] texts.

---

[32] Hamburg, St., H. B. Levy Collection, 143 JMI 1583. The title-page states that Pontremoli translated d'Holbach's work in Nice in 5615 (1854/5).

[33] D'Holbach's *Christianisme devoilé* in point of fact first appeared in London, in 1761, although the title-page of that edn. erroneously bears the date 1756. It was repub. in Amsterdam in 1766; and 4 further editions appeared there in 1767. Pontremoli seems to have translated from a copy of one of these last: see Naville (n. 10 above), p. 425. The Jewish equivalent of 1767 was 5527/8; 5573, which, by a slip, Pontremoli equates with 1767, corresponds to 1812/13.

[34] Hamburg MS (n. 32 above), translator's preface. The Hamburg MS is an incomplete translation, breaking off in the middle of chap. 12.

But the [Jewish controversialists] by dint of their wisdom completely defeat them by the truth inherent in their rejoinders, as for example in the *Niṣṣaḥon* books, the *Ḥizzuq 'Emunah*,[35] or the book entitled *Israel Vengé* by the former crypto-Jew Isaac Orobio; [I know,] for I myself translated it from French into Hebrew in my youth in Ivrea, in the year 5573 (1813) . . .[36]

I have succeeded in locating a copy of this translation in the Department of Manuscripts of the Hebrew University and National Library, executed by 'Samuel Ḥayyim Abram Barukh of the city of Acqui [Terme], in response to the desire of my respected father: Chieri, 25 *Tammuz* 5578 [29 July 1818]'.[37] The translation in headed: *'Niqmath Yisra'el* [*the Vengeance of Israel*] translated from French into our holy tongue by the *H*[*akham*] [*sic*] Rabbi Elisha Ḥanan'el Pontremoli.'

All that Pontremoli knew about Orobio de Castro and his work was derived from what the editor of *Israel Vengé* had to say about him in his introduction and from the bibliography published at the beginning of the century in Parma by G. B. de Rossi. In allusive language Pontremoli states 'the name of the sage Isaac Orobio is well known, as can be clearly seen from the [French] editor's introduction and from the number of his books listed by the advocate G. de Rossi, but I know of nothing stated about him in Hebrew publications'.[38]

---

[35] *Niṣṣaḥon* ('vanquishment') is the generic title for Hebrew works of Jewish apologetics written in dialogue form, the best known being the *Niṣṣaḥon yashan* (12th–13th cent.) between the emperor Henry II and the Jew Qalonymus, and the *Niṣṣaḥon* of Yom Ṭov Lippmann Mühlhausen, *c.* 1410. See O. S. Rankin, *Jewish Religious Polemic*, Edinburgh, 1956; *EJ* 6, pp. 889 f. The *Ḥizzuq 'emunah* ('Faith Strengthened') by the Karaite Jewish scholar Isaac Troki (*c.* 1533–*c.* 1594), first printed in 1681 by the anti-Jewish Johann Christoph Wagenseil in his *collectaneum* entitled *Tela ignea Satanae*, was accepted as a standard text-book of apologetics even by rabbanite Jews (cf. below n. 41).

[36] Ibid. (see n. 34 above). Ghirondi and Neppi (see n. 30 above) wrongly give the title of the book as *Niqmath yishma'el*. Pontremoli also translated into Hebrew Basnage's *Histoire des Juifs*, adding thereto polemical notes of his own; the holograph is in Cincinnati, HUC MS 856/7, JMI 26401–2. It is in 2 vols. containing 339 and 750 pages respectively. He likewise rendered into Hebrew 14 books of the Apocrypha, including Tobit and 1–2 Maccabees (New York, JTS L 731, JMI 23971).

[37] MS 8° 886, ff. 92, written in an Italian hand. Begins (f. 1ʳ⁻ᵛ) with the 'publisher's introduction', i.e. that in the French original, followed by Pontremoli's own 'translator's introduction' (ff. 1ʳ–3ʳ), and Orobio's tract (ff. 3ʳ–91ʳ). At the end stand a prayer of thanksgiving by the translator and an acrostic poem spelling out his full name Elisha Ḥanan'el Pontremoli (ff. 91ʳ–92ʳ). The copyist's colophon of Samuel Ḥayyim Barukh (f. 92ʳ) is followed, on the same leaf, by a note to the effect that it had [once?] had inserted a paper written by Tobias Barukh Pontremolo (*sic*) on the 14th day of the *'omer*, viz. 28 (*sic*: the correct equivalent is 29) *Nisan* 5568 (23 or 24 Apr. 1808), he being in mourning for his (unnamed) son who had died in prison in 'Tolin' (? = Turin, Torino) after living there continuously for 12 years. The unidentifiable Tobias Barukh Pontremoli was clearly related to the translator, and the note must be understood to have been written before Elisha Pontremoli translated Orobio's work in 1813.

[38] Ibid. ff. 1ʳ–2ʳ. The reference is to G. B. de Rossi's *Dizionario Storico degli Autori Ebrei e delle loro opere*, 2 vols. Parma 1802, see ii, p. 84.

Having come to appreciate the importance of Orobio, he decided that readers of Hebrew ought to know more about him and his writings:

So I said to myself, I shall put pen to paper and write about these profound things, in exact correspondence to the tenor of what is written by these Gentile [scholars]. I have, moreover, flavoured the introduction with a glimpse into the author['s life] so that the Jewish [Hebrew-reading] public may know what is already familiar to the Gentiles ... Of his writings, the only one which the Lord has seen fit to put in my way is the *Vengeance of Israel*, a work that is full to the brim of excellent and wholesome arguments; through it the Jew may come to know how to reply to his opponents, since the author has demolished faith in Jesus of Nazareth. The words of this book speak for themselves, and great credit redounds to him whose achievement it was to write it. I consequently thought that it would be to my own advantage to render it into Hebrew, so that it should no longer be a closed book as far as [Hebrew-reading] Jews are concerned: let it thus be open to the vision of all, and specifically those who do not know French...[39]

The Hebrew translation is, in general terms, a faithful one, although Pontremoli himself indicates in his introduction that he has himself elaborated in some passages according to his own understanding: 'wherever I have been able to add a touch by bringing biblical quotations into line with the original I have not failed so to do, and I have occasionally added something of my own in so far as God has enabled me, such additions being marked.'[40] (They are generally indicated by the abbreviation *he he* = *ha-ṣa'ir ha-ma'athiq*, 'mere translator['s note]'.)

Some of his additions consist of proofs adduced from rabbinic literature that reinforce Orobio's own contentions against the principles of Christianity.[41] Elsewhere he attempts to illuminate the historical background of events and ideas adumbrated by Orobio in brief. Thus, for example, he extends the scene when translating what Orobio had had to say about false messiahs with whose pretensions Jewry had had from time to time to deal:

Apart from what the author writes, we know quite certainly that others arose purporting to be the messiah (in Maimonides' time, as explained at length in the *Shevet Yehudah*, section 31), and they occasioned much evil to [various] Jewish communities. David Aldoir [*sic, l.* Alroy] in Maimonides' time, as can be seen in *Shevet Yehudah*, where is also told of another case at the beginning of the Islamic period; and again in the time of Rabbi Solomon b. Adret, and in Persia, too, see section 32. Finally Sabbatai Ṣevi together with Nathan of Gaza ... and they all met their deaths, since they were minus the traits which characterize the true messiah...[42]

---

[39] Ibid., f. 2ʳ.   [40] Ibid., f. 3ʳ.
[41] He cites Joseph Albo's *'Iqqarim* (f. 5ʳ), Maimonides' *Guide to the Perplexed* (f. 88ᵛ), Judah Ha-levi's *Kuzari* (ff. 59ʳ, 84ʳ), Levi b. Gershon (f. 65ʳ), David Qimḥi (ibid.), Isaac Abravanel (ff. 28ᵛ, 29ᵛ, 76ʳ, 89ᵛ), Samuel Laniado's *Keli yaqar* (ff. 64ʳ, 89ᵛ), Azariah dei Rossi's *Me'or 'eynayim* (f. 19ᵛ), and Isaac Troki's *Ḥizzuq 'emunah* (see above n. 35), (ff. 26ᵛ, 27ʳ⁻ᵛ).   [42] Ibid., 34ʳ, see ibn Verga's *Shevet yehudah*, pp. 74 f.

He provides particularly rich supplementation regarding Ferdinand the Catholic of Spain:

> There were five Spanish sovereigns called Ferdinand, but the one who persecuted the Jews was the fifth, surnamed the Catholic, son of Juan II of Aragon. The miscreant Isabella was a princess of Castile, and by virtue of marriage to her he gained the two kingdoms, fought successfully against Alfonso V of Portugal, and expelled both the Moors and the Jews from Spain. It was in his time that Columbus discovered a new world in America. Though much experienced in the art of politics, he was so eager to seek glory and extended sovereignty that he inflicted punitive burdens upon the very people whose shepherd he was supposed to be . . .[43]

Occasionally a personal note filters through his additions:

> I once heard [Gentiles] tell how a certain priest wanted to explain the secret of the trinity to the common folk of whom he had spiritual charge, and he resorted to comparison of the trinity with a trident. Although a trident has three prongs, if one uses its shaft or other butt to jab with, it is but one. He expounded all this *coram populo,* and everyone burst out laughing . . .[44]

An echo of criticism can be detected behind his note on Orobio's customary disregard of rabbinic sources. 'In this work the author omitted everything that might be appropriately adduced from the rabbis by way of rejoinder to the Gentiles, because he resorted in it to the best application of logic, and occasionally to biblical citation . . .'[45] Pontremoli himself occasionally adds references to midrashic literature that reinforce the point.[46]

He once appears actually to differ from his author and to correct him, when dissenting from the number of years assigned by Orobio to the period of the second temple. 'For its duration', he writes, 'see the *Shalsheleth ha-qabbalah* and *Me'or 'Eynayim.* Although Orobio gives the figure as 430 years I have not translated him, because of divergence of opinion.'[47]

And so it came about that a tiny fragment of Orobio's was translated into Hebrew from a secondary source. Although there must be considerable doubt as to whether this translation achieved very much in the way of circulation, it is in itself testimony to the interest which Orobio's writing was arousing amongst Jews even outside Holland more than a century after his death.

C: ENGLISH

In 1838 *Israel Vengé* was published in English, those who promoted its printing being themselves English Jews. In Orobio, they felt, they had found an educa-

---

[43] Ibid., f. 86ʳ⁻ᵛ, cf. also f. 26ʳ. When referring to events in Jewish history he relies on Abraham b. David's *Sepher ha-Qabbalah* (f. 20ᵛ), ibn Verga (see previous note), and the *Shalsheleth ha-Qabbalah* of Gedaliah ibn Yaḥya (ff. 19ʳ, 2ᵛ, 26ʳ). Once (f. 20ᵛ) he cites the *Histories* of Tacitus.

[44] Ibid., f. 76ʳ. [45] Ibid., f. 80ʳ. [46] Ibid., f. 88ʳ. [47] Ibid., f. 19ʳ.

Translations of Orobio's Works 463

tional source-book of the first order, well suited to meet the needs of Jewish youth growing up remote from the centres of intensity of traditional Judaism and exposed to the impact of Christian propaganda. They thought that the book would provide young people with an understanding of the Jewish religion, and of the rejoinders that it had to make to the basic claims of the Christian faith. The idea of making an English version available was conceived by Moses Mocatta (1768–1857), who himself translated several Hebrew works into English: the translator was G[race] A[guilar] (1816–47), an Anglo-Jewish writer of crypto-Jewish descent. It appeared in London in 1838 under the title *Israel Defended*.[48]

In her introduction, dated from Brighton in that year, she indicated that she had been at pains to moderate Isaac Orobio's acerbic tone, since the situation of Jews within the Christian world had changed since his time:

The different position which the children of Israel now occupy in the Christian world: the enlightened and liberal spirit with which they are regarded in this free and blessed island more particularly; the wide difference between the kindly charity of the Protestants and the bigoted cruelty of Catholicism; all these considerations have urged the translator to adopt a much milder tone of language towards the followers of Christ than that which pervades the original, a freedom which, she is well assured, will meet the approbation of coreligionsts.[49]

The title-page bears the words *Not Published*. In my opinion, this shows that the Jews of London wished to reassure the Christian majority that the book was intended merely for private circulation and they had no interest in proselytizing.

Grace Aguilar's version is very far from being faithful to the French recension which she used as her source. All passages which might have offended the minds of the Anglican community were rigorously excised.

Despite (or possibly because of) this, the Revd Alexander McCaul of Trinity College Dublin felt it necessary to publish a new edition in English in London, which came out in parts in 1839–40 under the title *Israel Avenged ... Translated and answered*. McCaul made a fresh and very faithful translation of the intro-

---

[48] Naville, p. 430, stated that there was an Eng. trans. pub. by R. Carlile in 1823, giving no further details. Professor R. Loewe informs me that Naville's statement is without foundation. On Moses Mocatta see V. D. Lipman, 'The Age of Emancipation', in V. D. Lipman (ed.), *Three Centuries of Anglo-Jewish History*, London, 1961, p. 103 n. 63, and *EJ* 12, 198. For Grace Aguilar see BethZion Lask Abrahams, 'Grace Aguilar: A Centenary Tribute', *TJHSE* 16, 1952, pp. 137 f., 140. J. Fürst's statement (*Bibliotheca Judaica*², Leipzig, 1863, iii, p. 54) that in 1839 there appeared an English version entitled *Israel Revenged* by Anna Maria Goldsmid, seems to rest upon a confusion: no such work is traceable in print.

[49] See translator's introd. pp. iv f. The parallel passages adduced above (n. 7) from *Israel Vengé* and its Spanish original may be further compared with Grace Aguilar's rendering of the same, p. 192, where she has added a piece of her own, formulated in a spirit of religious tolerance.

duction and the first two chapters of the French edition, attaching long and detailed rejoinders to every section, including the citation of Hebrew sources in the original. In his own preface he wrote as follows:

In the London Jewish translation the language of Orobio is confessedly moderated. It seems, however, fairer in reply to his argument, to give all due force to his words, and therefore a new and more literal translation is given.[50]

What McCaul has to say for his own part is formulated in acid tones, laced with a sneering provocativeness *vis-à-vis* Judaism in general and the English edition of 1838 in particular.[51]

[50] *Israel Avenged*, 1839, p. vii.
[51] See Friedenwald, *Jews and Medicine*, part ii, p. 456, who erroneously states that McCaul's edn. appeared in 1837.

APPENDIX H
Works Attributed to Orobio

A: *PROPUGNACULUM JUDAISMI*

Certain works, the identity of those responsible for which has not been adequately established, have been ascribed to Orobio de Castro. Thus it has been claimed that the *Propugnaculum Judaismi*, a book written by way of rejoinder to Grotius' strictures on Judaism in the fifth part of his *De Veritate Religionis Christianae*, was composed by none other than Orobio.[1]

In his book on the Sephardi Jewish poets and authors of Amsterdam, the poet Daniel Levi (Miguel) de Barrios devoted a special paragraph to the author of this work:

Dr Judah [*sic*] Lumbrozo, a celebrated scholar and president of the Council of the Grand Duke of Tuscany, migrated to Venice in order to be able to fulfil there the prescriptions of the holy Law. He practised medicine there, and composed a work in defence of the Torah—a volume of upwards of two hundred pages directed at contraverting the renowned Hugo Grotio, lecturer at the University of Utrecht.[2]

There is no doubt whatsoever that Judah Lumbrozo of Venice—regarding whom our knowledge is scanty—did in fact write the book with which we are concerned, during the first half of the seventeenth century.[3] His work was

---

[1] M. Mortara, *Indice Alfabetico dei Rabbini e Scritori Israeli*, Padua, 1886, p. 35 n. 2: 'da alcuni attribuito al Lombroso e da questi invece a Isac Orobio'. Mortara was followed by the article on Lombrozo in *JE* 8, p. 154, the German *Encyclopædia Judaica* 10, 1094; see J. Rosenthal in *'Aresheth* 2, 5720 (1960), p. 170.

[2] Daniel Levi de Barrios, 'Relación de los Poetas y Escritores Españoles de la Nación Judayca Amstelodama', *Triumpho* (copy in Amsterdam, *EH* 20 E 61), p. 56. See also Kayserling, *De Barrios*, 1889, p. 284.

[3] Most bibliographers who discuss Lombrozo give his first name as Jacob: J. Ch. Wolf, *Bibliotheca Hebraea*, i, Hamburg, 1715, p. 604 ff.; G. B. de Rossi, *Dizionario Storico degli autori Ebrei e delle loro opere*, ii, Parma, 1802, pp. 12 f.; Ghirondi–Neppi (App. G, n. 30), p. 201, no. 183; Carmoly, pp. 172 f.; Samuel Joseph Finn, *Keneseth yisra'el*, Warsaw, 1886, p. 553. C. Roth was correct in asserting that no confidence can be placed in the identification of *Jacob* Lombrozo, author of *Ḥesheq shelomoh* with *Judah* Lombrozo; he was, however, mistaken in saddling Wolf with the responsibility for the attribution to Orobio of the *Propugnaculum*. What Wolf wrote was the following: 'Idem contra librum V. Hugonis Grotiide Veritate Religionis Christianae, qui Iudaeis oppositus est, exaravit librum, quem dixit Propugnaculum Iudaismi ... Ejusdem scripti meminit Philippus Limborchius in Collatione cum erudito Iudaeo, qui et in comment. ad Acta Apostolorum v. c. p. 85 in epist. ad Hebraeos exceptionibus quibusdam ejus satisfacit. Antea vero in praefat. ad illum comment. ubi Iudae praenomine minus recte vocaretur, monuerat, se Lombrosii librum Ms. ab Isaaco Orobione nactum esse.'

known to Orobio, who indeed lent it to Limborch to peruse, and both he himself and Limborch referred to it in the course of their discussion. Lumbrozo's tract was never printed and I have not succeeded in tracing any manuscript of it, although some bibliographers have asserted that it was to be found in the possession of the Jews of Amsterdam.[4]

B: 'OROBIO AND BOLINGBROKE'

In 1770 there appeared in London a book in French with the title *Entretiens sur divers sujets d'histoire et de religion entre. Mylord Bolingbroke et Isaac d'Orobio, Rabin des Juifs Portugais à Amsterdam*. Examination of it reveals that it is simply a fourth edition of a book written by the French scholar Mathurin Veyssière de Lacroze. De Lacroze, who had been born in Nantes in 1661, on converting to Calvinism fled to Basle, and in 1711 he published in Amsterdam his *Entretiens sur divers sujets de literature, d'histoire et de critique et religion*.[5]

The book is divided into four dialogues between the author and a Sephardi Jew from Amsterdam, 'Moses Aboab', allegedly the grandson of Isaac Aboab—but he was undoubtedly a fictitious character. The dialogues are supposed to take place in Amsterdam, the author endeavouring to convince his conversationalist of the justification of Christianity and the Jew blandly accepting the Christian's contentions. The four dialogues are followed by a disquisition on atheism and contemporary atheists.[6] The work has no connection at all with Orobio de Castro, who at the date of its first appearance had long been dead. Orobio is even quoted occasionally in the body of the work, and the Jew is represented as showing him a marked respect.[7] The book ran into further editions in 1733, 1740, and 1770, the last being the edition here under discussion, in which the parties to the dialogue are represented as Bolingbroke and

---

[4] See Orobio, *apud* Limborch, *De Veritate Rel. Christ.*, p. 19: '... ut Doctor Lumbrozo in suo Propugnaculo Judaismi consitetur, et contra Grotium urget, etc.' and Limborch himself, p. 217: 'Doctor Lumbrozo, qui in suo Propugnaculo Iudaismi, ad articulum Grotii XVI, lib. V de Veritate Religionis Christianae, doctrinae Christianae originem non attribuit gentibus, aut graecis, sed Iudaeis.' For the circulation of the work in manuscript amongst the Amsterdam Jews see, *inter alios*, de Rossi and Finn (n. 3 above). Ghirondi–Neppi state that the work was written in Spanish, but this seems to me to be unfounded.

[5] See M. Jordan, *Histoire de la vie et des ouvrages de Mr. La Croze*, Amsterdam, 1741.

[6] The *Dissertation sur l'Atheisme et sur les Athées Modernes* occupies about half the book. In the very first dialogue the 'Jew' evinces an inclination to accept Christianity: 'Je crus seulement m'appercevoir qu'il avoit quelque inclination pour le Christianisme, et qu'il n'y avoit que des vues humaines qui l'empêchassent de l'embracer'; (edn. 1770, p. 3), and in the last he is convinced that he must do so: 'J'ai vu des choses qui m'engagent à faire désormais profession du Christianisme que j'ai déja interieurement embrassé, comme vous avez pu le connoître par les discours' (pp. 243 f.).

[7] e.g. ibid., p. 68: 'Notre Savant Orobio l'a déja dit dans une de ses réponses a M. Limborch, et vous trouverez ses paroles dans le livre que ce savant Homme a publié sous le titre de la Verité de la Religion Chrétienne.'

Works Attributed to Orobio

Isaac Orobio. Meanwhile an edition had also appeared in Dutch, published at Amsterdam in 1757: that edition contains no reference at all either to Orobio or to Bolingbroke, and even 'Aboab's' name is represented merely by the abbreviated cypher *Axxxx*.[8]

The question arises as to why the names of Isaac Orobio and Bolingbroke should have been introduced into the 1770 edition. Rosenthal is of the opinion that there is here a confusion between the disputation of Orobio with Philip van Limborch and that of Veyssière de Lacroze with 'Moses Aboab'.[9] That proposed explanation is however unsatisfactory. There could clearly have been no contact at all between Isaac Orobio and the English deist, who at the date of Orobio's death was but nine years old.[10] It is none the less possible that the appearance of this edition under so curious a title has something to do with the publication of *Israel Vengé* translated from Orobio by Baron d'Holbach in London in the same year. That anti-Christian tract evoked many an echo within the Christian community of western Europe: and conceivably the issue of Veyssière de Lacroze's work in London, in the form of a book describing a disputation to which Orobio is a party and is worsted, was a reaction by Christian circles concerned to use the *Entretiens* as a means of getting back at the author of *Israel Vengé*. But this still leaves unexplained why they should make use of the name of none other than Bolingbroke as the purported opponent of Orobio, despite the fact that the views of the English deist were very far removed from those of the true author of the book. The reason for the appearance of this fourth edition is consequently still shrouded in secrecy.

[8] I have located a copy of the Dutch version in Amsterdam, Bibl. Rosen., 1867 F 23: *Merkwaardig en zonderling Mond-Gesprek Tusschen en Gereformeerd Christen en een Portugeesche Jood*, Amsterdam, 1757. Compared with the original, this recension is abbreviated and is constructed out of only two of the dialogues.

[9] Rosenthal (n. 1 above).

[10] See M. Merril, *From Statesman to Philosopher: A Study in Bolingbroke's Deism*, New York, 1949; Ettinger, *De'iṣtim*, p. 204.

Bibliography

I ARCHIVAL HOLDINGS

A *Belgium*   *Abbreviation*

ANTWERP
Stadsarchief   Antwerp St.
PK 1072, 1074 *Natie van Portugal*
PK 53   *Liber Baptismatis Ecclesiae collegiatae et Parochialis Sancti Jacobi (1665–1672)*
PR 168   *Dopen en Huwelijken Parochia S. Philippi im Castronouo Antuerpiensi*

B *France*

BAYONNE
Archives Municipales   Bayonne Arch.
GG suppl. 4   *Baptèmes, paroisse Saint-Étienne d'Arribe Labaurd*

TOULOUSE
Université de Toulouse   Toulouse Univ.
Archive de la Faculté de Droit, reg. 9, 28

C *The Netherlands*

AMSTERDAM
(i) Archief der Gemeente Amsterdam   Amsterdam, AGA
Dopen, Trouwen, Begraven   DTB
Particuliere Archieven   PA
(1) PA 334   Amsterdam Portuguese Jewish Congretion
Nos. 19–20 *Livro dos Acordos da Nação e Ascamot*
  A. 5398–5540
  B. 5441–5472
Nos. 24, 24a, 25 *Memorial de advertencias*
Nos. 118–20 *Varios papeis de pleitos findados (1670–1815)*
No. 139 *Suplicas de Abraham y Jacob Pereyra*

Nos. 174–7 *'Manual'* (1653–1718)
No. 178 *Kladjournal 1677/78*
Nos. 215–21 *'Livro Longo'* (1663–1713)
Nos. 240–3 *'Livro grande'* (1653–1710)
No. 333 *Livro da Repartisão dos Lugares da Esnoga* (1687–1730)
No. 338 *Stukken betreffende plaatsen uitgegeven door parnassim 1675, 1687, etc.*
Nos. 382–6 *Ketubot. Livros I–VIII* (1673–1701)
No. 421 *Registro das Mulheres enterradas no Beth Haim a Ouderkerk desde o A° 1616*
No. 422 *Registro dos Homens enterrados no Beth Haim a Ouderkerk desde o A° 1616*
No. 423 *Kladlijsten voor een alfabetisch register op voornaam van de overledenen die begraven zijn te Ouderkerk* (1616–1846)
No. 518 *Livro dos testamentos* (1663—1733)
No. 520 *Testamentos e outros actos depositados em poder dos senhores do Mahamad* (1671–1778)
No. 616 *Antonio Alvares alias Joseph Israel Alvares, Testamento* (1694–1773)
Nos. 675–91 *Manuel Levi Duarte (testament 1699), 1713–1747 met retroacta*
No. 695 *Abraham Penso Felix. Testamento*
No. 738 *Joseph Henriques Medina alias Aaron Henriques Medina. Testamento*
No. 783 *Livro Grande de Legados de Abraham e Sara Pereira* (1659–1746)
No. 882 *Stukken betreffende de ban opgelegd aan Daniel de Prado en Daniel Ribera, 1658*
No. 916 *Livro de Bet Haim* (1680–1716)
No. 1051 *Termos de Talmud Torah e de Ets Haim* (5376–5488)
No. 1052 *Termos de Ets Haim* (5397–5488)
No. 1072 *Livro dos SS^{res} Thezoureiros da Santa Irmandade de Ets Haim*
No. 1073 *Registers van de broeders van de gebroederschap (Ets Haim) en van legatarissen, etc.* (1637–1902)
No. 1163 *Santa Companhia de dotar orfas e donzelas. Termos D* (1661–1735)
No. 1163 *Santa Companhia de dotar orfas e donzelas. Livro de irmãos* (1615–1956)

1. Archival Holdings

Abbreviation

No. 1186 *Honen Dalim. Reglementen, besluiten en ledenlijst (1625–1684)*
No. 1191 *Gemelut Hassadim. Reglementen, besluiten en administratie der contributiegelden, etc. (1666–1761)*
No. 1291 *Aby Jetomim (1648–1795)*

(2) PA 27 Amsterdam *Collegium Medicum* Amsterdam,
No. 20 *Series nominum doctorum medicinae* Coll. Med.

(3) Municipal Authority
1674 *Quohier van de 200ste Penning*

(4) Notarial Archives
No. 2904, 2907 A–B, 3700, 4077

(ii) Ets Haim Livraria Montezinos
MS 48 D 36 *Registro das Eleições feitas depois da união das Tres Quehilot*

D *Spain*

CUENCA
Archivo diocesano Cuenca AD
Leg. 462, No. 6341 *Proceso contra Mencia Fernández Núñez (1641)*
Leg. 462, No. 6346 *Documentos del Proceso contra Manuel Alvares (1641)*
Leg. 462, No. 6348 *Proceso contra Manuel Alvares (1641)*

MADRID
Archivo Histórico Nacional Madrid AHN
(1) Inquisition Section
Libro 693
Libro 1.123
Leg. 163, No. 14 *Inq. de Toledo: Copia del Proceso contra Gonzalo Luis (1640)*
Leg. 163, No. 15 *Inq. de Toledo: Copia del Proceso contra Isabel Luis (1640)*
Leg. 166, No. 8 *Inq. de Toledo: Declaração que hiço en tres de Março de 1664 Manuel de León, etc.*
Leg. 168, No. 2 *Inq. de Toledo: Copia del Proceso contra Andrés de Narvaez (1640)*
Leg. 181, No. 1 *Inq. de Toledo: Copia del Proceso contra Melchor Rodríguez (1640)*

Leg. 2067, No. 95 *Copia del Secuestro de bienes del Dr. Don Baltazar de Orovio (1654)*
Leg. 2067, No. 100 *Copia del Secuestro de bienes de Simón Rodríguez y Leonor Albarez, su mujer (1654)*
Leg. 2067, No. 101 *Copia del Secuestro de bienes de Beatriz Orobio y Biolante y Clara de Orovio, sus hijas (1654)*
Leg. 2987, A–B *Correspondencia entre el Tribunal de la Inquisición de Sevilla y la Suprema*
(2) Universities Section
402F, 421F, 430F, 446–449F, 491–495F *Matrículas*
Leg. 44–47, 53, 72, 74, 360, *Universidad*
1045–1046F *Colegio de la Madre de Dios de los Teólogos*

2 OTHER MANUSCRIPTS

A *England*

LONDON

(i) British Library   BL
Harley 3430 (Orobio, *Prevenciones Divinas, Respuesta a un Predicante Francés, Epístola Invectiva*)
Add. 40084 (Orobio, *sobre capítulo 53 de Izahias*)

(ii) Jews' College   JC
Montefiore 525 (Hirschfeld, *Cat.* 298) (Orobio, *Prevenciones Divinas, Epístola Invectiva*)
Montefiore 532 (Hirschfeld, *Cat.* 299) (Orobio, *Certamen contra Bredemburg*)

(iii) Wellcome Institute of the History of Medicine
3722   (Orobio, *Prevenciones Divinas*)

MANCHESTER
John Rylands University Library   Rylands
5 (Isaac Aboab, *Nishmath Ḥayyim*; Saul Levi Mortera, *Yisra'el . . . lo' ye'anesh be-'oneshi[n] niṣṣaḥi [n]*

OXFORD
Bodleian Library   Bodl.

2. Other Manuscripts

	Abbreviation

Opp. Add. Fol. 29 (Neubauer, *Cat.* 2471) (Orobio, *Prevenciones Divinas*)

Opp. Add. 4° 51 (Neubauer, 2475) (Orobio, *Tratado de las 70 semanas*)

Opp. Add. 4° 147 (Neubauer, 2472) a–b (Orobio, *Prevenciones Divinas*), c (Orobio, *Respuesta a un Predicante Francés, Epístola Invectiva*)

Opp. Add. 4° 148 (Neubauer, *Cat.* 2474) (Orobio, *sobre o capitulo 53 do Izahias*)

Opp. Add. 4° 150 (Neubauer, *Cat.* 2481, 1,2) (Abraham Cardozo, *Two polemical letters (Spanish)*)

Opp. Add. 8° 7 (Neubauer, *Cat.* 2473) (Orobio, *Prevenciones Divinas*)

Misc. 544 (Abraham Guer [de Cordova], *Fortaleza del judaísmo*)

B *France*

BORDEAUX

Bibliothèque Municipale   Bordeaux

347   (Orobio, French version of *Prevenciones Divinas*)

828   (Orobio, French version of *Contra Bredemburg*)

PARIS

(i) Bibliothèque Nationale   Paris BN

13351   (Orobio, *Dissertation sur le Messie*)

14928   (Orobio, French version of *Isaiah 53, Dissertation sur le Messie*)

ésp. 40–1 (Orobio, *Prevenciones Divinas, Respuesta ... Raymundo Lulio, Respuesta Apologética al Zepeda, Certamen Philosóphico, Respuesta a un predicante Francés, Epístola Invectiva, Carta Apologética, Carta al hijo de Prado*)

(ii) Bibliothèque Mazarine   Paris Maz.

1190   (Orobio, French version of *Isaiah 53*)

11494   (Orobio, *Dissertation sur le Messie*)

(iii) Bibliothèque de la Sorbonne   Paris Sorb.

761   (Orobio, *Dissertation sur le Messie*)

		Abbreviation

C *Germany*

HAMBURG
Stadtsbibliothek — Hamburg St.
Hebr. 85a (Steinschneider, *Cat.* 342) (Orobio, *Prevenciones Divinas*)
Hebr. 240a (Steinschneider, *Cat.* 343) (Orobio, *Tratado a un Cavallero Reformado*)

D *The Netherlands*

AMSTERDAM
(i) Sephardic Community, Ets Haim / Livraria Montezinos — Amsterdam *EH*

47 C 30	(Fuks-M., *Cat.* 440) (I. C. Belinfante, *Miscellaneous Hebrew Poems*)
48 A 1	(Fuks-M., *Cat.* 190) (Jonathan Guer, *Keset Jeonatan*, Portuguese translation)
48 A 9	(Fuks-M., *Cat.* 187) (Saul Levi Mortera, *Providencia de Dios*, original Portuguese text)
48 A 11	(Fuks-M., *Cat.* 423) (Moses Aguilar) (*Perguntas de Anveres, Explicação do capitulo 53 de Yesaya*(1), *Pergunta que fez Orobio*(1), *Pergunta da Jessiba de Veneza, Pergunta[s] que fez Orobio*(2), (3), (4), *Pergunta que se me fez, Discurso contra Calvino, Reposta sobre perguntas de Bayona, Explicasão do Cap. 53 de Yesias*(2))
48 A 12	(Fuks-M., *Cat.* 244) (Orobio, *Epístola Invectiva, Respuesta a un Predicante francés, Respuesta . . . de Lulio, Respuesta Apologética al Zepeda*)
48 A 21	(Not in Fuks-M., *Cat.*) (Orobio, *Respuesta a un Predicante francés, Carta contra Prado*)
48 A 23	(Not in Fuks-M., *Cat.*) (Orobio, *Epístola Invectiva, Carta contra Prado*)
48 B 1	(Fuks-M., *Cat.* 203) (Saul Levi Mortera, *Providencia de Dios*, Spanish translation)
48 B 5	(Fuks-M., *Cat.* 237) (Orobio, *Respuesta . . . Raymundo Lulio, Respuesta Apologética al Zepeda*)

2. Other Manuscripts

Abbreviation

48 B 6	(Fuks-M., *Cat.* 195) (Orobio, *Prevenciones Divinas*)
48 B 11 I	(Fuks-M., *Cat.* 449) (Jeonatan Guer, as 48
48 B 12	(Fuks-M., *Cat.* 238) (Orobio, *Epístola Invectiva, Respuesta ... Raymundo Lulio, Respuesta Apologética al Zepeda, Discurso sobre la Trinidad*)
48 B 13	(Fuks-M., *Cat.* 202) (Orobio, *Prevenciones Divinas*)
48 C 1/2	(Fuks-M., *Cat.* 219) (Orobio, *Prevenciones Divinas*)
48 C 3	(Fuks-M., *Cat.* 220) (Orobio, *Respuesta a un Predicante francés, Epístola Invectiva*)
48 C 4	(Fuks-M., *Cat.* 242) (Orobio, *Epístola Invectiva*)
48 C 5	(Fuks-M., *Cat.* 239) (Saul Levi Mortera, *Respuesta a las objeciones al Talmud*)
48 C 9	(Fuks-M., *Cat.* 223) (Saul Levi Mortera, *Preguntas que hizo un Clérigo de Ruan*)
48 C 10	(Fuks-M., *Cat.* 224) (Saul Levi Mortera, *Providencia de Dios*, Spanish translation)
48 C 11	(Fuks-M., *Cat.* 193) (Saul Levi Mortera, *Providencia de Dios*, Spanish translation)
48 C 12	(Fuks-M., *Cat.* 194) (Orobio, *Prevenciones Divinas, Respuesta a un Predicante francés, Epístola Invectiva*)
48 C 16	(Fuks-M., *Cat.* 245) (Orobio, *Certamen Philosóphico contra Bredemburg*)
48 C 21	(Fuks-M., *Cat.* 189) (Saul Levi Mortera, *Providencia de Dios*, Spanish translation)
48 C 24	(Fuks-M., *Cat.* 204) (Isaac Naar, *Discurso*)
48 D 6	(Fuks-M., *Cat.* 196) (Orobio, *Prevenciones Divinas, Respuesta a un Predicante francés, Respuesta ... Raymundo Lulio, Epístola Invectiva, Respuesta Apologética al Zepeda*)
48 D 9	(Fuks-M., *Cat.* 156) (Isaac Aboab, *Documentos para todo estado*)
48 D 16	(Fuks-M., *Cat.* 197) (Orobio, *Explicación del capítulo 53 del Ysaias*)
48 D 31	(Fuks-M., *Cat.* 46) (Abraham Pizarro, *Sermón en la Corte del Haya*)

		Abbreviation
48 D 38	(Fuks-M., *Cat.* 206) (Saul Levi Mortera, *Preguntas que hizo un Clérigo de Ruan, Obstáculos de la Religión christiana)*	
48 D 40	(Fuks-M., *Cat.* 232) (Saul Levi Mortera, *Respuesta a las objeciones al Talmud)*	
48 E 41	(Fuks-M., *Cat.* 218) (Saul Levi Mortera, *Preguntas* as 48 D 38)	
48 E 42	(Fuks-M., *Cat.* 234) (Orobio, *Respuesta Apologética al Zepeda)*	
49 A 1	(Fuks-M., *Cat.* 214) (Eliau Montalto, *Obras)*	
49 A 16	(Fuks-M., *Cat.* 207) (Orobio, *Respuesta a un Predicante francés)*	
49 A 17	(Fuks-M., *Cat.* 205) (Saul Levi Mortera, as 48 C 21)	
49 B 3	(Fuks-M., *Cat.* 231) (Saul Levi Mortera, as 48 D 40)	

(ii)	Universiteitsbibliotheek	Amsterdam Univ.
111 D 16/17	(Ph. Limborch, *Brieven*)	
Ba 255	(J. Locke, *Brieven aan Limborch*)	
I H 12	Orobio, *Prevenciones Divinas, Respuesta Apologética al Zepeda*)	
I H 13	(Orobio, *Prevenciones Divinas, Respuesta Apologética al Zepeda, Respuesta a un Predicante francés, Epístola Invectica*)	

(iii)	Universiteitsbibliotheek, Bibliotheca Rosenthaliana	Amsterdam Univ. Bibl. Rosen.
119	(Fuks-M., *Cat.* 254) (Isaac Aboab, *Documentos para todo estado*)	
459	(Fuks-M., *Cat.* 282) (Orobio, *Prevenciones Divinas*)	
631 1–5	(Cassuto Collection: not in Fuks-M. *Cat.*) (Orobio, *Prevenciones Divinas, Epístola Invectiva, Respuesta a un Predicante francés, Respuesta ... Raymundo Lulio, Respuesta Apologética al Zepeda*)	
(iv)	Private Collection (M. H. Gans) (Orobio, *Respuesta a un Predicante francés*)	Gans

2. Other Manuscripts

Abbreviation

LEIDEN
Universiteitsbibliotheek   Leiden
Pap. 15 (Jean Le Clerc, *Ad Ph. van Limburg*)

E *Israel*

JERUSALEM
University Library   Jerusalem Univ.
Heb. 8° 886   (Orobio, *'Israel Vengé'* [based on *Explicación de Ysaia 53* and *Prevenciones Divinas*, Hebrew translation)
Heb. 8° 2001 (Rabbinical *Responsa* from Palestine, Turkey, the Levant, and Italy)
Var. 282   (Orobio, *'Israel Vengé'*, see Heb. 8° 886)

F *Spain*

MADRID
Biblioteca Nacional   Madrid BN
18249 (Gayangos Collection: Roca, *Cat.* pp. 312 f.)
   (Orobio, *Respuesta a un Predicante francés, Epístola Invectiva, Prevenciones Divinas*)

G *United States of America*

NEW YORK
Jewish Theological Seminary of America   JTS
Adler 2359[1-3] (Adler, *Cat.* p. 53, Marx, *Cat.* 67)
   (Orobio, *Prevenciones Divinas, Respuesta a un Predicante francés, Epístola Invectiva*)
Sulzbacher Collection (Marx, *Cat.* 66) (Orobio, *Prevenciones Divinas*)

PHILADELPHIA
Library of the University of Pennsylvania   Penn Univ.
Lea 175 (Abraham Guer [de Cordova], *Fortaleza del judaísmo*)

3 AUTHORS: PRIMARY SOURCES

ABOAB, Emanuel, *Nomologia, o discursos legales*,   Aboab, Em.
Amsterdam, 1629

Bibliography

	Abbreviation
ABOAB, Isaac, *Sepher Nishmath Ḥayyim*, MS Rylands 5	Aboab, *NḤ*
—— *Parafrasis Comentado sobre el Pentateuco*, Amsterdam, 5441 [1681]	Aboab, *Pent.*
—— *Doutrina Particular*, Amsterdam, 1687	Aboab, *Dout.*
—— *Documentos para todo Estado e Ydade*, MSS Amsterdam St. 5445, 5446, Amsterdam Univ. Bibl. Rosen. 119, Amsterdam *EH* 48 D 9	Aboab, *Documentos*
ABOAB, Samuel, *Devar Shemu'el (Responsa)*, Venice, 5480 [1720]	Aboab, Sam.
ABRAVANEL, Isaac, *Yeshu'oth Meshiḥo*, edn. Königsberg, 1861	Abravanel, *YM*
—— *Ma'yeney Ha-yeshu'ah*, edn. Stettin, 5620 [1860]	Abravanel, *MH*
—— *Perush Torah Nevi'im u-kethuvim*, edn. Jaffa, 5714–20 [1954–60]	Abravanel, *Bibl.*
ABUDIENTE, Moses, *Fin de los Días*, Glückstadt, 5426 [1666]	Abudiente
AGRIPPA, Henricus Cornelius, *De incertitudine et vanitate scientiarum declamatio invectiva ex postrema authoris recognitione*, Cologne, 1575	Agrippa
AGUILAR, Moses Raphael, *Perguntas que me fizerão de Anveres; Breve explicação do Capitulo 53 de Yesaya; Pergunta que me fez o Doutor Orobio; Outra Pergunta da mesma Jessiba ou academia de Veneza; Pergunta que me fez o insigne Doutor Orobio; Pergunta do muy docto senhor Doutor Orobio; Pregunta que me fez o eminentissimo Senhor Doutor Orobio; Pergunta que se me fez; Breve discurso contra a doitrina de Calvino; Reposta e discurso sobre certas perguntas de Bayona; Explicasão do Cap. 53 de Yesaias, feita no Brazil*, MS Amsterdam, *EH* 48 A 11	Aguilar
AMELANDER, Menaḥem Man, *She'erith Yisra'el*, Amsterdam, 5503 [1743]	Amelander
Amsterdam, Collegium Medicum, *Privilegien, Willekeuren en Ordonnantien, Betreffende het Collegium Medicum Amstelaedamense*, Amsterdam, 1728	Amsterdam Coll. Med.
Amsterdam Synagogue, *see* Synagogue, Amsterdam	
[ARNAULD, Antoine], *La Logique, ou l'Art de Penser, contenant, outre les règles comunes, plusiers observations nouvelles, propres à former le jugement*, Amsterdam, 1775	Arnauld
BARRIOS, M. D. L. de, *See* DE BARRIOS	

3. Authors: Primary Sources

Abbreviation

BARROS, J. de, *See* DE BARROS
BASNAGE, J., *Histoire des Juifs depuis Jésus-Christ jusqu'à présent*, enlarged edn., The Hague, 1716 — Basnage
BAYLE, Pierre, *Dictionnaire historique et critique*, i–iv, Rotterdam, 1715 — Bayle
—— *Historical and Critical Dictionary, Selections*; trans., with... notes, R. H. Popkin, Indianapolis, 1965 — Bayle, *Selections*
BELINFANTE, Isaac Cohen, *Sepher Segullath Melakhim, Shirim we-shiroth*, 5528 [1768], MS Amsterdam *EH* 47 C 30 — Belinfante
BERNAL, A. N., *See Elogios*
CARDOSO, Abraham Michael, *Two letters* (Spanish), MS Bodl. Opp. Add. 4° 151 — A. M. Cardoso
CARDOSO, Isaac, *Philosophia Libera in Septem Libros distributa*, Venice, 1673 — Isaac Cardoso, *Philos.*
—— *Las Excelencias de los Hebreos*, Amsterdam, 1679 — Isaac Cardoso, *Excel.*

CLEMENTE, P. Claudio, *El Machiavelismo degollado por la Christiana sabiduría de España y Austria*, Alcalá, 1637 — Clemente
DA SILVA, Hezekiah, *Del Fundamento de nuestra Ley — sermón moral*, ed. M. B. Amzalak, Coimbra, 1925 — Amzalak, *da Silva*
DE BARRIOS, Miguel (Daniel Levi), *Flor de Apolo*, Brussels, 1665 — De Barrios, *Flor*
—— *Coro de las Musas*, Brussels, 1672 — De Barrios, *Coro*
—— *Imperio de Dios en la Harmonía del Mundo*, Brussels, 1673; 2nd edn., *s.l.e.a.* — De Barrios, *Imperio*
—— *Mediar extremos*, Amsterdam, 5437 [1677] — De Barrios, *Mediar*
—— *Respuesta panegírica a la carta que escribió el R. don José Penso Vega al Dr Ishac Orobio*, Amsterdam, 5437 [1677] — De Barrios, *Respuesta*
—— *Luna Opulenta de Holanda, en nubes que el Amor manda*, Amsterdam, 1680 — De Barrios, *Luna*
—— *Triumpho del Govierno Popular y de la Antigüedad Holandesa*, Amsterdam, 5443 [1683] (Copies located: BL 4033 aa 43, Amsterdam *EH*, 2 F 9, 2 F 81, 9 E 43, 20 E 61, Amsterdam Univ. Bibl. Rosen., 19 G 11, 19 G 12) — De Barrios, *Triumpho*
—— *Alegrías o Pinturas Lucientes de Hymeneo*, Amsterdam, 1686 — De Barrios, *Alegrías*
—— *Monte Hermoso de la Ley Divina*, Amsterdam, 5459 [1699] — De Barrios, *Monte Herm.*

Bibliography

	Abbreviation
DE BARRIOS, Miguel (Daniel Levi) *Contra la verdad no ay fuerça*, Amsterdam s.a.	De Barrios, *Contra Verdad*
—— *Desembozos de la verdad contra las máscaras del mundo*, s.l.e.a.	De Barrios, *Desembozos de Verdad*
—— *Metros Nobles*, s.l.e.a.	De Barrios, *Metros*
DE BARROS, João, *Ropicapnefma*, reproduction of 1532 edn., with notes etc. by I. S. Révah, 2 vols., Lisbon, 1952–5	De Barrios, *Ropicapnefma*
DE PINA, Manuel, *Chanças del ingenio y dislates de la Musa*, Amsterdam(?), 1656	De Pina
DE PINEDO, Moses, *Disputatio Medica Inauguralis: De Dysenteria Vera*, Leiden, 1685	De Pinedo
Elogios que zelozos dedicaron a la Felice memoria de Abraham Núñez Bernal, s.l.e.a.	Elogios Bernal
ENRÍQUEZ GÓMEZ, Antonio, *Academias Morales de las Musas*, Madrid, 1734	Enríquez Gómez
FÉNELON, M. de, P. LAMI and BOULLAIN-VILLIERS, *Réfutation des Erreurs de Benoit de Spinosa*, Brussels, 1731	Fénelon
FRANCO MENDES, D., *Memorias do Establecimiento e progresso dos judeos portuguezes e espanhoes nesta famosa cidade de Amsterdam*, ed. L. Fuks, R. G. Fuks Mansfeld and B. N. Teensma, *SR* 9, no. 2, July 1975	Franco Mendes, *Memorias*
GRANADA, Fray Luis de, *Obras*, I–III, Madrid, 1922	Granada
GROTIUS, Hugo, *De Jure belli ac pacis*, Amsterdam, 1720	Grotius, *Jure Belli*
—— *De Veritate Religionis Christianae*, London, 1813	Grotius, *Rel. Christ.*
—— *Remonstrantie nopende de ordre dije in de Landen van Hollandt ende Westerwrieslandt dijent gestelt op de joden*, ed. J. Meijer, Amsterdam, 1949	Grotius, *Remonstr.*
GUER (de Cordova), Abraham, *Fortaleza del judaísmo y confusión del Christianismo*, Penn Univ., MS Lea 175; *Fortaleza ... y confusión del extraño*, Bodl. MS Misc, 544	Guer. A., *Fort.*
GUER, Jonathan, *Keset Jeonatan*, Portuguese trans. by Samuel Abaz, 1665, Amsterdam *EH* 48 A 1, 48 B 11[1]	Guer. J., *Kes.*
HERRERA, Abraham Cohen, *Sepher Beth 'Elohim*, Hebrew trans. by Isaac Aboab, Amsterdam, 5415 [1655]	Herrera, *Beth 'El.*

3. Authors: Primary Sources

	Abbreviation
—— *Sepher Shaʻar Ha-Shamayim*, Hebrew trans. by Aboab, Amsterdam, 5415 [1655]	Herrera, *Sh. Hash.*
IBN VERGA, Solomon, *Shevet Yehudah*, ed. A. Shoḥat, Jerusalem, 5707 [1947]	Ibn Verga
ISAAC B. SHESHETH (Perfet), *Responsa*, Constantinople, 5307 [1547]	Is. b. Shesheth
JOSEPH HA-KOHEN, *Divrey ha-Yamin le-malkhuth Ṣarephath u-malkhuth beth ʼoṭoman ha-Togar*, Amsterdam, 5493 [1733]	Joseph Ha-Kohen, *Hist.*
—— *'Emeq Ha-Bakha'*, ed. M. H. Letteris, Vienna, 1852	Joseph Ha-Kohen, *'Emeq. Ha-B.*
JOSEPHUS, *Respuesta de Josepho contra Apion Alexandrino*, Spanish trans. Joseph Semah Arias, Amsterdam, 1687	Josephus (Arias)
LE CLERC, J., *Bibliothèque Universelle et Historique*, II, Amsterdam, 1686, VII, 1743	Le Clerc, *Bibl. Univ.*
—— *Bibliothèque Choisie*, XIX (1709), Amsterdam 1710, pp. 350–427	Le Clerc, *Bibl. Choisie*
—— *Ad Ph. van Limburg, 22 Febr. 1700*, MS Leiden Pap. 15	Le Clerc, *Ad Lim.*
LEÓN HEBREO, Jacob Judah, *Psalms. Qodesh hillulim, Las Alabanças de Santidad*, Traducción de los Psalmos, Amsterdam, 5431 [1671]	León Hebreo
LIMBORCH, Philip van, *De Veritate Religionis Christianae. Amica Collatio cum Erudito Judaeo*, Gouda, 1687	Limborch, *De Veritate Rel. Christ.*
—— *Historia Inquisitionis*, Amsterdam, 1692. Eng. trans. by Samuel Chandler, London, 1731	Limborch, *Inqu.*
—— *Brieven*, MS Amsterdam Univ. 111 D 16/17	Limborch, *Brieven*
—— *Catalogus Librorum quibus usus est ... Ph. à Limborch*, Amsterdam, 1712	Limborch, *Cat.*
—— *Armenianesimo e tolleranza nel Seicento olandese: il carteggio Ph. van Limborch, J. Le Clerc* [Latin text], ed. Luisa Simonutti, Accademia toscana di scienze e lettre 'La Columbaria', Studi, 70, Florence, 1984	Limborch, *Carteggio*
LOCKE, John, *Brieven aan Limborch*, MS Amsterdam Univ. Ba. 255	Locke
LULL, Ramón, *Arbol de la Ciencia*, Spanish trans. by Alonzo de Zepeda y Adrada, Brussels, 1664	Lull (Zep).
MENASSEH B. ISRAEL, *De la fragilidad humana*, Amsterdam, 1642	Menasseh b. Israel *Frag.*

	Abbreviation
MENASSEH B. ISRAEL, *Esperança de Israel*, Amsterdam, 1650	Menasseh b. Israel *Esp.*
—— *The Humble Addresses* . . . Amsterdam(?), 1651	Menasseh b. Israel *Addr.*
—— *'Even Yeqarah. Piedra Gloriosa o de la Estatua de Nebuchadnesar*, Amsterdam, 1655	Menasseh b. Israel *Piedra*
—— *Vindicia Judaeorum*, London, 1656	Menasseh b. Israel *Vind. Jud.*
MODENA, Leone da, *Ma'amar Maghen we-ṣinnah*, ed. A. Geiger, Breslau 5616 [1856]	Modena, *Mag.*
—— *Responsa, Ziqney Yehudah*, ed. S. Simonsohn, Jerusalem, 5716 [1956]	Modena, *Ziq. Yeh.*
MONTALTO, Eliau, *Obras do Doctor Eliau Montalto*, MS Amsterdam, *EH* 49 A 1	Montalto
MORTERA, Saul Levi, *Haṣṣa'ah 'asher be-shem yisra'el yekhunneh 'aph 'al pi she-'avar 'averoth ha-ḥamuroth she-ba-'olam lo' ye'anesh be-'oneshi[n] niṣṣaḥi[n]*, MS Rylands 5	Mortera, *Yisra'el she-'avar*
—— *Respuesta a las objeciones con que el Sinense injustamente calunia al Talmud*, MS Amsterdam, *EH* 48 B 3, 48 C 5, 48 D 40	Mortera, *Resp. obj. al Talmud*
—— *Preguntas que hizo un Clérigo de Ruan de Francia, a las quales respondió . . . Mortera*, MS Amsterdam, *EH* 48 C 9, 48 D 38, 48 E 41	Mortera, *Clérigo de Ruan*
—— *Providencia de Dios con Israel*, Portuguese original, MS Amsterdam, *EH* 48 A 9, Spanish translation, 48 B 1, 48 C 10, 48 C 11, 48 C 21, 49 A 17	Mortera, *Providencia*
—— *Obstáculos y oposiciones de la Religión christiana en Amsterdam*, MS Amsterdam, *EH* 48D 38	Mortera, *Obstáculos*
NAHAR, Isaac, *Discurso del . . . Ribi Ishac Naar*, MS Amsterdam, *EH* 48 C 24	Nahar
[NICERON, J. P.], *Mémoires pour servir à l'histoire des Hommes Illustrés dans la République des Lettres avec un Catalogue Raisonné de leurs Ouvrages*, XI, pp. 39–53, Paris, 1730	Niceron, *Mém.*
OROBIO DE CASTRO, Isaac (= Baltasar Alvarez). For works by Isaac Orobio de Castro preserved solely or mainly in manuscript, see above, Appendix E (indicated here by MS[S])	
—— *Epílogo de lo que passó en la peste de la ciudad de Málaga este año de 1637*, Málaga, 1637 (repr. above, Appendix B)	Orobio, *Peste Mál.*

3. Authors: Primary Sources

	Abbreviation
—— *Controvertitur Utrum Materialibus morbis in choantibus sanguinis missio revulsiva iuxta Hippocratis et Galeni dogmata per distantissimas venas effici debeat*, Seville, 1653	Orobio, *Sang. Miss.*
—— *Carta Apologética del Doctor Ishack Orobio de Castro al Doctor Prado*, MS	Orobio, *Cart. Apol.*
—— *Carta al hijo de el Doctor Prado*, MSS (The three codices are collated above, Appendix F)	Orobio, *Carta al hijo de Prado*
—— *Certamen Philosophicum, Propugnatae Veritatis Divinae ac Naturalis*, Amsterdam, 1703; MSS	Orobio, *Cert. Phil.*
—— *Epístola Invectiva contra Prado, un Philósopho Médico que dudava o no creía la verdad de la divina escriptura y pretendió encubrir su malicia con la afectada confessión de Dios y Ley de Naturaleza*, MSS	Orobio, *Epíst. Inv.*
—— *Explicación Paraphrástica del Capítulo 53 del Propheta Isaias*, MSS	Orobio, *Expl. Is. 53*
—— *Prevenciones Divinas contra la vana Idolatría de las Gentes*, MSS	Orobio, *Prev. Div.*
—— *Respuesta a una persona que dudava si el libro de Raymundo Lulio, nuevamente traducido y comentado por don Alonzo de Zepeda era intelligible, y si concluyan sus discursos*, MSS	Orobio, *Resp... Lul.*
—— *Respuesta Apologética al libro que escrivió Don Alonso de Zepeda que intituló Defensa de los términos y doctrina de Raymundo Lulio*, MSS	Orobio, *Resp. al Zep.*
—— *Respuesta a un escrito que prezentó un Predicante Francés a el Author contra la observancia de la Divina Ley de Mosseh*, MSS: Printed by M. B. Amzalak, Coimbra, 1925	Orobio, *Resp. Pred. franc.*
—— *Tratado en que se explica la prophecía de las 70 semanas*, MS	Orobio, *Setenta Sem.*
—— *Discurso sobre la Trinidad*, MS	Orobio, *Trin.*
Translations (18th–19th cents.), see above, Appendix G	
—— *Traité des preventions divines, etc.*, MS	
—— *Dissertation sur le Messié où l'on prouve qu'il n'est pas encore venu, etc.*, MSS	
—— *Explication du cinquante-troisième chapitre d'Isaïe*, MSS	
—— *La Divinité de Jésus-Christ détruite, ou commentaire ... sure le LIIIe chapitre d'Isaïe*, MSS	
—— *Israel Vengé, écrit ... Raphaël Isaac Ione*, MS;	

	Abbreviation
Printed, London, 1770, Paris, 1845; Eng. trans. (*Israel Defended* ...), London, 1838, and (*Israel Avenged*), A. McCaul, Dublin–London, 1839–40	
—— *Sepher Niqmath Yisra'el*, Hebrew trans. by Elisha Ḥanan'el Pontremoli, MS	
—— *Traduction de la prétendue démonstration proposée par Jean Bredembourg, etc.*, MS	
OROBIO A CASTRO, Moses, *Disputatio Medica Inauguralis: De Hydrope*, Leiden, 1678	M. Orobio, *Hydr.*
PABLO de S. Maria, of Burgos, *Scrutinium Scripturarum*, Paris(?), *c.* 1520	Paul of Burgos
PASCAL, Blaise, *Pensées*, ed. Ch. Marc Des Granges, Paris, 1951	Pascal
PAUL(O), *see* PABLO	
PEÑALOSA Y MONDRAGÓN, Benito de, *Libro de las excelencias del español*, Pamplona, 1629	Peñalosa
PENSO VEGA, Joseph, *Rumbos peligrosos*, Antwerp, 1683	Penso, *Rumbos*
—— *Discursos Académicos, Morales, Rethóricos y Sagrados, que recitó en la florida Academia de los Floridos*, Antwerp, 1658	Penso, *Floridos*
—— *'Asirey Ha-Tiqwah*, Amsterdam, 5423 [1663]	Penso, *'As. Ha-Tiq.*
PEREYRA, Abraham Israel, *La Certeza del Camino*, Amsterdam, 5426 [1666]	Pereyra, *Certeza*
—— *Espejo de la vanidad del mundo*, Amsterdam, 5431 [1671]	Pereyra, *Espejo*
PINA, David, *Disputatio Medica Inauguralis: De Pleuritide*, Leiden, 1678	Pina
PINTO DELGADO, João, *Poema de la Reina Ester; Lamentaciones del Profeta Jeremías; Historia de Rut y varias poesías*, Rouen, 1627 (Introd. by I. S. Révah, Lisbon, 1954)	Pinto Delgado
PIZARRO, Abraham Israel, *Sermón que predicó, ... en la Corte del Haya en la Lucidíssima Hesnoga del Señor Baron Suasso, a la fiesta del Hatam (sic) Beressith ... este año de 1702 ...* MS Amsterdam, *EH* 48 D 31	Pizarro
REBOLLEDO, Bernadino de, *Ocios*, Antwerp 1660	Rebolledo
Responsa, Qoves she'eloth u-teshuvoth u-pesaquin meḥakhmey 'ereṣ yisra'el we-ha-Mizraḥ turkhiya 'italia we-'od (Responsa and rabbinical decisions by authorities in Palestine, the Levant, Turkey, Italy, etc), MS Jerusalem Univ. Heb. 8° 2001	Responsa, Palestine, etc.

3. Authors: Primary Sources

	Abbreviation
SASPORTAS, Jacob, *'Ohel Ya'aqov* (Responsa), Amsterdam, 5497 [1737]	Sasportas, *Resp.*
—— *Ṣiṣath Novel Ṣevi*, ed. Y. Tishby, Jerusalem, 5714 [1954]	Sasportas, *Ṣiṣ. N. Ṣ.*
Sermoes ... Amsterdam ... 5435, See *Synagogue, Amsterdam*	
[SPINOZA, Benedictus], *Tractatus Theologico-Politicus*, Hamburg, 1670	Spinoza, *Tract. T.P.*
SPINOZA, Benedictus, *Opera Posthuma*, (Amsterdam), 1677	Spinoza, *Op. Post.*
—— *Opera*, ed. J. van Vloten and J. P. N. Land, 2 vols, The Hague 1882–83	Spinoza, *Opera*
Synagogue, Amsterdam, Sermoes que pregarão os Doctos Ingenios do K. K. de Talmud Torah desta Cidade de Amsterdam, no alegre estreamento e publica celebridade da Fabrica que se consagrou a Deos, para Caza de Oração, cuja entrada se festejou em Sabath Nahamu, Amsterdam, 5435 [1675]	Synagogue, *Serm.*
VÉLEZ DE GUEVARA, Luis, *El diablo cojuelo*, Madrid, 1641	Vélez de Guevara
VEYSSIÈRE DE LA CROZE, Maturin, *Entretiens sur divers sujets d'Histoire et de Religion entre Mylord Bolingbroke et Isaac d'Orobio, Rabin des Juifs Portugais à Amsterdam*, London, 1770	Veyssière, *Entre.*
[——] *Merkwaardig en zonderling mondgesprek tusschen een Gereformeerd Christen en een Portugeesche Jood*, trans. from the French, Amsterdam, 1757	Veyssière, *Mondgespr.*
VOLTAIRE, F., *Oeuvres Complètes*, XXXIV, Paris, 1827	Voltaire
ZACUTO, Abraham, *Sepher Yuḥasin Ha-Shalem*, ed. H. Filipowski, London and Edinburgh, 1857	Zacuto
ZEPEDA, Alonso de, *Defensa de los términos y doctrina de S. Raymundo Lullio sobre el misterio de S. S. S. Trinidad, contra cierto rescribente judío de la Sinagoga de Amsterdam*, Brussels, 1666	Zepeda, *Defensa*
ZURREÑO, Moses, *Discurso*, ed. M. B. Amzalak, 1925	Zurreño

4 AUTHORS: SCHOLARLY LITERATURE

AARON, R. I. *John Locke*[2], Oxford 1963	Aaron
ADLER, E. N., 'Documents sur les Marranes de Portugal et l'Espagne sous Philippe IV', *REJ* 48, 1904, pp. 1–28; 49, 1904, pp. 51–73; 50, 1905, pp.	Adler, *Doc.*

Bibliography

	Abbreviation

53–75, 211–37; 51, 1906, pp. 97–120, 251–64

—— *Auto de Fé and Jew*, Oxford, 1908 — Adler, *Auto de Fé*

—— *Catalogue of Hebrew Manuscripts in the Collection of E. N. Adler*, Cambridge, 1921 — Adler, *Cat.*

AESCOLY, A. Z., *'Ithon flandri 'al 'odoth Shabbethai Ṣevi'*, *Sepher Dinaburg*, Jerusalem, 5709 [1949], pp. 215–36 — Aescoly

AJO Y SAINZ DE ZÚÑIGA, C. M., *Historia de las Universidades hispánicas*, 8 vols., Madrid, 1957–72 — Ajo de Zúñiga

ALTKIRCH, E., *Maledictus und Benedictus*, Leipzig, 1924 — Altkirch

ALTMANN, A., 'Eternality of Punishment: A Theological Controversy within the Amsterdam Rabbinate in the Thirties of the Seventeenth Century', *PAAJR* 40, 1972, pp. 1–88 — Altmann

ALVES, F. M., *Os judeos no distrito de Bragança*, Bragança, 1925 — Alves

AMADOR DE LOS RÍOS, J., *Estudios Históricos y Literarios sobre los judíos de España*, Madrid, 1848 — Amador, *Estudios*

—— *Historia social, política y religiosa de los judíos de España y Portugal*, 3 vols., Madrid, 1875–6 — Amador, *Historia*

AMZALAK, M. B. *Joseph de la Vega e o seu livro Confusión de Confusiones*, Lisbon, 1925 — Amzalak, *Joseph de la Vega*

—— (Ed.), *Hisquijahu da Silva, Del Fundamento de nuestra Ley—Sermón Moral*, Coimbra, 1925 — Amzalak, *da Silva*

—— (Ed.), *Isaac Orobio de Castro, Respuesta a ... un Predicante Francés...*, Coimbra, 1925 — Amzalak, *Resp. Pred. franc.*

—— (Ed.), *Mosseh Zurreño, Discurso*, Lisbon, 1925 — Amzalak, *Zurreño*

—— *Abraham Israel Pereyra*, Lisbon, 1927 — Amzalak, *Pereyra*

ASSAF, S., 'Anusey Sepharad u-portugal be-saphruth ha-Teshuvoth', *Me'asseph Siyyon* 5, 5693 [1933], pp. 19–60 — Assaf, *'Anusey Sepharad*

—— *Be'oholey Ya'aqob*, Jerusalem, 5073 [1943] — Assaf, *Be'oholey Ya'aqob*

ASTON, T., (Ed.), *Crisis in Europe 1560–1660: Essays From Past and Present*, London, 1975 — Aston

AZEVEDO, L.d', *Historia dos Christãos Novos Portugueses*, Lisbon, 1921 (2nd edn., 1975) — Azevedo

BAER, Y. F., *Die Juden im christlichen Spanien*, 2 vols., Berlin 1929–36 — Baer, *Christ. Span.*

—— *A History of the Jews in Christian Spain*, Eng. trans.

4. Authors: Scholarly Literature

	Abbreviation
L. Schoffman, 2 vols., Philadelphia, 1966	
—— *Galut*, New York, 1947	Baer, *Galut*
BARBOSA MACHADO, D., *Biblioteca Lusitana Historica, Critica e Cronologica*, 3 vols., Lisbon, 1741–52	Barbosa Machado
BARBOT, J., *Chroniques de la Faculté de Médicine de Toulouse*, I (1229–1739), Toulouse, 1905	Barbot
BARBOUR, V., *Capitalism in Amsterdam in the 17th Century*, University of Michigan Press, 1966	Barbour
BARNETT, L. D., 'Two Documents of the Inquisition', *JQR* 15, 1924, pp. 213–39	Barnett
BARON, S. W., *A Social and Religious History of the Jews*^{2}, New York, London and Philadelphia, 1952– (vols. I–XVI–)	Baron, *Hist.*
—— 'John Calvin and the Jews', *Harry Austryn Wolfson Jubilee Volume*, Jerusalem, 1965, pp. 141–63. Repr. in Baron's collected articles, *Ancient and Medieval Jewish History*, ed. L. A. Feldman, New Brunswick 1972, pp. 338–52	Baron, *Calvin*
BATAILLON, M., *Erasmo y España*^{2}, Mexico, 1966	Bataillon
BEINART, M., '¿Cuándo llegaron los judíos a España?', *Estudios*, 3, 1961, pp. 5–32	Beinart, *Cuándo llegaron*
—— *Conversos on Trial*, Eng. trans. from the Hebrew edn., Jerusalem, 1981	Beinart, *on Trial*
—— *Te'udoth ha-'inquizisia—maqor le-toledoth ha-'anusim, Divrey ha-'aqademia ha-le-'umith ha-Yisre 'elith la-Madda'im*, 2, 5727 [1967], pp. 150–63	Beinart, *T'udoth*
—— (Ed.), *Be-'iqevoth megorashim wa-'anusim*, Source material for Seminar, The Hebrew University, Jerusalem, 5728 [1968]	Beinart, *Meg.*
—— *Ha-Yisshuv ha-Yehudi he-ḥadash bi-sepharad— reqa' meṣi'uth we-ha'arakhah*, Jerusalem, 5729 [1969]	Beinart, *Yisshuv Ḥadash*
—— 'Parashath ḥayyaw shel ben saloniqi shennithgalgel li-sepharad ba-Me'ah ha-sheva' 'esreh', *Sefunot*, 14, 5730–3 [1970–3], pp. 191–7	Beinart, *Ben saloniqi*
—— 'The Converso Community in 15th century Spain', and 'The Converso community in 16th and 17th century Spain', in *The Sephardi Heritage*, I, ed. R. D. Barnett, 1971, pp. 425–78	Beinart, *Conversos*
—— '*Ha-'inquizisia ha-Sepharadith ha-le'umith bi-*	Beinart, *'Inq. ḥuṣ*

	Abbreviation
phe'ullathahh mi-ḥuṣ li-gevuloth sepharad', Divrey Ha-Qongres ha-'olami ha-ḥamishi le-madda'ey ha-Yahduth, Jerusalem, 1972, pp. 55–73	Sepharad
BEINART, M., *Records of the Trials of the Spanish Inquisition in Ciudad Real*, vol. I (1483–5), vol. II (1494–1512), Jerusalem, 1974–7	Beinart, *Ciudad Real*
—— *'Ri'shoneyha shel london ha-Yehudith'*, Meḥqerey ha-Merqaz le-ḥeqer ha-folklor, 5, Jerusalem, 1975, pp. 11–25	Beinart, *London*
—— *'Halikhatham shel yehudim mi-Maroqo li-sepharad be-re'shith ha-Me'ah ha-Sheva' 'esreh'*, S. W. Baron Festschrift, Jerusalem, 5735 [1975], Hebrew section, pp. 15–39	Beinart, *Yehudey Maroqo*
—— *La Inquisición Española*, Buenos Aires, 1976	Beinart, *Inquisición*
—— 'The Jews in the Canary Islands: A Re-evaluation', *TJHSE* 25, 1977, pp. 48–86	Beinart, *Canary Islands*
—— *'Yeṣi'ath 'anusim me-ḥasi ha-'iy ha-'iveri ba-Me'oth ha-ḥamesh 'esrey—ha-Shesh 'esrey'*, Sepher ha-Zikkaron le-S. Nahon, Jerusalem, 5738 [1978], pp. 63–106	Beinart, *Yeṣi'ath 'anusim*
BELTRÁN DE HEREDIA, V., 'La faculdad de teología en la Universidad de Osuna', *Ciencia Tomista*, 49, 1934, pp. 145–73	Beltrán de Heredia
BENAYAHU, M., *'Yedi'oth me-'iṭalia u-me-holand 'al re'shithahh shel ha-Shabbetha'uth'*, Eretz Israel 4, Jerusalem, 5716 [1956], pp. 109–205	Benayahu, *Yedi'oth*
BEN-SASSON, H. H., 'The Reformation in Contemporary Jewish Eyes', *Proceedings of the Israel Academy of Sciences and Humanities*, iv, 1969/70, pp. 239–326	Ben-Sasson, *Reformation*
—— *'Galuth u-ge'ullah be-'eynaw shel dor goley sepharad'*, Sepher Yovel le-yishaq Baer, Jerusalem, 5721 [1961], pp. 216–27	Ben-Sasson, *Galuth u-ge'ullah*
—— *'Dor goley shepharad 'al 'aṣmo'*, Zion, 26, 5721 [1961], pp. 23–64	Ben-Sasson, *Goley sepharad*
—— *Toledoth 'am yisra'el biymey ha-Beynayim*, Tel Aviv, 5729 [1969]	Ben-Sasson, *Yemey ha-Beynayim*
BERNHEIMER, C., 'Some New Contributions to Abraham Cardoso's Biography', *JQR* 18, 1927/8, pp. 97–129	Bernheimer
BESSO, H. V., *Dramatic Literature of the Sephardic Jews of Amsterdam in the XVIIth and XVIIIth centuries*, New York, 1947	Besso

4. Authors: Scholarly Literature 489

	Abbreviation
BIDERMAN, S., and A. KASHER, '*Ḥerem spinoza*', *Qoloquium meyuḥad le-melo'th shalosh me'oth shanah le-motho shel barukh spinoza*, Tel Aviv University, 1977, pp. 31–58	Biderman and Kasher, *Ḥerem*
BLOOM, H. I., *The Economic Activities of the Jews of Amsterdam in the Seventeenth and Eighteenth Centuries*, Williamsport, 1937	Bloom
BOLIN, W., *Spinoza, Zeit–Leben–Werk*², Darmstadt and Leipzig, 1927	Bolin
BONNO, G., *Lettres inédites de le Clerc à Locke*, University of California, 1959	Bonno
BRUGMANS, H., and FRANK, A., *Geschiedenis der Joden in Nederland*, vol. I, Amsterdam, 1940	Brugmans and Frank
CAMPELO Y ALLUEVA, J., *Reseña histórica de la Universidad de Sevilla*, Seville, 1885	Campelo y Allueva
CARMOLY, E., *Histoire des Médecins Juifs anciens et modernes*, I, Brussels, 1844	Carmoly
CARO BAROJA, J., *Los judíos en la España Moderna y Contemporánea*, 3 vols., Madrid, 1962	Caro Baroja, *Judíos*
—— *La sociedad criptojudía en la corte de Felipe IV*, Madrid, 1963	Caro Baroja, *Sociedad criptoj.*
CARVALHO, J. de, 'Oróbio de Castro e o Espinosismo', *Mémorias da Academia das Ciencias de Lisboa. Classe de letras*, 2, pp. 183–300. Lisbon, 1937 (also separately printed)	Carvalho
CASSUTO, A., 'Aus dem ältesten Protokolbuch der Portugiesich-jüdischen Gemeinde in Hamburg', *JJLG* 7, 1908, pp. 1–54, 159–210; 8, 1910, pp. 227–90; 9, 1911, pp. 318–66; 10, 1913, pp. 255–95; 11, 1916, pp. 1–76; 12, 1920, pp. 55–118	Cassuto, *Protokolb. Hamburg*
—— 'Neue Funde zur ältesten Geschichte der portugiesischen Juden in Hamburg', *ZGJD* 3, 1931, pp. 58–72	Cassuto, *Neue Funde*
CASTRO, A., *Aspectos del vivir hispánico*², Madrid, 1970	Castro, A., *Aspectos*
—— *De la Edad Conflictiva*³, Madrid, 1972	Castro, A., *Edad Confl.*
COHEN, D. E., 'De vroegere Amsterdamsche joodsche Doctoren', *Nederlands Tijdschrift voor Geneeskunde*, 70, 1927, Part ii, no. 14	Cohen, D. E.
COHEN, M. M., *The Martyr: The Story of a Secret Jew and the Mexican Inquisition in the Sixteenth Century*, Philadelphia, 1973	Cohen, M. M.

	Abbreviation
CRANSTON, M., *John Locke, a Biography*, London, 1975	Cranston
DE CASTRO, D. H., *Keur van Grafsteenen op de Nederl. –Portug.–Israël. Begraafplaats te Ouderkerk aan den Amstel*, Leiden, 1883	De Castro D. H., *Grafsteenen*
DECLAREUIL, M., (Ed.), *VIIe Centenaire de la Fondation de l'Université de Toulouse 1229–1929*, Livre d'Or, Toulouse, 1931	Declareuil
DELEITO Y PIÑUELA, J., *La vida religiosa española bajo el cuarto Felipe*, Madrid, 1952	Deleito, *Vida relig.*
—— *También se divierte el Pueblo*, Madrid, 1954	Deleito, *Pueblo*
—— *El Rey se divierte*, Madrid, 1955	Deleito, *Rey*
DENUCE, J., 'Een geheime Synagoge te Antwerpen in de XVIe eeuw', *AA* 2, 1929, pp. 151–4	Denuce
DE ROSSI, G. B., *Biblioteca Judaica Antichristiana*, Parma, 1800	De Rossi, *Bibl. Antichr.*
—— *Dizionario Storico Degli Autori Ebrei e delle loro opere*, 2 vols., Parma, 1802	De Rossi, *Dizionario*
DEVÈZE M., *L'Espagne de Philippe IV (1621–1665)*, 2 vols., Paris, 1971	Devèze
DIBON, P., (Ed.), *Pierre Bayle, le Philosophe de Rotterdam*, Amsterdam, 1959	Dibon
DOMÍNGUEZ ORTIZ, A., 'El proceso inquisitorial de Juan Núñez Saravia, banquero de Felipe IV', *Hispania*, 61, 1955, pp. 559–81	Dom. Ortiz, *Saravia*
—— *La clase social de los conversos en Castilla en la edad moderna*, Madrid, 1955	Dom. Ortiz, *Conversos*
—— *Política y hacienda de Felipe IV*, Madrid, 1960	Dom. Ortiz, *Felipe IV*
—— *La Sociedad Española en el siglo XVII*, 2 vols., Madrid, 1964–70	Dom. Ortiz, *Sociedad Esp.*
—— *Los Judeoconversos en España y América*, Madrid, 1971	Dom. Ortiz, *Judeoconversos*
DOMÍNGUEZ ORTIZ, A., and F. AGUILAR PIÑAL, *Historia de Sevilla*, vol. IV, Seville, 1976	Dom. Ortiz and Ag. Piñal
DUNIN BORKOWSKI, S. van, *Spinoza*, vol. II part i, Münster, 1933	Dunin Borkowski
ELLIOT, J. H., *Imperial Spain, 1469–1716*, Pelican Books, 1970	Elliot, *Spain*
—— 'Self-Perception and Decline in Early Seventeenth-Century Spain', *Past and Present*, 74, 1977, pp. 41–61	Elliot, *Self-Perception*

4. Authors: Scholarly Literature

Abbreviation

EMMANUEL, I. S., 'Qesharim beyn qehilloth saloniqi we-'amsṭerdam', *Ganzakh Saloniqi, Qoves*, 1, Tel Aviv, 5721 [1961], pp. 24–33 — Emmanuel, *Saloniqi we-'Amsṭ.*

—— 'Siyyu'an shel qehilloth ha-Sepharadim be-'amsṭerdam we-qurasao le-"'ereṣ ha-Qedoshah" we-li-sephat', *Sefunot* 6, 5722 [1962], pp. 401–24 — Emmanuel, *Siyyu'an shel 'Amsṭ.*

—— 'Seventeenth-Century Brazilian Jewry: A Critical Review', *AJA* 14, 1964, pp. 32–65 — Emmanuel, *Brazilian Jewry*

—— 'Les Juifs de la Martinique et leurs coreligionnaires d'Amsterdam au XVIIᵉ siècle', *REJ* 123, 1964, pp. 511–16 — Emmanuel, *Martinique*

—— 'Yedi'oth ḥadashoth al ha-Qehillah ha-Portugezith me'amsṭerdam', *'Oṣar yehudey sepharad*, 6, 5723 [1963], pp. 160–82 — Emmanuel, *Yedi'oth*

EMMANUEL, I. S., and S. A., *History of the Jews of the Netherlands Antilles*, 2 vols., Cincinnati, 1970 — Emmanuel, I. S. and S. A., *Antilles*

ESAGUY, A. d', *Apontamentos da História da Medecina*, Lisbon, 1931 — Esaguy, *Hist. Med.*

—— 'Orobio de Castro', *RHMH* 2, Sept./Dec. 1948, pp. 15–19 — Esaguy, *Orobio de Castro*

ETTINGER, S., 'The Beginning of Change in the Attitude of European Society towards the Jews', *Scripta Hierosolymitana*, 7, 1961, pp. 192–219 — Ettinger, *Change*

—— 'Yehudim we-yahduth be-'eyney ha-De'istim ha-'angliyyim ba-Me'ah ha-Shemoneh 'esrey', *Zion*, 29, 5724 [1964], pp. 182–207 — Ettinger, *De'istim*

—— *Toledoth 'am yisra'el ba-'eth ha-ḥadashah*, Tel Aviv, 5729 [1969] — Ettinger, *Toledoth*

FARINELLI, A., *Marrano: Storia di un vituperio*, Geneva, 1925 — Farinelli

FISHLOCK, A. D. H., 'The Rabbinic Material in the "Ester" of Pinto Delgado', *JJS* 2, 1950, pp. 37–50 — Fishlock

FRANCÈS, M., *Spinoza dans les pays Neerlandais de la seconde moitié du XVIIᵉ siècle*, vol. I, Paris, 1937 — Francès

FRANCO MENDES, D. (*Ḥophshi*), 'Toledoth he-ḥakham ha-mepho'ar 'Orovyo zikhrono li-verakhah', *Ha-me'assef*, 5548 [1788], pp. 155–174 — Franco Mendes, *'Orovyo*

FRIEDENWALD, H., *The Jews and Medicine*, 2 vols., Baltimore, 1944 — Friedenwald, *Jews and Medicine*

—— *Jewish Luminaries in Medical History and a Catalogue of Works bearing on the Jews and Medicine from the Private Library of H. Friedenwald*, Baltimore, 1946 — Friedenwald, *Cat.*

Bibliography

	Abbreviation
FUKS, L., and R. G. FUKS-MANSFELD, *Hebrew and Judaic Manuscripts in Amsterdam Public Collections*, I, *Catalogue of the Bibliotheca Rosenthaliana University Library of Amsterdam*, Leiden, 1973	Fuks-M., *Ros.*
—— *Hebrew and Judaic Manuscripts in Amsterdam Public Collections*, II, *Catalogue of the Manuscripts of Ets Haim/Livraria Montezinos Sephardic Community of Amsterdam*, Leiden, 1975	Fuks-M., *EH*
—— (Eds.), 'D. Franco Mendes, *Memorias do Establecimiento e progreso dos judeos portuguezes e espanhoes nesta famosa cidade de Amsterdam*', with philological commentary etc. by B. N. Teensma, *SR* 9, no. 2, July 1975	Fuks-M., *Franco Mendes*
GANS, M. H. *Memorboek, Platenatlas van het leven der Joden in Nederland van de middeleeuwen tot 1940*, Baarn, 1971; Eng. edn., 1977.	Gans, *Memorb.*
GARCÍA PERES, D. *Catálogo razonado biográfico y bibliográfico de los autores portugueses que escribieron en castellano*, Madrid, 1890	García Peres
GATES, E. J., 'Three Gongoristic Poets: Anastasio Pantaleón de Ribera, Juan de Tamayo Salazar and Miguel de Barrios', *Estudios dedicados a Menéndez Pidal*, vol. II, Madrid, 1951, pp. 383–95	Gates
GAY, P., *The Enlightenment: An Interpretation*, vol. I, New York, 1973	Gay
GEBHARDT, C., *Die Schriften des Uriel da Costa*, Amsterdam, Heidelberg and London, 1922	Gebhardt, *Uriel da Costa*
—— 'Juan de Prado', *Chronicon Spinozanum*, 3, The Hague, 1923, pp. 269–91	Gebhardt, *Prado*
GEYL, P., *The Netherlands in the Seventeenth Century*, vols. I–II, London, 1961–4	Geyl, *Netherlands 17th Cent.*
—— *The Revolt of the Netherlands (1555–1609)*², London, 1962	Geyl, *Revolt*
—— *History of the Low Countries*, London, 1964	Geyl, *Low Countries*
GIGAS, E., *Grev Bernadino de Rebolledo, Spansk gesandt in Kjøbenhaven 1648–1659*, Copenhagen, 1883	Gigas
GLASER, E., 'Referencias antisemitas en la literatura peninsular de la Edad de Oro', *NRFH* 8, 1954, pp. 39–62	Glaser, *Ref. antisem.*
—— 'Invitation to intolerance: A Study of the Portuguese sermons preached at autos-da-fe', *HUCA* 27, 1956, pp. 327–85	Glaser, *Auto da fe sermons*

4. Authors: Scholarly Literature

Abbreviation

—— 'Two Notes on the Hispano-Jewish Poet Don Miguel de Barrios', *REJ* 124, 1965, pp. 201–11 — Glaser, *De Barrios*

—— *Portuguese Studies*, Paris, 1976 — Glaser, *Port. Studies*

GOTTHEIL, R. J. H., 'Gleanings from the Spanish and Portuguese Archives', *JQR* (OS) 14, 1901/2, pp. 80–95 — Gottheil, *Gleanings*

—— 'The Jews and the Spanish Inquisition (1622–1721)', *JQR* (OS) 15, 1902/3, pp. 182–250 — Gottheil, *Inquisition*

GRACIA BOIX, R., *Autos de Fe y Causas de la Inquisición de Córdoba*, Córdoba, 1983 — Gracia Boix

GRAETZ, H., 'Don Balthasar Isaak Orobio de Castro', *MGWJ* 16, 1867, pp. 321–30 — Graetz, *Orobio*

—— *Geschichte der Juden*, 11 vols., Leipzig, 1879–1911; Eng. trans. by Bella Löwy, 6 vols., Philadelphia 1891–8; Hebrew trans. by S. P. Rabinowitz, 1890–9 — Graetz, *Geschichte* (+ *Eng. trans., Heb. trans.*)

GREEN, O. H., *Spain and the Western Tradition*, 4 vols., Madison and Milwaukee, 1964 — Green

HALEY, K. H. D., *The Dutch in the Seventeenth Century*, London, 1972 — Haley

HALKIN, A. S., 'A *Contra Christianos* by a Marrano', *M. M. Kaplan Jubilee Volume*, New York, 1953, Eng. section pp. 399–416 — Halkin

HAMPSHIRE, S., *Spinoza*, London and Tonbridge, 1967 — Hampshire

HARRISON, A. W., *The Beginnings of Arminianism*, London, 1926 — Harrison

HAVER DROEZE, J. J., *Het Collegium Medicum Amstelaedamense 1637–1798*, Haarlem, 1921 — Haver Droeze

HAZARD, P., *La Crise de la conscience européenne*, Paris, 1935 — Hazard

HERCULANO, A., *Da origem e establecimiento da Inquisição em Portugal*, 3 vols., Lisbon, 1854–9 — Herculano

HERNÁNDEZ MOREJÓN, A., *Historia bibliográfica de la medicina española*, 7 vols., Madrid, 1842–52 — Hernández Morejón

HERRERO GARCÍA, M., *Ideas de los Españoles del siglo XVII*, Madrid, 1966 — Herrero García

HIRSCHFELD, H., *Descriptive Catalogue of the Hebrew MSS. of the Montefiore Library* [deposited in Jews' College, London], London, 1904 — Hirschfeld

HUIZINGA, J., *Dutch Civilisation in the Seventeenth Century and other essays*, sel. P. Geyl and F. W. N. Hugenholtz, New York and Evanston, 1969 — Huizinga

Bibliography

	Abbreviation
HUSIK, I., 'The Law of Nature, Grotius and the Bible', *HUCA* 2, 1925, pp. 381–417	Husik
JIMÉNEZ, A., *Historia de la Universidad Española*, Madrid, 1971	Jiménez
JOURDAIN, C., *L'Université de Toulouse au XVIIe siècle*, Paris, 1862	Jourdain
KAGAN, R. L., 'Universities in Castille 1500–1700', *Past and Present*, 49, 1970, pp. 44–71	Kagan, *Universities*
—— *Students and Society in Early Modern Spain*, Baltimore and London, 1974	Kagan, *Students*
KAMEN, H., *The Spanish Inquisition*, New York, 1965	Kamen
KAPLAN Y., 'Yaḥsahh shel hanhagath ha-Qehillah ha-Portugezith be-'amsterdam la-Tenu'ah ha-Shabbetha'ith, TK"H-TL"A', *Zion*, 39, 5734 [1947], pp. 198–216	Kaplan, *Shabbetha'uth*
—— 'R. sha'ul levi morṭera we-ḥibburo "te'anoth we-hassagoth neged ha-Dath ha-Noṣerith', *Meḥqarim 'al toledoth yahduth holand* 1, 5735 [1975], Jerusalem, pp. 9–31	Kaplan, *Morṭera*
—— 'Nueva información sobre la estancia de Juan de Prado en Amberes', *Sefarad*, 35, 1975, pp. 159–163	Kaplan, *Prado*
—— 'Meqomo shel ha-rav mosheh repha'el d'agilar be-masseketh kesharav im pelitey sepharad u-porṭugal ba-Me'ah ha-Sheva' 'esreh', *Divrey ha-Qongres ha-'olami ha-Shisshi le-madda'ey ha-Yahduth*, Jerusalem, 5736 [1976], vol. II, pp. 95–106	Kaplan, *d'Aguilar*
—— 'El testimonio de Baltasar Alvarez de Orobio sobre la peste de Málaga en 1637', *Helmantica*, 29, 1978, pp. 212–31	Kaplan, *peste de Málaga*
—— 'Studenṭim yehudim me-'amsterdam be-'universiṭath leiden ba-Me'ah ha-Sheva' 'esrey', *Meḥqarim 'al toledoth yehudey holand*, 2, 5739 [1979], Jerusalem, pp. 65–75	Kaplan, *Studenṭim be-leiden*
—— 'Qeliṭatham shel gerim ba-Qehilah ha-Portugezith be-'amsterdam ba-Me'ah ha-Y"Z- parashath lorenzo 'escudero', *Proceeding of the Seventh World Congress of Jewish Studies, History of the Jews in Europe*, Jerusalem, 1981, pp. 87–101	Kaplan, *Escudero*
KAHSER, A., and S. BIDERMAN, 'When was Spinoza banned?' *SR* 12, i, 1978, pp. 212–31	Kasher and Biderman, *Spinoza*
KATZ, J., *Exclusiveness and Tolerance: Studies in Jewish–Gentile Relations*, Scripta Judaica iii, Oxford, 1961	Katz, *Exclusiveness*

4. Authors: Scholarly Literature

	Abbreviation
—— 'Yisra'el 'aph 'al pi she-ḥaṭa' yisra'el hu', *Tarbiz* 27, 5718 [1958], pp. 203–17	Katz, *Yisra'el she-ḥaṭa*
—— 'Sheloshah mishpaṭim 'apologeṭi'im be-gilguleyhem', *Zion*, 23/24, 5718/19 [1958/59], pp. 174–93	Katz, *Mishp. 'apolog.*
—— *Tradition and Crisis*, New York, 1961	Katz, *Tradition and Crisis*
KAYSERLING, M., *Ein Feiertag in Madrid. Zur Geschichte der Spanisch-Portugiesischen Juden*, Berlin, 1859	Kayserling, *Madrid Feiertag*
—— *Sephardim. Romanische Poesien der Juden in Spanien*, Leipzig, 1859	Kayserling, *Sephardim*
—— 'Analekten zur Literatur der spanisch-portugiesischen Juden: Moses Raphael de Aguilar', *MGWJ* 9, 1860, pp. 397–400	Kayserling, *Aguilar*
—— *Geschichte der Juden in Portugal*, Leipzig, 1867	Kayserling, *Geschichte*
—— 'Une Historie de la littérature juive de Daniel Levi de Barrios', *REJ* 18, 1889, pp. 276–89; 32, 1896, pp. 88–101	Kayserling, *De Barrios*
—— *Biblioteca española-portugueza judaica*, Strasbourg 1890	Kayserling, *Biblioteca*
—— 'Notes sur la littérature de Juifs hispano-portugais', *REJ* 22, 1891, pp. 119–24	Kayserling, *Notes*
—— 'The Earliest Rabbis and Jewish Writers of America', *PAJHS* 3, 1895, pp. 13–20	Kayserling, *America*
—— 'R. yiṣḥaq abo'ab ha-Shelishi, toledothav we-shirav', *Hagoren* 3, 5662 [1902], pp. 155–74	Kayserling, *Isaac Aboab III*
KELLENBENZ, H., *Sephardim an der unteren Elbe*, Wiesbaden, 1958	Kellenbenz
KING, P., *The Life and letters of John Locke*², London, 1864	King, P., *Locke*
KING, W. F., *Prosa novelística y academias literarias en el siglo XVII*, Madrid, 1963	King, W. F.
KNIGHT, W. S., *Life and works of Hugo Grotius*, London, 1925	Knight
KOENEN, H. J., *Geschiedenis der Joden in Nederland*, Utrecht, 1843	Koenen
KOLAKOWSKI, L., *Chrétiens san église: la conscience religieuse et le lien confessionnal au XVII ͤ siècle*, French trans. from the Polish, Paris, 1969	Kolakowski
KUHN, A. K., 'Hugo Grotius and the Emancipation of the Jews in Holland', *PAJHS* 31, 1928, pp. 173–80	Kuhn

Bibliography

	Abbreviation
LAPEYRE, H., *Géographie de l'Espagne Morisque*, Paris, 1959	Lapeyre
LASCARIS COMNENO, C., *Colegios Mayores*, Madrid, 1952	Lascaris Comneno
LEA, H. C., *History of the Inquisition of Spain*, 4 vols., New York, 1907	Lea
LEMOS, M., *Amato Lusitano: a sua vida e sua obra*, Oporto, 1907	Lemos, *Am. Lusitano*
—— *Zacuto Lusitano*, Oporto, 1909	Lemos, *Zac. Lusitano*
LEVI, Z., *Spinoza u-musag ha-Yahduth*, Tel Aviv, 5732 [1972]	Levi
LIBERMAN, K., 'La Découverte d'une synagogue secrète à Anvers à la fin du dix-septième siècle', *REJ* 100, 1935, pp. 36–48	Liberman
LINZ, J. J., 'Intellectual Roles in Sixteenth and Seventeenth Century Spain', in S. N. Eisenstadt and S. R. Graubard (eds.), *Intellectuals and Tradition*, New York, 1973, part ii, pp. 59–108	Linz
LIVERMORE, H. V., *A History of Portugal*, Cambridge, 1947	Livermore
LLORCA, B., *La Inquisición en España*, Barcelona, 1954	Llorca
LYNCH, J., *Spain under the Habsburgs*, 2 vols., Oxford, 1964–9	Lynch
MADRE, A., *Die theologische Polemik gegen Raimundus Lullus*, Münster, 1973	Madre
MARAÑÓN, G., *El Conde-Duque de Olivares*⁴, Madrid, 1959	Marañón
MARAVALL, J. A., *La Teoría española del estado en el siglo XVII*, Madrid, 1944	Maravall, *Teoría del estado*
—— *Estudios de Historia del Pensamiento Español. Siglo XVII*, Madrid, 1975	Maravall, *Pensamiento esp.*
MARX, A., 'The Polemical Manuscripts in the Library of the Jewish Theological Seminary of America', *Studies in Jewish Bibliography and Related Subjects, In Memory of Abraham Solomon Freidus*, New York, 1929, pp. 247–78	Marx
MATUTE i LUQUIN, G., *Colección de los Autos Generales i Particulares de Fé, Celebrados por el Tribunal de la Inquisición de Córdoba*, Córdoba, s.a.	Matute i Luquin
MÉCHOULAN, H., 'L'Alterité juive dans la pensée espagnole (1550–1650)', *SR* 8, 1974, pp. 31–8,	Méchoulan, *Alterité juive*

4. Authors: Scholarly Literature

	Abbreviation
—— 'Nouveaux élements dans la controverse des status de pureté de sang en Espagne au XVIIᵉ siècle', *SR* 10, no. 2, 1976, pp. 142–50	Méchoulan, *pureté de sang*
—— 'Spinoza face à quelques textes d'origine marrane', *Raison Présente*, 43, 1977, pp. 13–24	Méchoulan, *Spinoza*
—— 'Quelques Remarques sur le Marranisme et la rupture spinoziste', *SR* 11, no. 2, 1977, pp. 113–25	Méchoulan, *Marranisme*
—— *Le Sang de l'autre ou l'honneur de Dieu*, Paris, 1979	Méchoulan, *Honneur de Dieu*
—— 'Un regard sur la pensée juive à Amsterdam au temps de Spinoza', *Cahiers Spinoza*, 3, 1979, pp. 51–66	Méchoulan, *pensée juive*
—— 'Le Herem à Amsterdam et l'excommunication de Spinoza', *Cahiers Spinoza*, 3, 1979, pp. 117–34	Méchoulan, *Herem*
MEIJER, J., *Encyclopaedia Sefardica Neerlandica*, 2 vols., Amsterdam, 1949–50	Meijer, *Enc.*
—— 'Hugo Grotius' *Remonstrantie*', *JSS* 17, 1955, pp. 91–104	Meijer, *Grotius*
MEINSMA, K. O., *Spinoza en zijn kring*, The Hague, 1896	Meinsma
MENDES DOS REMEDIOS, J., *Os Judeus em Portugal*, vol. I Coimbra, 1895, vol. II Lisbon, 1928	Mendes dos Remedios, *Judeus em Port.*
—— *Os Judeus Portugueses em Amsterdam*, Coimbra, 1911	Mendes dos Remedios, *Judeus em Amst.*
MENÉNDEZ Y PELAYO, M., *Historia de los Heterodoxos Españoles*, 5 vols., Santander, 1947	Menéndez y Pelayo, *Heterodoxos*
—— *La Ciencia Española*, 3 vols., Santander, 1953–54	Menéndez y Pelayo, *Ciencia*
MERRY Y COLÓN, M., *Del origen, fundación, privilegios y excelencias de la Universidad de Osuna*, Madrid, 1868	Merry y Colón
MOLCHO, J. R., '*Ha-Qehilloth ha-Sepharadiyyoth ba-Tephuṣoth: 'amsṭerdam'*, *'Oṣar yehudey sepharad*, 4, 1961, pp. 59–77	Molcho
M[ONTERO] DE E[SPINOSA], J. M., *Relación histórica de la judería de Sevilla, establecimiento de la inquisición en ella, su estinción y colección de los autos que llamaban de fé celebrados desde su erección*, Seville, 1849	Montero de Espinosa
MOORAT, S. A. J., *Catalogue of Western Manuscripts on Medicine and Science in the Wellcome Historical Medical Library*, 2 vols., London, 1973	Moorat

Bibliography

	Abbreviation
MOREL-FATIO, M. A., *Catalogue des manuscrits espagnoles et des manuscrits portugais* [de la Bibliothèque Nationale], Paris, 1892	Morel-Fat.
MURRAY, J. J., *Amsterdam in the Age of Rembrandt*, University of Oklahoma, 1967	Murray
NAHON, G., 'Les Sephardim, les Marranes, les inquisitions péninsulaires et leurs archives dans les travaux récents de I. S. Révah', *REJ* 132, 1973, pp. 5–48	Nahon, *Révah*
—— 'Les Rapports des communautés judeo-portugaises de France avec celle d'Amsterdam au XVIIe et XVIIIe siècles', *SR* 10, no. i, 1976, pp. 37–78, no. 2, pp. 175–88	Nahon, *Rapports France–Amst.*
—— 'Les Marranes espagnols et portugais et les communautés juives issues du marranisme dans l'historiographie récente (1960–1975)', *REJ* 136, 1977, pp. 297–367	Nahon, *Marranes*
—— 'Amsterdam, métropole occidentale des Sefarades au XVIIe siècle', *Cahiers Spinoza*, 3, 1979, pp. 15–50	Nahon, *Amsterdam*
NAUERT, Ch. G., jun., *Agrippa and the Crisis of Renaissance Thought*, Urbana, 1965	Nauert
NETANYAHU, B., *The Marranos of Spain from the late XIVth to the early XVth century*, New York, 1966	Netanyahu, *Marranos*
—— *Don Isaac Abravanel*[3], Philadelphia, 1972	Netanyahu, *Abravanel*
NEUBAUER, A., *Catalogue of the Hebrew Manuscripts in the Bodleian Library and in the College Libraries of Oxford*, 2 vols, Oxford, 1886, 1906	Neubauer, *Bodl. Cat.*
NEUBAUER, A., and S. R. DRIVER, *The Fifty-Third Chapter of Isaiah according to the Jewish Interpreters*, 2 vols., London and Oxford 1876–7; Repr., with Prolegomenon by Raphael Loewe, New York, 1969	Neubauer and Driver
OELMAN, T., 'Antonio Enríquez Gómez's, "*Romance al divin mártir, Judá Creyente*", Edited text with introduction', *JJS* 26, 1975, pp. 113–31	Oelman
OLLION, M. H., and T. J. DE BOER, *Lettres inédites de John Locke, à ses amis Nicholas Thoynard, Philippe van Limborch et Edward Clarke*, The Hague, 1912	Ollion and De Boer
PEETERS-FONTAINAS, J., *Bibliographie des impressions espagnols des Pays-Bas Méridionaux*, 2 vols., Nieuwkoop, 1965	Peeters-Fontainas

4. Authors: Scholarly Literature

	Abbreviation
PIETERSE, W. Ch., 'Enige eigenhandig geschreven brieven van de dichter-geschiedschrijver Daniel Levi de Barrios', *De Opbouw*, 16, no. 1, 1962, pp. 8	Pieterse, *Brieven van De Barrios*
—— 'De "Joodsche Natie" anno 1668 verzoekt belastingverlaging', *De Opbouw*, 19, no. 3, 1966, p. 177	Pieterse, *Joodsche Natie*
—— *Daniel Levi de Barrios als geschiedschrijver van de Portugees-Israelitische Gemeente te Amsterdam in zijn 'Triumpho del Govierno Popular'*, Amsterdam 1968	Pieterse, *De Barrios*
—— *Livro de Bet Haim do Kahal Kados de Bet Yahacob*. Original Text, Introd., notes, and index, Assen, 1970	Pieterse, *Livro de Bet Haim*
PINTA LLORENTE, M. de la, *Proceso criminal contra el hebraísta salmantino Martín Martínez de Cantalapiedra*, Madrid, 1946	Pinta Llorente, *Proceso*
—— *La Inquisición Española*, Madrid, 1948	Pinta Llorente, *Inquis. esp.*
—— *Las cárceles inquisitoriales españolas*, Madrid, 1949	Pinta Llorente, *Cárceles inquis.*
PLATZECK, E. W., *Raimund Lull. Sein Leben—seine Werke. Die Grundlagen seines Denkens*, 2 vols., Düsseldorf, 1962-4	Platzeck
POHL, H., *Die Portugiesen in Antwerpen (1567–1648): Zur Geschichte einer Minderheit*, Wiesbaden, 1977	Pohl
POLLOCK, F., *Spinoza: His Life and Philosophy*, London, 1899	Pollock
POPKIN, R. H., 'Pierre Bayle's place in 17th century Scepticism', *see* DIBON, pp. 1–19	Popkin, *Bayle and Scepticism*
—— *The History of Scepticism from Erasmus to Descartes*, rev. edn., New York, Evanston and London, 1964	Popkin, *Scepticism Erasmus–Descartes*
—— 'Scepticism, Theology and the Scientific Revolution in the Seventeenth Century', *Problems in the Philosophy of Science*, Amsterdam, 1968, pp. 1–28	Popkin, *Scientific Revolution*
—— 'The Historical Significance of Sephardic Judaism in 17th century Amsterdam', *The American Sephardi*, 5, nos. 1–2, 1971, pp. 18–27	Popkin, *Historical Significance*
—— 'The Marrano Theology of Isaac La Peyrère', *Studi Internazionali di Filosofia*, 5, 1973, pp. 97–125	Popkin, *Peyrère*
—— 'Menasseh ben Israel and Isaac La Peyrère', *SR* 8, no. 1, 1974, pp. 59–63	Popkin, *Men. b. I. and Peyrère*
—— 'The Development of Religious Scepticism and	Popkin, *Peyrère's*

	Abbreviation
the Influence of Isaac La Peyrère's Pre-Adamism and Bible Criticism', in R. R. Bolgar (ed.), *Classical Influences on European Culture, 1500–1700*, Cambridge, 1976, pp. 271–80	*Pre-Adamism*
——— *The History of Scepticism from Erasmus to Spinoza*, Berkeley, Los Angeles, London, 1979	Popkin, *Scepticism Erasmus-Spinoza*
See also BAYLE, *Selections*	
PRINS, F., 'Joden te Antwerpen in 1682–1694', *Bijdragen tot de Geschiedenis*, 28, 1937, pp. 166–74	Prins
RANUM, O. and P., (Eds.), *The Century of Louis XIV*, New York, Evanston, San Francisco, London, 1972	Ranum
RASHDALL, H., *The Universities of Europe in the Middle Ages*², 3 vols., Oxford, 1936	Rashdall
RÉVAH, I. S., 'Les Juifs et les courants spirituels espagnols au XVIᵉ siecle', *REJ* 103, 1938, pp. 97–101	Révah, *courants spirituels*
——— For *Ropicapnefma*, see DE BARROS	
——— 'Une Famille de "nouveaux-chrétiens": les Bocarro-Frances', *REJ* 116, 1957, pp. 73–87	Révah, *Bocarro-Frances*
——— 'Spinoza et les hérétiques de la communauté judéo-portugaise d'Amsterdam', *RHR* 154, 1958, pp. 173–218	Révah, *Spinoza*
——— *Spinoza et le Dr. Juan de Prado*, Paris and The Hague, 1959	Révah, *Spinoza et Prado*
——— 'Les Marranes', *REJ* 118, 1959/60, pp. 29–77	Révah, *Marranes*
——— 'Pour l'histoire des "Nouveaux-Chrétiens" portugais: La relation généalogique de I. de M. Aboab', *Boletim International de Bibliografia Luso-Brasileira* II, 1961, pp. 276–312	Révah, *généal. de I. Aboab*
——— 'Autobiographie d'un Marrane: Edition partielle d'un manuscrit de João (Moseh) Pinto Delgado', *REJ* 119, 1961, pp. 41–130 (*see also* PINTO DELGADO, João)	Révah, *Pinto Delgado*
——— 'La religion d'Uriel da Costa, Marrane de Porto', *RHR* 156, 1962, pp. 45–76	Révah, *Uriel da Costa*
——— 'Un pamphlet contre l'Inquisition d'Antonio Enríquez Gómez: la seconde partie de la "*Política Angélica*" Rouen 1647)', *REJ* 121, 1962, pp. 81–168	Révah, *A. Enríques Gómez*
——— 'Pour l'histoire des Marranes à Anvers: recensements de la "Nation Portugaise" de 1571 à 1666', *REJ* 122, 1963, pp. 123–47	Révah, *'Nation Port.' à Anvers*
——— 'La Playdoyer en faveur des "Nouveaux Chrétiens" de Licencié Martín González de	Révah, *M. González de Cellorigo*

4. Authors: Scholarly Literature

	Abbreviation
Cellorigo (Madrid 1619)', *REJ* 122, 1963, pp. 279–398	
—— 'Aux origines de la rupture Spinozienne: nouveaux documents sur l'incroyance dans la communauté Judéo-Portugaise à Amsterdam à l'époque de l'excommunication de Spinoza', *REJ* 123, 1964, pp. 359–431	Révah, *Rupture Spinozienne*
—— 'Les Écrivains Manuel de Pina et Miguel de Barrios et la censure de la communauté Judéo-Portugaise d'Amsterdam', *Tesoro de los Judíos Españoles*, vol. VIII, 1965, pp. 74–91	Révah, *Censure de la communauté*
—— 'Orobio de Castro et sa famille au prises avec l'Inquisition Espagnole', *BMGJWN* 9, 1965, pp. 87–90	Révah, *Orobio aux prises*
—— 'L'Hérésie Marrane dans l'Europe catholique de 15ᵉ au 18ᵉ siècle', in *Hérésies et sociétés dans l'Europe préindustrielle 15ᵉ–18ᵉ siècles*, ed. J. Le Goff, The Hague, 1968, pp. 327–37	Révah, *Hérésie Marrane*
—— 'Aux origines de la rupture spinozienne: nouvel examen des origines du déroulement et des conséquences de l'affaire Spinoza–Prado–Ribera', *ACF* 70, 1970, pp. 562–68; 71, 1971, pp. 574–87; 72, 1972, 641–53	Révah, *rupt. spin.*, *nouvel examen*
—— 'Les Marranes Portugais et l'Inquisition au XVIᵉ siècle', in *The Sephardi Heritage*, vol. I, ed. R. D. Barnett, London, 1971, pp. 479–526	Révah, *Marranes et l'Inquisition*
RIBEIRO dos SANTOS, A., 'Memorias da Litteratura sagrada dos judeus Portuguezes no seculo XVII', *Memorias de Litteratura Portugueza publicadas pela Academia Real das Sciencias de Lisboa*, vol. III, Lisbon, 1792, pp. 227–373	Ribeiro dos Santos
RIVKIN, E., *Leon de Modena and the Kol Sakhal*, Cincinnati, 1952	Rivkin
ROCA, P., *Catálogo de los Manuscritos que pertenecieron a D. Pascual de Gayangos, existentes hoy en la Biblioteca Nacional*, Madrid, 1904	Roca
RODRÍGUEZ de CASTRO, J. *Biblioteca española*, vol. I, Madrid, 1781	Rodríguez de Castro
RODRÍGUEZ MARÍN, F., 'Cervantes y la Universidad de Osuna', *Homenaje a Menéndez y Pelayo*, vol. II, Madrid, 1889, pp. 757–819	Rodríguez Marín
ROGENT, E., and E. DURÁN, *Bibliografía de les impressiones Lullianes*, Barcelona, 1927	Rogent and Durán

	Abbreviation
ROSENTHAL, J., 'Saphruth ha-Wikkuaḥ ha-'antinoserith 'ad soph ha-Me'ah ha-Shemoneh 'esreh', Aresheth, 2, 5720 [1960], pp. 130–79; 3, 5721 [1971], pp. 433–39	Rosenthal
ROTH, C., 'Immanuel Aboab's Proselytization of the Marranos', JQR 23, 1932, pp. 121–62	Roth, C., Immanuel Aboab's Proselytization
—— A Life of Menasseh ben Israel, Philadelphia, 1934	Roth, C., Men. b. I.
—— 'João Pinto Delgado—A Literary Disentanglement', MLR 30, 1935, pp. 19–25	Roth, C., João Pinto Delgado
—— 'Abraham Núñez Bernal et autres martyrs contemporains de l'Inquisition', REJ 100 bis, 1936, pp. 38–51	Roth, C., A. Núñez Bernal
—— 'The Jewish Ancestry of Michel de Montaigne', in C. Roth, Personalities and Events in Jewish History, Philadelphia, 1953, pp. 212–25 (Rep. from Revue des Cours et Conferences and Bulletin de la Societé des Amis de Montaigne, both 1937)	Roth, C., Michel de Montaigne
—— A History of the Marranos³, New York, 1966	Roth, C., Marranos
—— 'Dath u-marṭirologia beyn ha-'anusim', Milḥemeth qodesh u-marṭirologia be-toledoth yisra'el u-be-toledoth ha-'ammim, Jerusalem, 5728 [1968], pp. 93–105	Roth, C., Dath u-marṭirologia
ROTH, L. (=H. Y.), Spinoza, London, 1929 (repr., 1954)	Roth, L., Spinoza
ROWEN, H. H., The Low Countries in Early Modern Times: A Documentary History, New York, Evanston, San Francisco and London, 1972	Rowen
RUBENS, A., A Jewish Iconography, London, 1954; rev. ed., London, 1981	Rubens, Iconography (+ rev. edn.)
RUBIO, J., 'Notas sobre la vida y obras del Capitán Miguel de Barrios', MEAH 5, 1956, pp. 199–224	Rubio
RÚJULA Y DE OCHOTORENA, J., Indice de los Colegiales del Mayor de San Ildefonso y Menores de Alcalá, Madrid, 1946	Rújula de Ochotorena
RUSSELL, P. E., (Ed.), Spain: A Companion to Spanish Studies, London, 1973	Russell
SALOMON, H. P., 'New Light on the Portuguese Inquisition: The Second Reply to the Archbishop of Cranganore', SR 5, no. 2, 1971, pp. 178–86	Salomon, Reply to Cranganore
—— 'The Portuguese Inquisition and its Victims in the Light of Recent Polemics', JAPCS Summer–Fall 1971, pp. 19–28, 50–55	Salomon, Portuguese Inquisition

4. Authors: Scholarly Literature 503

	Abbreviation
—— 'The "De Pinto" Manuscript: A 17th century Marrano Family History', *SR* 9, no. 1, 1975, pp. 1–62	Salomon, *De Pinto MS*
—— 'Haham Saul Levi Morteira en de Portugese Nieuw-Christenen', *SR* 10, no. 2, 1976, pp. 127–41	Salomon, *Mortera*
SÁNCHEZ, J., *Academias literarias del siglo de Oro español*, Madrid, 1961	Sánchez
SARAIVA, A. J., *Inquisição e Cristãos-Novos*, Oporto, 1969	Saraiva
SCHOEPS, H. J., 'Isaak Orobio de Castros Religionsdisput mit Philipp van Limborch', *Judaica*, 2, 1946/7, pp. 89–105	Schoeps, *Orobios Disput mit Limborch*
—— 'Philosemitism in the Baroque Period', *JQR* 47, 1956/7, pp. 139–44	Schoeps, *Baroque Philosemitism*
—— *The Jewish Christian Argument*, trans. by D. E. Green, London, 1963	Schoeps, *Jewish Christian Argument*
SCHOLBERG, K. R. *La poesía religiosa de Miguel de Barrios*, Madrid, 1962(?)	Scholberg, *Poesía de M. de Barrios*
—— 'Miguel de Barrios and the Amsterdam Sephardic Community', *JQR* 53, 1962, pp. 120–59	Scholberg, *De Barrios and Amsterdam*
SCHOLEM, G., 'Liydi'ath ha-Shabbetha'uth mi-Tokh kithvey Cardozo', *Zion*, 7, 5702 [1942], pp. 12–17 (repr. in *Gilguley Shabbetha'uth*, pp. 274–97)	Scholem, *Shabbetha'uth be-kithvey Cardozo*
—— ''Iggereth 'avraham mikha'el Cardozo le-dayyaney 'izmir', *Zion*, 19, 5713 [1953], pp. 1–22	Scholem, *'Iggereth A. M. Cardozo*
—— *Sabbatai Sevi, The Mystical Messiah 1626–1676*, Eng. trans. by R. J. Z. Werblowsky, Princeton, 1973	Scholem, *Sabbatai Sevi*
—— *The Messianic Idea in Judaism*, New York, 1972	Scholem, *Messianic Idea*
—— *Meḥqarim u-meqoroth le-toledoth ha-Shabbetha'uth we-gilguleyha*, Jerusalem, 5734 [1974]	Scholem, *Gilguley Shabbetha'uth*
—— *Devarim be-go*, Tel Aviv, 5735 [1975]	Scholem, *Devarim be-go*
SCHWARZSCHILD, S. S., 'Do Noachites have to believe in Revelation?', *JQR* 52, 1962, pp. 297–308; 53, 1962, pp. 30–65	Schwarzschild
SEELIGMAN, S., 'Het Marranen-Probleem uit oekonomisch oogpunt', *BMGJWN* 3, 1925, pp. 1–36	Seeligman
SHMUELI, E., *Beyn 'emunah li-kephirah*, Tel Aviv, 5722 [1962]	Shmueli

	Abbreviation
SICROFF, A. A., *Les Controverses des statuts de pureté de sang en Espagne du XVe au XVIIIe siècle*, Paris, 1960	Sicroff
SILVA ROSA, J. S. da 'Over de verhouding tusschen Joden en niet-Joden in de Republik der Vereenigde Nederlanden gedurende de 17e en 18e eeuw', *NIW* nos. 5, 6, 7, 8, 9, 1922	Silva Rosa, *Joden en niet Joden*
—— 'De Indruk van Sabbatai Tsebi den valschen Messias te Amsterdam (1666)', *VA* Proefnummer, Jan. 1924, pp. 5–6	Silva Rosa, *Sabbatai Tsebi*
—— *Geschiedenis der Portugeesche Joden te Amsterdam 1593–1925*, Amsterdam, 1925	Silva Rosa, *Geschiedenis*
—— 'Van Marrano tot Joodsch Apologeet: Dr Isaac (Balthazar) Orobio de Castro (Omstr. 1620–1687)', *VA* 3, 1926, no. 27, pp. 6–9; no. 28, pp. 21–3	Silva Rosa, *Orobio de Castro*
—— 'Die Spanischen und Portugiesischen Gedruckten Judaica in der Bibliothek des Jüd. Port. Seminars "Ets Haim" in Amsterdam. Einer Ergänzung zu Kayserling *Biblioteca Española-Portugueza-Judaica*', *BMGJWN* 5, 1933, pp. 177–205	Silva Rosa, *Ergänzung zu Kayserling*
SLOUSCHZ, N., *Ha'anusim be-portugal*, Tel Aviv, 5692 [1932]	Slouschz
SMIT, W., 'Joden in Middelburg', *ZT* 18, 1968, pp. 8–18	Smit
SOKOLOW, N., *Barukh spinoza u-zemano. Midrash be-philosophia u-be-qoroth ha-'ittim*, Paris, 1929	Sokolow
SOLEDAD RUBIO, M., *El Colegio-Universidad de Osuna (1548–1824)*, Seville, 1976	Soledad Rubio
SONNE, I., 'Da Costa Studies', *JQR* 22, 1923, pp. 247–93	Sonne, *Da Costa*
—— 'Leon Modena and the Da Costa Circle in Amsterdam', *HUCA* 21, 1948, pp. 1–28	Sonne, *Leon de Modena*
STEINSCHNEIDER, M., *Catalog der Hebräischen Handschriften in der Stadtbibliothek zu Hamburg*, Hamburg, 1878	Steinschneider, *Hamburg Cat.*
STRAUSS, L., *Spinoza's Critique of Religion*, New York, 1965	Strauss
SWETCHINSKI, D., 'The Spanish Consul and the Jews of Amsterdam', in *Texts and Responses: Studies Presented to N. N. Glatzer on the Occasion of his Seventieth Birthday by his Students*, ed. M. A. Fishbane and P. R. Flohr, Leiden, 1975	Swetchinski
SZAJKOWSKI, Z., 'An Auto-Da-Fé against the Jews	Szajkowski,

4. Authors: Scholarly Literature

	Abbreviation
of Toulouse in 1685', *JQR* 49, 1958/9, pp. 278–81	*Toulouse Auto da fe*
—— 'Trade Relations of Marranos in France with the Iberian Peninsula', *JQR* 50, 1959/60, pp. 69–78	Szajkowski, *Marrano Trade*
—— 'The Marranos and Sephardim in France', *The Abraham Weiss Jubilee Volume*, New York, 1964, pp. 107–27	Szajkowski, *French Marranos and Sephardim*
TEENSMA, B. N., 'De levensgeschiedenis van Abraham Peregrino, alias Manuel Cardoso de Macedo', *SR* 10, no. 1, 1976, pp. 1–36	Teensma
TEICHER, J. L., 'Why was Spinoza banned?' *The Menorah Journal*, 45, 1957, pp. 41–60	Teicher
THOMAS, K., *Religion and the Decline of Magic*, Penguin Books, 1971	Thomas
TREVOR ROPER, H. R., *The European Witch-Craze of the Sixteenth and Seventeenth Centuries and other essays*, New York and Evanston, 1967	Trevor Roper
ULLMAN, S., *Geschichte der spanisch-portugiesischen Juden in Amsterdam*, Frankfurt, 1908	Ullman
VALBUENA PRAT, A., *La Vida Española en la Edad de Oro*, Barcelona, 1943	Valbuena Prat
VAN AGT, J. F., *Synagogen in Amsterdam*, The Hague, 1974	Van Agt
Van Asa, J., 'Seqirah 'al rophe'im yehudian be-holand', *Korot I*, no. 5–6, 5715 [1955], pp. 1–8	Van Asa
VAN DEN BERG, J., *Joden en Christenen in Nederland gedurende de zeventiende eeuw*, Kampen, 1962	Van den Berg
VAN DER HOEVEN, A. A. des, *De Joanne Clerico et Philippo à Limborch Dissertationes duae*, Amsterdam, 1843	Van der Hoeven
VAN PRAGG, J. A., *Gespleten Zielen*, Groningen, 1948; Spanish trans., 'Almas en litigio', *Clavileno* 1, Jan.–Feb., 1950, pp. 14–16.	Van Praag
VAZ DIAS, A. M., *Spinoza Mercator et Autodidactus*, The Hague, 1932	Vaz Dias
VINCES VIVES, J., *An Economic History of Spain*, Princeton, 1969	Vinces Vives
VRANKRIJKER, A. C. J. de, *Geschiedenis van de Belastingen*, Bussum, 1969	Vrankrijker
WADE, I. O., *The Clandestine Organization and Diffusion of Philosophic Ideas in France from 1700 to 1750*, Princeton, 1938	Wade
WILLEY, B., *The Seventeenth Century Background*, London, 1967	Willey

	Abbreviation
WILSON, C., *The Dutch Republic and the Civilization of the Seventeenth Century*, London, 1968	Wilson
WIZNITZER, A., 'The Merger Agreement and regulations of Congregation Talmud Torah of Amsterdam 1638–9', *HJ* 20, 1958, pp. 109–32	Wiznitzer, *Merger Agreement*
—— *Jews in Colonial Brazil*, New York, 1960	Wiznitzer, *Brazil*
WOLF, L., *Menasseh ben Israel's Mission to Oliver Cromwell*, London, 1901	Wolf, *Men. b. I. and Cromwell*
—— *Jews in the Canary Islands*, London, 1926	Wolf, *Canary Islands*
WOLFSON, H. A., *The Philosophy of Spinoza*, 2 vols., New York, 1948	Wolfson, *Spinoza*
YAARI, A., 'Yeshivath pereyra biyrushalayim u-veḥevron', in *Yerushalayim, Meḥqerey 'ereṣ yisra'el*, ed. M. Ish Shalom, M. Benayahu, A. Shoḥat, Jerusalem, 5713 [1953], pp. 185–202	Yaari
YARDENI, M., 'Yahduth wiyhudim be-'eyney ha-Golim ha-Protestantim ha-Ṣarephathiyyim she-be-holand', *Meḥqarim be-toledoth 'am yisra'el we-'ereṣ yisra'el le-zekher ṣevi 'avneri*, Haifa, 5730 [1970], pp. 163–85	Yardeni
YERUSHALMI, Y. H., *From Spanish Court to Italian Ghetto: Isaac Cardoso, a Study in Seventeenth-Century Marranism and Jewish Apologetics*, New York and London, 1971	Yerushalmi, *Isaac Cardoso*
—— 'Ha-'anusim ha-ḥozerim la-Yahduth ba-Me'ah ha-Sheva' 'esrey: haskalatham ha-Yehudith wehakhsharatham ha-naphsith', *Divrey ha-Qongres ha-'olami ha-ḥamishi le-madda'ey ha-Yahduth*, vol. 2, Jerusalem, 1972, pp. 201–209	Yerushalmi, *'Anusim hozerim*
—— 'Professing Jews in Post-Expulsion Spain and Portugal', *Salo Wittmayer Baron Jubilee Volume*, Eng. Section, vol. 2, Jerusalem, 1974, pp. 1023–58	Yerushalmi, *Professing Jews*
ZILVERBERG, S. B. J., *Geloof en Geweten in de zeventiende eeuw*, Bussum, 1971	Zilverberg
ZIMMELS, H. J., *Die Marranen in der Rabbinischen Literatur*, Berlin, 1932	Zimmels
ZUMTHOR, P., *Daily Life in Rembrandt's Holland*, New York, 1963	Zumthor

Name Index

Note: Spelling of names reflects modern orthographical practice

Abbas, Jacob 207
Abbas, Rebecca 421
Abbas, Sarah 207, 234 n
Abendana, Jacob 271
Abiatar, Emanuel *see* Benattar, Emanuel
Aboab, Benjamin 427
Aboab, Rabbi Emanuel 352 n, 371
Aboab, Rebecca 427
Aboab, Samuel 328 n
Aboab da Fonseca, Rabbi Isaac 197 n,
　205 n, 223 n, 311, 345
　rabbi of the congregation *Talmud Torah*
　　of Amsterdam 112, 229
　cabbalist 113, 333, 334
　attitude towards the Sabbatean
　　movement 221
　commentary on the Pentateuch 275,
　　312, 340
　polemic with Rabbi Mortera 333–4
Abraham Israel *see* Escudero, Alonso
Abrahams, Levi 206 n
Abravanel, Isaac 355 n, 365, 374 n
Abravanel, Judah (Leone Ebreo) 308
Abudiente, Jacob 331
Abudiente, Moses 219 n
Achehoven, Cornelis von 425
Acosta, José d' 321
Acosta, Uriel d' 121, 161, 312, 352 n
　strictures on Jewish tradition 114 n,
　　165 n, 345, 349–51, 379
　excommunication 276
　autobiography 277 n, 278–9
Agrippa von Nettesheim, Henricus
　Cornelius 319, 320
Aguesseau, Henri d' 106 n
Aguilar, Antonio de *see* Farhi, Isaac
Aguilar, Grace 464
Aguilar, Isaac Israel d' 111
Aguilar, Rabbi Moses Raphael d' 110,
　156, 161, 223 n, 331, 334 n, 342,
　344
　sojourn in Brazil 111
　rabbi of the congregation *Talmud Torah*
　　of Amsterdam 112, 221

member of the brotherhood *Kether
　Torah* 112
teacher at the yeshiba *'Eṣ Ḥayyim* 112
attitude towards the Sabbatean
　movement 112, 211
attitude towards Christianity 252, 261
writings 113, 251
letter to the crypto-Jews of Bayonne
　337
reply to crypto-Jews in Antwerp 367 n
Ahumada, Dr Pedro de 72
Almazán, Jacinto de 13
Almeida, Isaac d' 139 n, 332
Alsted, Johann Heinrich 238
Alting, Jacob 271
Alvares, Ana 25 n
Alvares, Bastián 25 n, 28, 30
Alvares, Fernando 34, 35, 59, 61, 62
Alvares, Isabel (grandmother of Prado,
　Juan de) 124 n
Alvares, Isabel (wife of Hurtado, Luis) 40
Alvares, Isabelica 25 n, 27, 28, 36, 38, 49,
　50
Alvares, Leonor (daughter of Luis,
　Santiago) 25 n, 27, 28, 36, 38, 40,
　49, 50
Alvares, Leonor (paternal grandmother of
　Orobio de Castro, Isaac) 1, 2, 25 n,
　28
Alvares, Luis 28, 30
Alvares, María (daughter of Bastián) 28,
　30
Alvares, María (wife of Castro, José de)
　28, 29 n
Alvares, Melchor *see* Orobio de Castro,
　Yaacov
Alvares, Mencia 38, 39
Alvares, Pedro 28, 30
Alvares de Castro, Domingo 96 n
Alvares de Castro, Leonor (wife of Luis,
　João) 2
Alvares de Orobio, Leonor (sister of
　Orobio de Castro, Isaac) 2, 3, 28,
　207

Name Index

Alvares de Orobio, Leonor *(cont.)*:
   wife of Simón Rodríguez de Monsanto 34 n, 57, 75
   trial at the Seville Inquisition 79, 82, 83, 89, 91
   imprisonment by the Inquisition 94
   public conversion to Judaism 106, 107 n
Alvares de Orobio, Manuel *see* Orobio de Castro, Abraham
Alvares de Tavara, Manuel *see* Zacuth, Abraham
Alvarez, Aaron 421
Alvarez, Ana (of Aguilar) 6
Alvarez, Beatriz 6 n
Alvarez, Diego 6
Alvarez, Francisco 6
Alvarez, Gabriel 206 n
Alvarez, Isabel (of Andújar) 6
Alvarez, Joseph Israel 292, 296 n, 297
Alvarez, Sarah 421
Alvarez Machado, Moses *see* Machado, Moses
Alvarez Machado, Rebecca 297 n, 421
Ambrose, St 182
Amelander, Menaḥem Man 1 n, 24 n, 87 n
Andrade, Jacob de 265 n
Antunes, David 373 n
Aquinas, Thomas 182, 236, 237 n, 314, 315
Arias, David *see* Arias de Fonseca, Esteban de
Arias de Fonseca, Esteban de (David) 335–6
Arias Luna, Dr Pablo 72
Arias Montano, Benito 235, 237, 238, 291 n
Aristotle 15, 119, 120, 121, 126, 138, 188, 300
   in the curriculum of Spanish universities 12, 15
   in Spanish neo-scholasticism 314
   Isaac Orobio's attitude towards 315, 349, 355, 358
Armand de Bourbon (Prince de Conti) 103, 104
Arminius, Jacobus 274
Armuñia (Armuña), Julio de 410, 412, 413
Arnauld, Antoine 168–9
Arriaga, Gonzalo de 237, 315
Athanasius 236

Athias, Abraham 226 n, 420
Athias, Immanuel 420
Athias, Joseph Raphael 293, 296 n, 420, 423, 428, 429
Athias, Moses 290 n
Athias, Raphael 425
Augustine, St 168, 182, 236, 238, 268
Avicenna 9, 68, 77
Avilar, Jacob Uzziel d' (Avilar Cardozo, Jacob d') 293, 296 n, 420, 421, 430
Ayala, Flor de 4 n, 51
Azevedo de Pas, Dr Moyses Salom 200 n

Báñez, Domingo (Dominicus) 180, 313
Barbosa, Diego 335
Barrios, Daniel Levi de (Barrios, Miguel de) v, 207 n, 208 n, 252, 296 n, 309, 311, 330, 331, 334, 340, 344, 360, 467
   captain in the Spanish army 224
   public conversion to Judaism in Leghorn 223
   married to Abigail de Pina 223
   attitude towards the Sabbatean movement 222–9, 373
   relations with Isaac Orobio 226, 229–34, 437
   relations with Juan de Prado 157–9, 265
   attitude towards Spinoza 265
   translation into Spanish of Isaac Orobio's book against Zepeda 184, 187, 227
   writings: *Flor de Apolo* 223, 226 n; *Coro de las Musas* 223, 225, 226; *Contra la verdad no hay fuerça* 226; *Imperio de Dios en la Harmonía del Mundo* 229, 230; *Respuesta panegírica* 232, 233
   sonnet in praise of Abraham Pereyra 221 n
   member of the *Academia de los Floridos* 289–95, 297–302, 418, 420–7
   punished by the *Talmud Torah* congregation 224, 338 n
   messianic vision 373–5
Barrios, Miguel de *see* Barrios, Daniel Levi de
Barrios, Simon de 290, 293, 294 n, 296 n, 297, 301, 420
Barros, João de 163
Basnage 1 n, 24 n, 103 n, 210 n, 455, 460 n
Bayle, Francois 100

Name Index

Bayle, Pierre vii, 263, 264 n, 265 n, 268 n, 269
Bellarmine, Robert 316 n
Belmonte, Manuel de *see* Nunes Belmonte, Isaac
Ben Israel, Rabbi Menasseh (Dias Soeiro, Manoel) v, 194 n, 251, 371, 455
  teacher at the yeshiba 'Eṣ Ḥayyim 112
  writings: *Esperança de Israel* 309 n; *Humble Address* 174, 370
  translation of Phocylides into Spanish 309
  works found in Limborch's library 275
  messianic expectations 366
Benattar (Abiatar), Emanuel 219, 222, 227
Bentivoglio, Giulio *see* Curiel, Moses
Benzemero, Isaac 336 n
Berahel, Jacob 423
Berahel, Rachel 423
Beuningen, Conrad van 194 n, 271
Blandon de Silva, Duarte 294, 296 n, 418
Boileau, Nicolas 104
Bolingbroke 466, 467
Borromeo, Jan Carlos 404
Boscán, Juan 16 n
Bossuet 104
Boullainvilliers, Charles 269
Bravo de Morales, Juan 11
Bredenburg, Johannes 151, 263–8, 277, 439, 440, 457
Brissot, Pierre 68
Broughton, Hugh 271 n
Browne, Edward 194
Browne, Thomas 194 n
Brunt Ambona, Georges 200 n
Bueno, Dr Aaron 202 n
Bueno, Dr Ephraim 202 n
Bueno de Aragão, Abraham 195
Bueno de Mesquita, David 290 n
Bueno de Mesquita, Jacob 205, 206
Bueno Henriques, Eliau 192 n

Caballero, Dr Pedro 47 n
Caballero de Los Olivos, Don Julio 81 n, 402, 410, 412, 413, 414, 415
Caldenn, Juan 61 n
Calderón de La Barca, Pedro 287, 291 n
Calvin, 114 n, 236, 238, 241 n, 261, 274, 308
Caminho, Esther *see* Cohen Camiña, Esther
Camões, Luis 309
Cano, Melchor 313

Capadose, Simhah 294 n
Caraffa, Giovanni Pietro (Pope Paul IV) 38 n
Cardillo de Villalpando, Gaspar 314
Cardoso, Abraham Michael 7 n, 221, 346, 380
  birthplace 27 n
  and the Sabbatean movement 210–19
  two letters in Spanish 210, 212–18, 228, 232
  proscription of his writings 233
  messianic theory 212–15, 342, 343
Cardoso, Isaac (brother of Abraham Michael) 371
  in Medina de Ríoseco 27 n
  and the 'Patient Christ' trials 4 n
  writings: *Philosophia Libera* 217, 268–9; *Las Excelencias de los Hebreos* 173, 174, 320, 337 n; 355 n, 372 n
  attitude towards the Sabbatean movement 210 n, 211–19
  on the nobility of the Jews 325
Caro, Rabbi Joseph 118 n, 119 n
Carracena, Marqués de 187
Carrascal de Prado, Martín 402, 417
Carreras y Coligo, José *see* Ribera, Daniel de
Carrillo, David 144
Carrillo, Isaac 293, 294 n, 296 n, 420, 423, 429, 430
Carrillo, Samuel 420
Cartagena, Alonso de 177 n
Carvalho, Judith 422
Carvalho, Rachel 422
Casares (Caçarez), Bartolomé de 410, 412, 413
Castillo, Raphael del (Montezinos, Raphael (Gabriel) Hezekiah) 293, 296 n, 297, 421, 423, 425
Castro, Antonio *see* Castro, Manuel
Castro, José de 25–9, 35–42, 45
Castro, Manuel (Antonio) de 83 n
Castro, Rabbi Mordecai de 112 n
Castro, Rodrigo de 35
Castro Tartas, Abraham de 111
Castro Tartas, David de 205, 206 n
Castro Tartas, Isaac de 111
Caturce 99
Cerda, Don Antonio Juan Luis de (duke of Medinaceli) 64, 65, 66
Cervantes, Miguel de 8
Cetina (Zetina), Don Gutierres de 402, 412, 413, 414

Name Index

Cetina (Zetina), Julio de 81 n, 402, 410, 411, 412, 413
Chaves, Jacob de 206 n, 293, 294 n, 296 n, 297, 421, 429
Chaves, Miguel 47 n
Chaves, Moses de 192 n, 421
Chaves Vaez, Moses 422
Chaves Vaez, Rebecca 422
Chilton Fantoni, Don Esteban 413
Chmielnicki 209
Christina (Queen of Sweden) 128
Claros, Francisco Antonio 75, 410
Clearchus 355 n
Clemente, Claudio 323
Cobirin, Solomon 206 n
Cocceius 238
Cohen, Isaac 206 n
Cohen, Nethanel 206 n
Cohen Camiña (Caminho), Esther 425
Cohen Camiña, Hannah 427
Cohen de Soza, Rachel 223
Cohen Herrera, Abraham 113, 333
Cohen Pimentel, Abraham 223 n
Colbert 100
Collins, Anthony 456 n
Confucius 121
Córdoba, don Antonio de 157
Córdoba, Francisco de 34
Correa, Dr Jorge 58
Coserans, Marques of 103
Covarrubias 308
Cromwell, Oliver 60, 174
Cruz, Pablo de la 51
Cudworth, Ralph 275
Cuevas, Dr 125
Cuperus, Frans *see* Kuyper, Frans
Curiel, Moses (Nunes da Costa, Jerónimo; Bentivoglio, Giulio) 203, 204 n, 292, 294 n, 296, 420, 421, 426, 428, 429
Cuyper, Frans *see* Kuyper, Frans

Damascius (Damasino) 236
Daniel Judah *see* Olivier y Fullana, don Nicolás de
Deodatus of St Blois 236
Desa, Catalina 40 n
Descartes 167, 265, 318 n, 319 n
D'Holbach, Baron 453, 454, 455, 456, 459, 467
Dias Soeiro, Manoel *see* Ben Israel, Rabbi Menasseh
Díaz, Raphael 290 n

Dirks, Simon *see* Franco Mendes, David
Doiley, Oliver 275
Domínguez Camacho, Sebastián 410, 412
Duarte, Constancia 423
Duarte, Isabel 420
Duarte de Tavora, Francisco 72, 74
Duns Scotus 12, 71, 166, 182, 236, 238, 315 n
Durand de St Pourçain 182, 237–8, 315

Encarnación, María de (la) 75
Enrique IV (king of Castile) 235 n
Enriques, Violante (of Bayonne) 30, 31
Enriques, Violante *see* Orobio de Castro, Leah
Enríquez, Manuel *see* Henríquez, Aaron
Enríquez, Daniel 144
Enríquez, Dr Duarte 335
Enríquez, Marianne 97
Enríquez, Violante 28
Enríquez Alvares, Daniel 28, 60
Enríquez Alvares, Duarte 28, 60, 61, 135 n
Enríquez Basurto, Diego 317 n
Enríquez Fonseca, Rodrigo 126 n
Enríquez Gómez, Antonio 317, 320
Enríquez Medina, Joseph *see* Medina, Aaron
Epiphanius 236
Episcopius, Simon 274, 275, 284
Erasmus 379
Ercilla, Alonso de 309 n
Ergas Henríquez, Jacob 193 n
Ernest August (duke of Calenberg and Hanover) 203
Escudero, Alonso (Lorenzo; Abraham Israel) 180, 181, 184–7
Espina, Alonso de 235 n, 236 n
Espinosa, Benjamin d' 420
Espinosa, Juan de 127
Espinosa, Pedro Marcos de 127
Espinosa, Rachel 420
Espinossa, Manuel de 416, 417
Estrella, Fray Diego de 310
Eusebius 236, 300
Eymeric (inquisitor of Aragon) 179

Faber, Jacobus *see* Le Fèvre, Jacques
Farhi, Isaac (Aguilar, Antonio de) 336
Farrar, Dr David 271 n, 352
Fénelon, M. de 269
Fernandes, Gonzalo 43, 44, 48

Name Index

Fernandes, Micia 2
Fernandes de Fonseca, Miguel 335
Fernández, Manuel 53
Fernández, Miguel 50
Fernández de Navarrete, Juan 177
Fernández de Valentín, Vasco 127
Fernández Núñez, Mencia *see* Orobio de Castro, Sarah
Fernández Paez, Diego 6 n
Fernández Pato, Luis 92
Fernelius (Fernel, Jean-François) 73 n
Ferrier, Augier 100
Fonseca, Dr Antonio de 127 n
Fonseca, Isabel de 262 n
Fonseca, Pedro de 313, 314
Francis of Assisi 20
Francisco (Franciscano), Felix 238
Franco, Fray Joseph 135 n
Franco da Silva, Jacob 195 n
Franco Mendes (Mendez), Abraham 190 n
Franco Mendes, David (Rodríguez Mendes, Simon; Dirks, Simon) 293, 294 n, 296 n, 297, 422, 423, 425, 428, 429
Franco Mendes, David (18th cent. writer) 1 n, 103, 210, 212, 289 n, 424
Franco Mendes, Rachel 297, 425
Frois, Dr Abraham (Abrahamus) Israel 200 n, 205 n, 293, 294 n, 296 n, 422
Fuente, Miguel de 11 n

Gabai Faro, David 192 n
Gabay Henríquez, Isaac 205 n
Gabbay Isidro, Jacob 293, 294 n, 296 n, 422, 429
Gabriel, Antonio *see* Mocatta, Moses ben Abraham
Galante, Moses 365 n
Galen 9, 69, 70, 71, 77, 410
Gama, Abraham 422
Gama, Jacob de (Mendez Gama, Jacob) 293, 296 n, 297, 422, 429, 430
Gamarra, don Esteban de 185
Gans, David 275
García Moreno, Sebastián 411, 412, 413, 414
García de Prados, Francisco 124, 125 n
García Zamora, Luis 124
Garcilaso de la Vega 16 n, 309 n
Gassendi 167, 320 n
George I (king of England) 203
Gil, Julio 414
Gobea, Gaspar de 28, 59, 60
Goes, Damião da 370 n
Gomarus, Franciscus 274 n
Gómez, Felipa 124
Gómez, Fernán 124 n
Gómez, Gracia 124
Gómez, Isabel 124
Gómez, Juana 127
Gómez, Martín 30, 31
Gómez, Simón 97
Gómez de Araujo, Abraham 309, 310 n
Gómez Bravo, Miguel 335
Gómez Moreno, Beatriz 425
Gómez Pereda, Gerónimo 88, 124
Gómez 'Romano', Francisco 124, 125, 126, 127, 128 n
Gómez Vittoria, Miguel 335
Gompertz, Reuben 206 n
Gonçales, Ana *see* Orobio, Hannah
Gonçales, Clara 40 n
Gonçales, Juan 40 n
Gonçalves, Ana 2, 3, 4 n, 5, 25 n
Gonçalves, Diogo 2, 3 n
Gonçalves, Isabel 25 n
Gonçalves, Joana 25 n
Góngora, Luis Argote de 301, 308, 309
Gontery 316 n
Gonzales, María 22 n
González, Francisca 28, 30
González, Gonzalo 28, 38
González de Alvelda (Aluelda), Alonso 413
González de Barriga (Varriga), Alonso 402, 410, 412
González de Cellorigo, Martín 175
Gracián, B. 308, 310 n
Graevius 285 n
Granada, Fray Luis de 237, 310
Granado, Dr Alonso de 71, 72 n
Graswinckel, Theodor 276
Gregorio de Valencia 313
Gregory IX (pope) 99
Groenwolt, Jacobus 385, 386
Grotius, Hugo 279, 284 n, 285, 358 n, 465
Guedelha (Gadella), Jacob 385 n, 438
Guenellon, Pieter 275
Guer, Jacob 249 n, 439
Guerra, Joseph 134, 417
Guevara, Pedro de 179, 180
Gunning, Peter 275
Gutierres (Gómez), Dr Abraham 205 n, 290, 293, 294 n, 296 n, 422, 428, 429

Gutierres, David 204
Ha-Cohen, Joseph 330 n
Halfon Ha-Levi, Rabbi Elijah (of Fürth) 458 n
Hamis Vaz, David 292, 294 n, 296 n, 297 n, 422, 423, 425, 429, 430
Hamis Vaz, Rachel 297 n, 425
Harvey, William 71
Henríquez, Aaron (Enríquez, Manuel; Nunes Enríquez, Aaron) 292, 296 n, 421, 422
Henríquez Faro, David 193 n
Heredia, Dr Pedro Miguel de 67, 68 n
Heredia, Phelipe de 417
Hernandes de Quirós, Pedro 309 n
Herrera, Miguel 53
Hilary of Poitiers 236
Hippocrates 9, 69, 77, 410
Hooghe, Romeyn de 421
Huarte de San Juan, Juan 309
Hulsius, Antonius 271
Hurtado, Luis 40 n
Huygens, Constantine 424

Ibn Verga, Solomon 340 n, 365, 366, 367 n, 370, 372 n
Ione, Raphael Isaac 456 n
Isidore of Seville 236

Jenkes, Henri 275
Jerome 182, 238, 291 n
Jessurun, Jacob 206 n
Jessurun, Joseph 205, 206
Jessurun, Reuel *see* Pina, Pablo de
Jessurun Espinosa, Daniel 205, 206
Jessurun Henríquez, Jacob 193 n
Jessurun Lobo, Joseph (Medina Lobo, Joseph) 292, 296 n, 423, 425, 428, 429, 430
Jessurun López, Jael 427
Jessurun López, Joseph 427
João II (king of Portugal) 369
Jon, François du (Junius) 238
Joseph, Aaron 206 n
Josephus 242, 255, 355 n
Judah Ha-Levi 320
Junius *see* Jon, François du
Jurieu, P. 271
Justin Martyr 236

Kuyper (Cuyper, Cuperus), Frans 264

La Fontaine 104

La Peyrère, Isaac 132, 133
Laínez, Fray José 77
Lamy, François 269
Lara, Manuel de 290, 293, 294 n, 296 n, 297, 418
Lavater 121
Le Clerk, Jean vii, 274, 275, 278
Le Fèvre, Jacques (Faber, Jacobus) 12
Leão, Justa de 25 n
Lemmerman, Abraham 263 n, 264
Lenglet Dufresnoy 269
León, David Judah 191
León, Esther de 208
León, Fray Luis de 237 n, 310
León (Templo), Jacob Judah 196 n, 275, 312
León, Manuel de 96
Leone Ebreo *see* Abravanel, Judah
Leopold III 292, 426
Levesque de Burigny, Jean 455
Levi, Emmanuel (Manuel) 292, 294 n, 296 n, 423
Levi, Joel 206 n
Levi, Moses 423
Levi, Rachel 423
Lima, Jacob 207 n
Lima, Solomon 207 n
Limborch, Philip van vii
  studies 274
  and the Dutch Remonstrants 274-5, 318
  library collection 275
  disputation with Bredenburg 265
  relations with John Locke 275
  letter to Theodor Graswinckel 276
  writings: *Historia Inquisitionis* 79, 86 n, 87 n, 93; friendly conversation (disputation) with Isaac Orobio 4, 133, 248, 253, 254 n, 270, 273-85, 316, 318, 358 n, 372, 452, 454, 455, 466, 467
Lipsuis 300
Lis, Francisco de *see* López Berahel, Abraham
Lobo, Eleonora Francisca de 159
Loçano, Alonso 47 n
Locke, John vii, 1 n, 87 n, 275, 277, 278, 285 n
Lopes, Rabbi Elijah 205 n
López, Damián 410, 416
López, Ginebra 40
López Berahel, Abraham (Lis, Francisco de) 292, 296 n, 420, 423, 429

López de Quirós, Isaac 220 n
López de Viloslada, Juan 52, 53
López Pinto, Michael 438, 439
López Quirós, Daniel 432, 434, 436, 438
López Quirós, David 434
López Rosa, Duarte *see* Rosa, Moses
Louis, Dr P. C. A. 68 n
Louis II de Bourbon (Prince de Condé)
  vii, 103, 104
Louis XIV vii, 103, 104, 239 n, 306 n
Lugo, Juan de 313
Luis, Benito 28, 31
Luis, Clara 28, 30 n
Luis, Enrique 28, 31
Luis, Gonzalo 25 n, 27, 28, 35–42, 45
Luis, Isabel 25, 27–35, 42, 45, 47, 48
Luis, João 2
Luis, Manuel 25 n, 28, 36
Luis, María (grandmother of Orobio de Castro, Abraham) 2
Luis, María (sister of Luis, Benito) 28, 31
Luis, Melchor 35
Luis, Santiago (Jacôme; brother of Alvares, Manuel) 25, 28, 31
  father 38 n
  children 36
  arrival in Spain 35
  escape from Spain 29
  escape from Málaga 41
  trial at the Cuenca Inquisition 27, 42–9, 55–6, 58–9, 62–3
  possession of a Jewish calendar in Spain 33
  circumcision 47
Luis, Tomé 31
Lull, Raymond (Lulio, Raymundo):
  proscription of his writings in Aragon 179
  rehabilitation by the Catholic kings 179–80
  Pedro Guevara's works on his philosophy 179
  Spanish translation of his *Arbor Scientiae* 179
  in A. de Zepeda's writings 179–81
  as subject of controversy between Isaac Orobio and Zepeda 181–9, 238, 253, 300, 385, 433–4
Lumbrozo, Abraham Hai 293, 296 n, 421, 424
Lumbrozo, Benjamin 424
Lumbrozo, Dr Judah 465, 466
Luque, Julio de 11 n
Luther, Martin 236, 238

Luzzatto, Rabbi Simḥah (Simone) 366 n, 370 n, 371 n

McCaul, Revd Alexander 463–4
Machado, Moses (Alvarez Machado, Moses) 292, 296 n, 297 n, 420, 421, 424, 429
Machiavelli, N. 322, 323
Machorro, Abraham 188, 431, 432, 433, 434, 435, 436, 438
Maharit *see* Trani, Rabbi Joseph Moses
Maimonides (Rabbi Moses Ben Maimon; Rambam) 214, 268, 320, 461
  on bleeding 68 n
  on the righteous amongst the gentiles 118–19, 356, 357
  writings found in Limborch's library 275
Majarres de Credia, don Pedro 414
Maldonado de Galdo, Francisco 51
Malebranche 167
Manoel (king of Portugal) 369
Manzanares, Gerónima de 52
Marchena, Jacob 139, 140, 143
Margarita María (daughter of Philip IV) 180
Mariana, Juan de 340 n
Marianne of Austria 180
Martínez, Miguel 47 n
Martini, Raymund 236 n
Marvell, Andrew 109
Mateos, Ana 51
Mazarin 104
Medici, Catherine de 100
Medici, Marie de 105 n
Medina, Aaron (Enríquez Medina, Joseph) 293, 294 n, 296 n, 297 n, 425
Medina, Solomon de 270 n
Medina Cardozo, Rachel de 428
Medina Lobo, Joseph *see* Jessurun Lobo, Joseph
Mendelssohn, Moses 121
Mendes, Isabel 28, 31
Mendes, Salvador 31
Mendes Brito, Francisco 336 n
Mendes Chumaceiro, Jacob 432
Mendes Franco, Melchor (Abraham) 422
Mendez de Almansa, Dr Aaron 200 n, 201 n
Mendez Gama, Jacob *see* Gama, Jacob de
Mercier, Barthélemy 455
Mersenne 167
Mesquita, Moshe de 190 n
Milano, Isaac 208, 234 n

Mocatta, Joseph (Nunes Marchena, Joseph) 292, 296 n, 297, 422, 425, 428, 429
Mocatta, Moses ben Abraham (Gabriel Antonio) 293, 294 n, 296 n, 297, 422, 425, 428, 429, 463
Mocatta, Moses (Nunes Marchena, Moses; son of Joseph) 293, 294 n, 296 n, 297, 301, 425, 428, 429, 430
Mocatta, Rachel 297, 422
Modena, Rabbi Judah Leone da 350, 352
Molcho, Rabbi Solomon 330 n
Molière 104
Molina, Gonçalves 99
Monsanto, Abraham Israel (Rodríguez de Monsanto, Simón):
  brother-in-law of Baltazar Orobio 28, 34, 76
  residence in Seville 56–7
  before the Seville Inquisition 66 n
  trial by the Seville Inquisition 79–82
  sequestration of property by the Inquisition 75 n
  residence in Cádiz 78
  sentence of confinement by the Inquisition 90–1
  arrival in Amsterdam 106
  public conversion to Judaism 107
Monsanto, Isaac 206 n
Monsanto, Jacob 139 n, 141
Monsanto, Rebecca 206
Montaigne, Michel de 321
Montalto, Dr Elijah 105 n, 251, 259, 262 n, 455 n
Monte, Jacob del *see* Soto, Jacob del
Montesinos, Fernando de 335
Montezinos, Raphael (Gabriel) Hezekiah *see* Castillo, Raphael del
Montezinos, Rebecca 421
Morales, Juan 374 n
More, Henry 275
Moreno, Abraham Shalom 425
Moreno, Gabriel 293, 294 n, 296 n, 425, 429, 430
Moreno, Dr Jacob 204, 425
Moreno Villacresess, García 402
Mortera, Rabbi Saul Levi 161, 336, 455 n
  and Dr Elijah Montalto's interment in Ouderkerk 105 n
  founder of the brotherhood *Kether Torah* 112, 426
  influence on Rabbi Moses Raphael d'Aguilar 113
  and Juan de Prado 137, 139–41, 166
  anti-Christian polemic 259
  attitude towards crypto-Jews 328, 329 n
  controversy with Rabbi Isaac Aboab da Fonseca 333 n, 334
  writings: controversy with Sixtus of Sienna 237 n; *Obstáculos y oposiciones de la Religión christiana* 312
Moses Ben Maimon, Rabbi *see* Maimonides
Moses ben Naḥman, Rabbi (Nahmanides; Ramban) 349
Moyano de Medina, Dr Juan 71, 72 n
Muli' Isma'il (sultan of Morocco) 427
Muñoz y Espinosa, Tomás 9
Musaphia, Dr Benjamin 112, 229

Nahar, Dr Isaac 112, 220, 222, 223 n, 254, 257 n, 340, 342, 343
Nahar, Jacob 432, 436, 437
Nahmanides *see* Moses ben Naḥman
Naigeon, Jacques 453, 454, 456
Narváez, Andrés de 25–35, 42, 45, 48
Narváez, Francisco de 28, 30
Nassi, Samuel 140, 141
Nathan of Gaza 217, 218, 228, 462
Nesplet, Hendrik 203
Netto, Rabbi Isaac 205 n
Nicholas de Lyre 237
Nicole, Pierre 104, 168 n
Nunes Belmonte, Isaac (Belmonte, Manuel de) 292, 296 n, 297, 301, 420, 426, 428, 430
Nunes da Costa, Jerónimo *see* Curiel, Moses
Nunes da Costa, Joseph 423
Nunes Enríquez, Aaron *see* Henríquez, Aaron
Nunes Marchena, Joseph *see* Mocatta, Joseph
Nunes Marchena, Moses *see* Mocatta, Moses
Núñez, Dr Alonso 404
Núñez, María 25 n, 27, 28, 36, 38, 40, 49, 50
Núñez, Violante *see* Orobio de Castro, Leah
Núñez, Violante (grandmother of Orobio de Castro, Sarah) 2
Núñez, Violante (maternal aunt of Orobio de Castro, Isaac) 4 n
Núñez Bernal, Abraham 139 n, 260, 332, 426

Núñez Bernal, Elijah 260 n
Núñez Bernal, Manuel 6 n
Núñez Carvalho, David 431, 433
Núñez da Costa, Duarte 335
Núñez de Acosta, Dr (Alonso) Duarte 71, 72 n, 77, 88
Núñez de Gobea, Simón 28, 54 n, 55 n, 60, 61 n
Núñez Enríquez, Pascual (Jacob) 75 n, 79, 82, 96, 97, 106, 107
Núñez Enríquez, Rebecca 301, 425
Núñez Enríquez, Rodrigo 425
Núñez Fernández, Rachel 226 n
Núñez Mendez, Jacob 107 n

Olivares, Conde Duque de 5
Oliveira, Selomoh de 112, 205 n
Olivier y Fullana, don Nicolás de (Daniel Judah) 226 n
Origen (Origines) 182, 374 n
Orobio, Clara de (Rachel; sister of Orobio de Castro, Isaac) 2
  trial by the Seville Inquisition 79, 82, 83, 85 n, 89, 91
  sequestration of property by the Inquisition 75 n
  imprisonment in the Inquisition gaol 94
  arrival in Amsterdam 106
  public conversion to Judaism 107
  marriage to Moses Barukh Pérez 107 n, 207
Orobio, Hannah (Isabel; Gonçales, Ana; sister of Orobio de Castro, Isaac) 2, 83 n
Orobio, Leonor de *see* Alvares de Orobio, Leonor
Orobio, Melchor de *see* Orobio de Castro, Yaacov
Orobio de Castro, Abraham (Alvares de Orobio, Manuel; father of Orobio de Castro, Isaac) 2, 28, 34, 35, 38 n, 78, 416
  brother of Santiago Luis 31
  married to Mencia Fernández 3
  children 3–4
  trial at the Cuenca Inquisition 25, 27, 29, 41–63
  observance of Jewish fasts and festivals 32, 43–4
  circumcision 47
  home in Cádiz 76 n
  escape from Spain 79, 82
  sojourn in France 96–7
  arrival in Amsterdam 106
  public conversion to Judaism 107
  death 109
Orobio de Castro, Abraham (Velasco, Alonso de; son of Orobio de Castro, Isaac) 107, 208, 304
Orobio de Castro, Esther (Pérez de la Peña, Isabel; wife of Orobio de Castro, Isaac) 414
  daughter of Francisco Pérez 67
  residence in Cádiz 75
  sojourn in Bayonne 98
  arrival in Amsterdam 106
  public conversion to Judaism 107
  tombstone in Ouderkerk 305, 306 n
Orobio de Castro, Hannah (daughter of Orobio de Castro, Isaac) 96, 107, 207
Orobio de Castro, Leah (Enriques, Violante; Núñez, Violante; sister of Orobio de Castro, Isaac) 2
  married to Pascual Núñez 75 n
  trial by the Seville Inquisition 79, 82, 83, 85, 86, 88, 91, 94
  arrival in Amsterdam 106
  public conversion to Judaism 107
Orobio de Castro, Moses (son of Orobio de Castro, Isaac):
  birth 95–6
  arrival in Amsterdam 106
  public conversion to Judaism 107
  student at the Leiden university 96 n, 200, 203
  member of the *Collegium Medicum* of Amsterdam 200, 205 n
  married to Sarah Abbas 207, 234 n
  brother of Abraham Orobio 208 n
  member of the *Academia de los Floridos* 290, 293, 297, 418
  member of the *Maskıl el Dal* brotherhood 294 n
  finta payment 296 n
  physician to the congregational poor in Amsterdam 304
  parnas of the Portuguese congregation in Amsterdam 428
  parnas of ʿEṣ Ḥayyim in Amsterdam 429
Orobio de Castro, Rachel *see* Orobio, Clara de
Orobio de Castro, Rebecca (daughter of Orobio de Castro, Isaac) 107, 207, 234 n

Orobio de Castro, Sarah (Fernández Núñez, Mencia; mother of Orobio de Castro, Isaac) 2, 28, 41, 50, 57, 63
  sister of Mateo Rodríguez Núñez 4
  married to Manuel Alvares 3
  children 3
  escape from Málaga to Seville 27, 46, 48, 49, 51–4
  home in Cádiz 76 n
  trial by the Seville Inquisition 79–85, 88–91, 94 n, 95
  arrival in Amsterdam 106
  public conversion to Judaism 107
  death 109
Orobio de Castro, Sarah (daughter of Orobio de Castro, Isaac) 107, 208
Orobio de Castro, Yaacov (Alvares, Melchor; Orobio, Melchor; brother of Orobio de Castro, Isaac) 2
  residence in Seville 57
  escape from Spain 79, 82
  burned in effigy by the Seville Inquisition 96, 97
  arrival in Amsterdam 106
  conversion to Judaism 107
  married to Rebbeca Monsanto 206, 207 n
  business activities in Amsterdam 207
Osorio, Gerónimo 370 n
Ostens, Jacob 266

Pablo de Santa María (Solomon Ha-Levi of Burgos):
  father of Alonso de Cartagena 177 n
  Scrutinium Scripturarum 114–15
  works read by Isaac Orobio 86, 87, 126 n, 236
  Isaac Orobio's questions about his biblical exegesis 114–15
  Isaac Orobio's polemics with 237, 246, 357 n
Pacheco, Dr 134
Pacheco, Isaac 141, 142
Padthuysen, Pieter 203
Paez, Adrien 61 n
Paez, Barbarrida 51
Pagninus 235, 238, 291 n
Paiba, Rachel de 199 n
Paracelsus 71
Pardo, Josiah 221, 229
Pascal 168, 169, 171
Paul IV (pope) 38 n
Paz, Jacob de 138
Paz, Sarah 427
Paz, Violante de 25–9, 35–41, 49, 50, 52, 54
Peña, Rachel de 422
Penso, Abraham 293, 294 n, 296 n, 297, 423, 426, 428, 429
Penso, (Felix) Isaac 112, 205 n, 426
Penso Alvarez, Rebecca 426
Penso de la Vega, Joseph:
  brother of Abraham Penso 293, 297, 426
  sojourn in Leghorn 426
  founder of the *Academia de los Sitibundos* in Leghorn 290, 426
  member of the *Academia de los Floridos* 232, 288–90, 293–5, 297–302, 427
  payment of *finta* 296 n
  client of Manuel Levi 423
  death 427
  writings: *Rumbos peligrosos* 289, 420, 426; *Discursos Académicos* 297–300, 302, 425; *'Asirey ha-Tiqvah* 426; *Triumfos del Aguila* 426; *Retrato de la Prudencia* 427; *Confusión de Confusiones* 427
Pereira, Joseph 431, 435, 436
Pereira, Samuel Israel 431, 435, 436
Pereyra, Aaron 297
Pereyra, Abraham Israel (Rodrigues Pereyra, Tomás) v
  residence in Madrid 220
  escape from Spain to Venice 220
  arrival in Amsterdam 220
  public conversion to Judaism 220
  questions on religious matters 122 n
  founder of a *yeshibah* in Hebron 220
  father of Moses Israel Pereyra 427
  messianic vision 375
  religious thought 322, 323, 333, 337, 338, 344, 345, 360, 364, 365
  influence of Spanish culture on him 310–11
  writings: *La Certeza del Camino* 220; *Espejo de la Vanidad del Mundo* 220, 226
Pereyra, Isaac Israel 427
Pereyra, Jacob Israel 122 n, 220 n, 424
Pereyra, Moses Israel 292, 294 n, 296–7, 423, 427, 428, 429, 430
Pereyra, Sarah 427
Pérez, Francisco 67, 78, 408, 410, 416, 417
Pérez, Dr Miguel 72

Name Index

Pérez, Moses Barukh 107 n, 207
Pérez, Tomás 47 n
Pérez de la Peña, Isabel see Orobio de Castro, Esther
Pérez de Maltranilla, Miguel 134, 145
Pérez de Montalbán 308
Pérez Ramírez, Luis 70, 71, 72 n, 73, 74
Perron, Jacques du 316 n
Pessoa, Abraham 427
Pessoa, Hannah 427
Pessoa, Isaac 293, 296 n, 427, 429
Pessoa, Moses 427
Philip III (king of Spain) 180, 286
Philip IV (king of Spain) 5 n, 20, 55 n, 67, 173, 180, 287, 288
Phocylides 309
Picard, B. 436
Pierce 284 n
Pieterzoon Beelthouwer, Jan 271
Pimentel, Domingo 127
Pina, Abigail de 223, 420
Pina, David de see Sarfati de Pina, David
Pina, Jacob (Manuel) de 129, 130, 144
Pina, Pablo de (Jessurun, Reuel) v
Pineda, Juan de 237
Pinheiro, Isaac 206
Pinheiro (Piñeiro), Dr Juan 126
Pinto, Gaspar 40 n
Pinto, Isaac de 205, 206
Pinto, Jacob de 205 n
Pinto, Sarah de 204
Pinto Delgado, Juan 308
Pizarro, Abraham Israel 309
Plato 349, 355
Pliny 300, 349
Pollak, Alexander 206 n
Pontremoli, Rabbi Elisha Ḥana 'el 457–61
Pontremoli, Ezra 458 n
Pontremoli, Tobias Barukh 460 n
Porphyry 12
Prado, David 136, 137, 154, 156, 177 n
Prado, Daniel de see Prado, Dr Juan de
Prado, Isaac de 207 n
Prado, Dr Juan de (Daniel de):
  family origin from Vila Flôr 123
  parents 124, 129
  student at Alcalá de Henares university 125
  student at *Madre de Dios* college 14, 125
  licensed as physician by the Toledo university 125
  in Lopera 124
  in Antequera 127
  and Spanish Inquisition 88
  observance of Jewish commandments in Spain 126, 127
  and deism 126, 132
  escape from Spain 127–8
  arrival in Hamburg 128
  public conversion to Judaism 128
  arrival in Amsterdam 128
  member of the *Collegium Medicum* of Amsterdam 128–9
  two poems in honour of Jacob de Pina 129
  conflict with the Portuguese community of Amsterdam 130–46
  public recantation in the synagogue 130–1
  friendship with Barukh Spinoza 133–5, 151
  relations with Daniel de Ribera 138–9
  enquiry of the Portuguese community against him 138–46
  excommunication 135
  residence in Antwerp 157–60
  death of first wife 158
  married to María Marcelina 159 n
  relationship with Eleonora Francisca Lobo 159
  disputation with Isaac Orobio vii, ix, 103, 104, 110, 118, 122–57, 169, 174–8, 179, 216, 217, 235, 240, 244, 248 n, 257, 266, 307, 315, 316, 329, 347, 354 n, 359, 360
  death 159
  and heterodoxy within the western Sephardi diaspora 161–6, 312
  on election of Israel by God 171, 174–8, 354 n
  Abraham Pereyra's criticism of 323
Prados, Felipa (Leah) de 124, 129
Pratensis, Felix 291 n

Quevedo y Villegas, Francisco de 287, 308–10
Queyrats, Jean de 100 n
Queyrats, Louis de 100, 101, 102
Quintanilla, Tomás de 78, 410, 416

Rabelais 99
Racine 104
Rambam see Maimonides
Ramban see Moses ben Naḥman, Rabbi
Ramírez, Lope 335

Ramírez Pina, Francisco 335
Rashi *see* Solomon Isaac
Rebolledo, Conde Bernardino de 128, 129
Reynoso, Dr Miguel 88, 134, 135 n, 204
Ribeiro Macedo, Duarte 230 n
Ribera, Daniel de (Carreras y Coligo, José) 137 n, 138–45
Ribera, Francisco de 309 n
Rieuwerts, Jan 55 n
Rivadeneyra, Pedro 323
Rocamora, Dr Isaac de (Rocamora, Fray Vicente) v, 202 n
Rocamora, Salomon 205 n
Rocha, Judith da 427
Rodrigues, Anna 2
Rodrigues, Diogo 4 n
Rodrigues, Felipe 40 n
Rodrigues, Jacôme 2
Rodrigues, João 2
Rodrigues, Lourenço 2
Rodrigues, Melchor (grandfather of Orobio de Castro, Isaac) 1, 2, 25 n, 28, 38 n
Rodrigues Lourenço, Antonio 2, 3, 4 n, 5
Rodrigues Pereyra, Tomás *see* Pereyra, Abraham Israel
Rodrigues Versinha, Balthazar 25 n
Rodríguez, Melchor (son of Luis, Santiago) 25 n, 27, 28, 36–42, 45
Rodríguez, Pedro *see* Sarmiento, Manuel
Rodríguez, Dr Pedro 262 n
Rodríguez, Sebastián 44 n, 45 n
Rodríguez Almeida, Francisco 66, 80 83 n
Rodríguez Cáseres, Jacob 226 n
Rodríguez da Costa, Jorge 336 n
Rodríguez de Mattos, Rachel 421
Rodríguez de Monsanto, Simón *see* Monsanto, Abraham Israel
Rodríguez Medina, Gaspar 425
Rodríguez Medina, Isabel 425
Rodríguez Mendes, Simon de *see* Franco Mendes, David
Rodríguez Monsanto, Isaac 203
Rodríguez Núñez, Mateo 4–6, 10, 28, 35, 53–6, 58–62
Rois Carion, Abraham 199 n
Rophe, Rabbi Meir ben Hiyya 220
Rosa, Conde de la 17, 18, 20
Rosa, Moses (López Rosa, Duarte) 290, 293, 296 n, 297, 301, 427
Rosa, Samuel 223, 297, 301, 427

Saavedra Fajardo 308
Sabbatai Ṣevi 112, 209
 opposition in Amsterdam to 210
 apostasy 211–12
 Abraham Michael Cardoso's defense of 212–14
 Isaac Cardoso's attitude towards 217
 Isaac Orobio's attitude towards 218–19, 221
 Abraham Pereyra's attitude towards 220, 222, 374–5
 Daniel Levi de Barrios's attitude towards 228–9, 231, 233, 273
 Philip van Limborch on 283
 Rabbi Elisha H. Pontremoli on 461
Salçedo, Dr Diego de 47 n
Sales, François de 291 n, 316 n
Salom, Selomoh 192 n
Salomons, Joseph 206 n
Sánchez, Francisco 100, 321
Sánchez, Matea
Santiago, Antonio de 30 n
Sarfati de Pina (Pina, David de) 96, 200 n, 203–5, 207, 271, 304
Sarmiento, Juan 25 n, 28
Sarmiento, Manuel (Rodríguez, Pedro) 25, 28, 29–41, 45, 48, 59
Sarmiento, Pedro 22 n
Saruco, Rabbi Isaac 205 n
Sasportas, Rabbi Jacob:
 rabbi in Hamburg 209
 on Rabbi Moses d'Aguilar's sabbatean beliefs 112, 211
 on sabbateanism in Amsterdam 209–12
 on Daniel Levi de Barrios 227–9
 teacher in *Tiph'eret Bahurim* 293, 421
 teacher in *'Eṣ Ḥayyim* 420
 Ṣiṣat Novel Ṣevi 209
Sceperus, Jacob 274
Semah, Rabbi Abraham 427
Semah, Dr Daniel 193 n, 206 n
Semah, Samuel 293, 294 n, 296 n, 427
Semah Fero, Jacob 190 n
Seneca 77, 308 n, 310, 311, 349, 404
Senior Coronel, Abraham 271
Serra, Manuel de 335
Serrano, Dr Diego Duarte 88, 126
Serrano de Vargas y Urueña, Juan 15 n, 387
Sextus Empiricus 316 n
Sheshet Perfet, Rabbi Isaac ben 326, 327
Sibiller, Francisco 23 n
Silva, Hezekiah da 365 n

Name Index

Silva, Michael de 290 n
Silva, Miguel de 309
Silva, Samuel da 161, 275
Silva Calbo, Simón de 88
Simon, Richard 132 n
Simons, Menno 236 n
Sixtus of Sienna 114 n, 236, 237
Socrates 300, 355
Solano y Robles, Fray Tomás 124 n, 133–4, 145, 243
Solomon Halevi of Burgos *see* Pablo de Santa María
Solomon Isaac, Rabbi (Rashi) 116, 237 n, 352
Solon 121
Soto, Clara 424
Soto, David del 421, 424
Soto, Fray Domingo de 12, 313
Soto, Gracia del 297, 421
Soto, Jacob del (Monte, Jacob del) 196, 197, 198, 199
Soto, Rachel del 297
Sotomayor, Antonio de 54, 63
Souza, Abraham de 210
Souza, Esther de 427
Spencer 278
Spinoza, Barukh:
  relations with Juan de Prado 131–5, 145, 160
  excommunication by the Portuguese community in Amsterdam 123, 129 n, 130–1, 133, 160, 379
  Isaac La Peyrère's influence on 132–3
  studies in Leiden 133
  settlement in Rijnsburg 151
  meeting with the Prince de Condé 104 n
  writings: *Renati des Cartes Principia Philosophiae* 151; *Tractatus Theologico-Politicus* 55 n, 132, 176, 263, 264, 266, 277; *Ethics* 151, 265
  arguments against Maimonides 118–19
  on the election of the Hebrews 176–7
  'Deus Sive Natura' 264
  political philosophy 322
  on antisemitism 371
  library collection 308
  and heterodoxy in western Sephardi diaspora 161, 312, 379
  Isaac Orobio's polemic with vii, 150, 151, 216, 263–9, 300, 307, 315
  Joh. Bredenburg's attitude towards 262–5

Daniel Levi de Barrios on 229 n
Philip van Limborch on 277
Abraham Pereyra on 323
Suares, Antonio 411
Suares, Mencia (of Ocaña) 22 n
Suárez, Francisco 180, 182, 237, 313, 315
Suasso y López, Isaac Israel 190 n, 423
Suasso y López, Rachel 423

Tapia, Pedro de 238
Tartas, Jacob 420
Tartas, Leah 420
Teixeira, Abraham (Diego) 128
Telles da Costa, Jacob 205 n
Telles Girón, Juan 8
Téllez Girón, Juan (duke of Osuna) 9
Templo, Jacob Judah León *see* León, Jacob Judah
Tenorio de León, Alvaro 71 n, 72
Tertullian 182, 236
Tillotson 284 n
Toland, John 456 n
Toledano, don Joseph 427
Toletus, Francisco 313
Torre, G. de la 269, 270, 440
Tostado, Alonso 237
Touro, Abraham de Judah 205, 206
Trani, Rabbi Joseph Moses (Maharit) 7 n
Tremelluis, Emanuel 238

Vaesa, Salvador de 52
Vaez, Deborah 223
Vaez de Castro, Pedro 24 n
Valera, Cipriano de 238
Valero, Miguel 47 n
Vallejo, Dr Alonso de 27, 43–52, 54–6, 62, 63
Valverde Horozco, Dr Diego de 69, 70, 71–4
Vásquez, Gabriel 9, 180, 182, 313, 315
Veene, Egbert 277 n
Vega, Esther de la 426
Vega, Manuel da 424
Velasco, Alonso de *see* Orobio de Castro, Abraham
Vélez de Guevara, L. 287, 301, 302 n
Vellozino, Isaac 205 n
Velthuysen, Lambert de 265, 266 n
Vera y Alarcón, don Lope de 336 n
Veron, François 316 n
Versé, Noel Aubert de 263 n, 264
Veyssière de La Croze, Mathurin 466, 467

Vieira, Joseph 208
Villegas, Isaac 293, 296 n, 301, 427
Villegas Selvago, Alonso de 77
Virgilio, P. 180
Vittoria, Francisco de 313
Vivien, Balthazar 223 n
Voltaire 453, 454, 456
Vondel, Justus van den 420
Vossius 238, 284 n

William III (king of England) 292, 424

Ximenes Cardozo, David 293, 294 n, 296 n, 301, 420, 423, 427
Ximenes de Cisneros, Cardinal Francisco 13

Zacuth, Abraham (Zacutus Lusitanus; Alvares de Tavara, Manuel) 73 n
Zacuto, Abraham 370 n
Zeno 300
Zepeda, Alonso de:
   translator of Raymond Lull's works 179–80
   portrait 385–6
   writings 179 n
   Propugnatio Terminorum 186
   meeting with Alonso Escudero 180–1, 184–5
   Isaac Orobio's polemic with 121, 181–9, 227, 230–2, 238, 253, 314, 315, 319, 320, 356, 372, 385, 433–4
Zetina, Don Gutierre(s) de *see* Cetina, Don Gutierre de
Zetina, Julio de *see* Cetina, Julio de
Zurreño, Moses 343, 344

Place Index

Acqui 460
Aguilar 6
Alcalá de Henares v, vi, 1 n, 8, 9, 11–15,
  18, 19, 23, 41, 51, 55 n, 58, 64, 65,
  67, 101, 102, 122, 124 n, 125, 126,
  133, 150, 180, 181, 200, 238, 314,
  346, 347, 387
Alcázar de San Juan 4
Alessandria 104
Almagro 25, 44
Amsterdam 73 n, 79, 105 n, 116, 139 n,
  143, 155, 184, 188, 217, 221, 245,
  249, 250, 263, 269, 358
  Arminians 274
  Daniel Levi de Barrios' residence
    222-3, 227
  Cabbala 162 n
  Catholics 243–4
  Collegium Medicum 102, 128–9, 200–5
  economic boom 191
  Hebrew press 111, 293
  Huguenot exiles 239, 241 n, 455
  Iberian crypto-Jews reverting to
    Judaism v, 22, 106–7, 149, 220, 308,
    309, 314, 335–8, 345, 373
  Jewish citizens 201–2
  Jewish literary academies 286–302
  Jewish printers 293, 420
  John Locke's sojourn 275
  Isaac Orobio's sojourn v, vi, vii, 22,
    106–9, 122, 123, 152, 179, 181, 194,
    200–8, 251, 266, 268, 349, 386
  Orobio's family residence 67 n, 95, 96,
    208
  Pérez de Maltranilla's stay 134, 145
  Isaac La Peyrère's visit 132
  Portuguese Jews 14, 88 n, 110, 118,
    128–30, 138, 146–8, 156–8, 189,
    198, 205–6, 219, 226, 252, 260, 262,
    265 n, 303–4, 307, 310–11, 313,
    322, 325, 326, 329, 331, 352, 360,
    362, 374, 379, 381, 420–7, 465
  printing centre of Sephardic
    prayerbooks 81 n
  printing press of Spanish and
  Portuguese books 230, 232, 238
  proselytes 180–1, 324
  rabbis 110–11, 228, 333, 343, 352, 456
  Sabbatean movement 209–11, 339,
    340 n, 376
  and Sephardi diaspora vii, 109
  Solano y Robles' stay 133, 145
  Barukh Spinoza's residence 135–6,
    145, 151, 176
  theological disputations between Jews
    and Christians 235, 239–40, 271–3,
    278 n, 285, 459
Andalusia 4, 6 n, 8, 14, 43, 64, 74, 75 n,
  88 n, 105, 107 n, 122, 223, 288, 302,
  340 n
Andújar 6, 30, 88 n, 107 n, 127
Annecy 291 n
Antequera 53, 127
Antwerp 5, 107, 187, 237 n, 265 n, 289,
  315, 420, 423, 426
  churches 159 n
  crypto-Jews 121 n, 337, 367 n
  'Portuguese nation' 157
  Juan de Prado's residence 123, 146,
    156, 157–9, 244
  university 138
Aragon 179, 462
Astorga 9
Athens 354, 360
Austria 180
Avila 237 n

Bailén 88 n
Barbados 420
Basle 466
Bayonne 293, 422, 425, 427, 431
  crypto-Jews 5, 29–32, 42, 48, 96, 337
  Baltazar Orobio's sojourn vii, 96–8
Beira 61 n
Beja 427
Beverwijk 156
Biarritz 98
Bohemia 369
Bordeaux 317 n, 321, 335
Bourges 104

Brabant 116, 156 n, 244
Braganza 24 n, 25 n, 31, 35, 36, 38–40, 61, 124
  crypto-Jews 1, 3 n, 37
  Baltazar Orobio's birthplace v, vi, 3, 12, 91, 414
Brazil 111, 138
Bruges 244
Brussels 144, 179, 180, 184, 186, 187, 225, 269, 338 n, 385
  Miguel de Barrios' books printed in 157, 223, 224, 226–8, 230 n
  university 138
Burgos 9, 86, 87, 114, 116, 177 n, 236, 246

Cabra 6 n
Cádiz 66, 72, 79, 81, 82, 84, 90, 335
  Baltazar Orobio's residence vii, 67, 91
  his house in 75–8, 402–17
Calahorra 9
Calatayud 321
Calatrava 27
Cambrai 269
Cambridge 275
Canary Islands 60, 134, 135 n
Cartagena 96
Casale Monferrato 458
Castile 4, 12, 53 n, 235 n, 369, 370 n, 462
Catalonia 9, 138, 186 n
Ceuta 78
Chantilly 104
Chieri 458
Coimbra 1, 3 n, 5, 313
Cologne 424
Copenhagen 128
Córdoba 56, 311
  Inquisition 6, 9, 80, 82, 83 n, 127, 226, 420
  Abraham Núñez Bernal burnt at the inquisitional stake 260, 332, 426
Cuenca:
  Inquisition 5, 27, 42–3, 48, 50–4, 55 n, 56, 59–63, 64, 83, 125, 127 n, 128 n
  surgeons 47 n
Curaçao 432

Dax 5, 25
Delft 272
Denmark 373
Djerba 214 n
Dordrecht 272
Dublin 464

Écija 58, 66
Egypt 312
England 145, 206 n, 227, 251, 275, 363, 420, 451
Enkhuizen 271

Ferrara 81 n
Flanders 30, 179, 180, 224, 226, 227
Florence 81, 287
France 283
  crypto-Jews 5, 25, 29–32, 96–7, 121 n, 317 n, 336, 425
  'fideistic scepticism', centre of 316
  Huguenots, flight of 239
  Jews 368–9
  Jewish apostates 339, 363
  Baltazar Orobio's sojourn in v, vii, 65, 95–105, 154, 169, 200, 240, 244
  diffusion of his writings there 269, 451, 454, 456–7
  war against Holland 206 n
Fundão 61 n
Fürth 458 n

Gallipoli 218
Gandia 8 n
Germany 287, 363, 369, 374, 382
Ghent 244
Glückstadt 5
Gouda 272, 274, 277
Granada:
  conquered by the Catholic kings 369
  Inquisition 27, 29, 37, 41–3, 46, 49, 50, 54–6, 59, 62, 127
  Jewish settlement 340 n
  university 10
Groningen 271
Guiana 78
Guimarães 46

Hague, The 185, 204, 265 n, 269, 310
Hamburg 122, 128–9, 146, 207, 208, 209, 310, 352 n
Hanover 373
Harderwijk 205 n, 422
Hebron 220
Holland 133, 135, 156, 223 n, 227, 451, 456 n, 463
  Huguenot exiles 239
  Jews 105, 118, 149, 260 n, 335, 344, 360
  Jewish physicians 202
  medical treatment 134 n

Place Index 523

philosophical circles 263
States General 272
theological disputations between Jews and Christians 115, 238, 455
war against France 206 n
Hungary 369

India 369
Italy 104, 113, 415, 424, 451, 457
  crypto-Jews, immigration of 30 n, 223
  Jews 251
  Jewish apostates 339, 363
  literary academies 286–7
  Abraham Pereyra's journey to 221
Ivrea 457–8

Jaén 4, 83 n, 88, 124, 125 n
Jerez de la Frontera 66, 72 n, 340
Jerusalem 219, 225, 247

Labastide 98
La Mancha 4, 53
Las Peñas 59
Languedoc 100, 104
Leghorn (Livorno) 223, 227, 232, 286, 288, 289, 290 n, 294 n, 426
Leiden 151, 279
  Calvinist preachers 272
  Jewish medical students 96 n, 200, 201 n, 203, 204 n, 207 n, 340 n
  Spinoza's studies in 133
  university 138, 274
Lima 126 n
Lisbon 46, 53, 77, 111, 287, 293, 410, 420, 422
Livorno *see* Leghorn
London 60, 199 n, 423, 425, 451, 464, 467
Lopera 88, 123–6
Lorca vii, 96

Madrid 52, 65, 77 n, 90, 179 n, 336, 422
  crypto-Jews 34, 55, 58, 84, 220
  Inquisition 30, 54, 62, 80, 88, 91, 93–5, 127, 133, 134, 243, 335
  trials of the 'Patient Christ' 4–5
Málaga:
  Alvares' family residence vi, 4, 10, 35, 36, 45, 51, 53, 55, 60, 63
  Alvares' family escape from 46, 48–9, 51, 52, 54
  crypto-Jews 25 n, 27, 30, 38–41, 50, 59 n

inquisitional commisary 51, 52, 62
Baltazar Orobio's falsely acknowledged birthplace 1 n
the plague of (1637) 15–23, 73, 75, 387–401
Manzanares 25, 59
Mauricia 111
Medina de Ríoseco 27, 40, 43, 46
Membrilla 34
Mexico 171
Middelburg 107 n, 207, 426
Miranda 38
Montilla 223, 311
Morocco 427

Nantes 105, 466
Naples 175 n, 287, 363
Nes 374 n
New Amsterdam (New York) 136 n
New Spain 78, 171, 405, 406
New York *see* New Amsterdam
Nice 458

Ocaña 22 n
Oporto 43, 46
Ostend 179 n
Osuna vi, 1 n, 8–15, 65
Ouderkerk v, 105 n, 106 n, 109, 198, 305, 306 n, 420–7

Palestine 196 n, 220, 255, 343
Palma de Majorca 180 n
Pamplona 335
Paris 104, 105 n, 155, 156, 458 n
Pernambuco 265 n
Peyrehorade 425
Piedmont 457, 458
Poland 363, 369, 374
Portugal 1, 27, 61 n, 111, 138, 143, 227, 309, 346, 380, 421, 422, 427, 462
  crypto-Jews vi, 33 n, 37, 40, 42, 43, 91, 92, 109, 120, 177, 314, 326, 331, 339, 342, 379; their emigration to France 98; their emigration to Holland v, 73 n, 105, 308, 358, 373; their emigration to Spain 5 n, 7, 12 n, 18, 50, 84 n, 338, 379
  Jews, exiles from Spain 370 n
  Jews, expulsion of the 369
  Jews, forced conversion 327
  Jews, emigration from viii
  'New-Christians', writings against the heresy of 162

Priego 6
Puerto Real 67, 408, 410, 416, 417

Remmich 424
Rijnsburg 151
Rome 128, 145, 183 n, 287, 427
Rotterdam 204, 263, 264, 266, 271, 343
Rouen 96 n, 334 n, 421, 423

St Jean de Luz 98
St Maur 269
Salamanca 9, 14 n, 24 n, 72, 237 n
Salonika 336 n
Sanlúcar de Barrameda 66, 71, 80, 81, 402, 414, 415
Santa Cruz de Mudela 27–32, 36, 45
Santander 9
Saragossa 9, 287
Savoy 457
Scotland 420
Segovia 317 n, 414
Seville 8
  Inquisition 6, 7, 27, 74, 75 n, 78, 79–97
  Baltazar Orobio's falsely acknowledged birthplace 1 n
  his residence v, vii, 56–8, 60, 62, 64–7
  his family's residence 46, 48, 49, 54, 57–8, 63, 64, 66
  physicians 71
  printing of medical books 69, 70, 77 n
  university v, 10, 64–5, 72, 101
s'Hertogenbosch 156 n
Sienna 114 n, 236, 237
Smyrna 212, 214
Spain 21, 35, 42, 43, 69, 102, 107, 127, 138, 158, 185, 283, 292, 317 n, 373, 374, 380, 426
  averroism among Jews 142 n
  crypto-Jews viii, 12, 33 n, 37, 39, 85, 109, 120, 122, 163, 212, 254 n, 308, 326, 331, 335–7, 339, 379
  crypto-Jewish emigrants 30, 88, 105, 215, 216 n, 220, 338, 343–6, 358, 378, 382
  crypto-Jewish emigrants to France 29, 31
  crypto-Jewish immigrants from Portugal 18, 25, 27, 36, 124
  decline of 172, 175
  deism in 126 n, 131, 132, 163
  Inquisition 139 n
  Jews 162, 179 n, 312, 340 n, 369

  expulsion from 162, 327, 369, 370 n, 462
  forced conversion of 363
  in the 17th century 7 n
  literary academies 286–7, 297, 302
  medical studies 10, 68
  messianism, Spanish 172–4, 177–8
  neo-stoicism 310
  nobility 65
  Baltazar Orobio's family's arrival 3–6
  his residence ix, 1, 114, 123, 148, 150, 154, 244, 250, 284, 329–30
  his emigration 95–6, 98
  physicians 67, 77 n
  plagues 16
  scepticism 321
  scholasticism 313–15
  Sephardic Jews' attitude towards 225–7, 308–15
  social thinking 325
  taxes 53 n
Surinam 421
Sweden 128

Tenerife 135 n
Tobago 223
Toledo 77 n
  Alvares' family residence 27
  Inquisition 22 n, 25, 29, 30 n, 34, 35, 42–3, 45–8, 55, 56, 59, 62, 96
  Jews, first settlement 340
  university 125
Toulouse 208
  auto-da-fé of (1685) 105, 106 n
  Baltazar Orobio's residence in 100–3, 169, 194 n, 200–1, 216, 240, 347
  university v, vii, 65, 97–105, 321, 347
Triana 93, 126
Tripoli 210 n, 211, 212, 214 n
Turin 460 n
Turkey 29
Tuscany 465

Utrecht 104 n, 138, 155, 274, 360, 422, 465
Utrera 72

Valdepeñas 25–9, 30 n, 31 n, 32, 34–7, 40, 44, 45, 59, 61 n
Valencia vii, 8 n, 9, 127 n, 404
Valenciennes 244
Valladolid 9, 12 n, 27, 80

Venice 30, 81 n, 217, 220, 268, 293, 352 n, 424, 465
Verona 173, 210 n, 211, 217, 219, 325, 427
Vila Flôr 123, 124
Villa Real 92

Wijk-aan-Zee (Weycke) 155, 156

Ypres 244

Zeeland 292, 423

Subject Index

Anabaptists 236, 252
Anglicanism, Anglicans 145
apostates, heretics 87, 114 n, 146, 235–8, 246
Arminians *see* Remonstrants
atheism, atheists 104, 133, 162, 165, 216, 264–7, 277
Augustinians 133–5, 243
autos-da-fé:
  in Coimbra 1
  in Córdoba 6, 260, 332, 420, 426
  in Lisbon 111 n
  in Seville 90, 91, 97, 317 n
  in Toledo 35, 42
  in Toulouse 106 n
averroism amongst crypto-Jews in Spain 142 n, 162

biblical exegesis in Spanish and Portuguese 339, 340, 341, 342, 343
biblical criticism 132, 166–7
brotherhoods, charitable and teaching confraternities in the Portuguese–Jewish community of Amsterdam:
  'Abodath Ḥesed 195, 198
  Biqqur Ḥolim 189–91, 195, 207 n, 304, 429
  Cautivos 429
  Dotar 430
  Gemiluth Ḥasadim 430
  Kether Torah 112
  Terra Santa 111, 429
  Vistiaria dos Talmidim 430

cabbala 113, 161, 179 n, 333
Calvinism, Calvinists 252
  in Amsterdam 235
  attitude towards Jews 202
  in France 100, 316 n
  in Holland 239
  Isaac Orobio's attitude towards 261–2
  on Portuguese Jewish heterodoxy 136
  and Remonstrants 274
  synods in the Dutch Republic 272
  theological disputations with Jews 239–42

Calvinist synods in Holland 272
Capuchins 20
Carmelites 8, 20, 115, 116, 238, 243, 244, 314, 452
Cartesians 167
Catholicism, Catholics 172, 252, 275
  in Amsterdam 243
  in Antwerp 146
  Armenian 84–5
  and Counter-Reformation 316
  crypto-Jews' attitude towards 82
  and 'fideistic scepticism' 316, 318
  Dutch Calvinists on 272
  Elijah Montalto on 259
  Rabbi Saul Levi Mortera on 260
  Isaac Orobio on 248, 259, 284, 456
cemetery in Ouderkerk, Portuguese–Jewish 105 n, 109, 198, 305–7, 420–8
Christianity, dissemination among the Jews of Holland 271, 272, 285
christological exegesis of the Bible 110 n, 114, 235, 241, 245–8, 251, 256, 257
citizenship of the Jews in Amsterdam, rights of 201, 202
collector (*tesorero*) of the *millones* 53, 55, 58, 63
Collegianten 266
Collegium Medicum of Amsterdam 102, 128, 200–5
congregations, Jewish:
  Ashkenazi, in Amsterdam 198
  Beth Israel, in Amsterdam 189
  Beth Jacob, in Amsterdam 189
  Magen Abraham, in Mauricia 111
  Neveh Shalom, in Amsterdam 189
  Portuguese–Jewish, in Hamburg 128–9, 146, 310
  Portuguese–Jewish, in The Hague 310
  Congregational *Talmud Torah* of Amsterdam 14, 106 n, 107, 110, 113, 128–30, 135, 138, 146, 156, 186, 189–96, 197, 209, 219, 220 n, 224, 226, 228, 245, 272, 273, 286, 309, 310
  great synagogue of 197, 205, 206, 302, 421

Portuguese–Jewish *(cont.):*
  old synagogue of 206
  regulations of 189, 190, 193–7, 198, 224, 272, 273, 338
Cristo de la Paciencia case 4, 5, 84 n
crypto-Jews:
  in Antwerp 114 n, 146, 157, 337
  changes of names on return to Judaism 77 n, 128, 129, 336
  Christian education and values among 7, 19–23, 38, 44, 45, 73, 76, 87, 97, 98, 378, 379, 380
  Christianity, attitude towards 22, 23, 34, 44, 45, 49, 82, 83, 253, 254
  circumcision of 7, 47, 84, 335, 336
  confiscations of property of 37, 42, 47, 62, 75 n, 78, 81, 82, 90, 402–17
  emigration from Portugal to Spain of 3, 4, 5 n, 12, 18, 29, 30, 35, 37, 39–40, 122, 124
  escape from Spain of 5, 6, 25–30, 41, 42, 45, 46, 79, 88, 96, 98, 122, 128, 321, 329
  expulsion from Toulouse of 98
  fasts among 32, 33, 38–41, 43, 44, 50, 80, 82, 87–9
  in France 5, 25, 29, 30, 32, 96, 98, 99, 335–7
  imprisonment after prosecution of 27, 35, 42, 63
  imprisonment in Spain for investigation of 37, 41, 79–84, 127
  Jewish education of 6, 7, 8, 46
  lecturers in universities 64, 65, 100, 101, 312
  messianic expectations of 373
  observance of the sabbath and holidays by 31–4, 36, 37, 38, 39, 40, 41, 43, 44, 45, 76, 81, 84, 89
  occupations and professions of 30, 31, 35, 36, 40 n, 53, 57–9, 67, 75, 78, 83 n, 88 n, 125
  perpetual imprisonment of 89–94
  physicians 58, 60, 65, 71, 72, 88, 125, 126, 127, 128, 134
  in Portugal 1, 3, 18, 37, 39, 122, 124, 326, 327, 328, 331
  practice of the Jewish commandments by 6, 7, 30–2, 36–41, 43, 44, 80, 81, 84–8, 124, 126, 127
  prayer-books among 80, 81
  prayers of 31, 32, 33, 37, 38, 80, 81
  private libraries of 75–7, 89
  refusal to eat non-kosher food by 39, 40, 44
  return to Judaism of 3, 4, 6, 7, 22, 29, 30, 73 n, 105–9, 121, 122, 128, 150, 162, 173, 175, 189, 215, 216, 220, 223, 226, 227, 313, 324, 325, 326, 329, 330, 334, 335, 338, 339, 343, 344–7, 349–53, 378–82
  in Spain 3, 6, 10, 12, 18, 22 n, 31, 32, 36, 39, 88, 122, 123, 212, 213, 220, 223, 226, 260, 312, 317 n, 326, 327, 328, 329, 331, 426

deism:
  Uriel d'Acosta's attitude towards 276
  in England 251, 456, 467
  in France 454
  and Iberian 'New-Christians' 379
  Juan de Prado's links with 88, 123, 126–7, 131–2, 147, 166
  and Sephardi heterodoxy 162–3, 165, 215, 381
Dominicans 64, 91, 180, 237, 238, 313, 379

Edict of Nantes 105, 239 n
election of Israel 161
  in Jewish–Christian theological disputations 279–82
  Isaac Orobio's defense of 171–2, 177–8, 353–6, 363
  Juan de Prado's rejection of 164–6, 171, 175, 177, 379
  in Spanish literature 172–3
  in Spinoza's thought 173–4, 380
  in western Sephardic thought 173–4, 380
encyclopaedists 251, 454
excommunication:
  of Uriel d'Acosta 276
  of David Arias 336
  of Abraham Bueno de Aragão 195
  of the heirs of Jacob del Soto 196–9
  of 'non-believers' of Sabbatai Sevi 210 n
  of Juan de Prado 14, 122–3, 135–8, 146–7, 148, 153, 154, 166
  of Barukh Spinoza 130–1
expulsion of Jews:
  from Portugal 369
  from Spain 327, 369

fideistic scepticism 167, 188 n, 316–18, 322, 347, 353

Subject Index

Franciscans 8, 9, 235 n, 237, 238, 243
governmental court of Holland, Jews before the 204
guilds of Amsterdam 201, 202, 420

Hebrew grammar-books in Portuguese 113 n
Hebrew learning in Spain 65, 66
Hebrew printing press of Amsterdam 111, 293, 420
hermetism, the hermetic school 186, 188, 319
Huguenots 238–42, 252, 255

immortality of the soul 113 n, 123, 142, 152, 160, 163, 166, 246, 275, 323
Inquisition in Portugal 1, 3, 25, 36, 111, 124, 329
Inquisition in Spain 3, 5, 6, 23, 25, 29, 122, 133, 139 n, 158, 160, 175, 176, 179, 226, 329, 402–17
  prison of the 42, 61, 79, 80, 82, 90, 92, 93, 127, 317 n
inquisitional tribunals in the Americas:
  in Lima 126 n
inquisitional tribunals in Portugal 1, 3
  in Coimbra 5
inquisitional tribunals in Spain:
  in Ciudad Real 22 n
  in Córdoba 80, 82, 127 n, 226, 260
  in Cuenca 5, 27, 42, 50–4, 56, 59, 62–4, 83, 125, 127 n
  in Granada 27, 29, 37, 42, 43, 49–54, 62, 127
  in Madrid 133, 134, 335
  physicians of the 7, 47, 74
  in Seville 6, 7, 27, 66 n, 74, 78–80, 82, 83, 84, 88–91, 93, 94, 96, 97, 127 n
  testimonies laid before the 6, 25, 27, 31–4, 42, 43, 80, 81, 82, 83, 96, 133, 134, 335, 336
  in Toledo 25, 27, 29, 34, 42–5, 47, 48, 56, 62, 96
  trials of the 25–63, 79–92
  in Valladolid 80
inquisitional investigations, tortures during 48, 84–8, 90 n
inquisitional punishments:
  banishment 91, 92
  burning 91, 139 n, 332
  burning in effigy 6, 96
  imprisonment 6
  wearing of the *sanbenito* 6, 35, 42, 62, 63, 90, 93, 95
Inquisitor General 54, 63, 94

Jansenists 167–9
Jesuits 38, 64, 78, 104, 180, 237, 313, 316 n, 321, 380

legal status of Jews in Amsterdam 201, 202
literary academies:
  in Europe 286, 287, 288
  in Spain 286, 287, 288, 297, 301, 302
literary academies of Jews:
  Academia de los Floridos, Amsterdam 234, 286–302, 418–30
  Academia de los Sitibundos, Amsterdam 232 n, 286, 288, 289, 290, 292, 294, 295, 426
  Academia de los Sitibundos, Leghorn 232, 286, 288, 289, 290, 294, 295, 426
literature:
  anti-Christian, in Spanish and Portuguese 114–17, 187, 188, 235–62, 312, 315, 316 n, 434–9
  apologetic, Jewish 22, 118, 173, 174, 245, 320, 336, 337, 361, 371, 372, 451–64
  belles lettres, crypto-Jewish 308, 317, 320
  belles lettres, Portuguese–Jewish in Amsterdam 129, 157, 158, 159, 223–7, 229–34, 289, 290, 297, 298, 299, 301, 309–12, 330, 331, 420, 423, 426, 427
  philosophical, of the Sephardi diaspora 113, 147, 151, 181–5, 186, 187, 188, 216, 217, 229, 230, 231, 263–70, 431–5, 439, 440, 441–50
  rabbinic, in Spanish and Portuguese 113, 327, 328
Lutherans 252

Ma'amad of the Portuguese community:
  in Amsterdam 129, 130, 135–9, 144, 145, 146, 147, 148, 154, 155, 156, 186, 189, 190–9, 205, 210, 223 n, 224, 229, 230 n, 233, 272 n, 273, 278, 296
  in Hamburg 146
Mennonites 236
messiah's apostasy 210–13

Subject Index

messianism:
  Daniel Levi de Barrios' attitude towards 228–9, 373–4
  in Abraham Michael Cardoso's thought 212–15, 342–3
  and Dutch Remonstrants 274–5
  in Jewish-Christian theological disputations 240, 272, 279–81, 283
  and millenarism 271
  in Isaac Orobio's writings 241, 246–8, 356–7, 375–7
  and sabbatean movement 210–21, 228–9, 373–5

natural law 121, 126, 127, 152, 163, 262, 348, 356, 358, 359
natural reason 117, 119, 152, 155, 166, 249, 260, 314, 356, 359
natural religion 88, 152
neo-scholastics 9, 310, 313–15, 321, 380
'New Christians' *see* crypto-Jews
Noahide commandments 117–20, 157, 356–7

occupations and professions of Jews in Holland:
  apothecaries 203 n
  bankers 292, 423
  merchants 107 n, 207, 208, 292, 293, 296, 420–7
  pedlars 206
  physicians 200–3, 206, 207, 293, 422
  printers 293, 420

philosophical arguments of the seventeenth century 179–89, 263–70
phlebotomy 57, 67–75, 77 n, 88 n
plagues in Spain 15–23, 51, 61 n
political and social views of Portuguese Jews 256, 257, 322–5
Portuguese community of Amsterdam:
  and Christianity 118, 155, 235, 241, 242, 243–8, 249 n, 252–62, 272, 273, 279, 280, 281, 282, 283, 314, 315, 316, 317, 323, 324, 332, 338, 339, 341, 358–62
  and crypto-Jews 117, 118, 120, 251, 326–43, 362
  heterodoxy in the 114, 118, 121–78, 312, 349–53, 362, 379, 380, 431, 433–4, 441–50
  and Islam 253, 283
  and the municipal authorities 194, 195, 198, 199, 292
  physicians in the 128, 129, 133, 134, 200–5, 207, 293, 304, 352, 422, 425
  poor of the 189, 190, 194, 195, 199, 293, 294 n, 296, 304
  private libraries in the 308
  rabbis of the 110, 112, 113, 130, 131, 137, 139–42, 145, 146, 147, 196, 197, 220–3, 227, 228, 229, 294, 295, 333, 334
  struggle against heterodoxy in the 114 n, 118, 122, 123, 129, 130, 131, 135–54, 155, 161, 162 n, 167, 169–71, 175, 176, 265 n, 322, 323, 362
predestination 274
private libraries 275
  of crypto-Jews 75–77, 89
  in the Portuguese community of Amsterdam 308
privileges of Portuguese merchants in France 97
proselytes, conversion 117, 118, 139, 180, 181, 249 n, 324, 325
purity of blood, Spanish regulations regarding the 10, 14, 19, 23, 174–5, 325

Quakers 252

religious arguments between Jews and Christians 115, 116, 181, 185, 186, 187, 188, 235–62, 270–85, 318, 323, 324, 375, 376, 381, 385, 386, 451–64
Remonstrants (Arminians) 79, 202, 252, 274–7, 279, 284, 285, 318
'righteous among the gentiles' 118–20, 156, 356–60

Sabbateanism, Sabbatean movement in Amsterdam 112, 209–34, 339, 373, 374
salvation of the soul 116, 126, 240, 275, 279, 280, 335, 337, 357
scepticism 100, 162, 167, 268 n, 316, 319–22
scholastics 180–3, 237, 266, 313–16, 320
scientific arguments in Spain 67–75, 88 n
scientific revolution of the seventeenth century 71, 166, 167

Subject Index

Sephardim and Ashkenazim in Amsterdam, relations between 195, 198
Socinians 236, 252, 274

taxes in Holland:
200ste Penning tax 204, 206
taxes in the Portuguese community of Amsterdam:
  on the cemetery at Ouderkerk 106 n
  on import and export in the Congregation *Talmud Torah* 207, 296
  on membership in the Congregation *Talmud Torah* 106 n, 129, 193 n, 206, 207 n, 296, 303
taxes in Spain:
  alcabala tax 46
  millones tax 53
  sisa tax 53
translations of Jewish literature into Spanish and Portuguese 109, 196 n

universities in France:
  Bourges 104
  Languedoc 100
  Toulouse 65, 98–102, 105, 200, 240, 321, 347
universities in Holland:
  Harderwijk 205 n, 422
  Leiden 96 n, 133, 138
  Jewish students at 138, 200, 201 n, 203, 204 n, 207 n, 340 n
universities in Portugal:
  Coimbra 313
universities in the Southern Low Countries:
  Antwerp 138
  Brussels 138
universities in Spain:
  Alcalá de Henares 1 n, 8, 12–15, 19, 23, 64, 65, 67, 101, 102, 122–6, 133, 150, 181, 200, 238, 314, 346
  curriculum 12, 14
  faculty of arts 8, 12, 125
  Gandia 8 n
  Granada 10
  Osuna 1 n, 8–13, 15, 65
  Salamanca 9, 14 n, 24 n, 72, 237 n
  Seville 10, 64, 65, 67, 69, 70, 71
  students 9, 10, 13, 14, 15, 126 n
  study of canonic law 8, 11
  study of civil law 8, 10
  study of medicine 8–15, 64, 65, 67, 68, 125, 127 n, 150
  study of philosophy 12, 125, 150, 180, 313–15
  study of theology 8, 13, 14, 180, 314
  Toledo 125
  university colleges 10, 13
  Valencia 9, 127 n
  Valladolid 9, 12 n

'world to come' 117–21, 138, 142, 155, 156, 161, 163, 261, 333, 334, 356, 357, 359–62

yeshibah *Hesed le 'Abraham* in Hebron 220
yeshibot in Amsterdam:
  'Abi Yethomim 294 n, 429
  'Es Hayyim 112, 191, 192, 193, 195, 207 n, 298 n, 420, 428
  Gemiluth Hasadim 111
  Honen Dallim 294 n
  Kether Shem Tob 294 n
  Kether Torah 426
  Maskil 'el Dal 207 n, 294 n, 429
  Temimey Derekh 207 n, 208 n, 294 n, 430
  Tiph'ereth Bahurim 293, 294 n, 421
  Torah 'Or 294 n, 345

www.ingramcontent.com/pod-product-compliance
Lightning Source LLC
Chambersburg PA
CBHW071703311025
34809CB00046B/3231